Bridgeport Public Library
1200 Johnson Ave.
Bridgeport, WV 26330
(304) 842-8248

People, Pooches and Problems

Understanding, Controlling and Correcting Problem Behavior in Your Dog

JOB MICHAEL EVANS with his Dalmation friend, Sport the spotted wonder dog.

People, Pooches and Problems

Understanding, Controlling and Correcting Problem Behavior in Your Dog

Job Michael Evans

Photography by Kevin Smith

Additional Photography by
Levon Mark, Lionel Shenken/Visual Productions,
Dealing with Dogs/Campbellville, Ontario
and
Dealing with Dogs/TV Ontario

636.7
EV15p

Howell Book House
IDG Books Worldwide, Inc.
An International Data Group Company
919 E. Hillsdale Boulevard
Suite 400
Foster City, CA 94404

Copyright ©1991 Job Michael Evans, 2001 Elaine Evans

All rights reserved. No part of this book may be reproduced or transmitted in
any form or by any means, electronic or mechanical, including photocopying,
recording, or by an information storage and retrieval system, without permission
in writing from the Publisher.

Howell Book House is a registered trademark of IDG Books Worldwide, Inc.

For general information on IDG Books Worldwide's books in the U.S., please
call our Consumer Customer Service department at 800-762-2974. For reseller
information, including discounts and premium sales, please call our Reseller
Customer Service department at 800-434-3422.

Library of Congress Cataloging-in-Publication Data

Evans, Job Michael.
    People, pooches & problems / Job Michael Evans ; photography by
Kevin Smith ; additional photography by Levon Mark ... [et al.]. -- People,
pooches and problems
        p. cm.
        ISBN 0-7645-6316-5
        1. Dogs--Training. – 2. Dogs--Behavior therapy. – 3. Dogs--Psychology. –
I. Title.
SF431 .E96 2001
636.7'0887--dc21   00-063449

Originally published in a hardcover edition by Howell Book House.

Cover design by Piper Kaufman
Cover illustrations by Ed Kim

To John Arcangeli

and in memory of
Charles Peter Hornek
and
Thomas Connor

Love lives on beyond "good-byes,"
The truth of us will never die,
Our spirits will shine long after we're gone,
And so the love lives on.
And so the love lives on.
—Barry Mann

Contents

Foreword

When I was asked to write a foreword for the paperback edition of Job Evans' classic book, *People, Pooches & Problems*, I had to initially stop and catch my breath. It had been a long time since I first met Job, who was instrumental in my "coming of age" as a dog trainer. On that day, I was still a teenager, a mere pup myself. As I stood in front of the door to his apartment on New York City's Upper East Side, my heart was in my throat. He had been asked to judge whether or not I had the potential to be a good dog trainer. All I remember of our first meeting was that he asked me very little. He gave me no direction as he watched me handle his dog. We discussed our mutual passions for teaching and for animals as we strolled through his neighborhood. I had not yet even heard of many of the legendary dog trainers I now collaborate with on a regular basis, but at that moment I felt the wing of Job embrace me and tuck me into the circle of dog lovers who are lucky enough to be called "dog trainers."

Over the next several years, Job was to become my mentor and my friend. Now, as I sit in front of my computer, I wish I could see his expression at the news that I have written several books of my own since that first meeting. And although it has been five years since Job passed away, in rereading his book (as I often have throughout the years), I noted that there isn't a word that could be dismissed as dated or unfair. What he taught me then still holds today: We must take a holistic approach when we work with "Recalcitrant Rovers." Naughty actions are never just the dog's fault; they are a result of how the dog and the owner are interacting. In this book, he promises no quick fixes, but offers an approach that examines all of the dynamics affecting dog behavior. In a style that is truly Job, he forces his readers, as he did his clients and friends, to ask themselves: Who are you to your dog? The answer to this question is the primary point Job urges you to discover.

Read this book, then reread it. The relationship between you and your dog will improve, and your life will be enriched. As Job taught me, it is the things we work hardest for that mean the most.

And Job's truths will never die.

I conclude this foreword with a letter to my friend, Job Michael Evans . . .

Dear Job,

I know in my heart that you're looking down and smiling at the influence you've had on dog owners everywhere. No one who ever met you or read one of your many books will forget your candor and your insistence on responsible dog ownership. If the dogs could, they would give you a 21-tail salute.

Your faithful followers

Sarah Hodgson

Katonah, New York

August 2000

Note to Readers

Before embarking on any behavioral program for your dog, take it to your veterinarian for a complete medical evaluation. Since many medical and behavioral problems can overlap, it is important that you rule out any physical causes for problem behavior in advance of behavioral therapy.

Acknowledgments

I HAVE LONG WANTED to write a book on problem dogs and problem owners, and I originally thought the whole process would be a downbeat affair entailing endless days of composing critical prose. I soon found out that even problems could be joked about—perhaps problems *should* be joked about even as solutions are sought—and that very rarely is a dog problem the end of the world anyway. Everyone who has read my other books knows that I take the human/canine bond quite seriously, but I've always been able to see the funny side of the relationship. One reason for that is I have surrounded myself with smart, funny, sensitive people from the world of dogs who have greatly aided my dog work and especially the completion of this book. I'd like to thank them here.

My love and thanks to John Arcangeli, who typed and "computerized" the whole tract. I don't understand computers. He does. He even likes them. He has a Dalmatian, Sport (so named because "That way everyone in the Bronx will think his name is Spot"), so he must be sane. Sport is pictured throughout the book doing various naughty things—of course all the shots are fakes (and if you believe that, I have a bridge I'd like to sell you).

I'm grateful also to Carol Lea Benjamin, dog trainer and writer *extraordinaire,* for encouragement and endearing support, as well as to trainers Jack and Wendy Volhard, Marie Ehrenberg, Don Arner, Michele Siegal, Terese Van Buren and the members of the Society of North American Dog Trainers, a pioneering group of which I am a proud member.

Several members of the veterinary community refer clients with problem dogs my way, and I thank Dr. Lewis Berman, Dr. Sally Haddock, Dr. Jane Bicks, Dr. Peter Kross, Dr. Stephanie Hazen and my good friend Dr. Myrna Milani.

I am also grateful to the convention staffs at the Ohio State Veterinary Medical Conference, the Michigan Veterinary Conference, and the Illinois State Veterinary Medical Association Conference who enlisted me for seminars several years running—I've learned as well as taught at these excellent conventions.

My thanks to the staff at the American Kennel Club library, especially the head librarian Roberta Vesley, as well as to the members of the Dog Writers' Association of America. My research at the AKC library and my contacts in DWAA greatly aided writing this book. My thanks to my editors at Howell Book House, especially Seymour Weiss.

In Canada, special thanks goes to trainer Judy Emmert, head of Dealing with Dogs in Campbellville, Ontario, and her assistant trainer Joanne Nimigan. Ms. Emmert's popular TV Ontario series of the same name flooded her school's switchboard with training inquiries—and generated many photographs for this book! Most of all, I am grateful for the friendship and support my "Canadian connection" has given me on professional and personal levels.

Sincere thanks to my photographers the late Kevin Smith, Levon Mark, Lionel Shenken/Visual Productions, Dealing with Dogs/Campbellville, Ontario, and Dealing with Dogs/TV Ontario and especially to my canine models that withstood hours of photographic sessions and sometimes had to take a fake correction to illustrate a point for readers. You should know that some, but by no means all, of the shots of dogs doing dastardly deeds contained herein had to be set up. My canine models are certainly not up for canonization, but I wouldn't want anyone to think that Dalmatians, Dobermans, Collies or any other breed shown are inherently "problem dogs." Finally, my thanks to over 7,000 clients over twenty years who made me laugh, made me cry, but for the most part listened intently, were open to being educated, identified difficulties, changed some aspects of their own behavior and thus became people without problem pooches.

Job Michael Evans
New York City

Introduction

B Y THE TIME this book sees publication I will be "celebrating" my twentieth year "in dogs." For that fact alone some people have remarked that I should have been committed. Perhaps they're right. But there's a difference between being committed and having a commitment. My commitment began in the early seventies at a monastery in upstate New York, and continued in Manhattan where I later opened my own dog training school.

During these two decades I calculate that I have individually interviewed over 7,000 clients with problem dogs. People, pooches and their problems have dominated my life. In the early years I interviewed my clients, took their dogs into the monastery kennels for boarding and training and then released the dogs to their owners with some "exit" lessons. I had no choice: I was cloistered and couldn't go to clients' homes. Later, in New York, I went directly into owners' homes to interview and train. I have carefully studied the methodology and psychology of how owners accept information and criticism about their dogs. This book is the culmination of too many years working with too many clients who own too many troubled canines. Yes, perhaps I *should* be committed.

The "flagship" chapter of this book is "A Radical Regimen for Recalcitrant Rovers," which I always abbreviate as the RRRR program. It's a twenty point "hit list" that is levied, or inflicted (the choice of verb is yours), on a problem dog and on a problem owner. The chapter is new to this book, but it did make the rounds in a very limited fashion in dog training clubs and within the veterinary community via my ubiquitous seminars. After hearing the RRRR in those seminars, many members of clubs or veterinary associations asked to reprint the RRRR for their clients. I agreed in a few cases because I wanted to "test market" the program nationwide. The response has been uniformly positive. The program works. It is a canine/human version of the tough love techniques recently popularized to correct failing teenage/parent relationships.

Seeing the results practical application of the RRRR garnered was a heartening experience. Earlier, when I would prescribe the program I always felt like the Big Meanie, called in to regiment the dog's life. But seeing others use it and have it work has taught me that what owners of problem dogs desperately need is succinct, concrete advice, dispensed in easy-to-remember steps. Trainers are sometimes ooververbal. I try to make the complex simple.

The second core chapter is "Setting Up Set-ups." I don't mean to sound dictatorial, but I would recommend that you read it and *study* it. An understanding of these two chapters is absolutely essential if you are to grasp the theoretical underpinnings for *People, Pooches & Problems.* The concept really isn't that difficult. I'll be asking you to use your creativity and ingenuity to trick your dog into being naughty so that you can correct bad behavior. In so far as you are adept at trickery (let's face it, who isn't?) and at keeping the small details of the RRRR in mind, you should have success. Imagine that you've somehow copped the starring role of The Joker from Jack Nicholson in the latest *Batman* sequel. The Joker, of course, is also a trickster.

Fumbles and Foibles

The problem with owners of many problem dogs is that they either think too little or too much of themselves. Softhearted placating-type owners tend to think too little of themselves. Their lack of self-esteem makes it hard for them to grasp that they can stage a successful set-up. They are not used to being assertive or tricking anybody into anything. Instead they "enjoy" pleading and cajoling others, including their dogs, in order to get cooperation. Bombastic blamer-type owners, on the other hand, think way too much of themselves. They enjoy entrapment techniques because the execution makes them feel powerful. A middle course needs to be charted so that the dog is truly fooled by the set-up but not abused in the process.

I like to think that I can chart that middle course. I *have* enjoyed success in my dealings with my own dogs and the dogs owned by my clients. But this was not always the case. I once was a placating, cajoling, sniveling, shy dog handler. My family and academic background didn't exactly provide me with successful dog handling skills. A peek into my own early life with dogs—or more appropriately *without* dogs—might give you perverse encouragement if you think you are the world's worst dog trainer. You think you are? You're wrong. I once was.

Few good dog trainers are born. Most are made. Some of the greatest trainers in the dog fancy once disliked dogs or at least were supremely indifferent toward them. Nothing, and I repeat, absolutely *nothing* in my back-

"No dogs in this house," Dr. Evans had decreed, and indeed how could a dog find a place amidst this horde? No, this isn't a shot of the extras from *The Ten Commandments;* instead it's a photo of myself at far left with my siblings.   *Author's photo*

ground slotted me for the career I now enjoy. Even as a child I was informed that dogs were out of the question. This was decreed early on. My heart-wrenching story might comfort you.

No Dogs in This House

"There will be no dogs in this house," Dr. Evans stated flatly, "It would not be psychologically good for the family—and besides, there are too many of you." We sat around the dinner table, my siblings and I, eleven of us, looking sadly at the floor, casting dejected gazes at each other. "Maybe one of us could leave," offered my brother John. "That will be enough," answered my father, "the subject is closed."

Well, we had tried again and failed. There would be no dog in the Evans household. And after Midnight and Lolita who could blame my father? Those two hadn't been shining examples of training.

We were allowed to procure two dogs during my years at home as "experiments"—and they were short-lived experiments. The first dog, Midnight, was a black Labrador from the pound who after being with us for three days ran out onto the highway and was squashed by the Good Humor truck. We were heartbroken—yet, we hadn't the slightest idea what we had done wrong. So much for Midnight.

Lolita the Loser

The next candidate, about three years later, was Lolita, also a pound mutt. She was some variety of exotic Afghan/Golden Retriever mix. The shelter personnel looked delighted and relieved when we picked her up and wasted no time attaching a leash to her and almost pushing us out the door into our car as soon as we had signed the necessary documents. My psychologist father had since proclaimed the family more "mature and stable" than at the time of the Midnight fiasco, and everyone expected Lolita to work out fine. On the way home, seven children cooed to Lolita, who licked back and looked demure.

When we arrived home, my father was in appointments. "In appointments" was a phrase that every Evans child understood as sacrosanct. Dr. Evans maintained his office in the home. We had to keep absolutely quiet when he was seeing clients. The office complex was in the lower level of the house, and we had to tiptoe above it. I spent my childhood in stockings.

Ever try to keep eleven children, a stressed mother, and a brand-new puppy quiet? Twice Dr. Evans stormed up from his office complaining about noise, at which point we would take Lolita outside to romp. Lolita would then run back inside the first available open door and invite us to catch her.

We remembered: The receptionist at the shelter had said something about Lolita being "hard to catch" because of her Afghan background. We began to discover what she meant. She had also warned us not to take the leash

4

off the first day under *any* circumstances. Naturally, the first thing we did was take the leash off.

Lolita tore into the house with all eleven kids in hot pursuit. But she was long gone. She whipped through the entire house knocking over china, vases, precious heirlooms, and descended to the lower level of the house. She ran through the waiting room door of the office complex (which my dad had left open after one of his complaining trips), crashed into my father's office and flung herself onto the laps of the troubled couple he was counseling. My father, shocked, lunged for her. Lolita freaked out, dodged his grasp, ran into a corner and before the stunned couple and an even more surprised psychologist, defecated. Dr. Evans tried to make a lame joke about this being part of the therapy but the couple was too busy gagging to hear him.

Lolita was immediately returned to the shelter. She was greeted by the not-too-surprised receptionist, who, barely looking up from her *National Enquirer,* remarked to a coworker, "Well, Lolita's back." We made our apologies. I stayed after everyone had filed out the door to pet Lolita one last time.

Our next pets were two swans that had clipped wings and nested on the lake our house was located on. They hated children of any age with a passion, and would occupy our backyard, which sloped down to the lake. If we tried to go out to play, the swans would charge at us, hissing. We tried goldfish but we didn't take care of the tank properly. They all got a strange fungus and died. I grew up petless.

Unrequited Love = Frustration

Throughout high school and college I went without dogs. The tragic experiences with Midnight and Lolita plus a run-in with a heavily fanged German Shepherd Dog had converted me into a confirmed dog hater. If this was the way it was with dogs, what good were they? It was a defense reaction, I now realize, but my feelings were acute at the time. Dogs and I did not mix. I did not bother them and I hoped they would not bother me. If I saw a dog coming down the street I crossed to the other side. I closed my eyes during dog food commercials. I refused to buy anything in the supermarket stored in the same aisle as dog foods.

I detested the way dogs ran freely all over the quadrangle at the University of Michigan, totally out of control, breeding indiscriminately, while their student masters studied on the grass or did the same as the dogs. Before I made friends with people, I first attempted to find out if they owned a dog. Probably precisely because of my inner conflict, dogs never failed to come up to me, stick their faces in mine, snort at me, lick me, nudge me, paw me, grope me and do all the things that dogs do when they want to push someone over the brink. "Go say hello to Michael," my dog-lover acquaintances would enjoin the mutts. "Give him a *big kiss.*" The dogs always obliged.

During that time, I was juggling my interest in monastic life with anthropological studies. I loved the sections in archeology that dealt with canine fossils. I was chronic. The monasteries I visited raised animals or pursued other agrarian interests, and I could see myself in that kind of work easily enough. After all, the cheese-producing cows would sleep in the barn and I would sleep in my cell. *That* I could handle. But after visiting twenty-two contemplative monasteries, I managed to find something wrong with all of them.

Monastic life at that time was in a crisis of renewal, and the changes were being badly bungled in many houses. I was looking for a small, family-type community where brothers were a closely-knit group who had simplified work life and a rich liturgical life. Many of the monasteries I visited numbered over twenty monks, and I dismissed them out of hand. A group that size would be too large to sustain the deep relationships between the monks I was looking for, and I knew I had to have to live the life happily. Others had work occupations that were not inspiring—one house made cement blocks for a living, another baked bread. I wanted to be outdoors, close to nature. To me at that time, dogs were not a part of nature. They were a domestic frill inserted into otherwise peaceful and sane households. After two years of methodically searching for the right monastery, I had narrowed my choices down to two. One monastery was hidden seventeen miles off the main road in a canyon in New Mexico, far from family and friends and in a climate and terrain that were unfamiliar to me. That eliminated it from consideration. The other monastery was in upstate New York.

The monastery was New Skete, a collection of wood frame buildings which had been constructed by the monks themselves. In the center of the complex was a stunningly beautiful, eight gold-domed, Russian-style church. The place was surrounded by 500 acres of wilderness—silent, mountainous, serene. The brothers were loving and gracious. The liturgical services were touching. The monastery observed the Byzantine rite—and the beauty of the chant, the figures of the black-robed monks wreathed in incense, the intensity of the icons swept me away. This would be home. But there was a rude shock: The monks of New Skete supported themselves primarily by breeding, raising and training *dogs*. And they bred German Shepherd Dogs.

An Animal Laboratory

New Skete crawled with dogs. When I entered the community in 1972, about twelve dogs were in the breeding program, and there was room for four or five dogs of other breeds that came for training. Only four years after inaugurating the breeding program, the monks had already made a small name for themselves, and luminaries in the dog fancy were visiting the monastery frequently, trying to impart as much of their knowledge as they could to the monks. One woman, Marie Leary, a pillar of the German Shepherd Dog breed, remarked that the monastery was "an animal laboratory." She went on to add that she would rather work with the monks than many other novices in the dog fancy, "because I know they're serious, they will be working with dogs for a long time, they will probably be famous."

6

The brothers were originally farmers. The farm years spanned 1966 to 1969 and at one time or another the monks had goats, chickens, pigs, Holsteins, Herefords, sheep and even pheasants. Without realizing it at the time, the monks were receiving a grass-roots education in animal psychology and behavior. The monks had a mascot dog, Kyr, a German Shepherd Dog who had "flunked out" at Seeing Eye school because of a problem with his pedigree papers. He was a beloved pet, but he either ran away or got lost, and the monks never saw him again.

The house was empty without a dog, and other animals just did not fill the bill. Besides, the farm had to be phased out. It was not financially feasible and the monks were moving to a new location twelve miles away, high on Two Top Mountain. Brother Thomas Dobush, who died in a tragic automobile accident in 1973, had thought seriously about a breeding program, partly as an experiment (insofar as Brother Thomas "experimented" with anything) and partly as a means of livelihood—especially now that the farm was being phased out.

He contacted prominent breeders, procured some bitches and, on a very small scale, began breeding litters. More and more professional breeders and trainers recognized his sincere interest, which was spreading quickly to other monks, and visited. They imparted their knowledge graciously and openly, which is invaluable in a field that is self-learned. I was overwhelmed with the current that seemed to flow between Brother Thomas and the resident dogs.

Brother Thomas began to train the dogs to live in the monastery as a group and maintain quiet and order. "I don't want them in kennels," he said. "A Shepherd's mind will rot in a kennel." But there could be no fighting within the monastery pack. Each dog was assigned to a brother who was primarily responsible for its care. The dogs came to dinner, and as the monks said grace, they fell into down-stays and waited out the meal. During the meal, the dogs would remain anchored, and if one got up, it was immediately ordered to lie down. The dogs placed themselves behind the horseshoe-style refectory table, flung out along the dining room walls as if by centrifugal force. Feeding the dogs from the table was absolutely taboo. Even though I was afraid of the dogs, and held onto some lingering resentment, I wanted to feed them. I believed that if I fed them the dogs would "like" me, and it was very important to be liked by the dogs if you wanted to stay at New Skete. It never occurred to me that most of the dogs were simply not *interested* in me. I was just another guest, and a kind of regal aloofness is, in fact, written into the temperament section of the Standard of the German Shepherd Dog breed.

During my first meal with the monks, while I was still staying in the guesthouse and petitioning to be accepted into the community, the dogs eyed me with detached curiosity, calmly watching me as I took my place at the table, but they did not break their down-stays in order to greet me. One, Bekky, snoozed softly, and the others licked their paws, groomed themselves, looked at each other but did not get up. Not one gazed at my plate or drooled. "Good God," I thought, "this is incredible." I had never seen dogs behave that way, with such mastery, such self-control, such quiet dignity and poise. I realized that many of my negative feelings toward dogs stemmed from the obnoxious-ness of *badly behaved* dogs who jumped up on me, or just didn't listen to anything I or their owners asked them to do. I began to think, for the first time, that maybe, just maybe, I could get to know and like dogs.

But as quickly as that thought entered my head, the old myths took over. Poised behind me were two large females, lying down a few short feet away, directly behind my chair. I couldn't turn around to see what they were doing without making a fool of myself in front of the other monks, but my nervous-ness mounted as I reflected on the myths and rules I had learned in childhood. These were German Shepherd Dogs. I half believed that before the meal was over, one of them would lunge at the table, steal a platter full of food and scamper away. But worse than this, German Shepherd Dogs *bite* people, sometimes even *eat* them. My mother had told me plainly: *Never* trespass on a German Shepherd Dog's territory. *Never* pet one. *Never* turn your back on one. Here I was, sitting, eating a meal, in a strange place, with strange people, with two German Shepherd Dogs lurking behind me. The end will be merciful and quick, I thought, I'll never know what hit me, and I forced another forkful of mashed potatoes down my dry throat.

Then the abbot checked to see if everyone was finished eating and rose to say the closing grace. The rest of the monks rose in unison, and we sang grace, but the dogs remained in position. When the last note was sung, the monks turned to their respective dogs and said, "OK!" and the dogs leapt up. Everyone was petting a dog, and a large self-assured bitch, Jesse, sauntered over and placed herself squarely in front of me. She did not jump, nudge or nuzzle, but she looked as if she definitely wanted something and wasn't going to move an inch until she got it. "Well, pet her," Brother Thomas said, "like this." And he took my hand and like a baby's moved my palm back and forth over the dog's forehead. We both laughed at my behavior and Jesse too seemed to be smiling. My defenses crumbled and I knelt down in front of her and ruffled the rich fur around her neck.

"You can't stay here unless you like dogs—or can get to like them," Brother Thomas commented. "Oh, that won't be any problem at all—no problem at all," I answered in the most blasé tone I could fake. "Good," he responded, "Maybe tomorrow you can help me with the training. We have two dogs brought in recently. One is a Labrador that soiled the house and the other is a Great Dane that bites."

My throat was dry again. A Great Dane that *bites.*

My Own Dog

I managed to stay out of the jaws of that Great Dane and began training other dogs. I was also given a personal dog to care for. She was a three-month-old German Shepherd puppy named Cita. She had been procured from a top breeder in Massachusetts and came from a long line of beautifully bred, even-tempered, exquisitely structured and genetically sound Shepherds. Even

The then Brother Isaac and the then Brother Job with puppies at New Skete Monastery. I finally had a "dog of my own" to spoil, and boy *did* I!   *Connie Vanacore*

Today, with my friend John Arcangeli and the spotted wonder, Sport.   *Eileen Evans*

now, after twenty years as a professional in the dog fancy—and remember, I *counsel* dog owners—I cannot tell you all of the stupid mistakes I made in attempting to raise my first dog. But, I will be publicly honest with you concerning my mistakes, if you will be privately honest with yourself concerning your relationship with your own dog. Is it a deal? I will tell you this: Within one month I had taken this otherwise sound, open, gracious puppy and turned her into a cringing mass of fetal jelly. Shy, unable to approach others, Cita was a wreck.

Brother Thomas came to me to have a serious discussion. He was a six-foot-two monk of Ukrainian background with a football player's build. He cut an imposing figure and was in charge of everything concerning the monastery dogs. He sat me down and told me in no uncertain terms that I was making a mess of my first dog. "Cita's littermate Cheer is doing fine," he said. Cheer lived five miles away at the convent of the Nuns of New Skete under the care of one of the sisters who had excellent handling skills. "The problem with Cita can't be genetic," Brother Thomas continued, "It must be environmental. There must be something in her environment that causes her to have these shy, spooky reactions. I think that something is *you.*"

He then went on to tell me that if Cita continued as she was she would never be able to be bred. She could never be shown to the public without embarrassment. The monastery prided itself on the temperamental excellence of its breeding stock. It was routine procedure to show prospective puppy owners the mother of the puppy proposed for them. Displaying Cita as she was would certainly not encourage adoption of her puppies. "I'll give you one month," Brother Thomas decreed. "During that time we'll watch and see how Cita does. If you make changes in the way you handle her, there is a chance that she can stay."

I sat silent and flabbergasted, filled with sadness. I had failed with my first dog. I asked Brother Thomas to please, please, please, tell me *everything* I wasn't doing to make Cita more sociable. "It's not so much the things that you *don't* do with Cita that make her respond so defectively," he replied. "It's specific things that you *do* that make her shy." Again I asked him to please, please, please, tell me all of the things that I was doing to cause the shyness.

Brother Thomas took a deep breath and looked at me wearily. "Well," he said, "I can tell some of the things that you do that have to stop if she's to improve, but frankly I can't tell you *all* of the things that you do that are detrimental."

"But why?" I asked. "Go ahead, tell me everything, I can take it."

"There are two reasons why I can't tell you everything. First of all I would have to follow you around the monastery day in and day out because there are so many little things that you do with Cita that are faulty and I would have to be by your side every minute to point them out. The second reason I can't tell you everything to do or not to do is that you are simply not emotionally prepared to understand or accept the information."

"Then tell me what you *can,* and I'll work on that," I said.

"OK, I'll tell you what I can," he replied. "But remember, one more month and then Cita goes to a new handler if her behavior doesn't change. . . ." Brother Thomas then launched in, "First of all, you have your hands on the dog all the time. You are constantly stroking and petting her. The two of you look like a couple going steady—and we're supposed to be celibates! My advice is to get your hands off Cita and pet her only when she deserves praise. Also, you have the dog on your bed all night. You know that is against monastery rules. We have small twin beds. We run a breeding program. The sheets get stained when the dogs are in heat. There's not enough room for both of you in the bed. Yet, you persist in this practice. How do I know? The brother who does the laundry has snitched on you. Get the dog off the bed."

Brother Thomas then cataloged over ten other specific "tips" that I had better follow if I didn't want Cita shipped off. I began to try to change my "love affair" with my puppy. I suppose I made some progress—but Brother Thomas was absolutely right: I was too emotionally bound up with the puppy to understand what I was doing. For instance, I'd be at community recreation talking over the day's activities with another one of the monks. All of the other brothers would have their dogs lying peacefully on down-stays some distance away from them. I, of course, would have Cita sitting right at my side, her adorable little head plopped in my lap, my hand fondling her forehead. I would hear footsteps from behind, and before I knew it the powerful arm of Brother Thomas would reach over my shoulder, grab my wrist and remove my hand from the dog.

Did Cita stay? Unfortunately, no. Unfortunately for *me* that is. Cita was sent to join Cheer at the convent. Brother Thomas wouldn't even let another one of the monks take charge of her. "We have to get this dog as far away from *you* as we can," he said bluntly. My first dog was sent to a nunnery. The shame! The humiliation! I was the only dogless monk in the monastery full of monks with dogs.

Within one month the sister in charge had changed Cita into a loving, outgoing adolescent who was shaping up to be a fine brood bitch. I had been a bad influence on my own dog. In this case, at least the dog could be rescued.

Most lay owners in the process of ruining a dog obviously do not live in monasteries under vows of obedience to superiors. There is no one to point out handling flaws or dictate changes. Even if a spouse were to point out handling foibles that would be the ruination of the dog, most probably the dog would still remain in the household. In a sense, Cita was very lucky to be able to get away from me. It's an old saying in the dog fancy—and a sad one—that very often one has to ruin a first dog before succeeding with others. I don't believe it *has* to be that way. If the neophyte owner is willing to get educated, it needn't be, unless the owner is psychologically or emotionally impaired. I was. I hope this book helps you not to be.

Public Confession: A Closer Look

Let's look at my situation a little closer—remember our "deal," I'll be publicly honest with you if you will be privately honest with yourself. What do you think was *really* going on between myself and Cita? What did Brother Thomas mean when he said that I was not "emotionally prepared" to accept the help that he would try to give me? Was the root of the Brother Job/Cita dilemma the various "things" I was doing or not doing with the puppy? Or was the true cause much deeper?

It has taken me years to figure this out, but I now believe that the real reason Cita got messed up and could not be rehabilitated—at least not by me—was that I was unintentionally *using* the dog to supply myself with a certain kind of support, love and affection one would normally expect only from a lover or spouse. In my case, I should have been looking for that kind of sustenance from the community and in my relationships with my brother-monks. I'll go even further. The truth of the matter is I should have been looking *inside myself* for affirmation and love. But the Job Michael Evans of 1972 was a very different person than he is today. He was, in fact, a shy, skinny, socially inept, twenty-one-year-old kid, with some serious communication problems. How many times have you heard the old saying: "Shy owner, shy dog"? I am living proof that this saying is often true.

The upshot? I think you can see the lesson clearly in my own story. Whenever you relate with a dog in a needy way, asking the dog to provide a kind of support that only another human can provide, or a kind of support that needs to be drawn from within, the dog inevitably breaks down behaviorally. The emotional and psychological stress is simply too great for an animal of another species. Faulty body language and insecure paralanguage miscue the dog and destroy the relationship. Dogs, naturally gracious, giving creatures that they are, attempt to accommodate us in our misguided needs, but inevitably they break under the strain. They cannot bridge the emotional gap between the species. We've put them in an emotional bind. They become shy, spooky, aggressive, destructive or simply frustrated.

A good experiment is to ask your closest friend to make mental notes for one week whenever you talk about your dog. If the name of a spouse or longed-for lover can be easily inserted whenever the dog's name is used, this might spell trouble. We must be extremely careful what we ask of our dogs. They are our charges and our responsibility. We are their stewards. They are also our friends, and we can be theirs. But they are not our mates or lovers. Believe me, I tried: It doesn't work. I hope that this "public confession" and this book helps you to examine and deepen your own friendship with your "best friend," and, if necessary, to balance that relationship.

A perfect balance once existed between the leader and the led—in fact, still exists, within the social structure of the domestic dog's nearest relative, the wolf. A look at wolf behavior is in order at this point. It will clear the air—and perhaps your head—for all that will follow.

1

Wolves and Dogs

PEOPLE WITH PROBLEM POOCHES should make an effort to get to know the dog's ancestor. It can be very helpful. There is an extraordinary amount of interest in wolves among dog owners these days. It's not that we're talking less about dogs and more about wolves—some observers say dog people talk too much, period—but that we're talking about *both* now. This is a heartening trend because the more we know about wolves, the more we can come to know about our canine pals.

This kind of thinking is now the dominant philosophical basis for most training texts. Most trainers now view the dog as a member of the pack, a social being, an animal that can be praised and disciplined using techniques modeled after those used in wolf packs. A number of dog trainers—but not all—persevere in their dogged insistence that a dog is a little machine-to-be-trained, and keep dishing out the usual folklorish, cookbook remedies for behavior problems. But the tide is turning against this kind of approach, and this is shown clearly by the popularity of training texts with a naturalistic approach. To learn more about your dog, learn more about wolves. And you can do this easily in many cities. If your city zoo keeps wolves, my advice is to put this book down *now* and hightail it to the zoo. Go ahead. If you really watch, you'll learn more about your dog there in one hour than I can teach you in ten.

My first experience with wolves happened when I was a member of that religious community and was sent, along with Brother Peter, on a fact-finding journey to St. Louis, Missouri, then the home of several canine endeavors of great interest. For one thing, Dr. Michael Fox lived there and was then teaching at Washington University. We went to meet him and his wolf, Tiny.

After a short talk with Dr. Fox, he told us we would soon be meeting Tiny, a large grey Timber wolf, and we piled into the backseat of his Datsun, presumably on our way to meet the wolf. We had driven about one mile when I noticed a long tongue out of the corner of my eye. The tongue was licking my ear. Thinking it was a dog, I instinctively reached around and put my arm around the animal without fully turning around. But it quickly became apparent that if this was a dog, it was a breed that I was wholly unfamiliar with, and a very large breed at that. I turned around and my eyes met a pair of wolf eyes. We were about five inches apart. The wily Dr. Fox had forgotten to tell us that Tiny was already present—and when he noticed what was happening, he commented, "We're on our way to a large park to take Tiny for a walk," and added, "You should feel complimented. She doesn't usually relate well to men right away—men have too much ego." I did feel complimented, but I also felt like someone who had been set up for a blind date—in this case it was a success. The illustrative point is that ego, indeed, does frighten animals, and especially wolves, and it was truly better to let Tiny introduce herself, rather than attempt a frontal approach. This is something to remember with some dogs, too, especially aggressive ones. Sometimes when I am training I try to set up a situation so that the aggressive dog can choose to come or not to come to me. If you show absolutely no reaction, and especially no eye contact, toward the aggression, and yet are positioned so that you can save yourself from an attack, many times the aggressive dog will come over to you. This can be the basis for a training relationship that will later include elements of control and discipline for aggression, which can be increased incrementally during the training process.

Wolves can show us the way in many training procedures and problems, but their input must be evaluated on the basis that they *are* in fact different from domestic dogs in many of their behavioral manifestations. A good illustration of this is the walk we took in the park with Tiny. Dr. Fox had her on a rope attached to a regular dog collar of the wide, flat variety. At one point Tiny spotted a Beagle romping around on a small knoll and expressed great interest in approaching the dog. We had tried to stay in areas of the park where people would not see us and be freaked out by the wolf, and where we would not disturb dog walkers, but here was this Beagle, totally unattended and totally enjoying itself by rolling around on something that looked exceptionally dead and probably exceptionally smelly. This was just too much for Tiny to resist and she made a beeline for the Beagle. She had Dr. Fox literally in tow, and I wondered inwardly why he didn't use a training collar on the wolf and simply give a leash correction to stop the lunging—a true trainer's thought. But instead, Fox controlled the situation by letting the wolf zip toward the dog, but slowing the wolf down by exerting steady but gentle pressure, and finally turning the wolf away by making a large arc. I later realized that it is simply futile to stop the prey reaction in an adult wolf—it can only be controlled by prevention or diversion, not by the kind of force we use as trainers of domestic dogs. The concept of "timing"—so extolled among trainers and so important to the training process—just doesn't have the same significance to a wolf. This ability to take tactile correction, to adapt to and understand carefully timed corrections, is one area where the domestic dog has branched off, behaviorally, from the wolf.

Nor can wolf pups be leash-trained in the same way as domestic dogs. This was explained verbally and graphically to me on a visit to Wolf Park, a nineteen-wolf research facility outside the little village of Battle Ground, Indiana. Pat Goodman, second in command to Erich Klinghammer, who heads the park, was working with six wolf pups, trying to accustom them to the leash without at the same time convincing them to hate it. "They need *some* kind of leash work," she said, "because they will at some point be in contact with the public because of the educational programs we have here. But most training texts are not helpful—you cannot use a choke chain and you cannot dictate a heeling pattern." We worked with some of the pups, Pat instinctively giving directional tugs on the leash, giving the wolf pups freedom, within limits. It was a joy to watch her, and to see the pups respond to direction. In some ways they reacted as many young pups react at the first experience with a leash. They stalled, they squawked, and then they came along. But the impetus provided by the trainer was totally different from the greater amount of pressure that could be exerted, and more quickly, by a trainer of a domestic dog. And wolf pups didn't really care if they "got it"—there was not the desire of the domestic dog in their eyes or in their reactions. I mentioned this to Pat Goodman and she replied, "Well, why should they care? They're wolves, not dogs." Her simple answer again batted the point home to me, and made me appreciate both the amazingly cooperative spirit of the domestic dog and the integrity of its progenitor.

During my visit to Wolf Park, I did see one area of wolf interaction that validated what I had previously written concerning discipline for dogs. Techniques like the Shakedown and the Alpha-Wolf Roll Over came to life for me in a new way when I saw the wolves demonstrate them on each other. These discipline techniques are detailed in *How to Be Your Dog's Best Friend* (Monks of New Skete, Little, Brown, 1978), but it was one thing to write about them and another thing to see them. Mostly, the wolves did variations on these techniques. For instance, a dominant wolf will not always throw a rival or pushy subordinate to the ground and pin it in a full rolled-over position. Most disagreements don't come to that, but the dominant wolf might use eye contact to "cast a wolf down" or simply approach and put its head over the withers of the wolf it intends to discipline. The message, however, is clear: If you don't stop your behavior, I will execute the full discipline technique.

There is a point here for dog owners who misunderstand the use of discipline. Once you have your dog in line, which may include having a few episodes with him over the behavioral transgression, the dog should know clearly that you will go through the whole process if necessary. Trouble is, many dog owners *do* go through heavy discipline when they could have gotten away with vocal control, eye contact and partial discipline and stopped any bad behavior neatly with just those. Because training texts must teach corrections in a rather literal way, due to the limitations of the medium, there is often no way to show dog owners how to modify, subdue and adapt discipline so that the dog and dog owner are not in a constant state of war. Again, the wolves can show us the way. Spend an afternoon at Wolf Park or at a zoo that houses wolves and watch for nothing except how social order is maintained. You'll be fascinated—and you'll have to watch closely, for it is happening. But rarely is discipline a big event, a prolonged encounter or an ongoing trauma. It is swift and sure—and when you discipline your dog it should be swift and sure. The dog should get the point, and the discipline should have a beginning, a middle and an end, and not last more than a few seconds. I recently got a call from someone who had read an article on discipline and proudly announced, "Well, I used all the techniques on Rascal. I took him into the den and we had it out for an hour." The owner may have felt he had accomplished something, but I'm sure the dog just felt it was a game—the equivalent of big-time wrestling, and great fun.

The study of wolves can help dog owners in many other more subtle ways. You can gain a deeper appreciation of canine anatomy by studying wolves. Look at their structure, the way they move, the gait, the stops, the drive behind even the slowest trot. Look at their heads, and especially at the eyes. It's not a good idea to stare at a wolf for a long time, but if the wolf isn't looking at you, try to take in the eyes. They are iridescent, luminous eyes, full of teaching ability and knowledge that can be tapped into only by intuition and patience. Look at the way the wolves hold themselves, also—quite different from domestic dogs, and not all are equally self-assured and composed. The main exercise should be just looking and watching, seeing, and even as the poet Rilke says, "inseeing."

Before you go, bone up—read Barry Holstun Lopez's *Of Wolves and Men,* David Mech's *The Wolf: The Ecology and Behavior of an Endangered Species,* Dr. Fox's *The Soul of the Wolf* and anything else on wolves you can get your hands on, especially if it is illustrated. And then go, watch, insee.

If you ever have the opportunity to visit with wolves directly, à la my encounter with Tiny, do accept the invitation. I had a recent encounter with four wolves at Wolf Park, where I was allowed to enter the wolf enclosure after being briefed in proper behavior and asked to sign a paper saying I would not sue the park for any damages sustained while with the wolves. It is a necessary precaution because wolves are wild animals and stupid humans can easily mislead them by faulty body signals and other quirks. I was asked not to wear any earrings (no problem). My beard was, however, a potential problem, but Dr. Klinghammer thought it was short enough to pass. Wolves like to grab on to anything that hangs out, and when they grab it, they might want it, and there will be little convincing them at that point, that they can't have it. The thing they want could be your beard, and by extension, your face. There were other precautions, and when I was fully prepared, Dr. Klinghammer, Pat Goodman and I entered the wolf enclosure. Dr. Klinghammer continued to lecture to fifteen visitors who sat on bleachers and who had come to participate in the raucous Wolf Howl nights held every Tuesday and Thursday.

As soon as we entered, the four wolves flung themselves at us in greeting, jumping up immediately to nibble my beard. The jump was a driving, hard-hitting landing, somewhat like being thrown a cement block—again, so different from the jump of the domestic dog. Even chronic jumpers tend to inhibit their jump a little when they meet a person of authority (most trainers can attest to this) but not these wolves. Once they jumped up, they stayed and they started to lick and nibble. It was wonderful, uninhibited, sustained licking—a full face bath. I wondered how to turn it off, and Pat Goodman indicated that I should place my hand over my cheek, rather than try to push the wolf away as one would a dog. We stayed for about twenty minutes, while Dr. Klingham-mer continued to talk to the crowd, explaining the dual myths currently plaguing wolves. On the one hand, there is the "Little Red Riding Hood" syndrome in which wolves are seen as evil and treacherous, and on the other hand the more recent, developing myth (shared by some dog people) that wolves are really just Boy Scouts in fur coats, "just like dogs" and incapable of harm. Neither is true, as I so clearly knew from my own experience.

We exited, carefully slipping out of the pen, and the wolves returned to the center of the enclosure. I felt absolutely honored to have been with them, and as I glanced back with an affectionate look, I caught the eye of one of the aged wolves, who had been especially welcoming and warm in her wolf way while I was in the pen. Our eyes locked for a few moments and through her I thanked all wolves for the gift of the dog, and most of all for being themselves.

Every wolf was born of a bitch. So too with every domestic dog. Most wolf and domestic canine youngsters are also raised by a bitch. She is the first leader figure: the Alpha. Even orphan wolf and dog youngsters carry in their genes an ardent desire to lead or be led. But, usually, the bitch in either species imparts the basics they need to know.

2

Bitch Basics

EXPERTS aren't absolutely sure about the lineage of the domestic dog, but we are next to certain that dogs descend from wolves, *Canis lupus*. Maybe there's *some* other blood mixed in, but as you read in the last chapter, if we take our behavioral cues from the wolf, it's hard to go wrong in making some comparisons between wolf and dog behavior. Wolves live in packs. In every wolf pack there is an *Alpha* or leader wolf. This wolf is the head honcho. However, I hasten to add that sometimes the Alpha wolf is a female. The Alpha keeps order in the pack and keeps members of the pack on friendly terms. Just because we've domesticated dogs does not mean that we have changed their desire to lead or be led. If you can't function as your dog's leader, you probably should reconsider dog ownership. If you can't handle the job because of a lack of leadership skills, your dog will try to assume the role. The result is trouble.

This isn't a moral choice on the part of the dog, it is a genetically dictated response. The dog is looking for leadership, but if it is absent, the dog will attempt to lead the pack itself. Even if you live alone with your dog, it will consider you "the pack." Of course, you want to be your dog's friend, but your friendship must always include elements of leadership and ongoing demands for obedience and cooperation.

A bitch controls her litter of puppies in somewhat the same way an Alpha wolf packs a wallop with its pack—usually through low growls, various kinds of eye contact and occasionally physical punishment. Recently there has been some criticism of dog writers like myself who watch wolves closely and adapt wolf maneuvers to domestic dog dealings. We've been called, and not always in a complimentary way, "wolf watchers," and the criticism is trotted out particularly when we pander punishment Alpha-wolf style. It's said that very little physical punishment actually goes on in wolf packs, so the comparison is unwarranted. But that's exactly the point: I'm not advocating punishment as a *way of life* with your dog, but rather as a valid occasional ploy you must pull to get rid of problem behavior—which is exactly the way punishment is used among the dog's wolf ancestors.

Eye-Eye Sir (or Ma'am)

A leader wolf stares down a packmate or a naughty puppy with a hard cold look that practically freezes the offender in its tracks. This stare is often teamed with a low growl. *Grrrrrrrrr.* The leader never barks, yodels, screeches or screams at this critical juncture, but instead will lock eyes with the culprit and emit a low serious tone. The eye contact will be sustained for just a few seconds, and then the leader will look away maintaining an aloof expression. It's a transparent minidrama from the point of wolf watchers, or those experienced in watching brood bitches, but most subordinate wolves and puppies learn to respect "the look."

I've emphasized eye contact in all my other books, and now I'd like to go into how to obtain it in some detail. Don't skip over this section if you have a problem dog. You may think that your dog already looks at you enough. Trust me—it probably looks at you only when it wants something, or thinks it will get it. Often, when I bring up the subject of eye contact to owners of problem dogs, they will immediately state, "Oh he looks at me all the time." Closer examination shows that the problem dog does, indeed, look at the owner "all the time," but that this same dog usually wants something all the time, and knows how to get it—by looking forlornly or demandingly at the owner. This is not the type of eye contact we want. Because eye contact between problem dog and problem owner is often used by the dog in a *manipulative* way, a new kind of eye contact must be practiced in a formal way using the following steps:

- Take the dog *alone* in a room. There should be no other person, no other dog around. Remember, I said *alone* with you, no matter how artificial that may seem. If there is another person or another dog in the room, the dog may use that person or pet as an excuse not to look at you. Suddenly, your spouse will become the most interesting person on the face of this earth or your dog will become suddenly entranced with your kitty cat—*anything* to avoid making eye contact with you.
- Put your dog on a leash and sit the dog in front of you. If your dog doesn't know the sit command, a little upward tension on the leash will tend to hold the dog in the sit position. You want your dog on leash, because if it isn't on leash, it is free to walk away. You'll be demanding eye contact and the dog will simply saunter off. The leash prevents this.

The first step in getting eye contact with your dog is to make sure all excess hair is trimmed back or held back in some fashion—otherwise you can't read your dog—and I wouldn't be so sure this dog could read you through that veil of hair! *Kevin Smith*

Hold your dog in the sit position by keeping some upward tension on the lead. Touch the dog's muzzle and immediately bring your finger up to your eyes—this rivets the dog's attention on you as Alpha.

Judy Emmert /
Dealing with Dogs/TV Ontario

20

Having your dog in the sit position is also important because when a dog is sitting it will tend to look up into your eyes. If the dog is standing it will tend to make eye contact (depending on its size) with your kneecaps or ankles, which don't have eyes.

- Now, holding your dog in the sit position with some upward tension on the leash if necessary, bend down and touch your index finger to the side of the dog's muzzle. Immediately bring that same finger up to your temple. The purpose is to help the dog orient on your eyes by following your finger up from its eyes to yours. Sometimes it helps to "quarter-frame" your eyes with your thumb and index finger, clearly indicating the portion of your face you want to highlight.

- Simultaneously with the muzzle touch, emit an animated sound (similar to the type one would use with a horse) and then add a sentence that includes the dog's name and a request for eye contact, such as "*Psst,* Tippy, look up here at me right now." The animated sound gets the dog's immediate attention, the dog's name makes the pet know that this means *it,* and the sentence helps the dog to "lock in" with your eyes even more solidly. Choose a *sentence* though, because just the phrase "Tippy, watch me," might not give some dogs enough time to make full eye contact. It is very important that after bending over to touch the dog's muzzle, you straighten up your body completely to a fully erect position. Get those shoulders back, to force the dog to make the effort to look up at you. You should not be bending over the dog at this point, pleading with the dog for eye contact, but rather have a fully entranced animal sitting at your feet literally craning its neck up toward you.

- Once you have three to four seconds of "sealed" eye contact, end the exercise with some light verbal, not physical, praise. A simple "good dog" will do. Don't go overboard with praise just because the dog locked in with your eyes. The message to your dog is "When I say look at me, you *look.* This is to be an accepted part of our relationship from now on, just as it was between you and your mother." And, I might add, just as it was, and still is, between the leader wolf and pack members.

- You should be in and out of the "eye contact room" within one or two *minutes.* The point is to trot the dog into the room, get eye contact and get out. *Dazzle* the dog. The speed with which you demand, and get, eye contact from the dog makes a deep impression on the dog and prepares it to give you eye contact quickly during the course of a set-up. Some dogs might seem a little shocked and even perturbed about being dragged into a room and made to lock eyes with their owners. But, believe me, a certain dramatic swiftness when practicing eye contact is very important. There is a scene in *To Sir with Love* in which Sidney Poitier propels a recalcitrant student out of the classroom and into the hall, makes eye contact with him, issues a growling

By practicing eye contact you'll get an "overflow" of it in your general relationship with your dog. Day by day you'll notice your dog looking up at you, as if he wants to be told what to do—or simply out of love for you. *Kevin Smith*

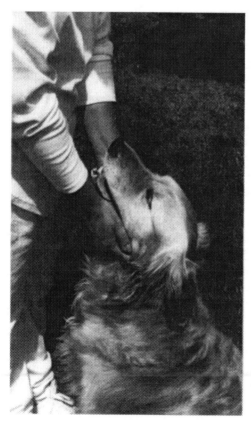

Occasionally there is a dog that simply refuses to make eye contact. Check all your techniques and if all else fails simply force the issue by cocking the dog's head up toward your eyes. Remember, hold the eye contact for only three to four seconds. *Dealing with Dogs/TV Ontario*

warning and then trots the student back to his seat. That student never misbehaves again in the film.

- By practicing eye contact, you'll start to get an overflow of it in your general relationship with your dog. Day by day, you will notice your dog looking up at you more responsibly, as if it wants to be told what to do. You'll find a corresponding *decrease* in manipulative eye contact designed to get you to give a treat, pet, walk or just drop whatever else you might have been doing and pay attention to Sweet Sam. Responsibility will replace manipulation, and one is just as satisfying to the dog as the other. In fact, many dogs become bored using manipulative eye contact because their owners respond *so* predictably. They welcome the challenge of responsible eye contact as taught herein, and their stress level is actually lowered because they no longer have to eye their owners into submission.

- Occasionally, there is a dog who won't make eye contact, even if the above structure is carefully adhered to. "He just won't give me eye contact" is a statement I sometimes hear from clients or at seminars. The usual complaint is that the dog simply looks away, looks at the ground or even at the sky, but avoids the owner's eyes. If this is happening double-check your timing and structure. Are you alone in a room with no distractions? Do you have a leash on your dog and are you holding the dog in the sit position? Are you nagging the dog in a whining tone of voice? You might try simply tilting the dog's head up toward your eyes by scooping one hand under its chin and using the other on its forehead for leverage. You might have to settle for a one or two second "lock" and call it a day. Whatever eye contact the dog grants you, don't engage in prolonged entreaties, begging the dog to look longer. This will only cheapen you in the dog's eyes and ruin the effect of swiftly granted eye contact. Ideally *you* look away first, breaking the "spell."

- Remember, the whole point is to leave the dog dazzled, thinking "What was *that* all about?" Don't worry if the dog appears bewildered—that is exactly the response you want, besides, of course, its undivided attention. The dog will find out later what "that" was all about when you use eye contact in steps one and four of set-ups. If you need to fine-tune set-up steps one or four, make sure you return to this section on eye contact.

No Collar, No Correction

You might think it is the height of stupidity for an owner to complain about a problem dog but have the dog walking around the house, constantly doing naughty things, without a collar on the dog. But it happens all the time. I've walked into literally hundreds of households where I am immediately jumped on, pummeled, goosed and occasionally bitten, but when I reach for

23

the dog's collar I find I am dealing with a nude dog. Of course, I can't give any kind of correction and the dog knows it. Owners of such collarless culprits have a bizarre array of excuses for why their dogs don't wear collars:

- *"It wrecks his fur."* It's interesting that clients with this excuse often possess beautifully groomed but badly behaved dogs. The interiors of their houses are often first-class in decor and style. The dog is seen as an ornament whose esthetic beauty must not be tampered with. This line of reasoning is simply ridiculous. Exquisitely groomed and coiffed canines at shows like New York's prestigious Westminster still wear collars. Go to a first-class pet store or get a top-notch dog supply catalog that describes which collar is best for which dog. But *do* get a collar on your dog, because you will never be able to stop bad behavior if your dog constantly runs away, dive-bombs under furniture and cheapens you with chases.
- *"He knows when it's on and only misbehaves when it's off."* The solution is simple. Leave the collar on whenever the dog is in your presence. The dog might not misbehave for a while because he "knows it's on," but, trust me, he will. Besides, you might have gained yourself a few days of peace simply because wearing the collar put the dog on good behavior.
- *"I'm afraid it will get caught on something."* OK, this *is* a possibility, but it's still not a valid excuse for having a collarless dog. Simply take the collar off when you leave the dog alone or unsupervised and put it on at other times.
- *"I like my dog to feel free."* How very sixties! I know this excuse sounds strange to some readers, but I hear it all the time; often from unreformed hippies or other antiestablishment types. Owners of such dogs often send their children to Montessori school, stock their kitchens with tofu and, yes, love their dogs deeply. Something about leather or metal irritates these owners. The thought of placing a collar on the dog is revolting. But all the love in the world won't help you to catch your dog, not to mention correct it, if it is smarting off. So take that red bandana off and put a real collar on.

Correct Collars

The type of collar is important. Assuming you've gotten over any fur or freedom hang-ups you might have had, choose a leather buckle collar for very young puppies or toy dogs and a training collar (sometimes commonly, but incorrectly, referred to as a "choke chain") for older or larger pets. Be sure that the collar is not too long. This is the most common mistake lay owners make in outfitting their dogs. Almost always the collar is too large or too long. I've seen training collars on Cocker Spaniels that belonged on Great Danes, and I've seen collars on Great Danes that belonged on Shetland ponies. Every

This collar is too long. It might do for a Great Dane, but not this Dalmatian. Make sure the training collar is no more than two to three inches oversize when pulled tight.   *Kevin Smith*

inch of "slack" on a collar delays a corrective jerk on it by one or two seconds!

I prefer a metal collar with pounded flat links. If the links are pounded flat and not rounded the collar will have smooth clean action that tightens and telegraphs a correction swiftly. Nylon training collars are OK, too, especially if coat damage is a major concern. Whichever type you choose, make sure that the collar is no more than two or three inches oversize when it is pulled tight on the dog's neck. Since most dogs have foreheads that are wider than their snouts it's likely that the collar will be very snug passing over the dog's head. It also means that the collar might be hard to remove unless you bring the collar up to the dog's ears. Gently fold each ear under the collar, working it over the dog's forehead. By the way, using the scruff of your dog's neck as a "collar" is not acceptable, especially when correcting a dog, even though the bitch used the scruff this way. The bitch used her mouth, grasping the scruff of the pup's neck with an inhibited bite, but in a way that tightened the neck skin similar to the way a training collar does. You cannot possibly duplicate this bitch technique effectively because you cannot use your mouth to grab your dog. Well, I suppose you could try—and you're going to get a lot of laughs. So use your collar or the shake technique (of which more later) instead. Mastering bitch basics doesn't mean that we have to duplicate everything that mom did exactly. We can use our human ingenuity, plus properly fitted equipment, to train and discipline effectively.

The *width* of the collar is also important and also often ignored. A thin jewelry-type training collar—even one with pounded flat links and good, clean action—will be useless in correcting a large dog. Conversely, a collar that is too wide will "clunk up" on a small dog and deliver a correction that is too harsh. Again, visit a quality pet store or peruse a good supply catalog.

Putting the collar on correctly is essential, otherwise the collar can't "telegraph and teach." Stand with your dog at your left side and with both hands dangle the collar in front of its muzzle. When you hang the collar in front of the dog's face it will look like the letter P turned sideways. The rounded part of the P will be facing the floor. Take a careful look at the photograph in this chapter. Of course, if you are using a simple buckle collar you don't have to worry about this aspect, but you do have to be sure that the collar is snug. When the collar is pulled sharply, be sure it absolutely cannot pass over the dog's head. There's nothing worse than a failed set-up that went awry because of a malfunctioning collar—except of course a dog who is injured because an owner used a collar that was too large and tragically slips off.

The Terrific Tab

Just as some parents fail to keep tabs on their children, some dog owners fail to keep tabs on their dogs. Now that you have a collar on your dog (you do, I hope, have a collar on your dog after the lecture I've given you), I want to go one step further and suggest that you put a "tab" leash on your dog. The concept is very simple: Take a leash and snap it on your dog's collar. Now take a pair of scissors and cut the leash off so that it droops down to touch the floor when your dog is standing. That's your "tab." Don't make the tab too long, otherwise the dog might get tangled up in it. Although this might mean you have to cut up a good leash, it is well worth the sacrifice. Now you will have a way to get your dog if it starts to act up or act out. It doesn't matter if the dog looks like a fool walking around with the tab on—get one on, pronto.

If your dog decides to chew the tab, you might have to get a metal chain leash, have a locksmith cut it off and attach that to your dog's collar. It's amazing, but my clients often find myriad reasons for not attaching a tab to their dogs. That's why I mention attaching a metal tab if necessary. Whatever tab you choose, get one on your problem dog immediately and leave it on for the next two weeks.

That's right, for the next *two weeks*. Take the tab off when the dog is alone, but whenever someone is in the household the tab should be immediately attached. No ifs, ands or buts. You never know when the dog might act up. Just instruct everybody in the family that Tippy has to be tabbed to ticket taboo behavior.

That's the purpose of the tab: It helps you to get a "grip" on your dog when it's naughty. For instance, if Chuckles steals a Frito and dives under a table, you can more easily retrieve the dog and discipline it if you have a tab to grab. If Tippy is enamored of charging at the sliding glass door that faces out onto the street and barking at anyone who passes by with another dog, the tab will enable you to come from behind and haul the dog off its assault. If Conrad is in the habit of sending you around and around through the kitchen, dining room and living room (all of which form a circular route), the tab will help to short-circuit Conrad's circuit because you can grab the dog more easily if the tab is flailing behind it. You couldn't if you had nothing but a collar to grasp.

Cheap Chases

By the way, problem dogs love to cheapen their owners by sending them on circular chases. They seem to get a kick out of it. Because many homes and apartments are set up with a free-flowing layout, the "route" is easy for the dog to memorize (any idiot could do it) and the dog delights in having the owner chase it around and around. Many owners actually think this type of track meet is funny, but I can assure you every lap you and your dog run cheapens you in the eyes of the dog—especially if the dog is clenching something that it's stolen from you. I must stress that if you think the chase is funny, and you prefer not to believe that you are being cheapened, you will probably not have the necessary motivation to correct problem behaviors that stem from these very chases. Remember, *chases cheapen owners.* So, if you laugh during a chase the dog will sense your weakness and perceive your inability at leadership. You might very well have the dog that you want. In this case see the chapter "Do You Have the Dog You Want?"

But, if you've truly had it with chase scenes, you will readily see the value of the tab leash. It makes corrections so much swifter and efficient. After a while the dog begins to realize that you have a way to retrieve it even when it runs for its traditional hiding places, ones that were previously inaccessible to you. Owners of extremely crafty dogs might need to put a very long tab on the dog, and might need the services of a private trainer. Oh, by the way, tie a *knot* two or three inches from the end of the tab so that if you grab it midchase the tab doesn't slip *pffft* through your grasp. The knot also helps if you need to plant your foot on the tab.

The Shake

I hope all you ever need to correct your dog will be eye contact, a low tone of voice and perhaps a tab leash. But, if you're reading this book, chances are those ploys haven't worked. You might have to employ some physical bitch basics. A mother dog would grab her puppies by the scruff of the neck and give a very sharp shake. The shake wouldn't last more than two or three seconds, tops, and the bitch would use an inhibited bite so as not to puncture the skin of the scruff. I believe you should simply *invert* the procedure. Grab from underneath the dog's neck, then elevate the dog and shake firmly. I don't want you to mimic the bitch exactly in her scruff shake because I do not want your puppy or dog to become hand shy. Approaching with your hands underneath the dog's neck is less threatening.

The way the shake is executed is extremely important. Interloop your fingers underneath your dog's collar and at the same time gather up some of the skin underneath your dog's neck. Now, suddenly lift your dog's front paws up off the ground while at the same time shoving your dog's backbone into the ground like a stake. This sudden, swift, upward thrust and downward stab startles many dogs into submission. It also makes certain that the dog's center of gravity is in the lower third of its body, which will enable you to dangle the front paws in the air as you shake. The front paws don't have to be more than one or two inches off the ground. The point is to simply disorient the dog in the front while at the same time pinning the dog firmly to the ground in the rear.

The shake should be "Al Capone" style, in and out toward your body, not side to side, and should not be exaggerated or flamboyant. Remember, just because you are getting physical doesn't mean you are allowed to get loud or violent. No screaming or shrieking! Keep your voice low and growllike as you shake and don't go over three or four *seconds* of shaking. I repeat: No screaming. In our culture most of us are trained that when we get physical, we can get loud. This applies more to the Western male of the human species than to many females, and probably comes from cultural indoctrination pertaining to sports that involve physical contact. But among dogs the opposite is true. When a bitch gets physical with her puppies she uses a very low growl, if she uses any growl at all, and the growl is very quiet, almost spookingly quiet, yet

28

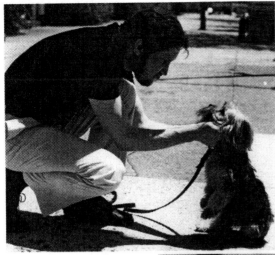

An effective shake: Interloop your fingers under the dog's collar, "plant" the dog into a sit, lift the front feet slightly off the ground and give an "Al Capone"-type shake. Remember, keep the correction short and humane—no screaming and no hysterics!
Charles Hornek

An ineffective shake: The dog is not being grasped firmly and it is climbing up on its owner—and probably thinks the whole ritual is funny. Compare this dog's eye expression with the Yorkie's above. You'll see submission and respect. Here you see play and even dominance.
Kevin Smith

The swat is more drastic than the shake and is reserved for big canine crimes: aggression, constant destructive chewing, housetraining infractions in older dogs and other "mortal sins." Remember, always go for the softest correction possible, but don't cheat your dog if you know you need to get tougher. *Charles Hornek*

29

firm. It's often difficult for humans—especially some macho males—to comprehend that loudness and extreme physicality doesn't mean that their authority will be respected. Welcome to a new species, mister macho, you've met your match, and you'll have to quiet down and calm down or resign yourself to an ongoing battle with your dog. The shake is never successful when overdone: Drama, surprise and timing are the keys.

The Swat

A more serious way of disciplining your dog is a swat under the chin. It's often easiest to stand with the dog on your left side so that your right hand can deliver the swat and your left hand can grasp the dog's collar. This correction stems from a basic correction by the bitch in which she swatted the puppy on the head or shoulders, usually with her paw (although I have seen bitches discipline large litters of puppies with their *tails* as well as their paws and mouth). We are again simply *inverting* the bitch's swat so as not to produce hand shyness in the disciplined dog.

How hard is the swat? Well, since the correction is more drastic than the shake, usually if you don't get a response like closed eyes or a yelp from your dog, the correction just wasn't hard enough. The swat is more immediate and startling than the shake. There are some dogs who will accept the swat but not the shake and vice versa. Many owners opt for the shake instead of the swat because they do not like the idea of striking their dogs. I sympathize with you, but must stress that sometimes the time it takes to put the dog into position to give the shake enables the dog to squirm away and the correction loses impact. The swat is much more immediate and forceful. Yet, it is fully valid because it is bitchlike. You do your dog a disservice if you use the more delayed shake when a firm, quick, startling swat is what the situation really calls for. This is especially true in the case of disciplining aggressive dogs. The problem, of course, is that often only an experienced trainer can effectively swat such a dog under the chin without getting bitten. If this is the case with your dog, you need to employ a trainer, or simply use collar and leash corrections. In other cases, especially with young puppies, the shake or only the slightest swat will effectively deliver your message. In general, it's best to always go for the *softest correction possible.* But you'll cheat your dog if you refrain from getting tougher when soft corrections are not working.

The Centering Spot

There is a special spot on your dog's head. Tapping it may help you warn your dog out of bad behavior *before* you have to deliver a physical correction. Massaging it will help calm your dog. I call it the "centering spot." It is located on your dog's forehead just above his two eyes. Perhaps your own mother tapped this spot on your forehead before you entered a store or another area where she thought you might act up. Mine did! I find tapping the spot to be quite powerful in warning dogs out of problem behavior. Several firm taps on the centering spot seem to focus many dogs and make them more appreciative of warnings and directions. In staging set-ups for bad behavior you'll notice that I stress the concept of emphasizing *phonics*—key syllables that need to be accentuated when giving the dog a warning or a reprimand. This is precisely when the centering spot should be tapped with your joined thumb and index finger, as in "Don't even *think* (tap) about it, *Spot* (tap), and I *mean* (tap) it!" Tapping the centering spot helps you to literally tap the warning or reprimand into your dog's brain.

It's interesting that this spot is called a Chakra point in Far Eastern religions. For instance, a Hindu woman will draw a spot on her forehead in this precise location to show that she is "centered"—meaning that, in that culture and religion, she has a husband and family. Jews at the Western Wall in Jerusalem routinely press their foreheads to the wall in prayer, melding the centering spot and the stones of the wall together. Christians, while in deep prayer, often bow their heads and press their enclosed fingers to this same spot. Look at a cross section of a dog's brain and the human brain—in other words, if you cut open the two brains like melons and lie them side by side—and a trained observer can see that there really is very little difference. The center, toward the front, is where both species feel emotions like love, hate, guilt or shame. Could it be that our dogs share with us a common centering spot? I certainly believe so, and have found that tapping this spot as a warning or a reprimand certainly seems to center many dogs. Of course, there is no way to scientifically prove such a theory. But, you didn't buy this book to read scientific theory—you bought it to tap into the lived experience of a longtime trainer. I can only tell you that the centering spot is the niftiest spot I've found on a dog's body—and not just for disciplinary purposes. It's amazing how many dogs go into practically a trancelike state, similar to hypnosis, when this spot is *massaged* as a form of praise, rather than tapped. Try this spot out for discipline *or* praise and you'll see what I mean. By the way, this is a spot I've seen many bitches "kiss" on their puppies. That's another bitch basic.

Some Final Cautions about Folklore Remedies

Responding like a bitch does not mean getting overly harsh with your dog! Practices such as hanging dogs by the leash, kicking them, throttling them and otherwise abusing them are inhumane, ill-advised and simply deprive the dog from learning anything. Usually, these "corrections" are manifestations of human anger, period! Anytime a dog is fighting for its life, for the basic right to *breathe,* that dog cannot possibly *think out* what it's done to deserve such a correction. It's a correction without any connection—quite apart from the deplorable "quality" of the correction itself.

Dogs are also often repositioned or restrained instead of corrected, and this can send mixed messages to the offender. Typical examples: the aggressive dog who is simply restrained lest it attack another dog or a human, or the obedience dog who breaks a sit-stay or down-stay and is simply repositioned in the correct space without any scolding.

The use of food in training is, of course, a controversial topic. In my opinion, you will not convince your dog to regard you as pack leader by the use of food. Verbal and physical praise are quite sufficient as rewards, and no bitch ever corrected a puppy by promising or withdrawing food. Funny—a full review of the existing literature shows food training to be a relatively recent phenomenon. It was rare twenty years ago. Your dog should work for you because it loves you, is bonded with you and wants to please. Let me tell you a super secret: Dogs are the greatest opportunists on the face of God's earth, and they are *thrilled* to get food for doing simple things they know they could do easily without food incentives. But please remember that dogs are also the most benign, forgiving, gracious creatures on the face of God's earth, and they will forgive you and perform, even if they don't get that cheese ball.

In short, if a correction is so harsh that you yourself can't imagine learning anything from it, the correction is probably incorrect folklore. If the advice has an air of finality behind it and doesn't allow for the fact that the dog and owner can revamp behavior, it's probably incorrect folklore. And, if you are advised to simply *reposition, restrain* or *feed* your dog rather than correct it, you might just have won the folklore lottery.

Finally, with the exception of overly harsh corrections, there seems to be a reaction from certain quarters against physical punishment in training—in some instances, a deep prejudice. But physical punishment *is* an acceptable way of dealing with unacceptable behavior in dogs and any good brood bitch can attest to it by her actions. Bitches physically punish their pups when they need to, and have no moral qualms about doing so.

If we are to master bitch basics, we might have to examine our attitudes toward physical punishment. While physical punishment is rarely needed, it is occasionally called for, and while "becoming a bitch" might not be acceptable in dealing with fellow humans, it is appreciated by your dog—after all, they do it among themselves, and have for almost 15,000 years. Don't worry that your dog will "hate you" if you get physical. Remember, its mother already got physical, and the problem might be that no one else has, at least not in a way that allows the dog to connect a correction with a connection. Remember, hands down, prevention beats correction. Read on.

3

Prevention or Correction?

YOU'VE ALL HEARD the saying "An ounce of prevention is worth a pound of cure," and only a fool would disagree. Books on problem behavior in dogs abound with preventative tips that can be used to circumvent dog difficulties such as not coming when called, pulling on leash, destructive chewing and a host of other maladies. I'll give you a hit list at the end of this chapter of preliminary maneuvers that you can employ to circumvent such problems. But first things first. Chances are that if you are reading this book you might be past the point of prevention and feel "condemned" to correcting your dog. Well, don't. Correction can be more difficult, to be sure, but there's nothing immoral about it! Besides, if I *only* preached prevention you'd join the ranks of frustrated dog owners who buy books in hopes of finding out how to stop bad behavior in its tracks, only to be told what you *should have* done, not what you need to *do now*.

You'll find that the emphasis in this book is on correction and not prevention. This certainly doesn't mean that I don't care about prevention. Along with the tips I'll give you for preventing problems, you'll find instructions galore in my other books, especially in *The Evans Guide for Housetraining Your Dog* and *The Evans Guide for Civilized City Canines*. But for some readers of this book, it might be too late for prevention. Again, it's not exactly a kindness for an author to list preventative measures that *should* have been taken months or even years ago. The owner of a problem dog who has moved past prevention and needs immediate correction is then left in the lurch. As distraught owners read over everything that *should* have been done, they sink deeper and deeper into despair. They accuse themselves of having blown it and can decide that it's too late to do *anything* now. They start up an internal mantra that goes something like "I *should* have done X when Rascal was Y years old, but I didn't, so now Rascal does Z. . . . I *should* have . . . I *should* have . . . I *should* have."

Psychological Put-downs

In fact, some problem owners love to look back at what they should have done or what could have been. Placating owners, especially, enjoy this type of self-castigation. It's a way of blaming themselves for the dog's problems. It adds a seemingly wonderful sense of hopelessness about the overall situation and justifies inactivity and even despair. Many owners of problem dogs have a love affair with despair. It's at least predictable.

The psychological roots of "should have" mind games reach down too deeply for me to analyze, but I can assure you the paralysis that results will do absolutely nothing to correct your dog. In my opinion, unless a dog is genetically defective, seriously ill or pathologically violent, it is *never* too late to attempt correcting problem behavior. First step: Give up all "should haves." Owners who enjoy reciting the "should have" litany need to find another form of prayer. They should instead meditate on staging sterling set-ups that will help eliminate undesirable behavior. I'll help you with factual information and with a theoretical framework that defeats most dog problems. I can offer you encouragement, sympathy and support. But if your personal psychological problems entrap you in the past, or if you actually enjoy beating yourself up because of what you should have done and didn't, you might be unable to appreciate the information or inspiration presented here. If you are caught in this game of psychologically putting yourself down, please realize that I mention it not to make you feel even worse, but so that you can realize that there are limits to what can be accomplished in a book on people, pooches and problems. While some reviewers have noted an emphasis on human psychology in my writings, I prefer to leave therapy to therapists. If you need one, get one.

Don't torture yourself as you read over the following preventative tips. Chances are, you didn't do a lot of the things listed, but there is still plenty that you can do now. Read over the list, which is presented in shorthand style, and as you bump into techniques that *should have* been employed, simply note them and use a given tip if possible. But if you can't use a tip because of a dog's age or the severity of its behavior, don't blame yourself, just resolve to do better next time. You can read the list to help you with your next puppy. If you are a far-sighted owner of a new puppy or a young "secondhand" dog, you're in for a real treat because most of the following tips are best begun during puppyhood.

Make sure your puppy thinks the world of *you*— so it'll want to come to *you*. Begin indoors using a hallway that will "funnel" the pup toward you. Remember: positive body language, positive tone of voice and positive eye contact!

Judy Emmert/
Dealing with Dogs/
TV Ontario

The best preventative measure to guard against your dog jumping is to never let the puppy begin to jump up. No matter how "cute" you think the behavior is, you can't have it both ways.

Judy Emmert/
Dealing with Dogs/
TV Ontario

PERFECT PROBLEM PREVENTION

Coming When Called

I believe that obedience to the word "come" is not completely a purely mechanistic response on the part of the dog but rather a manifestation of what the dog thinks of its *owner.* Your dog's opinion of you begins to be formed in puppyhood. In short, if the dog thinks you are somebody *worth* coming to, it'll come when called. If it thinks you are a littermate, or a complete bimbo, it won't. The preventative trick, then, is to teach your dog from the beginning that you are the star of the universe—its at least. Beginning as early as nine or ten weeks of age (when most puppies start to gain full depth perception) have a short five-minute "following" session with your pup. Your pup has a natural inclination to follow you, so maximize on this. Trace a simple figure eight, being careful to shuffle instead of walk, especially if your pup really hangs in close. You don't want to trample it! Pat your leg and move sideways suddenly, saying "come" as you do. Stoop and turn toward the pup after you say the command so that the pup winds up sitting in front of you. Praise heartily, but not for a lengthy period of time. Repeat another figure eight. Move sideways again, stoop and call.

Walk a straight line with your pup, but suddenly put yourself into reverse and walk four giant steps backward. The pup will probably forge ahead and it will take a few seconds until it notices you aren't by its side. As the pup turns to locate you, stoop and simultaneously say the dog's name and the word "come." Repeat three times.

When your pup is playing in an open field or wherever its play area may be, do not call and then immediately confine it. This will only teach the pup that when called it is always confined: end of play period. "Shucks," the pup will think, "I just won't come the next time." Instead, call the pup and then release it to play again. Every play session should be a little different—sometimes the pup gets leashed and/or confined on the first recall, sometimes on the fifth, sometimes on the third. Variety is the spice of successful recall training.

Another good tip: Have the puppy sleep in the bedroom. This increases bonding, which is the basis for steady recalls. When I cowrote *How to Be Your Dog's Best Friend* with the monks of New Skete, this was the first chapter I penned. In fact, "Where Is Your Dog This Evening?" was my first effort at any dog writing. Having the dog sleep in the bedroom might seem unconnected with success in the recall, but since your dog is coming to *somebody,* and granting the dog access to your personal "den" really makes you look like somebody super, it makes sense that recall rewards would be reaped from this simple practice.

Remember, if your pooch is past the puppy stage and is having a recall problem, begin immediately to retrain using the methods in chapter 18, "To Come or Not to Come." The follow-me preventative method won't be of much value, but use the in-bedroom sleep and the don't-call-and-always-confine methods.

Jumping Up

The best preventative measure to guard against your dog jumping up on you or others is to never let the puppy jump up on you or anyone else to begin with. This applies no matter how cute you or others think the behavior is. Teach the pup early on that you will only praise it if it presents itself in front of you for affection—never if it mauls you. See chapter 14, "Praise Problems"—the corrective measures can be used on pups as well. If you simply never encourage the behavior, you'll have very little reason to haul out heavy corrections for jumping up. Remember, no one else thinks the jumping is cute—even if they say they do. Trust me, they're lying.

Avoiding Aggression

Few dogs just wake up one morning and decide to turn on their owners. Unless the dog is genetically defective, the build-up to aggression is much slower, and thus more difficult for the indulgent or uneducated owner to detect. But there are things you can avoid. Don't play tug-of-war games with your puppy with *any* object. There is a new strain of thought in some training circles that says that such games are OK, and that dogs are *naturally* somewhat aggressive. I don't buy the argument. Dogs live in a specific culture— ours. They must not use their mouths on anything except their food and their toys. Making exceptions only results in double messages and a lack of boundaries, which the dog senses are changeable. Do not encourage any growling, overbarking, tug-of-war games or violent roughhousing no matter how much the pup seems to enjoy it, no matter how much the breeder may tell you that such activities are "normal" to that given breed. You are simply increasing the chances that you will wind up with a biter.

Socialize the *hell* out of your puppy or secondhand dog. Excuse the "French," but I repeat, socialize the hell out of your dog. The statement isn't really that far off or that risqué—for living with an aggressive dog *is* hell, and early socialization and exposure are the keys to avoiding such a state. Get your pup out to shopping malls, plazas, train or bus stops and other people-congested places early on. Park the dog in a sit. Keep some upward tension on the leash to hold the dog in the sit position, and when greeters approach (as they will, if you park yourselves long enough) *loosen up* on the leash and allow interaction between parties. Don't keep the leash tight—this telegraphs anxiety right down the leash into the insecure dog's cranium. If the dog jumps on the person, correct it. If the dog retreats, scoot it around from behind you and issue the sit-stay command with a strong flash of your hand in front of the dog's face. Allowing early retreats can produce a "fear biter" later on. And, if the young pup should growl or exhibit any aggression, *send the dog to the stars* with a firm swat under the chin. Blunt? Not at all. This is where it all starts, this is where canine aggression is born—and all too often the owner is the midwife. This is where it needs to be aborted. Your pup must know from the beginning that growling at, lunging at, snarling at or barking at *anyone* or *anything* without your express permission is *unacceptable* behavior.

Resolve from puppyhood on that whatever (short of physical abuse) someone else might do to your pooch does not justify any aggression on its part. If you make this a house rule, and an absolute dictum, you will not be psychologically swayed when a weird guest or set of circumstances seem to trigger Alfred to be aggressive. Instead, without even trying to figure out what is "bothering" poor Alfred, you will go into immediate corrective action. Alfred will learn to keep his aggression to himself, where it belongs. Most of all, examine your own motivations in getting a dog. If the dog was procured simply to provide a "service" for you such as protection, you might unintentionally have created an atmosphere that encourages overprotection. This is an old, well-known scenario among professionals in dogs. Usually the script features a placater-type "soft" owner who is scared of crime, a given neighborhood or life itself, and procures a large dog of a protection-oriented breed. However, if the original motivation was a desire for companionship rather than protection, the relationship would be off to a better start. In no other behavior problem do the psychological undercurrents in the owner's mind turn the tide of events as they do in problems of canine aggression. Your motivations, needs, desires and expectations as an owner plus your determination or lack of determination to seek out early training are pivotal here. If you don't want a grouch, train early and train hard.

Circumventing Chewing

If you want a puppy who will go through only a natural chewing and teething stage and then keep its mouth to itself, find a reputable breeder who puts his money where his mouth is. In other words, if you buy a quality puppy from a quality breeder, it's my firm belief that the temperamentally sound pup can easily assimilate corrections for chewing—even corrections after the fact. Brain power comes out of good breeding. The smarter puppy can more easily be humanely corrected early on.

Avoid the temptation to provide the newcomer with zillions of chew toys. You will unintentionally teach the pup that *everything* is a potentially chewable item. Obviously, do not let the pup chew on *you* at all. It's a small step for the pup to deduce that if it's OK to chew on you, it's OK to chew on your belongings.

A smart owner will also avoid the temptation to make a production number out of saying hello or good-bye to the pup. If you make these really commonplace daily events into high-powered or heart-wrenching scenes you'll simply set the dog up to become frustrated. Of course, the classic release valve for frustration in puppies is to chew—often a scent-soaked item—in order to get "closer" to the owner and relieve anxiety. When you leave, give the pup a brief pat, and when you return, no matter how excited the dog is, simply say a sweet, sincere hello and go about your day. No, the puppy will not hate you for playing it cool—and you'll be doing yourself and the pup a favor.

If the pup is chewing on something unacceptable, reprimand it in a growllike tone, but don't feel you have to immediately run and shove an acceptable item in its mouth—and do *not* praise it simply because it stops chewing on the illegal item. If you want to offer an alternative after reprimanding your dog for inappropriate chewing, offer the acceptable item only 50 percent of the time. The rest of the time let the pup learn to inhibit its own chewing compulsions. Remember, you won't be home to pop an "OK" item into its mouth all the time. At those times, the pup will have to seek one out itself or simply wait and chew nothing.

Be careful about toys. Don't buy or offer any that have a squeaker that can come dislodged. Certain breeds, especially some of the terriers, love to "kill" such toys; there are squeak toys available that have inverted noise makers that cannot be swallowed. Also, please, no foam or supersoft toys, and obviously, no old shoes or items of clothing from your wardrobe. The puppy can't tell the difference between old, beaten-up tennies and Guccis, B.V.D. underwear or Calvin Kleins.

Shunning Shyness

If you have a brand-new puppy that is acting extremely shy, my advice to you is to immediately, as in *now,* call the breeder and discuss the situation. Instead of calling with vague complaints of shyness, make a list prior to the call as to the *specific* instances of shyness. This will give the breeder something to go on, and will enable him or her to distinguish between what is a matter of the pup simply adjusting to life in a new environment and without its littermates and true genetic shyness. I stress immediate action because genetic shyness is the hardest to "train out" or modify, and even with training, such a dog may always be a management problem. It would be better to return the pup and start anew. There's also a chance that a mismatch has occurred and a shy person has wound up with a shy puppy—which is always a prescription for disaster. While you should know when to return the pup, it is also imperative that the breeder learn proper placement procedure.

Problems of shyness call for remedies similar to those used for discouraging aggression. Socialize your puppy or secondhand dog early on. Again, get out to shopping malls, train or bus stops—wherever people congregate or pass by—and just park yourselves. Keep some upward tension on the lead and sit the dog on your left—the tension will hold the dog in the sit. However, do *not* choke the dog with tension on the lead, and if someone approaches, *loosen* the lead, but do not allow the shy dog to retreat behind you. Often, your leash manipulation will be a combination of tightening and loosening the lead in order to keep the shy dog who wants to retreat in place, yet not telegraphing anxiety down the lead by having it too tight. Obviously, owners of shy dogs need to enroll in obedience class as soon as possible. The trick—and the hardest part—of getting your dog to shun shyness is to be tough and not to coddle the shy dog at all. If shyness has already set in, set-ups are in order, and you will need obedience training in order to execute them. So, off to class with the two of you!

Lying Down

In *The Evans Guide for Housetraining Your Dog* I detailed a method for getting your potentially messy canine resting comfortably by your side—before the dog has learned the words "down" or "stay." Besides the housetraining benefits, the technique has many other dividends. Be sure your pup is at least four months old before trying this technique. Attach a six-foot-lead to your pup, and bring the dog around to the side of a chair. It's best to start with a dining room chair rather than a low-slung couch, as the height of the chair will discourage the dog from bothering you. Take the other end of the lead and place it underneath your buttocks. Push your pup down to the ground. Measure out just as much lead as the dog needs in order to hit the dust—that's your goal. Correct the dog for any naughtiness. If the pup jumps up on you, whip the leash down hard and say, "No!" If the pup pulls on the leash, your dead weight will stop the dog from pulling any further. If the dog bites on the leash, whip the leash diagonally up and toward your body and say, "No!" No nonsense during this quiet time. Sooner or later, the dog will start to figure out that it might as well lie down—as you allow no other alternatives. I suggest having a young puppy hold such a thirty-minute down (yes, that's *thirty minutes*), beginning at age four months, forever. Yes, I repeat, *forever.* That's right, one thirty-minute down a day for *life* beginning at age four months. This must be an owner-enforced down—not just a time when the pup or older dog is snoozing and lying down anyway. Naturally, as you train commands, you will not have to sit on a leash anymore. But, for now, anchor your dog with the dead weight of your body. Trust me, you'll be investing in a solid future of steady, unwavering "free-lance"—that is, off leash—long downs, because your dog will already be comfortable holding the position for a lengthy period of time. Later you'll be able to use this expertise on your dog's part to take it to many, many places you would otherwise not even *think* of taking it— because you will be confident that you can "park" your dog. In short, park early and save later!

Walking Nicely on a Lead

Early leash training is the key. Your initial method can be quite simple. Attach a six-foot leash to your puppy's collar. Be sure the pup is at least four months old and wearing a buckle collar, not a choke collar. Drop the lead. Let your pup walk around like this for ten minutes each day. At some point, the pup will step on the lead and "correct" itself. The pup will look startled. Do not praise or coddle the pup at this point even if it screams when it steps on its own lead. Since you are not holding the lead, you will not look like the bad guy who choked the pup. It's amazing how quickly many pups learn on their own to somehow (there are a variety of methods) keep that lead over to the left or right side of their bodies—rather than get zapped by stepping on it yet again. Of course, this is exactly what we want: to have a pup that respects the lead. Go one week using this method. In week two, come from behind and gently pick up the lead and walk a few steps with the pup. You might also simply stop, without correcting the pup with a huge tug. As early as the fifth month, teaching a more formal "heel" can and should be started. Do it in class or from a book, but do it.

"Preaching to the Damned"

I recently told a fellow trainer that I was going to include a section on prevention in this book because I didn't want to simply offer corrective tactics. "Besides," I added, fantasizing, "perhaps, just perhaps, there will be new owners of puppies far-sighted enough to invest in a book on problem behavior just *in case* they ever have problems." "Magical thinking," my trainer friend replied. "Owners don't turn to problem books until they have one. Every puppy owner thinks—at least for the first two months—that everything their puppy does is saintly or just a *little bit* naughty. A section stressing prevention will be preaching to the converted, and the rest of the book will be preaching to the damned." I disagree. I do not consider naive puppy owners "converted" to anything except infatuation and romance. Nor do I consider an owner of a problem dog "damned." If this chapter caught you at the right time, great. Use the material presented here and you might not need the rest of the text, but you can never be sure. Remember, most dogs, no matter how preventatively trained, socialized, schooled, disciplined and educated, will *try everything at least once.* At least you'll be ready to administer corrections armed with the rest of this manual.

For those of you with older, terribly naughty or even criminal canines, you have a choice: You can read over this chapter and use the fact that you might not have done (or had the *chance* to do) this, that or another technique, and collapse into despair and inertia or catatonia, or you can say to yourself, "So what about the past and what I or somebody else did or didn't do? I have the dog I have the way it is today—and if I want a better dog I can build one. I can train, or I can complain.

4

A Worthy Cause

E VERY PROBLEM POOCH has a *reason* for misbehaving. Dogs do not sit around deliberately trying to think of how they can thwart their owners. There usually is a *cause* for bad behavior. Experienced trainers learn not only to evaluate actual bad behavior but to ask, "What is *driving* or *motivating* this problem dog?" Inexperienced owners, however, concentrate only on the *symptoms* or *results* of the unpleasant behavior. They just want to get rid of the unpleasant aspects of the behavior as soon as possible: If the dog continues to have a *cause* that it thinks is a worthy one for doing something obnoxious, that's the *dog's* business, and not something many owners want to be bothered about.

In fact, this book itself concentrates on alleviating the symptoms and the results of bad behavior by staging set-ups to weed them out. But, we must never forget the fact that the dog has reasons for the way it acts. Unless the underlying causes of bad behavior are addressed, set-ups can be staged until the cows come home, but the dog may still misbehave. So before designing a set-up, ask yourself: "*Why* is my dog misbehaving?" Let's look at some examples.

- Let's say your dog barks when you leave your apartment. In fact, it does more than bark. The dog yodels, screams, shrieks and screeches so dramatically that your neighbors are ready to lynch you both. A set-up to alleviate these intense vocalizations is easy enough to concoct. You would issue a warning to the dog as you leave, exit, explode back into the apartment at the first whimper, humanely discipline the dog verbally and/or physically, repeat your warning and leave again. Set-up steps 1, 2, 3, 4, 5. Simple, eh?

Let's look into this situation a little more deeply. If you are in the habit of trying to soothe your dog out of barking when you leave the house, coddling it, cooing to it gently and pleading with it not to bark, you might be in fact setting up a situation that will *encourage* the dog to bark. You will be intensifying the natural anxiety the dog feels when you, its pack leader, abandons it. This "separation anxiety" is the cause of the barking. The resulting operatic performance is just the result or a *symptom* of the real problem. Since you can't avoid leaving home (after all, someone's got to buy the dog food), thus alleviating separation anxiety completely, you can at least alleviate the dog's stress by avoiding overly dramatic hellos or good-byes. For more on overbarking, see the sections that deal with separation anxiety elsewhere in the book. For the purposes of this chapter, I think you can readily see how very important it is to look for the underlying cause of the barking rather than just correcting the dog for it. If you continue to emotionally overload the dog when leaving, and only stage a set-up to correct the barking, chances are the set-up will fail—or the dog will express anxiety in a different way. For instance, it might start to engage in destructive chewing, bed wetting, or even self-mutilation. You will have corrected a symptom but not the cause.

- Or let's say your dog has gotten into the habit of leg-lifting on everything when you are away from the house. A set-up to correct the symptoms of this problem is also easily devised. You would issue a warning upon leaving, return later, discipline if there is evidence of leg-lifting, reissue the warning and leave again. As simple as set-up steps 1, 2, 3, 4? Not necessarily. But again, let's look a little more deeply into the matter. There might be several causes—worthy ones in the dog's eyes—for the leg-lifting. For instance, let's say you simply haven't walked the dog enough, or on schedule, and its bladder is bursting. That seems to me to be a worthy cause for letting loose! Or let's say you leave a large amount of water for your dog when you leave home. Out of anxiety, some dogs drink a lot of water immediately after their owners leave, not realizing that they will have to "hold it" for several more hours. Or, let's say that your relationship with your dog is so corroded that the dog has you permanently slotted as submissive, and leg-lifts to establish territory and maintain its dominance over you.

Unless you identify and address underlying causes your set-ups will probably foul-up. You could get the dog emptied out and walked on schedule. You could leave less water, or leave a bowl of ice-cubes that will melt down slowly, preventing your dog from tanking up out of anxiety. If you sense that your whole relationship with your dog is marked by such a lack of leadership that this is the cause of the leg-lifting, you could place the dog on the Radical Regimen for Recalcitrant Rovers (RRRR). The point is, unless you identify the cause or causes for the objectionable behavior, simply staging set-ups probably won't stop it. Remember that sometimes there are several causes for a given canine behavior and all of them have to be identified and, if possible, alleviated.

All for the Cause

I mention the concept of cause and effect at an early point in this book for a good reason: Domineering "blamer" owners with problem dogs are often thrilled to learn how to stage set-ups to correct the *results* of bad behavior but don't want to take the time to look into what *causes* it. The relationship with the dog then becomes a battle in which the dog has to submit to set-up after set-up and is sometimes literally beaten into submission. Symptoms and results of bad behavior are corrected, but the dog continues to live on a level of supreme frustration.

That said, and those owners warned, I will also say that sometimes it's just not possible to fully address the cause of bad behavior. For instance, most owners have to leave their dogs alone, at least temporarily, so the basic cause for some overbarking and destructive chewing *can't* be changed. The problem behavior must still be corrected. Or consider, for instance, a genetically defective dog. The genes cannot be manipulated. If genetic defects are the root cause of shyness or aggression, set-ups might help only to a degree. The root cause of the difficulties can't be considered or corrected because it is untouchable. But it's still almost always worth trying to correct the bad behavior itself. But not knowing the cause, or not being able to allay it, can prevent full rehabilitation.

Trainer Tips

Often, a professional trainer will know very well what the cause of undesirable behavior might be but will mention it only in passing and immediately concoct remedies to stop whatever it is the dog does that is annoying. This is OK as far as it goes. After all, you *are* paying the trainer or specialist for some relief. However, a good trainer will not only provide you with specific techniques and tips for specific problems, but will help you to understand what is driving the dog—in short, the cause of the problem. You will then have a much deeper understanding of your dog's dilemma.

Remember, though, not to get obsessed with the cause of the bad behavior. Sometimes you will just not be able to change it. Very often a good trainer will, while mentioning the underlying cause of the bad behavior, appear to downplay it, and will want to get right to work on the symptoms and results of the behavior. This is not necessarily an oversight or an evasion. The trainer is, after all, employed by you to eliminate problem behavior—with your cooperation, of course. Give it.

On the other hand, beware of trainers or behaviorists who discuss *only* the causes of behavior, but never help with remedies for the problems themselves. It is of no use for a professional to come into your home and reveal to

44

you that your dog overbarks when you leave because of separation anxiety, collect a fee and leave. You will be a poorer person who still has a barking dog. This syndrome is especially common among professionals who have received only academic training and have little or no direct training experience with real, live problem dogs. A diagnosis will be dished out, but little else. Diagnosis without direction spells disaster.

A Human Analogy

Just as domineering blamer-type owners could care less about the cause of a problem, placater-type owners will use the cause as an excuse not to correct the problem behavior itself. I've had some clients who actually seem to *enjoy* the frustration of not being able to alleviate an underlying cause of a bad behavior and feel it is "unfair" to the dog to correct the manifestations of bad behavior when nothing can be done about the cause for it. While I sympathize to a degree, once a sincere effort has been made to research the cause of the dog's behavior, I feel it is a disservice to simply give up on the dog or give the dog tacit permission to continue irksome behavior.

Let me paint my philosophy concerning cause and effect in canines by giving you a *human* example of how a leader figure might confront the phenomenon. Let's say you are a parole officer. You have a sixteen-year-old client: a criminal who steals, specifically, items from stores. This client was assigned to you after being caught and sentenced to community service and to counseling sessions with you. You delve into your client's background in order to understand and help this young person more completely. You ask many, many questions trying to find out the *cause* for the shoplifting. You learn that your client comes from an impoverished background, is a member of a disadvantaged minority group, grew up in a ghetto and hung around with friends who are also fond of filching. You begin to understand that peer pressure, racism and classism are all possible causes for the stealing. Some of these causes can be changed and some cannot—at least not by you alone. What should you do? Sympathize and tell the person it's OK to steal because of everything he's endured? Tell the youngster to try to "cut down" on shoplifting "just a little"? Of course not! Instead, you are going to tell your client that if there is any more stealing, you will, in your capacity as parole officer and leader figure, correct the behavior with punishment and incarceration. You might appear to be unsympathetic to the underlying causes for the behavior, but you know you are doing the right thing.

The above situation mirrors the attitude I have toward problem dogs. If a dog is displaying unacceptable behavior I am sensitive to possible causes for the behavior, but I will not allow the dog to continue with it. In my early days of dog training I made excuses for problem dogs because they had solid reasons for doing what they did. Now I walk a middle course. I try to examine the cause, without *over*examining it, and go directly to work on the problem itself.

I suppose one could say that the original, root cause for all of the problems that we experience with our dogs is that we ourselves domesticated them. Perhaps we should have left them to their own devices in the wild. But we *did* domesticate them, didn't we? So, it is our responsibility, as their stewards and leaders, to make them as comfortable as possible in human society, in return for the great deal they give us. It's also our responsibility to correct them humanely if they abuse the covenant we made with them thousands of years ago. For better or worse, we are together, we two species. We might not always understand the other's causes and reasons, but we are honor-bound to compromise, and, if necessary, correct.

5

Do You Have the Dog You Want?

OFTEN terribly troublesome dog behavior problems result from an owner allowing eighty zillion little problems to go unchecked. Well, at least the *owner* perceives the little problems as insignificant. Little incidents of bad behavior are excused because the infractions really aren't that bothersome. Worse yet, an owner might think that some of the small-time naughtiness is comical and cute. These are the same owners who go into catatonic shock when they read over the twenty points of my Radical Regimen for Recalcitrant Rovers. About ten of the twenty points in the RRRR program mention various forms of obnoxiousness that dogs engage in that many owners think are cute. Some owners read the RRRR and think that I am telling them not to allow their dog to be cute anymore. This disappoints them deeply. In short, there are owners who really don't want to change bad behavior. They think the project is too overwhelming and will squash the personality of the dog. Essentially, these owners have the dog they want. Here are some examples.

- Munchkin loved stealing Fritos from the coffee table. He had done it for years. He does it in front of his owners. He does it in front of guests. And of course he does it when he's left alone in a Frito-filled room. It took some sleuthing to have the owners even reveal this instance of major bad behavior. I asked, *"Does your dog do anything you know in*

Do you have the dog you want? Are you "unintentionally" training in bad behavior? This owner enjoys feeding her "favorite" crackers and cheese.

Judy Emmert/
Dealing with Dogs/
TV Ontario

It's party time! Now the "favorite" is joined by dog number two. On with the festivities.

Judy Emmert/
Dealing with Dogs/
TV Ontario

Suddenly the phone rings in another room and our owner is called away....
Do you have the dog you want?

Judy Emmert/
Dealing with Dogs/
TV Ontario

your heart is naughty but you still find funny?" Both husband and wife looked down toward the floor with embarrassed grins on their faces, hesitating to answer. Finally the husband raised his eyes sheepishly toward me and said, "Well, there's this Frito thing . . ." And both the husband and wife burst out laughing. They thought the behavior was cute. But there's only one problem. The reason I was sitting across from them, employed as their trainer, was that Munchkin recently lunged at the husband when he tried to retrieve a piece of steak that had fallen from his plate onto the dining room floor. Munchkin, who naturally resided during meals under the table (instead of off to the side on a down-stay where he belonged), felt that the piece of steak had been delivered from heaven expressly for him. "Will he turn on us?" the wife asked. "No," I answered, "but you'll have to stop laughing at his Frito stealing or he'll be filching much more than pieces of steak." The wife couldn't see the connection between Frito filching and the mounting aggression of the dog. She had the dog she wanted.

- Chuckles was a "humper." He belonged to a twenty-six-year-old single man. And of course wasn't neutered. All this owner had to do was cross his legs and angle his kneecap in a certain provocative way and Cocker Spaniel Chuckles promptly mounted it. The owner would then swing his crossed leg as Chuckles grasped his calf in his entwined paws and enjoyed the "ride." Chuckle's sexual mounting became a kind of party tradition. The gentleman was even asked by his friends to bring Chuckles along for various "shows" around the city. When the owner called me to explain the problem, at first I thought it was a prank call or a joke, especially when he became rather graphic in his description of Chuckle's escapades. "What do you think this is, a porn line?" I asked. The owner then explained that it was indeed a serious problem. He revealed that recently, when he tried to scrape Chuckles off his leg in order to get up and answer the phone, Chuckles had growled at him. I explained that the first step in eliminating this problem would be a change in attitude. The owner could no longer laugh at, enjoy or condone *any* sexual mounting. Later I found out that the owner had stopped the mounting for a while. He was afraid the dog would turn on him. But Chuckles had resumed his "appearances" around town and the client had not followed my instructions to neuter him. After Chuckles growled at him a second time the owner called me to complain. After double-checking to see whether my previous advice had been followed, I said simply, "I don't think there's much more I can do for you. I think you have the dog you want."

- Muffin was a "nudge." She liked to gently push her mistress on the leg, on the arm, even on her rear end. Muffin's favorite nudge maneuver was to wait until her owner was holding the morning paper with one hand and a cup of coffee with the other. Muffin would circle behind and stick her head underneath her owner's armpit, nudging the owner's arm upward. The owner had learned, after being scalded a few times, to fill her coffee cup up only halfway. She thought Muffin's behavior was cute. Of course I didn't even find out about the morning scenario until I carefully interviewed the owner and asked my famous question: "Does your dog do anything you know in your heart is naughty but you still find funny?" Why was I called in for a consultation? Three times in the last week Muffin had destroyed the morning paper. Ripped it up into a million tiny pieces. Nothing else, just the morning paper. On those same mornings, it turned out, the owner had not had coffee and had read the paper with *both* hands, depriving Muffin of her morning nudge. Muffin was jealous of the attention paid to the paper. The nudgery had to stop or the destruction would continue and probably expand in scope. This owner immediately saw the connection between the small instance of bad behavior that she thought was cute (nudgery) and the larger problem that was potentially developing. She did a set-up to trick Muffin into nudging (it wasn't hard to do). The owner ceased to think that the behavior was cute, and on a deeper level, she decided that she really didn't have the dog she wanted.

- Conrad constantly hurried his owners. When it was time to go out for a walk he would start dancing around a full half hour before the owner even picked up the leash. Something as simple as the owner getting up and turning off the TV would set off Conrad's whirling dervish act. Conrad was a 120-pound Saint Bernard. The more Conrad whirled, barked and crashed around the apartment the faster the owner hurried to get him out for a walk. Conrad would then drag his owner to the park where he was immediately unleashed and allowed to tear about like a madman. The neighbors had even gotten into the habit of watching these Ben Hur chariot race walks for sheer enjoyment. The owner, and indeed the whole neighborhood, thought the behavior was cute. Only by asking my famous question did I find out about the dog's "hurry up" routine—the owner had simply asked me to teach his dog to heel, but obviously much more behavior modification was needed. You see, Conrad had finally floored his owner on the way to the park and the owner had a broken nose to prove it.

All of the above forms of cuteness are actually forms of *dominance.* When Munchkin steals, Chuckles humps, Muffin nudges or Conrad dances, they are *leading* their owners. These dogs immediately understood their owner's laughter as *submission,* because of the way dogs interpret light, lilting, whiney sounds. These seemingly insignificant actions fed directly into the development of more serious behavior problems. From the point of view of a trained trainer, "terminal cuteness" in a dog, especially if it is encouraged and condoned by the owner, quite predictably backfires. But many owners can't see the connection. And some of these owners already have the dog they want.

It really goes quite deep: Small infractions allowed to slip by lead to bigger problems. But the bigger problems can't be solved until the small infractions are identified and stopped. But that can't happen if the owner insists on seeing the small infractions as cute. It all comes back to the fact that the owner has to have a change of heart and a new view of the dog's behavior. This psychological mind shift can only occur when owners really decide, once and for all, that they don't have the dog they want, and they are going to do something about it. Sadly, it sometimes takes a bite, a growl, some thievery or one nudge too many before some owners reach that point. Then they hire me, and I tell them that the big problem they *think* is the problem isn't the only problem, just the tip of the iceberg of little "cute" problems they will have to correct.

Well, Do You . . . ?

If you are reading this book there's a big chance that you have a problem dog or know one. Ask yourself, "Do I have the dog I want?" Then reflect on everything, and I mean *everything,* the dog does during the day, especially those actions that you think are cute. Could they really be forms of dominance? And do you really want to eliminate them? This is the first, essential step in stopping a big behavior problem: revamping the way you view the little things your dog does.

Do you have the dog you want? If you've decided after reading this chapter that you don't, and you really want to create a dog you *would* want, get busy training and stop complaining. Get busy educating and stop bellyaching. Go into action setting up set-ups to cancel out behaviors that you once thought, but no longer think, are comical.

Remember, you can't have it both ways. You can't let slip by zillions of incidents of dominant behavior and justify them as funny when nobody else thinks so. The first step in getting rid of problem behavior in a dog is not working on the dog, but working on yourself.

On the other hand, if you *do* have the dog you want, I suppose that's OK, too. Live with it that way. Just don't endanger me or others. And don't invite me to visit your Frito-less house where all that will happen to me is that my knee will be raped, my coffee spilled and my feet trampled by your thieving, oversexed, pushy or hyperactive canine controller. So live like a hermit with your problem pooch, since no one will want to visit. You'll be lonely, frustrated and controlled by a dog that you will probably grow to dislike. But you *will* have one consolation: You'll have the dog you want.

6

Do Dogs Feel Guilt
or Shame?

WHEN I TEACH SEMINARS in the United States and Canada I often conduct an informal poll of the audience. Without necessarily telling them in advance my own feelings, I ask them if they feel dogs can understand being disciplined after the fact for wrongdoing. I ask them to raise their hands if they've ever disciplined their dogs after "criminal" canine activity. I don't want my opinion to prejudice their vote, and I don't want the feelings of others around them to sway their vote, so I ask the seminar participants to close their eyes before the poll.

Then I ask them: "How many of you have ever disciplined your dog after the fact—you came home and found defecation, urination or something chewed or stolen, and disciplined your dog?" Regardless of what they have read in dog training books 90 percent of the audience always raise their hands. To verify what I am seeing I usually ask one or two participants to open their eyes and look around the room.

Then I ask, "Of those who raised your hands, how many of you feel that disciplining your dog after the fact had the desired effect. In other words, the dog didn't do the same naughty thing again, or at least not so quickly?" Of the 90 percent who had their hands up for the first question about 80 percent keep their hands in the air. In short, dog owners routinely discipline their dogs after the fact and claim success, but most dog training books instruct against this. Why this discrepancy?

Time Games

When I was researching my housetraining tract, *The Evans Guide for Housetraining Your Dog,* I spent hours at the American Kennel Club library poring over everything that had ever been written on the topic. Different prescriptions were dispensed pertaining to the amount of time that can pass between a canine offense and a human correction. Many authors simply said disciplining a dog after the fact is totally taboo and should *never* be done. The theory, of course, is that dogs live in the here and now and can't remember the wrong they have done.

That was one extreme. Then the "time games" began. Various authors stated that a dog *can* be disciplined after the fact but only if not more than two or three or four or ten or even 15 minutes had passed between crime and correction. Interesting, isn't it? Who interviewed the dogs to find out exactly what time span they can comprehend? And if the dogs *were* interviewed, who got interviewed? Dalmatians? Chow Chows? Pekingese? Basenjis? (I hasten to add that Basenjis can't bark, so they could hardly talk, let alone confess.)

The time games became so bizarre that in one book an author suggested that you could still discipline your dog for defecation if you discovered it later on—but only if it was still *warm.* Now, how can you tell if the mess is still warm? Should you *touch* it? Should you put a meat thermometer in it? And if you do, what is the correct temperature reading? Medium? Medium rare? Well done? It all gets a little ridiculous and tedious, doesn't it? Ridiculous *and* tedious. Tedious researching it, tedious writing about it here, perhaps tedious reading it and certainly tedious and frustrating for anyone who has to live with a dog who supposedly "can't be disciplined after the fact."

I'm spending time going over what's in the existing literature because disciplining dogs after the fact is one of the most controversial areas in dog behavior and training. During my research I found only three major authors who condoned it. Everyone else said no to the idea or started playing those silly time games. But 90 percent of the reading audience disagrees with them according to my informal polls. Noted author Carol Benjamin *(Mother Knows Best, Dog Problems)* talks about the concept of "evidence." If you have evidence you can convict your dog of a crime. I like to use the word "proof." The concept is similar. In fact, I've discovered that many guide dog trainers routinely advise their blind clients to discipline their dogs for infractions discovered after the fact. Guide dogs might appear to be saints, but they are still dogs and occasionally forget themselves. But the blind master might not discover a chewed pillow until a sighted person brings it to his or her attention. The guide dog who has "sinned" is reprimanded humanely even after the fact. Are "regular" dogs incapable of comprehending what a guide dog can comprehend? Is it possible that we have sold our dogs short in terms of their capacity for understanding discipline after the fact?

Why It Works: Some Background

Before I tell you how, when, where and why to discipline after the fact, bear with me while I give you a little more background on why it so often works. I decided to do some private research, and asked my psychologist father to educate me on the etiology of "guilt" and "shame." What he said, and what I do with the information when it comes to disciplining dogs, might help you to correct your problem pooch.

First, understand that we are going to be talking about guilt and shame in their purer, more primitive forms. Wise parents bring guilt and shame out of the closet. We should do as much for our dogs. Here we go.

Guilt, as experienced in humans, can begin around age five to seven (rarely before) and operates as a kind of undercurrent. *Guilt* doesn't exactly wash over a person every minute of the day, but nevertheless keeps the person in a state of sadness and confusion. *Shame,* on the other hand, is a much more immediate phenomenon, and shame is always felt, and felt deeply. Think about how often you've heard people say, "I was so embarrassed I could have crawled under a table" or "I felt so ashamed I could have died!" Interesting how we humans feel so ashamed about being shamed that we often invoke life or death comparisons—"I could have *died!*" You might be guilty all your life, but you are *shamed* for a moment—even if the moment seems like an eternity. Got the difference?

Now, given what we know about dogs and how they like to live life in the here and now—being much smarter than we stupid humans—I would venture to say that dogs cannot experience ongoing guilt, but they can be made to feel shame, or to feel ashamed. That's why I believe in carefully structured discipline after the fact—because the dog *can* be shamed. In fact, there is one breed—the Pharoah Hound—that *blushes* when excited or reprimanded.

The difference between guilt and shame hinges on *discovery.* You can be guilty all day or all year, but you are shamed when you are discovered. Someone could be having, for instance, and extramarital affair, and feel very guilty about it, but the guilt doesn't exactly stop the affair from continuing. But if your mate *discovers* you in bed with your lover, you are bound to feel more ashamed than guilty, for the moment at least. That's why it's so important to keep your cool and not scream when you discover evidence of wrongdoing on the part of your dog. More on that soon.

The distinction between guilt and shame is important. If you understand it you will be able to give corrections with connections. Don't kid yourself for one minute that your dog feels an ongoing sense of guilt over what it did or even plans to do. Your dog can be made to feel shame but it's unacquainted with guilt. Guilt is a human invention stemming from human culture—dogs couldn't care less about it. Just think in terms of simple shame, the kind of shame you felt when you were less than five. Little children are incapable of feeling guilty, but they *can* be shamed. Dogs are like little kids in this respect. They too can be shamed, but they do not feel guilt.

People who want their dogs to feel ongoing guilt—and there are many—like to say, "He does it all for spite," and then they will usually add, "He knows when he's done wrong" or "He knows he's guilty" when all the dog is doing is looking ashamed. Watch what you think about your dog and certainly what you say about it, because if you really believe your dog is "guilty" and "does it all for spite" rather than simply showing shame and frustration, you will tend to deal with your pet on a moral plane. You'll then get very angry and abusive rather than dealing out fair, calm corrections that clarify issues for the dog rather than confuse them.

Follow these steps:

1. If you come home and you find evidence of defecation, urination or something chewed or stolen, you can try disciplining after the fact if you have "proof"—but you must not react to the proof until you get the dog *to* the proof. In other words, don't explode into the house and scream or whine at your dog. The dog will simply run away and you will *think* you have corrected it. I assure you, you have not. Instead, say nothing. Go get the dog. The dog may still flinch when you approach. That's because your body language is hard to disguise, and perhaps you have a past history of screaming at the proof before getting the dog to the proof. Just approach the dog calmly even if it flinches.

2. Without saying anything yet, bring the dog by the collar over to the proof. If the proof is a chewed or stolen item, pick it up and brandish it in front of the dog's face, softly but firmly scolding the dog. Remember you want to mimic the growl of the bitch in your tonality. *Grrrrrrrrrrrrr.* For really recalcitrant thieves use the swat-under-the-chin correction.

3. If the proof is defecation or urination the method is slightly different. Of course you can't pick it up, so simply tilt the dog's head down toward the mistake *without* shoving the dog's nose in it. With your other hand point to the mistake and give your growl reprimand. Again, for older dogs who consistently fall off the housetraining wagon, the swat correction may be in order at this juncture.

4. Now, trot your dog to the desired area for defecation or urination, unless this is impossible. If the proof was a chewed item, or if the dog eliminated, but it is simply not possible to march the dog to the desired area for elimination, simply isolate the dog. Return and clean up the mess, using vinegar and water (50/50) for housetraining accidents (*never* ammonia). Don't let the dog see you cleaning up. Your body language looks submissive as you kneel, grovel, scrape and scrub, and that won't win you any Brownie points in the dog's eyes.

5. Leave the dog in isolation for thirty minutes. If it barks, yodels or screams when isolated you will have to correct it for that also. Isolation after serious canine crimes such as destructive chewing or inap-

propriate elimination is necessary. These infractions are almost always attempts on the part of the dog to claim territory within the household. By isolating the dog you are telling it, "This small room or crate is all you get, and if you chew my things or soil my house, you'll be confined. The rest of the territory is *mine* and I, as the Alpha figure, simply grant you access to it. You make a mistake on *my* territory—Boom!—you get disciplined and demoted in territory." Don't worry that isolating the dog will make it "hate its crate" or a particular room. As Carol Benjamin says, "when your mother sent you to your room after you caused trouble, it didn't make you hate your room." I'd only add that perhaps it made you "hate" your mother—for a while—but maybe you didn't misbehave so soon afterward!

Some Qualifications

If your dog continues to commit crimes while you are away, and certainly if it does the same naughty things right in front of you, and you've tried disciplining the dog after the fact and/or during the act, your dog is probably telling you that for some reason it simply cannot understand the corrections. Double-check your corrective style by rereading chapter 11, "Why Set-ups Sometimes Foul Up," and simply arrange the dog's life so that it does not have access to your personal belongings. Also see chapter 12, "Creative Avoidance," and practice it for two to three weeks. This will probably mean more confinement or the use of a crate. There are some dogs who simply cannot be shamed—during or after an act of mischief—but this is rare.

Finally, remember to keep your cool when disciplining during the fact or after the fact. No screaming! No hysterics! This is correction time, not Oscar time. No Academy Awards are being presented for Most Dramatic Canine Correction. Your on-site growling sentence should never be longer than three to four *seconds*. Remember, dignity is never despised by dogs, it is always respected. Yelling at your dog is a good way to cheapen yourself. The dog can tell that you've lost your cool. Your lack of control doesn't elevate your Alpha status, and may make the dog escalate into violence. On the other hand, if your correction is too soft, or if you break down laughing because you think what the dog did was cute, the dog will understand the signals you send as submissive. Wimpy owners often have to act angry even if they aren't.

Many dog writers have not and will not take the risk of going out on a limb and discussing discipline after the fact, even if they themselves do it at home with their own dogs and have raised their hands during my poll (and some have). But I am not ashamed to bring up shame in dogs. I'd be ashamed if I didn't. I suppose there is always a chance that some domineering owners will unfairly and overharshly discipline their dogs. They will reap what they sow. The dog will continue to defecate or destroy, and these owners will continue to believe that the dog is guilty. My responsibility as a dog trainer and writer is to bring to you my *lived* experience with dogs and share with you what has worked for me and many others, not just deal in theory and abstraction. If dogs cannot be shamed, and truly cannot understand discipline after the fact, why does it so often work so well for so many owners and so many dogs?

If you've got a problem pooch that acts up only when you are gone, and you've been wondering if and when you can correct such a dog—take heart, you often can. But hold the thought—and the discipline—let's take a look at *you* first.

We may never know for certain whether dogs feel guilt or shame. My personal observation is that the cannot feel guilt but can be shamed. *Kevin Smith*

7

Your Owner Personality or How to Drive Your Dog Nuts in Five Days or Less

DID YOU KNOW you can drive your dog bonkers simply by being who you are? If that sounds like an insult, please don't take it that way. As you now know, I drove my first dog stark, raving crazy simply by being the shy, nervous personality I used to be. She was an open, friendly, outgoing three-month-old German Shepherd puppy when she was placed in my care at the beginning of 1972. By mid-1972 she had picked up on my insecurities and resembled fetal jelly more than the happy puppy she started as. I was a first-class placater with my new charge and projected my personality onto her.

I've since owned many more dogs. While I still have my handling foibles, I have been able to learn enough about them to avoid frying more canine brains. Ironically, a system I developed to help other trainers and dog-owner counselors classify owner personalities has helped me to stare down my own faults. I first introduced this classification system in *The Evans Guide for Counseling Dog Owners.* That book is geared to the professional, who, in any capacity, has to talk with dog owners. In this book, I'll talk more informally about owner personalities. They are the placater, the blamer, the computer, the distractor and the leveler.

These classifications are the terms of the late Virginia Satir, a pioneer in the field of family therapy. I first met Dr. Satir when I was about ten years old and she did a series of seminars with my father, who was also doing family therapy. Satir says that placating, computing, distracting or leveling are near-universal patterns of communication people use with each other in order to avoid the threat of rejection or elicit obedience and cooperation—in other words, to get what they want. I theorize that people also employ these ploys to get what they want from their dogs.

- You can *placate,* so the dog doesn't get mad at you, so the dog will perceive you as being "fair," with the hope of getting obedience and cooperation.
- You can *blame* the dog, so that it will regard you as strong, in control and not to be trifled with.
- You can *compute,* be very logical, orderly, concise and unfeeling, and hope that the dog will see the eminent "sanity" of your approach.
- You can *distract* yourself and others from the dog and its problems and just ignore bad behavior as if it were not there.
- You can *level* with your dog, acting as leader, steward and Alpha, while at the same time deepening your friendship with your dog.

It's important that you diagnose your owner personality because it often influences your "paralanguage": the emotional overtones your dog ascribes to the way that you sound. And the way you sound, the tonalities that you use in your speech, are often directly influenced by your owner personality. If you placate, you will tend to whine at your dog, and the dog will regard you as a littermate, an equal, a peer. Your set-ups for bad behavior will lack authority because your underlying owner personality is not taken seriously by the dog. If you blame, your voice will tend to be either too loud, with accompanying oververbalization, or hard, tight, succinct but tense, and the dog will fight this misuse of leadership. Your set-ups will be overproduced, possibly hysterical and bombastic, and will only frighten, not teach. If you compute, your voice will probably be dry, flat, unanimated and clinically cold. Your set-ups will be technically accurate but their staging will lack the drama and surprise that are essential. If you distract, you will be in an ongoing state of ambivalence about the dog, and your voice will be lilting, sing-songish and lacking in authority. Your set-ups will be flops. If your paralanguage is off, the dog will tend to regard you as a littermate instead of a leader, as a bimbo rather than the boss and, in extreme cases, as an ass rather than an Alpha.

It sounds complex but it really isn't. How you think of yourself inevitably influences how you sound to others—and to your dog. Sound like a wimp and you'll probably get taken advantage of. Boss others around and you'll get into fights. Try to be superlogical and Murphy's Law—If anything can go wrong, it will—will get you every time. And simply ignoring life or distracting yourself from it will lead nowhere.

The Placater

A large percentage of problem dog owners are placaters. They are over-verbal with their dogs and talk in long, whiney sentences. They plead with the dog to "be good" and their whining tonalities are usually decoded by dogs as the sound of a littermate. Whines, wimpers and yelps are infantile sounds that littermates make among themselves when they are cold, hungry, lonely or stressed in some way. Most placaters don't even realize that they are whining at their dogs.

If you are a placater you are probably enamored of the word "but" and the phrase "if only," as in

- "But he won't *listen.*"
- "But I *tried* that."
- "If only I had gotten a Maltese instead of a Rotteweiler."
- "If only I had gone to that third obedience class, maybe he wouldn't still pull me down the street."
- "If only I had *tried* harder, I could have changed the rainwater into wine, but I didn't *try* hard enough."

When I train trainers in seminars I play recordings of placaters taped during counseling sessions. The words "but" and "if only" can be heard frequently on the tapes. Placaters are basically passive and these terms give them excuses for not going into action. In extreme cases placaters reduce themselves to food ploys in order to gain even a shred of obedience from their dogs. The dog will only come, lie down, sit or simply leave the owner alone when a food reward is offered.

Placaters have low self-esteem and do not see themselves in a leadership role with the dog. The placater wants to be friends with everyone. But dogs want more than friendship: They want leadership.

How to Help Yourself

If you are a placater your first task is to educate yourself concerning the concept of paralanguage. Just reading this book is a good start, but because books don't talk it might also be therapeutic to simply listen to yourself as you deal with your dog. Studies show that a full 35 percent of dog owners talk to their dogs *all day* as if they were fellow human beings. I'm willing to bet that at least 90 percent of that 35 percent are placaters. Because some of the problem behavior your dog exhibits might stem from its hearing faulty para-language too often during the regular course of a day, my suggestion is to simply not talk to the dog without reason for one month. Save speaking to your dog for commands or for giving praise when it is truly warranted. If you are a placater, simply drop point number twenty in chapter 9's RRRR program—no jingle for your dog. Your placating has probably already jangled its nerves. When the dog experiences long stretches of silence interspersed only with occasional command words and praise phrases, its attitude toward you will change. At first the dog might be bewildered, but it will soon learn to listen more intently. After all, something you have to say might actually be important! The benefit for you is that, even unbeknownst to yourself, you will find yourself placating and pleading less, and will inevitably move more toward the owner personality of the leveler.

You have a great advantage if you are a placater. It is very likely that you have a self-deprecating sense of humor. You're capable of laughing at yourself and you should choose educational tools that are funny, sympathetic to your stance but offer no-nonsense advice. Placaters like to laugh, especially at themselves and this is OK as long as there is also some education going on. While I hope that this book is funny enough and sympathetic enough for a placater to learn new ways of handling the dog, and at the same time have a good hoot, I realize that other books might be welcomed also.

Finally, in order to help yourself pull out of placating, remember not to be too rough on yourself. Besides choosing funny yet helpful training books, choose a trainer who does not criticize you directly or harshly. Know why? As a placater, you will tend to simply agree with the criticism, but simple agreement, simple acquiescence, will not necessarily mean that you have learned anything, only that you have acquiesced to the criticism in an attempt to placate the trainer! Placating can become a vicious cycle that carries over from how you relate with your dog into how you relate with those trying to help you with the dog. The untrained trainer doesn't realize that the key to effective criticism, especially with a placater, lies in humor and technique. Luckily, it is usually easy to find a funny dog trainer who will help you without clobbering you with direct criticisms. The reason for this (and this is a closet secret in the dog fancy) is that many trainers are former placaters!

The Blamer

The blamer is a faultfinder, a boss and a dictator—but the sad thing is that the blamer doesn't know it. Blamers feel that they are superior and like to use all-encompassing terms like "always," "never" and "all" when describing their dogs.

- "Tippy *always* disobeys."
- "He *never* comes when he is called."
- "He does it *all* for spite."

As a blamer you will probably catch yourself using such drastic terminology. Be honest with yourself and you will probably admit that you often begin sentences with the dog's name or the personal pronoun that pertains to the dog. By putting the dog's name first in a sentence, or at least somewhere in the sentence, it enables you to blame the dog more effectively. You probably aren't even aware that you do this. It might just be part of your overall personality. As the character Ouiser Boudreaux says in *Steel Magnolias,* "I'm not crazy. I've just been in a bad mood for forty years." However, you should realize that such an overall stance in life is bound to have ramifications for your dog. Dog problems are very rarely the fault of the dog alone. They are almost always the result of human/dog interaction.

If you are a blamer you might have trouble in obedience classes or with a trainer because you will tend to criticize everything being taught. You will come into class or engage a private trainer with a know-it-all attitude that will, in fact, thwart the very help you are seeking. Because you will question every technique and move the trainer makes, you will probably not do your homework in between classes and will fall behind the rest of the group. Then you will blame the trainer or the other members of the class. What blamers have to realize about themselves is that they almost always blame everyone else for their dogs' bad behavior rather than themselves. Blamers always assume they are never the one causing any of the problems.

How to Help Yourself

If you recognize yourself as a blamer you should probably realize that you might have a set of problems more complex than can be handled in this book. That's for you, or your therapist, to diagnose. I hasten to add that in some cases of extreme blaming the result is a battered dog. There is a grim ecology present in the households of some blamers. It tallies like this: Husband beats wife; wife beats children; oldest child beats youngest child; youngest child beats dog. In this case, professional help is needed.

Usually, however, things have not gotten that bad. For a blamer, sometimes a simple examination of conscience and a commitment to training will do. You might take ten to twenty minutes before each training session with your dog to meditate or at least sit quietly. Read over your training lesson and rehearse in your mind what you plan to do with your dog that session. Resolve in advance that you will not become testy or agitated if the dog doesn't respond just as you would like. Blamers often have short fuses and bring incredible tension and nervous energy into training sessions. Of course the dog picks this up. The session turns into a shambles. Blamers often laugh at the idea of meditating, but they are exactly the persons who could profit from it. Blamers are often really very insecure and unhappy persons underneath the difficult exterior that is presented to the public. But the dog, even a dog the blamer deems "stupid," often sees through this mask and sees a person who needs to be secure and safe and needs a friend. Unfortunately, many blamers get into such dominance fights with their canine charges that they never decipher the truce messages that the dog telegraphs.

Blamers should be especially sensitive toward trainers. If you've decoded yourself as a blamer, even if you have to bite your tongue, give the trainer a chance to explain fully any technique that will help you. You don't have to like or love your trainer, or for that matter a training book you might read, just try to be civil and empathetic with the trainer's or book's goals. One more closet secret: Some dog trainers are former blamers!

The Computer

This personality is very reasonable, very correct, calm, cool and collected. This owner could be compared to an actual computer. The vocal tonality is dry, flat, a monotone. If you've ever heard a voice-activated computer "talk" you have an idea of the vocal quality. Dogs, however, adore vocal modulations, especially a higher pitched voice for praise and a lowered voice for reprimands. The computer offers none of this. Computers very carefully choose their words and actions. Giving praise is a supreme difficulty because the computer is rigid physically and mentally.

Computers love to read and memorize training books. They expect everything that is said in the book to be the gospel truth and allow the author little or no leeway. They often view dogs as little robots who can be ordered about if only all the right words are said at just the right time. Sometimes professionals in the hard sciences exhibit computer traits. Lawyers, especially, often take a linear, computerish view of life. The syndrome also occurs among some physicians and even veterinarians. I am not announcing anything new—medical schools now have to teach physicians bedside manners while lawyers flood seminars that promise to teach them kinder negotiating skills and simple human warmth.

However, computers have several good points going for them. When they seek out training they usually listen very carefully to everything the trainer has to say. They do the prescribed homework with their dog between private sessions or classes. If they are not sure about something, they ask. Correct information is extremely important to the computer. Just as proper data must be fed into a mechanical computer in order for a project to be successful, the human computer doesn't feel he can train his dog successfully unless he has proper data. In the computer's world life goes like this: First there is A and after A is, of course, B. Then we proceed naturally to C, followed by, of course, D. Order. Logic. Correct sequence.

The problem with this world view is that dogs don't necessarily operate this way. The dog might say instead, "No, no, no—we're *starting* at B. Then we're going back to A. But, I'm not sure—we might go on to C." This of course throws the computer for a loop. The computer becomes especially frustrated if a training book states an A-B-C-D scenario, and then the dog performs otherwise. That's why my philosophy of dog writing is never to say, "Do *this*, and your dog will never do *that* again." Instead, I allow for more leeway in dog/human interactions and will suggest, "Try this, try this and try this. If that doesn't work, then try this, this and this." I don't kid myself that training texts can be absolutely accurate or exact, no matter how badly computers desire them to be.

You might wonder why a computer gets a dog at all. I think I've finally figured it out. Computers want to recapture a side of themselves that they sense they have sacrificed. One accusation hurled at dog people to "explain" why we keep dogs is the old chestnut that says the dogs are simply our substitute kids. This criticism is often levied by non–dog owners. But there might be some truth to it. A look at the dog fancy *will* reveal a large number of single persons and childless couples. But a second look quickly reveals the presence of many families with children who also choose to keep one or more dogs. Perhaps the real reason that people keep a dog is not so much as a substitute kid, but instead as a way to get back to the kid in themselves—the free, open, honest person who gave spontaneous unconditional love to all, who loved to play (in fact, *lived* to play) and who led a carefree life. The dog is both an actual manifestation and a cultural icon of these traits. This was, in fact, Freud's reasoning behind why people get dogs and I think it is accurate. The personality type that has most sacrificed the kid in itself is the computer. And computers know it. They sense that the kid inside is "on vacation" or might even be dead— that's why they get a dog. So you see, the motivation behind the computer's acquiring a dog is really quite healthy. While the behavior toward the dog might *seem* cold and distant, computers are really quite taken with their dogs and love their pets.

How to Help Yourself

If you've diagnosed yourself as a computer, you need to get into a training class and watch good dog handlers in action. Watch the instructor and the better handlers in the class. Listen to the amount of praise they give and instead of judging them as gushy Pollyannas, watch how the faces of the dogs light up and how obedience to commands picks up. You might ask the instructor to work with your dog, which might be somewhat surprised at being handled in a vivacious way. Even if you feel uncomfortable about praising your dog, give it a sincere try. Remember the inner reason you got your dog to begin with was to free yourself to enjoy life more fully through and with your friend. You owe your dog not only training, but sincere praise, tons of warmth and gratitude for all it has given you.

The Distractor

We've all met off-the-wall dog owners—people who seem unaware that they have a badly behaved dog. We see such owners being dragged down the street, or we see them driving along with a horde of unruly ruffians boomeranging around the back of the car, sometimes occupying the passenger side of the front seat—or even the driver's seat—barking wildly, totally out of control. Meanwhile the owners will be listening to the radio, talking to friends or simply humming to themselves—anything to distract themselves from the shenanigans of the dogs.

Obedience class instructors know distractors well. They are the members of the class who, even after several sessions, still do not have their dogs under even minimal control. While all the placaters, blamers and computers in the class will have begun correcting their personality foibles and paralanguage problems, and have their dogs sitting calmly, the distractor has a rotating pooch and a dislocated arm.

Distractors love to give double or even triple commands that confuse the dog. Double commands are phrases like "sit down" or "c'mon heel." Since "sit" and "down" are two distinct body positions, there is no way a dog can adopt both at the same time. "C'mon" might be used as a term of encouragement, but it is also a word that sounds suspiciously like "come"—which means that the dog should present itself directly in front of your body. It's awfully hard for the dog to do that if it's trying to stay by your side to heel. Watch out for double commands, especially if you are a distractor.

I once had a distractor as a client who, even after repeated admonitions, persisted in giving double and even triple commands. During our last lesson together I asked her to do some off-leash work with the dog, a Cocker Spaniel, who was standing about ten feet in front of her. "Tell the dog to sit," I said. My client said "sit" in a wimpy voice that the dog totally ignored. The client looked to me and I told her to give the command again. Using the same ineffective tonality she whined at the dog, "Sit downnnnn." Again the dog stood staring at her with a blank expression on its face. My client stamped her foot in exasperation and again looked to me for advice. I told her to give the command once again. This time she got angry and bellowed at the Cocker, *"C'mon, sit down!"* At this point the dog went into a full crouch. The front portion of his body was slightly more elevated than the rear, which he dragged on the ground as he began to crawl subserviently toward his mistress. He looked like a guerrilla snaking along the jungle floor. The frustrated distractor threw up her hands, stamped her feet again, turned to me and said, "See, he's stupid. He doesn't know his words!" "Excuse me," I replied, "He knows his words very well. He's coming, sitting and lying down. You *did* give three commands. That's his version of it." The distractor now looked totally baffled, and I thought to myself, "This is a damn smart dog. He's found a way to obey all three commands. He probably figures, 'I don't know what she wants—I'll give her a little of everything and see if she'll leave me alone.' "

How to Help Yourself

First, try not to do more than one thing at a time when you are working with your dog. Distractors need to meditate a bit before starting a training session and clear their minds of all distractions. Take the phone off the hook, drive to a quiet area, do whatever you have to do to concentrate on the training session alone and not be drawn away from it. While in general I do not like the idea of sending the dog away to a training camp to be educated, distractors sometimes need a break from their dogs. Just be sure if you do this that the same trainer who takes your dog in releases the dog to you. Consistency is very important in your training efforts because, let's face it, you're distracted and have a lot on your mind. Finally, if you have diagnosed yourself as a distractor and do not currently own a dog but are simply thinking of getting one, *don't.* Wait until the elements of your scattered life fall together more cohesively so that you can offer a dog the consistency and leadership it deserves. Try goldfish, but don't forget to feed them.

The Leveler

A leveler offers to the dog friendship *and* leadership. The voice is controlled and reasonable. The relationship between the dog and the leveler is honest. The dog clearly sees the leveler as the Alpha figure in its life and responds happily. Some owners are natural-born levelers and others are reformed placaters, blamers, computers or distractors who assimilated correct handling from a book or picked up paralanguage skills by listening to and observing levelers interacting with their dogs. There are three hallmarks of the leveling response:

1. When giving an active command or praising the dog, the leveler's voice will tend to rise higher in tonality—without whining or yelling. For instance, a praise phrase like "good boy" will be delivered in an animated tonality more like "Goooooood boy!" A command word that needs an active response such as "Come!" will be delivered in a slightly elevated tone. Dog's like voice modulation and respond well to it. The opposite is also true.

2. When giving a static command or reprimanding the dog, the leveler's voice will tend to sink lower in tonality—without yelling. For example, a command word such as "stay" will be delivered in a deep or "husky" tone of voice rather than a light one. The darkened tonality will definitely suggest to the dog that no movement is desired. A discipline phrase or a reprimand will also be delivered in a lower tone. Again, some levelers adopt these tonalities quite naturally and others learn from experience. Don't worry if you have a naturally high voice. It's the *difference* between the way you normally sound and the higher or lower voice modulations that will impress the dog. Just remember: active command or praise go higher, static command or reprimand go lower.

3. When reprimanding the dog, levelers do not yell. Instead, the leveler will change tonality but not increase volume. If you yell, the dog will literally start to structure reality around your yelling. The dog will reason that you don't really mean it unless you yell. Since dogs do know the difference between the two species, it becomes noticeable after a while that the two-legged members are addressed in normal conversational tones, while members of the four-legged species are yelled at. In short, if you yell enough, you will simply produce a dog

that will literally learn to *wait* for you to yell. Levelers don't yell. They level with their dogs using paralanguage that the dog understands.

So, that's it, our rundown of owner personalities. In my experience, 50 percent of owners placate their dogs, 30 percent blame their dogs, 15 percent compute with their dogs and just .5 percent distract themselves from their dogs. That leaves only 4.5 percent of owners who, without any work, reading or education will naturally level with their dogs. It should be quite clear that for most of us, dog training skills are *learned* skills. And we should be thankful they *can* be learned, otherwise our dogs would be doomed to living in a bizarre world where they are constantly placated into obedience, blamed for every-thing, overreasoned with, forced to decipher distractions they cannot under-stand or simply ignored. Once again, remember, your owner personality influ-ences your paralanguage, and your use of paralanguage will give you problems or peace.

8

Look, See, Observe, Memorize, Insee

I T'S A BIG STEP for owners to admit that they are a placater, blamer, computer or distractor. It's an even bigger admission to allow that because of these personality problems one's perceptive abilities might be limited. But inability to see clearly and fully lies at the root of many pooch/people problems.

It's amazing the number of clients I've had over the years who claim that erratic behavior on the part of their dog is totally unpredictable, unexplainable and spontaneous. I'll hear, "She just explodes over nothing and tries to bite people," or "He steals my things so quickly there is just nothing I can do about it." Owners of problem dogs often have a vested interest in believing, and getting other people to believe, that their dogs misbehave so quickly, so suddenly that nothing can be done to even anticipate the bad behavior. After all, if this is the case, then the owner is excused from doing anything about the misbehavior. An owner can justifiably claim difficulty in arranging a set-up if the dog truly engages in completely unprovoked, unexplainable behavior. Then it's back to complaining or off to the pound with the dog. But, as trainers have said for years, "Train, don't complain." I'd only add, "Set up. Don't screw up."

Part of training your dog is to open your eyes and go beyond simply looking at your dog to *seeing* its behavior. The fact is, many owners of problem dogs can't even see what's right in front of them. Their dogs will already be lunging, growling or snapping at somebody before they even consider verbally, not to mention physically, reprimanding the dog. These owners can't see the dog escalating into aggression or some other form of bad behavior because they literally don't know what to look for. Once educated as to the signs of upcoming aggression you might think that these owners would be faster on the draw and able to discipline their dogs more speedily. But the problem goes even deeper than lack of education as to trouble signals. Trouble signs can be memorized—but if your vision is impaired, we're in trouble.

The sad fact is, not only do many owners of problem dogs not know what danger signs to look for, they don't know how to look, period. The situation becomes quite serious because the owner is blind to seeing the true nature of the problem dog's behavior. Some trainers simply drill these owners and their dogs in obedience commands, forgetting that the owner's basic ability to perceive visual reality may be retarded.

If that sounds like a severe judgment, it's meant to be. In an era of endless remote-control options for practically every aspect of life—including selecting a TV channel or activating the coffee maker from bed—our ability to sit still and look, see and observe has been extremely compromised. This lack presents serious difficulties for our dogs because the core of all animal study is the ability to *truly observe* the animal's behavior. Owners of problem dogs are not exempt; in fact, they need such skills even more than other owners.

The eminent naturalist Konrad Lorenz once noted, "You must love the animal you are studying, and in order to love it, you must go beyond just looking at it." This seemingly innocent and obvious statement caused an uproar among academic naturalists, who were used to quantifying animals and delivering the behaviorist's party line—that animals are just little machines and it is a waste of time to speculate about things we can't catalog, and far better to limit our study to what we *can* see: the input, the stimulus, the response. Konrad Lorenz, talking about "loving the animals you are studying," blew some academics away. The man must be a romantic, a hedonist, a communist or something worse.

But decades after Lorenz made his statement about loving animals we are really not much better off in our ways of dealing with animals—including dogs, although we will protest to high heaven that we do love them. We stammer and stutter and stamp our feet and say again and again, "We *do* love them. We do, we do, we do!" The problem, however, is an inverse one for dog people. I accept all that stuttering and stammering and stamping of feet. I know that most dog owners and professionals *do* love dogs—but I am far from convinced that the majority of lay persons or even professionals know how to *study* a dog.

The Steps to Inseeing

Most of us never get much past the point of *looking* at something or somebody. But if you do, you are on your way to a visual adventure that will enrich your life and enable you to stop problem behavior by recognizing it promptly. You will, for the first time, be able to see your dog!

Here's an example of what I mean: Let's say you're driving home from work one day. It's a regular, old, run-of-the-mill day. Nothing special about it. You come to an intersection and stop at the red light. You stop at this same red light 365 days a year, sometimes twice in one day. But today, perhaps because the sun is exceptionally bright, you turn toward a building on your left and notice some ornamentation on the roof of the building. It suddenly strikes you that you've never quite noticed that ornamentation before. Congratulations! You've just graduated one step from looking to *seeing* what has been right in front of you for days and even years.

Most people would simply drive on at this point, perhaps vaguely noting that they should take more time to stop and look at the world around them. But because you want to embark on a visual adventure, *you* won't simply drive on. Instead, you pull over to the side of the road, get out of your car, cross the street and look even more carefully at the ornamentation. You notice that it is baroque in style and you recall your college art history courses. You notice the interplay between the sunlight and the ornamentation. You see the shadows the ornamentation casts on the rest of the roof. You note some pigeons strutting near the ornamentation. Congratulations! You've just gone one step further from looking to seeing to *observing*. Observation takes more time, you note, but you're grateful you've taken the time because the image of the ornamentation stays clearly in your mind even as you walk back to your car.

Now, if you were to pursue this visual adventure even further, you would, when you came to the next stoplight, be able to close your eyes and still see the ornamentation just as it was a moment ago. Your mind's eye has *memorized* it. If you were determined to take this exercise even further, perhaps you would go home, sit down and write something about the ornamentation. Everyone comes to this last step of *inseeing* in their own personal way. Perhaps you would write a poem about the building or its ornamentation. Maybe you would make a journal entry about the ornamentation, discussing its meaning to you—if only that noticing the ornamentation clearly indicates that you have to take more time to stop and truly look, see, observe, memorize what you've observed and try to insee.

Try this exercise at the next intersection you commonly cross. Better yet, try it with your dog. Try it first when the dog is just hanging around doing nothing. Then you can graduate to the more complex activity of observing your dog in action. Remember, if you do not know what you are looking at, you will never be able to anticipate bad behavior and issue an advance warning as step one of a set-up. Sometimes issuing an advance warning is impossible anyway, no matter how acute your observation skills are, but many times it is the owner's inability to see danger signals and signs that makes a set-up foul up. This is where a professional trainer with a trained eye can be of great help.

The Payoff

There is another payoff in perfecting your visual skills. You will fall more deeply in love with your dog insofar as you go beyond simply looking at him or her. With a little discipline you will be able to reach new levels of observation that will culminate in beautiful moments of inseeing. Inseeing is a term originated by the poet Rilke. I chose to reproduce his definition at the beginning of *How to Be Your Dog's Best Friend* (Little, Brown, 1978), which I coauthored while with the Monks of New Skete. Brother Nil, then a monk at New Skete monastery and a German classics scholar, conducted a series of talks on Rilke for the monks and alerted me to this quote about dogs:

> I love inseeing. Can you imagine with me how glorious it is to insee, for example, a dog as one passes by. *Insee* (I don't mean in-spect, which is only a kind of human gymnastic, by means of which one immediately comes out again on the other side of the dog, regarding it merely, so to speak, as a window upon the humanity lying behind it, not that.)—but to let oneself precisely into the dog's very center, the point from which it becomes a dog, the place in it where God, as it were, would have sat down for a moment when the dog was finished, in order to watch it under the influence of its first embarrassments and inspirations and to know that it was good, that nothing was lacking, that it could have not been better made. . . . Laugh though you may, dear confidant, if I am to tell you *where* my all-greatest feeling, my world-feeling, my earthly bliss was to be found, I must confess to you: it was to be found time and again, here and there, in such timeless moments of this divine inseeing.
>
> Rainer Maria Rilke, *New Poems,* translated by J. B. Leishman (Berkeley, Calif.: North Point Press, 1977)

At the time I became acquainted with this quote and the concept of inseeing, I had been appointed head trainer of the monastery German Shepherd Dogs and began boarding and training recalcitrants of all breeds dumped off at the monastery kennels for "rehabilitation." I had only been training for about one year. I hardly even knew what I was looking at when I encountered criminal canine behavior. I certainly didn't know how to see it for what it was, truly observe it, memorize what I had observed and write up a program to help a distraught owner eliminate the behavior. Inseeing, I thought, was truly a distant, and maybe even an unreachable, goal. But at least I knew there *was* a goal to strive for. Now you do, too.

I started to do daily exercises, such as the one we've discussed in this chapter, with the monastery dogs and with inanimate objects out in the woods. Slowly my perceptional abilities developed. With a little practice yours will, too. So don't feel frustrated if you can only inspect and not insee. In fact, even perfecting your ability to inspect your dog's actions will help you to set up sterling set-ups. Inseeing will most probably be reserved for more contemplative, quiet, nondemanding times with your dog. Those "timeless moments of inseeing" Rilke mentioned will deepen your relationship with your dog and balance off those times when you have to inspect its behavior and stage a set-up to change it. But it all starts with *you* and your ability to look, see, observe, memorize and insee.

You might wonder if your dog needs to perfect *its* ability to truly see *you*. Trust me—your dog watches you more closely than you'll ever watch it. After all, it's got little else to do except eat, behave, or misbehave, play with its toys, go for walks—and watch your every move. It's *we* who don't see, not them!

9

RRRR:

A Radical Regimen

for Recalcitrant Rovers

$\mathbf{Y}$OU KNOW that presiding over every wolf pack there is a leader, or Alpha wolf, who keeps order within the pack. This wolf informs other wolves about their status on a particular day, about how well they are doing and about how poorly they are doing. Depending on the Alpha's style of leadership, its role might be that of a dictator or a guide, or the Alpha might adopt either of these roles at different times. All subordinate wolves look to this Alpha for leadership and direction.

You also know that domestication has not nullified in the dog this ardent need to lead or be led. While dogs are light-years distant from wolves in some respects, in other matters they still resemble wolves closely—especially in their need for an Alpha figure to guide them, and failing the presence of such a guide, the desire to assume the position themselves. For your dog, there should be absolutely no question as to who is the Alpha figure in its life. You are, or more accurately, you'd better be!

Trainers often express these theories of Alpha leadership to their class and private clients in crude ways that accentuate the "control" the owner must gain to be the "boss." Trainers will often say, "Let him know who's boss!" and then hand out a few folklore corrections to whatever problem is at hand.

Copyright © 1987, courtesy The Pet Clinic, Salem, Oregon

Trouble is, just applying those few corrections—even if they do seem to address the behavior problem at hand—will not by itself elevate the wimpy owner to anything approximating Alpha status in the naughty dog's mind. In fact, the dog might rebel fiercely, getting into a dominance fight with the owner, or simply correcting itself on one set of problems (say, destructive chewing) and substituting another (soiling in the house instead of chewing). A few folklore corrections down the pike and the owner is *still* not Alpha.

Often a more holistic approach to bad behavior is called for—a hit list of changes that are imposed on the dog in order to rattle its brains, disturb the status quo and slot the owner in the starring role as Ms. or Mr. Alpha once and for all. Little things add up. Just as it was probably a plethora of little infractions, little slips, little forms of naughtiness that allowed the situation between dog and owner to deteriorate, it will be a series of little changes and renovations that will bring the relationship back into sync and stop the problem behavior. The *specific* problem areas can be restructured via set-ups, but more on that later.

No Quick Fixes

If you are the owner of a problem dog, please reflect on the above comments before reading on. You probably would prefer a quick-fix solution from this book—just one or two techniques that will cancel whatever behavior problem you are now putting up with from your dog. I must say to you: It's not that easy or simple. With few exceptions, your problems with your dog, at root, are *relational*. The dog probably fancies itself as the Alpha. Or it doesn't know who is or doesn't care or doesn't want to know. Whatever the case, you're not it! You might be regarded as a friend, as a companion, as a littermate, as a lover or as all of the above, but you're not regarded, at least not fully, as the Alpha. To grab that role, you have to take a radical approach to your problem dog. I am going to suggest twenty different ruses you can pull to convince your pushy dog that you are the boss.

This more holistic approach is rather new in dealing with dog behavior problems, but not totally new. Until rather recently, trainers tended to hand out 1-2-3 remedies to behavioral inquiries, without addressing the underlying malaise that affects the owner/dog relationship. Lately, there have been some heartening efforts toward a more all-encompassing approach that help owners to identify problems, solve them *and* restructure their relationship with the dog. Carol Lea Benjamin's "Alpha Primer" (*American Kennel Gazette,* November 1986) is an excellent example of this, as is the chapter on behavior problems in *Training Your Dog* by Joachim Volhard and Gail Tamases Fisher (Howell Book House, 1983). Both programs are designed to help you up your Alpha status. My RRRR program—Radical Regimen for Recalcitrant Rovers—is similar, with my own personal flourishes, gathered from too many years of experience with too many problem dogs and too many problem owners. I offer my RRRR program to you with my sympathy and support.

Have your dog hold one thirty-minute down each day. These can be done during dinner. If your dog doesn't yet know a long down, sit on the leash, measuring out just as much as the dog needs to "crash." *Judy Emmert/Dealing with Dogs/TV Ontario*

Should your dog sleep on the bed? Not if it needs the RRRR— problem dogs do not belong on their owners' beds. You'll look like littermates. *Judy Emmert/Dealing with Dogs/TV Ontario*

76

Some final tips before the hit list: Don't modify the program until the behavior problem stops. Obviously, act on the behavior problem itself using sensible and humane set-ups, but add the RRRR program if you are experiencing any of the following:

Housetraining problems
Destructive chewing
Digging
Chasing people
Chasing cars
Jumping up
Overbarking
Aggression
Biting
Fighting with other dogs
Not coming when called
Predation

These are all *major* behavioral problems and they call for a *radical* approach. Apply the following program for the dog who is exhibiting any of the above problems and apply it for *one solid month.*

1. Give your dog two obedience sessions a day practicing whatever exercises the dog knows. These sessions should be ten to twenty minutes long. Do not praise physically during this session. Use only verbal praise and keep the session moving. Give commands quickly, dazzle the dog.
2. Have two formal eye-contact sessions with your dog each day. Problem dogs look at their owners only when they feel like it. Up the eye contact. Practice formally. Put a leash on. Sit the dog. Step around in front and animate the dog, saying, "Watch me. I want your attention *right now,*" in a low growling tone of voice. Do not yell. You want three to five seconds (*not* minutes) of locked, sealed eye contact. Once you get this moment, end with light *verbal* praise. See "Bitch Basics" for more details on eye contact.
3. Have your dog hold one thirty-minute down each day. This is very important. These downs can be done during television shows, dinner, reading or any time that works for you. Enforce it! If your dog doesn't know the down, teach it immediately, as well as the stay command. For now, sit on the leash and measure out only as much as the dog needs to hit the dust. If the dog jumps up on you, whip the leash down hard with a "No!" If the dog stress-whines, give the dog a slap under the chin and say "No!" If the dog bites the leash, whip it diagonally out of its mouth. During this time no petting, no toys, no soothing, no *nothing.* Long downs make you look Alpha. Consult chapter 13 concerning teaching the "long down."

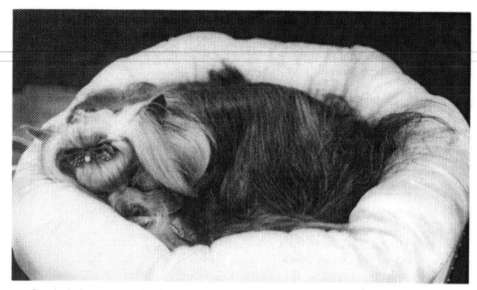

But don't demote your dog from the bedroom altogether. Instead, provide your pooch with comfortable sleeping accommodations of its own. *Kevin Smith*

Enough exercise is essential! How much is enough? Consult point number five in RRRR. Dogs that aren't exercised enough often resemble hummingbirds in the house. *Kevin Smith*

4. Move your dog into the bedroom for overnight sleeping. Read the chapter "Where Is Your Dog This Evening?" in *How to Be Your Dog's Best Friend* by the Monks of New Skete. This simple step has tremendous bonding effects. Remember, in the bedroom, *off the bed.* Problem dogs do not belong on beds. You'll look like littermates—but you want to look Alpha, remember? If the dog jumps up on the bed, tie the dog to the foot of the bed.

5. Exercise is very important. Problem dogs usually don't get enough *aerobic, sustained* exercise, which is what they need to calm them down. Putting the dog out in the backyard for three hours is no solution—it isn't exercising, it's exercising and resting, or just resting, period. Use a leash and jog or run with your dog. Sometimes the dog can be made to run alongside a bike. Keep moving. A good guide: for a small dog, ¼ mile, no stopping, four times a week; for a medium-size dog, ½ mile, no stopping, four times a week; for a large dog, 1 mile, no stopping, four times a week. I'm not even asking you to run with your dog every day. And a mile can go by quite quickly. Obviously, if your veterinarian advises against exercise for your particular dog, you'll have to skip this step.

6. Whenever you leave home, leave the radio on—easy-listening music, not rock or talk shows. Stressed tones of voice usually keep dogs on edge, and talk shows feature people who call in with problems and stresses.

7. Feed two times a day, if possible in the early morning and the early afternoon. Place the food down and leave it ten to fifteen minutes. Leave the dog and the food alone in a quiet room. Then return and pick up the food even if the dog hasn't finished. Do not make a thing out of the dog not eating—you may be engaging in faulty paralanguage and encouraging the dog *not* to eat even as you try to get it *to* eat (see "Nutrition Notes"). This method of feeding keeps food in the dog's stomach during its waking hours, eliminating hunger tension and giving you more of a chance for a calmer dog.

8. Reevaluate the diet. In my opinion high-quality meat-meal-based rations surpass soy-based rations. Drop all people food from the dog's diet. Your dog knows it was your food and sharing it with him doesn't make you look Alpha. When your dog doesn't have problems, you can slip in some people food, but not now. Remember, little things add up—usually to big problems. And never, ever add anything to the food after you've placed it down—not because you forgot an ingredient, not because you want to encourage the dog to eat. The dog will simply learn to wait until something yummy is added, and again, you won't look Alpha.

9. Give absolutely no food treats for one month. Yes, that's right, zero treats! Owners often place themselves in a subordinate position vis-à-vis the dog by giving too many treats or giving them in the wrong way.

Tighten food controls if your dog is on the Radical Regimen. Stop all treats for one month, drop all people food from the diet and insist on a short sit-stay before the gang chows down.

*Judy Emmert/
Dealing with Dogs/
TV Ontario*

Tug-of-war is taboo! It is not "cute." You're teaching your dog it's OK to bite down hard. Here, the Cocker is learning that the leash—which it should consider a symbol of the owner's authority—is really just a plaything.   *Judy Emmert/Dealing with Dogs/TV Ontario*

Stop for one month. If your dog's problems clear up and the month has passed, give one treat a day only if the dog sits. Never give a free treat carte blanche—make the dog do something for the treat. But nothing for one month. For more nutrition nuggets, see "Nutrition Notes."

10. Stop petting, stroking or fondling your problem dog for minutes, not to mention hours, at a time. Get your hands off the dog and pet for only seven to ten seconds and only if you've told the dog to sit or down. I know you love your dog, but love isn't enough. If it were, you wouldn't be having the behavior problem you're having. What your dog needs from you now to help it out of its behavioral jam is scratch-type petting, quick and light, not seductive stroking. It would shock most dog owners, but problem dogs are often pooped from petting, yet they oblige and stay for it because they're addicted to it.

11. Don't allow the dog to go before you in or out of a door. Make the dog wait by giving the stay command or at least go together. If you allow the dog to barge in or out of the door before you, you're telling it something pretty powerful about who controls the territory. The dog will say, "I do. After all, I always go *first,* and that wimp goes second." If this happens three or four times a day, the dog really gets to stake a claim to the territory it enters first, with ensuing problems. Some examples: The dog is allowed to barge out onto the street and has a problem fighting other dogs. Aren't you setting the stage for the fighting by allowing the barge? The dog chews destructively when the owner is not home. If you routinely let the dog crash into the house before you, aren't you telegraphing to it that the home is its territory—to chew up, to trash, to rearrange at whim? Don't allow the dog to go before you in or out of territory! Again, little things add up, usually to big problems. If that phrase is beginning to sound like a mantra in this chapter, I'm getting through.

12. Pick up all the dog's toys and leave one, perhaps its favorite, out. That's all the dog gets for one month. When a month passes and the problems clear, add one toy a week.

13. Stop playing any and all tug-of-war games. When you let go you look subordinate, and you're teaching the dog to bite down hard while in your presence. You're OKing serious mouth play. A no-no for a problem dog. Play only fetch and if the dog doesn't bring the object back to you and release it, get up and walk away.

14. If you have to have the dog move because it is in the way, make the dog *move.* Don't refrain from doing something or step over the dog because you don't want to bother it. If you're Alpha, you can go where you want when you want. Even if you want to change the channels and the dog is in front of the TV, make it move. Believe me, if you don't, the dog will notice. Little things add up.

15. Resolve to stop yelling at your dog and instead speak in a low tone of voice. If you yell, the dog will learn to wait for you to yell. Change your tonality, not your volume. Most problem dogs are yelled and screamed at. Most have tuned their owners out and learn to wait for louder and louder yelling until they finally don't hear their owners at all. If you've been tuned out, don't yell, change your tonality. You'll probably find you have to couple a physical correction with your lowered tone of voice to get the dog to tune back to your station on the dial—radio station Alpha. So don't hesitate to use a shake, a swat under the chin or a leash correction if necessary. But stop yelling.

16. If your dog knows the down command—really knows it—pull a surprise down on this problem dog once a week. For instance, you're in the kitchen doing dishes and you hear Rover waltz in. Wheel on him, give both the hand and vocal signal and command for *down!* Recalcitrant Rover will probably look shocked, and then do it. If not, you'll have to enforce it. The surprise element is the key. Remember, just once a week. Each down is a notch on your Alpha belt, and combined with your daily long downs you'll look like Evita Peron—which is how your dog needs to see you right now.

17. If your dog is aggressive, immediately employ a private trainer to work with you in your home. Please don't wait. One session can work wonders. The situation could get out of control. It certainly won't get better without training. Your dog is just growling, you say? You're in trouble—big trouble. *A growl is a bite that just hasn't connected yet.* Don't delude yourself. Call a trainer—yesterday! Institute RRRR immediately, even before the trainer gets there to tell you what to do specifically for the aggression. You'll make his or her task easier if the RRRR is on a roll. Read over my "open letter" later in this book in "Aggressive Advice."

18. If you have a shy or aggressive dog, neuter the dog right away. Male or female. Right away. Don't even think of breeding the dog. The problem could be partially genetic. The spay or neuter operation could help calm the dog and, in my experience, is a card you should play regardless of the age of the dog. The only exception is a very old dog who cannot risk the surgery. Otherwise, in my opinion, this step is merited and could be of great help.

19. Whatever the problem is, be sure you understand the *specific* corrections for it outlined by your trainer or in this book. Apply these techniques as well as the RRRR. You'll find that instituting the RRRR rarely interferes with specific corrective techniques and almost always aids their effect. I've had many clients who did nothing about specific problems such as chewing or aggression (usually because they were too busy, too tired or too scared to act on the problem itself) but *did* begin the RRRR program, and the problem

lessened and in some cases disappeared. I won't promise you that, but you will find the RRRR will greatly aid your specific corrections for whatever problem plagues your dog.

20. Finally, to balance the harshness of the RRRR program, create a little jingle for your dog. This jingle can be based on a popular television ad, and should be light, lilting and friendly—sometimes just substituting your dog's name where the product name was in the jingle will achieve the desired effect. Sing the jingle to your dog once a day—even from afar. I've used jingles from a variety of ads. Just sing it out to your dog once a day—and make eye contact. And don't go over ten seconds. It's a jingle not an aria. Your dog will know, and it's your way of saying, "Yes, you bratty boob, I still love you, even though for now you're living under this Radical Regimen for a Recalcitrant Rover!"

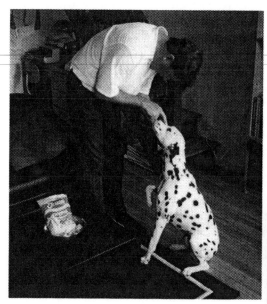

The Frito Filcher gets an advance warning with a distinctive phrase and a couple of taps on the "centering spot."

Kevin Smith

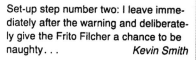

Set-up step number two: I leave immediately after the warning and deliberately give the Frito Filcher a chance to be naughty... *Kevin Smith*

... and of course the Frito Filcher readily obliges.

Kevin Smith

10

Setting Up Set-ups

IF YOU READ the RRRR and winced, you might go into catatonic shock after this chapter. Sit down and take a deep breath. Set yourself up to learn about set-ups. Still there? Let's go.

Remember the Iran-Contra affair? Remember Abscam? Remember Watergate? All these events were set-ups, sting operations of one sort or another designed to achieve a secret or not-so-secret goal. You don't have to be a politician to set up a set-up. You can simply be a frustrated dog owner using your superior thinking ability and creative powers.

What's a set-up? A set-up is a deliberately concocted event in which a given bad behavior is elicited from the dog. The difference between a set-up and real life is that the owner is physically, psychologically and environmentally prepared to correct the dog. Read the above sentence again. This sentence is the core of this book. Remember, you are smarter than your dog, and if you understand what a set-up is, you can outsmart your dog and eliminate problems. The steps of a set-up are

1. Issue an advance warning.
2. Deliberately give the dog a chance to be naughty.
3. Deliver verbal and/or physical discipline.
4. Reissue the warning phrase.
5. Give the dog another chance to be naughty.

Let's go over the steps in detail using a sample behavior problem.

1. *Issue an Advance Warning*

Advance warnings are very important. Unfortunately most people don't think enough in advance to give one. For instance, an owner might know darn well that when Fritos are left out on the coffee table Fido will filch them. Yet this owner will consistently place a bowl of Fritos on said coffee table and leave the room to shower in preparation for a party, hoping against hope that maybe, just *maybe* Fido won't steal the Fritos just this time. Of course Fido *does*. If you want to do a set-up for a Frito freak you must realize that every time you have put Fritos out and then left the room without saying anything you were *training*. You were training Fido that Fritos would be put out and nothing would be said. You were overtrusting and unintentionally training your dog to steal Fritos.

Now all that's going to change. Your days of saying nothing are over. Take a bowl of Fritos and get your dog's undivided attention. Use eye contact and as you place the Fritos down on the coffee table stare your dog down and issue an advance warning in a low, growling tone. Emphasize a few select phonics in your phrase ("OK, *Fido,* you *filch* those *Fritos* and you'll *fry*"). Don't worry about the words of your sentence. Other than its own name, which should be included, the words won't matter much to the dog. The phonics do. Emphasizing key phonetical sounds strengthens the sentence and helps the dog to remember the warning. This is important because you will use this same sentence later on in the set-up. Again, don't get hung up on the literal meaning of the words of warning. The sentence in this case could just as easily be, "OK, *Fido,* mushrooms, mushrooms, *mush*rooms, *Fritos, mush*rooms." But do emphasize three or four phonetical sounds in the warning.

2. *Deliberately Give the Dog a Chance to Be Naughty*

Now you leave the room to shower. Remember, there is no law that says you are not allowed to stop at the doorway just before you disappear from sight, stare down Fido and issue your advance warning again. You are going to give your dog a chance to steal the Fritos. Of course you're not really going to go take a shower. But it may be necessary to have your bathrobe on and a towel flung over your shoulder to trick the dog into thinking that you are. Instead, you simply go around the corner or two doors down the hall (whatever distance is necessary to convince the dog the coast is clear) and wait to hear the crunch of corn chips. This step is usually easy, but can involve fine points of trickery in order to elicit the bad behavior. Be creative! If you think long and hard enough it's usually possible to get the dog to misbehave.

3. *Deliver Verbal and/or Physical Discipline*

As soon as you hear Fido eating the Fritos or, worse, hear the bowl crash to the floor, you charge, and I mean *charge* back into the room, grab Fido,

I'm hiding out at the top of the stairs. When I hear the first crunch of corn chips I head downstairs, *pronto*. "Oh, my God, he's coming *back*! I'm caught!" *Kevin Smith*

The Filcher is focused on the Fritos . . . *Kevin Smith*

. . . and humanely disciplined with a swat under the chin.
 Kevin Smith

87

sit Fido, brandish some Fritos in front of Fido's face and give a firm swat under the chin, or in the case of a puppy a simple shake correction. This sounds easier than it may turn out to be if you haven't thought out this step of your set-up in advance. In anticipation of the chase that will probably ensue after you charge back into the room, you will certainly want to have put a collar or even a short tab leash on the dog so that the dog can be immediately retrieved if it dives under the buffet or runs to a corner. Of course, you've closed off the rest of the house to lessen the dog's options and eliminate all avenues of escape. Remember, chases cheapen owners. Even if you catch your dog after a prolonged chase, your physical correction might be lost on the dog because it is too delayed. So think this step out in advance so that you are environmentally prepared to act as Alpha—a quick, fully in control Alpha.

"Environmental preparation" is important. It is amazing how many owners will perform the first two steps of a set-up nicely enough but fail to think out this step. Think out the set-up in advance. What are the possible ways the dog can elude you and your correction? What do you have to do to prepare the environment so that you come out as top dog?

4. *Reissue the Warning Phrase*

You've caught your canine criminal in the act and disciplined said criminal. Now you haul out the same phrase you used in step number one, emphasizing the *same* phonics. Very often step number four will need to be teamed simultaneously with step number three. In our case of the Frito fracas this means that the warning phrase needs to be delivered at the same time the dog is shaken or swatted. Remember, no screaming, no whining and no laughing. A low, serious growllike tone is what you want. Remember to punch out those phonics. "OK, *Fido,* you *filch* those *Fritos* and you'll *fry.*" By reissuing the phrase you help your dog to understand you meant business when you used the phrase the *first* time. The whole point of a set-up is to get your dog to the point where warning phrases alone stop bad behavior. You can get to the point where you can even shorten the phrase as time goes by, simply saying, for instance, "Fritos, *fry,*" when you leave the room the first time. Further along, the dog should internalize the correction and give up Frito filching completely, even if no warning is issued. Great goal, eh?

5. *Give the Dog Another Chance to Be Naughty*

Guess what? We're not done with our set-up quite yet. We want to truly test the dog. So, after steps three and four are executed, go back to step one and again deliver the warning phrase. Now leave the room again. Move! You want to leave again while the correction is still fresh in the dog's mind. Reissue your warning and go into hiding again. If the dog filches Fritos again, go back to step three.

Maybe all you can gain with a first-time set-up of this sort is one or two

Set-up step number four: The same warning I gave in advance of the wrong-doing is repeated as I depart. *Kevin Smith*

Another sample set-up: The problem is that the dog jumps and barks when the intercom signals the arrival of guests. Downstairs, a decoy "guest" buzzes once every thirty seconds five to ten times. *Levon Mark*

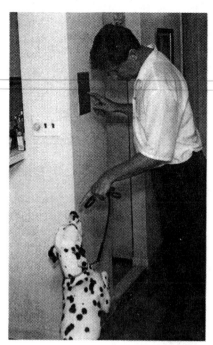

Meanwhile, instead of hurrying to admit the guest, I discipline the squealer and only then buzz the guest in. The guest knows there might be a wait because all of this is prearranged.   *Kevin Smith*

The dog is placed on a sit-stay, and instead of watching the entering guest, I watch the dog—ready to promptly correct the barking with the shake or swat correction and the jumping up with the three-part jumping correction.
     Kevin Smith

The guests are admitted and stay for a few minutes. They then leave but return a few minutes later and repeat the whole set-up.   *Kevin Smith*

minutes during which the dog doesn't steal any more Fritos. That's progress. Tomorrow is another day and you can try another set-up. You will gain more time with each set-up until the dog understands that items, even food, placed on the coffee table belong to *you*.

Frequency and Fairness

How often do you try a set-up? My usual answer to clients is "until one works." However, some owner discretion is necessary. Some harsh, blamer owners will do thirty set-ups in one day. In the above case, the owner of the Frito freak, in an attempt to proof the set-up even more, might go to the ridiculous extreme of "setting the dog up" to not even *look* at Fritos when taken into the corner deli! The owner might sit the dog at the deli door, deliver the warning phrase, trot the dog inside, deliberately glide the dog past the Fritos and rudely yank the dog away. This is taking the idea of a set-up too far. The dog stole Fritos only at home, not in the store. I mean, really, let's be fair.

But there are some owners who worry about whether the whole idea behind set-ups is fair to the dog. Of course, there will always be instances of possible overkill, like the one mentioned above. But, in general, set-ups are much more fair to your dog than the pressure the dog feels from being constantly nagged, cajoled or overtrusted. It is more humane to stage one successful set-up than to constantly browbeat your dog about bad behavior.

Sometimes the concepts of frequency and fairness are intertwined. Just as it's unfair to overuse set-ups, it is also unfair to underutilize them by not staging enough set-ups. Don't think your dog is rehabilitated after one set-up. Staging the same set-up thirty times in one day might be appropriate for a rare dog. But for most dogs one set-up a day is the limit.

Now using what we've learned here, look over the following worksheets. Included are the set-up steps and another sample behavior problem. Just get acquainted with the worksheets for now. Then go on to the next chapter, "Why Set-ups Sometimes Foul Up." If you're skipping around in this book and were attracted by the worksheets, my advice is to go back to the beginning of the text rather than risk staging a poor set-up because of lack of information. Then if future problems crop up, you will find you will be able to go directly to the worksheets to script your set-ups. Use a pencil so that you can use the worksheets over and over again.

Use a pencil when filling out the form as you may want to erase and rework the form later for additional or new problems that may arise. Better yet, make copies of the worksheets. If you do not have a specific problem in mind, make one up. Remember, practice makes perfect. The more experience you have in thinking about set-ups, the better you will be at implementing them. Good luck!

My problem pooch has the following problem: (Briefly outline the problem behavior, e.g., My dog attacks other dogs it passes on the street.)

_____

_____

_____

_____

Pause now and review the steps in a set-up. They are:

1. *Issue an advance warning,* using eye contact if possible and a distinctive phrase, e.g., *"Tippy, you touch that other dog and you're DEAD."* Be sure to include the dog's name in the phrase.
2. *Deliberately give the dog a chance to be naughty,* e.g., glide Tippy right into the path of another dog, loosen the leash and pray that Tippy will start a fight.
3. *Deliver verbal and/or physical discipline,* e.g., Tippy gets a firm swat under the chin.
4. *Reissue the warning phrase,* e.g., "Well, excuuuuuuse me, *Tippy,* I said you *touch* that other *dog* and you're *dead!"*
5. *Give the dog another chance to be naughty,* e.g., you hang a wheelie as you complete step 4 and catch up with the dog Tippy just molested and glide Tippy past the dog again.

Now, using the following worksheet, notate the steps of your set-up for your problem. If you made copies you can place them side by side if you need to refer back to the steps or example.

People, Pooches & Problems
Worksheet 2

My Set-up:

1. _____

_____

_____

_____

2. _____

_____

_____

_____

3. _____

_____

_____

_____

4. _____

_____

_____

_____

5. _____

_____

_____

_____

Will you put your problem pooch on the RRRR for one month? __yes __no

If not, why not?_____

Is there a reason a set-up won't work? __yes __no

If yes, why? No evidence to facilitate discipline after the fact; corrections cannot be given quickly enough; firm enough corrections cannot be given; dog is stupid, etc. See next chapter.

_____

_____

_____

_____

_____

_____

_____

_____

_____

_____

_____

_____

_____

_____

_____

_____

_____

People, Pooches & Problems
Worksheet 3

If for any reason you cannot figure out how to set up a set-up on your own, you need to pick a partner. It's preferable to pick someone who does not live with you or your dog as he or she will be more objective and exact in designing a set-up. However, in a crunch, a family member, spouse, boyfriend, girlfriend or significant other will do. Have this person read the chapters "RRRR" and "Setting Up Set-ups."

This worksheet is for your partner to use to critique your set-up. Partners: Be frank and helpful in your comments. Point out any gaps in the five steps. Look carefully to any stated reasons why the set-up won't work and decide whether you agree or disagree as to whether the dog should or should not be put on the RRRR. Good luck! Remember, two heads are better than one.

Partner critique: _____

_____

_____

_____

_____

_____

_____

_____

_____

_____

_____

_____

_____

_____

_____

11

Why Set-ups Sometimes Foul Up

WE'VE SAID A LOT about set-ups so far, and you might think that they are miraculously fail-safe and, well, "set." But no set-up is perfect. No sting operation *always* stings. And doing one set-up doesn't necessarily mean that your dog will never act up again.

Let's review some of the reasons set-ups sometimes foul up. You can refer back to this section if your set-up goes awry. Remember, though, not to use the following complications as excuses not to correct your canine criminal. You'll see in most instances these qualifications don't foul up the set-up irredeemably. These flukes force you to fine-tune your set-up just as the FBI has to fine-tune sting operations. Remember, Abscam took a lot of thought and planning. (For that matter so did Watergate!) Trickery, however well intended, isn't easy. You owe it to your dog to put as much time into designing, and if necessary redesigning, your set-up as the cops put into Abscam and the criminals put into Watergate. Here are the potential areas where set-ups foul up.

The dog is just too young for set-ups. In this case you might have to wait things out. Practice "creative avoidance" by using confinement or a crate and give the dog more time until your canine Dorothy makes it out of Oz. This potential foul-up occurs most frequently when owners try to set up very young dogs for chewing or housebreaking problems and the puppy is simply too young to assimilate the information imparted in a set-up. You certainly should not be setting up, for instance, a three- or four-month-old puppy to destructively chew or soil. The puppy is too young, the set-up is unfair and you should simply confine, confine, confine the puppy or have it under your direct supervision. Be fair to the young.

The correction is too soft. For wimpy owners with dominant dogs, this is far and away the most common reason their set-ups foul up. Some examples: The owner of an aggressive dog might simply *restrain* the dog from lunging, charging or biting when what Jack the Ripper really needs is a good strong slap under the chin. Or, the owner of a lunatic lunger may simply give ineffective jerks on the training collar, or even not have one on the dog, rather than giving an effective pop and snap on the collar. In my years of dog training I find that the running themes marking ineffective physical correction are, in a nutshell: The owner will *restrain* the dog instead of correcting it, or the owner will simply *reposition* the dog instead of correcting it. Double-check your set-up for this foul-up and be honest with yourself: Are you sure you were correcting your dog firmly enough? Are you restraining the dog or repositioning it instead of correcting it?

The correction is too slow. After youth and lack of force, owner slowness tops the hit parade of excuses and potential foul-ups. Examples include using the shake correction when the swat could be delivered more quickly. Another form of owner slowness is simply verbally *nagging* the dog to "be good" and *then* finally delivering a physical correction that unfortunately might as well be five years late. There will always be owners who, because of lack of physical dexterity or coordination, cannot deliver corrections quickly enough. Their timing will be forever off and the dog will always explode, cheat, chew, lie or steal faster than they can correct, or so they think. These souls need help in the form of a private trainer. But let me tell you something: It's a lot cheaper to try to speed yourself up and weed this foul-up out of your set-up than to pay a high training bill. I sympathize with you—I used to be one of the slowpokes, but with coaching from my training mentors, I learned just how *fast* "fast" really is. Often, one session with a professional trainer will help you to duplicate the correct speed for the set-up.

The owner is too loud. Even if the dog is old enough, and the owner fast enough and forceful enough, some set-ups still foul up because the owner becomes a screaming banshee. This will often happen during part four of the set-up (when the owner is supposed to repeat the warning phrase), and the owner (in an attempt to make sure that he or she "got through" to the dog) will bellow so loudly that the set-up fouls up. If you yell, the dog then focuses on the *correction* rather than the *connection* that you want it to make. For instance, if you find an "accident" and scream at your dog—even if you are properly executing discipline after the fact—your screaming will simply make the dog focus on *you* instead of its shame. Be sure to read chapter 6, "Do Dogs Feel Guilt or Shame?" for more on this. Screaming makes any shame the dog might feel turn into pure fear and the desire to flee. If your set-ups make your dog freeze or take flight, the chances are you're too loud. Your voice can be hard and firm but you mustn't yell or shriek. Remember the gentle growl of the bitch directed at a naughty puppy: *Grrrrrrrrrrrrrrrrrrrr.* Growl softly and carry no big sticks! And please, no rolled-up newspapers: first-class folklore— no bitch ever disciplined a puppy with a rolled-up newspaper!

There is no proof and some proof is needed to shame the dog. An example is the theft of food, when the theft includes complete digestion of the desired "proof." Another example is destructive chewing. Perhaps you don't even know *what's* been chewed—until days later when you miss it or need it. But, by then, the object of the dog's desire has been completely ingested. There is no proof to justify discipline after the fact. In fact, you might have to wait for the elimination stage of the digestive process before you recognize what you're missing. What can you do when proof is needed and you can't get any proof to convict the dog? You can think, and think hard. After all, we are supposed to be smarter than them. Is there any way you can trick the dog into leaving a trail or even a smidgen of evidence?

I once had a client who had a devious Dalmatian that inhaled whatever it could find on the kitchen counter. The Dalmatian had also learned to open the refrigerator, which it investigated when the counters were bare. Of course, the dog did all of these things when the owner wasn't home. The owner finally got tired of counter climbing and refrigerator raids and devised a set-up under my guidance. The dog was "invited" to steal peanut butter mounded on a dinner plate. Dogs tend to ingest peanut butter rather slowly. My perverse sense of humor found this quite satisfying. So, some of the peanut butter would be left stuck to the plate. We would have the proof we needed. We came back after a short stroll. The dinner plate was smashed on the kitchen floor with just enough proof stuck to it to give the Dalmatian a correction with a connection. The dog was walking around trying to scrape the peanut butter off the roof of its mouth, and was brought to the evidence, disciplined and isolated. Score: Humans, 1, Dalmatians, 0. By the way, use creamy not chunky. It sticks to the plate better.

The stimulus cannot be repeated, it is too specific. This is often the situation in cases of aggression. You need to get the dog grouchy, but often the stimulus or stimuli that set the dog off cannot be reproduced in order to secure a set-up. For instance, if your dog growls at other dogs when passing them, it might not be easy to get the cooperation of another owner and have them glide their dog past yours so that you can correct your dog. After all, people may not want to cooperate, no matter how badly *you* want to do your set-up. The solution may have to be using people and their dogs without them knowing they are being used. This might demand your securing the services of a professional. A professional will have the timing to make sure no other person or dog gets hurt.

Sometimes owners will claim they cannot give an advance warning, or even do a set-up at all, because the dog "just explodes." Or they will claim that they don't even know what the stimulus *is* that sets off the dog. But un- provoked, unexplainable and unannounced attacks by dogs are very rare. Usually the dog is responding to a given stimulus, and *is* announcing way in advance its intentions. The owner simply cannot read the dog's signals. For more on this, see chapter 17, "Aggressive Advice," and try to find a way to read the signs of aggression more quickly and repeat the stimulus.

The dog cannot give up his Alpha status so quickly. In this case the owner might be trying to do set-ups too soon. Instead of doing set-ups for specific problems, wait awhile and let the Radical Regimen for Recalcitrant Rovers kick in. Follow point ten *strictly* and give only earned praise. See what develops, wait and pray. Go two weeks like this and then try set-ups again. The RRRR will change your relationship with the dog and quite possibly soften your problem pooch, preparing the dog to accept set-ups.

The dog is mentally or genetically defective. Don't laugh—it does happen. But it is very rare. Occasionally there are dogs that are so "stupid" that they can't figure out the five parts of the set-up. This is not to be confused with *owners* who cannot comprehend the five steps of a set-up! There are also dogs who will rather stupidly fight through the correction step of the set-ups. Check yourself: Are you being too loud, too soft, too slow or too hard in your corrections? Remember, if you are too hard some dogs with active defense reflexes will simply go completely on the defensive and fight the correction. This is not the same as stupidity. Usually these dogs are quite smart. They just fake stupidity.

Dogs that are genetically defective are another matter. Sometimes genetic defects predetermine not only the physical health of the dog, but the dog's mental health as well. This is sometimes the case with "puppy mill" produce or dogs from "backyard breeders." In my opinion, even a genetically defective dog is worth working with, and worth staging set-ups for, because the alternatives are pretty grim. Of course, if you don't yet have a dog, my advice is to procure one only after being *interviewed* by a reputable breeder who uses Puppy Aptitude Testing (PAT) to evaluate temperament. That's the only sure way to skirt genetic behavioral defects, and even this method isn't 100 percent effective.

Set-ups that foul up usually mean that the owner is too slow, too loud, too soft or too hard. Or perhaps the stimuli can't be repeated and really needs to be repeated for that particular dog, or the dog is too bossy, too stupid or too genetically weak to assimilate the information and discipline.

In my experience—and my records show this—80 percent of the time the set-up doesn't "take" because of *owner softness or slowness.* When skills improve, the set-up usually kicks in successfully. Remember, part of owner slowness is simply not doing enough set-ups over a long period of time.

If you think your set-ups foul up because of disciplinary softness on your part, remember, while you should always go for the softest correction possible, if continual failed set-ups are happening the dog is probably informing you that you can get tougher. Heed the message. Get tougher.

My records show that 5 percent of the aggressive dogs I've worked with will simply not relinquish their Alpha status. The bond between themselves and their owners is so corrupted, so out of kilter, so entangled with the owner as a submissive party that the dog cannot be corrected or shamed any longer. These dogs usually bite their owners or other family members and will continue to do so even after training is attempted. They usually have to be euthanized. My records also show that another 5 percent of aggressive dogs are too slow, too stupid or genetically defective, thus preventing them from understanding the corrective and informational content of set-ups. But in 90 percent of cases of canine aggression I have found that if a dog is smart enough to have the organizational and mental skills required to run a human household via dominance, canine stupidity usually is *not* the issue. Human stupidity, lack of education and lack of motivation usually *are* the issues. Once in a while, everyone, dogs and humans alike, need some time out to make set-ups work out. As I always urge, read on.

12

Creative Avoidance

 TIME OUT! This is a phrase you've probably yelled when in the midst of a heated argument with someone. Perhaps you felt you just needed a breather so that a criticism could sink in, or needed time to think over a response. Sometimes in canine/human relations similar time-outs are necessary. A given canine conundrum can become so complicated and convoluted that both owner and dog feel lost at sea. It is sometimes necessary to simply let some time go by so that a particular form of bad behavior is simply *avoided,* not allowed to happen, somehow circumvented, *before* trying to correct the naughtiness. This is what I call "creative avoidance." By simply avoiding triggering the dog's bad behavior, sometimes an atmosphere is created in which the dog will accept correction. Many times this will entail simply establishing a moratorium period on a given bad behavior so that it just can't take place at all. Some examples:

 • Mary Kratzmiller had a Labrador Retriever who was in the habit of not coming when called. This behavior had been going on for at least one year. The routine was this: Mary would routinely let the dog out in the morning to relieve itself, which the dog promptly did. But the Lab would then encircle the house three times, like clockwork, and disappear into the neighboring woods. Mary would helplessly call the Labrador from her porch, standing in her bathrobe and fluffy slippers. Sometimes her Lab would even grant her the favor of glancing back at her for two seconds and would then, of course, gallivant off into the woods. The behavior had become so patterned in that even immediate training for the recall would not turn the situation around. A moratorium period had to be put into place—some creative avoidance practiced—while at the same time the dog entered formal obedience training. We had to buy some time to let the dog forget about the morning ritual of running away and begin to teach the word "come." "Does that mean that I'll have to take him out on a leash every morning to let him do his business?" Mary asked. "I guess so," I answered, "or you'll have to get an aerial runner chain and string it between the house and a tree and hook him onto that. Or maybe one of the kids will have to walk him. But under no circumstances can this dog be allowed to run away from you." Every time in the past Mary had said the word "come" and the dog had disobeyed, Mary was *training* the dog that the word "come" meant "Stay where you are or run the other way." It takes a *long time* for a dog to forget such mistraining and apply a new meaning to an old word. I usually recommend a moratorium period of six weeks for dogs who do not come when called. For more on this, see chapter 18, "To Come or Not to Come."

• Twinkles was an unaltered Yorkshire Terrier. He had a habit of leg-lifting every place he desired, including on the sides of the sofa, the bed and even his owner's leg. While it was easy enough to stage a set-up for such behavior (and we did), I recommended that Twinkles first be neutered and then strictly confined to a crate whenever the owner was not home. The bulk of the sprinkling that went on occurred at that time. But the owner wanted to start work on the problem right away and was enthusiastic about the idea of set-ups and discipline after the fact—perhaps *too* enthusiastic. Because the behavior was long-standing, and because it would take a few weeks for the benefits of the neutering to kick in, some creative avoidance was in order. We set it up so that Twinkles resided in a crate so small he would have to lie in his own urine if he let loose. He refrained, and after two weeks of strict confinement (and the neutering operation) the owner staged a set-up. She left the house with an advance warning, returned, disciplined if Twinkles had urinated and then repeated the process. Twinkles tightened up after just one set-up. It was probably the combination of neutering, crating and the actual set-up that helped Twinkles become a little star. But creative avoidance also played a role in this success story.

No Cop-out

Twinkles' owner asked me at one point, "Aren't we just *avoiding* the problem by neutering and crating him?" I replied, "Yes, in a sense we are, but we need to let a little time pass during which Twinkles adjusts to the hormonal changes of the neutering and to strict crating. He has to learn to correct himself, so to speak, from within, by simply learning to hold his own urine." This owner was gung-ho on discipline. So the idea of "setting Twinkles up" was a genuine thrill. But she had been using the classic folklore technique of striking Twinkles on the rump with a rolled-up newspaper. I explained that no bitch would use a rolled-up newspaper as an implement for discipline, and demonstrated correct discipline techniques. The owner was still ready to really go to town on Twinkles. But it was still too soon. Instead, creative avoidance was employed and success achieved.

I'm a strong advocate of getting on your dog's case if it is flubbing up behaviorally. But you should also know that often stalling correction is OK as well—as long as during the stall period the dog simply cannot do whatever naughty thing it was doing. Creative avoidance does *not* mean that you let bad behavior go on unchecked. It simply means that you structure the dog's environment, schedule or exposure to suggestive stimuli to avoid triggering the bad behavior you will later correct.

Creative avoidance is not a cop-out. Some hard-line trainers may say it is more productive to go after all problem behaviors immediately, but this presents several problems. Some strong, dominant dogs will not accept immediate correction for specific faults. They will often retaliate against their owners. Softer dogs might simply crumple under discipline and begin to submissively urinate, nervously shake or simply avoid their owners by hiding from them. A structured waiting period during which the problem behavior is avoided gives owner and dog a cooling-off period. Trainers who go after problem behavior with heavy corrections without giving a second thought to the benefits of creative avoidance often wind up treating only the symptoms and not the cause of the problem. For more on this, see chapter 4, "A Worthy Cause."

Often, if set-ups continually fail, it is an indication that a little creative avoidance is in order. Back off, refrain from disciplining and try to think out some ways that you can simply avoid triggering the bad behavior. During this period of time, I'd suggest putting your dog on my Radical Regimen for Recalcitrant Rovers for one month. This will begin to change the relationship between you and your dog and make the dog more open to correction for a specific problem—if only because it forgets old behavior patterns.

Creative Avoidance Forever?

Some *permanent* forms of creative avoidance are frankly necessary and inevitable for most dog owners. For instance, no matter how well-trained your dog may be, it's probably unwise to leave a pot roast cooling on the edge of the kitchen counter with your dog in the kitchen unattended. The temptation is simply too great, and most owners learn to avoid such a challenge. I *suppose* you could stage a set-up and trick the dog into stealing the roast, but why waste the time (and the roast) when it's just as easy to place the roast on top of the refrigerator or simply leave it in the oven? Some owners with several dogs simply have to use crates as tools of creative avoidance, so that individual dogs can get special attention or proper nutrition, or just to avoid tripping over too many dogs. This form of avoidance is fine as long as the dogs do not live out their entire lives in crates, and as long as the crates are not used as a cop-out or a way of avoiding correcting bad behavior.

Finally, the break provided by a period of creative avoidance gives the emotionally upset, distraught owner a chance to think out how to concoct a perfectly structured, nonhysterical, instructive set-up to stop bad behavior. Domineering owners might feel that a waiting period prevents them from reforming their dogs pronto, but it is precisely these owners who will tend to get too loud and too bossy when they attempt corrections. Just because, by reading this book, you have the knowledge of how to set-up and correct your dog does not mean that you have to *use* that knowledge right away. Unless the problem behavior is a threat to life and limb, time is probably on your side. If you find repeated corrections fail, try creative avoidance for one to three weeks and then stage a sterling set-up. During this time-out period, begin to teach, or *reteach,* your dog essential words that will help you to stage set-ups— words your dog can live by.

13

Words Dogs Live By

EVERY GOOD DOG needs to know the words "heel," "sit," "stay," "come" and "down" to function reasonably in human society. Of course, a well-trained dog can learn to understand forty words or more, but if your dog doesn't know at least these five basic words you should consider it a functional illiterate. The difference between canine illiteracy and the human version is that your dog is hardly responsible for its own lack of knowledge. Bluntly, it's your fault. It is every owner's responsibility to teach the dog these five basic words, either at home with the aid of a book or the help of a private trainer or in obedience class.

Magical Thinking

Teaching your dog words will, however, be useless unless those words are usable in real-life situations. Please don't assume that your dog knows a command if it only obeys the command some of the time. For instance, if your dog comes to you when you happen to call its name while you're fixing its morning meal or sees you brandishing a treat, but disobeys the same command when it is running around a baseball field and you call, I'm sorry to inform you, but your dog simply doesn't know how to come when called. The dog might have an acquaintance with the word, but it does not *know* the word. It is not a word the dog lives by. Yet, many dog owners caught in just such a jam would swear to high heaven that their dog *does* know how to come when called. I note this misperception on the part of dog owners because this magical thinking is one of the most common reasons that dog training doesn't take with some dogs. The misguided owner thinks that the dog already knows certain words when the dog just *doesn't*.

The problem with this lack of education—again, purely the fault of owner negligence—is that many set-ups involve the use of one, two or even three command words in order to succeed. For instance, let's say your dog has a problem shying away from children. You decide to follow the five steps outlined in the set-up chapter to conquer, or at least lessen, this problem. First, bravo to you for going even this far in your efforts!

So, following the set-up scenario, you arrange for a trip to the local playground at recess time. You know you can trick probably half a dozen or, more likely, one zillion kids into attempting to relate with Shy Sam. You park yourselves on the fringes of the playground and, sure enough, children start to approach to solicit attention from Sam. Naturally (big surprise), Sam backs away behind you to hide from his young admirers. You haul Sam forward out into "reality" every time he does. You warn him, following the set-up scenario, and at one point realizing that even shyness can be disciplined, you give him a good shake, tap his centering spot and start the set-up process again. But Sam keeps retreating. What's wrong here? What's crucial, and what's missing, is the issuance of, and obedience to, the command word "stay." Each time the kids approach, the word and signal for stay should be given to the dog. Technically, if Sam really, truly *knows* the word, he will not be able to retreat behind you—if only because he fears being reprimanded for disobeying the stay command. But since Sam doesn't know stay, he can't be given the command, and the set-up fouls up. When your dog has no words to live by, it can quite literally be doomed.

When you first introduce a word, teach it in a quiet environment. This is what Sam's owner had to do before a set-up succeeded. If you can't practice at home try to find a quiet nook outside in which to teach each word. Graduate to more hectic areas. You will see your dog begin to comprehend each word. A light will go on in your dog's eyes—that special light of recognition and obedience. As soon as you see that "light" that's your signal to up-scale your training environment to one that will have more distractions to throw your dog off the word. It's important to "proof" each word as fully as possible, especially for shy or aggressive dogs.

Equipment

I prefer a metal collar with pounded, flat links. If the links are pounded flat and not rounded, the action of the collar tends to be quicker. Just run your hand across the collar after laying it flat on the store counter. Form your hand into a fist and pass the collar over it. Snap it on your wrist. Is the action quick, clean? Nylon collars are fine, too, but they tend to stretch with use and are harder to locate on the neck of a speeding dog who is taking you on a goose chase. The tighter the collar rides on the dog's neck, the more effective it usually is—but even properly fitted collars tend to sink down the dog's neck.

When a training collar is placed on your dog properly it will look like the letter P turned sideways. *Charles Hornek*

The solution might be to purchase a nylon "snap-around" collar that is clipped high on your pet's neck, yet still has training collar action and speed. It might take some searching to locate such collars. Try your speciality pet store or a dog-ware catalog. I have used such snap-around collars on dogs who would otherwise have needed a prong collar and have had good results. The secret, of course, is that the collar stays hiked up on the dog's neck, which makes even small corrections or restraints more effective.

Some owners are enamored of harnesses. I think, at least in most cases, harnesses belong on horses. Occasionally there is a dog with a trachea problem or other medical malady that simply makes the use of any kind of neck collar impossible. But many owners simply use harnesses because Fifi fidgeted once when a neck collar was put on. Usually the harnessed dog just spins around like a yo-yo at the end of the leash, and it becomes impossible to give quick corrections—and possible only to restrain the dog from getting in trouble.

When a training collar is placed on your dog properly, it will look like the letter P turned sideways. Stand with your dog on your left side, make your collar into a P shape and pass it over the dog's head. There should be only two or three inches of extension when the collar is pulled tight. If you are using a snap-around collar, there will, of course, be less extension, but you should be able to run your index finger all the way around the inside of the collar in a smooth motion.

Lastly, you need a good leash, one that fits comfortably in your palm yet is not so wide that you cannot manipulate it with your fingers. Chain leashes are hard on the hands, and the weight of the leash decimates the corrective tug by the time it reaches the dog's neck. I prefer a leash of braided construction made of leather with no sewn parts. With this kind of leash, there is nothing to break, and strong corrections can be given without worry.

Heeling

Set-ups for dogs who lunge at other dogs, snarf up garbage or simply pull ahead are next to impossible to concoct with any success unless your dog has an acquaintance with the word "heel." This is the word your dog must live by if your set-up is to succeed. The word "heel" means pretty much what it says—that your dog should be at your heel, precisely with its withers (shoulders) at your left heel. Why the left? There is probably no absolute reason except that many people are right-handed and all dogs are creatures of habit and prefer predictability.

As for the word "heel" it's a somewhat funny word to many people. At first they feel somewhat uncomfortable saying it to a dog because they've never said it before. In fact, most trainers don't know why we use this particular word. The reason is that phonetically "heel" simply doesn't sound like any of the other five command words. Take a moment and say all of the five basic words aloud and you'll see that they each sound very different. In fact, if you place your fingers over your mouth and clearly pronounce heel, sit, stay, come

In heeling, the dog is on your left side. Keep your hands palm down on the leash—you will then have full power of your forearm to "check" the dog toward your thigh if the dog breaks the heel.

Judy Emmert/
Dealing with Dogs/TV Ontario

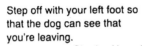

Step off with your left foot so that the dog can see that you're leaving.

Charles Hornek

This is the proper heeling position. Settle for nothing less. Remember, you might have to use heeling someday in a set-up so you'll want to teach it right and teach it *tight* from the beginning.

Dealing with Dogs/
TV Ontario

and down you can feel in your own fingers the difference between the words. Proper enunciation of the words is important and, as we've discussed before, screeching commands is absolutely forbidden. Just as chases cheapen owners, there is no quicker way to cheapen yourself in a dog's eyes than to scream command words or reprimands.

Remember the tips concerning vocalizations in the RRRR: When giving a command or reprimanding the dog, change your tonality by lowering it but do not change the volume of your voice. If the command is for an active exercise, pitch your voice slightly higher (heel, come) or slightly lower for static commands (down, stay, sit). Simply put, just remember if the word involves movement, up your voice. If it doesn't, lower your voice.

In heeling, the dog is at your left-hand side. Keep your hands palm down on the leash so that you will have the full power of your forearm to tug the dog in toward your thigh for a correction. You will find that the inside portion of your left wrist does a lot of slapping against your outer left thigh; after years of training I have a permanent bruise on mine to prove this. Keep the collar up high around the dog's neck with the rounded rings of the collar rotated underneath the ear closest to you. Step off with your left foot, saying, "Rascal, heel." Try to remember to use your left foot so that your dog can see that you're leaving. If the dog lags or lunges ahead give a sharp correction in toward your left thigh. Make this a smart snap, not a restrained choking action. Snap that leash! Pop that training collar! Zip that dog in toward your thigh—that's the key to good heeling. Restraining your dog by keeping tension on the lead will only result in a standoff. Use plenty of praise as you strut, and when you stop, sit your dog next to you by simultaneously pulling up on the leash in and up toward your chest, and if necessary push down on the dog's rump. You'll find that in time just a slight snap of the leash up and slightly in toward you will telegraph a sit through your dog's backbone.

The Automatic Sit

Part of the heeling process—and one that is essential for successful set-ups—is drilling your dog in the automatic sit. This means that when you stop for any reason, at any time, rain or shine, your dog is to sit smartly alongside your left leg. This technique can be trained in when you are teaching the heel. Many dogs just sit naturally when the owner stops and if yours does, you're lucky—you were just spared a slipped disk. But if yours doesn't, pull up slightly on the training collar one or two seconds before you actually stop. If necessary, transfer your right hand to the base of the leash. Then your left hand will be free to guide the dog's bottom into a sit as your right hand jerks the collar up. If you don't make this hand transfer you'll find that your arms crisscross, forming an uncomfortable X. You will probably not be able to execute the maneuver.

Drill your dog. Take five steps ahead and then insist on a sit. Take another five steps. Sit the dog again, and so on. Don't say the word "sit"—just get the dog into the position. If you say the word continually the dog will simply learn to wait for you to say the command word. The dog will think that it should remain standing until you say "sit." You will then be condemned to saying "sit" every time you stop. But, especially if you own a problem dog who is a hooligan on heel, you will want the assurance that the automatic sit is subliminally solid in the dog's brain. That way, if your lunatic lunger suddenly comes upon another dog, squirrel, pigeon or other distraction, you can rest assured that as you screech to a stop the dog's training dictates "sit" before its instincts dictate "score!" Insist on the automatic sit—it is not simply ornamental. You will feel so relieved knowing that your dog glides into a solid sit when you stop—so that you do not have to be dragged or pulled about. Be careful about double commands like "sit down" or "c'mon, heel" while practicing heeling. Remember, "down" and "sit" will very shortly be distinct words meaning desired actions. Don't confuse your dog. Use "let's go" as a term of encouragement instead.

OK

"OK" is used when you want to release your dog from strict heeling to relieve itself, to play with another dog, to sniff around or as part of a set-up to trick the dog into bad behavior. I simply don't believe that a dog should pull you to where it likes to eliminate, play or sniff. Dogs that yank their owners around are displaying dominance. Instead, I believe in an either/or proposition, which means that *you* heel your dog where you want it to engage in any of these activities, and then *you* release the dog from the heel command with a clearly pronounced "OK!" Your palms will be flat down on the leash, but at this point, turn your hand around and dramatically push the leash forward, clearly indicating that the loose lead means that your dog gets more freedom. For instance, let's say that your dog is on heel and you want to do a set-up for garbaging. Garbaging, of course, means that your dog likes to snarf up objects on the street and perceives itself to be a vacuum cleaner. When you pass a particularly attractive gob of garbage you simply issue the OK command, issue an advance warning and push the leash out to release your dog from the heel. If you are really lucky, the dog begins to gobble garbage, at which point you reprimand your dog, repeat the warning and double back over the same gob of garbage. If your dog dips its head again, you repeat the set-up steps again.

Finally, remember that it is absolutely essential for problem dogs and problem owners to begin the heeling process *indoors.* You cannot allow your dog to yank you out of the front door, yank you across the front yard, yank you into the car, yank you out of the car and then ask your dog to heel down the smartest avenue in town. If you consistently allow a dog to precede you in or out of territory you are telling the dog a whole heck of a lot about who owns the territory. Your dog will simply surmise, "I do. After all, I go first. The dummy I'm dragging goes second."

Please remember that dogs do not think in terms of addresses, street names, your reputation or—for that matter—what you may be trying to accomplish via a set-up. Instead they think in primitive terms of *territory*—and who owns the territory is dictated by who gets to go first. City owners encounter particular problems involving heeling because their dogs live—at least outdoors—almost exclusively on leash. Urban owners will find a lengthy explanation of the intricacies of city heeling—probably the fullest explanation in print—in *The Evans Guide for Civilized City Canines*.

Sit and Stay

You might find that you've taught the word sit at the same time you were teaching the heel just by tightening up on the lead. If you're not so lucky, or if you've decided to teach "sit" first, which is perfectly OK, use three fingers pressed together in a curved motion over the dog's head as you say "sit." The dog's rump will sink as it follows the motion of your hand.

Attach a leash to teach the sit command. Start from the heel position, with the dog on your left. Keep the leash absolutely straight up and down. There should be a slight amount of tension on the lead. Hold the taut lead with your left hand and bring your right hand down in front of the dog's face with your hand just slightly cupped closed. Now, as your hand nears the dog's eyes, flash it open, fingers closed, and say "stay." Step in front of the dog. If the dog moves, give a zip on the leash and repeat. If the dog stays, praise and return to the heel position. Now go halfway around your dog, return and go all the way around. Say "stay" each time you leave and flash the stay signal in your dog's face. Now loosen the tension on the lead and widen the distance you go away from the dog. Repeat the above steps until you can walk completely around your dog using a six-foot leash with the dog not moving.

That little "flash flourish" to your stay signal is very important. It makes the signal more dramatic and makes more of an impression on the dog. While most trainers use a flattened hand with no flashing movement, I prefer the sudden burst of fingers. I picked up this training technique by watching old clips of Diana Ross and the Supremes singing "Stop! In the Name of Love" and flashing their hands at the audience in their dynamic dance routines. It was effective for audiences then and it's effective for dogs now. Dogs do stop and stay in place!—if not in the name of love, then in the name of obedience.

Proofing the Sit-Stay

I like a proofing method found in *Training Your Dog: The Step-by-Step Manual* by Joachim Volhard and Gail Tamases Fisher (Howell Book House, 1983). They suggest the following to get the sit-stay tight and superreliable, and a supertight sit-stay is essential in staging many set-ups. From the heel position, signal and command "stay." Walk three feet in front of your dog and turn to face it. Your left hand is at your midsection and the right hand is ready

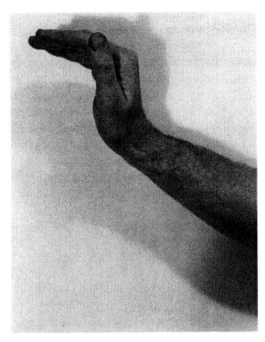

Use a "flash flourish" when giving the hand signal for "stay." Cup your hand slightly...
Charles Hornek

... and then open your hand. Keep your fingers together.
Charles Hornek

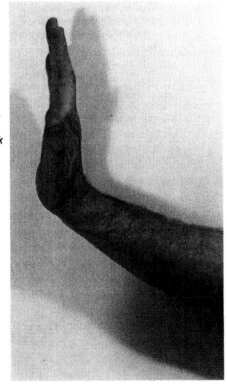

Teach a solid stay for successful set-ups! From the heel position, signal and command "stay."

Judy Emmert/
Dealing with Dogs/
TV Ontario

Walk in front of your dog and be ready with your left hand to "zip" the dog if it breaks the stay.

Judy Emmert/
Dealing with Dogs/
TV Ontario

Loosen the tension on the lead and widen the distance you go away from the dog.
Judy Emmert/
Dealing with Dogs/
TV Ontario

The tug test: Gently pull the dog toward you while reissuing the verbal and visual commands.

Dealing with Dogs/TV Ontario

to reinforce the stay. With as little body or hand motion as possible, apply slight pressure toward you on the collar. This is accomplished by folding a few more inches of the leash into your left hand. If the dog begins to come to you, reinforce the command by slapping the leash with your right hand, repeating "stay." This "tug test," as I've dubbed it, forces the dog to give primacy to the word and the signal and not the distraction of your pulling toward you. It really forces the dog into a mode of deductive reasoning, making it think out, indeed, that words mean what they say in spite of distractions. In this case the distraction emanates from you via the slight tug (don't go over three to five seconds of slight pressure) but out on the streets of Metropolis, the distractions will assault you from all sides without your being able to control them. Better to proof the exercise inside first, and then hit the streets for these progressions to a solid sit-stay. By the way, be sure to keep your fingers closed when flashing your "Supremes" signal. The air holes in an open hand make a slight difference to the dog in terms of the overall blocking effect. Don't use your dog's name while teaching the sit-stay and don't praise physically until the tug test is successfully completed. You'll just break the flow of the progressions and switch the dog into a play mode when you want it in a work mode.

At first the sit-stay looks rather frivolous. Heeling and the down look far more important and many an owner considers the sit-stay marginally valuable. Besides, with all that flashing of signals and saying of "stay" it's boring to teach—and what if I hardly use it anyway? I sympathize, but I disagree. I agree that the sit-stay can be boring to teach and that the progressions can appear Sesame Street-ish and even exasperating. But they are necessary. I once confessed this to a client with whom I was discussing the sit-stay exercise. I used the term "Sesame Street-ish" to describe the steps involved in teaching a good sit-stay. The client turned out to be the originator of the children's show *Sesame Street.* It was not my first taste of shoe leather, even though the series' creator thought it quite funny. You'll need sit-stays for successful set-ups and to successfully socialize your dog.

Welcoming the Wanderers

The fact is, there are a myriad of uses for the sit-stay. The first and most obvious is greeting people when they come to your home. This is where all hell often breaks loose. First the admittance bell is intoned from the street or by the doorman or concierge or the doorbell rings. This primes the dog that someone is going to come through the door momentarily. The dog then begins organizing its welcome, usually by spinning around the house or apartment at full speed, yapping its head off, chasing its tail and generally going nuts. The owner screams, "No! No! No!" but to no avail.

By the time the person actually arrives at the door the dog has entered the Twilight Zone. The neighbors upstairs and downstairs are phoning or pounding on the floor or ceiling. "Shut that @#$%#!#@! mutt up or we'll have you evicted!" You hurry to open the door and admit your guest, hoping

Another way to "proof" the sit-stay is to jump up and down and clap in front of the dog—correct *quickly* if necessary.

Dealing with Dogs/
TV Ontario

The jinx for jumping: a nifty three-part correction that can be used whether the dog jumps on yourself *or* others.   *Kevin Smith*

that once he or she is inside and settled, Screechy will shut up. And sometimes the dog does (but sometimes it doesn't). The pounding on the ceiling stops and all is peaceful and serene again.

Not quite. Although the barking, yapping and yodeling have subsided your dog is now scaling your guest's body in ardent passion. If you are *really* a spaced-out owner, unconcerned with what your dog is doing to others, you will make the usual excuses:

- "He's just friendly!"
- "That's funny, he's never done that before."
- "Just let him jump on you for a while and maybe he'll calm down."
- "He just wants a little love."
- "He only bites if you push him down."
- "Don't worry, his paws are clean."

Well, my God in Heaven above, my friend, how very rude of you! You wouldn't allow your child to behave this way toward a guest, so why are you allowing such behavior in your dog? Did you really invite your friend over for a mauling? Do you really expect the grocery clerk to keep delivering foodstuffs to a house where he is molested by a dog? What about Aunt Matilda's best nylons, now torn to shreds? When you've worked for Calvin Klein, as I have, you learn that not everybody likes to be jumped on when he or she is wearing fine clothing, especially not by a dog that just came in from the rainy streets. Stop all excuses. Your salvation is a solid sit-stay.

The Jinx for Jumping

Here's your correction for jumping; in shorthand, then I'll elaborate.

1. Whip down *hard* on the collar, tab leash or leash and say *no*.
2. Pull on the collar, tab or leash, say *sit*.
3. Flash the stay signal in your dog's face, say *stay*.

You should understand that refusal to sit or stay or spring-jumping on guests is not just love, it is canine dominance. Attempts to seek love can indeed be exercises in dominance; ask anyone who has suffered a relationship that went down the tubes. So don't put up with jumping, no matter how cute you think it is, no matter how small your dog is and no matter how much guests tell you *they* think the jumping is cute. I can assure you, they are lying. Outside they are saying, "Oh, how cute, he likes me," and inside they are saying, "Get this creature off me this instant." Since they will most probably not administer the correction it is up to you to step in from behind and remove the canine clinger from your guest's body. Snap the collar up smartly and issue your verbal stay command and the stay flash. Now, have the guest pet the dog again, right away. If the dog jumps again, readminister the correction.

The best ruse you can pull on your dog to teach it to greet guests is to stage a set-up in which a family member and then a less familiar guest show up at the door. The difference between a set-up and real life is that you will be prepared to correct your dog. Attach a short tab leash for your set-ups so that you will have more than flying fur to grab if the dog breaks the sit-stay. Quite obviously, you will issue the stay command to your dog *before* you open the door. It's perfectly OK, during the set-up, to slam the door in the "guest's" face (he or she will understand this is a set-up) and correct your dog. The point you want your dog to get is that persons are not admitted until the dog is seated and under control.

I'm not saying that guests arriving is easy for most dogs—but set-ups pave the way to success. You might try a dry-run set-up without any person at the door. Put your dog on leash and station it at least four feet from the door. Issue your advance warning. Don't let the dog crowd the door. You will need that space for admitting your guest. Get your dog into a sit and deliver the stay command. Open the door halfway. Correct your dog with an upward snap if it moves. Close the door. Reissue the command and open the door all the way. Close it. Reissue the command and open the door all the way and ring the doorbell or buzzer. If the dog breaks the stay (and believe me this is Waterloo for many dogs that have been unintentionally trained to freak out when the doorbell rings), stage a set-up as a peopleless dry run. You can gradually build up to a set-up with a real person, and then really real people!

The above teaching techniques and corrections apply equally to meetings on the street or in a lobby. Passersby often make it difficult, especially on owners of smaller cute breeds. They will greet the dog and then, when it jumps up, actually hold the dog up on its hind legs, supporting the paws. Very few if any will ask your dog to sit before petting it, and of course, every time the dog jumps up on someone and is supported, the behavior is OKed. So since you can't train the people you meet in chance encounters not to hold your dog up, you must train your dog. If the dog is jumping up on someone who does not know or will not use the three-part correction outlined above, then *you* will have to step in from behind and grasp the leash to yank your dog off firmly, sit the dog and flash the stay. Remember, only three words should come out of your mouth when you administer the jump correction: no, sit and stay. Recapping:

Verbal sequence: no, sit, stay.
Physical sequence: pull down, pull up, flash stay signal.

What too often transpires is a ton of verbiage that just confuses the dog: "*No! Off,* Tippy. Gosh darn you bad dog get the @#$% *off* that man. Oh, I'm sorry. Tippy, *off,* down, no! Stop!" No dog can make sense of such oververbalization, so remember just three words coupled with the physical sequence of the correction. Don't say *anything* else. It should now be obvious that the words "sit" and "stay" are not at all ornamental but essential words for your dog to live by.

Long Stays

Teach your dog to hold the stay for longer and longer periods of time. Issue the command and let out the extension of your lead. Turn sideways and count to sixty. Return and praise. Correct with a "No!" and a snap of the lead if your dog breaks the stay during that time period. Now turn your back to your dog and watch your dog in a mirror. Keep a hand cupped under your leash ready to snap it up if the dog moves. The purpose of this exercise is to teach your dog to hold the sit-stay even when you appear unable to correct the dog if it breaks.

Now take it to the streets. Go window-shopping using a display window that features mirrors or reflects the dog's image nicely. Set your dog up on the sidewalk (leave room for passersby) and issue the command. Window-shop, but watch your dog in the reflection. The faster you correct breaks, the faster your dog is going to learn a rock-steady sit-stay. A technique I often use with my canine students is to set the dog up facing a restaurant window. Most restaurants display both the menu and their reviews in the window. Simply pretend to read the menu or the review or both, but of course, really watch your canine student's sit-stay in the reflection.

Sometimes I really *do* read the menu, and while I'm reading a rave review or drooling over reports of an establishment's perfect chateaubriand, duckling, baby lamb chops (I could go on and on, but I won't), my dog will be wandering around aimlessly, having broken the stay who knows how long ago. Pick badly rated restaurants that get boring reviews!

Try to build up to five to ten minutes on your long stays. The time period can seem like an eternity, so pick a place where you can read a review, take in a view or window-shop to proof your dog. Remember, the lesson for your dog is very important here. You are teaching it that it has to do what you say, when you say it, for *as long* as you say it. This is invaluable practice in teaching your dog to be patient in stores and on the street and also prepares the dog to hold the long down.

Recently I was helping a client proof her dog's store-stays in a drugstore and we wandered into an area of the store with large cardboard boxes. I assumed they were baby diapers and after putting the dog on a sit-stay began to read the instructions on the box aloud as a distraction to the dog. Suffice it to say that the box contained not diapers but another paper product used by women. Another taste of shoe leather for the naive ex-monk.

Stoop and Scoop Sit-Stays: Elimination without Exhaustion

It can be very difficult to stoop and scoop the feces of a dog that is dragging you away from or even *into* the very excrement you are attempting to remove. No wonder so many dog owners cheat on the laws of their locales and run away from elimination sites. The solution, again, is a solid sit-stay.

Wait until your dog has eliminated fully, and then place it in a firm sit-stay. Stoop and scoop. It helps if you have previously staged a fake stoop-and-scoop session during which you are picking up a stone, gravel, garbage or even nothing, in order to proof the dog's sit-stay. So your set-up sequence would be: Sit your dog after elimination; issue a warning, "Sam, don't move, stay!"; now stoop, scoop. If Sam breaks, correct immediately, reissue the same warning emphasizing the phonetic sounds—"I said, *Sam, stay,* and I *mean* it!"—and stoop and scoop again. Remember, when you bend over, your body language looks pretty subservient and inviting, and your dog doesn't necessarily know that you are obeying the city law and retrieving waste. Truth be told, your dog could care less. All it sees is a bending human who *appears* to be inviting the dog to come, play, cavort or even stomp on the very feces you are trying to remove.

It's never surprising to me why this type of set-up is readily agreed to by my city clients, whereas they might object to other set-ups they see as "too strict." The fact is, picking up after your pet, while the law of the land, might not be the thrill of your life, but a lunging maniac pulling you into and through elimination won't increase your desire to perform this task. You don't have to be played the fool—you can obey the law and perform this essential service without losing a shred of your, or your dog's, dignity. Practice and teach a solid stoop and scoop sit-stay. Then do a few set-ups. You'll be soon home free.

Down

The down is also taught from the heel position, with the dog already seated. There is a sensitive spot on your dog's back that is analogous to the spot behind your knees. Pressure here can fold the dog into the down position. Put your left hand on the dog's shoulder blades (properly called the scapula) and with your thumb and index finger trace down the scapula to where the spinal column begins. You will find an indentation there into which your thumb and finger will fit readily. For those more experienced with canine anatomy, the "secret spot" is the upper thoracic vertebrae. Push gently forward and down on this spot. Most dogs will go down readily, but if there is resistance, lift one or both front legs and say "down." Add a hand signal as you say "down," with your finger (right hand) pointing to the ground.

The Long Down or "Coma on Command"

For a trained canine a good, solid down is the essence of being civilized. Now that you've got your dog going down on command, getting into the actual physical position of all fours flat on the floor, you are at a very critical and important juncture in your training efforts. The reason this moment is so important is that you can royally goof up right now and train your dog to give you only short minidowns unless you *insist* on a long down. Insist? Yes, as in i-n-s-i-s-t!

How long? Well, I'm going to ask you to go for the big time: thirty minutes. OK—I hear you screaming with laughter. "Thirty *minutes?*" you might be saying. "My sweet monster has never hit the dust for longer than thirty *seconds!*" Or you might be not just a Doubting Thomas but also a Sympathetic Sam, who feels thirty minutes is too lo-o-o-ng of a down. After all, what if your dog has to amuse, feed or relieve itself during those thirty minutes? Too bad! There are twenty-three-and-a-half hours left in the day for your dog to pursue those activities. Right now, *you* need some quiet time, too—and the long down is your way to get it. Besides, there are hidden benefits to this exercise your dog doesn't have to even know about.

Don't expect to get much coaching about long downs if you are taking your dog to the typical obedience class. Unfortunately, long downs are rarely taught in classes. What *is* taught are three- to five-minute minidowns because these are all that are needed for the obedience trial competition. Not withstanding, a three-minute down is next to useless in real life. You can *do* something with thirty minutes and the dog can be easily convinced to extend the time once it's passed the thirty-minute threshold.

Don't attempt a thirty-minute down until your dog goes into a down reliably without your touching the special spot and/or offering paw assistance. When you are getting the down response to just your finger signal, and when you can flash a "Supremes" stay signal in your dog's face, rise and walk slowly around your dog (keep a hand cocked over the dog's back to correct it if it rises), *then,* and only then, are you ready to try out thirty minutes. I stress again, though, don't train-in too many short downs, releasing the dog with praise, because you may never get the long down.

Don't Tread on Me!

Where you position your dog when you ask for a thirty-minute down is important. I'd advise you to avoid placing the dog directly underfoot or in passageways. Directly underfoot is a bad choice because if you so much as cross your legs with an inexperienced dog trying to hold a long down at your feet, the dog will probably interpret the movement as a threat or as permission to move. Also, with your dog camped out at your feet, you cannot make effective eye contact to correct the dog if it breaks from the down, and probably more important, you are going to find your hand stroking your dog, which will only make it more difficult for the dog to stay down and not rise and solicit more praise. Be fair to your dog. I'm not saying that your dog can *never* lie at your feet, but if you are counting on a canine to commit itself to a long down it's better to *recess the dog from your body.*

For committed long downs always think in terms of centrifugal force—put the dog against the wall and out of a passageway. Dogs do not like to be told to lie down and stay in a passageway. They know that passageways are where the humans walk and they are worried about getting stepped on. Little dogs really fret about this (cats are almost phobic about passageways). All dogs psyche out the passageways in a room the minute they enter it, and when they

Teach the down from the heel position with the dog seated. Pressure on the "special spot" on your dog's back will help ease it down. Give the hand signal simultaneously. The spot is usually easily located on larger dogs.
Dealing with Dogs/TV Ontario

On smaller dogs the spot may only need pressure with your thumb and index finger.
Charles Hornek

If there is resistance, lift one or both legs and ease the dog down. *Judy Emmert/ Dealing with Dogs/ TV Ontario*

want a silent snooze will often select a spot against a wall or at least in an out-of-the-way area. Sometimes dominant, bratty, bossy dogs will deliberately plop themselves in passageways to make their owners step over them. If you own this type of dictator, it's even *more* important that you place your dog on long downs out of the mainstream of traffic. Wherever you go with your dog for the lifetime of your pet—even if you are in unfamiliar surroundings—check out the room from the point of view of the dog in terms of where the passageways are. See why this exercise if often not taught in a class setting? You need a real room to train real long downs, but even if this exercise wasn't introduced in class or in the books you've read, select your spot and read on.

Tough-Love Corrections

Got your dog positioned in a proper spot? OK—attach your six-foot leash and string it out from your dog's side toward wherever you'll be sitting. Now down your dog. Flash your stay signal in your dog's face. Stroll to your seat—that's it, keep a strict eye on your pooch and immediately wheel on the dog and say, "No! Down! Stay!" if the dog rises. Remember, no screaming. Just darken your voice; change your tonality, not your volume. You did get to your seat and the dog didn't break down? Great. Have a seat, but *as you sit* flash another courtesy stay at your dog just so it doesn't misread your body language and think that your sinking down is permission to come. Don't look at the dog, but keep an eye on it. Staring will invite the dog to negotiate with your eyes—which are full of weakness and worry at this point because you really, really *don't* believe that the dog is going to stay there for thirty whole minutes, do you?

Well, it is. You are going to make it. You're going to make the dog stay because you know that even though this exercise looks like a terrible limitation on the dog's freedom right now, this long down will really be its liberation if the two of you really get this exercise, well, down. Why? Because you will be able to take your dog many more places because you will know that you can, in essence, park it. So you have to be strict.

Here's your corrective sequence if your dog breaks down (and believe me they all do).

- *At the first break,* say, "No. Down. Stay!" On the word "no" raise your finger up as in a warning, on "down" throw that raised finger down dramatically and on "stay" flash the stay signal at your dog. No excess verbiage. No screaming. If the dog hits the dust again, fine—but don't say "good." Say nothing. The dog isn't doing anything good—it's correcting a command issued a while ago that it goofed up. If the dog tries to bolt out of the room, step on the leash and reposition the dog in the exact same spot.
- *At the second break,* repeat the above sequence, but even if the dog drops back into place go and give the dog the shake or the swat

correction. Strict? Yes, but totally humane and in the dog's best interests—if you do not get physical, the dog will simply continue to rise and fall, rise and fall, with your rising from your seat to reposition the dog. Some dogs will actually come to enjoy being shoved down again and again and making you get up and sit down, get up and sit down—a sort of canine musical chairs.

- *At the third break,* repeat the verbal correction and the physical one, and then in silence tie your dog to an immovable object like a chair leg. Tie your tether tightly and *short*—so short the dog cannot rise to sit. Do this in silence. Return to your seat, complete the thirty-minute down.

Through this corrective sequence you tell your dog how important this exercise is to you, and that you will not give in and let it walk around at will, nor will you give in and use your crate as a cop-out or throw the dog in another room or cheapen yourself by yelling and screaming until finally, finally, the dog leaves you alone. You are through with yelling and screeching. You are through with avoidance, casting your dog off to another room. You are teaching, not tolerating your dog.

Review these long-down rules:

1. Don't place your dog underfoot.
2. Don't place your dog in a passageway.
3. Leave the leash *on* in case the dog decides to split—at least until you are confident it won't.
4. Don't look at the dog during the long down—but keep an eye peeled on it.

Proofing the Long Down

Proofing means weeding the kinks out of an obedience exercise so the dog knows that the word really means what it says. Proofing means upsetting situations in which the dog is tempted to break its down and decides not to or gets corrected if it does. Proofing means tying the long down into the structure of real life. Proofing means letting the dog know that it has to do *what* you say *when* you say it for *as long* as you say it—whatever "it" is. Including "down."

Proof your long down against four distractions: movement, going out of sight, food and friends. Here's how:

- To proof against movement, flash a courtesy stay from your seat and move to another chair, adding a second courtesy stay as you sit again. I call these extra flash stays "courtesy stays" because they are just that—forms of politeness to the dog so that it doesn't think the stay is over. You'll find you need fewer and fewer courtesy stays because the dog will settle into the down (especially if you do one or more thirty-minute downs each day). But at first they will be necessary. Try throwing a magazine up in the air and saying and flashing "stay" just as you do. Or "accidentally" spill a dish of candy on the floor with an accompanying "stay." You get the idea. Be creative.

- Snap a set of keys on your dog's collar (just use the bolt of the leash). Return to your seat. Now rise and flash a courtesy stay. Leave the room and flash one more courtesy stay just as you disappear from sight. Listen carefully. If the keys jingle, your dog is cheating. From the room you exited to, say, "No. Down. Stay." If the keys stop, your dog listened. If they keep rattling, the dog is still moving. Return and replace the dog in its spot. Repeat going out of the room and follow the same corrective sequence outlined earlier. Crafty, aren't we?

- Don't try to do your first thirty-minute down during Thanksgiving dinner. The canine mind goes nutzola around food, so start with a glass of water and a cracker at the dining room table with your dog properly positioned on the down. But eat the cracker *slowly*, savoring every bite. Slurp the water. Get ready to go through your corrective sequence. Remember, at some point you are going to have noisy eaters as guests, if not already in residence. Proof that long down! Don't forget the alfresco dining situation. Proof these by simply ordering a drink or an appetizer at an outdoor restaurant. Be sure to check in advance if dogs are admitted—often they are, at least in the outdoor portion of the establishment.

- Finally, most dogs, even dogs who have performed spectacular long downs and resisted movement, food and disappearing owners, will fail miserably to stay parked in the presence of your friends. The dog just senses that you are not going to be as strict in front of your friends and that all bets are off. Since you'll really want to use the long down when friends come over—especially friends who may not appreciate being mauled by your Malamute or nuzzled by your New-foundland—proof the down by inviting over an understanding friend who will sit in total silence as you correct your dog. It usually takes one or two proofings but, believe me, most dogs then reason: *"Every-one* is in on this long down business. The only way I get in on things that happen around here is come in, say hello, find the nearest wall and plop myself."

Your release word for a long down is simply pronounced "OK!" Don't say "come," because we don't want the dog resting on the down but inwardly thinking any minute you'll say "come" and this stupid exercise will be over. Praise your dog nicely after a successful long down. Make it know how very pleased you are that it's done the greatest obedience exercise of all—the one that shows its deepest respect for you as leader, the one that allows you to take it to baseball games, dog shows, libraries, outdoor restaurants, even, in some cases, church—the hard-to-achieve but blessed-to-have long down!

The long down is the culmination of all of the other exercises. It produces deep dignity in the dog, respect for the owner in the dog and reverence for the dog in the owner. It is the crowning achievement that elevates mere obedience training to the level of etiquette and manners. While you must be strict in teaching it, don't deprive your dog of learning the long down.

A praise problem: Excessive stroking and fondling sometimes backfire when the dog comes to expect longer and longer stroke sessions. *Kevin Smith*

14

Praise Problems

DOGS LOVE PRAISE so much that you wouldn't think it could conceivably be any problem for them. But sometimes it is, mainly because we humans misunderstand its use. Praise is *absolutely essential* to a healthy dog/owner relationship. Any book concentrating on problem behavior will inevitably put more emphasis on corrective techniques and discipline than on praise. Indeed, some problem dogs deserving radical therapy need to earn *all* of their praise simply because they have become accustomed to "stealing" large amounts of it from their owners. Once an owner realizes that dishing out praise for nothing can backfire and result in problem behavior, the owner often tightens up and goes to another extreme: "OK—no praise for you, Bozo!"

Antipraise owners have an ambivalent relationship with the concept of praise. They may feel it is unnecessary and will spoil the dog. The real problem, of course, has very little to do with the dog and everything to do with an uptight owner. If you are the type of person who is basically a sad sack and finds it difficult to give encouragement and praise, you should rethink dog ownership.

On the other hand, you might be an owner who simply gives too much praise or gives it at the wrong time. One problem with praise results when it is too high-powered, too bombastic or too sweet and whiney in tonality. Placating owners especially have to guard against whimpering praise at their dogs. Rather than feeling congratulated the dog simply feels placated. Blamer owners have to be wary of praise that is too loud because it can actually frighten the dog.

I've seen placaters, for instance, call their dogs and then fawn over them in such whimpering tones that the dogs will simply collapse at their feet and, sometimes, squat or even flip over and submissively urinate. Then there is the dog that looks truly bewildered and somewhat berated as its owner bellows out "GOOD BOY" because the dog obeyed some simple command. Praise that is too high-powered or too bellicose often makes a dog switch out of the "work" mode and snap into a "play" mode. If this happens the dog can lose concentration and certainly doesn't remember what specific action it is being praised for.

Bubbles Belong in Champagne

When I began training dogs I received contradictory information regarding the intensity and vivaciousness that should accompany praise. One trainer who tutored me insisted on using a lot of what she called "bubbles" while training. What this meant was that one flitted around the training area constantly singing praise to the dog, even for the smallest positive actions. Training sessions with this trainer resembled the opening moments of *The Lawrence Welk Show.* So I tried her technique. My perception was that the dogs saw through my "act" and seemed more puzzled than pleased by this type of praise. The bubbles went flat quickly. My main mentor, Brother Thomas, certainly believed in praise, but used it in a more constructive way. He would, for instance, praise with just the words "good boy" or "good girl" and he pronounced those phrases in a way similar to that of a sergeant telling a soldier "at ease." The dogs seemed to respond more quickly and efficiently. Training sessions went more smoothly. Because the dogs were not distracted by the praise, they learned more in a shorter period of time. I think, therefore, that parceling out praise is best during actual training sessions.

Meanwhile, off the training field, just hanging around the house with the dogs, Brother Thomas would toss out praise to them constantly. He had a personal jingle for almost every dog, which he would sing when the dog was doing nothing but being itself. This use of praise—which on the surface can seem like a misuse—kept all of the monastery dogs in a friendly frame of mind toward Brother Thomas. While overtly "good" actions, such as obeyed commands, received simple and succinct praise and praise during actual training sessions seemed parsimoniously doled out, the balancing factor was the joy and affection expressed in the silly jingles and personalized songs during other parts of the day. The philosophy I learned from this was that when actually training a dog, it's not good to overload the dog's circuits with praise that borders on frivolity, but during the bulk of the day other types of praise should be used to make the dog feel welcome and appreciated. This philosophy has stood me in good stead. Often, even during an initial training session, I will parcel out praise. I train as though the dog already knows the exercise. This type of praise challenges the dog and at the same time rewards it.

Getting Physical

Physicality in praise is, of course, also important. Very often praise that includes an excessive amount of stroking or fondling backfires when the dog comes to expect longer and longer "stroke sessions." I like to concentrate physical praise on the centering spot on the dog's forehead. Often the lightest touch of your index finger, a gentle massage with your thumb or even a kiss planted on the centering spot will have an almost magical effect. Because this spot is so important to so many dogs, *where* the physical praise is given intensifies its effect. Yet, how many times have you seen a trainer *kiss* a dog's forehead as a form of physical praise? Not many times, I'm willing to bet. Contrary to the lyrics of the famous song, a kiss is not always "just a kiss."

Another super stroke spot is the sternum—that protruding breast bone that juts out especially when your dog is sitting. A brief stroke or scratch on or around the sternum keeps the dog happy yet "on" to the learning task at hand. From the heel position it's easy with many dogs to, with your left hand, deliver praise to this sensitive spot.

Inappropriate Praise

Another praise problem is the misuse of praise in which the dog is praised for simply refraining from bad behavior. This is a source of great confusion for many lay owners. A typical situation: Let's say you're reading quietly in the living room and suddenly you notice that your four-month-old chocolate Labrador Retriever has started to munch on the cable TV wire. You haul out your best "bitchy," growllike sentence and quietly pronounce, "Rascal, get your mouth off that right now and I *mean* it." Bravo for you. You didn't yell. You didn't scream. Rascal stops chewing on the TV cord. But now you blow it. You turn to Rascal and in the sweetest possible tones coo, "Goooooood boy. Now, don't touch that wire again, pleeeeeeeaze." To complicate matters, you go over to Rascal and give him a chew toy while continuing the praise. What's wrong here?

What's wrong is that Rascal doesn't deserve or need any praise for simply refraining from doing something bad. It would be far better to say nothing after the reprimand and simply return to your reading. If Rascal were to resume chewing the cable wire, sterner action, such as a shake correction, is warranted. The idea of giving the dog an appropriate chew item sounds like a worthy one, but this too could backfire. If Rascal always has something appropriate shoved in his mouth whenever he chews on something inappropriate, what will happen when Rascal chews destructively and the owner is not home to pull off the switch? Bite your tongue if necessary, but make it a cardinal rule to never praise your dog for simply refraining from unacceptable behavior—most especially if it's engaged in such behavior time and again. Considerable canine confusion can result.

I am a cheerleader for crates—but constant or careless crating is a cop-out.
Lionel Shenken/Visual Productions

15

The Crate as Cop-out

I'VE ALWAYS been a cheerleader for crates. I've used them when housetraining my own dogs and recommended them to others for myriad reasons. There is absolutely nothing wrong with crating your puppy or older dog. Most dogs accept crating because they are, at heart, den animals. Wolf progeny are born in a den, a cave or some similar shelter. The mother keeps the den clean by consuming all the body wastes produced by her children. When wolf pups grow older she starts to send them outside for defecation and urination. The youngsters soon learn that it is important to keep their enclosed area clean. Otherwise, they will quickly incur the wrath of their mother and this they do not wish to do. Using a crate, then, is historically and scientifically valid because the crate environment simply replaces the den environment.

Crates are manufactured in different styles, such as a pressed fiberglass model used by the airlines and wire models, available at most pet stores. I usually suggest that owners invest in an airline crate because it can be used in the back of a car or on a plane if it becomes necessary to travel with your dog. Sometimes behavorial difficulties make this model the best choice. If you have a chronic leg lifter, avoid the wire crate because your dog can simply aim its urine outside the crate. An airline crate is better because then Squirt will have to sit and simmer in his own urine. On the other hand, if your dog has a severe problem with destructive chewing stemming from severe anxiety at the prospect of being separated from you, the wire model might be a better choice because the dog doesn't feel so cut off from you and shunted away. The dog can see you leave and simply resign itself to the fact. There are crate rental services in many cities so you can try both models.

The Crate Craze

There's been a real revolution in the dog training community in terms of the use of crates. Twenty-five years ago they were hardly mentioned in dog training literature. Now it is *de rigueur* to recommend them for everything from housetraining to much more complex behavior problems. I find some problems in this emphasis on crating. I guess I wonder what dog owners did to control their dogs prior to today's crate craze. For instance, if the dog is getting in your hair, simply driving you nuts, it's extremely tempting and convenient to crate the dog—and this is routinely recommended by trainers. Old-timers who grew up in the fancy, not using crates at all or using them on a very limited basis, would solve this problem by training the dog to go to its place, lie down and stay. If every time your dog bothers you, you simply pop the dog into a crate, what, I ask, are you *teaching* the dog? Are you not teaching it that whenever it starts driving you bananas it will be confined in its private quarters? Aren't you also communicating to the dog that you have no way to control it except by confinement? Further, could you actually be *rewarding* the dog for bad behavior—especially if it adores its crate?

Many crate connoisseurs will readily admit that if, in a moment when the dog is engaged in frenetic activity, they were to say, "OK, Conrad, go to your place and lie down and stay," Conrad would simply stare at them as if they were out of their minds—and of course continue whirling around the house. So then, it's off to the crate. What is really needed for dog *and* owner is instruction in, and insistence on, a long down. What will these owners do if they ever need to anchor their dogs in a crateless situation? They will be in a real bind, forced to simply restrain or reposition their dogs. Many dogs sense this loss of control. They can see that the handy, dandy crate is nowhere to be seen. This is a perfect example of the "rewards" reaped when the crate is used as a cop-out.

If you *do* use a crate make sure you've also taught your dog good, solid obedience commands. Remember, use the crate when you *are* at home; do not simply deposit the dog in it when you leave. If you crate the dog only when you are gone this can lead to separation anxiety, whining in the crate and clawing at the metal grating to achieve escape. It's a good idea to teach your dog to go to its crate, lie down in it and stay there while leaving the crate door *open*. When you release the dog from the crate, just ignore it for a few moments. If you are too enthusiastic when releasing it from the crate you might be unintentionally training the dog to badger you for earlier and earlier release. This can lead to barking and stress whining when you are away.

Special Crate Conundrums

A small number of dogs absolutely *refuse* to be crated. They will urinate and/or defecate on themselves while in their crates. They lie in their refuse and seem to enjoy it. There are others who will become absolutely crazed when confined to a crate and will even bend the metal bars of the crate with their teeth to try to get out. Often these dogs simply need to be decrated but still confined. They do better in a larger area.

If the problem concerning crating has to do with soiling, the crate is probably too big. You'll have to get a smaller crate or shrink the area by loading up half of the crate with an indestructible yet safe object. Remember, though, some pet store puppies are used to sitting in their own wastes. Shrinking the crate won't matter, so in this instance you should decrate the puppy or older dog and use baby gates to confine the dog to one room.

Crate That Crate!

Frankly, my idea of how to use a crate in dog training consists of employing it as a tool during the housetraining process, and then folding it up and putting it away in a closet or the rear of the car so that the dog can travel in it. I think the crate gets used as an excuse by many owners who do not want to invest the time in training good, solid sit-stays and down-stays. I do not think it is anthropomorphic to suggest that the dog senses a lack of control on the part of the owner when no crate is available for confinement. The desire to stay still in one place is first instilled in the dog by teaching command words, such as "sit," "down" and "stay." These words can then be strung together and the concept of *place* added to the command, as in, "Go to your *place* and lie *down* and *stay.*" If the dog only stays still when confronted by the three walls and grate of a crate this desire will never flow from *within* the dog. Yes, by not using the crate as a cop-out and by making your dog do one or two thirty-minute downs a day, your dog will begin to "sense" when to go away and plant itself, sometimes before you even issue a command. Trained dogs seem to develop a sixth sense of when you want to be left alone. They come to know that if they don't make the decision to lie down on their own, you will probably tell them to do it anyway. These dogs start to realize that they are never crated, yelled at, tethered or banished to another room if they simply take their place in the family circle and lie down quietly. This is no less than we would expect from a well-behaved child. It is not wrong to ask and expect as much from your dog. Teach a good, solid long down using the techniques in this book. If crating is abused your dog will never learn to think out its downs for itself. The crate then becomes a cop-out and the joy of owning a well-trained dog is greatly diminished. Train, don't just crate and complain. You want to be your dog's leader and friend, not its warden.

16

Our Own
"Urine Analysis"

NOW, I'M GOING TO TALK about urine. Shocked? Don't be. Doctors regularly run urinalysis tests on their human patients, so it's about time a dog trainer analyzed the role of urine analysis for dogs and their owners. Many owners simply do not realize the overwhelming power of dog urine as a tool of dominance. The novelist J. R. Ackerly wrote, "Dogs see with their noses and write their history in urine." I can only agree. If you have a dog that is leg-lifting, anointing your couch or squatting on your bed, you have a dominant dog trying to write his personal history on your personal stationery. With the possible exception of submissive urination (more on that later) inappropriate urination is almost always, in my experience, an expression of dominance by the dog—an attempt to gain or regain Alpha status in the household. You see, dogs have an easy life—if they see it, they sniff it, if they like it, they lick it and sometimes if they love it, they wet on it. That's the truth, short and not so sweet.

It's helpful to know a bit about the composition of urine itself. While urine may look clear or just sport a simple yellowish hue, it is a complicated substance. It is made up of water, proteins, uric acid, urea, amino acids, salts, several inorganic compounds and—guess what—ammonia. That's why it is foolish to clean up urine with ammonia or any dog cleaner that contains it. And, believe me, almost 75 percent of the cleaners I've researched contain a healthy dose of ammonia. Ammonia is a compound of urine: You will be compounding your problem, adding, in essence, urine over urine if you use ammonia to clean up housetraining accidents or other urine deposits.

Why then, do so many doggie cleaners contain ammonia? Well, I figure it this way. Maybe either the manufacturers of such products know that the product will backfire on the owners who use it and just don't care, or they ascribe to the more-is-better theory that pervades the American consciousness. You know what I'm talking about—the doctor told you to take one pill a day, so you take *two* figuring you'll get better faster. So the owner uses *twice* as much ammonia doggie cleaner thinking that it will stop Yuri from urinating once and for all. Yuri then urinates ubiquitously. Solution? Go buy *more* of the same ammonia-based "cure." A classic catch-22. I like catch-22's in novels, not in dog training!

There are scent substances called *pheromones* in the dog's urine—they are also present in feces—and these substances tell the dog that it's OK to eliminate in that same area again. The best way to kill off these naughty pheromones is to *acidify* them out of existence. The cleaning fluid I've always used is 50 percent white vinegar and 50 percent water. You can cut the vinegar to 25 percent if you're worried about whitening out a colored carpet, but one caution: Do *not* sponge with vinegar on marble floors, as the vinegar will discolor the marble. So what should you do if you have marble floors and your dog lays a load or places a puddle on the floor? Simply clean with a *swipe* of vinegar and then *immediately* clean up the vinegar with water. Frankly, if you can afford marble floors you probably have a maid who needs this information more than you do.

Bed Wetters

My clients often call ranting and raving because their pooch has wet the bed—not its bed, theirs. I've had clients so disgusted with this practice that they were ready to hang the dog at high noon, feeling that the dog was morally depraved and perverted to do such a thing. I always assure these souls that there are pooch perversions far worse than this one and the dog isn't acting in a morally deficient way, anyway. It's just marking territory—probably territory it wants from *you*. It often begins by having the dog up on the bed, or even under the covers, and never informing the dog that getting on the bed is a *privilege* you grant, not a *right* it holds, and that you can elevate the dog or demote it from the bed on whim.

Many dogs urinate on things they are trying to claim from another dog or person. Male dogs especially do this, but I've known plenty of bitches who do it, too. Remember what I said about the use of urine as a tool of dominance? If you think of urine here as a canine attempt to gain the bed, you've got the right idea. My advice, then, is to teach your dog that the bed is a place it gets invited up to, not a landing platform that it can hurdle itself onto whenever it wants.

If you have a bed wetter, immediately demote the dog from the bed for one month. If necessary tie the dog to the foot of the bed or to the table nearest you. You'll then be able to reach down and pet the dog if you'd like, and you can yank the leash, *hard,* if it pipes up to protest being demoted—which it probably will. After one month, you can begin teaching your dog the difference between having the privilege of being on the bed and seeing it as an inalienable right. Put a tab leash on and leave your dog free. As soon as it hurls itself onto the bed, grab the tab and send the dog *sailing* off the bed. Don't let go of the tab. When the dog lands, give it a good shakedown and scold firmly—but not loudly. Release the tab and if the dog tries it again, repeat the process. This time use a swat to cap off your correction. Remember, if you don't cap off the correction with the shake or the swat you have *not* corrected your dog, you have simply *repositioned* it. And many dogs will make repositioning into a game—forcing you to reposition and reposition until you are about to go nuts. So be sure to give the shake or swat correction after the first repositioning. Chuckles is to stay off the bed for one month. If he's lost his "chuckle"—too bad. He'll rediscover it, on the floor.

After demoting Chuckles from the bed (remember, for one month) you pull a fast one. One night while you are quietly reading in bed or watching TV, call Chuckles (who is now snoozing on the rug, resigned to being on the floor) and say, "Hey Chuckles, *come up here* on the bed." Emphasize the words "come" and "up here" as these are the new commands you're teaching. Pat the bed invitingly. At this point Chuckles will look at you with a perplexed look. The dog doesn't know this new command, and certainly doesn't trust your invitation even if it *does* understand your meaning. So repeat the command and again pat the bed encouragingly. Most probably the dog will approach the bed hesitantly and then place one paw up. Encourage the dog. There are some brazen pooches who, even after being demoted for one month, will hurl themselves up on the bed readily. Whatever happens, praise your dog once it hits the bed. Let the dog quiet down for a few minutes. Now, pointing your index finger toward the ground, announce, "Chuckles, get *off* the bed." At this point Chuckles will look at you like you're out of your mind.

But of course you're not. So *gently,* not too forcefully this time, guide Chuckles off the bed, repeating the command phrase and emphasizing the word "off." Now repeat all of the above until you have Chuckles jumping on or off the bed at your command. Congratulations, you've just taught your dog that being on the bed is a privilege you grant, not its supreme right. If you had a bed wetter I am willing to bet that the problem will never reoccur. And if you have a lover or spouse, they may be extremely happy. Also, whether you know it or not, you just staged a stealing set-up.

If your dog wets its *own* bed, and believe me this is not uncommon behavior, simply take the bed away for two weeks and let the dog sleep on the floor or provide a towel. Clean the bed with vinegar and water, if you can. Many dogs will wet their own beds. I usually advise owners not to invest big bucks in elaborate beds at first. Buy a simple bean-bag style bed instead or just use a towel or a rug until Fido proves trustworthy. The Louis XIV canopy bed can wait.

Illegal Leg-lifting

Do you recall when I mentioned that urine is the "ink" that dogs use to write their history? If you have a leg-lifter you have a dog who is a very active historian; it is writing a book! Follow the step-by-step approach for disciplining inappropriate urination outlined in the chapter "Do Dogs Feel Guilt or Shame?" Illegal leg-lifting can often be disciplined even after the fact because the pheromones still "stink" to the dog. Visually, the dog can often still see the stain. If you have a shred of proof I would give discipline after the fact a try.

Remember, leg-lifting is almost always an attempt on the part of the dog to dominate the owner. First, have your veterinarian rule out any medical problems. Put the dog on the Radical Regimen for Recalcitrant Rovers (RRRR) right away. In most cases leg-lifters need to be neutered. Put aside any emotional qualms or anthropomorphic projections you may have concerning neutering. Simply have the operation performed. You'll be doing your dog a big favor. If I seem blunt or curt in my advice to neuter the chronic leg-lifter you'll have to understand that after seventeen years of patiently explaining the benefits of neutering to clients who appear to think the operation will be performed on *them* and not the dog, I'm just bone tired. Every single behavioral and medical study clearly indicates that neutering is in order and can help ease or eliminate this problem. If you want to cheat, and not neuter, and only want to discipline your dog and put it on the RRRR, I certainly can't stop you. It's a free country and you're welcome to do as you like—but don't blame me if your dog continues to squirt the staircase or baptize your bedroom.

Tighten the Controls

Besides neutering, there are a few other aspects of your leg-lifter's behavior you'll have to control. Don't let Squirt spray the neighborhood. Some leg-lifters are unintentionally trained that urinating in the house is OK when owners allow them to leg-lift ten, twenty, even thirty times during each walk—and, of course, heartily praise each outdoor spray. Limit your dog to only three or four urinations by using the methods detailed in the section on heeling in chapter 13. City owners might also consult my book *The Evans Guide for Civilized City Canines,* which has an extremely well-detailed section on city heeling. Rather than letting the dog pull you from pillar to post, *you* release the dog from heel for urination.

Second, limit your dog's water intake by simply offering water three or four times a day rather than leaving it down all the time. Remember, what goes in, must come out, and if your dog tanks up after each walk it's more difficult for it to exercise control. If you have to leave a leg-lifter alone, leave a bowl full of ice cubes instead of water. They will melt down gradually and "ration out" the water. Some chronic leg-lifters will not agree with discipline and will need to be crated. But some recalcitrants, if crated in open-air crates, will simply squirt their urine outside the crate. What these dogs need, as unpleasant as it might sound, is to sit and stew in their own you-know-what. Get an enclosed airline crate so that if the dog lifts its leg, the urine will drip down and the dog will have to sit in it—something most dogs prefer not to do.

You can check with your veterinarian about drugs that might help Squirt stop squirting. Progestin therapy can sometimes be useful for dogs with this problem, and the veterinarian may have other drugs in his or her arsenal that you should consider. But remember, you will have to train the behavior out by doing set-ups during the period of time that you are using a given drug. If the problem is behavioral, drugs alone won't cure it.

Concocting a set-up to limit leg-lifting is really quite simple. You simply pretend to leave the house, issuing an advance warning. Hide so the dog can't see you but you can see it. The moment the "lift" commences, charge, and I mean *charge,* to your leg-lifter, discipline, repeat the warning and leave again. If it's not possible to position yourself so you can catch the dog right in the act, simply leave for as long a period as you think it will take for Squirt to leave some proof. Use your worksheets to design a set-up, and remember to seal off as much of the house as possible so that when you administer discipline you will not be cheapened by a chase.

Submissive Urination

Submissive urination is a completely different matter. It occurs when the dog is highly excited and feels that the owner is dominant. It is often an attempt on the part of the dog to *please* the owner. The response is out of the dog's control and usually corrects with maturity.

If you are having a problem with a submissive wetter *don't punish the dog.* This will only worsen the problem. It is still possible to do a set-up, skipping the discipline step. The first thing to identify in setting up this kind of set-up is *when* the behavior tends to occur. The most frequent times that submissive urination occur are

- When the owner arrives home and greets the dog too effusively
- When the owner disciplines the dog
- When the owner catches the dog after a chase
- When the owner argues with another human—even on the phone
- When friends greet the dog after coming onto the owner's territory

If the problem occurs when greeting the dog it's important that you do *not* touch the dog. Avoid eye contact during these times and pass the dog as if it does not exist. Try to avoid approaching the dog directly and instead pass the dog on its side. Don't hover over the dog when saying hello or good-bye. It's also a good idea to take this type of dog to obedience school. Here the dog will learn the words "sit" and "stay" and you can use these words in your set-ups. Obedience training will also instill a certain confidence that will help the submissive dog.

Staging Set-ups for Submissive Squatters

If your dog has a problem with submissive urination and tends to exhibit the behavior when you come home from work and overaffectionately greet the dog, your set-up would be scripted as follows:

You might think you have to skip step one, the advance warning, because you won't be home to issue any warning since you will be coming back from being away. Not so. You can gently, and I mean *gently,* issue the warning as you *enter* the house, without making eye contact or touching the dog. When the dog squats, which you'll be looking for out of the corner of your eye, softly repeat the warning without physically disciplining the dog. Then, immediately hang a wheelie and leave the house again, coming back perhaps five or ten minutes later and repeating all of the above.

The next time you do a set-up perhaps you would touch one finger to the dog's forehead, bending your knees to reach down to the dog, not hovering over the dog. You would still avoid eye contact and perhaps just say "Hello," and then give the warning phrase. In future set-ups, increase the physical contact.

You can also dry your dog out for the set-up by limiting water beforehand. This might give you an edge for success. Submissive urination is no picnic, but it can be treated by carefully staged set-ups. Again, I urge you to use your worksheets to script the set-up. Especially for this problem, a set-up has to be finely tuned.

Finally, I must stress again that my records and consultations clearly show that various urination infractions are the number one "closet" problem among dog owners. Owners often fail to connect urination problems with other ongoing difficulties the dog may be having, such as aggression and destructive chewing. But in reading this "urine analysis" I hope you now clearly see the importance of correcting your dog for all forms of illegal urination. Please don't think that occasional "mistakes" can be ignored or tolerated because "It really isn't much of a problem." It *is* a problem, and one that is often intimately connected with whatever "big problem" the dog is having. If you don't eradicate illegal urination you won't eradicate that big problem either. By illegally urinating, your dog is writing its history, and part of that history is what the dog thinks of *you.* Your dog is sending you a message when it inappropriately urinates and (with the exception of submissive urination) that message could be, "P___ on you." Fill in the blanks.

17

Aggressive Advice: An Open Letter to the Owners of Canine Terrorists

Dear beleaguered friend,

If you are living with a canine terrorist who lunges, growls, snaps, snarls or bites other humans or other dogs, this letter is for you. You must know the frustration experienced by government officials, security personnel and airline pilots. As with human manifestations of terrorism, canine attacks often seem to come out of nowhere. The aggression often appears to be totally unprovoked and unexplainable. Just as an airliner can be suddenly taken over by a thug, some canine terrorists seem to take over a household and hold their owners hostage.

What you should know is that, just as governments with good intelligence agencies often detect signs of impending terrorist action, a skilled trainer and an educated owner *can* decipher the signs of upcoming aggression from a dog. In fact, even while the dog is being aggressive correction *is* possible. Remember Entebbe? Israel essentially concocted a set-up, a sting operation to save its citizens held hostage in Uganda. President Carter tried and failed to rescue U.S. hostages from Iran; the set-up fouled up, but at least he tried. You *can* stage set-ups to stop your canine terrorist and rescue innocent human hostages. The first step is to get out of denial and into action by setting up a plan of action. You need to reason out the context of your dog's aggression.

In fact, very few incidents of canine aggression are unexplainable or unprovoked. Aggression is almost always *context specific*. That means that when your dog flies off the handle it has a *reason* for doing so. The dog has probably been placed in a specific context of psychological and environmental influences that trigger the aggression. You need to find out what these influences are. But first, some background.

In this open letter to you, the troubled owner of an aggressive dog, I need to deliver up-front aggressive advice. I'd like to share with you my thoughts about what society thinks of aggressive dogs and what you yourself must do to spare yourself society's wrath. You see, people have pretty much *had it* with aggressive dogs. You only have to look at the incredible number of city and state "dangerous dog" laws that have been enacted over the last ten years, the Pit-Bull controversy and the enactment of legislation banning certain breeds from certain places to realize that there is *zero* public sympathy left for aggressive dogs and their unfortunate owners. There are an estimated 3.5 million dog bites each year in the United States. Most of these bites occur in the spring or summer, but the seasonal differences disappear in states like Hawaii or Florida where the weather is more temperate all year. Children ages five to fourteen are most likely to be bitten, and boys between those ages are twice as likely as girls to suffer injury. Such a statistic readily shows that there is no small amount of cultural conditioning—especially macho cultural training foisted on young boys—behind some of the bites. In short, young boys often tease aggressive dogs and get themselves nailed in the process. We can't necessarily do anything to change the way youngsters are culturally conditioned, and because a child teases your dog it still does not justify your dog biting that child. You must do your best to train your dog to be better behaved than some children! Again, remember the trend in society is definitely away from any kind of support or sympathy for you and your grouchy dog. Stop blaming society, "unfair" laws and teasing kids. Train, don't complain.

A Dreamworld of Denial

Now that you realize that you won't win any popularity contests, and that a large number of people would just as soon see your canine Jack the Ripper imprisoned or even eliminated, instead of pouting because nobody likes you or your dog, engage in an examination of conscience. Owners of aggressive dogs often live in a dreamworld of denial, a twilight zone of rationalizations and excuses for their dog's bad behavior. They are often afraid of the dog themselves, terrified that the dog may turn on them next and feel powerless and hopeless. Perhaps you feel that there is not much you can do about the aggressive behavior except avoid the instances that trigger it—and so you structure your life around skirting situations that will make your dog angry and you unpopular. It's a difficult task to break out of this dreamworld of denial and stop your tendency to avoid rather than confront your dog's aggression, but it *is* possible to do so, but only, I repeat *only*, if you are sufficiently *motivated* to do so.

It is more difficult to motivate someone in print than in person, but I'll give it a try. Let me talk to you in the same way I have spoken with hundreds of clients with aggressive dogs over the last nineteen years. As a first step let's take a fearless, honest look at exactly what alternatives you have with the dog. Here are the four options that I know of for the owner of an aggressive dog.

1. Live with the behavior the way that it is.
2. Try to train the behavior out of the dog.
3. Give the dog to somebody else.
4. Euthanize the dog.

Options, Options, Options

Now let's take a look at each one of these options individually. By virtue of the fact that you are reading this book and this specific chapter, something tells me that probably option number one is not a possibility for you any longer. You probably don't want to live with the behavior the way it is. Perhaps you have visible evidence of this choice in the form of a bite mark on yourself or someone in your family. To "live with the behavior the way it is" might also be something you've been doing for several months or even years, hoping that the dog's aggression was just a phase it was going through and would outgrow. But as the days and months have gone by you've come to see that the aggression only gets worse, not better. Your excuses for it have grown more numerous, but sound, even to yourself, more and more hollow and evasive. You know that you have to break out of that dreamworld of denial. So this option is not viable for you. Now, as corny as this sounds, I want you to take a pencil and cross out option number one on the list. Go ahead, cross it out.

Alternative number two, trying to train the behavior out, might leave you excited, hopeful, skeptical or all of the above. When I discuss this option with my clients excitement is often the initial response. They ask me, "Is it really possible to stop the aggression?" My reply to them and to you is a qualified "yes." Many aggressive dogs *can* be rehabilitated, but only with the cooperation of a motivated owner, sufficiently committed to the task. The rehabilitation will consist of placing the dog on the Radical Regimen for Recalcitrant Rovers, and I ask my clients to read over the regimen right at this point. That's not a bad idea for you either. Just stop reading here and flip back to chapter 9. Read over all twenty points of the regimen, and ask yourself whether you are committed to following it completely. Adherence to the

RRRR will mean major life-style changes for your dog and possibly for you. The Radical Regimen will be the *platform* on which you will stage set-ups to rehabilitate your recalcitrant. If you honestly can't see yourself following the RRRR, get your pencil and cross out number two in the list above. Go ahead, flip to the RRRR, read it over, determine whether you can "obey" the twenty points and then cross out or leave standing option number two.

Option number three, giving the dog to somebody else, might seem mighty attractive. "After all," you might reason, "if it only had a country home where it could run and play and get all that energy out of its system maybe the dog would be so *tired* it wouldn't have the *energy* to bite anyone." Magical thinking. As if energy or lack of it ever determined who gets bit when. Or you might reason that if your dog just didn't have to see so many black people, white people or purple people perhaps it would never growl at another member of those groups again. Or maybe your dog growls and lunges at people who wear funny hats or cheap perfume. If you could find it a hatless home with unscented owners maybe it wouldn't get so grouchy. Maybe, maybe, maybe. Maybe if . . . If only . . . A dreamworld of denial. A twilight zone of excuses for excuses for excuses. See the syndrome?

Trouble is, life in a country home, even if the dog gets a Jane Fonda workout each day, might also include the possibility of visits from black, white or purple people in funny hats wearing cheap perfume. Sooner or later the stimulus that sets your dog snarling is bound to appear. An added difficulty is that the new owner won't necessarily know all the different people, places and things to avoid in order not to trigger the aggression. There is a strong likelihood that the new owner will unwarily walk right into a dangerous situation. The result can be injury to that person and others. I'm sure you wouldn't want that on your conscience. So it becomes increasingly obvious why giving the dog to somebody else is not a viable alternative. In most cases it would be far better for *you* to keep the dog, try training and walk into situations that might set off an aggressive response fully aware that you are setting the dog up to misbehave and fully prepared to discipline it. Once again: Stage set-ups. Train, don't complain.

There is another problem in giving your aggressive dog—or any problem dog—to a new owner. It's one you might not have thought about yet. The second owner and the dog will be new to each other. They will not have had the time to bond and feel deeply about each other. In short, the new owner will not be in love with the dog the way that you most probably are—or at least once were. Tolerance often flows out of love. Love for another can be the birthplace for motivation. The new owner will have little tolerance or sympathy for the dog's bad behavior and scant motivation to try to modify it through training. Most probably the new owner will simply transfer the dog to yet another owner. Or take option number four. We'll discuss that option next, but if you see the insanity of taking option number three (unless you know a hermit in Antarctica who wants a dog) go back and cross out option number three from the list.

Option number four, euthanize the dog, is a prospect that horrifies many owners. However, there is a small number of owners, especially those enduring life with an unpredictable, violent dog, who will see euthanizing the dog as a viable option. While most owners really want to give training a try, hoping that the behavior can be eliminated, there are some owners who have simply had it with the dog. These owners often try to get professionals such as veterinarians or trainers to support them in their decision to put the dog to sleep. I suppose this is understandable, but no trainer or veterinarian can ethically indicate that this alternative is the only one to be followed without a full discussion of the other three alternatives. In fact, the American Veterinary Medical Association has published ethical standards dealing with this question. It is not the veterinarian's mission to decide anything in this area for the client. Whatever is done is, after all, your decision, and the ultimate authority to make that decision rests with you.

I *never* indicate euthanasia as the desired option, but rather lead the client to examine *all* the alternatives and take responsibility for the final decision. Sometimes an owner simply euthanizes an aggressive dog without any attempt at training the behavior out or, if that isn't possible, at least educating themselves as to what they might have done wrong with the dog that helped set the stage for the aggression. Very often what then happens is these owners procure another dog and repeat the whole sad process again. Sometimes the second dog is even *more* aggressive than the dog that preceded it. It's sad to say, but often the trauma of the decision to euthanize the dog helps the inadequate owner face personality difficulties and lack of leadership skills more squarely. If this is done honestly, even if the dog is beyond repair, frequently the second owner/dog relationship is much better.

That said, it's far more common that owners do *not* want to play this final card and will readily cross this option off the list. If you've made the decision that option number four is *verboten,* turn back and cross it out. Still, it's a good idea to look at this alternative because it *is* a possibility. Just looking at the option can be cathartic in and of itself. If you decide it is not a viable possibility you can look back at our list of four alternatives and see that probably your only option is to try training. There may still come a time when you are forced to accept option number four and put your dog to sleep because perhaps training doesn't work. But at least if that sad day comes you can assure yourself that you did everything in your power to change your dog's behavior through training, and correct any handling errors on your own part. I know that's not much of a consolation, but some consolation is better than no consolation at all. At least you will be able to say that you yanked yourself out of self-pity and denial and really tried to reeducate your dog. There are some people who think that self-pity is better than none, but they probably aren't reading this open letter.

To sum up: Most probably you have crossed out options number one and three and are left with options two or four. You've decided you cannot live with the behavior the way it is any longer and that it is impractical, unethical and unthinkable to simply transfer the dog to somebody else. You are left with the options of either training your dog or euthanizing your dog. In short, train the dog or kill the dog. That's blunt, and perhaps even hurtful to some of you, but it's probably accurate—and again, as much as it may hurt to hear such a statement, it's a lot better than denial and despair. Right? Whoever lived richly, fully in denial or despair? Not you. So, let's gear up for action.

Going into Action

If you've decided to try training, great! You've chosen option number two. The first thing you must realize is that there is the strong possibility that you might need the help of a private trainer. Do not take the aggressive dog to a dog training class. Such dogs don't belong in class but rather need private, in-home training. Place your dog on the Radical Regimen for Recalcitrant Rovers right away, following all twenty points *to the letter*. This program will begin to change your relationship with your dog and set the stage for successful set-ups.

If it's absolutely *impossible* to hire a private trainer—and you've checked with your veterinarian for a referral and come up with no leads—you can try the following program on your own. However, I must add that I can in no way take responsibility for your personal safety or the safety of others if you opt to try to train your aggressive dog all alone. Working with an aggressive dog, even if it is a personal pet, can be potentially dangerous. This book can only give you a skeleton plan at best. It's simply not possible for me to diagnose in print what type of aggressive behavior your dog exhibits. If you do want to wing it the first step is to try to get an idea of what type or types of aggression your dog displays. Aggressive behavior can fall under any of the following classifications, or it may fall under several. Here's a checklist:

Fear-induced
Learned
Pain-induced
Territorial
Interspecies (dog fighting)
A response to teasing (by children *or* adults)
Genetically predisposed
Jealousy related
The result of brain disorders (petite or grand mal seizures, biochemical, lesions, infections, etc.)
A response to medications
Focused on other animals (predation on chickens, cows, deer, etc.)

It should be obvious that your first stop with any aggressive dog is the veterinary office. Make sure, absolutely sure, that there are no neurological problems that may be contributing to the aggression. Get a second opinion if necessary.

Fear-induced and territorial aggression are by far the most common and easiest to categorize. They are often also the easiest to stage set-ups for because they are so predictable. A good way to figure out which categories of aggression your dog exhibits is to simply write down in short paragraph form everything you can remember about the last growling, lunging or biting incident. Take the time to do this now before going any further in this chapter. Just write down who was involved in the incident, where and when it happened and how long the "action" lasted. Don't try to justify or explain the dog's behavior. Just write down here the bare bones of what happened.

_____

_____

_____

_____

_____

_____

_____

_____

Now, reading over your description and looking over the checklist, try to classify the aggression. If you're truly baffled show somebody who does not know the dog your description and the above listing of aggression categories. You want to get a handle on the *type* of aggression because this information will help you to design set-ups.

If writing a description of the last episode doesn't seem to help, try this: Sit down and write as full a description as you can of a typical day with your dog. Begin from the time you get up in the morning until the dog is snoozing at night. Again, don't try to diagnose or justify the dog's behavior. Just write down everything it does during the day—good and bad. If you have a problem dog, the description of the day might be weighted on the negative end, but that's OK. The important thing for right now is to simply get the description down.

Well, I get up in the morning and_____

_____

_____

_____

_____

_____

_____

_____

Here's a sample description written by one of my clients describing the typical day of King, a one-and-a-half-year-old unneutered Doberman male:

> Well, when I get up in the morning I have to get up very carefully. Why? Well I don't want to wake up King because he'll growl at me if he doesn't get to sleep until at least eight-thirty. King sleeps between me and my husband in bed. I get out of bed quietly and get dressed quickly. I go downstairs and eat breakfast in a hurry because he'll be up any minute and it's impossible to keep food on the table when he's around. He just takes whatever he wants from the table. I have to make sure the bathroom door is shut because otherwise he takes the end of the toilet paper and starts running around the house with it and wraps it around everything.
>
> Also I have to have his food dish down and ready when he gets downstairs because for some reason he doesn't like me offering him his food. He doesn't like anyone near his food dish. I have to watch the kids carefully because if they let him out when they run for the bus stop he'll terrorize all the kids at the stop. So I let one kid out at a time, and I throw a hunk of meat into the next room to distract King. He doesn't like to be brushed either, so usually there is a lot of vacuuming to be done around here. But that's a problem, too, because King attacks the vacuum cleaner. I had to rent a post office box rather than have the "scene" with the mailman every day. He's already bitten him once. I go to the drugstore to get the daily paper rather than risk the life of that poor paperboy. It has to be a fast trip because King gets lonely easily and will rip up the house if I'm gone for more than a half hour. So you see, I've had to make a few adjustments in order to live with this dog.

If you've read the chapters leading up to this one and are getting the point of this book, as you read the above description you were probably ticking off various set-ups that could be staged to correct King's terrorist ways. Of course you were also saying to yourself, "Oh, that's disgusting." Or, "I would never let a dog of *mine* do that." But if you *aren't* getting the point of this book, astonishment and amazement might have been your only reactions. Readers who are in tune with my message will not waste time being surprised at King's shenanigans, but instead will be anxious to go into action to modify his behavior. I mention this because many owners of problem dogs seem to almost *enjoy* being astonished at just how bad their dog can be. A stupid waste of time and energy. Train, don't complain!

Easy Set-ups First

Let's work on King's problems. Your battle plan should be to stage the easiest set-ups first. From the description given above it's obvious that there are over fifteen possible set-ups that can be staged. The easiest ones are, of course, the set-ups where it would be most difficult for King to retaliate physically. In short, set-ups we won't get bit staging! Put on your thinking cap and think along with me. What are the easy set-ups that can be staged right away? Try these:

- Get King out of the bed! This is accomplished easily enough and doesn't have to involve a fight with the dog. Simply tether King to the foot of the bed without giving him enough lead extension to hurl himself on top of it. Another solution would be to use a crate in the bedroom. Remember that part of the RRRR is to let the dog sleep in the bedroom but not in the bed. Because the in-bedroom sleep increases or preserves owner/dog bonding, we don't want to demote King from the bedroom completely, but rather teach him his place in it.
- For food stealing and toilet paper unraveling, mousetraps can be used. A mousetrap can be placed strategically on the toilet paper so that it goes off when King investigates. However, King should *not* see his owner set the trap. A fake plate for breakfast can be set for a fictitious child, perhaps complete with muffin and mousetrap. Remember, we are trying to stage the easy set-ups first and for a dog of this type, that means avoiding getting bit. It is not "cheating" to practice some creative avoidance or use mousetraps so that the environment itself appears to discipline the dog.
- King's problem with having his food offered to him or barging out the door for the bus stop can be remedied by beginning to teach a good, solid sit-stay. A set-up can be staged dramatizing a fake school day morning, perhaps on a Saturday, during which the children could be employed to run for the bus stop while King practices his stays and gets corrected if he fails to stay.
- A simple set-up will vanquish the vacuum cleaner vexations. Place King on a sit and stay (or hold some upper tension on the lead to hold him in place if he doesn't know the sit-stay) and issue your warning phrase. "OK, King, you *touch* this vacuum and you're *dead.*" Now follow out the traditional steps for a set-up. Flick the switch of the vacuum on for just two seconds. Of course King will probably break his sit-stay and lunge for the vacuum. You know what to do. Grab King and give him a firm shake correction, a swat under the chin. If neither of these is possible because of a chance of physical injury from the dog, give him a firm collar correction. Repeat the warning and the stimulus, this time turning the vacuum on for perhaps three seconds. Repeat the correction if necessary, but if King decides to refrain from

attacking the vacuum, end the set-up for now. *Do not praise the dog for not attacking the vacuum.* He isn't doing anything good, he is simply refraining from being bad. There's a difference, and he knows it. You've just had a success, if only a three-second one. Remember, every time in the past the vacuum has been attacked has been a failure. Nothing succeeds like success, and nothing fails like failure. So take your small success for today and build on it tomorrow. You can try for five seconds then, until you are vacuuming in peace.

Similar set-ups can be concocted to solve the problems of grooming King or leaving him alone and coming home to destruction. For the latter problem it's probably OK to try discipline after the fact as outlined in the chapter "Do Dogs Feel Guilt or Shame?" It's my opinion that a dog like King is probably quite capable of understanding discipline after the fact if it is correctly administered. After all, this is a dog who has a good enough memory that he can remember to sleep until eight-thirty and still make it downstairs in time to essentially run all the morning activities of the household. This is a dog with organizational skills galore, a *smart* animal, a whiz, in fact, although his owner considered him stupid.

Save the Worst for Last

The more difficult set-ups will have to wait awhile. In this case we had to wait two weeks for the RRRR to kick in and begin to change the owner/dog relationship. Needless to say, several points of the RRRR directly addressed the overall situation between King and his owner. The dog was on the bed, there was too much indulgent petting, too many treats, but too little obedience training, earned praise and respect for the owner. If you have a dog like King, a strong, large, dominant dog, I'd advise you to practice creative avoidance, institute the RRRR and then start the simpler set-ups.

On the other hand, if you're working with a professional trainer or if your particular canine monster is cooperating fabulously on the easier set-ups, you can go for broke and try some harder ones. Looking back at the earlier description of King's behavior, there are several more difficult set-ups.

King's malevolence toward the mailman will need a carefully concocted set-up. It will take owner motivation, speed and stamina. It will also take a considerable amount of environmental preparation. Needless to say, such a set-up needs to be thought out and even *written out* in advance, in much the same way a director would plot out a crucial scene in his directorial notes. I've always suggested that my clients write out a script for the harder set-ups in advance. Here's what King's owner came up with.

One of King's problems is barking at the mailman, and if he has access to him, charging at him. I now realize that every time in the past King has done this and the mailman runs away it reinforces the bad behavior. King thinks that he is chasing the mailman away. Also, every time in the past I have not issued an advance warning to King, and instead hope against hope that maybe, just maybe, today he won't bark at or chase the mailman, I have been party to unintentionally training him to do just that. I am happy to announce that those days are over. Instead, I will do a set-up with the mailman. I'll speak with him a few houses away and ask him to pause for a few moments after delivering the mail. I will have the house closed off in advance so that King cannot run away from me. I'll attach a short tab leash to his collar so that I can grab him and discipline him when he even *looks hard* at the mailman. I will not wait until he disappears into that never-never land of crazed barking. If I can catch King's eyes growing serious and "hard" as he stares down the mailman I'll issue an advance warning *then*.

Another difficult set-up is, of course, the situation concerning newspaper delivery. This gambit would involve careful preparation because we would not want the newspaper boy to be injured. King may have to be on a twenty-foot rope or leash, and an adult might have to play newspaper boy. Of course it's understandable that when a stranger throws an object like a newspaper into a dominant dog's territory, the dog exhibits territorial aggression. Understandable, but not acceptable. Some owners might decide to stage all of the above set-ups and continue to pick up the daily paper at the drugstore. That sounds like an OK compromise to me—an acceptable form of creative avoidance.

My tendency as a trainer, however, would be to go for the gold and reform King's bad behavior from A to Z. However, I stress again that too many set-ups staged too quickly will force some dogs to retaliate, with the risk of personal injury to their owners or others. Further, often after the RRRR is put into play and set-ups begin, sometimes the behavior of the dog will become *worse*—at least for a while. Clients are often amazed at this phenomena, especially because they themselves are suddenly so motivated and dedicated to correcting bad behavior.

But there's nothing really strange about this bad behavior backlash. From the dog's point of view it is a perfectly natural response to a changing situation. What the dog is saying to the owner in colloquial terms is

> OK, *bimbo* . . . look here: Whether you knew it or not we had things set up around here so that I was the head honcho. I ran the household, I slept where I wanted, I ate what I wanted, I chased, growled and lunged at who I wanted—when I wanted. When I said "move" you moved. Now you're telling me all that is changed? That I'm not sleeping on the bed anymore, I have to obey words you say like "stay," I have to earn all my praise and I can't touch the toilet paper, any food that's not mine, the vacuum cleaner, the grooming brush, the mailman or the paperboy. *Well, don't expect me to buy it, Bimbo!*"

It's quite natural and normal for the dog to fight through some initial corrections. This is a phase you'll have to live through with the dog. But if you're going it alone in your training efforts, following the RRRR and the advice in this chapter, and the backlash period lasts longer than one week, it is clearly indicated that you need the help of a trainer. Get one. However, many dogs do not experience any backlash reaction at all and are happy to give up their dominant role in the household.

In Search of Sinister Signs

It should be obvious that in order to stage a sterling set-up it's necessary to be able to decode what the dog is feeling in order to issue an advance warning or deliver a well-timed correction. Many owners simply are not acquainted with or cannot see the signs of impending aggression. A rundown is in order. The following signs of aggression must be *memorized* in advance and watched for extra carefully, otherwise the set-up will foul up because of delays.

- *Hackles:* A dog makes itself look larger by raising hair along the back of its neck and spine, called hackles. There are muscles underneath these hairs that the dog can use to make them stand up dramatically. This is a first-class sign of imminent aggression. Unless the dog is a trained employee of a police force or the military—which I'm willing to bet your dog isn't—in my opinion a dog with raised hackles is exhibiting aggression and should be *disciplined.* Yet I've seen owners who are deep in denial simply try to smooth the hackles down by petting them! The aggressive dog is thus *rewarded* for its belligerence, and the behavior is trained *in,* good and tight. You should *never* bring a hand in contact with an aggressive dog when it is exhibiting aggression unless it is with the intent to discipline the dog. Any other contact, even the slightest touch, can be misinterpreted by the dog as a reward.
- *Ears:* A dog will also sometimes prick its ears forward, as if listening intently for something, when it is feeling aggressive. This is another classic sign of belligerence.
- *Legs:* Some dogs will tighten their front and back legs, firming up their overall stance, seemingly bracing themselves for an attack.
- *Tail:* The tail-set of the dog will often change so that the tail is held straight out from the rump rather than drooped down or held high. It is quite possible that the straight-out tail will also be wagging. This confuses many lay owners because lay dog wisdom has indoctrinated the public with the idea that a wagging tail indicates a happy dog. It can be easy to misread a signal. Why would a dog raise its hackles, prick its ears forward, firm up its stance, growl and at the same time wag its tail? Probably because it *likes* the reactions it is getting and is *enjoying* itself in its aggressive display.
- *Vocalization:* Obviously any growl, even a low, barely audible one, is an indicator of escalating aggression. Pronounced barking and snarling are even worse. Dogs emitting such sounds should, in my opinion, be sent to the stars with a firm swat under the chin, or, if that's not possible, a superstern collar correction.
- *Eyes:* Watching the dog's eyes is probably the best way to decode aggression because changes in the eyes often *precede* some or all of the above signs. Specifically, the dog's eyes will get "hard." Sometimes the eyes will glaze over and sometimes not, but the general look will be serious, fixed and unblinking. Do not stare at a dog who looks like this.

Watch for sinister signs of aggression. This Cocker is defending its bone, which the cat happened to walk over. A vigilant owner would issue a warning *now*.

Judy Emmert/Dealing with Dogs/TV Ontario

Instead, the dog chases the cat into another room and corners it. Now he *really* needs to be corrected.

Judy Emmert/Dealing with Dogs/TV Ontario

Simply try to get a moment of eye contact and then launch into the steps of your set-up. If you cannot understand what I mean by "the look" and you own an aggressive dog, please find a trainer or other professional who can indicate it to you in person. Occasionally, depending on breed type or the personality of a given dog, the *only* sign of imminent insanity will be this slight change from softness to hardness in the dog's eyes. This is why it is so important to read your dog's eyes, or find someone who can.

Breed Idiosyncrasies

Sometimes because of the "design" of a particular breed you will be deprived of seeing one or more of the above signs. For instance, if you're dealing with an aggressive Rhodesian Ridgeback, it's senseless to watch for raised hackles because the hackles are always raised. If the canine criminal is a Pembroke Welsh Corgi, it's silly to watch for a straightened out tail because this is a tailless breed. Some breeds, like Old English Sheepdogs, Australian Shepherds and some Benji-type mixes will not prick their ears forward, at least not in a way noticeable to laymen. An aggressive Irish Setter or Golden Retriever may sport so much feathering on the legs that any stiffening of the limbs will be difficult to see. Finally, some dogs simply growl so inaudibly (or not at all) that even a concert microphone wouldn't pick up the sound. All of this points to the absolute necessity of being able to read your grouchy dog's *eyes,* while at the same time mentally cataloging all of the other signs and then warning and/or correcting the dog speedily. Obviously, it is essential that any hair covering the eyes be clipped off or groomed and held back. Experienced trainers know that sometimes all of the above manifestations of aggression appear within *two* to *three seconds,* and that response time is critical. The point here is, don't feel guilty or stupid if your layperson's eye is not as quick as a professional's eye.

Does It Have to Be a Dog-Eat-Dog World?

Interspecies aggression—dogs fighting other dogs—is probably the most misunderstood form of canine combat. Owners make several mistakes. They try to decide who started a given fight and often discipline the *wrong* dog. The dog who exhibits overt aggression, such as a growl or an attack, gets clobbered. However, it takes two to tango. Very often, the more silent dog "began" the fight by casting a hard look toward the second dog. The owner then explodes into the room and wails on the dog who responded with a growl, snap or lunge. This teaches dog number one to perfect its hard stares to trigger increasingly quicker reactions from the more vocal dog. Sometimes the dog with the hard stare is comforted.

Things become even more complicated when the two fighters are separated, even if both are disciplined. This plays right into the dogs' paws! They

It doesn't have to be a dog-eat-dog world. There are friendly or neutral interactions like this one . . .
Levon Mark

. . . or there are interactions that go overboard—when even the "submissive" dog exhibits aggression. If they live in the same household, both dogs should be disciplined, not separated, and placed on a long down.
Judy Emmert/
Dealing with Dogs/
TV Ontario

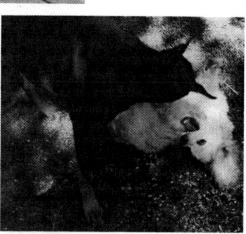

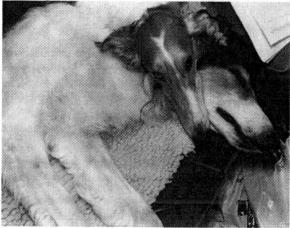

By ditching denial, elevating your Alpha status and concocting set-ups that demonstrate that you are "top dog," even arch enemies can sometimes become kissing cousins.
Kevin Smith

156

wanted to get at each other, but failing that, they'd like to be separated from each other. Owners cooperate beautifully by hauling off the fighters into separate corners, or worse, completely separate portions of the house. This is understandable because, after all, if the dogs are left in the same room, they will simply resume fighting, right? Wrong. Not if you remain and make each dog hold a long down. If the dogs don't know the down, tether them *tight* a few feet apart and make them stay in your presence for thirty minutes.

The message one dog is giving the other is: "Look *you,* I don't like your *ugly* face. Maybe I like you sometimes, some days, but right now, for reasons of my own, I don't like your mug. And the best thing that could happen is for me to rip it apart. Failing that, at least get your ugly mug off my territory and out of here." And of course in trots the owner and separates the dogs. The dogs still win.

Instead the message the dogs should receive from the owner is: "Look you two (or three, or four, whatever the number of fighters is), you may not like each other and you don't have to. But you must tolerate each other, and if you fight, I will discipline you—harshly. In fact, I'll even set you up to fight, and if you do, you'll still have me to answer to. Think of it this way, guys: The fleeting, momentary rush you'll get from fighting with each other will be so miniscule compared to the horrendous price you'll have to pay from me, that it just doesn't seem worth the fight, now does it?"

Faced with that ultimatum, most dogs start to inhibit their aggression toward each other, if only to avoid incurring the wrath of the owner. If you have a house full of scrappers, immediately put all resident dogs on the RRRR. That's right—*all* of the dogs. The dogs who are seemingly innocent of starting fights (remember, you could be dead wrong in this assumption) will simply have to pay a price for the more overt fighters. It's simply not practical to place only one or two dogs on the Radical Regimen since it is an overall life program—and placing one dog on it and not another could well inspire jealousy. Look over the twenty points and you'll see why the program must be leveled on all resident pooches.

If the fighting is really out of control, practice creative avoidance for a few weeks until the RRRR starts to kick in. Then try a set-up with the help of an assistant. Be sure to have the gladiators wearing tab leashes in advance, so that you will have a way to separate them and discipline them if a scrap ensues. It's nearly impossible to discipline two dogs at once, so you may have to reprimand one while stepping on the leash of the other until you can get to it. If the fighting is so intense that the dogs turn on *you* if you try to intervene with discipline, your problem is indeed serious and you need the help of a professional trainer, *in* your household. But get ready—some trainers will advise you to discipline only the dominant dog, without spending enough time to see just who is being dominant in which ways. Other trainers may suggest letting the dogs work it out—to the tune of a walloping vet bill due to injuries they inflict on each other, and possibly you.

My experience comes from eleven years living in a household, New Skete

Monastery, with twenty to twenty-five in-house German Shepherd Dogs—all of whom got along, including, yes, males. The dogs knew the rules about fighting. They would have us to answer to if they even looked cross-eyed at each other! I also take my cue from my parents. I come from a large family—eleven children. Yes, it was a big litter. My psychologist father and my savvy mother usually ended fights over an object by removing the desired object from both the children fighting over it—without wasting one second to see who "rightfully" deserved it. Instead we were *both* reprimanded and sent to the kitchen to scrub the floor or clean the cupboards. In silence. The point was, of course, to substitute a productive, creative activity for the destructive and definitely uncreative one we had been engaged in. We had the cleanest kitchen floor and cupboards in the state of Michigan. The training took. All eleven of us are extremely close with each other. We fought, but we don't *fight*.

Drugs

A word about the use of drugs with aggressive dogs. Sometimes they can be quite useful if the right drug and the right dosage are used. Some behaviorists like to use tranquilizing drugs such as Valium or Librium to calm the dog. I do not. Since these drugs depress the central nervous system it is more difficult for a dog under their influence to think out the steps of a set-up. These drugs can wear out in effectiveness or, occasionally, be so effective that the owner will complain of a drugged dog, no longer aggressive but one that more closely resembles a possum than the dog they once knew.

The drug that I have had the most success with is megestrol acetate, commonly dispensed as Ovaban. This hormonal drug was originally developed to control estrus (heat) in females, but given in higher or varied doses seems to have a calming effect, without tranquilizing, on some aggressive dogs. Veterinarians and behaviorists have reported amazing results using this drug in treating behavior problems, *as long as the drug is administered concurrently with ongoing behavior modification training.* In other words, a good veterinarian will not prescribe Ovaban, or any drug meant to effect aggressive behavior, without at the same time prescribing a good trainer or specialist.

Ovaban and similar drugs are not cure-alls. If they were, there would be no aggressive dogs left to bother anybody. Progestins are currently the single most effective chemical therapeutic agent for problem behavior in dogs. The problems that are most responsive to the medication are

- Attacking other males without obvious provocation
- Urine marking in the house when the behavior is clearly not a reflection of inadequate housetraining
- Mounting of other dogs, people or inanimate objects when the mounting is not a reflection of puppy play
- Roaming

Notice that fear-induced and territorial aggression are not listed, but my experience with these forms of aggression has been that set-ups sometimes go more smoothly when Ovaban is used. My professional criteria for using or not using a drug is this: If I can concoct and stage a successful set-up and begin to rehabilitate the dog, but the owner cannot, whether because of lack of motivation, stamina or long-standing subordinate status in the dog's eyes, drug therapy is worth a try. The effect of the drug might mellow the dog sufficiently to think out the set-up and accept the correction. If on the other hand, a professional cannot attempt to educate the dog without being injured, usually the only possibility is to prescribe the RRRR for a while, avoid triggering the dog's aggression, wait and see what develops and try set-ups at a later time. The dosage I suggest for Ovaban is the one suggested by the manufacturer, Schering, for behavior problem management. Some behaviorists use very high doses, but there can be side effects. Consult your veterinarian if you think drug therapy will help you in training your dog.

Finally, I know this letter may have been rough reading for some of you, especially those who own and still love a grouchy dog. But after years of dealing with owners of aggressive dogs, and several bites down the line, I have the battle scars to prove that bluntness pays off. I have seen many aggressive dogs who have been rehabilitated go on to lead happy lives and give great pleasure to their owners. Good luck in your training efforts and your attempts to lead your dog from grouchiness to graciousness.

My very best,

Michael Evans

Job Michael Evans

18

To Come or
Not to Come

NEXT TO HAVING a grouchy, aggressive dog, there is nothing worse than owning a dog who will not come when called. Owners of such vagabonds have to live in constant fear that they will lose control over their dog, that the dog will get hit by a car, lost or stolen. It's a supreme difficulty to live life with such an animal. As usual, my sympathy and now my advice.

Of course I have to immediately jump to the defense of the dog. First, has the dog ever really been *taught* the recall? Some owners simply assume that the dog knows how to come when called, when they have never spent one iota of time teaching the dog the actual word. When the dog was a puppy, the owner reasons, it seemed to always come when called. But now that the dog is older, it doesn't anymore. This is delusionary thinking. Puppies have a natural tendency to *follow* their owners. This tag-along propensity can last up to the fourth or even fifth month, when the puppy becomes more mature and independent and begins to go its own way, responding less and less to the word "come." Perhaps during the following phase the owner just happened to say the word "come" in an animated tone. The puppy hugged the owners leg closely. This certainly looked like a valid come to many lay owners. But all the puppy was doing was following. When a dog gets older it has to learn the word "come" through formal training. Here's how:

- First, teach a good solid sit-stay. Be sure your dog knows how to sit and stay in one place before you begin teaching the recall. Start from the heel position. Attach a twenty-foot leash to your dog, issue the stay command and signal and, holding one end of the leash in your left hand, walk directly out from the dog the extension of the lead.
- Walk away from the dog, don't back away. This will only make you look hesitant and make the dog break its sit-stay. Keep an eye peeled over your shoulder and if the dog breaks the stay command, spin around quickly, flash the stay signal again and scold, "No, *stay!*" If the dog doesn't replant itself, get the dog and take it back to the *exact same spot* where it broke the sit-stay. Repeat the above process.
- When you reach the end of the twenty-foot lead, turn smoothly, genuflect, fling open your arms wide, smile and clearly command, "Rascal, *come.*" If the dog doesn't start toward you, give a pop on the leash to get it started. If it does start toward you, start to praise in a higher-pitched, but not whiney, voice. It doesn't matter much *what* you say, as long as it is genuine praise. However, *don't* say the slang term "c'mon" within your praise phrases, because you will be repeating a command the dog is already obeying.
- For owners of young puppies or older, "green" dogs who have never formally learned the recall, I usually suggest seven such recalls a day, building up to off-leash trustworthiness.

A Running Away Remedy

Of course preventative training as described above is easier than corrective action, but if your dog has been schooled in the recall and is simply running away or staring at you when you say the word "come," it probably does not perceive you as its leader. Sound blunt? Well, sometimes the truth hurts. Recall problems are, in my experience, most frequently *relational* problems. Something is wrong in the relationship between the dog and the owner. Specifically, the dog does not view the owner as Alpha. You see, the dog is coming to *somebody,* and you'd better *be* somebody to that dog if you want it to come to you. Makes sense, doesn't it? If you're viewed by the dog as an insignificant presence, a casual friend or, worse yet, a complete nothing, then there is no underlying reason for the dog to obey the command. In short, the underpinning for the recall is the relationship.

I mention this right at the beginning of our discussion because very frequently owners do not think of recall difficulties as *relational* but rather *mechanical.* Such owners drill, drill, drill their dogs in the recall in a mechanistic fashion, often making the dog hate the command in the process. Meanwhile, nothing is done to change the dog's perception of the owner. The dog still looks for the first opportunity to split, and when it does, the owner becomes even more enraged.

If this scenario sounds familiar, and you have the humility to admit that,

During the six-week moratorium on any off-leash freedom, you can "umbilical cord" the dog to your body to keep it near. This exercise also has bonding benefits—which you can cash in on later.

Dealing with Dogs/
TV Ontario

During the moratorium, practice formal recalls. Issue the stay and walk out unfurling a twenty-foot leash. *Charles Hornek*

just perhaps, your dog refuses the recall because of relational problems, I offer again my sympathy and the following advice:

- Immediately, as in *yesterday,* put the dog on the RRRR program for one month. You will see the dog grow in respect for you during this month.

- On the same day that you institute the RRRR begin a six-week moratorium on any and all off-leash freedom. That's right, six *weeks.* Under no circumstances should you say the word "come" to your dog and not be in position to correct your dog if it doesn't obey the command. Remember, every time in the past you said the word "come" and your dog either stopped and stared at you or ran the other way, you were *training.* Whether you knew it or not, you were unintentionally training the dog that the word "come" meant to stand and stare at you or to run the other way. It takes a dog a *long time* to forget that kind of unintentional training and ascribe a new meaning, the *correct* meaning, to an abused word. Don't worry, though, the dog *can* relearn the word. It simply needs this moratorium period to forget the bad associations attached to it.

- Remember also that dogs that run away usually have some place to go. If your runaway is an "overnighter" that disappears for hours on end, or even all night, there is a very strong chance that the dog has memorized a route it follows. It will take six weeks for the dog to forget its itinerary and for the scent substances called *pheromones,* which are found in urine and feces and were left to mark the route, to die off. So don't cheat on the six-week period. Arrange your dog's life so that it simply does not hear the word "come" without having to obey it. The six-week moratorium period is not a punishment for you or your dog. Instead, it's a beneficial period for both of you.

- During the six-week moratorium period, practice seven formal recalls a day in an enclosed area. Leave a twenty-foot leash on the dog in order to get it if it bounds off, then graduate on week two to a six-foot leash. These are formal recalls in which you place the dog on a sit-stay, walk away and use a full complement of positive body language, positive tone of voice and positive eye contact. Do all seven recalls one right after the other, and make your praise short and snappy in between each recall. Don't overpraise. The dog will tend to focus on praise that interrupts the flow of recalls. All seven recalls should only take fourteen minutes.

- Remember positive body language! Lower one knee completely to the ground, balancing yourself with your other leg. Open your arms extra wide to funnel the dog in toward you. Sometimes, while holding your arms outstretched, pointing your index finger in toward your chest helps to orient the dog to come directly to you. The top portion of your body should be erect. Under no circumstances should you stand and

Positive body language! Lower one knee to the ground—Catholic or not, *genuflect*. Open your arms wide. Use another dog or person as a distraction.   *Levon Mark*

If you are ring-bound get ring ready by "straightening up" your body language in some sessions. Don't forget to employ a decoy person.
Dealing with Dogs/
TV Ontario

Graduate to free-lance recalls. Spring a recall on your dog when it's distracted. Be sure the leash is in your favor so you can correct quickly.
Levon Mark

164

simply bend over at the waist. This stance does not give the full impact of the "genuflection." When I use that term, I am not trying to be funny. Think it over: Catholics genuflect in church to honor a spiritual friend they want to have "come" to them. Your dog will also read these sentiments in your body language.

- Your tone of voice is important. Cough out the word "come" with an emphasis on the *co* portion of the word. Place your dog's name before the command. Remember also light, lilting praise as your dog proceeds toward you, but *do not* say "c'mon" as an encouragement word.
- Your eye contact should be gentle and encouraging. You should look at your dog throughout the recall. As the dog arrives in front of you, rise slowly so that you are fully erect. This will tend to make the dog sit in front of you because your height is imposing. The dog will cast its eyes upward to meet yours. Make sure that you are looking down to meet its glance at this point. Your four eyeballs should *lock*. In this meeting of eyes there is also a meeting of minds. There will be a sense of completion to the recall process, which, from the dog's point of view, includes the launch, the transition toward you and the arrival at your feet. Each of these segments demands sustained eye contact.

Free-lance Recalls

After two weeks practicing seven formal recalls as described above, you and your dog are ready to free-lance. Take your dog to the *same* enclosed area you have been using to practice the more rigid recalls. Take along a paperback book as well and a twenty-foot leash or rope. Take your dog to the middle of the area, tell the dog to sit, but *do not* say "stay." Guess what? You are now going to stage a set-up to see if your dog has begun to relearn the word "come."

Please don't simply detach the leash and let your dog run around the area. Instead, leave the leash on, sit your dog, tap the centering spot and issue a serious, but not scolding, warning. "OK, Tippy, I want you to *come* when I *call.*" Tap the centering spot lightly on the words "come" and "call." Now, without issuing a stay command, and after making one last check to make sure that the area you are working in is fully enclosed, drop the leash. Turn, walk ten feet away from your dog. Turn halfway back around to your dog. Pretend to ignore the dog, but keep an eye on it. Hoist your paperback toward your face and pretend to read. If you'd like, you can begin to stroll around randomly. Keep one eye peeled on your dog.

You might see some amazing reactions. Many dogs will simply sit stock-still, thinking that you simply forgot to say the word "stay." They will be afraid to move in one direction or another because they are not quite sure what you are up to. Besides, many dogs are also still in a state of shock from practicing seven formal recalls and living under the RRRR for the last week. Don't worry, though, if you saunter about long enough and pretend to read your book long enough your dog will begin to move about.

You are going to spring a recall on your dog. Wait for a moment until the position of the leash is in your favor. When your dog starts to move around, either following you or going away from you, try to position yourself so that the dog is facing away from you but the end of the twenty-foot leash is at your feet. This might involve walking swiftly toward the end of the leash if the dog is moving away from you. If the dog is hugging close and following you, you can suddenly go into reverse and start walking backward. Hopefully your follower will forge ahead. The end of the leash will wind up at your feet, in short, in your favor.

"In your favor" for what, you might ask? For delivering a correction, of course. If you've mastered the steps of a set-up, you can see that we are now on step number two. We are giving the dog a chance to be naughty and *not* come, but we are fully prepared to correct. So, now, in your most animated voice, issue the come command. "Tippy, *come!*" If Tippy voluntarily turns toward you and starts in your direction, begin your praise chant and complete the recall by rising and making eye contact as you did when practicing formally. When the dog arrives, praise for just a few seconds, release your dog again, do not say "stay" and continue sauntering about and reading. Try once again to get the leash in your favor, and spring another free-lance recall on your dog. If you're on a roll, do seven such recalls and then call it a day.

If the dog does not come to you, grab the end of the twenty-foot leash and *propel* the dog toward you with a firm jerk on the leash, simultaneously repeating the command. Make the dog finish out the recall even if you have to reel it in like a fish. Give very little praise. Instead, sit the dog, don't say "stay," reissue your warning phrase. Drop the leash and try another free-lance recall. For the dog who does not voluntarily come and ignores you or tries to run the other way, further free-lance recalls should be practiced. The elements of surprise and timing are essential. With the leash in your favor, try to spring the recall command on the dog, especially when it is fully involved sniffing leaves or socializing with another dog. You must teach the dog that it must listen for the come command and obey it *even* when it is distracted. The dog must learn that the word "come" applies at all times, in every place. Some dogs who have been drilled on only formal recalls never learn this. Practicing free-lance recalls helps change the dog's perception. *Always,* dog, *everywhere.*

Risk Taking

After one week of free-lance recalls using the twenty-foot leash, begin one week of free-lance recalls using a six-foot leash. You will now be on week four of the program (see the chart on page 170). You should still be working in enclosed areas, but they do not have to be the same ones you were using before. Getting the leash in your favor will now be much more difficult, simply because it is so short. Don't forget: Don't say "stay," issue your warning, including tapping the centering spot. You will have to surmise for yourself how your dog is doing. You will also have to be quick on your feet in order to get up behind the shortened leash, or at least within striking distance of it in order to give corrections. Most dogs at this point will be voluntarily turning toward their owners when they hear their name and the command. After all, this *is* week four of the RRRR. Many recalls have been practiced, both formal and free-lance style. The dog has begun, through the RRRR and practicing recalls, to regard you as a somebody worth coming to.

If the dog is crafty enough to sense that you cannot control it as easily on the six-foot leash as on the twenty-foot leash, and returns to its old ways, go back to week one of practicing seven formal recalls a day. Don't be disappointed if this happens. Perhaps you goldbricked in practicing recalls earlier, or perhaps your dog just needs more time. Perhaps the RRRR wasn't followed to the letter. Check and double-check.

But, if you *have* been successful with six-foot-leash free-lance recalls, you know what tactic comes next. You've got it—put your dog on a short *tab* leash and practice free-lance recalls as described above. Again, don't forget your advance warning! At this point the tab is simply for safety's sake and to enable you to give some sort of correction if the dog does not return to you. You will have to go and get your dog because there will be no leash to use for correction. If you must do this, the dog should be given a firm shake. Place the dog on a stay and snap on the twenty-foot leash, which you've brought along just for this occasion. Make the dog do seven formal recalls. You'd be wise to return to week number three at this point and practice free-lance recalls for one more week using a twenty-foot leash. On the other hand, if everything goes smoothly, and your dog returns to you on command, tab leash gaily flapping in the wind, go on to the finals.

Reaping Recall Rewards

When five weeks of the six-week moratorium have been completed, you're ready for the big league. Unless it is illegal to do so, take your completely leashless and tabless dog to a large, unenclosed area that is as free of distractions as possible. Sit your dog, give your advance warning and release your dog. Say a prayer, rub your lucky charm and call your dog. Remember, stoop and smile! Get those arms open wide to receive your friend. Praise heartily as your dog bounds in toward you. Positive body language! Positive tone of voice! Positive eye contact!

But if by chance your dog does not come at this juncture, you must have a battle plan. Memorize these steps in advance of releasing your leashless, tabless dog in an unenclosed area. You will have to have each step firmly in mind in case the dog does not come:

- If you've genuflected once and you have called your dog and it has not responded, rise and wait for another moment of eye contact from your dog. Sink to the ground again *just as the dog looks at you* and simultaneously call the dog. Your command and your genuflection should be timed as exactly as possible with the first moment the dog looks at you. Don't stoop down before the dog makes eye contact with you because this may make you look submissive, and don't genuflect too late because the dog will have looked away already. Hit the moment just right. There is a powerful, orienting effect on the dog that hearkens back to previous training.

- If your dog still does not come, try genuflecting again. But, if your dog *still* doesn't come after the second attempt, you have a decision to make. If you think you can get your dog, *go and get it.* You might have to chase the dog down, corner it or have an assistant trap it. Once you get the dog, deliver the shake correction, the swat correction, shove it into a sit, repeat the warning phrase, snap on a six-foot leash (or use your arm for a leash) and put the dog through seven formal recalls. Do not drop the leash and do not praise. The reason for this strict discipline is that your dog has just goofed royally. After all the practicing you've both done, after weeks on the Radical Regimen, the dog has committed a major gaffe. Go back to week two and resume practice on the twenty-foot lead.

- Let's say that the dog has not come after two attempts at the recall. But you also realize that you cannot possibly get to the dog to discipline it. Perhaps the area is too large. Or perhaps the dog is too fast and you are too slow. Whatever the case, you have another decision to make. It's possible to get the dog to *follow* you. Wait for a third moment of eye contact. Instead of stooping down and calling the dog, swivel around dramatically and begin to walk *away* slowly. Hunch your shoulders humbly toward the ground, hang your head and look depressed. You will be anyway. If the dog follows you, calculate your chances of grabbing it. Perhaps you can get it to follow you into an enclosed area. Perhaps it follows closely enough that you can lunge and grab it. If you think you have a chance, make the attempt. Once you've got your recalcitrant, shove the dog into a sit, give the shake and swat and practice seven formal recalls on the spot. Go back to practicing on a twenty-foot leash. Don't worry about justifying discipline for a dog who *followed* you. It's perfectly allowable because the dog *didn't* come to you. It followed you. There is a difference, and the dog knows it. After all, the way you have been teaching the recall, both on a formal and a free-lance level, for so many weeks dictated that the dog present itself in *front* of you and make eye contact, *not* follow behind you.

- Let's say the situation is really bad. After two attempts at the recall your dog will not come to you. You have also determined that you cannot trap or capture it. Attempts at tricking the dog into following you have failed. Well, my friend, you just have to get your dog however you have to get it. Enlist the help of friends, open your car or your house door, use a butterfly net—whatever you have to do, but under no circumstances should such a dog be trusted again. Go *all the way back* to week one of this program, reinstitute the RRRR and begin again.

So, that's it, my answer to the ongoing query in the heart of every dog, "To come or not to come?" If some of the numerical prescriptions suggested in this chapter, such as one week for this, two weeks for that, sound arbitrary, trust me. Over the years I've fiddled with this program and fine-tuned it. I sincerely want you to have a dog that comes when called. I want you to live with the peace and security you deserve. I also want your dog to be able to enjoy its life fully. For most dogs, unless it is legally proscribed, that enjoyment includes rip-roaring times gallivanting about in open fields, on the beach or in the woods. I know the absolute thrill I get watching my Dalmatian, Sport, chase down waves on the beach or wildly chasing his tennis ball in a city playground. These are the times when he really gets to be himself, and he is a real fun-loving character. But I also have the security, and so does he, that when I open my arms and say his name, he faithfully returns. Through training, he has answered *for himself* the question "To come or not to come?" and his answer is *yes!*

Running Away Remedy Chart

	Moratorium on any off-leash freedom?	Formal and/or free-lance recalls?	How many recalls?	Where?
Week one	Yes, strict	Formal	Seven each day	In enclosed environment, using 20-foot leash.
Week two	Yes, strict	Formal	Seven each day	In enclosed area, using 6-foot leash. Vary locations.
Week three	Yes, except for practice	Formal *and* free-lance	Seven of each type, each day	Same enclosed areas, using 20-foot leash.
Week four	Yes, except for practice	Formal *and* free-lance	Seven of each type, each day	*New* enclosed areas, using 6-foot leash.
Week five	Yes, except for practice	Formal *and* free-lance	Seven of each type, each day	Same enclosed areas as in week four; *tab* leash on the dog.
Week six	No, unless necessary to backtrack because of goofs	Free-lance	Seven each day	Unenclosed but safe area (unless illegal), leashless, tabless dog.

End Program

Live Life Securely
with a Dog That Comes Reliably

19

Nutrition Notes

I HAVE already written extensively about nutrition in my other books—some say too extensively. I am deeply concerned about how nutrition affects behavior. Dr. Paul Pemberton, an Australian veterinarian, did a study in which he showed that in order for a dog to be successfully trained a nutritious diet is a must. It must be high in usable protein and in use at least three to four weeks *before* the onset of training, thus enabling the dog's brain to work in all its complexity. When you examine the chapter on set-ups it should be readily apparent that it is important for the dog to be able to think out the content of the set-up. The nutritional status of the dog influences its ability to decode what you are trying to teach it.

To briefly summarize what I have previously written about nutrition: I believe that canned foods should be used in moderation and semimoist foods not used at all. Nonfixed-formula dry foods should be carefully evaluated because it might not be possible for the dog to eat enough of the food to get the promised amount of protein, and protein works the brain. Obviously I prefer the so-called speciality foods. These are dry foods that are made in small amounts and usually have a 3:2 ratio of protein to fat. As an example, a food that is 30 percent protein should contain 20 percent fat. In my opinion this 3:2 rule is a benchmark for a quality specialty food. The correlation between the two percentages is important because there must be easily digestible fat, and enough fat to supply energy to *use* the protein with just enough fat left over for a nice shiny coat. Yet there must not be so much fat left over that it becomes the source of other problems such as large stools, obesity, an overly greasy coat or, worse yet, medical problems such as a fatty liver. Use a specialty food with good quality control and a terrific track record. This means selecting a specialty food that has been in production for at least seven years. Because the dog food industry is changing faster than ever before, it is impossible to indicate specific brands, but if you use the 3:2 protein to fat guideline and do a little research at your local pet supply or food outlet (which may involve calling some of the 800 numbers listed on the backs of different bags), you should be able to zero in on the best food for your dog.

Let's talk about nutrition as it pertains to particular behavior problems. My comments here might help to illuminate the decisive role proper nutrition can play in behavior modification. Remember, you can concoct a sterling set-up, but if your nutrition is a no-no the results will be no-go!

Housetraining

If owners of new puppies or older dogs who have "fallen off the wagon" simply remembered that what goes in has to come out, the housetraining process would be greatly simplified. Canned foods in particular present major problems. These foods are 50 to 78 percent water, and added to the water that a growing puppy already drinks, it's harder for the puppy to "hold." Canned foods also contain ingredients like iron oxide and dyes that are not digestible and irritate the lining of the intestine, making mistakes more likely. Again, use canned foods only as a flavoring for a quality dry ration. Hold the line at one, two or three *teaspoons* added to the dry ration. No more!

Specialty foods usually contain a fibrous substance such as beet pulp, bran, corn cobs or even peanut husks that help the growing puppy or older off-the-wagon dog to maintain control. This gives the possible house soiler more time to alert the owner or simply make it to the desired spot for elimination. No one knows how much time is gained when a dog eats a food with a felicitious fiber substance, but my experience has been that even if only one minute is gained, it's worth feeding that food. Yet it never ceases to amaze me how many otherwise educated owners will be in the thick of the housetraining task and yet feed their charges foods with no fiber, and worse, foods with ingredients that will actually trigger on-the-spot elimination. You wouldn't try to toilet train your kid on prunes, so why try to housetrain your dog on junk food?

I also have a big beef with breeders who intelligently recommend specialty foods but then send their clients home with elaborate instructions to add supplements like B and C vitamins, coat conditioners or dairy products. All of these additions can cause diarrhea. The addition of these substances to the diet should be held off until the housetraining process is over. I stress again that what goes in has to come out, and it is often the *owner's* choice, not the dog's, as to whether what comes out is deposited decently or destructively.

Aggression

The favorite food of all aggressive dogs is whatever you're eating. Grouches are adept at conning their owners and others into surrendering their food or giving excessive treats. Point nine of the RRRR says cut off all treats for the problem dog. Don't take this advice lightly. *No treats.* Also remember not to feed your doggie dictator any people food—even if you are adding it to its normal ration as flavoring. The dog knows that it was once yours—after all the dog smelled it when you prepared it for yourself—and it's important that the Alpha does not share food with a subordinate, at least not a problem subordinate.

Because set-ups for aggressive dogs often demand split-second timing and fully engage the dog's mind, it is important that the dog's nutritional life be sound. The hypothalamus, the gland that to a degree controls behavior, must be calm and regulated. In my experience the higher quality foods are beneficial in this respect, as long as the dog is properly exercised. I also feel that *two* daily feedings keep aggressive dogs calmer. Try feeding one meal in the early morning and one in the afternoon so that food is kept in the dog's stomach during its waking hours and the hypothalamus kept happier.

It's possible that a trainer will recommend the use of food treats to facilitate a set-up that will help your aggressive dog. As long as the previously stated food rules of the RRRR are adhered to, and as long as the treat is used only *within* the set-up, give the ploy a chance. Sometimes food works as a training tactic for aggressive dogs. However, some aggressive dogs can no longer be manipulated with food, even if they know how to manipulate to *get* food. If food fails, clearly it needs to be removed from the set-up. Trust your trainer, but you owe it to him or her to state in advance whether you have abused food in your relationship with your dog by feeding the dog from the table or bribing the dog with treats, or if the dog has a history of stealing food or displaying aggression when eating food.

A quick tip to breeders: Computer analysis of my client records reveals a direct correlation between large litter size and later problems with aggressive displays toward owners while the dog is eating food. Perhaps this problem has early roots stemming from too few available feeding plans during early weaning. The pups soon learn to jostle each other around the food pan, the dominant pups getting the lion's share of food. These pups later turn out to be food grouches and food guarders. Breeders can help by providing one pan for every four puppies, thus eliminating fanatical food fights—and later problems for owners. However, if you do own a food grouch, don't hesitate to devise a set-up to correct the problem unless you can simply use creative avoidance to circumvent it. Sometimes it's simply not worth the effort to correct feistiness over food, especially if the problem is isolated, infrequent, easily avoided and doesn't connect up with other displays of aggression. A good trainer can usually decode whether or not it's essential to correct an aggressive dog over food or simply leave the dog alone when it eats.

Jumping Up

A dog with a jumping up problem often receives double messages from its owner when the owner allows the dog to jump for a treat but forbids the dog to jump otherwise. If you have a jumper you must realize that you can't have it both ways. The dog must be taught to sit and stay for *all* treats. In fact, if the dog is a serious jumper you should put it on the RRRR program, which will forbid the dog any treats for one month anyway. After the jumping subsides and you are "allowed" to reoffer treats, try to curve your hand above and over the dog when offering the treat. If the treat is held too closely to your body the dog will be more tempted to jump up on you than if your hand is extended and curved downward.

Be sure that children do not tease the jumping dog with food. Kids sometimes enjoy running around, enticing the dog to grab food from their hands. This can result in serious accidents and calls for parental supervision. If this type of teasing and play isn't curtailed the dog could become a spring jumper—and I don't mean the season, but rather a dog that springs into the air so quickly that most lay owners will simply not be able to correct the dog fast enough. Remember, jumping up is not simply a search for love and attention, but also a form of dominance.

Destructive Chewing

There is considerable anecdotal information from trainers and behaviorists that poor-quality foods containing high levels of red or yellow dyes are connected with the development of destructive chewing. Semimoist foods seem to be the main culprits, but it might not just be the dyes and preservatives that produce canine "beavers." It could very well be that these foods do not have any natural crunchiness that allows the dog to alleviate some of the natural desire to chew hard objects. Again, a diet of specialty foods would be in order.

Don't make the tragic mistake of rewarding your dog for not chewing by offering food treats, especially if the reward is given after the fact. The dog simply won't get the connection. Destructive chewers can also be helped by feeding them two or even three meals a day. Keep that hypothalamus happy!

Not Coming

Obviously, never offer your dog a treat as a bribe to get it to come to you. This sound advice has been in training for decades, but a recent spate of food-oriented training books advises that it's OK to break this once cardinal prohibition in training. The theory is, of course, that the food treat can be used early on as an inducement to get the dog to come and later can be phased out. This is nice on paper but overlooks the fact that in daily life food is often abused by the owner (with the best of intentions) and the acquisition of it becomes a major obsession for even younger dogs.

Just as housetraining difficulties are, in my opinion, the biggest closet secret amongst dog people, bribing dogs with food to get them to come when called probably ranks as the second most prevalent "dirty little secret." Very few owners—especially professional dog handlers—are proud of the fact, or will even admit (except under experienced cross-examination), that the only way they can get their dog to come is via food bribery. Of course this *isn't* anything to be proud of, but rather something to be concerned about, because often a dog who won't come ends up as a dead dog. What I am saying is that food bribery is much more widespread than is generally acknowledged and many owners feel trapped and terrified. After all, they have to get the dog *somehow.* Yet they are ashamed that they have to use food to do it.

If you are stuck with this problem, follow the directions in the chapter "To Come or Not to Come" carefully. Photocopy the training chart and put it on your refrigerator door so that you'll be sure to follow the program exactly. Turn to the RRRR and apply that program immediately. If you follow both training regimens at the same time, you can stop food bribery as of today, because your dog simply will not be away from you to cause you to cheapen yourself by proffering a treat, and the RRRR forbids all treats anyway. Presto: You've won round one!

You can see from these nutrition notes that intentional or unintentional misuse of food aids and abets many major behavioral problems. There are probably deep psychological reasons why humans enjoy offering dogs food so much. It is a deep-seated human need to be liked and loved. Many of us are taught in childhood that the way to a dog's heart is through its stomach. I disagree. The true way to a dog's heart is via friendship and leadership.

20

In the Trenches: Inside Information for Individuals "in Dogs"

VETERINARIANS, groomers, boarding kennel operators, obedience class instructors and, of course, trainers are on the front lines in the battle against problem dogs. A look at the articles in trade and professional journals or even a cursory glance at speaker lineups at professional conferences readily confirms this "in the trenches" mentality. Veterinarians sometimes risk limb and even life dealing with upset, aggressive patients—not to mention upset, aggressive human clients. Every groomer has a particular dog whose arrival at the shop is a dreaded event and sometimes a day-long ordeal. Boarding kennel operators sometimes feel more like wardens of maximum security prisons or supervisors in mental institutions for the criminally insane—depending on the particular batch of dogs occupying the kennel at a particular moment. Obedience class instructors may never know who in the lineup of students will strike.

Professional trainers have it worse. I've given my fellow trainers a separate chapter. They are employed to change the dog's behavior and thus place themselves in the direct line of fire for assaults. Years ago, I applied for disability insurance. After a review of my application the company told me that my rate would be the highest. I was in "group four." Other occupations represented in group four are fire fighters, high-rise construction workers, theatrical stunt performers and lion tamers. I rest my case.

Seminars for groomers now routinely feature speakers on canine behavior—usually behavior that involves attempts at biting (usually a groomer). I often teach canine behavior at various veterinary conferences. The draw for my talks at the Michigan Veterinary Conference, for instance, was over 700 veterinarians and technicians. At the Ohio State conference, over 1,000 practitioners flooded the conference hall. Simultaneous surgical and clinical presentations drew far fewer attendees. Obviously, behavior has come of age and is receiving the attention it has always deserved. But the explanation might be much simpler—professionals are tired of being bitten! I don't blame them.

Aggression is by far the biggest problem for those "in dogs." But first things first. The perspective of the given professional is also important. Of the groups mentioned, only trainers have the specific task of training dogs and counseling owners. Naturally, veterinarians, groomers and boarding kennel operators are often asked for advice, but their attitude toward giving it should include the realization that they are not necessarily qualified to dispense it. All too often these professionals overstep the boundaries of their chosen fields in a sincere attempt to help clients who have a canine behavior problem. But true training and correct counseling involve interviewing skills, the ability to catalog information and intricate instructional skills that assure that clients fully *understand* what is being taught. It's next to impossible to employ these procedures correctly over an exam table in a clinic setting, over a grooming table with an unruly dog or at a boarding kennel when perhaps all the dog wants is to get *out* of the kennel, into the car and home. Also—and this is very important—clients in such settings are usually not *paying* for the proffered advice, and thus do not necessarily fully appreciate it.

Just as I do not groom dogs, board them or perform clinical or surgical procedures on them, other professionals should not assume to train them. Besides the fact that the quality of the advice can be shoddy, the well-meaning professional puts an unnecessary pressure on himself or herself. Inevitably this lessens the quality of their primary service. It's hard enough to be in dogs in any capacity and not get bitten, pummeled, goosed, dragged, barked at, wet or otherwise assaulted *yourself*—so why complicate matters by playing trainer unless you are one?

The advice included here, then, is intended to help professionals in given fields protect *themselves* and their employees. It is intended to help them run their clinics or businesses in a smooth fashion. The chapter for trainers is also geared in this fashion, but since trainers also need information on how to advise clients, I have added some "people tips" and I would suggest they also read *The Evans Guide for Counseling Dog Owners.*

Veterinarians: Viciousness and Vexations

Veterinarians do not want to become disabled veterans. They should take time to consider the concept of *territoriality* in dogs. A lack of appreciation for how territoriality operates in the canine mind is the root cause for many unpleasant incidents in clinic settings. Dominant or aggressive dogs often claim territory as they go. It's a moving concept of territory that includes protection of the dog itself, the owner and as much as a six- to ten-foot area around the dog and owner. So when a dog barges into your waiting room, dragging its owner behind, that dog has already claimed your clinic. Smell trouble? Your sense of smell is excellent.

There's not much you can do to prevent this with a first-time client, but if the practice continues, the receptionist or the veterinarian can inform the client that barging makes the dog feel that it is boss. Frequently, it's better if the aggressive or extremely unruly dog is removed from the waiting room, and its owner, and placed in a holding pen in the rear of the clinic. A diplomatic way of approaching this separation is to say, "One of the jobs your dog thinks it has is to protect you. If you are not around, there will be nobody to protect, and it might be easier for us to give the dog proper care." Naturally, what *isn't* being mentioned is that a dog that feels it has to protect its owner in a veterinary waiting room, where there is no threat to life or limb, probably has a pretty mixed-up, leaderless relationship with said owner—but then again, we're not being employed to train the dog that's in this situation, just treat it.

It's far better for the practitioner to be in the exam room *before* the aggressive dog enters. While this is the opposite of usual procedure, it makes eminent sense, given the territoriality of most dogs. Naturally, if it's the first time you've ever seen a given patient, you will have no way of setting this up in advance. But if the patient is a known troublemaker, try to arrange to be in the exam room so that the aggressive dog perceives *you* as having claimed it already. The alternative is to stuff the unruly dog and ineffective owner into the exam room (often to maintain peace in the waiting area) and then let them "comfort" each other. The owner then lets the dog "get used" to the room by sniffing (claiming) everything in it, and soothes the dog with faulty paralanguage and body language—cooing to and fondling the dog. By the time the poor veterinarian enters the room the dog feels perfectly at home and ready to go into action. It is on guard: "This exam room is *mine!*" Reversing the usual procedure throws the dog off guard—it's entered *your* turf.

Some troublesome dogs are better treated on the floor, but it's touch and go and has to be evaluated on the spot, for other dogs are disoriented by being elevated onto an exam table and thus more manageable. With the advent of mechanically operated tables that rise to the desired height with a minimum of motion or noise, some happy compromises can be made.

My advice to veterinarians if they even slightly suspect that a patient will become aggressive is to muzzle the dog. While, in general, muzzling *increases* tension in dogs and encourages resistance, the fact is you have procedures to perform, treatment to give and time limits. The medical exam must be completed. If a trainer muzzles a dog, it is simply a stopgap measure, but for a veterinarian to do so is simply sane and right. Remember, in every single case in which a veterinarian has brought suit against an owner for being bitten, the veterinarian has lost. Bites are considered occupational hazards and litigation is a lost cause. Self-protection, advance planning and psyching out each client and patient behaviorally are the only safeguards available.

Remember also, it is quite feasible that trusted clients can sue *you* if *they* are bitten by their own dog—if they can prove that the veterinarian placed them in a situation that insured that a bite would take place. Malpractice suits of this nature are on the rise. I know we live in a litigious society, but some instances are truly sick, tasteless cheap shots at well-meaning vets. It seems incredible, but owners of known aggressive dogs have actually collected hard cash because they were bit while the veterinarian tried to help their untrained, unruly pets. The cases I've studied show that there is almost always a history of aggression by the dog and a corresponding lack of leadership and neglect of obedience training by the owner. This again points up the necessity—and possibly money-saving value—of veterinarians clearly advising such owners to secure training early on. The suggestion should be backed up by giving the client the actual phone numbers of prospective trainers, and this should then be noted on the patient's chart. If training is not pursued, and the dog later acts up during an exam and bites the owner, the veterinarian will have an excellent line of defense since he or she *did* suggest training.

I usually advise veterinarians to schedule known agitators for the early morning hours, when the waiting room is less crowded, the clinic quieter and the practitioner's patience highest. Also, there is absolutely nothing wrong with refusing to treat an aggressive dog unless it is properly restrained. "Properly restrained" might mean that you will have to *insist* that the owner leave the dog's presence so that his or her negative thought waves, body language and paralanguage aren't affecting the patient. A technician (or two or three!) can then be called in to restrain the dog. A metal ring screwed securely into the wall can be handy because the dog's leash can be passed through it and the dog pulled toward the wall. The dog's head will now be tethered and the remaining task is to simply block in the rear end. A tech can work the rear end and another can keep the leash taut so that the dog cannot wheel around and retaliate. It's sad when veterinarians and technicians have to engage in such tactics. After all, they studied animal medicine, not rodeo routines. The absent owner should be informed, not of every difficult detail that was involved in securing the dog for treatment, but certainly that treatment was a torture and training is strongly indicated.

If you are presented with an older, grouchy patient, trying to sell training can be difficult—especially if the owner is content with the dog as it is or too lazy to seek out help. With young puppies, the best course is prevention. Ask, "What are you planning to do about training?" during the very first examination. Be sure to button your lip and let the client answer. Don't just say, "Are

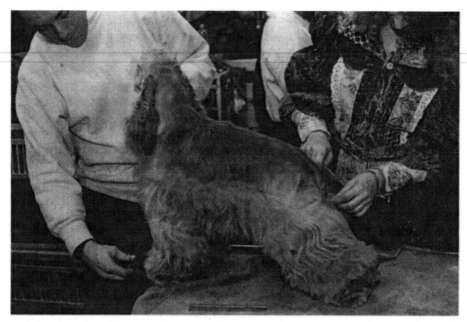

Frontal control by one person often enables a veterinarian or groomer to "work the rear" more effectively. The dog cannot whirl around as easily. *Kevin Smith*

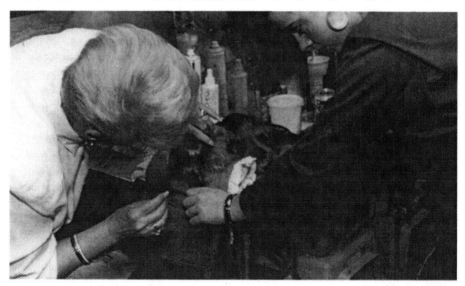

Groomers are "in the trenches" with a great motivation: They just want the dog to look beautiful! *Kevin Smith*

you going to train this dog?" because the answer will, of course, be "yes." What the client means is that the dog will be trained to sit for a treat at home: end of "training." The former wording places the client on the spot and indicates that there is something to be *done, they* have to do it and you know they *should.* Remember, clients view the veterinarian with deep respect. Since you are probably the first contact who speaks with authority concerning the dog, you owe it to your clients to indicate early training. The long-term benefit will be a patient that, hopefully, lives for many years. Note: Trained, unstressed dogs live longer than stressed-out dogs. Trained dogs are a joy to have at the clinic—in the waiting room or on the table. Moreover, such an early suggestion clearly shows the client that you are concerned with the *whole* dog, body and mind. The AVMA has targeted behavior as an area that needs more attention from rank-and-file practitioners. Bravo for your heeding the call.

Doom and Groom: Trouble on the Table

I've met many groomers who are closet trainers—but not many trainers who are closet groomers. In short, groomers are often behaviorally oriented but behaviorally uneducated—a situation that can be remedied—while most trainers would rather pick up a dinner tab than a grooming brush. More communication is desperately needed between the two groups.

Groomers are in the trenches like no one else, because sometimes they have to battle to confer beauty on a beast! Groomers sometimes overstep the boundaries of good sense by refusing to restrain or muzzle an unruly canine customer, and instead tranquilizing or harshly disciplining a dog. If you want to take the risk, that's regrettable, but most groomers agree that more flies are caught by honey than vinegar. Groomers, you can throw all my previous admonitions about not using food aside. While I do not suggest the use of food for standard training, we need to remember that in this case, the dog is the customer, not a student. Your job is to make the dog look beautiful, and if food helps, use food.

The traditional grooming table is really quite nicely designed from a behavioral standpoint, so use it. The metal bar allows the groomer to "string up" a dog so that the head is held high—and biting attempts thwarted. Just be sure to watch the dog's rear end, as, even if properly tensioned in the overhang bar, many smaller dogs can easily rotate, sending themselves into a panic. Often an assistant can be at table side, with hands palm down on the table edge, not restraining the dog but ready to if necessary. Some dogs allow grooming if they feel they are being *watched* but are *not* restrained. Read over the chapter on aggression in this book and watch for the classic hardness of the eyes. This is when a well-timed "No!" can be of great value—minus any physical discipline. Some aggressive dogs do better if left to sit and stew in a crate or holding pen while observing other dogs being groomed.

Naturally, grooming the head and shoulders presents the biggest problem when dealing with "the ungroomables." In extreme cases, it's not unacceptable to let the owner do the grooming under your direction. The tool can be passed to you without much fanfare and you can add a few strokes before completing the job. The next session, perhaps one side of the face can be done by the owner and the other by yourself. Advise owners of known or potential menaces to feed only one-half the normal ration if you plan to use food as bribery for cooperation. Remember, aggressive dogs do not like sudden movements. Try to have all clippers, scissors and other implements laid out in advance so that opening drawers, slamming cupboard doors and any delays can be avoided.

There are some groomers who have enough experience to incorporate elements of training, via a set-up, into the grooming procedure—if only in order to complete the task at hand. Follow the steps for a set-up listed earlier. A typical set-up would include warning the potential grouch *as you pick up the first tool,* retreating immediately if there is a snap or other retaliation (a growl should suffice) and *quickly* yanking the tether that is attached to the overhang bar. Repeat the process if necessary, but try food first, set-ups second. You do not have to have a love affair or leadership role with this little (or huge) monster. You just have to get the dog groomed nicely and out of your life—at least until the next appointment.

Quiet soothes and often mystifies aggressive or bouncy dogs. Grooming shops are, unfortunately, sometimes the rivals of rock concerts for decibel output. Especially if you run a drop-off-and-pick-up service, a shop full of screamers can be an everyday fact of life. If there is a quiet nook you can escape to, even if it means going into a backyard, do so. Dominant dogs tend to like noise and confusion, as the humans then become distracted and exhibit erratic body language that is easily decoded as a threat. Sometimes a simple walk around the block or building on leash will display the dominance needed to change some hellions into demure devils. While most trainers would not trade places with most groomers, many groomers would make excellent trainers. If you find yourself training more than grooming, consider a career change—we trainers need all the soldiers on the front lines we can get!

Boarding Kennel Operators: The Keepers and the Kept

The biggest problem boarding kennel operators face besides aggressive clients is, of course, aggressive dogs. I used to run the boarding/training kennel at New Skete Monastery. The monks had developed a reputation for being able to rehabilitate aggressive dogs. Unfortunately, because of our cloistered status we were unable to go directly into the lion's lair so to speak—the domicile of the aggressive dog. Instead, owners simply deposited such dogs with us and after a careful interview would fly off to Rome or Tahiti while we were left with a kennel full of dogs resembling the ones in Stephen King's *Cujo.*

Just realizing the fact that the kennel will often be populated by problem dogs somehow helps the boarding kennel operator deal with the issue. There is always a chance that a given boarder will be aggressive. Perhaps even as

182

Boarding kennel proprietors should not underestimate the value of a well-timed "No!"—especially to squelch fence-fighting. *Judy Emmert/Dealing with Dogs/TV Ontario*

many as one out of ten dogs will exhibit aggression while in your care, so some coaching is in order. Aggressive dogs do not endure stress well. They are often neurotically dependent on their owners and do not want to transfer their love or loyalty to anyone else—and certainly not to you, bozo! Trouble is, if you run a boarding kennel, you are *ipso facto*—at least to a degree—asking dogs to be dependent on you. The aggressive dog doesn't want this transfer to take place and will marshall all its forces to prevent you from taking over. The scene is set for problems early on in the dog/owner interactions, before the dog even reaches your doorstep.

Owners have often been cooing to, coddling and generally placating the hell out of their aggressive dogs for days, even weeks, before the dog gets to you. If you have contact with the owner before the dog arrives, especially when the owner is actually preparing to leave on a trip, tell the owner to hide all signs of imminent leave-taking from the dog. Suitcases should be packed on the sly, housecleaning done normally and even the discussion of the upcoming boarding avoided. After all, an owner chitchatting on the phone in a nervous, worried way, constantly interjecting the dog's name, is being listened to by the dog—which does know its name and recognizes the worried tonalities. The boarding, instead, should be sprung on the dominant dog with little preparatory fanfare. On many levels, aggressive dogs don't like sudden surprises, but this ploy is a "structured" surprise that will have payback potential. The dog will simply not have time to rev itself up into a frenzy about the upcoming separation.

When owner and dog arrive at the kennel, it's best—although not always possible—to separate the two on neutral territory. A good place is halfway between the owner's car and your entrance way. Second best is to separate the two within the kennel. Unfortunately, since aggressive dogs claim territory as they move, the dog may already have claimed your kennel. If the dog had claimed the parking lot it's not as bad—after all it won't be camping out there. If you take some time to explain what it is you'd like to do, most owners will be willing to accommodate you. Whichever site is chosen, have the owner hand the leash to you. Do not reach toward the owner or dog and simply take over—this could result in a bite. Remember, the aggressive dog is set on defending three things: itself, its owner and the territory it has just claimed.

Preregistration phone interviewing is very desirable in preventing incidents with aggressive dogs in a boarding kennel situation. Watch out for code sayings like "Just leave him alone and he'll be fine," or "She just gets a little uptight sometimes and gets grouchy," or "Whatever you do, don't corner him." These statements are all dead giveaways that you have a problem pooch coming in. A code system can be developed listing dogs that are to be suspected of acting up on arrival.

Remember, you cannot afford to get bitten. You make your living with your hands, and if the aggressive dog gets in one good zap, your authority is lessened. Plan out in advance just how you are going to whisk "little Hitler" back into the kennel. Be sure to have passageway doors propped open in advance because dominant dogs often take advantage of passageways and act up—and act out—in them. There is a way of taking the dog from the owner and having it ensconced in its kennel so smoothly that the dog literally doesn't know what has taken place. This beats trying to "make friends" with the dog while the owner coos to it, unintentionally informing the dog that you are the warden of this "lockup" and not a friend at all.

Once the dog is placed (or plopped) in its kennel, simply leave the grouch alone. Don't try to make friends or warm up to the dog. On the other hand, if the dog is growling at you, issue a stern "No!" and then quickly look away aloofly. Some dogs will stop growling, others will continue, but you will have employed a bitch basic that registers with the dog. Even seasoned boarding kennel operators sometimes underestimate the power of a well-timed "No!" accompanied with a withering stare and the aloof look away. In my kennel, I often stopped fence-fighters using this method and sometimes a squirt bottle. Aggressive dogs love to fence-fight, and often need to be placed on the end of the line so that they have only one partner, preferably a submissive dog who does not care to fence-fight or will simply ignore the dog. Turn to your older, more experienced boarders for this invaluable service.

There are some boarding kennels that simply do not accept aggressive dogs. After all, in most cases, you are not being employed to untrain the aggression anyway. There are also some boarding kennels that find that aggressive dogs do better if handled by female employees. Women seem to telegraph less ego than many macho men. While I've mentioned the value of a well-timed verbal reprimand, sheer force usually will not make the dog accept its fate with equanimity. Try to assign female employees to care for such dogs, as long as direct physical contact with the dog can be avoided. If not, be certain they possess the necessary skills.

When interviewing owners of dogs being admitted to the monastery boarding/training kennel, I was often informed that a given aggressive dog "hated men." The owners often volunteered this information innocently, then suddenly realized that a monastery is an all-male community. While often I felt like replying, "Thanks for nothing," I kept my monastic cool and usually replied that monks are gentler than most men—and in general, monks are. Knowing that aggressive boarders often calm down when cared for by a woman, I would be sure to give that particular dog a good look at myself in full monastic habit. That usually smoothed the psycho's psyche. I'm sure the dog thought I was an exceptionally ugly woman in a black dress!

21

The Trials of Trainers

IF VETERINARIANS, groomers and boarding kennel operators are in the trenches in the war with problem pooches, trainers are truly on the front lines—minus any protective trench. While medically treating, grooming or boarding a difficult dog can be potentially dangerous, only trainers are charged with the task of changing the behavior of the dog. As if this isn't enough, trainers also deal with the dog's owners in a counseling setting. The trials of trainers include burnout, sexism and tolerating repetition—and it's these dilemmas, and others, I'd like to address. Trainers, prick up your ears, this is for you from me.

Tolerating Repetition

How can a trainer manage the monotony of repetition? How does one learn to tolerate it? I learned a lot about repetition during my years at New Skete Monastery where we sang Matins, Vespers and other services day in, day out, 365 days a year, with small changes in the service except for perhaps a feast day song. After eleven years of that, I might be crazy or I might be able to offer you some tips on tolerating repetition. Because I don't want to face the first prosect, however true it may be, I'll opt for the second and offer some help.

1. Facing down the fact that repetition is, well, repetitious is the first step in tolerating it. Of course you are going to be called in for countless housetraining consultations, and of course it will be boring

to dish out the same advice each time. On the other hand, even though housetraining consultations will be among the most boring and repetitious you will face, your client desperately needs the information, otherwise he or she will sour on the dog and get rid of it because it is "dirty." The way I get through such consultations is to remind myself that if I fail to be informative, lively, caring and complete, the dog's death will possibly be on my hands. Drastic? Not really. Try it, it works.

2. Some advice books on repetition will counsel you to focus your attention elsewhere in the room or off the subject of repetition. This is absolutely bogus, false and potentially hurtful advice for private trainers. *Never* do this. No matter what the effort, keep you attention fixed on the client and dog—especially if it is an aggressive dog. Trying to divert yourself to spare yourself boredom is a losing game and you will be mauled in the process.

3. Instead, try to rearrange your material, perhaps explaining eye contact last instead of first, even if it seems more natural to open a consultation stressing its importance. There are some clients who simply want the cold info on crating, confinement, schedules, foods, etc., rather than a lot of philosophical verbiage. Feel free, when repetition is unrewarding, to depart from your standard, rehearsed speech. You'll give yourself the break you need, but be sure to provide all pertinent information within the consultation, if only rearranged.

4. I have another trick for you from my monastery days. Since we followed the Eastern rite, the services were rich, ornate, mystical, inspiring and *long*. Indeed, the Russian Orthodox have a standing joke that all churchgoers develop legs of steel since standing is the preferred position during worship. No matter how much you love a particular religious rite—or your dog training and counseling sessions—the fact that the sessions are lengthy can be bothersome, especially if material is old hat. I used to tell myself during a particularly arduous service, "This service can only go forward, it cannot go backward." It was my way of reassuring myself that time does, indeed, pass, despite the timeless quality of some services. It can be your way of enduring a session during which a client prattles on endlessly about the dog's faults or virtues, or surviving an interview where careful interviewing and note taking is essential. Repeat it like a mantra to yourself: "This session can only go forward, it can't go backward." Know what? You'll probably free yourself from feeling trapped by time and have a better session for it.

5. On the other hand, some private trainers cook their own gooses by simply trying to give too much during a session. An initial session, in my opinion, should not last more than two hours, even if the dog has severe problems. After a while, clients simply feel overwhelmed

with information, even if you leave everything in writing, and even if you are a laid-back, low-key counselor. I'm quite the opposite, I'm told, and I have learned to trim my goods to the necessary essentials so that I don't leave clients with their head spinning. Other trainers feel that the more they give, give, give, the more they talk, the more information they impart, the more they are doing quality work. Not necessarily so. Much depends on your delivery style, the educational level of the client and how much you can endure repeating yourself for such a long time. "Trimming your goods" by having a fellow trainer sit in on your sessions and offer frank evaluations of what to cut and what to add can be invaluable in helping you tolerate repetition.

6. Finally, it may seem odd to include a section on repetition as a "trial" trainers endure, but I've identified it as one of the major causes of burnout among private trainers. More on burnout follows. The sooner a private trainer develops techniques against repetition before being bored by it, the better. And who knows, tomorrow you may get a new, *exciting* student for training—like a Rottweiler that waits until you are settled for twenty minutes and *then* attacks your buttocks as you rise, rather that than three Maltese who defecate behind couches—all of course owned by separate persons, and all three consultations, of course, on the same day. You'll be thankful for the Rottie problem—*if* you avoid that butt bite.

Trainer Burnout

Burnout has been getting a lot of press over the last few years, and its sister, rustout, isn't far behind. Burnout, even in the dictionary, means, simply, *exhaustion;* rustout means you're nearing burnout. If you've experienced burnout, or are nearing rustout or burnout as a trainer, this section is for you.

First, let's face reality. Learning for dogs and for people is stressful. If you've ever studied for an exam, the probability was that you were under pressure and had a strained, uptight and tension-filled expression on your face. Learning isn't easy, and teaching is *worse!* So just take it as a given that training pooches and people is going to involve looking at stressed, depressed and even ugly canine and human faces. I mention this because it is the virtual sea of sad-sack faces that gets to a good many trainers and seminar givers. "They all look just, I don't know how to say it, so *out* of it," one trainer told me about her classes. Well, it's the teacher's responsibility to infuse the class with so much energy that the participants no longer look so out of it—but in doing so the teacher can readily burnout.

It takes a lot out of a person to consistently go into a class setting, see private clients, welcome newcomers to a veterinary practice or work at an animal shelter and *not* burnout within one to five years. If this person also tries to juggle a show or obedience career, the chances of burnout are much higher, since by virtue of the way trials and shows are set up they produce only a fraction of winners and a plethora of losers.

In reality, losing or winning doesn't really stop burnout. It is a syndrome that affects winners and losers, and in fact, consistent losing may be a blessing in disguise, motivating you to make decisions to curtail activities that *would* have led to burnout. Burnout victims often don't realize one important rule: You can't do it all.

Upon entering the dog game, many newcomers will attempt to conquer every aspect of the fancy—showing in obedience and confirmation on the weekends (often with the ubiquitous RV complete with appropriate decals), training all week (maybe running classes), plus volunteering at the local Humane Society (very laudable) and perhaps penning a column for the local newspaper or club newsletter. In between all this they fit in a KPT class, the fly-ball team and hosting the club's monthly meeting every so often.

Then there is the phone. Very few dog people learn to curtail their phone chatter, ringside verbiage being the only other vocalistics they have an even harder time refraining from. Phone consultations can quickly lead to burnout. The facts are: Phone consultations take an extraordinary amount of time as the caller feels he or she has your OK to prattle on forever; phone calls effectively prohibit you from doing anything else; finally, they *don't work* if you attempt to give advice via them, which of course adds to your feelings of ineffectiveness (a classic sign of burnout). You simply can't help someone over the phone with a dog problem because you must usually see the owner and dog interact. Simply saying, "I'm so sorry, but I can't see you and your dog together, so I'm sure you'll understand why I can't be of any help to you over the phone," seems to be a near impossible statement for many trainers to croak out.

Of course, preventative medicine is the best response to the problem of burnout. Making a decision early on to limit your time on the phone when it comes to doggie matters, carefully charting your activities and involving yourself in only the activities you can realistically handle are, of course, the best ways to avoid burnout.

But for most of us, burnout will be there before rational thought is. Here are some signs of burnout for the dog trainer and some remedies:

- *You have to teach a class or see a client, but you just don't care about it.* A classic sign of burnout is not caring about anything—yet, you do . . . of course you do. If you absolutely *can't* get out of teaching or seeing that client (and preferably take a vacation—more on that in a second), just focus on the dogs. Pick out a comical canine face and play to it—perhaps use that dog as a demo dog. *Fake it,* for that night, and then reevaluate your priorities.
- *You are confronted with a complex behavior problem (like aggression or destructive chewing) and your mind goes blank, even though you*

know what you need to say. Burnout frustrates giving complex information in a logical sequence—even if you know your materials and remedies! Don't be frustrated with yourself. Your inability to think straight about a situation you are perhaps well versed on is symptomatic of exhaustion and a signal for rest. Give the client the best outline you can—often writing it out will help your mind to focus—and personalize it for the client. Now, heed the warning. The very next day, cancel all unnecessary appointments and rest. Do not take phone calls. If you don't have an answering machine, get one (preferably *not* voice activated, but with a prescribed message time limit). Don't worry, you're *not* losing your mind, and you don't have to bone up on what to do for house soiling problems—you're just bone tired. You're burned-out.

- *You come home from class (or a private client or from the shelter or veterinary office) and you break down and cry. Or perhaps you cry while on the job—and you can't figure out any reason.* You're really burned-out—unless the crying is the result of some other kind of stress. Assuming everything is A-OK at home and otherwise, the crying could be a reaction to stress. Wash your face (always a good temporary remedy) and go back to work—for that day. After work, talk to your boss (if it's yourself, sit yourself down and have a talk with yourself) and explain that you are overworked or at least overextended. You most probably will not get fired. You will most probably get a few days off (or give yourself a few days off if you're the boss). But that's not enough.

- *After a few days off you feel just as strung out, tensed up, preyed upon and awful as you did before you had the respite.* Get a newspaper or job placement tabloid and look for the nearest seminar or expert on stress and/or time management. You need to learn how to handle stress and organize your time and to set priorities. The fact that the brief vacation didn't help clearly signals that more work must be done if you are to escape burnout.

- *You got bitten in class or while seeing a private client.* Chances are, your timing was off, unless you simply are not skilled in handling such dogs. Were you overtired? Preoccupied? Overextended? In an extraordinarily perceptive and honest piece in the February 1986 *Off-Lead* magazine, veteran trainer Roy Hunter recounted a time when he had suffered from jet lag and "started a brand-new training class at 9:30 A.M." the next morning. He wound up getting zapped by a small dog that spun itself around enough to also injure itself. His observations are to be well noted. *Never* work with an aggressive dog when you are tired or out-of-sorts, and have the wisdom and humility of Mr. Hunter to admit that such was the case—and give yourself a rest.

- *Try to get into the habit of taking short three-to-four-day vacations several times a year instead of one long two-or-three-week vacation.* (Of course if you can get that length of time, too, go for it!) I've found that people who work with dogs often do better under this system. Short vacations spaced periodically will give you something to look forward to, and be sure that they are at least three days long (one or two days are too short). If you are self-employed (many trainers are) these should be easy enough to arrange; in fact, they might be more desirable than closing down completely for two or three weeks.

Above all, don't laugh at burnout or make light of it in any way—many do, thinking, "it won't hit me." It *can* hit you, very easily, and a healthy respect for burnout and related syndromes can help you prevent it in the first place. Protect yourself from burnout and you'll also be protecting the dogs you train as well as their owners.

Sexism in Dog Training

Didn't that subhead grab you? I thought it would. But the fact is, dog trainers confront sexism on the job constantly and discuss it among themselves frequently. Yet I've never seen a mention of it in print. It's time to remedy the situation.

Women suffer the most from sexism. Almost every female trainer has a story about how some butch male resented her handling his dog, or assured her in advance that she would never be able to handle anything larger than a Pekingese. One trainer in New York City told this story:

I walked into the house, and the husband was lying on the couch watching a football game. The dog, a German Shepherd Dog, was running around the dining room with a kitchen towel in his mouth, shaking it frantically. The wife was in hot pursuit, trying to retrieve her dish towel, do the dishes, answer the phone, which was ringing, and let me in all at the same time. As soon as the husband noticed me, he lifted his head ever so slightly and said in a low drawl, "Oh, you're the trainer? I was expecting a man. You'll never be able to do anything with *him.*" Indicating, of course, that this lowly female would never be able to rehabilitate such a male maniac.

Some men will seem subtly proud of their male dog's naughtiness, and "agree" to training for the sake of the wife's sanity. The truth is, they have no idea of how to control the dog and most of their attempts to do so have met with outright rebellion. Now, here is this *woman* who is going to shape things up. It's everything some men can do to hide their interior humiliation.

How do you handle such binds? First, don't be insulted. Sexism is endemic in our society. There are still double standards, especially in dog training, even though so many famous trainers have been women. Respond by educating. To "You'll never be able to do anything with *him,*" respond by laughing and saying, "Well, have *you?* Maybe we can try together." Push through the implications and elevate the situation to a new level—and begin training.

191

Sometimes it's impossible to involve a husband in training. This has frequently happened to me, even though I agitate to have the whole family present at all sessions and particularly at the opening session. In one recent situation I was called in to solve a housetraining problem coupled with destructive chewing. I sat down at the kitchen table with the wife, and the husband was (you guessed it) watching a football game on TV, beer in hand. I asked Mrs. Travolinni (not her real name) if Mr. Travolinni would join us, and she replied, "Good God, no—don't bother him, he's mad enough at the dog as it is." Mr. Travolinni did get up, though, to come over to the table to coach us. "Now, you listen to him carefully, honey," he said, "and get to the bottom of this messing in the house." He then returned to his post at the television. Housetraining and picking up after the destructive dog were strictly women's work.

I had sized up the situation and decided to use it to my own advantage. We set up a program for housetraining that night and agreed to start active training the next session, beginning with the heel. Mr. Travolinni again stopped by the table when I arrived, after grabbing a beer from the fridge, and was headed back to you-know-where. I stopped him though when I said, "Mr. Travolinni, today we are going to start some of the more *active* phases of training, starting with the heeling, phases of training when more *control* must be exerted. . . ." For the key words "active" and "control" I cast a quick glance at Mrs. Travolinni, who looked down at the table smiling. She knew exactly what I was doing, and she didn't care: She wanted to get the dog trainer and her husband involved. Mr. Travolinni appeared suddenly concerned, and in a low voice asked me, "Well, do you need help? I mean, do you think she can handle it?" I replied that I'm sure that *both* of them would make fine handlers, and we went out for the session together. Then, as Mr. Travolinni worked on the heel (he was terrible, by the way), I gave him all the information on housetraining and destructive chewing I had given his wife earlier. He never missed another session, although I had to plan our appointments around the NFL games.

The classic situation where sexism rears its head is when the dog trainer suggests neutering a male dog. Spaying a female is rarely a mental problem for men or women, but the specter of castrating a male is reason for a crisis. The reaction on the part of some men is so visceral that I've had men immediately cross their legs when I introduce the idea. I've been told by female trainers that the reaction is even worse when they suggest the surgery. I plow right through this reaction without even noting it. I do not have time to deal with the emotional issues right away, although I do back up and talk about them later.

My first priority is education about neutering. I explain what the studies (especially the one conducted by Dr. Benjamin Hart, University of California at Davis) have shown about neutering as a tool in behavior therapy, and explain that male dogs secrete testosterone in *two* locations (testicles and adrenal glands) and that only one production zone is being removed. While this is not clinically kosher, because the greater amount of the hormone *is* produced in the testicles, it is one way of taking the sting out of my suggestion. I also explain other health benefits resulting from the operation, such as the elimination of prostate cancer. I explain all this slowly, absolutely calmly, even though I know my client's head is spinning with emotional distress. Then I back up and ask my client's feeling on the matter. Their emotionality then hits the solid wall of education I've laid down. Every trainer has had difficulty with this one. As public education increases, the problem will lessen, and it will be easier to suggest neutering and talk about it calmly.

Some sexism exists within the professional training community itself, although I am not aware of any inordinate degree. In general, men and women participate in obedience competition on an equal basis, and collaboration between male and female trainers is good. In fact, compared with other dog-related fields—veterinary medicine for example—training is remarkably free of discrimination and sexism. A man will just as readily pick up a book by Wynn Strickland Carlson to gain knowledge and information as a woman will use a book written by William Campbell. We don't look at whether the author or seminar or clinic lecturer is a man or a woman—we look to see how they train dogs. The many husband-and-wife trainer teams present in the dog-training field are also an inspiration to us all and wonderful examples of cooperation and mutual respect.

When it comes to sexism, a trainer's major problems and hurdles remain the attitudes of clients, which are, in turn, a product of the society at large. While these attitudes can sometimes hinder us in our work, and occasionally make it impossible to work with some clients, they are responses that people in other helping fields have to deal with also, and handled with humor and tact, can be overcome.

Rhythm, Timing and Training

Most trainers develop a sense of timing quickly, but few develop perfect or near-perfect timing. What's timing? To most trainers it is the ability to move with the dog and to deliver praise or correction (usually via the leash, but not always) at just the right moment—and the right moment from the *dog's* point of view, not the trainer's. This usually involves speeding up bodily movements and tightening up hand, forearm and leg coordination so that praise or correction registers with the dog in split seconds. Most trainers are too slow at the start of their careers. They do not realize how quickly they can work a dog, and how much vocal animation is needed. But occasionally—rarely, but occasionally—a trainer will be *too* quick for the dog, and will need to learn timing by slowing down. When a trainer has good timing, he or she is in tune with the dog and there is a seemingly effortless flow of energy and communication between them.

I have heard "perfect" timing described as everything from "dancing with the dog" to "as wonderful as good sex," and I'd have to agree with both statements. Timing cannot be *learned* from a book or an article—the importance of timing can only be *pointed out* in print. The budding trainer needs to be directed to other sources to learn more about it. The number one source for learning timing is a trainer who has it. The only way you will learn whether she or he has it is to observe her or him in action with dogs. Some trainers have wonderful timing on static exercises (like sit-stay) and horrendous timing on active exercises (like the heel). This search for learning will involve seminar and clinic attendance and general snooping around. Even then, don't make the foolish mistake of asking the trainer with perfect timing to "impart" his or her secret to you. Timing comes from within, and the trainer, no matter how dearly he or she may like to share it with you (and remember many do *not* want to share it with you), simply cannot "give" it to you. All you can do is watch, listen, *try* to move your body like the trainer does. One hint: When you see a trainer with perfect timing, or at least timing you admire, *stop looking at the dog.* Look only at the *trainer* for at least twenty minutes, imagining yourself as the dog. Watch the trainer's hands, watch his or her eyes, study the way the trainer holds the torso (very important). Watch the whole body of the trainer, the neck, the way the head is held. Don't just watch the extremities—many beginning trainers get hung up on what to do with their hands, and they forget that the hand is connected to a forearm, which in turn is connected to an arm, a shoulder, etc. All of these are communicating something to the dog. Remember: Watch the trainer's *eyes!*

Remember, too, that the concept of timing has also to do with other essential questions: What *time* of the day is it? What is the *timing* of the dog's meals? What *time* in the dog's life span is it? And on and on. Consider the overall *concept* of time when perfecting your timing.

Where does timing come from? Even though I've clearly indicated that timing can be learned, acquired, perfect or near-perfect timing, in my opinion, flows out of an innate sense of rhythm, specifically, *musical* rhythm. Take a man like the late Jack Godsil. I had the benefit of an extended, one-on-one personal clinic with him. Here was a man who was essentially a ballet artist who trained dogs. This man was grace in action, as on his toes in his given craft as Baryshnikov is in his. He was an accomplished guitarist—and it's no surprise. He was able to time his training moves because of an innate sense of rhythm, coupled with a good frame (it always helps to look imposing) and a certain quiet charm and poise that dogs, well, just *felt.*

This gift of rhythm is the underpinning of many trainers' sense of timing. Don't be fooled—the timing was developed, worked hard for, by observation, study, trial and error. But to some degree the sense of timing flowed out of rhythm, which is a gift, an inborn drive, a desire to be at one with a "beat."

Can you develop what may be a dormant sense of rhythm that may lead to better timing and better training? Sure! Why not take a swing at it? I've known of trainers who play march music while they train, timing automatic sits during heeling patterns to an oompah-pah beat. I know one trainer who trains to a waltz, "The Blue Danube" or other 3/4 rhythm pieces. Then I know of some trainers who play disco, although the steady, pounding 4/4, 120-beats-per-minute drive of most disco songs may make it hard to train most breeds, I know of Dobermans trained to disco. Disco Dobes, in other words.

All kidding aside—do what you can to free yourself to hear life's beat, usually heard most clearly in music, and to develop whatever rhythmic abilities you have. Out of that will flow timing, and out of that, happy, well-trained dogs. And what does rhythm *itself* flow out of? Well, the philosophers have a lot to say on that. Some say that musical rhythm developed not just out of humankind's urge to entertain itself, but out of a longing for a hookup with a more universal rhythm that first shaped our world. Scientists would call this a "life force" and religious people would call it "God's rhythm." Is it any surprise that the evolutionary theory widely accepted now is called the "big bang"?—a pretty rhythmic phrase if you ask me! As a trainer, you are in touch with life's rhythm, expressed in and through yourself and in and through another living being—the dog. It is a great opportunity, something that might be thought of as granted only to artists, but available to all of us who work with dogs, for trainers are artists also.

Competition or Craziness?

One problem I deal with constantly in seminars, on the phone and in working sessions is the complaint about the "ring-wise" dog. The seemingly malicious dog that runs out of the obedience ring during the recall or the off-lead heeling process, but always performs well at home. In fact, if you are to believe the stories, the dog in question always performs *perfectly* at home. Just as lay dog owners have tons and tons of folklore and mythology they hold dear concerning their pets, so do professional obedience persons. And one of those myths we want to hold on to is this nonsense about the ring-wise dog. You see, such thinking makes mistakes very understandable: We can project the blame onto the dog. But who is really to blame?

Paralanguage is the original tongue of your dog—the sublanguage it learned while still in the litter. The puppy's mother growled at it to assert her Alpha role, but littermates whined at it—and this whining was a signal of distress, loneliness or separation from the mother. The mother *never* whined at her puppies—only littermates whine at each other. In this book we've talked about the placating owner who tries to cajole his or her dog into good behavior by using a whining tone of voice. This placating behavior often becomes a general life stance toward the dog, keeping the dog in an infantile state and in a type of low-grade distress, since the owner is read, by the dog, as a littermate talking about littermate concerns. Remember, littermates don't perform for each other—they just play with each other. Obedience competition is not play. It is work. It can be fun, but it is not play.

But the dog owned by a placating owner can quite possibly perceive the whole obedience ritual as pure play, especially if the owner alternates the play with some Alpha leader-type behavior in the form of corrections. "You'd better play—or else." This effectively screws up signals enough so that the dog plays until no corrections can be given. Further, often the placating owner will do an about-face on the dog on the way to the trial. These owners turn on their dogs on the way to the trial site and begin to blame or scold the dog in an effort to get the dog ready to perform perfectly in the ring. All this does is make the dog wary of the ring. The dog is bewildered at this sudden sense of "command" and presence from an owner viewed, essentially, as a bimbo and a wimp who loves to play. "Why the sudden switch?" the dog wonders.

Conversely, owners who *blame* their dogs as a way of relating to them (see description of the blamer in chapter 7) will often pull an about-face on their dogs and try to *placate* their dogs into good behavior (performance) just before they enter the ring. ("Pleeeeeze Tippy, pleeeeze do the off-lead heeling, okaaaaay. Pleeeeze.") These owners do *not,* by any stretch of the imagination, talk with their dogs this way the other 364 days of the year. Why blame the dogs for being totally bewildered, strung-out, absolutely spaced-out because of *our* faulty paralanguage, *our* abrupt about-faces? Again, the problem lies within the relationship itself, the faulty relationship between dog and owner, and the tension the owner brings into the ring.

It is standard practice for obedience competitors to refrain from feeding their dogs prior to a trial. I disagree. Be sure to feed your dog something before a trial. Remember, there is a center in your dog's brain called the hypothalamus. It controls behavior, to a degree. If you feed your dog normally other days of the year and then cut off food on the one day you want *top* performance, thus "hyperventilating" the hypothalamus, it's small wonder that your dog is edgy when entering the ring. The rationale for *not* feeding is that if the dog eliminates in the ring, the team will be excused and disqualified. If you're concerned about this, try feeding just one-half the dog's normal ration before a show. But *do* feed.

Obedience competitors can visualize success in much the same way Olympic athletes do. Right before you go into the ring, calm yourself and close your eyes. Envision the ring ritual and recall successful practice sessions. Reach down and massage the centering spot on your dog's forehead with your thumb. Breathe. Breathe deeply. Now, go out there and knock 'em dead!

Two other problems affect clear thinking on the ring-wise syndrome. First, some owners think the real problem lies in the area of technique, and secondly, some owners think their dogs are simply too intelligent and are bored with AKC obedience work. Again, we have more human-centered, anthropomorphic thinking. Technique certainly *is* important, but some seminar givers would have their participants think that if they would just hold the little finger of the left (or right) hand one millimeter lower (or higher) during off-lead heeling, then the dog would not run out of the ring (or wander, or go lick the steward, or go to a spectator with a hot dog, or whatever it is the ring-wise dog does). The distraught owner is thus offered a cure by technique that effectively lets him or her off the hook in terms of examining underlying problems. When I bring up the subject of relational problems, owners of ring-wise dogs often tell me that this is *not* what they want to hear. What they want to hear is that they were holding the third finger of their left hand slightly off where it should have been (depending on whose information they are following) and *that's* the real reason Tippy didn't complete the recall. That's easier to stomach. A mechanical problem is often easier to solve than a relational one.

The my-dog-is-too-intelligent-for-this-stuff school of thought is a kissing cousin to the above syndrome. A recent piece in *Off-Lead* magazine details the escapades of yet another ring-wise dog that thwarts her owner at every turn because she is a German Shepherd Dog and thus too intelligent for AKC ritual. At one point the owner reports having turned on the dog after a particularly poor performance and said, "I hope you're satisfied!" One wonders what kind of paralanguage roller coaster this Shepherd rides before and after each show, and just how very deeply it must affect her.

Professional obedience people get a good deal of laughter out of this ring-wise business. If the problem stayed on the level of laughter, I'd have no complaints. Of course there is always a bad day for almost any dog, even if the paralanguage is completely kosher, even if the owner has good technique and wonderful timing. But the laughter most often blames the dog, ascribing to the dog that failed spiteful motives that are purely human projections and consequently a great source of confusion for the dog. That's the really sad part—the blaming and the subsequent stress for the blamed dog. And all because we'd rather spend time figuring out why our dogs are ring-wise than why they are wise to us.

What to Do When You Walk In

What do you do when you enter the household of an ineffective owner with an unruly, bratty dog? It never ceases to amaze me how crazy and off-the-wall the dogs (and some of the owners) are during that first session. There is a variety of often-used approaches. If any of these sound familiar, you are not alone.

- Trying to calm the dog down by petting it
- Ignoring the problem dog and going on with your work
- Screaming over the pronounced barking and/or defending yourself from physical maulings, pummelings, goosings, shovings and other forms of canine abuse

I've tried them all, too. They don't work. The fact is, most private trainers need to take a behavior case history during that first session, and to try to do so with a canine terrorist trying to hijack the session can be torture. By the way, if you are not in the habit of taking a complete behavior history and you call yourself a private trainer, you are probably undertraining and undercounseling. For forms, guidance and process see the classic *Behavior*

Problems in Dogs by William E. Campbell (American Veterinary Publications, 1975), or my own *The Evans Guide for Counseling Dog Owners*.

In my book I state that it is preferable if the dog is *not* present at the first session, as owners tend to lie less about their pooch when it is not physically present. Further, the absence of the unruly dog helps facilitate the interview process. However, I wrote that portion of the book when I was fresh out of New Skete Monastery, where I had an office for interviewing clients and a convenient kennel in which to stuff their crazed canines. If you have no such facility, and if you work in your clients' homes, you will not have this option.

In fact, this was exactly the situation I confronted when I started my business in New York. I would arrive at a household and immediately the dog would begin to molest me. There was a temptation to immediately correct the dog for jumping up, nipping or whatever canine crime it was committing, but I've always refrained from administering a correction until I have had an opportunity to explain my theory and interview the owner. Some private trainers *do* correct dogs right away, and I can only say that while the dogs' owners might be impressed with the efficacy of a jumping-up correction, they will *not* mentally catalog it (since they are stunned and in awe of your ability) and they most definitely will not like you for "manhandling" their dog so immediately. "Ego" trainers who want to "get the dog in line" quickly might disagree, but we should never forget that our work is 80 percent people work and only 20 percent dog work. Correcting a dog too quickly and too harshly will not endear you to your client, and if your client does not *like* you, you might as well pack up your training collars and leashes and go home.

Since I suffer from an inferiority complex, I have always been concerned with getting people to like me first and teaching them later. I have seen brusque, even brutish trainers enter a household or open a class by walloping an unruly dog with such force that the owners, to a man and to a woman, simply cringe. Believe me, that trainer has cashed in his or her chips when it comes to the trust of the clients. Of course, lay clients are in awe of us, so they don't say anything, but you will have hurt them deeply if you correct their dogs too soon.

What to do then? I can only offer my own procedure, developed over six years and three thousand clients in Manhattan. In each and every case, I was in the home of the dog's owner.

Here is my procedure:

1. Greet the owner *first,* even if the dog is crazed. Make direct eye contact with both unless the dog is aggressive. Smile, smile, smile— yes, that means smile even if the dog has slammed itself into a part of your anatomy that is especially sensitive. Male private trainers are now nodding their heads in sympathy at this statement. *Do not* correct the dog.

2. Ask if there is a *table* where you can sit and talk. Some owners will instinctively guide you to the living room. This will not work. You need a table in order to do your case history. You also need a table because you need a higher chair in order to sit on a leash to get a certain spoiled monster to lie down, pronto.

3. You have to get the dog quieted down fast in order to do your interview. If you hold the leash, you will give the dog enough slack so that the dog will fool around. Many dogs only see a leash when it is time to go outside and will immediately go into high gear when it is produced. This is especially true of city dogs. Just get the leash on and then sit on it. Yes, sit on it.

4. Measure out only as much lead as the dog needs in order to lie down, no more. You can estimate by simply pushing the dog down once to see how much leash is necessary. Do not say "down"—there is no sense in giving a command to an untrained dog until it has begun to learn the word, and believe me, if the dog you have tethered really knew "down," you wouldn't be there.

5. The dog will start to test its options. If it jumps up on you, snap the leash down smartly, saying "no." By now you should be into your interview, which should distract the owner, who is sitting opposite you. Yes, you *can* interview and snap a leash at the same time, and if you can't, get out of private training fast, as most of the work of a private trainer involves doing more than one thing at a time. If the dog chews on the leash, snap the leash diagonally up toward your body. When the dog pulls against the dead weight of your body it will become quickly apparent that the object (your body) is immovable, and, like most of us do when straining to move an impossibly heavy object, the dog will give up trying.

6. With this method, and as long as the private trainer cancels all unacceptable options such as jumping up, chewing on the leash, crying, whining or yodeling, most dogs calm down and hit the dust within ten to twenty minutes, many sooner. Some real recalcitrants and hyper types will remain standing or sitting, but at least they will not bother you. They will often simply stare at you in disbelief. This is an excellent moment to make some piercing, mean, frozen-eyed eye contact and then look away with aloofness and continue your interview. In fact, this is the exact look a bitch would have given a puppy that was bothering her while she tried to do something other than pay attention to the pup. If the dog does hit the dust quickly, *do not praise.* No command was given, no command was fulfilled, thus no praise is warranted. The dog simply figured out the options (basically, none) and deduced that it was smarter, more convenient, safer and certainly more restful to lie down while you do one heck of a job taking one heck of a complete behavior case history—the taking of which will enable you to become the Sherlock Holmes the owner hired you to

be and quickly solve the canine crime presented. At least with this method you can do so with style and grace. Try it—it works!

What to Do When You Walk Out

It's one thing for a trainer to know what to do or not do when walking *into* a client's house, but what do you do if you have to walk *out?* Sooner or later every trainer meets a difficult client who blames everybody but himself or herself for the dog's problems—including the dog's trainer. These clients are usually blamers. It sounds perverse but there are people who will call in a trainer, pay hard cash and yet deliberately thwart the trainer in his or her efforts to help. Such souls are really very insecure and lonely people beneath the haughty and superior facade they present to the world.

When I need to terminate a client—a given individual I sincerely feel that I do not want to work with—I indicate this *immediately.* I listen to the first strong gut feeling that registers inside myself, because without client cooperation and trust there is little or nothing I can do to help the dog. In my early years of training I ignored such gut feelings hoping that the difficult client would become less manipulative and more cooperative in time. Unfortunately, this rarely happens. My advice to trainers is to listen to that inner voice. If it tells you that a relationship with a client won't work, terminate that client. Do this immediately, as soon as you get the feeling.

How? Simply look your client directly in the eye and say, "I'm sorry but this session isn't going well. I'm afraid I'm not the trainer for you." That's it! You needn't say anything else. Simply wait for a reaction and if the client seems to be in agreement, immediately collect your training materials and exit. However, many clients will express surprise and even shock, especially if they are quite aware that they have been behaving obnoxiously. If, and I mean *if,* you sense the client is sincere, you might mention that client cooperation is essential if the dog is to be helped. Pause again and wait for another response. If the client becomes apologetic or repentant, you can then make the decision whether to continue.

Most of all, don't take such situations personally. Difficult clients are usually difficult with everyone, and you're no exception. Of course you will feel sorry for the dog, but perhaps the client will behave more civilly with another trainer. However, *do not* refer such clients to fellow trainers. Let these clients find other trainers on their own. If you do decide to continue the relationship and are a trainer with some experience, please remember that you probably have worked with problem clients in the past—and successfully. There is a tendency to forget this fact. Every time a troublemaker comes into a trainer's life it feels like the *first* time. Of course it isn't. As long as the air is cleared immediately and proper boundaries set up, most difficult clients will respond to consistent, firm friendliness.

In my twenty years of training I've had to terminate only fifteen clients out of over seven thousand. One particularly nasty woman, the owner of a

Maltese bitch with the habit of redecorating her Fifth Avenue apartment with the results of Nature's calls, drove me so batty that I called my own father to ask him to search his library of psychological books and journals and send me anything he had on difficult people. He informed me that he would have to photocopy half his library. Instead, I flew home to Michigan and did research with my psychologist pop for one week. I felt better after that, but I still had to leave the *lady*—and her poor Maltese.

22

A Panoply of Problems

S TAGING STERLING SET-UPS should be sufficient in your attempts to rid your pooch of problems. Sometimes, however, a set-up can be enhanced by using other methods specifically related to the problem at hand. I'll detail these "extras" in this chapter and I hope these added steps will insure eradication of problems. We'll round out the chapter with questions concerning a variety of canine conundrums.

Jumping Up

You now know how to concoct a set-up to put the jinx on jumping up. All you have to do is trick your dog into doing it and administer the three-part correction: Whip the tab or leash down *forcefully* and say *"no,"* pull up on the tab or leash and say *"sit,"* flash the stay signal in your dog's face and say *"stay."* Naturally it helps if you have been teaching your dog the sit-stay. So if you have a jumper, go immediately to the section on the sit-stay and begin teaching these words.

Now that you know what to do to stop the jumping up it's important that we take a moment to examine what you absolutely should *not* do when a dog is jumping. First of all, under no circumstances should you hold the dog up by its front paws with your hands since this will be taken as approval of the action. One ineffective correction for jumping that has been dished out for years is to firmly grasp the dog's paws in your hands and squeeze them tight or pinch between the dog's toes. By the time owners of jumpers get their hands positioned correctly and learn to squeeze the paws hard enough, the dog has interpreted the fact that the owner is supporting it as approval for its action.

Another mistake owners make is to simply turn away as the dog is jumping. At the same time the person being jumped on usually whines "no" or "stop it." Two things are wrong here. First of all, the body language is incorrect. Turning away looks like exposure of the flank to a dog. Did you ever watch two dogs playing in a field? The submissive dog will roll over and expose its belly or flank, saying, "you win." The submissive dog will also whine or whimper at the same time—precisely what people unintentionally do when jumped on. The faulty body language and paralanguage then says to the dog—at least in the way the dog interprets what it sees and hears—"Please jump on me again," which, of course, the dog does. So don't turn away and don't appear to whine. Get that tab or leash—or, if all the dog has on is a collar, get that—and whip it down hard, saying, "No!" Some owners of chronic jumpers might have to literally scrape the dog off of themselves so forcefully, in a firm downward yank, that they may feel that they have lost control and hurt the dog. If you're such an owner, don't worry—you're probably showing just as much force as the situation really merits. Remember, if the dog is jumping on someone else who does not know, or will not execute the correction, the same correction is still administered—by you.

Another classic goof that owners of jumpers make is to say the wrong words for a correction. I once purchased a classic sweat shirt at an obedience trial. The front of the shirt is covered with muddy dog paws, and the words "Down, boy, down" are emblazoned on it. "Down" is not the correct correction word here since the word "down" means, or should mean, that the dog is to recline on the floor. "Off," "no" or even "scoobie-doobie-do" would be more appropriate—anything but "down." Professional obedience people, the saleswoman told me, readily got the joke behind the sweat shirt—few lay persons did.

One last point: There is a tendency when administering jump corrections to concentrate on the person the dog is jumping on. This is a normal reaction because, of course, one is terribly embarrassed that one's dog is accosting another person. The trouble is, concentrating on the person being jumped on will distract you from yanking the leash down firmly and delivering a correction concisely. This is when a set-up can be of great help—because during a set-up, since it is preplanned, and hopefully because the jumped-on person is preenlisted, you need not pay special attention to your assistant and act apologetically. Instead, you can deliver a sharp correction with sufficient speed to startle your dog. Remember, your dog, if it is a confirmed jumper, has already become used to your delayed reaction as you apologize, explain, snivel out excuses and even offer to mend destroyed or soiled clothing—even as your dog clenches onto the offended person. So concentrate on correcting your dog *immediately* rather than paying attention to the person, place or thing it scales. A good technique—especially if your dog seemingly spring jumps onto people—is to simply watch your dog's two front paws. If both paws are off the ground, that's the beginning of a jump. If you concentrate on the two front paws, and on nothing else, you will be able to jinx most jumping.

Destructive Chewing

You can stage set-ups until the cows come home to cure your dog of destructive chewing, but if you don't examine the problem holistically, the set-ups might not take. Be especially careful about how you say hello and good-bye to your chewer. Overemotional hellos and good-byes keep the dog on edge. If you make a big production out of leaving, the dog will be ready to tumble into an emotional black hole by the time the door clicks shut in its face. It will chew to alleviate owner-induced frustration. On the other hand, if your dog is overanxiously awaiting the sacred moment when you arrive home—because this moment is when it is petted and fussed over the most—the dog may decide to munch down on valuables just before you get home. God forbid that you are held up enroute and Fido's sacred rite is postponed. Don't make a thing over greetings and departures. When you leave, present Rascal with a toy—a special toy. Keep the toy up out of the dog's reach and preferably out of sight. This toy is offered only when you leave the house. When you are actually ready to leave, and not before, sit your dog, make eye contact and in a friendly, but not anxious, voice tell your dog to watch the house, and just as you leave, scent the toy by rubbing it firmly on your palm or, still better, put some of your saliva on it. As you exit, offer this toy. If your dog doesn't grasp it in its mouth, simply drop it nearby. If your dog gets frustrated when you are gone, it may decide to masticate on this toy rather than on forbidden objects. The ploy works with some dogs and has no effect on others—but it's worth a try, and to a degree justifies correcting the dog even after the fact (but remember, you must have some proof to convict the dog) since you did, after all, provide a chewing option in the form of the scented toy.

When you return, greet your dog calmly. A simple hello should suffice. Of course, whether you have been gone twenty minutes or two hours the dog will inveigle you to put more "umph" into your greeting. Don't give in. Keep it simple. If you are returning home after staging a set-up, skip any greeting at all and simply search for proof. If there isn't any, say a simple hello and go on with your life. If there is, follow the instructions in the chapter "Do Dogs Feel Guilt or Shame?"

Besides staging set-ups, it's a good idea to try to make the environment itself look like it is disciplining the dog. You can use substances like Tabasco sauce, bitter apple or cayenne pepper (Vaseline applied to the surface first makes the pepper stick better). Jalapeño peppers are my favorite—but wear gloves when rubbing them on surfaces you do not want chewed. Mousetraps are an old trainer's ploy and can be set and placed on couches, chairs and other surfaces. Obviously, don't put bait in the trap! This is training, not torture. I once had a client who did put bait in the mousetraps she set on the couch—she figured using bait would speed up the training process.

I'd suggest blitzing your dog with set-ups when you can grab a free day. Leave with a proper good-bye and offer the scented toy. Stay away for just fifteen minutes. Return, check for proof and if you find some, discipline. Leave again, this time for a half hour. Return, check for proof and discipline if necessary. Leave again for one hour. Start adding half-hour increments and try to build up to two hours during your first blitz. Each time you leave, offer the scented toy, but each time you return, pick the toy up. The length of the interval between leave-takings should be only about ten to fifteen minutes. The point of the blitz—much like the bombing in England—is to stun the dog into accepting several hellos and good-byes from an Alpha figure. By coming and going so fast and frequently you are telling the dog that you are the leader who comes and goes from the den at will—and it is the subordinate who must hold the fort and behave. Remember, underplay all hellos and good-byes. If the dog "flunks" a section of the blitz, stay home for fifteen minutes and then repeat that part of the blitz again and call it a day. You can always try to build up to a longer time span another day. The blitz is best done on a free day, obviously, and this also accomplishes something else—it tells the dog that even on free days you might have to come and go—and it still cannot, must not, chew your belongings. You see, especially for some "weekend dogs"—dogs that see their owners basically in the evenings or on weekends—the contrast between when the owner is home and when the owner is absent is just too stark and must be minimized. When you are home, the dog feels like it is the center of the universe, and probably is. But when you are gone, the dog feels demoted to nothingness. The solution is to lessen the contrast, and this is done by leave-takings on weekends and during the evening.

You ultimate goal should be an adult dog that can be left to freely roam most of the house and not chew inappropriately. While I have nothing against crating destructive chewers, this goal will never be achieved using a crate—unless the crate is phased out over time. Obviously, young puppies have to be confined and are too young for blitzing. But older chewers, if simply crated, never learn to respect the house. Crate if you must, but when it's blitz time allow the dog house freedom, room by room. For instance, start the first blitz in a relatively chew-proof room like a bathroom or the kitchen, and then add a room each time you stage a blitz—but don't add more than one room at a time and don't add any rooms at all if the blitz bombs. Is there a risk factor in staging blitzes? Of course! It's not "cute" to try this technique and come home to a wrecked room. On the other hand, most dogs quickly become responsible and seem to appreciate freedom to move about more liberally, even if they can't munch at will. If your dog absolutely refuses to cease chewing, and you really feel that you have staged fair, humane, yet forceful set-ups, then you must simply practice creative avoidance for one month. Crate or otherwise confine the chewer for one month, and then grab a free day and blitz away. It goes without saying that such a recalcitrant should be placed on the RRRR program for one month.

Finally, don't feel guilty that you have to leave Rascal alone at times. Someone has to go out and work in order to buy the dog food—and it certainly can't be Rascal, can it? You have a life to live, friends to see and places to go. Besides, you are the Alpha, and even a mother wolf leaves the den to search out food or simply to take care of her own needs. Your dog is your dog, not your Siamese twin—for that matter, not even your identical twin, although it's spooky how many dogs look like their owners!

Housetraining

Getting your puppy or dog to realize that cleanliness is next to godliness can be accomplished by following the ACCESS plan I outlined in my book *The Evans Guide for Housetraining Your Dog*.

A   is for *Alpha*—that's you.

C   is for *Corrections*—that's what you give.

C   is also for *Confinement*—that's what you provide.

E   is for *Establish*.

S   is for a *Schedule* (which is what you establish).

S   is also for *Selecting* a dog food that will aid you in getting your dog housetrained.

You know all about how to be Alpha already, so remember to establish eye contact formally twice a day as previously described. Correct your dog for housetraining mistakes by quietly taking the dog to the proof itself, sitting the dog, focusing his eyes (*not* his nose) on the proof and delivering the shake or swat correction. Remember, no screaming and no overphysicality! If correction after the fact doesn't work don't just keep disciplining! Confine the dog in a crate or a small room and try another housetraining set-up later.

Stick to your schedule of walks and select a food that will help, not hinder, housetraining. Stay away from unlabeled generic foods, dairy products and superoily foods. Remember, what goes in comes out!

I've found that most owners who tolerate unhousetrained dogs either trust the dog too soon and too much, granting the dog more area than it can really handle, or they just cheat on the ACCESS plan and then blame the dog for goofing up. An exception is the dog that is physically ill. If you are having any problem with housetraining, get the dog to a veterinarian! After that, assuming your dog has a clean bill of health, I'd offer you my tips here, my book on the subject and my sympathy! Don't worry though, given time and consistency, most dogs *do* clean up their acts.

Dear Job: Questions—and Some Answers

Here is a potpourri of questions about various pooches and their problems. These are actual questions that I have fielded over the years in seminars and via letters and phone calls—although I hasten to add that I do not make it a habit to reply to unsolicited inquiries via phone or the mail. At seminars the questions were either asked aloud and taped or submitted in writing at the podium. Questions concerning elimination problems (which owners consider a "dirty" topic and thus kept closeted) and questions about shyness (surprise, surprise!) were almost never asked aloud. Knowing owner psychology after twenty years in this field, I understand this reluctance, especially on these two topics. This is precisely why I've always provided seminar participants with the option of submitting written questions. This has paid off for myself as well: I believe I get a truer reading of the problems really bothering owners, much in the same way a priest will eventually hear everything in confession. Anonymity sometimes aids truth.

I deliberately have not arranged these questions in any precise topical order, but rather mixed them up because often problems overlap and owners of problem dogs—always on the lookout for a quick-fix solution—have a tendency to falsely categorize their dog's difficulties. Nor have I changed the wording of the questions as transcribed from the tapes or question cards. Often the wording and phrasing of a question give an insight into the owner's psychology. So plow on through—you'll find problems of interest everywhere.

I have two nine-month-old Sheltie females (littermates). One is submissive and one is dominant. When we pay attention to the submissive one, the dominant one will start attacking her. How do we train the dominant dog not to attack the submissive dog?

First, I am always suspicious when owners decree who is dominant and who is submissive among their pets. My expeirence, more often than not, is that a substantial amount of owner miscalculation fouls up any set-up that might be concocted to stop such fighting. I would urge you to drop such classifications and instead place both dogs on the RRRR as soon as possible. Separate the dogs for one week using crates, confinement or whatever type of creative avoidance measures necessary. After one week on the RRRR the dogs will sense a change in the household atmosphere and you will be ready to stage a set-up. Put tabs on both dogs, deliver your warning with eye contact, discipline if necessary and *do not* separate the dogs if there is an outbreak of fighting. Instead, place them on down-stays if they know this exercise. If they don't know how to hold a long down, get busy teaching it pronto using the techniques in this book. If the dogs don't know the down-stay, simply tether them three or four feet apart in the same room after the fight. Even if you have to stand between them during this time and rediscipline them, *don't separate the dogs.* This is what they want! Since Shelties are a small breed and slight of build, you might be able to handle this set-up on your own. If you have the slightest suspicion that you will need some assistance make certain to procure it before staging the set-up. Good luck in your efforts and let's hope for serene Shelties.

You talk a lot about owner personality types such as the placater and blamer. Can one personality type be "pushed" into another by sheer frustration over a dog problem?

Babies and dogs can be great pals—especially if the dog knows a solid long down and there is proper parental supervision. *Judy Emmert/Dealing with Dogs/TV Ontario*

Of course, it happens all the time. The most common scenario is for a placater to become a blamer. As the dog's problems get worse and worse, usually because of continued placating and lack of leadership, the owner reaches a point of feeling trapped and begins to blame the dog for anything and everything. The switch doesn't happen overnight but is rather a gradual change, yet it is still extremely confusing for the dog. If you feel you've reached this juncture, don't simply back up into your original placting mode, but instead read over the section on *leveling* with your dog and try to avoid extremes of placating or blaming completely. Actually, your evolution is a plus because usually placaters who become blamers *are* developing some leadership skills and Alpha attitudes, if only by accident.

Could you please discuss how to introduce a newborn baby into the household? We have a one-year-old Golden.

First be certain to have taught your dog the long down. Being able to tell your dog to go to its place and stay will be essential. You wouldn't think that an ex-monk would know a lot about babies, but I am also the oldest boy from a family of eleven children. My mother was never *not* pregnant. I was four feet tall before I ever saw her face. I know that baby care involves rituals that are easily interrupted by a cavorting canine. If your dog doesn't know the long down you will find yourself constantly banishing the dog to the backyard or to a crate—which tells the dog that it doesn't rate anymore and can produce jealousy. By using the long down the dog can be included in household life, not excluded. Before your baby arrives practice long downs in the room that is planned as the nursery. It's a good idea to dry-run diaper a large baby doll, watching Rascal out of the corner of your eye for any breaks in the down-stay. Follow the corrective sequence for long down breaks that you'll find in this book.

The long down can also be used to let the baby socialize with the dog. You can stage set-ups by gently warning your dog to be nice, placing the dog on a long down and then placing the baby next to the dog. You can kneel nearby or even lie down with your child and dog to let them relate. If your dog uses its mouth or paws in too rough a fashion on the baby a slight swat under the chin or on the dog's paw itself should show the dog that gentleness is mandatory. Check with your veterinarian to be certain your dog doesn't harbor any parasites or other contagious diseases that the child can contract, and if your child has been ill, inquire with the pediatrician along the same lines.

How do you select a private trainer if you have a problem dog? How do you determine who is qualified? How do you determine if a person's methods are humane and sensible before hiring him or her?

Since training is an unlicensed field it is quite possible to hire a poor trainer. There have been some attempts to regulate the profession, but as of this writing, no definitve structures have been set up. So buyer beware are the watchwords for anyone looking for a trainer. Here are some hints. First, any decent private trainer will begin by taking a behavior case history—carefully interviewing you about your dog's problems as well as your needs and desires in training. Some class trainers now do this also. Bravo for them! Beware of trainers who skip this step or simply do an oral interview and do not take any notes. Even longtime trainers simply cannot remember what each client and student needs unless they write it down.

For a referral, begin by asking your veterinarian. Veterinarians have a vested interest in affiliating with good trainers because they are queried so often about behavioral matters, yet often do not have the time or skill to provide full answers. No veterinarian will remain associated, however loosely, with a trainer who consistently turns in bad results or if clients complain about the trainer's services. And believe me, the veterinarian will be the first to hear about any poor quality services. Don't worry—if you are the skeptical type— that there is any "arrangement" between the trainer and the veterinarian. Veterinarians are forbidden by the ethical guidelines of the American Veterinary Medical Association from taking any kickbacks for referrals. This is still another safeguard for you.

Do you feel comfortable with the trainer? Some persons prefer to work with a male trainer, some with a female. When you ask questions about the trainer's background—and you should—are answers clear and concise? Has the trainer published? While this is not absolutely necessary, if the trainer has authored a book or has written for training trade journals, there is more of a chance that he or she has been up for peer review and taken the criticisms and compliments publication usually brings.

You might also ask about methods over the phone—without expecting a detailed account of every method the trainer uses. Ask also if the trainer has worked with dogs of your breed, and be especially wary of negative comments concerning any breed. Be careful, too, of the unfortunately ubiquitous sales verb "guarantee." "We guarantee results!" some ads will scream. This is patent nonsense. Your dog is not a robot you are sending into a repair shop to be fine-tuned. It is a thinking, feeling, living being that has a relationship with a leader figure—hopefully you. Since there are three parties involved in the training process, yourself, your trainer and your dog, I fail to see how one party can guarantee the performance of the others. If all three parties cooperate and are willing to learn, change, identify problems and restructure life to alleviate those problems, training most often succeeds.

I have a one-year-old Border Collie. If I hadn't already named him I would have called him Saint because he practically is one. I know you're probably saying, "Oh sure, sure," Mr. Evans, but I really haven't had any sizeable problems with him. I've taken him to obedience school and feel my leadership is "in place" in his mind. I'm wondering about one thing though. I'm heading into a career period when I'll have to be away for longer periods of time. I understand about staging set-ups and your suggestions for blitzing the dog to correct destructive chewing—but is there anything else I can do to circumvent chewing? A kind of "preemptive strike"?

Yes. You can teach your dog avoidance of *verboten* items by leading him to the objects and issuing a *light* reprimand. Begin by placing your Border Collie on lead and making eye contact. Lightly touch his centering spot so that he will know that he should concentrate. Now calmly lead him to forbidden objects and make those objects attractive. For instance, let's say you fear that he might undo the fringe on an Oriental carpet. Take him to the carpet fringe, lift the end of the carpet about a foot in front of his face, wiggle the fringe enticingly and say, "No! Don't touch," or some similar phrase. Be sure to use the same phrase you would use to reprimand the dog for chewing something inappropriate if he did it when you weren't home.

Have handy the special scented toy discussed in the section on destructive chewing—the toy you usually would give your dog only when you are leaving. Right after your gentle reprimand, offer the dog that toy. He might take it or he might ignore it. If he takes it, praise him and let him chew or lick it for a few seconds, then move on to another no-no knickknack. If your dog looks bewildered and doesn't take the acceptable toy, simply lead him on to a few more items and call it a day. If you don't want your dog on the couch when you're gone, lead him over to the couch, sit him, lift one paw up onto the couch and give it a light but firm tap. Be sure to run several such sessions by your dog before you start to leave the household for longer periods of time—but, and this is important—don't center the dog's attention on more than five forbidden items a session, otherwise you'll overload his circuits and confuse him.

You've done so many things properly already—taking your dog to school, establishing yourself as Alpha and getting a preliminary understanding of set-ups—that you hopefully won't have any problem. One last tip: Dogs who engage in destructive chewing almost always lack aerobic, sustained exercise, the kind that truly dissipates excess energy. Especially with this breed, exercise is important, so don't shortchange your dog in this area. Frankly, you sound like the type of owner who never will.

What are your suggestions for staging a set-up for a digging dog? My backyard resembles a nuclear bomb test site.

First, my sympathy. Secondly, this advice: I hope you are being fair with your dog and leaving it in the house as much as possible. People who banish dogs to backyards usually wind up with yards that look like yours. I also hope that you've had your dog in school so that it has some words to live by, such as "down," so that it can be, in fact, a member of the household. When owners complain of this problem, my first thought is always "Why is this dog outside anyway?" Assuming all of the above is kosher, my advice would be to put the dog on the RRRR program for one month and practice creative avoidance for the first two weeks of that one month. In other words, simply do not leave the dog alone to dig. This might involve using a crate or confining the dog inside for two weeks. Once the RRRR kicks in, reestablishing your leadership, and once practicing creative avoidance has bought you and your dog some time and simply broken the daily habit of digging, you can grab a free day and blitz your dog for digging.

Take your dog to the back door and sit the dog. Issue an advance warning touching the centering spot and using eye contact. Release your dog to the backyard and hide out in the house, peering out a window secretively. At the first suggestions of digging—in other words, when the dog's paw starts to scrape dirt—heave a large handful of boulder-type marbles at the dog. Naturally, you'll have these ready to go in a bowl near the back door, which of course you've left slightly ajar for quick opening. BBs work well, too, but often don't deliver a strong enough correction. You should have a tab leash on your dog as well. Charge out toward the dog just as you throw the marbles, get the dog, give a good shake. Sit the dog at the excavation spot—do all of this quickly yet calmly—and take one paw and scrape it on the earth as if the dog is digging. Give the paw a good swat—and quickly lead the dog back to the back door. Reissue your warning, again using the centering spot: "Sport, I *told* you not to *dig!*" Now release the dog again. A nice flourish is to show the dog a handful of marbles just as it is (now dejectedly) marching out to the backyard. Hide again and observe. Repeat the process and extend the blitz by leaving the house for fifteen minutes, returning and checking for excavation, disciplining if necessary and leaving for a half hour, building up to two hours.

Again, your sequence in shorthand would be: Issue advance warning, release dog, hide out, if digging commences heave marbles, *charge!,* grab tab, shake dog, sit dog, scrape paw on ground, swat paw, race back to house, sit dog, reissue warning using *same* warning phrase and emphasizing same phonics, brandish marbles and show them to dog, rerelease dog and repeat all of the above, lengthening the period of time you leave the dog alone.

Finally, if you don't have an enclosed backyard, you'll have to use a leash longer than a tab to get your dog when you charge out—and frankly, if you don't have an enclosed backyard your dog has no business being left alone unattended there anyway. There are some other old ruses that might, I repeat, *might,* work and they are worth listing: You can try filling in the holes, but first bury some of your dog's feces about three inches underneath the top of the soil. Mousetraps set near the holes sometimes work, as do unpleasant lotions and potions such as Tabasco sauce—although the ground tends to simply soak up whatever potion is applied. Further, these ploys often simply convince the dog to shift earth-moving ventures to another portion of the lawn. It's my feeling that the discipline should come directly from the owner, but you can't go wrong if you try the above measures as well.

Are Dalmatians stupid? Everyone says so. Can they even understand a set-up? Aren't there breed differences to be taken into consideration in staging set-ups for bad behavior—or even using them at all? If you don't want to answer this question to the whole seminar group, you can contact me in Room #347. I'm staying in the same hotel as you.

Let me quote directly from my taped answer to this submitted-secretly-at-the-podium question: "First, folks, this is an actual question submitted today by an actual person. I am going to have it framed. No, I cannot rendezvous

212

with this person in room number 347. Yes, I will answer the question, not in private but to the whole seminar group. This is a funny, but ignorant, question. The only smart part of the question, I'd like to think, is the suggestion at the end! Dalmatians are not stupid. Further, this person obviously doesn't realize that I *have* one! Most people just assume that I have a German Shepherd Dog, I suppose, because I was once with the Monks of New Skete, who are famous for raising them. But no, my friend, wherever you are in the audience—and I think I can pick you out because there is only one crimson face in this sea of people—I have one of those 'stupid Dals.'

"In my opinion most breed qualifications are bunk when it comes to correcting problem behavior. I repeat, *bunk.* I find that, more often than not, owners simply use what they have heard about a given breed as an excuse to settle for a less-than-well-behaved dog, as a cop-out against taking the time to stage set-ups or even simply train their dogs in the basic words every dog needs to know. There is no such thing as a dog that cannot learn to heel, sit, stay, down itself and hold a long down. No such domestic canine exists unless it is medically or psychologically impaired—and this is very rare. If a given dog can learn those words, that same dog can, in my opinion, understand a correction and its connection. The foil, however, as we know, is an owner who has already decreed in advance that dogs of a given breed are dumb. This is a form of *blaming,* a way of hanging the dog without a fair trial. Of course there are breed idiosyncrasies, small behavioral quirks, that can be noted. For instance, it might be harder for a Siberian Husky or a Terrier to understand a set-up meant to eliminate digging, since a Siberian may really like to dig a cooling hole, and Terriers, by virtue of the fact that their very name comes from the Latin word for "earth," certainly like to burrow. Sight hounds and coursing hounds might be a tad more difficult to teach the recall to, and large, protection-oriented breeds might have a propensity to defend territory. But all of these are simply traits, not dictums, and can be modified, indeed must be modified in order for a given dog to fit into a given situation. I doubt whether the person who asked this question truly believes that Dalmatians are stupid or that any breed is impossible. Instead, most probably this person is issuing a cry for help—in his or her own peculiar way—because the person is frustrated by a problem dog. But the problem really isn't the dog, nor the dog's breed, is it? The 'problem' is registered in room number 347. So I've changed my mind: I'd be pleased to have dinner with you tonight. Let's see what we can work out together." (By the way, readers, when I read back the question to the group I changed the room number to protect the party involved. I used my own room number instead. I got a call later that night from a seminar participant who didn't recognize my voice and said I had a lot of nerve trying to see Mr. Evans alone.)

Here's the problem: My dog is working on his CDX, but I'm afraid he'll never earn it. As you know part of the "obedience ritual" to earn that title (Companion Dog Excellent) is that the dog has to hold a sit-stay and a down-stay while the

A set-up for an obedience foul-up: disobeying during the long sit. Warn the crash-landing Collie by tapping the "centering spot." *Levon Mark*

Immediately give the verbal command and visual signal for "stay."
Levon Mark

Devise a method to watch from afar, and when the dog begins to sink into a down, quickly return.

Levon Mark

handler is out of sight. This exercise is taken as a group and therein lies the problem. During the long sit my Collie lies down, goes into a play bow and starts to solicit attention from the other dogs! If they ignore him, he simply goes into a full down, ruining the exercise. I've tried everything. I've gone back and simply repositioned him without scolding. I've gone back and scolded him and I've even stationed helpers nearby behind him so that he always feels that someone will correct him if he breaks the sit-stay. He will never earn this title at this rate. I've heard of this problem with other Collies. Is it specific to the breed?

It *is* possible and preferable to stage a set-up for this problem and I'll tell you how. But before I do I need to tell you that my gut feeling is that something more serious is happening here than just a simple mistake on the dog's part. Let me simply ask some questions—questions every owner with such a so-called ring-wise dog should mull over.

You mention several times what the *dog* does that is wrong. You say twice—in a short question—that "he" won't earn the title at this rate. "He" won't earn the title? What about "we?" I thought obedience training involved teamwork. Is it possible that you are *drill, drill, drilling* your dog in this and other exercises to the point that he just doesn't give a good gosh darn about the whole ritual? My advice is to back off and employ some creative avoidance here. Simply *don't* train your dog at all for two weeks. Play fetch, go for long walks in the woods, go for a run on the beach, but other than usual household training, don't do any formal obedience training. Just enjoy each other.

I know this sounds anthropomorphic, but I firmly believe that many competition dogs can tell when they are being "used" to further an owner's goals. They pick it up via owner paralanguage and body language—especially before and after obedience trials. The owner, of course, in an attempt to deflect this "criticism" from the dog makes his or her goals the dog's goals, thus, "He will never earn the title at this rate." What if the dog just doesn't *want* to "earn" the title? Why does he have to "earn" it? What if you are pushing for it too hard? Very, very few professional obedience persons ask these kind of questions, often because they are fixated on achieving goals—goals that they have neatly transferred to the dog. The moratorium period on formal training will show your dog another side of yourself that your Collie might miss. A change in his psychological attitude might be what you need to correct this problem. So it's time to call "time-out!" and relax and reflect.

However, you'll still have to stage a set-up for the specific problem. After the two-week no-training period has passed, stage a set-up as follows: Leave your dog with a light warning, using a distinctive phrase, "OK, Tommy, you *sink* and you're *dead,*" emphasizing *sink* and *dead.* Remember, the phrase could be, "OK, Tommy, *mushrooms,* mushrooms, *mushrooms,* zucchini, mushrooms," just as long as it is consistent and does not include an obedience word. Tap the centering spot as you deliver your warning phrase. Now give the stay command and leave. Remember, there is no law that says that just before you disappear from sight you cannot reissue the warning command again. Of course, you will be secretly watching the dog from afar. Perhaps you

Do not simply reposition the dog into the sit. Instead, give the Collie a good shake and stern scolding—but no hysterics! Quickly reissue the command "stay" simultaneously with the visual signal and leave again.

Levon Mark

Remember, as you leave to disappear from sight again, there is no law that says you can't give a *second* warning—just be sure to use the same phrase consistently, emphasizing the same words.

Levon Mark

could try hiding behind the high jump, peering out at your dog through the slats. This is a nifty ploy because jumps are set up in various rings at trials, and your dog may never know which one you are hiding behind. As soon as your dog sinks into the play bow, charge back, repeat the warning phrase emphasizing the same phonics, give your dog a good shake correction, then reposition the Collie into the sit. Give the stay command again. Move! There should be a smooth, strict flow to this scenario. Don't go back and negotiate with the dog about its "fall from grace"—just repeat the warning phrase, discipline and get out of sight again.

The missing ingredient in your previous recipe was that you did not issue a warning, but instead hoped against hope that maybe, just maybe, this time the dog wouldn't sink into the play bow or simply crash. Repositioning the dog without any reprimand made the ritual into a game—and repositioning a dog is not correcting a dog. Finally, this dog obviously feels a need to solicit attention from other dogs, even in formal circumstances. Does he get to play with other dogs? Or is the only time he relates to members of his own species in such matches or trials? Try to let him play more around other dogs, cutting the play sessions midcourse and immediately going into an obedience exercise. If, on the other hand, your dog really does get to relate with other dogs frequently, he is simply playing "Mister Congeniality" with too much fervor and the set-up should show him that such an award, while awarded at beauty pageants, is definitely not awarded at obedience trials, and never to males in either circumstance.

I have a shy dog. She is fearful of loud noises, sudden moves, practically anything spontaneous. I am afraid she will become a fear biter, as she is already growling at people. What can I do? By the way, I'm shy, too.

(This question, like a good many queries I receive on shyness, was not asked aloud during the seminar but instead submitted in writing and placed on the podium during a break. Characteristically, the handwriting is extremely small, barely legible and scrunched. My purpose in pointing this out is not to criticize, but rather to point out that if an owner is underconfident—shy—often the dog will be, too. As a joke, I'll often say, "OK, who submitted this question? Stand up!" If one cannot joke about one's shyness, I believe that person will remain forever shy. I am shy outside of seminars, people are surprised to find out. But I can laugh about it, and my dogs aren't shy. Funny, but not shy.)

Forgive me in advance for being blunt but I'm concerned about this owner and dog. You don't have just a shy dog, you have an aggressive dog as well. You are in potential trouble unless you start training pronto. Put this dog on the RRRR today. Immediately read over the RRRR chapter and my open letter to owners of aggressive dogs in this book, then come back to this answer. Back already? I hope you read those chapters. I know you were probably protesting, "But why am I reading this, the dog's *shy,* not aggressive," but, my friend, if a dog is growling, that's aggression in my book, and aggression that could lead to a bite. No one will care, once bitten, that your dog is shy.

The bite will feel the same to them. So tackle the aggression first. From this moment forth, it is simply unacceptable for your dog to growl at anyone or anything. Repeat: Unacceptable. You must firmly discipline any such actions. Remember, often with shy dogs the corrections need not be very harsh. Indeed, you may get away with only stern leash corrections, but if the aggression is pronounced, regardless of the cause, stop it in its tracks.

Bear in mind that I understand that your dog may be, in fact, shy. But first things first. We have to stop the aggression and simultaneously socialize the dog out of shyness. The first step in rehabilitating any shy dog is to teach the dog a rock-solid, proofed, secure sit-stay and down-stay. If these commands are taught and adequately proofed the dog will be forced to face the prospect of disobeying a command word in order to cater to shyness. You will need these words, "down," "sit" and especially "stay" to stage set-ups for shyness. These words must be tight in the dog's brain. These words must be proofed. You can use these words to conquer shyness. At first the dog may only "do" the word in order not to incur your wrath—even as people pet it—but the word "stay" will save this dog. Does your dog *really* know "stay"?

Begin by having some guests over, seated in your living room. Let the dog see the guests enter the home, insisting on a sit-stay at the door. The guests need not touch the dog, but rather can simply nod, say a sweet (but not too sweet) "Hello, Shy Sam" and proceed to the living room. Bring your dog in and place the dog on a long down. If the dog doesn't yet know the long down get busy teaching it today using the methods in this book, and for now simply sit on the leash to keep Sam anchored. Have some conversation. Don't talk about the dog—shy dogs, like most, know their names and can tell when the name is interwoven into stressed, whiney paralanguage. Just ignore the dog, even if the dog is straining to get away, run and hide. Don't allow this, and don't touch the dog at all, unless it is to discipline obnoxious whining. After fifteen minutes, have the guests leave.

The next day repeat the process adding a warning to Shy Sam not to be shy. Remember, consistent phrase, tap the centering spot, make eye contact. Let the guests stay a half hour with no interaction with the dog. The following day, repeat all of the above, but leave a six-foot lead on your dog. Enclose the dog in the room and simply pass the lead around to each guest. In this Round Robin Recall the dog is called from person to person and praised. If the dog stalls, the person should haul the dog in firmly, but not pet the dog. If there is stalling or any sign of aggression, all praise must cease immediately. Only one person at a time should praise the dog, and if the dog clings to the owner, the owner should stare the dog down, issue a stern "No!" and look aloofly away. Try to blitz the shy dog with such set-ups for fourteen days. But, as the New Agers say, "Don't push the river." Once you have obtained the set-up goal for that day, call it a day. You can always stage another set-up tomorrow. Naturally, there is a risk factor in such set-ups, and if you feel that they would result in friends being bitten, you simply *must* secure the help of a qualified trainer or behaviorist right away. Shyness always gets worse, not better, unless checked by training, so don't delay. Good luck! At the risk of being presumptuous, you might seriously consider some assertiveness training for yourself. Most cities offer such services. Perhaps you are afraid to get tough with your shy dog because you yourself are shy. I fully identify because I am, off-stage. Even one session might work wonders. I'd suggest books on the topic, but my experience is that shy owners read them submissively and need personal confidence building.

My husband and I are concerned for our four-year-old son. We have a six-year-old, mixed breed, spayed female who constantly runs after him, nipping and trying to bowl him over. Worse though, and this is what we are really concerned about, three days ago the dog growled at our son when he approached us while we were still in bed. It was a Saturday morning and we wanted to sleep late, but our son knows that he can come into the bedroom then so that one of us can get up and turn on the TV for him. However, he also has a problem—pretty typical with children his age, I think—of trying to get into bed with us at night. Following a therapist's instructions, we simply walk or carry him back to his own bed each time he tries to get in ours. We tried simply telling our son to go back to his bed, but that didn't work. Our dog sleeps on our bed, always has since the time she was a puppy. The growling incident was on the morning after we had to escort our son back to his bed about six times. What can we do about our dog's behavior, and, while you're at it, any tips for our son's behavior!?

Some maids don't do windows—I don't do kids. But I do do dogs and I can assure you that there is a kid/dog interplay here that is essential for you to understand. Since your dog probably thinks of herself as number three in the family hierarchy (for that matter, maybe she even thinks she's number one), she definitely thinks that the "new puppy"—your son—is number four—and should stay in his place. You confirm this faulty notion each time you lead your son back to his sleeping quarters, even if you do so calmly. The dog watches this carefully and probably with a great deal of satisfaction; after all, she's been on the bed for six years. Who is this interloper? And, no, the dog does not necessarily know that this is your son, whom you love and cherish. Nor would she necessarily care if she did know. The dog probably feels that her place in the family hierarchy is threatened, or at least changing, and wants to preserve the status quo. So, obviously, get the dog *off* the bed, *pronto*. You will probably have to tether her to prevent her from trying to fling herself on the bed. Do not demote the dog from the bedroom, just off the bed.

Let your son have a walk session with the dog on leash. This can establish even a small child as an Alpha figure who has some leadership skills. If these two ploys don't work, and if within two days there is still hostility, place the dog on the RRRR program and leave her on it for one month. Put a short tab leash on the dog right away and be quick to grab it and deliver a *stern* leash correction if the dog chases or corrals your son—at this juncture all of this is aggression, not just simple play, and must be stopped. Don't just yell at the dog from afar, go and give a physical correction.

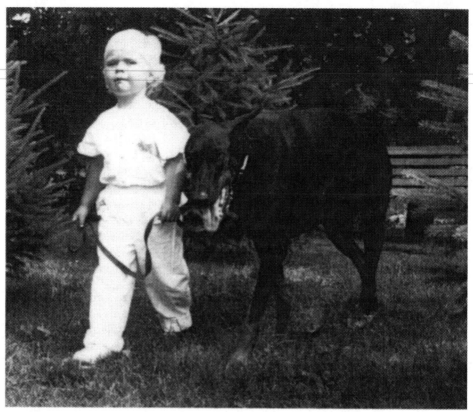

A child can establish some dominance over a dog by having a parentally supervised walk on-leash. This also increases the child's self-confidence and introduces the ideas of training and discipline.

Dealing with Dogs/TV Ontario

One night of obedience class can be structured so that the children are included. The kids hold the leash, seemingly "in control," but only mimic the adult's commands and signals—a kind of obedience "Simon Says" game.

Lionel Shenken/Visual Productions

You can concoct a set-up by issuing a warning and then releasing the dog near your son at a time when you know the child is bound to be playful or cavorting about. Zap the dog by grabbing the tab and disciplining if things get too rough, reissue the warning and release the dog again. Naturally, parental supervision of the child is a must. No tail yanking, ear pulling or other roughhousing should be allowed, and a four-year-old is old enough to understand being told to cease such behavior.

Chances are, in your efforts to allow the two to become friends, you've unintentionally allowed too much rough play. It's time to tighten up the controls now, before an unfortunate accident happens. Meanwhile, even if you wind up putting the dog on the supertough RRRR, you have my permission to modify it slightly by adding this step: Twice a week, each of the adults should take your pet for a long walk, alone, just you and the dog. The other parent can stay at home with your son. This will show your dog that you still love her and care enough for her to give her her own personal time alone with you. If there are woods nearby, try going there for the walk, even if it has to be on leash. This adds to the sense of intimacy the dog will feel with you. Good luck!

I've had it! I don't have a dog, I have a Hoover vacuum cleaner! I'm so frustrated I could scream! Well, let me back up. What I have is a garbager. I live in New York, and every walk I take with my dog, a five-year-old Cairn Terrier, is a trial because she snarffs up anything and everything she sees on the street. I yank the leash up hard, sometimes raising her front two feet off the ground, and scream, "Drop it!" and sometimes she does, but two seconds later she just snarffs up something else. It's a wonder she hasn't gotten sick from the filth she sucks up, or had a chicken bone caught in her throat. And don't ask me to just walk her where there isn't any trash on the street. This is New York! Oh, I forgot, you live here, too . . . well, then, you already know. . . .

I know you are trying your best with your Hoover, and I appreciate your attempts. There are several reasons success has eluded you. When you yank the dog up and away from "treats" you are simply *repositioning* the dog, not correcting the dog. Because the dog drops the trash doesn't mean that the Cairn will not try to pick up the next piece. Your walks have become games, and unpleasant to boot. I would advise you to stage a set-up that will involve issuing a warning, and then deliberately gliding your dog over some choice tidbit of trash. You should have no problem finding trash—I fully agree that even in the better areas of our city, it abounds.

Take your dog out on a proper training collar and a six-foot lead. Don't allow the dog to barge out of your building before you, as this only sets up an atmosphere that will make the tendency to garbage greater. Once you see the refuse you intend to use, stop about ten feet in front of it. Sit your dog. Tap the centering spot and deliver your warning, emphasizing key phonetics, "OK, Rascal, you *touch* that *trash* and you're *dead!*" Now glide over the garbage. I know you're shocked—after all, you've probably made it a habit to steer clear of as much garbage as possible, which means that in New York you probably look like a drunk walking a dog as you weave all over the sidewalk trying to avoid trash. Now here I am telling you to walk Rascal right over trash! The reason, of course, is so you can let Rascal garbage.

Watch for the moment her head dips to snarff and yank the leash up, *hard*. Now lean down and give Rascal a firm tap under the chin. Don't use the shake for this problem—the delay time is too long and the correction will be lost on the dog. If, by chance, the Cairn has already chomped down on the garbage and has it in her mouth, don't wrestle with her by sticking your fingers down her throat and trying to scrape the garbage out. Some "vacuum" dogs actually *like* this kind of interaction and consider it part of the game, especially if they sometimes manage to swallow the tidbit anyway. Instead, if the trash is of sufficient size, grab the end of it and yank the *dog* away from the trash, holding the trash steady, not vice versa. If the piece of garbage is too small to hold steady and yank the dog away from, try this: Place your left hand over the dog's snout, slipping a finger of that hand under the collar so as not to lose the dog. Place your right hand, palm up, under the dog's mouth and cup your thumb and index finger into the dog's mouth near the incisors. Firmly shake the dog's head downward to expel the trash. This method limits hand interaction with the dog's mouth and lessens the chance that the dog will interpret attempts to remove garbage from its mouth as a game and a challenge.

Regardless of whether the dog dropped the trash or had to have it removed, don't forget to give the disciplinary swat, immediately reissue the warning and heel forward. Now double back quickly, repeating the warning, and glide over the *same* trash. If the dog still garbages, chances are your initial correction was too slow or too soft.

Finally, you're right—garbaging isn't cute, there are real health risks involved. If the problem continues, you might have to call in a trainer—although most owners can rehabilitate "Hoovers" (sounds like a new breed, doesn't it?) themselves without too much difficulty. If you do need a trainer, and this is the only problem you have with your dog, one or, at most, two sessions should be all you need.

Bayou, my eleven-month-old Golden Retriever, has been baring his teeth and snarling at me and at other people since he was seven weeks old. Usually he does this when he is verbally corrected for his extremely destructive behavior or when he is touched (brushing, toweling him dry, pulling him off furniture). He has never actually bitten anyone. I obtained Bayou at age seven weeks from a reputable breeder and have contacted the breeder several times about his behavior. The breeder claims that there is no problem with the dog and just tells me to be firmer with him. My veterinarian has examined Bayou and ruled out medical causes for this behavior. Bayou was neutered at seven months but his behavior did not improve. He also attended obedience school for ten weeks and was the worst in his class. Bayou can be very sweet when he wants to be but I don't really feel I can trust him. I would appreciate any suggestions you can give me.

First, something that should be obvious to all, Bayou and, probably more importantly, Bayou's owner need to work with a qualified trainer or animal behavior consultant *in the owner's home.* While I'm happy the owner sought out obedience training, the class atmosphere is too hectic, even in well-run classes, to center in on the problems of a growling, snarling dog. In fact, obedience class training might have made the situation *worse,* especially since Bayou did not do well and probably got into tons of little dominance fights with the owner when they attempted to do the assigned homework between classes. An intelligent class instructor would have indicated this to Bayou's owner (it was probably apparent after the first class) and directed them to private training. Perhaps because the dog was so young, the instructor just thought the bad behavior would get better in time.

But all that's water over the dam now. I mention it for the sake of obedience class instructors who admit and keep aggressive dogs in their classes. You are doing the dog and the owner no favor. They should be directed to a private trainer or specialist. Often problems of aggression are easily treatable, and even one private session can work wonders. The dog can then come back to class or continue with the private training.

Since this was a written submitted question, there are many questions I need to ask the owner. I would need to interview Bayou's owner quite extensively. For now I'll just speculate since I can't interview owners during a seminar or as they read a book anyway.

While aggressive behavior is not generally genetically predisposed in Golden Retrievers, it does crop up occasionally. I would need to ascertain for sure if the puppy truly began displaying aggression at age *seven weeks.* Unless the breeder placed the pup at six weeks (a sign of an uninformed breeder), that means that the pup was exhibiting aggression from the time of placement! Yet the owner says that the dog was procured from a reputable breeder. My response to all this is simply, "Hmmmmm . . ." Very interesting, wouldn't you say? Why didn't the breeder catch it? Aggression in a seven-week-old Golden? Remarkable. Why didn't the breeder see the signs of aggression before placement? Or is this *owner* hyperbole—obvious and intentional exaggeration to impress me with the urgency of the problem? In order to ascertain this, and thus distinguish whether this problem has a genetic base or is owner-related, I would have to have the owner in a situation where I could ask him or her many questions. There are ways of asking trick questions so that the truth comes out.

If I were able to conduct a complete interview and work with the dog, and *if* the owner's statement that the dog was aggressive with him or her *and* others from seven weeks of age on was true, I would say there is a strong case that the dog is genetically defective. That will make rehabilitation and subsequent management very difficult. I would then counsel the owner to return the dog to the breeder if possible, or if the owner refused to be separated from the dog I would set up a program similar to the one that follows, with the provision and warning that the dog will always be a management problem.

I highly suspect, however, that this case is not one of genetically predisposed aggression but one of owner mismanagement. Let's face it, friends: You have to really *work at it* to produce a Golden Retriever that is genetically aggressive and "baring his teeth and snarling" at age seven weeks!

If the owner has intentionally or unintentionally bungled the leadership role I would prescribe the following:

1. Immediately employ a qualified trainer or specialist to help you in your home. The trainer will help you to devise set-ups so that the bad behavior is elicited from Bayou and can be corrected.

2. Since the dog has a problem with physical contact, all corrections must be distanced—collar corrections while the dog is on a leash or tab, which should be on whenever the owner is home. The owner should *not* use the shake or swat corrections I usually suggest. This is one of the exceptions to using those techniques.

3. I would advise the owner to immediately institute (the verb is correct) the RRRR program.

4. The private trainer or specialist *must* be sure to educate the owner as to *paralanguage*—indicating clearly that any stressed or whimpering tones of voice will simply demote the owner to littermate status in the dog's eyes. Some playacting might be necessary here and a lot of humor. I can assure the trainer that the academic approach will backfire here. Don't be afraid to mimic the littermate sounds and instruct the owner as to why these sounds, this paralanguage, will be misinterpreted by the dog and will lower the owner to littermate status in the dog's eyes. (By the way, as a quick aside to the trainer or behaviorist who might get this case—this is a blamer owner. I'm almost certain of it. Worse, he or she is also a placater. The dog gets placated and the breeder—and probably any trainer who gets called in—gets blamed. Tricky.)

5. Finally, the owner has to be taught how to refrain from *escalating* incidents when going after the dog for destructive behavior or grooming—often owners tense up, put tension on the lead (*if* they have one on to begin with) and create an atmosphere of high anxiety that the dog learns to anticipate and fight. Good luck to both client and trainer!

My dog chases cars. Not every car that passes by, only some. She also gets carsick on every ride. What can I do? How can I break her of these habits?

If this dog was not hanging around outside, undoubtedly off leash and unsupervised, such a problem would never develop. Get the dog in the house pronto, except for elimination and on-leash walks. If you are ever going to be able to trust her outside, even under your supervision, you must institute a moratorium period on any and all off-leash outdoors freedom. Break the car-chasing cycle! Do this for two weeks and then you can try a set-up. I'll describe one in a second, but, I hasten to add, if you simply let the dog return to an outdoors-all-the-time, unconfined life-style, you will probably *never* break the dog of car chasing. Instead, your dog will break something else: her neck, her leg, her back—get the picture?

After the moratorium period has passed (and during that time you should also be practicing formal recalls as described in the chapter "To Come or Not to Come"), you can stage a set-up. Put a six-foot lead on your dog and simply let the dog walk around the house with it on for two full days. You need to secure the help of a neighbor and another family member in order to stage this set-up. The neighbor will drive the car the dog will chase, and you will be hiding in that car. The family member, preferably the person in the family the dog thinks of as the second Alpha figure, will deliver the advance warning. Coordinate with each other as to the time the car will *slowly* pass the house. This can be announced by strategic horn honks just before the car will appear. At this point the helper sits the chaser, taps the centering spot, makes eye contact and delivers the warning, "OK, Road Runner, you chase that *car* and you're *dead.*" The helper then releases the dog and returns to the house, surreptitiously peering out. The decoy car should then roll by at a slow, enticing pace. The main Alpha figure should be hidden in the backseat, ready to charge out, grab Road Runner, who of course is wearing the six-foot lead it's gotten used to, and give two or three disciplinary swats under the chin. Yes, swats. In my opinion, this car-chasing problem is big-time and deserves the swat, not just the shake. Big canine crimes are better disciplined with the swat—especially when they involve a threat to the dog's own life or to the lives of others—as this crime definitely does.

The car driver may have to break suddenly, so be sure that you stage the set-up for a time when the road is not busy, and be sure that the driver announces to the person secluded in the car exactly when the breaks will be applied. If you do not manage to catch the dog for discipline, the indoors helper, who will be watching secretly, should simply prop open the house door. The dog will probably run inside, where that person can deliver the discipline or, better yet, trot the dog quickly back out to the scene of the crime and let the main Alpha discipline at car side. Repeat the process again, securing the help of still another neighbor in a different make car. At the start of the set-up, the two decoy cars can be parked together a short distance away. After the first part of the set-up, once discipline has been delivered, Alpha number one turns the dog over to Alpha number two and hitches a ride to decoy car number two with the driver of decoy car number one. Got it? Need three decoy cars? Well, get them.

I've found neighbors are only too willing to help with this ruse—as their cars are often the very ones being chased. They would rather participate in a set-up than run the gauntlet every day and risk injuring the dog or themselves. Owners of car chasers are often also owners of in-car howlers. They have gotten used to such behavior from their dogs inside and outside of cars. What they rudely don't consider or have any sensitivity about is the sheer panic almost all other drivers experience when the car is charged by a chaser. It's literally impossible to tell if the dog in at the side of the car or under it, and most drivers tense up terribly and swerve around dangerously, endangering themselves and others.

If you are fast enough exiting the decoy cars, your dog should be totally *shocked* to find you coming after it. The element of surprise, and the fact that the correction comes from a leader figure, puts the shine on this set-up. You might have to have a practice dry run minus a dog, so that driver, discipliner and house helper can coordinate their movements. One last point: During the two-week moratorium period, don't allow the dog to urinate or defecate anywhere near where the car chasing occurs. In other words, if the chasing happens in the front yard, confine all elimination to the backyard. Dogs claim territory by eliminating on it, and the chances are the dog thinks the front yard and thus the road and the "big shiny dogs" that "run by" there belong to it. If you believe in the myth that a dog "needs to be outdoors" or "needs to enjoy the country air," at the risk of sounding blunt—you are misinformed. Properly socialized, your dog is a pack animal that would far prefer being inside with the rest of the pack. But it might not know that this is best for it. It's up to the pack leader (that's you) to inform the dog what's best. As for fresh country air, unless you live in the Arctic, these days the air is most probably fresher indoors rather than outdoors.

For the second problem, set-ups minus discipline still work. Begin with short rides, gradually building up to longer ones. If the dog gets sick in the car, do not discipline the dog. Try not feeding the dog anything for two or three hours before a short drive out and then back into the driveway. That's all—not even around the block; do that tomorrow. The next day, drive a half mile, and the day after that, one mile. Ask your veterinarian about drugs that can help with this problem. If you have dual car conundrums—your dog chases cars and gets sick in them—you'll probably resolve the second problem by staging a set-up as described above for the first problem. The car-chasing set-up will deglamorize cars in your dog's mind and connect your authority and Alphahood up with the very presence of an automobile. This may very well aid in composing your dog inside cars.

I am going to Europe and am considering sending my two-year-old Rhodesian Ridgeback to a boarding kennel that also offers a training course. He has problems with destructive chewing and is still not 100 percent on his housetraining. Do you think the training will be successful in stopping these problems? He'd be at the kennel for almost one month.

I doubt that the type of training your dog will receive at a training kennel will include correction of chewing and housetraining problems. Since your dog will be kenneled, with only acceptable toys, how will he even have access to unacceptable chew objects in order to make mistakes and get corrected? As for housetraining, think about the word itself: *house*training. Seems to me the procedure is best accomplished in someone's *house,* specifically, yours. It is not just a mechanical process but rather has to do with how the owner is viewed by the dog, which food is offered, adopting a schedule, discerning whether the dog can be disciplined after the fact and then disciplining correctly. This can hardly be accomplished in a boarding kennel setting.

On the other hand, your dog most likely *will* learn the basic command words, and if his trainers take the time necessary to train *you* to train your dog, this will be beneficial in terms of the way the dog views you. Be sure to be carefully interviewed as to your needs and desires in training when you drop your dog off, and be sure that the trainer who takes your dog into the kennel is the same trainer who will give you an exit lesson when you come to call for your dog. The idea sounds workable, especially since you are going to Europe and need to board your dog anyway, but don't expect your dog to come home a saint. As William E. Campbell says, "I've worked with a few thousand problem-dog owners who have hustled their little 'Caesars' off to obedience classes or called for private instruction with the idea that what the dogs need is just 'a little training.' In truth, that's too easy; too much like a free lunch. The shoe is on the wrong foot. It's the owners who need the training, along with a change in their perspective and attitude and, hence, a change in *their* behavior, which will be followed by a change in their dogs' behavior."

My dog goes berserk when there is a thunderstorm. I mean absolutely nuts. As in off the wall. I've tried confinement and she screams in her crate. I've tried drugs, all under veterinary supervision. She fights through every drug she's ingested. The veterinarian says it is a behavioral problem. Around July 4th, she begins to freak out over firecrackers. What can I do other than move to the Sahara Desert or try to find a country that never celebrates anything with firecrackers?

Every July 4th, my answering machine is flooded with hysterical calls from owners on the battlefield. For some reason, especially in Brooklyn, Queens and the rest of the USA (other than the island of Manhattan), firecrackers are as American as Mom and apple pie. Funny, nothing similar occurs in Canada on July 1st (Dominion Day) or in other countries—although dogs in Greece suffer shell shock each Easter.

Often in the background I'll hear a dog screeching and bombs detonating. Occasionally, I can't even hear the distraught owner's voice. Usually this is because the owner is cradling the upset dog in his or her arms, and the dog's vocalizations outdo the owners.

The biggest mistake owners make is trying to soothe their puppy or older dog out of being fearful of such sounds. This usually begins in puppyhood. It doesn't take long for the dog to realize, "Mommy and Daddy pay lots of attention to me if I just act frightened during a storm or on the Fourth—and besides, I really *am* frightened . . . well, sometimes." It's interesting that many such coddled dogs simply do not freak out (at least not as much) when a storm comes up or a firecracker goes off and Mommy and Daddy are not home. Many scared dogs simply find a niche—behind a couch, in their crate or down in the basement—and wait things out. So if your pet has such a niche, I'd say let the dog retreat to it. Stop any petting or comforting of the dog. You will simply unintentionally train the dog's fear *in,* tighter and tighter.

There are some tape recordings and phonograph records of storms and firecrackers that are touted as a cure for storm shyness or Fourth freakouts. I've tried them but never had much success with them, but they are worth a try as a desensitizing ploy. In my experience, the tapes or records just can't reproduce the sound of thunder or firecrackers with enough decibels or suddenness to simulate the real happenings. Then, too, lightning (especially heat lightning flashes) usually *precedes* the sound of thunder, so the preconditioned dog takes its cue to get ready to freak from the lightning flash, which many dogs can perceive even if you draw all the blinds. Again, I'm for anything that works. Not everything works with every dog, so the tapes might be worth a try.

If you decide on such sound effects and you find that your dog is doing no better, just leave the dog alone. If, on the other hand, the dog engages in destructive behavior, runs about too much or screeches bloody murder, you owe it to your dog to lessen its stress by disciplining it and placing the dog on a long down. Your dog must know that even during a storm, even when firecrackers go off, hysterical behavior is simply unacceptable and you believe it can do better.

Sometimes a dog will become so hysterical during a storm or another disturbance—especially if coddling is cut off—that the dog resembles a person at a funeral who is so deeply grieved that he or she is out of control. It's standard policy in some cultures to give this person a good shake, or even a slight slap on the cheek, just to bring the person back to reality. The bereaved one is then advised to sit and relax. If your dog flies out of control, this type of action may be necessary, and the long down-stay is the equivalent of having your dog "sit and relax."

OK—I've listened all day and I think I've come up with fifty-five different set-ups for fifty-five different problems my dogs have. So, thank you. But I have a problem I'll bet even you can't stage a set-up for. It's overbarking, and I don't mean one overbarking dog, I mean seven. They live partially in the house and partially in an outdoor kennel in runs. When someone comes to the door, all hell breaks loose. It resembles the psychiatric ward in One Flew Over the Cuckoo's Nest. *If they are out in their kennels and I pick up the telephone (they can see if I'm on the phone by looking in the kitchen window) all seven go nutzoid. One trainer told me that this was jealousy. He said they probably think I'm holding and talking sweetly to another dog because the phone is held close and has what looks to them like a tail. That's a cute explanation, but it doesn't help me to stop the problem. Actually, it's not so far off the mark. Come to think of it, I'm usually talking to my mother, and she can be a bitch. If you can solve this one, Job, I'll cook you dinner. And, yes, they are Terriers. I know you're probably thinking, "Well, she deserves everything she gets."*

No, I don't think that. Instead, I was thinking, this woman deserves the very best, because you seem to have a lovely sense of humor, and despite some problems (most of which you feel you can alleviate or eradicate), I just sense that you deeply love your dogs. Some people think staging set-ups is mean or unfair, but this just isn't so, because the motivation for staging them comes out of love. Indeed, parent to child, owner to dog, discipline *is* love.

So you've already taken an important step just by listening to the seminar today and doing some work on yourself. If you do those fifty-five other set-ups (really fifty-five?!), you might find that much of the overbarking simply subsides. But—never one to avoid direct advice—let me describe some sample set-ups for your specific problems.

For the in-house doorbell vocalistics, you are going to have to teach each dog a rock-steady stay at the front door. Take each dog, one by one, for just three minutes a day and run the Volhard sit-stay progressions past the dog near the front door. You'll find them described in "Words Dogs Live By." On day two, have a helper ring the doorbell as you run each individual dog through these paces. Get ready, the dogs will freak out and you'll have to be superstrict about enforcing the stay *and* disciplining any barking.

On day three, admit the person to the house, again working with only one dog at a time. Enforce the no-bark rule. If you secure the help of an assistant who knows in advance that you will enforce the stay and discipline barking if necessary, you will not have to worry about greeting the person or being ashamed as you correct the dogs.

If you feel that individual dogs are controlling their barking, stage a set-up employing a helper and working, on leads, with two dogs. Start with the leader Alpha dog and the most subordinate dog in the "pack." You most probably know who's who. If you don't, which is unlikely but possible, ask a knowledgeable dog person who knows your dogs. They'll tell you who's who. Since other members of the pack will tend to mimic the top dog, you can cash in on disciplining it and having it filter down to the others. This type of mimic behavior is called *allelomimetic* behavior and can be a great aid in staging set-ups. Now work inward into the pack order, staging the next set-up with the second most authoritative dog and the next up in submissiveness. Your next step would be to do a sting operation using a helper and the four or even five most cooperative (which means newly silent) dogs. Set-up schedules are touch-and-go, and you have to set the pace according to how quickly the dogs learn that silence is golden.

If your dogs participate in a lot of random, sporadic, spook-type barking (for instance, at perfectly acceptable outdoor noises, at household machines, etc.) you must stop it all. Some dogs have been unintentionally taught to live just on the edge of a bark and are constantly "on." I think this is one heck of a stressful life-style for any dog, and the amount of stress such noisemakers will experience by being disciplined for inappropriate barking is really nothing compared to the ongoing stress of feeling that they have to be ready to "spook-bark" at anything that is in the least unusual.

Don't worry that you'll destroy the protection potential of the dogs and that they will suddenly become mute and never bark when undesirable intruders threaten. They will, trust me. You will be simply teaching them discrimination and poise rather than condoning random overbarking. Besides, even if they do inhibit their barking somewhat, by virtue of the fact that you are asking this question, you seem to be saying that this would be perfectly fine with you! But don't worry, especially with Terriers, a propensity to bark comes in the genetic bargain. The propensity for it simply has to be shaped and controlled.

For run barking when the dogs are confined, you might try verbal corrections and a squirt gun filled with water and lemon juice. A plant-misting bottle with the squirter dialed to deliver a sharp spray rather than a mist is often better than a squirt gun—it shoots a longer distance. The trouble with a set-up here is that the corrections would be delayed as you fiddle with the gates to get to the dogs. But it's still worth a try to stage one. The sequence would be: Start with one dog, warn, tap centering spot and leave a tab lead on, confine in kennel, leave, charge back and discipline if barking, rewarn and repeat. Use the worksheets found earlier in chapter 10 of this book.

Owners of overbarkers need to map out in writing their set-ups because it's so easy to lose one's cool in the face of such yodeling, screeching, yapping and general confusion. Don't bark back at the dogs! Screaming *"No! No! No-no-no-no!"* is faulty paralanguage and will make you sound exactly like the barking dogs, even if you use the word "no." Even if the dogs really know the word "no," they will opt for the paralanguage and bark back. All eight of you will simply have a bark-fest. Keep your voice low and firm and go into action. The dogs will learn quickly that you mean business.

I have really been "at it." I have really laid down the law with my aggressive dog. And I have been making headway—a lot of headway. I had "misdiagnosed" his aggression as shyness and he really was just damn overprotective, precisely, of me. So we have been on the RRRR for about three weeks. I realize that the program is as much for myself as for my dog. Now, however, we have entered a period (about the last two days) during which my dog's behavior has gotten even worse. He's been making so much improvement—now this. What gives?

Here's what gives. Your dog has reached a point of rebellion. It's quite understandable—and explains why sometimes bad behavior becomes even *worse* once any kind of behavioral therapy is begun. This regression often mystifies owners, since they assume that once they clamp down, the dog will quiet down. Not so simple. At the risk of sounding anthropomorphic, let me paraphrase it from the dog's point of view: "OK, bozo, what is this RRRR business? Whether you know it or not, we had life set up a certain way around here. Basically, I was in charge. Now you tell me that *you* are Alpha, that I can't get on the bed, can't finagle any treats, can't get petted unless I earn the praise, can't have any people food, can't do this, can't do that. What am I?—*grounded* like some rebellious teenage kid? Well, don't expect me to buy it! I'm going to do everything I can to get things back to the status quo—the way things used to be. And don't you try to stop me, bozo!"

Your "reply" to this little tantrum/speech (although there needn't really be any at all) is to say, "That's right, you've got it just right—ride it out." You need to hang in there. You're doing many things right, and this rebellion period will pass. Again, if you think about it from the dog's point of view, it's all quite understandable, if unenjoyable. So just stick to your guns and hang on for better times, sweet times you and your dog will enjoy together.

I have lost my dog and I am heartbroken. I heard you say once in a seminar, "If dogs don't go to heaven, then I don't want to go there." That comment helped me, in fact, made me cry, and I noticed that many around me were crying also. Many of us have been through the death of a dog, it seems—really, I guess we should expect it, after all, dogs just don't live as long as we do. Still, I feel so empty, alone . . . can you say anything to me . . . will I ever see my beloved friend again?

I do believe you will. As far as I have been able to determine, with the exception of some radical, fundamentalist sects, no major Christian or Jewish denomination has ever issued a definitive pronouncement about what happens to animals after death. You are free, regardless of your religious preference, to believe what you will.

I would say the following to comfort you. First, feel sad and don't be ashamed of it. Of course you are sad and there's nothing wrong with that—it's quite natural. I really, *really* worry about owners who lose pets and do not feel sad or grieve. Among professional dog people, I've seen this stoic reaction often. It's as if the dog was a member of a livestock herd, a commodity to be traded, bartered, sold. I think this is one reason lay owners often feel so gypped when they turn to some breeders or trainers for comfort after the death of a dog and run up against a brick wall of "unemotion."

I've written elsewhere about how to deal with the death of a dog. Over a decade ago, the first dog writing I ever penned, the book I coauthored with the Monks of New Skete, *How to Be Your Dog's Best Friend,* dealt with this issue for perhaps the first time. Now it is standard for authors to address this all-important question. Thank God, for, after all, death is part of life.

Still, I find myself floundering, hemming and hawing as to what exactly to say. I once read in the excellent Barbara Walter's book *How to Talk to Practically Anyone about Practically Anything* that sometimes (oftentimes, she implied) the best thing one can do for the bereaved is to listen and say, "I know, I know . . ." The stupidest things to say, she says, are "I know exactly how you feel" (because you don't), or worse, "Everything will be all right" (it isn't and it won't be).

Just keeping it simple and saying "I know" seems like sound advice even now—even in the new age during which we've been tutored on how to accept death. I suppose Elisabeth Kübler-Ross started this trend when she mapped out the stages she observed in terminal patients nearing the end: shock, denial, anger, bargaining and, finally, acceptance. Neat, huh? Trouble is, what Kübler-Ross reported were simply *descriptions* of what she had observed in near-death patients—but the descriptive quickly became *prescriptive,* especially at the hands of her disciples.

The fact is, very few persons want to face death squarely, not the death of their dog and certainly not their own! We live in a death-denying, seemingly death-defying culture. But all reasonable dog owners know that, unless they are very old themselves and own a younger dog, most probably their dog will die during their lifetime. So for many a dog's death places the mourner squarely in the face of the incredible mystery of death itself—for perhaps the first time. Scary stuff—especially when others, insensitive to the death of a dog (and the other losses and potential losses it signifies), caution the bereaved to "get over it," because, after all, "it was only a *dog.*" Neat, huh? And the death-denying culture we live in "wins" once again, if only by default. The grieving owner is left to sort out emotions all alone.

I think that the Kübler-Ross paradigm is accurate, to a degree. But not everyone goes though similar stages in confronting death—their dog's or their own—and mourners shouldn't be expected to follow a script, however in vogue. For some owners, the death of a dog is instead a roller coaster of events and emotions. This is especially true if the dog has been euthanized because of behavioral difficulties. The fear, guilt and incredible distress an owner can feel in such a situation is lessened only by the fact that if the dog were allowed to live, serious harm might have befallen many innocent souls. But the owner is often too distraught to see this fact, and that's understandable.

So don't feel you *have* to go through any prescribed stages, and don't be critical of yourself for feeling so blue. Deliberately try to stay away from insensitive souls who make silly comments that minimize or trivialize your grief. On the other hand, if after two or three months you are still deep in grief, perhaps you should seek out some counseling. It's quite possible that the loss of your dog is bringing to the foreground other losses that you might have experienced in the past and for one reason or another refused to acknowledge or simply squelched down in yourself. This type of delayed-reaction grief is very common, but if worked on, it can help you grow. As a positive action, you might consider making a memorial donation to an organization that helps animals. The Delta Society (321 Burnett Ave. South, Third Floor, Renton, Wash. 98055) or the Morris Animal Foundation (45 Inverness Dr. East, Englewood, Colo. 80112) or your local humane society are all good possibilities.

Something strange has happened in my household. I recently lost Copper, my oldest Golden Retriever. He was nine years old and pretty much ruled the roost vis-à-vis the other dogs in the household. I have four others, all Goldens. All are bitches of various ages. Copper had been under observation at my vet's office but he rallied and came home. Two days later he took a turn for the worse. I was upstairs cleaning and suddenly felt an urge to go down to the kitchen. I found him dead in the kitchen, on his favorite rug. All of the other dogs were surrounding him in a semicircle—they looked like someone had put them all on sit-stays, and when I entered the room they all continued to look down at Copper. It was like a wake; they all looked extremely sad. Are dogs aware of the death of another dog? If they are, does this mean that they have religious sensibilities?

I just can't get over coming upon that scene. Although I was devastated when I realized Copper was dead, I was somehow comforted by the way the "family" had gathered. What do you think?

I think that you were blessed to see all of your dogs at a very private, special moment. The hand of God had just touched Copper and you were lucky enough to be passing by. Yes, I believe that dogs can grieve. They must experience emotional pain when such a prominent member of the pack passes away. I also believe that the dogs probably sensed that Copper was weakening, and perhaps expected his death. It's interesting how they were all so strangely quiet, although gathered together, and that even upstairs you felt drawn to the scene. I have had similar experiences myself. While I know you are sad about Copper's death, you can know, practically for certain, that your dogs join you in grief.

The thing to do now is to make all of the remaining dogs as secure and happy as possible. When one owns a "colony" of dogs (in behavioral terms, this is what you have) there is a tendency to do everything en masse. Especially now, take each dog for a long walk, in the woods if possible, alone—just the two of you. This will reassure each dog and help them to reorder the pack—with you as the featured Alpha. Strange as this may sound, put each dog through its obedience paces—as mind work helps to lessen grief. Your question is not at all out of line and is, in fact, quite sensitive. You are a very lucky person and you sound like a top-notch owner and steward. Your dogs are lucky to have you to lead and love them.

In Closing

So now we come to the end of the subject. Well, almost. I'm glad I've answered these questions about death submitted at seminars, because this is an inevitability almost all owners will have to face. Of course, besides not wanting to face the pain of loss, the real problem behind our unwillingness to deal with the issue of pet loss is our tremendous fear of our *own* eventual death. Yet, as far as I know, three out of every three people on this earth will die, so there is no escape. Here, our dogs can teach us an invaluable lesson about facing reality and about living one day at a time and cherishing each day. While I believe that dogs grieve and feel loss, and perhaps sense that they themselves will die, I don't think they obsess on it or become preoccupied with it. They live life, as fully as they can, one day at a time. They are an inspiration for us all, in life and in death. They can teach us much about what we need to know about love—if we let them and if we are open to their message and to the message of all nature. As the wise monk Father Zosima said in Dostoevsky's *The Brothers Karamazov*

> Love the animals: God has given them the beginnings of thought and untroubled joy. So do not disturb their joy, do not torment them, do not deprive them of their well-being, do not work against God's intent. Man, do not pride yourself

on your superiority to the animals, for they are without sin, while you, with all your greatness, you defile the earth wherever you appear and leave an ignoble trail behind you—and that is true, alas, for almost every one of us!

Love God's creation, love every atom of it separately, and love it also as a whole; love every green leaf, every ray of God's light; love the animals and the plants and love every inanimate object. If you come to love all things, you will perceive God's mystery in all things; once you have perceived it, you will understand it better and better every day. And finally you will love the whole world with a total, universal love.

Bibliography

HERE IS an annotated bibliography of books that concentrate on problem dogs—and their owners. I have not included standard training books that simply teach the obedience exercises and do not address problems. The information in the following books usually complements advice in this book. The novice seeking to stage sterling set-ups can find helpful tips galore—and the *professional* trainer owes it to himself or herself and to clients to be fully informed on just who has advised what, and when, for dealing with behavior problems. Accordingly, I've added two books at the end of this list that are somewhat archaic in style and technique, but will be of interest to professionals who wish to get a broader, historical overview of how people have "put up" with problem pooches.

Benjamin, Carol Lea. *Dog Problems.* 1981. Howell Book House, 866 Third Ave., New York, N.Y. 10022.

Benjamin, probably our finest dog writer, has a sound theory: Anticipate problems with your dog, and if you already have them, don't remain passive about them. Practically every problem is handled: chewing, digging, aggression, shyness, car sickness and more. Highly recommended.

———. *Mother Knows Best: The Natural Way to Train Your Dog.* 1985. Howell Book House.

Another top-notch book, the key chapter for owners of problem pooches is chapter 7, "Trouble-shooting." Geared more to the puppy owner than *Dog Problems,* it's a book that trainers try to get new owners to read before problems occur.

————. *Second-Hand Dog: How to Turn Yours into a First-Rate Pet.* 1988. Howell Book House.

If you've adopted a dog from a shelter, this is the book for you. Included is the excellent "Alpha Primer" that has similarities to the Radical Regimen detailed in this text. Again, as in all Ms. Benjamin's writings, the emphasis is on the dog/owner relationship and the quality of leadership in that bond.

Campbell, William E. *Behavior Problems in Dogs.* 1975. American Veterinary Publications, Drawer KK, Santa Barbara, Calif. 93102.

The chapter "Problem Owners and Characteristics" is classic—and completely turns the tables around from the "blame-the-dog" approach found in many books. Get ready: Hardly anyone escapes criticism. But you'll love Campbell's breezy style and valuable tips. The book is a must-read for professionals who, in any capacity, must deal with problem dogs or problem owners. A companion volume, *Owner's Guide to Better Behavior in Dogs and Cats,* appeared in 1986 and is geared to the lay person. This is a pioneering, essential author.

Evans, Job Michael. *How to Be Your Dog's Best Friend* (with the Monks of New Skete). 1978. Little, Brown & Co., 34 Beacon St., Boston, Mass. 03410.

————. *The Evans Guide for Counseling Dog Owners.* 1985. Howell Book House, 866 Third Ave., New York, N.Y. 10022.

————. *The Evans Guide for Housetraining Your Dog.* 1987. Howell Book House.

————. *The Evans Guide for Civilized City Canines.* 1988. Howell Book House.

Since these books have been alluded to in the text, I'll simply say if you are a first-time owner you'll love what I always refer to as "the Monks' book" (although I wrote forty of the forty-four chapters). If you have a dog that has fallen off the housetraining wagon, read the housetraining guide—pronto! If you live in a town with more than one stoplight, *Civilized City Canines* will be of great help, and if you must talk to dog owners in any capacity—veterinarian, breeder, trainer or concerned friend—*Counseling Dog Owners* is the guide for you.

Hart, Benjamin L, and Lynette A. Hart. *Canine and Feline Behavioral Therapy.* 1985. Lea & Febiger, 600 Washington Sq., Philadelphia, Pa. 19106.

This academic guide is long on observation and short on specific, workable tips to aid the owner of a problem dog—and some of the protocols would try the patience of a saint—but it is, nevertheless, worth a look-see, especially for professionals.

Holmes, John. *The Family Dog.* 1957. Popular Dogs, 17-21 Conway St., London, W1P6JD.

I have always admired the way the English write about dogs. Invariably UK authors are blunt, strict about "proper" behavior in dogs, yet loving and caring. There is a good section here on various problems, including one Holmes simply calls "pestering." This means, of course, the dog that bothers its owner by constantly wanting to play ball, catch a stick, get a treat or just get praised for looking cute. Holmes doesn't sympathize with this kind of canine pest. "Any tendency to develop a 'thing' about anything should be discouraged in the dog or corrected before it becomes established." Bravo!

Milani, Myrna M., DVM. *The Invisible Leash.* 1985. New American Library, 1633 Broadway, New York, N.Y. 10019.

Dr. Milani has a six-step procedure for sizing up and solving many problems. First, recognize that probably the "bad" behavior is normal, then define the problem, list all possible solutions, collect information, select the best solutions and then evaluate the results. Sound too neat? Give this book a good examination and together with the understanding you'll gain, you'll feel a calm—your dog isn't out to "get you" after all.

———. *The Weekend Dog.* 1984. Rawson Associates, 866 Third Ave., New York, N.Y. 10022.

Have a dog you see only nights and weekends? Don't hang your head in shame—such an arrangement *can* work—but some problems are bound to crop up. They are all covered here, including separation anxiety, housetraining, nutrition, even a chapter on "Sex and the Weekend Dog." That should peak your interest. An excellent book.

Quakenbush, Jamie, MSW. *When Your Pet Dies: How to Cope with Your Feelings.* 1985. Simon & Schuster, 1230 Avenue of the Americas, New York, N.Y. 10020.

Is the death of a dog not the ultimate "pooch problem"? Truly it is, but there is no conceivable set-up that can be concocted to avoid it. Here, in a moving text, is a guide to acceptance of the event, or even the eventuality. A section entitled "In Spite of It All, We Miss Him Terribly" details the emotions surrounding the death of a biting dog—by owner decision, and may be of help to those facing this difficult juncture.

Siegal, Mordecai, with Matthew Margolis. *When Good Dogs Do Bad Things.* 1986. Little, Brown & Co., 34 Beacon St., Boston, Mass. 03410.

There is a directory of problems in this book that is as exhaustive as any in print, and a variety of solutions and steps that will aid you in setting up set-ups. It's well written, concise and has an appealing format.

Smith, Dr. M. L. *Eliminate on Command.* 1984. Masterworks, Inc., P.O. Box 901, Friday Harbor, Wash. 98250.

The no-frills title means exactly what it says—you can convince your dog to defecate or urinate practically on a dime. Who would want such a service? Try millions of city dog owners who must stand shivering waiting and waiting for their pooch to answer the call, or for that matter anyone who wants to speed up this process to enjoy more quality time with their dog—and that includes all of us.

Tucker, Michael. *Solving Your Dog Problems.* 1987. Howell Book House, 866 Third Ave., New York, N.Y. 10022.

While this book resorts to the old ploy of labeling dogs instead of owners ("The Clever Dog," "The Difficult Dog"), it contains solid tips for better behavior and should be examined. Aggression, car chasing, chewing and show-ring problems (which are often disregarded in other books) are covered.

Veterinary Clinics of North America. Small Animal Practice series: *Animal Behavior* (November 1982) and *The Human-Companion Animal Bond* (March 1985). W. B. Saunders, W. Washington Sq., Philadelphia, Pa. 19105.

These two somewhat technical volumes will be of interest to specialists and trainers and cover various behavior problems, mostly from an academic perspective. Authors like Drs. Borchelt, Voith, Hart, Houpt, Tuber and Wolski are represented in the volume on behavior. Articles by Drs. Bustad, McCulloch, Marder and Beck are offered in the human/animal bond issue. These are important names in the academic area of behavior studies and professionals especially will find much of interest here.

Volhard, Joachim, and Gail Tamases Fisher. *Training Your Dog: The Step-by-Step Manual.* 1983. Howell Book House, 866 Third Ave., New York, N.Y. 10022.

While this excellent training book concentrates on the nuts and bolts of training the traditional exercises, it does address behavior problems in one top-notch chapter. Professionals will also be interested in a companion volume, *Teaching Dog Obedience Classes*, for which I wrote the foreword (also Howell Book House).

Finally, two older books I came across at the AKC library, which is an invaluable resource to all interested in canine behavior and is located at 51 Madison Ave., New York, N.Y. 10010, 20th Fl., phone (212)696-8245. These two gems, while full of misinformation, can be read to get an overview of how techniques have changed over the years and how ethics, cultural influences and even sexism have affected dog training and problem solving.

Woodhouse, Barbara. *Difficult Dogs.* 1950. Faber & Faber Ltd., 24 Russell Sq., London, WC1.

While the late Ms. Woodhouse was controversial within the dog training community, she *could* write, and in a charming, if somewhat bratty, style. While many of the actual training techniques are old school, her view of owners is accurate. "I would very much like to hear what some dogs think of their owners," she declares. "I have a horrid suspicion it would not be too complimentary." Meanwhile, with a few exceptions, modern-day dog writing avoids criticizing dog owners—after all, they might get psychologically depressed. Woodhouse never gave a whit about that. By the way, English dog writers adore the adjective "horrid."

Badcock, Lt. Col. G. H. *Disobedient Dogs, and Other Matters.* 1933. Herbert Jenkins Ltd., 3 York St., London, SW1.

Another English author, Lieutenant Badcock is full of opinions, some of which have merit, but many of which truly betray the "state of the art" at that time. On Terriers: "Of all the mischievous varmints, except perhaps a Labrador puppy, Terriers of all breeds are the worst. I think one of the troubles of dogs in after years of being such nuisances to other people is the fact that their owners allowed them to run riot too long." So much for Terriers! But wait, Badcock has opinions on *people,* too. Lady Kitty Ritson, who wrote the foreword, warns us that "Col. Badcock has little opinion of the female 'handler.' I am convinced he wrote this book with the 'females of the species' in mind. I can hardly blame him. The average woman is a terror with dogs, for either she shouts at them (generally eliciting no response) or she nags them . . . a disobedient dog is a horrid dog, and dogs are never horrid of their own free will, it is some human who has made them so." I would have loved to be a fly on the wall during a blind date between Ms. Woodhouse and Lieutenant Badcock! But I doubt any such event ever occurred.

Most of all, enjoy your reading!

Index

239

240

Introduction

A CAREGIVER'S STORY

In hindsight, the symptoms of Alzheimer's disease began for Dad much earlier than any of us were willing to admit. My first reactions were complete and total denial.

One day Mom called frantically to say Dad had gone out in the car to run errands, and still hadn't come home. Sure enough, he was lost and was trying to find his way home all day.

Slowly, I watched my dad get worse. The words seemed to slip away. He could not put together a full sentence. He could not button his shirt. He couldn't work the remote control and he started to talk about going "home" when he was already there with my mom.

I knew something was wrong, but I couldn't bear to think that my dad could have Alzheimer's disease.

This was when I became sad and angry. I often woke up in the middle of the night, crying. I cried in the shower. I cried every time I left his apartment. I missed him. I wanted to be able to talk to him and have him understand. I had many things going on in my life, which he would have been so excited about. I felt it was so unfair. This man did not deserve Alzheimer's disease. Does anyone?

One morning, as I lay in bed crying, it hit me. If he knew that people were caring for him, he would hate it. But no one deserved to be taken care of more. Maybe this was God's way of paying my father back for all the good he had done in his lifetime. I suddenly felt so much better. I realized that this was our chance. I knew that from here on in, it wasn't about being sad for my loss. It was going to be about providing him with the best care and the most dignity possible. It was going to be about taking care of Dad in the same loving way that he had taken care of so many people during his lifetime.

Jackie M., Highland Park, Ill.

When a person you know or love gets Alzheimer's disease or other dementias, everything changes. Devastating is the day when your most intimate friend or lifemate no longer recognizes you. Heart-breaking is the first time your well-educated and successful father can no longer remember how to brush his teeth. Frightening is the call from the corner grocery that Mom is there and can't find her way home.

As a caregiver, you will likely struggle to understand the full impact of dementia; it's easy to become overwhelmed.

Despite years of research and a worldwide effort, there is still no cure for these diseases. Meanwhile, someone is being diagnosed every seven seconds, according to the Alzheimer's Association.

People generally want to stay in their home for as long as possible and people with dementia feel the same way. Their family caregivers also often desire to have them at home.

This guide has been designed as a quick and easy resource to help give you – the family caregiver – the confidence and skills you need to care for a parent, spouse, extended family member or friend with dementia at home.

OVERVIEW OF DEMENTIA

Dementia is a group of illnesses that affect memory and the ability to recall information. Dementia also leads to confusion, which affects personality and social behavior. Dementia can impact judgment, thinking, behavior, language and the ability to perform everyday tasks. There are many types of dementia, but the most common is Alzheimer's disease.

Dementia impacts all five senses. The diseases can affect field of vision and depth perception. What's more, the impact of aging already may be taking a toll on those areas. The abilities to see and understand are at the core of dementia, so when hearing loss is also present the person's condition is further challenged. The inability to see or hear adequately denies or distorts the processing of information by the already challenged brain.

The causes of dementia are not fully understood; however, most experts agree there are likely many factors at work. The greatest risk factor for dementia is growing older, but a progressive dementia, such as Alzheimer's disease, is NOT a normal part of aging. Other risk factors may include family history, cardiovascular disease and a history of head trauma or concussions.

Some researchers think lifestyle could matter as much as family history. All of us may be able to lower the odds of developing a dementia or delaying its onset by exercising, eating well, staying socially active and embracing life-long learning. In other words, using our brains!

STAGES OF DEMENTIA

Most experts agree that dementia does progress in stages, but symptoms will vary greatly from person to person. Not everyone will experience the same symptoms or progress at the same rate.

People in the early stages of dementia are still functioning well and require minimal assistance and cues. They may have memory lapses and forget familiar words or become confused in familiar places. In the early stages, they may have trouble handling money and bills, and experience mood or personality changes.

Symptoms in the middle stages become more pronounced and challenging for the family to handle. There is also an increase in memory loss and confusion. The person may have trouble recognizing family and friends, repeat stories, and have difficulty carrying out tasks that have multiple steps.

The late stage of dementia is when full-time care is typically needed. This can be the most difficult stage for the family caregiver. The person with dementia may have lost the ability to recognize herself or her family, can no longer communicate and needs total assistance with personal care.

To ensure proper diagnosis, it's important to seek assistance from a medical professional. A complete work-up can rule out treatable diseases, inform you about medications that could help a family member, and give you a better understanding of the disease. The earlier you acknowledge the symptoms, make a game plan and get help, the better.

SYMPTOMS OF ALZHEIMER'S DISEASE AND DEMENTIA

According to the Alzheimer's Association, the most common symptoms of Alzheimer's disease include:

- Memory loss that disrupts daily life
- Difficulty completing familiar tasks
- Challenges with planning and problem-solving
- Confusion with time and place
- Trouble understanding visual images and spatial relationships
- Misplacing things and losing the ability to retrace steps
- Decreased or poor judgment
- Withdrawal from work or social activities
- Changes in mood or personality
- Problems with speaking and writing

If you've ever had a migraine headache, you know that it's not the disorder itself that causes havoc – it's the symptoms you have to live through that disrupt your day or night. People with migraines commonly experience blurred vision and strange smells, and/or have extreme pain and nausea. Similarly, it's the symptoms of dementia that create such an emotionally, physically and financially stressful experience for families. It can be helpful to think about **two categories** of symptoms: **memory** and **behavior** symptoms.

Confusion is an example of a **memory** or cognitive symptom. If a person becomes confused about the day of the week, that may cause frustration for the one with dementia, but would result in no harm. However, if the confusion is causing that individual to forget to pay bills, it can result in serious issues or even make your family member vulnerable to scams.

An example of a **behavior** symptom is wandering. Wandering away from home can have an unfortunate outcome. Some behavioral symptoms may put the safety of the person or others at risk, while others symptoms can be frustrating and difficult.

The following chart provides a general ranking of these behaviors in terms of frustration, difficulty and danger.

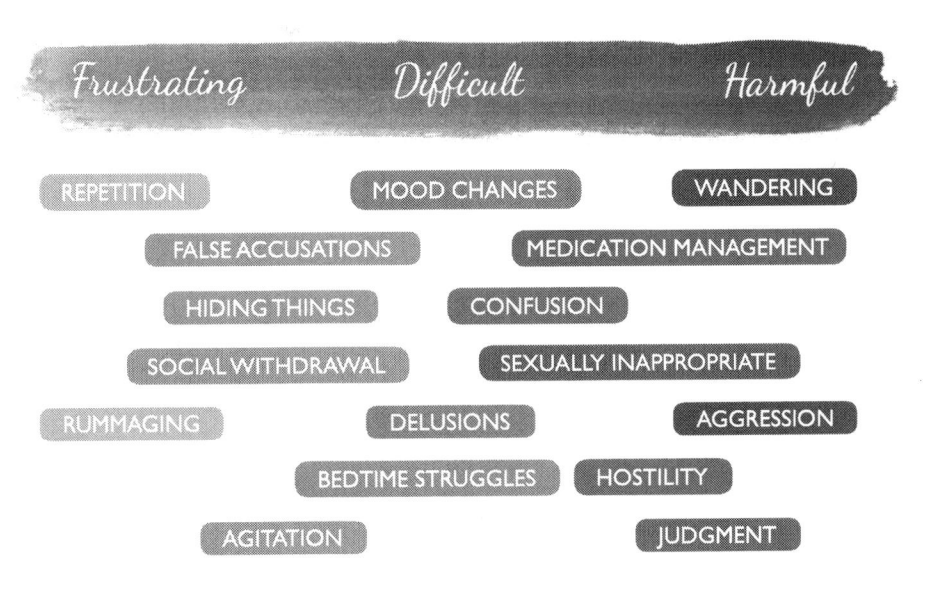

Frustrating — Difficult — Harmful

- REPETITION
- MOOD CHANGES
- WANDERING
- FALSE ACCUSATIONS
- MEDICATION MANAGEMENT
- HIDING THINGS
- CONFUSION
- SOCIAL WITHDRAWAL
- SEXUALLY INAPPROPRIATE
- RUMMAGING
- DELUSIONS
- AGGRESSION
- BEDTIME STRUGGLES
- HOSTILITY
- AGITATION
- JUDGMENT

This book will focus on both **memory** and **behavior** symptoms that family caregivers often need help with, including common personal care activities. Each of these chapters will offer plenty of care approaches and prevention tips, and begin with a relevant and moving real-life family caregiver story. The chapters are as follows:

- Aggression and Anger
- Agitation and Anxiety
- Bedtime Struggles and Sleep Problems
- Confusion and Memory Loss
- Delusions
- False Accusations and Paranoia
- Hiding/Misplacing Things/Rummaging
- Hostility
- Judgment (problems with decision-making and problem-solving)
- Medication Mismanagement
- Mood Changes
- Repetition
- Sexually Inappropriate Behavior
- Social Withdrawal
- Wandering

In general, behaviors usually arise when a person has an unmet need. Because language is often affected by dementia, people with this disease may "tell" you about their needs or issues by "showing" you. By acting in a certain way, they may be trying to communicate what they want or need. By "listening to what they do," it's possible to understand and manage that unmet need.

Quick Check: Are they...?

If your family member exhibits any behavioral symptoms, using the list below may provide clues for you to offer effective support.

EMOTIONAL
Bored
Sad
Tired
Embarrassed
Affectionate
Feeling Supported
Stressed
Afraid
Frustrated
Valued
Lacking Trust
Feeling Unsafe

SOCIAL
Unable to Talk
Feeling Left Out
Lacking Relationships
Accepting of Changes
Isolated
Lonely

PHYSICAL
Hot or Cold
Wearing Restricting Clothing
In Pain
Hungry
Thirsty
Sheltered

ENVIRONMENTAL
In a Noisy Room
In a Crowded Area
In New or Different Surroundings
Living with Clutter
Over-Stimulated
Living with Poor Lighting
Introduced to Strangers

APPROACHING CARE AT HOME

With dementia affecting the core cognitive functions of a person, providing care will not always be easy. One of the most crucial things to understand is that as a caregiver, you will have to make changes to maintain the person's quality of life, as well as your own.

Being present in their world, validating and reassuring the person, and serving and supporting are ways to ease the care situation. For example, when the person with dementia is talking about her mother, who is deceased, your role is to validate her feelings rather than bring her back to "reality" about her mother. By being in their moment, you will have a better opportunity for successful caregiving.

This may require you to tell a "therapeutic lie" or go along with the person in his or her confusion to avoid upsetting the situation. For example, if you are trying to get Dad to bathe and you know he used to be in the Army, you may encourage him to get into the shower because the "colonel is coming by for an inspection in 30 minutes." By using this technique to smooth over a brief moment of confusion, you are helping long term. The result of poor hygiene would have negative effects on several areas of Dad's life, so convincing him to bathe is of the utmost importance.

It is also important to understand your family member's life story to help you with the caregiving experience. This allows you to personalize the care you give and engage that individual in a meaningful life. Knowing the person's life story also will help you with behavioral symptoms.

Putting the person and his or her needs at the center of the caregiving experience is the key to this approach. When you try to provide care on your schedule or by your method, this may not always coincide with the person receiving care, which leads to frustration for both the individual and caregiver. With the uncertainty of this disease, flexibility will be important.

You may already know a lot about your family member or close friend and just need to refresh your memory. Or, if it's an extended family member for whom you are caring, you may need to go on a fact-finding mission. Simple steps to take include:

*   Asking the person questions
*   Observing their surroundings, including knowing their routines
*   Asking family members and friends questions

Recording this information is important so that you can review and refer back as needed. A journal, a notebook or your computer will suffice to keep the information.

Some common themes when gathering data include:

*   Likes, Preferences and Routines
*   Family
*   Childhood
*   Growing Up and Culture
*   Adult Life
*   Big Events

Your family member's "likes" along with his or her routines are important to honor as you provide care. Remembering if they prefer a bath rather than a shower can make this a smoother task. Or recalling that the person has a cup of tea every night before bed can make the bedtime ritual relaxed and less stressful.

Narrow down a short list of that person's life experiences, so if any agitation occurs, you can quickly turn to these themes for a possible solution.

TECHNIQUES

Here are the essential techniques to help you manage care at home.

REDIRECT

Redirect means "changing directions." Changing the topic or mood from bad to good and creating a more positive and safe result are the objectives.

For instance, if your family member asks or says the same thing over and over, such as, "What time is it?" or "I want to go home," you could use their personal information and redirect to a favorite subject or activity. The redirect technique is effective in managing many situations.

APOLOGIZE AND TAKE THE BLAME

Apologizing or taking the blame takes the attention off the person. The individual may calm down if he or she believes a situation was not their fault. Even when it isn't your fault, an apology sometimes solves the problem and allows you to regroup and move on to a more positive situation. It is often best to offer a simple apology, "I'm sorry I misunderstood you."

PHYSICALLY REMOVE THE PERSON OR CHANGE THE ENVIRONMENT

People can become agitated, upset or overly focused on something in their environment. For example, they may become upset because there are too many clothes in the closet or want to use potentially dangerous power tools in the garage simply because they are in plain sight. Move distracting, disturbing or potentially harmful things out of the way and simplify the environment where possible.

GIVE SIMPLE CHOICES

Offering simple choices helps the person feel in control. Someone with dementia may feel he or she has no control over life. If the person refuses to do something and becomes angry, offering simple choices

may help calm him or her and restore control. Asking, for example, "Would you like eggs or cereal for breakfast?" may work better than merely setting down a bowl of corn flakes.

ENGAGE IN MEANINGFUL ACTIVITIES

Research supports the importance of meaningful activities. Mental, physical and social activities can create positive emotional responses that diminish stress and anxiety for the person with dementia. Participating in activities helps the person feel a sense of purpose and accomplishment, even if it is as simple as answering a trivia question or making a successful trip to the grocery store.

You may have to try various approaches and use these techniques multiple times. When you use one technique and do not have success, try it again in a few minutes using a different approach.

Do not get discouraged. This quick and easy resource includes guidance on supportive approaches, proven techniques, and plenty of tips and strategies from experts and family caregivers like you. Within the following chapters, you will find specifics on how to react, and tips to try as you respond and communicate.

You won't have to read this guide from cover-to-cover to get what you need. Rather, go to the section that features information about the situation you're dealing with on a given day, and you'll find workable solutions to help make your life easier.

Before we delve into the alphabetized chapters of the most common issues that family caregivers face when caring for someone with dementia, we want to address the day-to-day personal care activities that could be becoming more difficult.

Personal Care Activities

Personal care activities are tasks that most of us take for granted, but ones that can be particularly difficult when a person has dementia. When your family member needs assistance with these types of activities, it also conveys the message that they are no longer able to care for themselves.

This loss of independence can be very difficult to accept for both you and your family member. Personal care can be a complicated task for the person living with dementia because there are numerous steps and choices. The tasks of bathing, dressing, eating and using the bathroom involve motor skills, adequate vision, sequencing, memory recall and decision-making.

At any support group or family meeting, one of the most talked about subjects is **bathing**. Those with dementia often resist bathing. Families may struggle to get a shower or bath accomplished and keep the person with dementia clean. Oftentimes Mom won't remember why she should be bathing, may be modest or shy about disrobing, have some discomfort or pain from arthritis, be afraid of falling or just simply resist.

Families often notice something is wrong with Mom and Dad when their appearance and **dressing** habits change. Mom, who had always been so neat and "put together," now is wearing the same stained blouse or has many layers of clothing on at one time. Dressing is a very personal and private activity for most of us. Many people have never dressed or undressed in front of another person and this can be an uncomfortable experience.

Eating and **drinking** habits may change with dementia. Some may want to eat all the time or not at all. A declining sense of smell may affect the person's ability to taste. Getting Mom or Dad to drink enough liquids to stay hydrated may be a difficult task as well. As the disease progresses, even swallowing could become a problem. In that case, be sure to consult your physician to get medical advice on how to

safely prepare food. Mom may still try to use the stove or prepare food on her own (which can become unsafe over time). Eventually she could lose the ability to fix her own meals. These changes make ensuring a family member has the proper nutrition as the disease progresses a growing challenge.

Incontinence could also affect a person with dementia. For example, he could forget to go, not recognize the toilet, urinate in an inappropriate place or have trouble unfastening his pants. There can be medical reasons for this, including urinary tract infections or side effects from medicines, but more often than not incontinence comes from the decline in memory and thinking.

BEING THE CAREGIVER

Having to care for a parent or family member in these personal ways can be difficult physically and emotionally. Take time to adjust so that you are comfortable in this new role. Some people never become fully comfortable and feel guilty when they cannot do it. Read on to gain a better understanding to determine if this is a role meant for you.

When helping a family member with dementia through personal care activities, effective communication is the key. Remain calm, supportive and confident, keep an even tone of voice and use non-threatening body language. Encourage independence by letting Dad do as much as he can by assisting from a distance.

Go slowly and move at Dad's pace. If you appear annoyed, this may cause him to feel ashamed, depressed, anxious and embarrassed. Always try to reassure Dad and let him know you will protect his privacy during these personal activities. For example, cover him with a blanket while undressing or close the door and blinds in his room.

Another way to help preserve Mom's dignity is to have a familiar person, preferably of the same sex, assist with these activities. The following **care approaches** will offer ideas on how to navigate your journey through personal care. Employ some creativity as you ease into this role.

CARE APPROACHES

ROUTINES AND PREFERENCES

- Set a regular time for bathing. Do things the same way and at the same time each day. Change routines only when they're not working.

- Try to maintain his personal style. If Dad wore khakis and a golf shirt every day, asking him to wear blue jeans and t-shirts may confuse him.

- Continue food traditions for as long as possible. For example, make Grandma's pasta sauce and ask her to help. If she is unable, have her sit near and watch, assisting if she can.

- Have a routine for taking Mom to the bathroom and stick to it as closely as possible. For example, take her to the bathroom every three hours or so during the day. Don't wait for Mom to ask. Say, "Mom, the bathroom is down the hall. Let's go."

MODIFY AND SIMPLIFY THE TASK

- If you can't convince Dad to take a shower or a bath, try getting by with a sponge bath. Consider alternatives such as no-rinse bathing wipes and dry shampoo.

- Try breaking the task into simple, manageable steps and doing them one at a time. For example, "Step into the shower now." "Let's get your hair wet." "Put some soap in your hand." "Rub it on your hair." Reassure Mom each time she completes a step.

- If you need to cut Dad's food for him, do it out of his sight line to help preserve his dignity.

- Keep the table setting simple and avoid patterned dishes, placemats and tablecloths. Patterns can be confusing as vision worsens, or distracting when you need Mom to eat.

- Consider serving just one dish or food at a time. For example, if you're having soup and sandwiches, serve the soup first and then the sandwich. Limit the number of utensils and serve small portions.

- Go with clothing and shoes that are easy to slip on, such as those with Velcro fasteners. Select fabrics that don't require ironing.

USE CONTRAST

- Look to create contrast on the dinner plate. Mom may not be able to see turkey, potatoes and cauliflower on a white plate. Consider a colored plate.

- Depending on the color of the bedspread, if you lay out clothes they may blend in. Either lay out a white sheet over the bedspread or hang clothes against a contrasting background.

SIMPLE CHOICES

- Give Mom choices. Ask, "Would you like to take a bath or a shower?" or "Do you want a bath now or after breakfast?"

- Offer a choice between a white shirt and a blue shirt.

- Ask, "Would you like to go out for lunch today, Dad, or stay in for leftovers?"

BE DESCRIPTIVE AND GIVE CUES

- Make sure to explain the task to Mom before beginning to help reduce confusion. For instance, "Mom, first I will blow dry your hair on low heat. Then we will pull it back in your favorite barrette."

- Continue to give details of the task while it's happening, using short, simple, but descriptive words. "Grandpa, take your comb and run it through your hair."

- If Dad doesn't recognize what he is eating, describe each item on his plate.

- Use familiar and respectful words to describe objects and actions. For example, refer to incontinence products as briefs rather than diapers.

- Cueing or reminding may help the person get dressed independently. "Dad, it's almost time for church. Shall we start to get dressed?" Or say, "Mom, I need to go to the bathroom. Do you need to go as well?"

- Lay out articles of clothing in sequence on the bed. They should be arranged in the order that they are meant to be put on.

- Use helpful language. For example, "Dinner is in a few minutes. Will you help me set the table?"

- Tap into Mom's life story to plan activities that would cue her to want to shower and change clothes. For example, getting dirt on her pants after gardening may help convince her to shower and put on clean clothes.

CREATE PLEASANT DIVERSIONS AND REWARDS

- Start the bath time with something Mom enjoys, such as having her back scrubbed. She then may allow you to assist with other areas.

- Create a spa-like atmosphere at bath time. Buy Mom's favorite lavender soaps and lotions to help create a pleasing experience.

- Setting the mood in advance will make for a more pleasant experience for you and your family member. Try soothing music.

- Offering a reward may help convince her to get in the shower. "After you shower, Mom, we will go to the park to feed the ducks." Or "Mom, once you finish eating dinner, let's go for an ice cream cone."

- Offer praise when a task has been completed successfully. That helps build self-esteem. For example, "Grandma, you look great today. Wonderful job picking out that beautiful sweater."

THREE TIMES, THREE WAYS

- If you're having trouble convincing your spouse to take a shower, first say, "Honey, it's time for a shower." If he resists, try a second time and say, "If you shower now, you'll be done just in time to read the morning paper." Finally, if he continues to resist, schedule an event. Say, "Sweetheart, church is today. Remember, you always like to shower before church."

- If Mom doesn't want to eat lunch, first say, "Mom, breakfast was four hours ago. Is your tummy growling?" Next, try, "Mom, you didn't eat much at breakfast, so let's have lunch. You need a good meal so you have energy for our walk later." A third try could be, "Mom, we are having your favorite chicken salad sandwiches for lunch. Come and eat."

MODEL

- If Mom is unsure what to do with her utensils, show her by picking up your spoon to eat the pudding. If that doesn't work, put the spoon in her hand and guide her hand to her mouth.

- Instead of brushing the crumbs off Grandpa's shirt, pretend you're brushing crumbs off your shirt, hoping he will follow your lead.

- If Mom is not drinking enough liquids, try enticing her by saying, "Gee, I'm thirsty, Mom. Lemonade sounds good." Or, "My mouth is sure dry. I could use some lemonade."

- If you are assisting with tooth brushing, ask Dad to stand in front of a mirror while you help from behind, so he can still see what he's doing.

APOLOGIZE, TAKE THE BLAME

- If Dad becomes frustrated during dinner because he can't chew his food, apologize and take the blame. "I'm sorry that I served you this tough piece of meat, Dad. I should have cooked it better."

- To ease embarrassment of an accident, blame it on an external factor. For example, "Mom, I am sorry about your accident. Next time I will buy pants with fewer buttons."

PREVENTION

Flexibility and the opportunity to adapt are the "name of the game" when caring for a family member with dementia. Planning for success as well as looking ahead could help you avoid frustration and save time. Writing down observations about a family member's daily routine may help you identify triggers that could lead to fewer accidents and frustrations. By trying these ideas below, you can learn to be proactive with your approaches to care.

PLAN AHEAD

- When it's bath time, gather all supplies including soft towels, scented soaps and shampoo. Baby shampoo, which won't sting Mom's eyes, is a good option. Remove clutter and make sure the path to the bathroom is clear. Lay out everything you need – towels, washcloths, soap, shampoo, fresh clothes – and then just gently lead Mom to the shower and walk her through the process, assisting when needed.

- Make sure the bath or shower water is not too hot or too cold. Pay attention to the temperature in the room as well to ensure that Mom is comfortable.

- Leave the bathroom door open and the toilet cover up when not in use so it is obvious that the toilet is vacant.

- At mealtimes, use a plastic tablecloth or placemats for easier clean-up. Ask Mom to wear an apron to protect her clothing.

- Include finger foods on your daily menu such as small sandwiches, and sliced fruits and vegetables.

- If Dad is incontinent, safeguard mattresses and furniture with protective covers. This will help with clean-up.

- Try replacing underwear in his drawers with disposable briefs.

- When preparing for an outing with Grandpa, know in advance where the restrooms are located. Have him wear simple, easy-to-remove clothing and take along an extra set in case of an accident.

- Group Mom's clothes into outfits. When she can grab one hanger with pants and a shirt, she will feel confident in her selection.

KEEP A JOURNAL

- Watch for any signs that Dad may need to go to the bathroom, such as fidgeting, restlessness, hiding behind furniture or pulling at his clothes.

- Understanding when, where and why accidents happen can help you avoid them. Writing down these triggers could also help.

- Journal possible irritants for Mom such as coffee, alcohol, some citrus and fizzy drinks.

- Notice and record changes in Grandma's appetite. Keep a food dairy, including spices and other details of items that could irritate Mom's digestion.

- Observe the time of day when your spouse has the most energy and schedule the more complicated tasks, such as bathing, at that time.

ADAPT

- A shower chair can help if Mom's mobility is limited and she has trouble standing. Add grab bars in the shower.

- For some people, buttons, snaps, hooks, zippers and belt buckles are too difficult to manage. Try replacing with Velcro fasteners – they're easier for you and Dad.

- Slip-on shoes can help Dad continue to complete this task on his own. Make sure shoes have non-skid soles.

- Select clothing that is washable and doesn't need ironing.

- Mom may lose her taste for what she once loved, or develop other food preferences. Have a variety of healthy snacks and other options on hand for her.

- Adapt tableware. Use a bowl, for instance, instead of a plate to make eating easier. Cups with lids and straws will help ensure fewer spills.

THINK CREATIVELY

- Ask for Mom's help trying out a new soap or lotion.

- If you're struggling to convince Dad to get dressed, present him with a gift. Wrap up new or even existing clothing. When he opens the present, ask him to try it on to see if it fits.

- If your spouse is wearing the same outfit day after day, know that it is not uncommon. Rather than trying to reason with him to change, it's often better to buy a few of the same outfits so you can have some of his favorite ensembles clean and ready to go at all times.

- If Grandma is having trouble with her bowels and digestion, offer her fiber-rich foods such as apples or green vegetables.

- If Dad isn't eating, turn mealtime into an event. For example, plan a family dinner gathering just because it's Flag Day!

- If Mom has lost the ability to use closets and drawers, hang clean clothes on doorknobs, scatter clean socks and underwear around the room, and keep shoes in plain sight.

DOCTOR'S ORDERS

- Routine dental checkups and daily oral health care to keep the mouth and teeth healthy will be important. Make sure dentures fit properly.

- Regular vision tests and having his glasses checked will help keep Dad independent longer.

- Talk with her doctors. A physician can advise about the best ways to get adequate nutrition, including when to use supplements like protein shakes. In addition, there are a number of medications on the market for urinary incontinence.

Memory and Behavior Symptoms of Dementia

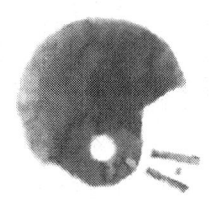

AGGRESSION AND ANGER

Even at the very end, Daddy always tried to make other people laugh and smile. But Dad really became aggressive when you pushed him to do something he didn't want to do: mainly with personal hygiene things. Taking over his bathing and incontinence needs was an invasion on his natural dignity and robbed what little independence he still had.

That last year, it got to be more and more difficult to change his clothing, or to shave or bathe him. His caregivers started giving him bed baths because he'd become so combative in the shower.

We would encourage him to eat and take him for walks (in his wheelchair). I would sing to him as a method to decrease his combativeness during personal hygiene care. He loved the Redskins, so I would sing the Redskins fight song and get him to make eye contact with me and sing along. His participatory singing allowed him to focus on something he loved and could still perform at some level. Advanced dementia made it difficult for him to concentrate on more than one thing concurrently, so the music was a perfect diversionary tactic. For Daddy, music could really soothe his soul.

— Liza H., Richmond, Va.

WHY DOES THIS HAPPEN?

There's nothing more difficult or unsettling than seeing a parent become angry or aggressive when you're trying to help. Aggression is a verbal or physical lashing out toward another person.

People with dementia may become angry for a variety of reasons. A person with this disease who becomes angry has many frustrations because of things that were once easy he can no longer do. Because Dad's brain isn't functioning normally, the one way he can communicate his wishes is through aggression. The clear message from Dad: "Stop what you are doing!"

For example, if you start to undress him in preparation for a bath or to clean him – as Liza found – and he doesn't understand your intent, or has a fear of bathing, he is going to try to stop you with his words and sometimes with actions.

Your approach is important in restoring calm. So are certain strategies and techniques, such as the ones Liza used. You may feel afraid, threatened or shocked by the aggression, but you can gain confidence and success with changes to your approach.

(Emotional • Social • Physical • Environmental)

Does the person have an unmet need that is causing the memory or behavioral symptom?

CARE APPROACHES

* When Mom or Dad is angry, arguing with them may escalate the situation. Validate their feelings and try to gain understanding so you can restore order.

- Give Dad what he wants as long as it's not dangerous. Apologize and take the blame even to help defuse the situation.

- Stay calm. Because you had good intentions, you may feel afraid or shocked by the aggression, but try not to express this through your body language. Let your face show genuine concern.

- Try to keep your voice tone even and polite. Grandpa is still an adult and if you try to boss him, this could be insulting.

- Check your body posture. Keep your hands at your sides or, if seated, in your lap. Stand or sit at the same level as Dad so that your relationship is equal. If you have backed off, wait for an invitation to approach.

- Slow down! Mom may need time to adjust to your physical presence in the room, and if you are rushed, she will become more confused.

- Make sure Mom sees or hears you before you touch her, so trying rattling some papers or softly clear your throat. Make eye contact with Mom. An unexpected approach and touch could be very upsetting to her.

- Greet her by name and perhaps talk about the weather or the picture on her wall.

- Step back out of harm's way (even leave the room for a few minutes if necessary) and take a few deep breaths. Sometimes simply letting things cool down works wonders.

- Be sensitive to privacy. The person with dementia may be uncomfortable during care tasks like bathing, dressing and toileting. Always have a towel, or clothing within reach to offer your family member. Or even consider looking away to help them feel more comfortable.

- Create moments of pleasure before beginning a task. Your spouse might be much more willing to get dressed in the morning after a refreshing cup of coffee or tea and a muffin.

- When it's time to help Mom dress, realize she may not see a need for changing her clothes. Appeal to her vanity and give her a reason, like telling her she will want to look nice for her visitors.

- Sometimes "bribery" works. For instance, after a bath promise a cup of cocoa or a snack.

- Give simple choices. Instead of asking Dad to wear a clean shirt, give him the choice between the blue shirt or the yellow shirt.

- If there are several people in the kitchen, for example, have the caregiver Mom trusts most stay with her. Ask all others to withdraw.

- Remove valuable and breakable objects. You wouldn't want a family heirloom to become broken or damaged.

- Once a person who is upset begins to calm down, refer to their life story to redirect to a more enjoyable activity such as:

  - A walk

  - Soothing music

  - Painting a picture

  - Watching a video

  - A useful job such as washing dishes or potting a plant

  - Mixing, measuring and pouring ingredients for a favorite recipe

STARTING THE CONVERSATION

When communicating with a person who is angry, tone of voice, volume, pace and inflection are crucial for the conversation as well as speaking with confidence and using supportive language. When you offer simple choices or take the blame, you are validating feelings and reassuring the individual with dementia.

"I'm here for you, Dad. We will get through this together. The nice, hot shower will be over before you know it."

"Dad, I know you're frustrated that you can't remember the date today. This must be hard for you."

"I am sorry that I upset you," or "I didn't mean to upset you; I was just trying to help."

"Hey, I've gotten pretty good at making the bed. Let me help you out."

"I can see you are uncomfortable in that sweater. Let me get you a different one."

"Do you want to brush your teeth first or wash your face?"

"Mom, once you are done in the bathroom, I will get you some hot tea before bed."

PREVENTION

Following are tips to consider to help prevent these actions from occurring again.

- **LEARN WHAT UPSETS YOUR DAD BY INVOLVING THE WHOLE FAMILY IF NECESSARY AND CREATE A JOURNAL.** It shouldn't take much detective work to discover when angry and aggressive actions occur. Understand when/where/why the angry episode occurred (for example, TV show, neighbor visiting, and reminder of something in the past) and avoid these situations in the future. Refer to this journal often and update as the disease progresses.

- **LOOK FOR WAYS TO SIMPLIFY TASKS.** People often become frustrated and then angry by being unable to complete simple tasks they used to do easily like buttoning a shirt or tying shoelaces. Substitute pull-on polo shirts with fewer buttons or a front fastening zipper and slip-on or Velcro fastening shoes.

AGITATION AND ANXIETY

Dad would get that look in his eyes: Nobody's home. His eyes would glaze over and he'd get more dazed and antsy. We didn't get it then, but having him deal with crowds was a trigger.

For example, we'd take him Christmas shopping, and he'd kick the racks. So we now avoid situations with large crowds. One time, we were all standing in the kitchen making dinner and he came in and acted like we were all in a huddle. Because Dad was a football coach in his younger days, he started calling out plays. By letting him go with his past memory, his mood began to lighten. Later that night, he just sat alone staring at the fire for hours, so calm. He seemed like he was having a nice, quiet time.

— Tessa S., Friendswood, Texas

WHY DOES THIS HAPPEN?

Dad's agitation and anxiety can upset the entire family. Anxiety is experiencing worry, uneasiness or nervousness, while agitation is the physical result of that anxiety. Dad may be restless, fidgety, unable to sleep well, unable to concentrate on tasks and may pace (walk to the point of exhaustion).

With Tessa's father, large crowds were the trigger to the anxiety and agitation. With others, it could be the seemingly smallest things, such as a book out of place.

When Tessa's family understood Dad's trigger, they knew how to respond. You can do the same when you understand what's causing agitation and anxiety with your family member.

(Emotional • Social • Physical • Environmental)

Does the person have an unmet need that is causing the memory or behavioral symptom?

CARE APPROACHES

* Anxiety often comes from an environment that is too stimulating or too boring. Try de-cluttering the counters or brightening the kitchen table with flowers from the garden.

* Frustration and agitation may come from noise or glare from TV or loud music. Learn Dad's trigger point and avoid it in the future.

* Create a calm space for Mom to go to when she is upset. Make sure she recognizes her favorite things in this place, such as a porch swing surrounded by the flowers she planted.

- Be aware of what's in Mom's line of vision. Sit in her favorite chair. Is the flickering TV screen, which changes at least every few seconds, upsetting her?

- Make sure Grandma has enough light for reading by her favorite chair. Low lighting could trigger agitation and anxiety.

- Create a change of scenery. Rather than serving your spouse lunch on a TV tray in the family room where he sits most of the day, serve lunch at the kitchen table.

- Try a gentle touch. Many love having their hands held, an arm stroked, or a back rubbed. Know what pleases Mom and provide it.

- Your loving voice can provide much comfort when your family member is agitated. Long after a person forgets your name, he or she will react to the familiar sound of your voice.

- Knowing Dad's preferences and routines can make a big difference. For example, if Dad prefers a bath rather than a shower, make sure to accommodate this to avoid upsetting him.

- Refocus the person's attention. If your spouse is anxious about an upcoming doctor's appointment that is hours or even days away, assure her that you will get there in time. For now, redirect her to an activity such as planting flowers or creating a painting. Food and drink can be great distractors, too.

- When Mom is anxious, try offering comfort from a beloved family pet or grandchildren. Look at a coffee table picture book.

- Fresh air and nature can have a positive impact. Go outdoors for a walk whenever possible, preferably in your favorite neighborhood garden or park.

- Everybody likes a good laugh. Show a funny YouTube video or read the comics in the Sunday paper to ease her agitation.

- Give Mom a chance to feel useful. Have her do simple tasks such as sweeping a walkway or folding towels or napkins.

- Providing something familiar can be calming. Some women may hang onto purses or spoons. Some men may like to jingle coins or keys in a pocket, or keep a newspaper under an arm.

- If your family member is pacing, ask if you could join in the walk. From there look for an opportunity to suggest you both sit down.

- If Mom gets easily flustered when faced with decisions, simplify her choices. Ask Mom if she would like to have oatmeal or toast for breakfast, two of her favorites.

- Be prepared. If Dad has low blood sugar and you are headed for a long doctor's appointment, be sure to take healthy snacks.

STARTING THE CONVERSATION

Your body language can have a big impact on the situation. If you're relaxed and calm, this will show in your face, posture and the tone of your voice. When you empathize with how your mother is feeling, she will calm down from the reassurance.

*"We'll get to the doctor's appointment in time, Mom.
How about a cup of tea first?"*

. . . .

*"I can see you're concerned about the pile of papers and
I am too. Let me clean that up."*

. . . .

*"I know you're missing your mother. Tell me your favorite
story about her."*

. . . .

*"President Eisenhower was a great man. What did you
like best about him?"*

. . . .

*"Mom, I know that summer is your favorite time of year.
Do you know tomorrow is the first day of summer? Let's make
a list of some fun things to do when it gets hot."*

. . . .

*"I can only imagine how hard this must be for you;
but I'm here, and I'll stick with you."*

. . . .

*"I am sorry that I upset you. Let's listen to some music
and try to take the bath later."*

. . . .

"Dad, would you like milk or cranberry juice with your dinner?"

PREVENTION

Following are tips to consider to help prevent these actions from occurring again.

- **WORK AS A FAMILY TO COME UP WITH SOLUTIONS.** For example, try visiting in pairs or at different times of the day to help minimize anxiety. Determine potential solutions together.

- **KEEP A FOOD DIARY.** Caffeine and sugar intake could be affecting Dad's agitation and anxiety.

- **PLAN AHEAD AND DON'T OVER-SCHEDULE.** Be sensitive to your spouse's most alert and most tired times of day and plan accordingly.

- **OBSERVE PATTERNS IN MOM'S BEHAVIOR.** For example, if Mom always cooked dinner at 5 p.m., engage her in mealtime activities at that time of day to help prevent agitation.

BEDTIME STRUGGLES AND SLEEP PROBLEMS

My dad would get up, he'd turn on the light and that would wake my mom up. She'd try to get him back to bed and then he'd say that he was hungry. That would go on for 20 or 30 minutes and then finally she'd get him back to bed and an hour later it would start all over again.

If he didn't turn on the light, she wouldn't wake up and he would wander out of the room. Then he wouldn't know where he was and he'd bellow for her. So she'd wake up with her heart pounding, wondering what had happened and where he was.

Mom was so embarrassed, she wouldn't tell us what was going on, but things got better when she reached out for help.

— Debbie O., Eugene, Ore.

WHY DOES THIS HAPPEN?

Nighttime can be challenging and even more so for caregivers like Debbie and her family. We all tend to wear out by the end of the day, but you may notice that Dad's symptoms can appear to worsen in the late afternoon and evenings. People with dementia might also confuse day and nighttime, causing sleep disturbances.

Be sure the person has been evaluated by a physician for the common causes of sleep disturbances that often come with age, such as sleep apnea, restless leg syndrome and side effects of medications.

Also, reflect on your family member's day. If he's not sleeping at night, it could be because he is sleeping all afternoon. Finding meaningful activities throughout the day can help prevent excessive napping.

Remember, when the person isn't sleeping, neither is the caregiver; none of us can continue to be successful caregivers without enough sleep. Be sure to reach out like Debbie's mother did, before exhaustion sets in.

(Emotional • Social • Physical • Environmental)

Does the person have an unmet need that is causing the memory or behavioral symptom?

CARE APPROACHES

- Try encouraging your family member to get up a little earlier each day. The longer he is awake and engaged, the more likely a sound night's sleep will result.

- Engage Mom in physical activities such as gardening, walking and helping with housework. Even light exercise or walking around the mall can help ensure Mom is comfortably tired at day's end.

- By providing adequate fluids to your family member, you decrease the risks of nighttime leg cramps and other discomforts.

- To avoid Dad feeling overstuffed and uncomfortable in the evening – which could keep him from a sound sleep – serve the last meal in the early evening and watch portion sizes.

- Tune into what Mom is reading and viewing. Limit the news, because stories about car accidents and bombings may cause a person with dementia to dream and even obsess about these terrible things.

- Understand Dad's sleep preferences and accommodate. If Dad always had a night light, keep one going in his room. If he doesn't like a lot of covers, make sure the room is warm.

- Check out things from Mom's point of view. Lie on the bed. Does a bright light shine in through the window all night? Does a mirror reflect light and cause shadows that could be alarming to her?

- Make sure the mattress is comfortable and the bedding is inviting. Does the mattress provide support without being too hard? Does your spouse have a favorite quilt, blanket or pillow?

- If bathing is what Mom always did at night, it's OK to modify this task with a simple wash-up of face and hands before bed. That's easier for everyone.

- Wind down at the end of the day with simple tasks such as rolling yarn or looking through a picture book of favorite things. Continue to re-direct the person to nighttime routines and activities.

- Build excitement for the next day. Keep a dry erase board in a place where your spouse can see it. Put the day and the date, and a list of what you will be doing, noting that a good night's rest will be needed.

- Make bedtime a pleasant experience. Offer a foot, hand or backrub. Tuck Mom in with a hug and a kiss.

- Provide a favorite soothing and familiar classical piece or a lullaby. Try adding night-time sounds such as crickets.

- Tell a favorite story from Mom's childhood or recite a popular family prayer.

- Install rope lighting on baseboards or small night lights from Dad's room to the bathroom to guide him. This may help ease confusion when Dad is looking for the bathroom in the middle of the night.

STARTING THE CONVERSATION

Comforting phrases can help set the mood for bedtime. You can help ease Mom's bedtime anxieties by planning ahead, cueing appropriate activities at the right times and providing comforting touches.

"Here's the bathroom, Mom. You head in and I'll wait for you."

If it's bedtime, say: "I'm really tired. You must be, too. Let's go to bed now."

"Why don't we dim the lights, turn down the TV and read a bit before bedtime."

"We did a lot of work in the garden today and need to get some rest."

"We're going out tomorrow to have coffee with your best friend, so we need to get to bed now."

"Why don't I rub this nice, warm lotion onto your hands, Dad. Then let's say a prayer."

"Would you like hot milk or herbal tea before bed?"

PREVENTION

Following are tips to consider to help prevent these actions from occurring again.

- **TRY TO DEVELOP A SLEEP SCHEDULE.** Sticking to the same bed time and getting up at the same time each day can help with sleep issues. Even schedule a 30-minute nap after lunch each day if necessary. This could help you and Dad.

- **UNDERSTAND YOUR SPOUSE'S MEDICATIONS AND THE POSSIBLE EFFECTS ON SLEEP.** Some medications can cause either drowsiness or excitability.

- **LIMIT CAFFEINE.** Determine if any of Mom's foods, such as chocolate, have caffeine. Offer coffee or chocolate earlier in the day to avoid keeping Mom up at night.

- **CONSIDER SAFETY PRECAUTIONS TO ENSURE YOUR PEACE OF MIND AND A RESTFUL SLEEP.** A monitor can alert you if Mom wakes up. If she is at risk for wandering, you could alarm doors and windows, and install special locks.

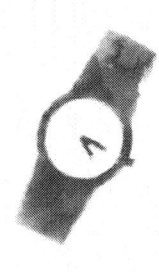

CONFUSION AND MEMORY LOSS

It's a new day every fifteen minutes for Mom. She's at the point now that, by the time you can finish your second sentence, she's re-asking you the question you were answering in your first sentence. She tells stories from the past, but she re-casts the players.

She had lung cancer two years ago and is in remission, but she'll still say things like, "When I get over this cancer . . ."

We do not argue with her when she says something wrong. We just leave it alone because she's not hurting anyone.

— Sharon S., Mabank, Texas

WHY DOES THIS HAPPEN?

Confusion is one of the primary symptoms of dementia. Confusion tends to affect Mom's personality and social behavior, whereas memory loss affects her ability to recall. Just like Sharon's mother, those with dementia confuse past and present, and cannot always reason things out.

Memory loss is what initiates the confusion. While you can't fix it, you can do important things to help your family member work around some of these problems. It is important that everyone understands these symptoms and develops consistent strategies that support Mom.

The confusion impacts the whole family, since it makes it harder to communicate and get everyday tasks accomplished. She may say, "I need the thing with the handle, the thing for my head." This could mean she wants her hairbrush. Or, she may struggle for the right word and come up with something close, like "my push" instead of "my brush."

Remember that the person with dementia always makes sense to herself. It's up to us to figure out the message. By understanding some of the basic problems Mom is dealing with, you can organize your approach and the environment to reduce stress and help her be more self-sufficient.

(Emotional • Social • Physical • Environmental)

Does the person have an unmet need that is causing the memory or behavioral symptom?

CARE APPROACHES

- Don't argue with Mom if she's wrong. If she thinks you are her sister instead of her daughter, just go with it. Reassure her that she is loved and well-cared for.

- Be more descriptive in your explanations. Describe the day in simpler terms. Instead of saying its 7 a.m., explain that it's breakfast time or morning.

- Speak simply with short sentences, without being condescending. Avoid unnecessary details in daily conversation.

- Learn to be a creative listener. If you are having problems understanding what he is trying to say, listen closely. If you still can't understand, apologize and ask him to repeat.

- Confusion can cause Mom to misidentify certain articles. For example, she may be confused about what to do with a spoon. Start by demonstrating and lifting the spoon to your own mouth.

- Break down daily tasks such as dressing into simple steps. Lay out clothing for the day with the underwear on top of his clothes so that is the first thing he puts on.

- When Mom is confused by daily tasks, use the "your hand under their hand" technique to guide her through a task such as washing hair.

- Simplify the space to help Grandpa succeed. In the bathroom, for example, clear the countertop and shelves. Then lay out just the towel, wash cloth and a measured amount of shower gel or soap.

- Visual cues can help support your point. If you want to talk to Mom about the dress that she will be wearing to the wedding, get it out of the closet and show her.

- Be sure to use elements of her life story to provide cues, such as offering her a favorite beverage, singing familiar songs or practicing past routines. Or redirect to a meaningful activity, such as helping you prepare dinner. This can help her feel more anchored to the day and less confused.

- Undertake activities in rooms that are smaller and quiet. If you're scrapbooking with Mom, leave the distractions of the living room and go to a corner of the dining room where she can focus.

- Reduce the "extra" noise in the home. Having the TV on while the family is chatting or eating dinner should be avoided. The unnecessary extra stimuli could cause confusion.

- Engage Mom in activities that will help keep her mind active, such as word games, puzzles and trivia.

- Allow enough time. If you ask Dad if he prefers to go for a walk or read the paper, give him time to answer. Dad's brain impairment may force him to process information more slowly.

- Changes to Dad's day may increase confusion, so try to keep them to a minimum. If the washer breaks down, schedule the repairman during Dad's naptime to minimize confusion.

STARTING THE CONVERSATION

Confusion is at the heart of dementia. It impacts every area of a person's life. It's common for people to get distracted, lose one's train of thought, misidentify objects and be unable to retrieve words. So your ability to communicate is key. Limit input, learn to be a patient, good, creative listener, use visual cues, and demonstrate and simplify to help Mom understand and preserve her dignity.

If Mom says, "I'm waiting for Dad to pick me up," and Dad is deceased, say: "Tell me again about how you and Dad first met."

. . . .

If Dad says, "We just sold the car last week," but it's been five years, say: "I hope the new owner still loves the car as much as we did."

. . . .

Don't say, "We took Charlie the dog to the vet today for his shots and annual check-up," say "Charlie saw the dog doctor. He's feeling great!"

. . . .

Say: "Good morning! It's time for breakfast," instead of "It's 7 a.m. Get up."

. . . .

Say: "Let's brush your teeth, Dad, with the toothbrush." If he is confused, say: "Your toothbrush is in the cup next to the sink." If he is still confused say, "Let's brush together." (Hold the brush up to your mouth and make the brushing motion.)

. . . .

If Mom is confused about the task of folding towels say, "I'm sorry, Mom. I shouldn't have asked you to fold the towels when I knew you were tired."

. . . .

Say, "Dad, it's time for your usual cup of tea before bed."

PREVENTION

Following are tips to consider to help prevent these actions from occurring again.

- **IT'S GOOD TO OCCASIONALLY PAUSE AND THINK ABOUT THE IMPACT OF DEMENTIA ON DAD'S LIFE.** Put yourself in his shoes. What has his life been like and what has he lost?

- **CONSIDER YOUR HOME LAYOUT.** For example, have the children's bedrooms, playroom and computer in the basement or at the opposite end of the house.

- **MAINTAIN AN ORGANIZED HOME FREE OF CLUTTER.** Keep the closet clean and group outfits to help Dad make easy selections and remain independent.

- **KEEP A JOURNAL WITH TRIGGERS FOR MOM'S CONFUSION.** It's hard to plan for unexpected disruptions, but maintaining a daily log could help you understand what prompts confusion.

DELUSIONS

My mom lived alone but within five minutes of our home. One night she called me, crying and very frightened. In the background, I could hear loud music and a lot of talking. Mom told me that there were strangers in the house and they wouldn't leave.

My husband and I immediately headed over, calling 911 as we drove. When we approached her home, the sirens were coming up fast behind us. I called Mom to let her know we were there.

When she answered the phone, all was quiet. Mom told me that the strangers had left. I asked her how she got them out and she proudly said "I turned off the TV." Just then, the police, fire and ambulances pulled in directly behind us. The emergency workers treated her with respect and told her she did a good job getting the people to leave.

— Betty K., Peachtree City, Ga.

WHY DOES THIS HAPPEN?

If Mom is insisting that there are strangers in the house, like Betty's mother, she may be experiencing a delusion – a fixed, false idea.

There are a variety of potential causes for this condition including changes in the brain that occur as a result of dementia. While these issues can be frightening for the entire family – like Betty's story – there are strategies and techniques that can provide a solution for the family caregiver.

As Betty and her family discovered, reacting calmly can help defuse the situation and preserve a person's dignity.

(Emotional • Social • Physical • Environmental)

Does the person have an unmet need that is causing the memory or behavioral symptom?

CARE APPROACHES

* In any occurrence react calmly, don't argue or try to reason or deny the experience. Reassure your family member that you are there with her and will help.

* Enter her reality. If Mom believes she is a young mother with toddlers, go along with that reality in a non-committal way by discussing how toddlers can be difficult. Redirect Mom to a favorite activity such as baking a cake.

* Understand Dad's triggers for delusions. For example, if he watched a violent TV show, he could think the bad guys are in the house. Turn the channel or redirect to a reading activity.

- If Dad says he is seeing strange lights, it may be an eye condition associated with aging. Be sure to have his vision and hearing checked regularly.

- Check the environment for inadequate lighting, shadows, reflections and glare. These may trigger delusions in a person with dementia.

- If Mom is concerned that her food tastes differently or is spoiled, take a step back and consider that certain medications may have caused her taste buds to change. Try to eat with Mom regularly to address her concerns.

- Helping Mom stay connected to the areas in life that she knew and loved could help minimize delusions. For example, if Mom was a housewife, keeping her engaged making dinner each night could help her stay in touch with the reality she once knew.

- If your spouse needs to move to a care community, take along pictures, furnishings, plants, etc., that can help him feel more at home and avoid confusion and delusions.

STARTING THE CONVERSATION

The biggest challenge of dealing with a delusion is to want to dismiss or correct it and bring the person back to reality As long as the delusion is not causing harm, don't argue or try to reason or deny, just go with it. Redirect to a meaningful activity or physically remove the person from the situation.

If Mom says, "There's a man outside," say "He's just passing by. Let's go have some lunch."

. . . .

"Mom, tell me more about what you see outside. Let's go sit down and discuss this over tea."

. . . .

"Would it help if I sat with you? May I hold your hand?"

. . . .

If Dad sees a cat in his bed, say: "Let's sit in the living room and I will have Billy, your grandson, remove it."

. . . .

"I see how this is scary for you. I am here with you, Grandpa."

. . . .

She may say, "My mother (deceased) came to visit today." Say: "I'm sure you had a wonderful visit!"

PREVENTION

Following are tips to consider to help prevent these actions from occurring again.

* **TO UNDERSTAND WHY A DELUSION IS OCCURRING, SEEK A DOCTOR'S EVALUATION.** This will determine if the cause is, for example, a medication reaction or brain damage.

* **BE OBSERVANT.** Look for signs of bladder infection, constipation, skin changes, thirst, weight loss, sudden sleeplessness or heightened anxiety. Keep a journal to track anything that may cause a delusion.

* **INVOLVE FAMILY AND FRIENDS TO HELP COME UP WITH CREATIVE SOLUTIONS.** Remember, you're not in this alone. Identify those with skills to best support her and involve them in her care.

FALSE ACCUSATIONS
AND PARANOIA

With Mom, this journey has had its ups and downs. Sometimes she is lucid and she can say how scary this is for her. Other times she just gets mad. She's suspicious we're trying to run her life. For whatever reason, she would become attached to grocery bags, for example. I've gotten kicked out of the room for trying to recycle them.

What we do is, we'll pick a room and say, "Hey, Mom, let's reorganize this room." We'll get her to tell stories about the things we find. Little by little, we're making some progress. But sometimes we'll be halfway through and she'll ask, "Why are you taking my things?" When that happens, we have to stop, right there, and change direction.

— Mary M., Albuquerque, N.M.

WHY DOES THIS HAPPEN?

Imagine what it would be like to not know what is happening around you. Or what if you couldn't recognize everyone in your life?

Paranoia is a condition that develops, partly through fear, as the symptoms of dementia set in. As Mom loses the ability to recognize family, friends or home, a struggle develops within her to make sense of it and hold on to things, places and people.

That's why Mary's mother became paranoid and accused the family of taking her things when all they were doing was organizing and recycling.

(Emotional • Social • Physical • Environmental)

Does the person have an unmet need that is causing the memory or behavioral symptom?

CARE APPROACHES

- Redirect Dad to a game of gin rummy or try to interest him in a walk to the park to see the geese.

- If Mom accuses you of moving her favorite vase, even if you didn't do that, calmly apologize and take the blame. Reassure her and try to change the subject.

- If someone else is accused, stay calm and look for an opportunity to change the subject. When you have the opportunity, take the accused person aside and explain the situation while Mom is distracted.

- Keep Mom's close friends up to date about her situation so that during social outings they won't show concern.

- Provide your family member with a small amount of money to keep in her purse if she is used to having some money on hand.

- If your spouse wants to carry around an old pair of keys because he thinks they are his car keys, go with it. It may comfort him or he may feel he is keeping things safe.

- As the disease progresses, it's so important to keep the environment familiar. If you need to make a change in his living arrangement or environment, make sure he is always surrounded by the things that he loves and recognizes.

- Designate an area in the home where Mom's favorite personal items are accessible, and label them.

- To avoid Dad losing his glasses, keep the house in tidy order. A clean environment will help make keeping track of items more efficient.

- Paranoia comes from fear and confusion. If she needs to buy a new dress, take her to the store in the morning when there are fewer crowds.

- Get spare sets of important items for him, such as eyeglasses or hearing aids. This will make replacement faster and easier.

- Try to re-direct your family member if he or she is feeling suspicious or nervous. If Dad loves watching sports, have him help you make some popcorn for you both to enjoy while watching the afternoon baseball game.

- Before discounting Mom's accusation, check out the facts. After all, older adults can be easy targets for scams.

STARTING THE CONVERSATION

If Mom is accusing you of something she thinks you've done or taken, the natural reaction will be to get defensive. The disease is robbing Mom of her life and this might be a way she is trying to exert some control. Don't take it personally. Reassure and validate her feelings, and encourage positive thoughts. Remember you're not going to win an argument, so apologizing and taking the blame is likely your best bet.

"This must be difficult for you. We'll get through it together."

. . . .

"Isn't it wonderful that we have each other and that I can help out!"

. . . .

"Dad, I'm sorry you are upset. Your doctor told you that you have some memory loss. Here is your wallet."

. . . .

"Mom, I understand that you're frustrated that you can't find your favorite earrings. It's upsetting when you think you've lost a treasured possession. Let's go look for them together."

. . . .

"Dad, I know you're frustrated with me. Let me show you that your shoes are in the bedroom."

. . . .

"Mom, I know the ringing phone makes you nervous. I've asked the pharmacy to call my number instead of yours. I will take care of everything."

PREVENTION

Following are tips to consider to help prevent these actions from occurring again.

- **KEEP A JOURNAL TO DETERMINE IF THERE ARE TIMES OF DAY OR SITUATIONS THAT CAN CAUSE MOM TO BECOME PARANOID.** For example, Mom could get nervous with all the questions she's asked at the doctor's office. Your journal notes will remind you that Mom likes to play cards. So take a deck along with you to the next appointment.

- **TALK WITH OTHER FAMILY MEMBERS ABOUT A SAFE PLACE TO STORE VALUABLES.** This allows for your family to all agree and know the location if they need to retrieve items to show Mom.

- **LOOK FOR WAYS TO HELP MOM MAINTAIN CONTROL OF AS MUCH IN HER LIFE AS SHE IS CAPABLE OF DOING.** If you're going to move her summer clothes to the basement closet, make sure she knows and ask her to help. That can keep her from feeling she is losing her independence.

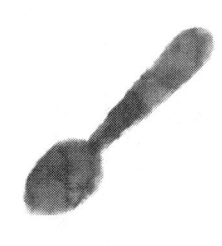

HIDING/MISPLACING THINGS/RUMMAGING

When my husband and I moved in with my in-laws, we learned early on we couldn't leave my mother-in-law home by herself. We'd go to church and when we'd come back she'd have put all the trash in the recycling bin and vice versa. One time we got home and she'd taken all the teaspoons out of the drawer and hidden them. We looked for them everywhere.

Then three or four days later, back they were in the drawer where they belong. I never know what tomorrow will bring, but we try to find the humor in everything.

—Alinda L., Bettendorf, Iowa

WHY DOES THIS HAPPEN?

When Mom hides things – like Alinda's family experienced – she may not realize what the items are or that they belong to someone else. She is not intentionally trying to hide an important item such as teaspoons. Because of her disease, she just doesn't understand.

Rummaging through cupboards and drawers is something Dad may do out of boredom. He may feel a sense of loss at times and may react by searching for things. His confused efforts may demonstrate his emotional losses. He also may be hoarding or hiding his things in an effort to keep his familiar possessions safe.

We know that unmet needs may contribute to these actions, so trying to understand the cause behind them will help you deal with the issue.

(Emotional • Social • Physical • Environmental)

Does the person have an unmet need that is causing the memory or behavioral symptom?

CARE APPROACHES

• If items go missing, react calmly. Mom will either have forgotten that she moved them in the first place or where she put them. If questioned, she may become upset, angry or feel that you are accusing her unfairly. Assume that she is just trying to keep these items safe and together look for the missing items.

• Help Dad maintain a regular routine. Give him things to do during the day to reinforce that routine. Perhaps ask for his assistance caring for the family dog. He could help feed and walk the dog at the same times each day.

- Lock up any valuables such as jewelry, checkbooks, important papers, keys and credit cards. Install locks on cupboards and drawers, if necessary.

- Keep an eye on the daily mail. If important mail starts to disappear, consider getting a post office box or change the address to your home for important items.

- Encourage positive rummaging. Put together a purse with lots of things for Mom or a tool box with nuts and bolts for Dad. Find a set of cards or poker chips and ask Dad to organize or sort by suit or color. Ask your spouse to sort a drawer of socks and find matched pairs.

- Observe Dad to determine if he is hiding items. The next time he can't find his hearing aid, you'll know where to look. Note this in your journal for the benefit of other family members.

- If hiding things becomes a big problem, consider installing a surveillance camera in the home.

- Regularly check the trash before it is put out. You will avoid the stress of an important item being thrown away. Keep trash cans covered and out of sight.

- Get an extra set of things such as Dad's favorite baseball cap or Mom's TV remote control. This will make replacement faster and easier.

STARTING THE CONVERSATION

When things go missing, panic and frustration are the natural responses. Maintain your composure and try not to show your frustration or irritation. Dad could become anxious, especially if he has no memory or understanding of what's missing. It's easier to just apologize and take the blame and redirect him into a meaningful activity.

"Dad, I'm sorry we can't find your book. I'll look for it later.
I am sure it will turn up."

. . . .

"Dad, I probably misplaced the remote control myself.
Don't worry, I'll find it."

. . . .

"Dad, it looks like you're looking for something in the drawer.
Can I help you?"

. . . .

"Mom, your scarf is not in this drawer. Why don't we
take a walk and look for it later."

. . . .

"Let's leave your glasses on your dresser, Mom, where we
know we can both find them."

. . . .

"Mom, I know you're upset you can't find your make-up compact.
Let's go to the store and get a new one!"

PREVENTION

Following are tips to consider to help prevent these actions from occurring again.

- **TO HELP PREVENT THE FRUSTRATION OF LOST ITEMS, SET ASIDE TIME TO GET ORGANIZED.** Straighten cupboards, de-clutter drawers and keep only the essentials. Take time to donate unused items to charity to maintain a clutter-free environment.

- **PLAN OUT MEANINGFUL ACTIVITIES BEFORE EACH DAY TO HELP AVOID BOREDOM.** Assign Mom simple household tasks such as dusting furniture or folding clothes, taking a walk or building a memory book. A schedule and routine could help keep her engaged in the day.

- **HELP YOUR SPOUSE SUCCEED IN HIS ENVIRONMENT.** Labeling drawers and cupboards when he is resting or sleeping, for example, will provide cues and help him have successful days.

HOSTILITY

My brother was diagnosed with Alzheimer's disease on his 59th birthday. During the first couple of years there were moments of strong anger, blaming the world for his illness and becoming verbally mean. My brother, a driver's education teacher, was accustomed to giving instructions and taking control of the car when teaching students.

Sometimes we'd be driving and he'd reach over and pull up the emergency brake. He thought he was testing or teaching me like his students. Once we were returning home on a winter's night and the roads were very slippery. He pulled up the emergency brake and put us into a slide right in front of an oncoming vehicle. I corrected the car, pulled over and tried to explain to him what had just happened. He denied that he had put our lives in danger; he had no sense of reality. He became angry, threw his hands up and got out of the car. He started walking and we followed behind until he'd walked off his anger and hostility. In the future, when he would try to distract me while I was driving, I would ask someone close to him to intervene or I would pull over again and allow him the opportunity to walk. Because of knee surgeries, sitting in the back seat was not an option.

— Joe V., Columbus, Wis.

WHY DOES THIS HAPPEN?

Joe's brother became hostile or belligerent because he had lost the ability to understand or remember. Keep in mind that Joe's brother had years of experience where he helped others by intervening in their driving. He is going back to those experiences and believes he's helping someone drive. It's important for families to understand the disease is the culprit.

Let's face it, dementia changes everything, including the person with the disease. He may be pleasantly confused or become agitated and challenging. His opposition or resistance and negative attitude all are expressions of his confusion. Understanding the person's life story can help you manage through these actions.

(Emotional • Social • Physical • Environmental)

Does the person have an unmet need that is causing the memory or behavioral symptom?

CARE APPROACHES

* Your demeanor and a confident and helpful tone will show in your face and voice. When Mom opposes your request, keep your body relaxed and your tone of voice even.

* When something upsets Dad, keep your emotions in check. If you insist that Dad change his shirt for example, he will resist. Step away and try approaching Dad later to change his shirt.

* Hostility is masking what Grandpa does not know. For example, he may not know the last time he washed and changed clothes. To curtail the hostility, apologize and take the blame, even if it's not your fault.

- Opposition is a sign that Dad knows he is losing control. Set the environment up for success. For instance, if you are going for a walk, have his shoes and coat ready by the door.

- Involve Dad in easy decisions about his day. This can be as simple as asking his opinion about the color of shirt he would like to wear. Anything that can engage him in the decision-making process about his life will help.

- Routines and rituals are useful. These activities will help him feel that rhythm in life. If Dad watched "Jeopardy" every afternoon, make sure he still has the opportunity to do that.

- Bring up a pleasant or favorite subject like his hole-in-one on the golf course or his famous barbecues. This could completely change his mood.

- Create happy and meaningful moments. Keep Mom busy doing things she likes, such as sorting the mail or clipping coupons.

- If hostility leads to an outburst, look for opportunities to lighten the mood. Changing the subject or diverting attention may calm the situation. For example, if you try to remove old newspapers and Mom becomes resistant and hostile, leave the papers and invite her to the kitchen for some lemonade.

STARTING THE CONVERSATION

If you've always been close to Dad, you could be an easy target for his opposition. Those with dementia often lash out in frustration at the ones they care about most. Sometimes you just need to let Dad vent. Try to empathize and focus on his feelings rather than the negative actions that he's exhibiting. Often the less said, the better.

"Dad, I know you're upset with me now. When you're ready to talk, I'm here for you."

"Mom, I'm sorry I stepped in to tie your shoes. I thought you needed help, but I should have asked."

"Dad, I know it's hard to wait for your grandson to mow the lawn. While he's on his way, tell me about growing up in South Dakota."

"We are going to church soon. Let's do your shower before we go."

"I am sorry this is happening. I can see you are upset. Can we sit and talk about it?"

"Mom, I know you're really good at baking chocolate cakes. But why don't I help so you can show me your secrets."

PREVENTION

Following are tips to consider to help prevent these actions from occurring again.

- **INVOLVE THE FAMILY TO LEARN ABOUT THE BEST APPROACHES TO KEEP DAD CALM.** Journaling could help identify a particular rocking chair that soothes, a blanket, a favorite dessert or a person who has a calming effect.

- **DETERMINE MOM'S "HOT BUTTONS" TO MINIMIZE HOSTILITY.** If you know Mom hates broccoli, look for other healthy vegetable options.

- **FOCUS ON SIMPLIFYING THE ENVIRONMENT TO HELP PREVENT OUTBURSTS.** If Dad "loses" sweaters, pants etc. and his room is messy, then tidy up his space. Organize Mom's hanging closet to display fewer choices and transfer items to a hamper. Label shelves and cabinets and have just essential items in the bathroom. Put an entire outfit on one hanger.

JUDGMENT

Mom called upset one day because my father was going to buy a new car with only $10,000 in the bank. When Dad came home from the dealer, he told us he was signing the papers the next day and he was paying cash.

When we tried to argue and reason that if he used all the money to buy a car, there wouldn't be any money left for him and Mom to live and eat. He said "It's my money and I'll do whatever I want with it," while my mom just sat there and cried. We talked to Mom about appointing a power of attorney, and that was the turning point. The next day, she put a stop on their account and that was the first step in taking over their affairs.

— Stephanie R., Gettysburg, Pa.

WHY DOES THIS HAPPEN?

Dementia often impacts not only memory, but also insight and judgment. In trying to maintain control, Stephanie's father nearly drained their bank account. Judgment problems could put Dad at risk in many areas of his life.

From the inability to select appropriate clothing for the weather to responding to a sweepstakes offer in the mail, judgment problems could make Dad extremely vulnerable. It's important for family members to try to find ways to shield him and to protect the family's interests, as Stephanie's family did.

(Emotional • Social • Physical • Environmental)

Does the person have an unmet need that is causing the memory or behavioral symptom?

CARE APPROACHES

- If Dad is vulnerable to phone scams, turn the ringer off on the telephone.

- If Dad is answering the phone, learn who he's speaking with. Scammers target older adults because they are thought to be more trusting. When Dad is napping, put his name and number on the Do-Not-Call Registry.

- Look for unusual activity. For example, large volumes of unsolicited mail addressed to Mom could mean that her personal information is in jeopardy. Consider a P.O. Box or having mail sent to your address. Check the outgoing mail with her writing on it.

- Befriend Grandma's neighbors and ask if they would be willing to help keep an eye out for suspicious activity and strangers.

- Perform daily activity checks on Dad's accounts and be prepared to cancel or curtail his credit cards and checking accounts, if necessary.

- If he has always had the habit of keeping rolls of cash, give him notes in smaller denominations. A wad of $1 bills may keep him satisfied and will not break the bank.

- Be aware of Dad's purchases and keep them visible. Dad may not have been acting recklessly or extravagantly in his spending. He may have forgotten that he has purchased certain items and will repeatedly buy the same thing. Keep an eye out for receipts and return items if necessary.

- Observe Mom with visitors – new friends and even old friends. Make sure they know that Mom could be giving away items of value when she is confused. Keep trinkets or baked goods in the freezer to give to family, friends and neighbors who drop by so that Mom doesn't risk giving away valuables.

- If Mom tries to give away a valuable, it might be time to store those in a locked box.

- Sit down with Dad and discuss his charitable giving and develop a plan together. Post it on the refrigerator and help him stick with it.

- Help protect Dad's dignity and self-esteem by including him as much as possible in decisions that affect his life. Hold a monthly "meeting" with Dad to go over his bills and statements.

- Make safety a priority. Be confident in knowing that drastic measures are often necessary to protect the person. For example, if Dad still wants to drive the car but can't remember where the store is, you may need to take away the keys. If he still insists, telling him the car has broken down may help.

STARTING THE CONVERSATION

Poor judgment might be one of the first things you notice in your family member with dementia. This difficult action could lead to role reversal, where you are now the protector, ensuring that Dad is safe. During this transition time, it's important to be helpful and positive while reassuring Dad through important decisions that impact his life.

"You've always done a great job with your bills, Dad. Let's work together and get things organized."

. . . .

"Dad, the bank wants us to be very careful with our accounts and keep everything private, OK?"

. . . .

"You know, Mom, there are greedy people out there. I won't let them take advantage of you so I put your name on the Do-Not-Call Registry."

. . . .

"May I please help you with your checkbook?"

. . . .

"Thank you for allowing me to play a role in your care."

. . . .

"Things in the world have changed so much, Dad. I understand your frustration. Let me take care of paying your property taxes."

PREVENTION

Following are tips to consider to help prevent these actions from occurring again.

- **TAKE TIME TO ASSESS THE HOME FOR SAFETY ISSUES.** Sharp objects in the kitchen (like knives), medications that are unsecured and chemicals under the sink or in the garage could be dangerous for someone with poor judgment.

- **TAKE PROACTIVE STEPS TO WORK WITH MOM'S LEGAL AND FINANCIAL ADVISORS.** Arrange for a Durable Power of Attorney, preferably appointing a close family member.

MEDICATION MISMANAGEMENT

My first clue was when Mom took her blood pressure medication twice because she'd forgotten to take it. I'd visit my Mom and when she'd go to stand up, she'd almost pass out. I'd take her blood pressure and it was so low, I just knew. Sure enough, I'd check the bathroom where she would sort out her medication for the day in a little custard cup, and the whole days' pills would be gone.

It wasn't too long after that, when she had her first fall, that I stepped in and started managing Mom's medications. The way I see it, my mother took care of me and now it's my turn to take care of her.

— Henry P., Mesa, Ariz.

WHY DOES THIS HAPPEN?

Aging adults often take multiple medications. Add to that the confusion that dementia may cause, as Henry's family discovered, and you have a recipe for disaster.

Mismanaging medications can lead to side effects such as drowsiness, irritability and insomnia. Accompanied with dementia, this situation could diminish a person's quality of life.

More than anything, you need to help your family member make sure she is taking her medications correctly. This will help prevent medication mishaps and adverse drug interactions.

(Emotional • Social • Physical • Environmental)

Does the person have an unmet need that is causing the memory or behavioral symptom?

CARE APPROACHES

- If Mom can no longer be an advocate for herself, you will need to be her eyes and ears. Work with her doctor, and learn the drug's purpose and possible side effects.

- Try faxing questions to her doctor prior to an appointment to ensure all your questions are answered.

- Maintain open communication with your spouse's pharmacist. This will help to reduce the risk of medication interactions.

- If a family member is having difficulty swallowing, ask the pharmacist if the medicine is available as a liquid or if you can crush it and add to a pudding or sauce that he likes.

- If Dad takes medications multiple times during the day, you may need to call and remind him or leave notes.

- Observe your family member for any potential side effects. She may be unable to understand, recognize, make the connection or describe the changes she feels.

- Mom may become confused when taking multiple pills. She could try to spit them out. Stay with her and make sure she swallows the pills. Check sinks, toilets and trash cans as well.

STARTING THE CONVERSATION

Medication management is an important part of Mom's quality of life. Dementia could cause Mom to confuse prescriptions and forget to take medications. Clear communication can help make sure she's safe. Start with a positive facial expression, use clear words and avoid over-explaining. Point to the medication and demonstrate how to take the pills all while giving step-by-step directions.

"I'm going to help you with your pills. Let's start with the first one."

. . . .

Say, "Here is your pill," rather than "Your prescription is on the counter."

. . . .

"Here's the white pill. Place it in your hand. Put it on your tongue. Take a drink of water."

. . . .

"This pill helps your heart, Mom."

. . . .

"You need to take these pills, Dad, to keep you feeling good."

PREVENTION

Following are tips to consider to help prevent these actions from occurring again.

- **STORE MEDICINES SAFELY.** A pill organizer can help. Find them at any pharmacy.

- **REVIEW THE LIST OF MEDICATIONS WITH YOUR PHARMACIST AND DOCTOR REGULARLY.** Does Mom need to take every pill? Reducing unnecessary medications can simplify your caregiving experience.

- **KEEP A MEDICATION TRACKER.** Record times, doses, the doctor who ordered the medication and any side effects or symptoms of each prescription Mom is taking. Note if she should avoid certain foods or take medicines on an empty stomach. Be sure to include over-the-counter medicines. Keep a list on your computer and a hard copy in a safe place at home. Carry a list in your purse or wallet.

- **READ ABOUT MEDICATIONS.** Ask for literature about each medication that your family member is taking and refer to it as needed for any questions.

MOOD CHANGES

My mother-in-law, who has dementia, lived with me, my husband and two small children for two years. She could be in the best mood — calm and happy — until we tried to help her get dressed or give her medications. "I don't need your help," she would say. "I've been doing this all my life."

If we attempted to encourage her to change outfits after wearing the same one for two days, her mood would change suddenly when she realized she was forgetting. If we could distract her by sitting outside on a nice day or inviting her to watch her favorite TV show, her happy mood would quickly return.

— Julie D., Winnipeg, Manitoba

WHY DOES THIS HAPPEN?

Throughout the progression of dementia, mood changes may occur and sometimes can be a complete surprise, as Julie observed with her mother-in-law. Your family member may experience difficult mental, emotional and even physical challenges that cause these increasing mood changes.

When a person can't remember or is constantly confused she may be frustrated, fearful and even fighting the changes. It's no wonder that mood swings are a common problem among those who have dementia.

It is wise to accept and anticipate that dementia is the cause of the mood changes. Avoid thinking that she is having personality changes. Separate her, the person you know and care about, from the disease and its symptoms.

(Emotional • Social • Physical • Environmental)

Does the person have an unmet need that is causing the memory or behavioral symptom?

CARE APPROACHES

- Maintain and establish new routines if necessary. By filling Mom's day with set activities, she won't be so prone to mood changes. When Mom understands that after breakfast she always reads the paper and gets dressed for the day, she knows what's coming next.

- If you tell Mom to get dressed she may become overwhelmed by the multiple steps involved in the task. Break it into simple steps, such as taking Mom to the closet and deciding on an outfit for the day.

- Asking Dad what he wants for dinner requires a lot of thinking. Why not give him a choice between meatloaf or chicken and noodles?

- Simplifying his living space will help. Avoid clutter, label his closet shelves, reduce items in cupboards and on his countertops.

- Keeping her physical environment constant and calm will help minimize mood swings. Turn down the TV volume if it's distracting. Keep redecorating to a minimum.

- If Grandma's in a bad mood, ask her to help with simple tasks around the house. By clipping coupons, polishing shoes, sorting socks or folding laundry, she will likely feel useful.

- If a mood change occurs, redirect Dad to a meaningful activity, such as walking the family dog around the block.

- Avoid stress as much as possible. If you think Mom would get nervous about an upcoming family reunion, tell her about it just a few days beforehand and keep details to a minimum.

- If Dad is upset about missing his favorite TV show, apologize and give a reason, like dinner was started a little late. This may lighten his mood.

- Pay Mom a compliment or offer praise to make her smile and improve her mood.

- Sometimes laughter is the best medicine. Looks for ways to inject humor into Dad's day, like watching old episodes of the "Three Stooges."

STARTING THE CONVERSATION

Mood changes can impact anyone involved in Mom's care. By controlling your own emotions, you can help prevent mood changes from ruining everyone's day and may even improve your family member's mood. When Mom is in a bad mood, try to limit her choices and keep the conversation simple.

"I'm excited about the family reunion tomorrow, Mom," instead of "The family reunion starts tomorrow, Mom, we need to pick out your dress, do your nails and get your hair done."

. . . .

"Would you like oatmeal or cream of wheat today for breakfast?"

. . . .

"Mom, I'm sorry I rushed you during your shower. Next time we'll start earlier."

. . . .

"I know you hate to go to the eye doctor, but let's get an ice cream cone afterwards."

. . . .

"Boy, Dad, I can't find the matches to any of these socks. You've always been good at this. Would you help me sort them, please?"

. . . .

"Dad, I know you're down today and really missing Mom. I miss her too. Let's go look at the photo album."

PREVENTION

Following are tips to consider to help prevent these actions from occurring again.

- **BE MINDFUL OF DAD'S SCHEDULE AND ADAPT IF NECESSARY.** For example, the whole process of bathing and dressing involves a certain level of energy to accomplish these once-routine tasks. Schedule them during the time of day when he is most calm, hydrated, free of hunger pangs and has some energy.

- **MOODS CAN BE DIFFICULT TO PREDICT, SO KEEP A JOURNAL OF WHAT'S CAUSING THESE CHANGES AND THEIR TRIGGERS.** Understand that your family member's abilities can change on a daily basis, so be prepared to assist.

- **TALK TO THE DOCTOR ABOUT YOUR SPOUSE'S MOOD CHANGES.** It will be important for your doctor to understand if she is losing weight, crying or sleeping too much, which could be signs of depression.

REPETITION

I was about 10 years old when I realized something was happening to my great-grandmother that I couldn't explain. When I was at their house, it seemed like Mimi was always going back to the places she had just cleaned and cleaning them again.

She compulsively applied her makeup and nail polish all day until her face and nails were caked half an inch thick.

My great-grandpa would go around behind her and "fix things." Whenever our family was together, we just went with this repetitive behavior.

— Kelly R., Charlottesville, Va.

WHY DOES THIS HAPPEN?

Because of Mom's memory loss, she could repeat the same phrase, question or task over and over again. While this behavior is not likely dangerous, it can be frustrating for you and other family members. Or puzzling for children, as Kelly discovered.

You might notice that Dad is going through the same actions from his prior work or interests, for example. This could indicate that Dad might be missing some structure in his life. Or this action could represent boredom. Discovering the causes of Dad's behavior could help cut down on the repetitive actions.

(Emotional • Social • Physical • Environmental)

Does the person have an unmet need that is causing the memory or behavioral symptom?

CARE APPROACHES

- Encourage Grandma to find the answer to the question she keeps repeating. For example, if she keeps asking the time, make sure a clock is visible to her. A digital clock is easier for people with dementia to understand.

- Dad may become anxious about future events such as an outing, which can lead to repeated questioning. When Dad has an upcoming appointment or event to attend, he may keep asking, "When do we leave?" Avoid mentioning the trip until a short time before it takes place.

- If Dad is continually asking to go home even if he is living with close family, reassure him that he is safe and loved. Find something in his environment that reminds him of home, or look at a photo album.

- Try letting the repetitive actions run their course without trying to "hush" him. Repetition is thought to be a comfort measure similar to physically rocking back and forth.

- Ask Grandma to tell you more about her concerns. Sometimes just drawing out the conversation can stop the repetition.

- If Mom is using repetitive phrases or movements, this can be due to noisy or stressful surroundings, or boredom. Redirect her to the kitchen for a snack, for example.

- Keep Dad engaged in meaningful activities he once enjoyed. Perhaps there was a hobby such as painting that he loved that you could re-direct him to.

- If Mom is constantly drumming her nails on the table, give her something to occupy her hands such as a ball of yarn.

- Try distracting Mom with her favorite treat or playing her favorite song when she is repeating words or questions.

- If Mom becomes fixated on an object in the room, distract her and remove it. If it's something that cannot be moved, lead Mom into the bedroom to fold clothes.

STARTING THE CONVERSATION

Repetitive actions can really test a family caregiver's patience. However, Mom can't help that she can't remember. Successful communication could help ease Mom's worries and frustrations. Listen for clues to understanding Mom's actions then try redirecting her to a different topic. Your tone of voice and body language will help set the stage for a great day.

"Mom, you keep getting your shoes out of the closet then putting them away. Are you anxious about the doctor's appointment today?"

. . . .

"Mom, you keep asking me what's for dinner and it is still several hours away. Why don't we have an apple?"

. . . .

"I'm sorry if I seem frustrated today, Mom. I am just having a bad day. Let's make some tea."

. . . .

"Dad, you keep pacing by the door. I know you're nervous about what time your sister is coming. She'll be here soon!"

. . . .

"Dad, 'Wheel of Fortune' is on in a few hours. In the meantime, let's do the word search from the paper today."

PREVENTION

Following are tips to consider to help prevent these actions from occurring again.

- **TUNE IN TO DAD'S DAILY ROUTINES.** For example, be consistent with walks, pet care and TV shows.

- **IDENTIFY AND STEER DAD TOWARD A FEW OF HIS KEY DISTRACTIONS THAT COULD HELP TO CHANGE HIS COURSE.** Find a CD with his favorite song, locate his favorite book in the bookcase and set out a photo of his prize-winning fisherman's catch.

- **SURROUNDING HIM WITH LOVE AND ATTENTION CAN HELP EASE REPETITIVE ACTIONS.** Have family and friends around to support him and visit.

- **KEEP YOUR JOURNAL CURRENT WITH CLUES THAT COULD LEAD TO DAD'S REPETITIVE ACTIONS.** Understanding those triggers can help you prevent the repetition.

SEXUALLY INAPPROPRIATE BEHAVIOR

Dad wanted to invite his brother, who has dementia, over for lunch. So I volunteered to help prepare the meal. When I greeted him, we hugged. But to my surprise, the hug lingered while he ran his hands down my back.

I didn't know how to react so I changed the subject. Then, as I was bringing lunch to the table, my uncle commented about my pretty legs. After the second incident, I realized this was not the action of my uncle, but the disease. I went back to the kitchen and took a few deep breaths. As the day went on, I was prepared to distract my uncle if anything happened again.

— Anonymous

WHY DOES THIS HAPPEN?

Dementia can reduce a person's inhibitions, which may expose his private thoughts, feelings and behaviors of a personal nature, including sex. That's what this family was observing. These actions are symptoms of the disease and sometimes the person is just looking for a human connection.

He may use language that people have never heard him use before and which seems very out of character. Or, he may have impaired impulse control. For example, your family member, who may have always been reserved, could begin to remove his clothes in public. Such behaviors are not only embarrassing to watch, they could jeopardize the person's dignity and safety. Understanding that this is the disease talking and not the person will help you cope.

(Emotional • Social • Physical • Environmental)

Does the person have an unmet need that is causing the memory or behavioral symptom?

CARE APPROACHES

- With this being a sensitive situation, try not to panic. The more upset you become, the more upset Dad will become. Remain calm with relaxed body language.

- If Dad comes out for breakfast without his pants, it may not be a sexual gesture. He may just have forgotten how to get dressed. Direct him to the bedroom and help him get dressed.

- Stand near the bathroom with Grandma's clothing when she is getting dressed. Be ready to cover her if she comes out undressed.

- Make sure clothing is easy to get on and off. Consider Velcro rather than buttons.

- If Dad is making an inappropriate comment to a restaurant server, redirect him by telling him the specials for the day or asking what he wants to drink.

- Look for new things to do together. Teach Dad a new board game or song to re-direct if he is acting inappropriately.

- Some people with dementia crave textures like soft fleece or cotton. If Dad becomes fidgety try having him hold a pillow, a stuffed animal, a blanket or even a squeeze stress ball.

- Give Mom more attention. She needs to know you are there as she goes through this sometimes-frightening journey.

- Sitting or kneeling with Dad on the same level may reduce his fidgeting. Then try holding his hand or offering him something else to hold.

STARTING THE CONVERSATION

Inappropriate behavior can fluster a family caregiver and may put you on edge, anticipating that it could happen at any time. Knowing the disease is causing the action and not the person, your best strategy is to preserve his dignity. A confident and understanding attitude will help you divert the situation without embarrassing your family member.

"Dad, instead of fidgeting with your zipper, do you have to go to the bathroom? If not, can you help me fold clothes?"

"Dad, don't touch Mom while she's trying to nap. Let's go into the living room and turn on the TV. What would you like to watch?"

"Dad, are you too warm? Is that why you're taking off your shirt?" "Let's leave your shirt on since it's cold," rather than, "Quit taking off your shirt!"

"Dad, she is really pretty, but she is very busy answering the phone. Let's go sit down and read a magazine while waiting for the doctor."

PREVENTION

Following are tips to consider to help prevent these actions from occurring again.

- **REASSURE YOUR SPOUSE REGULARLY.** He may be experiencing a need to be touched by another human. The disease is causing him to express it in the only way he knows how. Hold his hand, massage his shoulders or give him a hug.

- **BE AWARE OF DAD'S CLOTHING CHOICES.** If he is too hot, his underwear too tight or the material of his shirt scratching his skin, he may try to disrobe.

- **PRACTICE AND ROLE-PLAY THE CONVERSATION.** Because this is such a sensitive subject, you'll want to be prepared to avoid embarrassment and preserve their self-esteem. Choose your words and practice how you will re-direct. Role-play with another family member so you are confident and prepared in the future.

SOCIAL WITHDRAWAL

Dad would get into silent moods, not looking at or talking to Mom for the entire day. He still had days when he was lucid and responsive, so the silent days caused Mom to worry that he was slipping away entirely. One evening, when I stopped at my folks' house, Mom warned me that it had been "one of those days," so I told Mom to get out of the house to clear her head.

There was a baseball game on, so if Dad wanted to watch the game and not talk, that was fine with me. An hour or so of complete silence had passed before he turned to me and said, "Where's my Butterfingers?" That's his all-time favorite candy. When Mom came home, I assured her that he was still in there and we laughed about the only three words he spoke all day.

It occurred to me on my way home that if Dad were to die overnight, his last spoken word would be "Butterfingers." I circled back to my parents' house and awakened my sleeping Dad to tell him I loved him. I asked him if he loved me too so that those words would be his last words if he were to die suddenly.

— Dan W., Omaha, Neb.

WHY DOES THIS HAPPEN?

Socialization has many benefits. But for the person with dementia, it's safer just to stay home. They could be nervous about forgetting a name or failing to recognize an important person in their life.

Social withdrawal also can be caused by a desire to avoid embarrassment and having his friends see him struggling. Most people know that dementia is not "going away," so depression may set in, which might be what Dan's family was seeing with their father.

By being patient and finding simple, joyful moments, Dan and his family were still able to connect with their loved one.

(Emotional • Social • Physical • Environmental)

Does the person have an unmet need that is causing the memory or behavioral symptom?

CARE APPROACHES

- Dementia could be difficult for Dad's friends. Surround him with friends who best understand and can support him. Help organize a cookout in the back yard for those kinds of supportive friends.

- Reassure your family member that you will go with him for lunch with his friends to offer support if needed.

- One of the benefits of socializing is a good laugh. If Dad is apprehensive about going out with friends, put on a favorite movie that always makes him smile and laugh.

- Every home has a social hub, whether it's the kitchen, the family room or the back yard. Make sure your spouse is always present and included in conversations and family activities.

- Plan outings with extended family and friends. He may be reluctant to go to the family reunion, so ask his brother or another trusted relative to attend with him. Or plan smaller outings with relatives.

- During a large family barbecue, remind family members that it would be best to try to talk with him one-on-one in a quiet room so as not to overwhelm him.

- Plan appropriate activities that won't make Mom anxious. When the grandkids are over, instead of playing board games, ask her to hold the garden hose while they are watering flowers.

- Try asking Mom to be social in different ways. If she says "no" when you try to schedule a lunch, suggest that you invite one friend over to the house instead. If that doesn't work, suggest you call her friend on the phone later that afternoon.

- To encourage social activities, use Mom's life story to uncover meaningful outings. If she always got her nails done, schedule this activity and invite her good friend along, too.

- Work on building meaningful memories together. If she doesn't already have a scrapbook, go looking for pictures that represent various stages in her life. Ask about the people and places that were important to her.

STARTING THE CONVERSATION

Isolation may only worsen dementia and lead to depression. As a caregiver, you almost need to be a cheerleader for your family member, always encouraging her to stay socially active. Remember what Mom has always liked to do and talk openly with her about continuing those interests.

"I'd be so happy if you would come with me to the church picnic," rather than, "Would you like to go to the church picnic?"

. . . .

"Mom, I know you didn't want to go to lunch with Shirley. But Shirley wants to see you because she has some important news. Let's get your coat."

. . . .

"If you don't want to go to coffee with the guys today, let's walk around the block and see your old friend Joe."

. . . .

"Mom, I know you're nervous about going to bridge club. Let me go with you and be your coach."

. . . .

"Dad, why don't you come into the kitchen and join in the conversation. Tell us one of your famous fishing stories."

. . . .

"Mom, should we go out to lunch with your sister or have her over to the house?"

PREVENTION

Following are tips to consider to help prevent these actions from occurring again.

- **SET UP A MONTHLY SOCIAL SCHEDULE FOR YOUR FAMILY MEMBER.** Encourage Mom's friends, relatives and neighbors to get together once a month for a visit. Keep it on the same day each month. Keep a calendar in Mom's view to see all her upcoming social commitments.

- **OBSERVE GRANDPA'S REACTION TO DIFFERENT PEOPLE.** Does his face light up when he sees a certain friend or family member? Consider recording thoughts and feelings about what you have learned and what you know works for your family member.

- **UNDERSTAND THE PERSON'S LIFE STORY.** Did he go to lunch with friends? Did she talk on the phone with family? Did he like to entertain the grandkids? By maintaining his regular social activities, Dad will still feel connected.

WANDERING

When my husband started wandering, he would always go to the fire station that was four houses down. When I realized this, I went to the station with a picture of him and I gave them my name, address and phone number.

The firemen would take him to the break room and get him a cup of coffee while they called me. One Sunday morning, I discovered he was gone and the firemen hadn't seen him. Turns out he'd gone to church, and in his pajamas.

Then there was that one time when he tried to go out in my blouse and my cropped pants. I laughed so hard and he was so proud he could still make me laugh.

— *Evelyn H., Texas City, Texas*

WHY DOES THIS HAPPEN?

Many people with dementia pace or roam, perhaps out of nervous energy or because they are looking for things to do. Your spouse also may be trying to fulfill a physical need such as thirst, hunger, using the bathroom or exercise. This behavior can become more serious, however, if a person with dementia tries to leave, like Evelyn's husband.

Once you identify what he is trying to achieve, you can start to find ways to deal with the underlying issue. This could reduce your frustration and worry, and help him retain his independence.

(Emotional • Social • Physical • Environmental)

Does the person have an unmet need that is causing the memory or behavioral symptom?

CARE APPROACHES

- Make a path in the home where it is safe and comfortable for Mom to wander or pace. Closing off certain parts of a room or locking doors can help you achieve this goal. Such paths also can be created outdoors – in a garden, for example.

- Simplify the environment. Relocate decorative furniture such as the small antique flower stand. Use only a few larger pieces of furniture that are solid in color.

- Remove items that could be difficult to see, such as glass figurines, small picture frames and vases. De-cluttering the main living spaces can help Dad move about freely.

- Install barriers and fences in the yard to help ensure that Mom doesn't wander into unsafe territory or away from home. Place large flowerpots near a small opening.

- Create inviting areas. For example, Grandma's garden could have a bench, bird feeders and garden ornaments. When she is enjoying herself, this may stop her from wandering further.

- If Dad is determined to leave, try not to confront him, as this could be upsetting. Try to get him to put on appropriate clothing. Accompany him and then divert his attention so that you can both return.

- If Mom is trying to leave, re-direct her into a household activity, such as folding laundry, or a past hobby she may have enjoyed, such as gardening.

- Carve out 20 minutes a day for regular exercise to minimize restlessness. A supervised walk around the park will help relieve her agitation, anxiety and boredom.

- If Dad is wandering, try to get out for a car ride. A change in scenery and fresh air may help.

- When taking Dad on an outing, try to pick places that are less crowded; for example, the neighborhood coffee shop rather than a large supply store.

STARTING THE CONVERSATION

Although wandering is frightening, there's usually an underlying cause that communication could help you figure out and stop. Approaching the situation cautiously, being ready with a diversion and reassuring the family member will make this behavior less scary for everyone.

"Dad, can I join you on that walk?" or "Where are you headed?"

. . . .

"Mom, I know you're anxious to get to the store. Let's sit down and make a list first."

. . . .

"Mom, I notice that you keep walking to the window and looking out at the garden. Let's go buy a few pansies, your favorite flower, and you can help me plant them."

. . . .

"Dad, I notice that you keep pacing between your bedroom and the coat closet. It's OK. I'll remind you when it's time to meet your friends and go with you."

. . . .

"Mom, I see you're on the neighbor's porch swing. Aren't her flowers beautiful? Come back over to your house and I will get us some lemonade."

. . . .

"I'm sorry we didn't get out for our walk today since it was raining. I waited too long. Why don't we go for a car ride instead?"

PREVENTION

Following are tips to consider to help prevent these actions from occurring again.

- **BE PREPARED IF YOUR LOVED ONE WANDERS OR BECOMES LOST.** Make sure Dad has a piece of identification always on him or consider an ID bracelet. You may sew identification into his jacket near the collar so that it is not easily removed. Always have a current photo available if you need to report him lost or missing.

- **EDUCATE OTHERS.** Tell local shop owners and trusted neighbors about his disease and give them your contact details and a current photo.

- **SAFETY-PROOF YOUR HOME.** Position locks high or low on the door, in an unfamiliar location. A "stop" sign or "do not enter" sign on exit doors and stairwells may help.

- **KEEP A JOURNAL FOR A COUPLE OF WEEKS TO HELP IDENTIFY – AND REMOVE – ANY TRIGGERS.** Try to find out if his walking has a purpose; don't presume that he is wandering. He may be trying to get to work, for example.

- **ENSURE CONSTANT SUPERVISION.** People who wander need constant supervision to be safe. This is not something you should try to do alone for extended periods of time. Accept help.

Help for the Caregiver

It's likely you have discovered that one of the challenging aspects of caring for someone with dementia is managing the many emotions that often come with caregiving. It's important to discuss the common emotions people experience and why they happen. The following practical suggestions may help not only to manage the emotions, but also to prevent future problems. Besides, feeling less stressed and happier often leads to being a more patient caregiver. So everyone wins!

COMMON EMOTIONS THAT CAREGIVERS EXPERIENCE

Family caregivers report experiencing many emotions when caring for someone with dementia. Take a look at the list of emotions below and see how many you have felt in the last day, week, or perhaps month.

- AGITATION
- ANGER
- ANXIETY
- COMPASSION
- DEPRESSION
- EMBARRASSMENT
- FEAR

- FRUSTRATION
- GRIEF
- GUILT
- HAPPINESS
- HELPLESSNESS
- IMPATIENCE
- LOVE

- REACTIVE
- RELAXED
- RELIEF
- RESENTMENT
- SADNESS

As you look at the list, you may find you are experiencing several sometimes conflicting emotions at the same time; for example, love and frustration. And you may be feeling a certain emotion a little bit or very intensely. If you are angry and don't deal with that emotion, it may grow to be rage. That's one of the reasons it is important to take the time to identify your emotions.

Take a moment to journal the emotions you are feeling right now.

Many people think emotions are either "good" or "bad." The truth is emotions just are; it is what we DO with our emotions, how we handle them, that has either a positive or negative impact on our lives and on the lives of people we love. The first step in better managing emotions is to identify what we are feeling.

THE CAUSES

Many factors can affect our emotional state. Think about what could be contributing to your feelings. Begin by reading the list below and ask yourself if any of these may be impacting how you are feeling now. For example, are you completely exhausted? If so, and you are feeling stressed or anxious, it is very likely that this is contributing to your feelings. As you are trying to understand the causes of your emotions, maintain an attitude of curiosity rather than judgment. For example, "I wonder what might be contributing to me feeling angry today," is more helpful than scolding yourself for feeling angry!

Below are some examples of things that could be influencing your emotions.

- Your siblings or other family members are not supporting you or pulling their fair share.

- You have no family nearby to offer support and help with caring for your parent.

- The family is at odds on how best to support and care for Mom or Dad at home. Or your support team (family) has been distant most of your life.

- Your relationship with Mom or Dad has been strained over the years, but now they need your help.

- Because of the dementia, your relationship with Mom or Dad has changed, and there is tension because of the change in roles.

- If you are caring for a spouse who has the tendency to wander, worrying if they will leave in the middle of the night is causing you many sleepless nights, leading to exhaustion.

- You are working full time and managing your own household and family.

- You are overwhelmed with responsibility and Mom's dementia diagnosis leaves you feeling hopeless and depressed.

- You have a chronic condition, such as osteoporosis, that causes you to have pain most days.

- With all the other responsibilities in your life, exercise and nutrition have fallen off the priority list.

Take some time to journal what may be affecting your emotions.

After you have discovered a few of the causes, next consider these three questions:

- Why do I have no control over this situation?

- What can I control about the situation?

- What can I influence or impact?

As you answer each of these three questions, you may find that the only control you have is how you think and react to the situation. You also may realize that you can influence the situation. For example, Dad may be frustrated because you have to help him get dressed in the morning. Well, it's hard to change Dad's emotion, but if you took a few proactive steps to set Dad up for success, like put pants and a matching shirt on the same hanger or lay his clothes out in order of how they go on, you can then just assist from a distance if needed. So, Dad feels a sense of independence, and lessens his frustration.

After doing this exercise, you can start to train your brain to spend time focusing only on what you can impact and let the worry go.

MANAGING EMOTIONS

Now that you have identified your emotions and some of the causes, here are some additional tips on managing those emotions.

- **KEEP A JOURNAL TO IDENTIFY WHAT YOU ARE FEELING.** Before you can better manage your emotions, you need to know what you are feeling. Sometimes we get so busy in our lives that we don't tune into our own emotional signals. By writing down what is going on and what you are feeling, it can help you tap into your emotions.

- **TALK WITH A FRIEND.** Sometimes talking with someone who knows and loves us can help us figure out what we are feeling.

- **FIND A SUPPORT GROUP.** Look to your local faith community or Alzheimer's support group. You may find people who are also caring for someone with dementia. They can offer emotional support and additional tips for care.

- **GET HELP!** If there is a specific task that is difficult, consider asking someone else to do it. For example, if bath time becomes a struggle every time, you may find that Mom will be more cooperative with someone other than you assisting her.

- **DON'T BE AFRAID TO ASK.** How many times do you hear from your family or friends, "What can I do to help?" Well, consider taking them up on the offer or asking for help. And be creative as to where you ask for the help. What if you had a friend organize a team of people to bring over dinner once a week? Or is there a friend who could help with carpool activities?

- **TAKE A BREAK.** Respite care, or a break, is not just a "nice" thing, it is a necessity when caregiving for someone with dementia. You wouldn't expect your cell phone to work without recharging it, so why would you think you are able to provide endless caregiving without a break? You need to recharge, too! However, not every break has to be a week-long vacation.

- **BEGIN WITH A MINI-VACATION!** Start by writing down a list of things you enjoy doing. The list might include reading, watching TV, having coffee with a friend, talking with a friend on the phone, exercising, taking a walk, listening to music, sitting outside, cooking, crossword puzzles or any number of other things. Then, take one or two 15-minute mini-breaks each day to do something on your list. The goal is to build up the number and length of the breaks over time.

- **BE INTENTIONAL WITH YOUR BREAKS.** When you are a caregiver, planning ahead is important. Plan out your breaks, too. Pause and think about all the areas in your life. We all have basic needs that include physical, emotional, creative, social, mental or intellectual and spiritual. So each day, try to make sure you are balanced and taking breaks that will fill those needs. For example, when Dad is napping, do your 15 minutes on the treadmill. Or when Dad is watching his favorite show, read your book. Invite a friend over for lunch one day with you and Dad. When you are feeling balanced and meeting your needs, you will likely come back refreshed and better able to deal with the emotions that usually accompany caregiving.

- **TAKE CARE OF YOURSELF.** We all know that we should probably be taking better care of ourselves. Most of us know that getting enough sleep, attending to our medical care, eating well, exercising, having enough social support and doing things that help us enjoy life are key to good "self" care. Good self care contributes to our emotional well-being and helps us better manage stress and the other emotions that accompany caregiving.

- **ATTITUDE IS EVERYTHING.** The one thing all of us can do to feel better emotionally is to be aware of how we think about a situation. For example, do you believe that you have to do it all alone as a caregiver? Many caregivers have that belief and it makes them feel like a failure when they can't manage everything alone! Changing

your attitude to, "Mom needs the best care," instead of "I must provide all the care," might mean that several people – including professionals – are involved in the care team.

- **LET IT GO.** Ask yourself if something is worth the battle – if it really matters? Often when you step back and look at a situation, what seems very important in the short run won't matter in the long run. For example, if your father is wearing clothes that don't match, it isn't harming him and, since he is at home, it really doesn't matter. By asking yourself this question, it will likely prevent you from getting upset about things you can just let go.

- **USE THIS BOOK AS A RESOURCE.** It is full of practical solutions. For example, if you find you are increasingly frustrated because your father will only wear the same shirt every day, consider buying several shirts exactly like the one he wants to wear. In this way, he will be happy that he can wear the same shirt, and you will no longer be frustrated by the situation.

Look to the following section for other resources to help you in your caregiving journey.

Resources

FREE ALZHEIMER'S & OTHER DEMENTIAS DAILY COMPANION APP

Access these tips and resources on the go by downloading an extension of this book in the app store.

Benefits and features include:

- Tips for dealing with Alzheimer's and other dementia-related situations

- 24-hour caregiving assistance available via toll-free phone number or email

- Access to caregiver resources

- Caregivers sharing their own advice

- Ability to access all the solutions and tips without internet connectivity

DOWNLOAD THE APP

Go to **http://app.ConfidencetoCare.com**

Or scan the QR code at left with your mobile phone.

ORGANIZATIONS

AARP
601 E St. NW
Washington, DC 20049
member@aarp.org
www.aarp.org
Tel: 888-OUR-AARP (888-687-2277)

ALZHEIMER'S ASSOCIATION
225 North Michigan Ave., Floor 17
Chicago, IL 60601-7633
info@alz.org
http://www.alz.org
Tel: 312-335-8700 / 1-800-272-3900 (24-hour helpline)
TDD: 312-335-5886
Fax: 866.699.1246

**ALZHEIMER'S DISEASE EDUCATION AND REFERRAL CENTER
(ADEAR) - NATIONAL INSTITUTE ON AGING**
P.O. Box 8250
Silver Spring, MD 20907-8250
adear@nia.nih.gov
http://www.nia.nih.gov/alzheimers
Tel: 800-438-4380
Fax: 301-495-3334

ALZHEIMER'S DISEASE INTERNATIONAL
64 Great Suffolk Street
London • SE1 0BL • UK
info@alz.co.uk
http://www.alz.co.uk/
Tel: +44 20 79810880
Fax: +44 20 79282357

ALZHEIMER'S FOUNDATION OF AMERICA

322 Eighth Ave., 7th Floor
New York, NY 10001
info@alzfdn.org
http://www.alzfdn.org
Tel: 866-AFA-8484 (866-232-8484)
Fax: 646-638-1546

AMERICAN GERIATRICS SOCIETY

40 Fulton St., 18th Floor
New York, NY 10038
info.amger@americangeriatrics.org
http://www.americangeriatrics.org/
Tel: 212-308-1414
Fax: 212-832-8646

CAREGIVER ACTION NETWORK

10400 Connecticut Ave., Suite 500
Kensington, MD 20895-3944
info@caregiveraction.org
http://www.caregiveraction.org
Tel: 800-896-3650
Fax: 301-942-2302

FAMILY CAREGIVER ALLIANCE/ NATIONAL CENTER ON CAREGIVING

785 Market St., Suite 750
San Francisco, CA 94103
info@caregiver.org
http://www.caregiver.org
Tel: 415-434-3388 / 800-445-8106
Fax: 415-434-3508

HOME CARE ASSOCIATION OF AMERICA

941 East 86th St., Suite 270
Indianapolis, IN 46240
info@homecareaoa.org
http://www.homecareaoa.org/
Tel: 317-663-3637
Fax: 317-663-3640

HOME INSTEAD SENIOR CARE® NETWORK'S GLOBAL HEADQUARTERS

13323 California St.
Omaha, NE 68154
Tel: 888-484-5759
Fax: 402-498-5757
www.HomeInstead.com
www.HelpforAlzheimersFamilies.com
www.CaregiverStress.com

HOSPICE AND PALLIATIVE NURSES ASSOCIATION

One Penn Center West, Suite 229
Pittsburgh, PA 15276
hpna@hpna.org
http://www.hpna.org/
Tel: 412-787-9301
Fax: 412-787-9305

LEWY BODY DEMENTIA ASSOCIATION

912 Killian Hill Road, S.W.
Lilburn, GA 30047
lbda@lbda.org
http://www.lbda.org
Tel: 404-935-6444
LBD / Caregiver Link: 800-539-9767
Fax: 480-422-5434

NATIONAL ALLIANCE FOR CAREGIVING
4720 Montgomery Lane, 2nd Floor
Bethesda, MD 20814
http://www.caregiving.org/
Tel: 301-718-8444
Fax: 301-951-9067

NATIONAL ASSOCIATION FOR HOME CARE & HOSPICE
228 Seventh Str. SE
Washington, DC 20003
hospice@nahc.org
http://www.nahc.org/
Tel: 202-547-7424
Fax: 202-547-3540

CAREGIVER ACTION NETWORK
10400 Connecticut Ave., Suite 500
Kensington, MD 20895-3944
info@caregiveraction.org
http://www.caregiveraction.org
Tel: 800-896-3650
Fax: 301-942-2302

NATIONAL HOSPICE AND PALLIATIVE CARE ORGANIZATION / NATL. HOSPICE FOUNDATION
1731 King St.
Alexandria, VA 22314
nhpco_info@nhpco.org
http://www.nhpco.org
Tel: 703-837-1500
Helpline: 800-658-8898
Fax: 703-837-1233

NATIONAL INSTITUTE OF MENTAL HEALTH (NIMH)
NATIONAL INSTITUTES OF HEALTH, DHHS
6001 Executive Blvd., Rm. 8184, MSC 9663
Bethesda, MD 20892-9663
nimhinfo@nih.gov
http://www.nimh.nih.gov
Tel: 301-443-4513 / 866-615-6464 / 301-443-8431 (TTY)
Fax: 301-443-4279

NATIONAL INSTITUTE ON AGING
Building 31, Room 5C27
31 Center Drive, MSC 2292
Bethesda, MD 20892

NIA INFORMATION CENTER
niaic@nia.nih.gov
Phone: 800-222-2225
TTY: 800-222-4225

NATIONAL RESPITE NETWORK AND RESOURCE CENTER
4016 Oxford St.
Annandale, VA 22003
http://www.archrespite.org
Tel: 703-256-2084
Fax: 703-256-0541

WELL SPOUSE ASSOCIATION
63 West Main St., Suite H
Freehold, NJ 07728
info@wellspouse.org
http://www.wellspouse.org
Tel: 800-838-0879 / 732-577-8899
Fax: 732-577-8644

PUBLICATIONS

A Dignified Life, The Best Friend's Approach to Alzheimer's Care, A Guide for Family Caregivers, by Virginia Bell, M.S.W. and David Troxel, M.P.H.; http://www.amazon.com/dp/075730060X

Activities of Daily Living – an ADL Guide for Alzheimer's Care, by Kathy Laurenhue, M.A.; http://www.amazon.com/Activities-Daily-Living-Guide-Alzheimers/dp/097863621X

Alzheimer's Basic Caregiving – an ABC Guide, by Kathy Laurenhue, M.A.; http://www.amazon.com/Alzheimers-Basic-Caregiving-ABC-Guide/dp/0978636201

"Alzheimer's Disease Fact Sheet," National Institute on Aging; http://www.nia.nih.gov/alzheimers/publication/alzheimers-disease-fact-sheet

"Alzheimer's Disease: Unraveling the Mystery," National Institute on Aging; http://www.nia.nih.gov/alzheimers/publication/alzheimers-disease-unraveling-mystery

Alzheimer's Early Stages: First Steps for Family, Friends and Caregivers, by Daniel Kuhn, M.S.W.; http://www.amazon.com/Alzheimers-Early-Stages-Friends-Caregivers/dp/0897933974

"Care ADvantage®," for caregivers of people with Alzheimer's Disease and related illnesses (free quarterly publication), Spring 2013 issue, "It's Personal" (see the 2nd scenario: how you know when it is time to relocate a person to a long-term care facility), page 20; http://www.afacareadvantage.org/

"Caring for a Person with Alzheimer's Disease, Words to Know," National Institute on Aging; http://www.nia.nih.gov/alzheimers/publication/caring-person-alzheimers-disease/words-know

"Caring for a Person with Alzheimer's Disease, Understanding How AD Changes People – Challenges and Coping Strategies," National Institute on Aging; http://www.nia.nih.gov/alzheimers/publication/caring-person-ad/understanding-how-ad-changes-people-challenges-and-coping

"Caring for a Person with Alzheimer's Disease," Your Easy-to-Use Guide from the National Institute on Aging; http://www.nia.nih.gov/sites/default/files/caring_for_a_person_with_alzheimers_disease_0.pdf

"Dementia: Hope Through Research," National Institute of Neurological Disorders and Stroke; http://www.ninds.nih.gov/disorders/dementias/detail_dementia.htm

"Home Safety for People with Alzheimer's Disease," National Institute on Aging; http://www.nia.nih.gov/alzheimers/publication/home-safety-people-alzheimers-disease

Stages of Senior Care, Your Step-by-Step Guide to Making the Best Decisions, by Paul and Lori Hogan, Founders of Home Instead Senior Care; http://www.stagesofseniorcare.com/

Strength for the Moment, An Inspirational Book for Family Caregivers, by Lori Hogan; http://www.strengthfortheMoment.com/

Understanding Difficult Behaviors: Some Practical Suggestions for Coping With Alzheimer's Disease and Related Illnesses [Paperback], by Anne Robinson, Beth Spencer and Laurie White; http://www.amazon.com/Understanding-Difficult-Behaviors-Suggestions-Alzheimers/dp/9991249508

"What Happens Next?," A booklet about being diagnosed with Alzheimer's disease or a related disorder, National Institute on Aging; http://www.nia.nih.gov/sites/default/files/84206ADEARWhatHappensNextEarlyStageBookletab09OCT01_0.pdf

Journal

. . . .

Write down your caregiving experiences.

_____ / _____ / _____
Date

WHAT HAPPENED TODAY?

WAS IT CAUSED BY AN EMOTIONAL, SOCIAL, PHYSICAL OR ENVIRONMENTAL FACTOR?

HOW CAN IT BE PREVENTED TOMORROW?

NOTES

HOW CAN IT BE PREVENTED TOMORROW?

WAS IT CAUSED BY AN EMOTIONAL, SOCIAL, PHYSICAL OR ENVIRONMENTAL FACTOR?

WHAT HAPPENED TODAY?

Date
___ / ___ / ___

HOW CAN IT BE PREVENTED TOMORROW?

WAS IT CAUSED BY AN EMOTIONAL, SOCIAL, PHYSICAL
OR ENVIRONMENTAL FACTOR?

WHAT HAPPENED TODAY?

Date ___ / ___ / ___

_____ / _____ / _____
Date

WHAT HAPPENED TODAY?

WAS IT CAUSED BY AN EMOTIONAL, SOCIAL, PHYSICAL OR ENVIRONMENTAL FACTOR?

HOW CAN IT BE PREVENTED TOMORROW?

HOW CAN IT BE PREVENTED TOMORROW?

WAS IT CAUSED BY AN EMOTIONAL, SOCIAL, PHYSICAL, OR ENVIRONMENTAL FACTOR?

WHAT HAPPENED TODAY?

Date

___ / ___ / ___

_____ / _____ / _____
Date

WHAT HAPPENED TODAY?

WAS IT CAUSED BY AN EMOTIONAL, SOCIAL, PHYSICAL OR ENVIRONMENTAL FACTOR?

HOW CAN IT BE PREVENTED TOMORROW?

Date

_____ / _____ / _____

WHAT HAPPENED TODAY?

WAS IT CAUSED BY AN EMOTIONAL, SOCIAL, PHYSICAL OR ENVIRONMENTAL FACTOR?

HOW CAN IT BE PREVENTED TOMORROW?

Date ___/___/___

WHAT HAPPENED TODAY?

_____
_____
_____
_____
_____

WAS IT CAUSED BY AN EMOTIONAL, SOCIAL, PHYSICAL OR ENVIRONMENTAL FACTOR?

_____
_____
_____
_____
_____

HOW CAN IT BE PREVENTED TOMORROW?

_____
_____
_____
_____
_____

Date ___ / ___ / ___

WHAT HAPPENED TODAY?

WAS IT CAUSED BY AN EMOTIONAL, SOCIAL, PHYSICAL OR ENVIRONMENTAL FACTOR?

HOW CAN IT BE PREVENTED TOMORROW?

_____ / _____ / _____
Date

WHAT HAPPENED TODAY?

WAS IT CAUSED BY AN EMOTIONAL, SOCIAL, PHYSICAL OR ENVIRONMENTAL FACTOR?

HOW CAN IT BE PREVENTED TOMORROW?

Date _____ / _____ / _____

WHAT HAPPENED TODAY?

_____

_____

_____

_____

_____

WAS IT CAUSED BY AN EMOTIONAL, SOCIAL, PHYSICAL OR ENVIRONMENTAL FACTOR?

_____

_____

_____

_____

_____

HOW CAN IT BE PREVENTED TOMORROW?

_____

_____

_____

_____

_____

Date

___ / ___ / ___

WHAT HAPPENED TODAY?

WAS IT CAUSED BY AN EMOTIONAL, SOCIAL, PHYSICAL OR ENVIRONMENTAL FACTOR?

HOW CAN IT BE PREVENTED TOMORROW?

_____ / _____ / _____
Date

WHAT HAPPENED TODAY?

WAS IT CAUSED BY AN EMOTIONAL, SOCIAL, PHYSICAL OR ENVIRONMENTAL FACTOR?

HOW CAN IT BE PREVENTED TOMORROW?

HOW CAN IT BE PREVENTED TOMORROW?

WAS IT CAUSED BY AN EMOTIONAL, SOCIAL, PHYSICAL
OR ENVIRONMENTAL FACTOR?

WHAT HAPPENED TODAY?

Date ___ / ___ / ___

HOW CAN IT BE PREVENTED TOMORROW?

WAS IT CAUSED BY AN EMOTIONAL, SOCIAL, PHYSICAL
OR ENVIRONMENTAL FACTOR?

WHAT HAPPENED TODAY?

Date
___/___/___

HOW CAN IT BE PREVENTED TOMORROW?

WAS IT CAUSED BY AN EMOTIONAL, SOCIAL, PHYSICAL OR ENVIRONMENTAL FACTOR?

WHAT HAPPENED TODAY?

Date ___/___/___

_____ / _____ / _____
Date

WHAT HAPPENED TODAY?

WAS IT CAUSED BY AN EMOTIONAL, SOCIAL, PHYSICAL OR ENVIRONMENTAL FACTOR?

HOW CAN IT BE PREVENTED TOMORROW?

NOTES

HOW CAN IT BE PREVENTED TOMORROW?

WAS IT CAUSED BY AN EMOTIONAL, SOCIAL, PHYSICAL
OR ENVIRONMENTAL FACTOR?

WHAT HAPPENED TODAY?

_____ / _____ / _____
Date

_____ / _____ / _____

Date

WHAT HAPPENED TODAY?

WAS IT CAUSED BY AN EMOTIONAL, SOCIAL, PHYSICAL OR ENVIRONMENTAL FACTOR?

HOW CAN IT BE PREVENTED TOMORROW?

Date ___ / ___ / ___

WHAT HAPPENED TODAY?

WAS IT CAUSED BY AN EMOTIONAL, SOCIAL, PHYSICAL OR ENVIRONMENTAL FACTOR?

HOW CAN IT BE PREVENTED TOMORROW?

About Molly Carpenter

Author, speaker, trainer and family caregiver. Molly Carpenter, M.A., brings years of personal and professional senior care experience and training to families dealing with dementia care. Her passionate interest in older adults started early – as a high school student working in an adult day care program – and continues as an adult and a professional. The reality of caregiving is never far from her experience due to her work in skilled nursing facilities, adult day care centers and continuum of care communities.

In her current role, Carpenter works with a team responsible for ensuring that the Home Instead Senior Care® network's 60,000 caregivers worldwide have the resources necessary to effectively provide quality care in the home and understand the importance of their work enhancing the lives of those they serve. This combined background makes her uniquely qualified to author a book designed specifically to help family caregivers provide care to those with dementia in the home.

Carpenter's work as part of the team that developed a person-centered approach to Alzheimer's care has been adopted and adapted globally and is critical to the success of the Home Instead care approach for people with Alzheimer's and dementia. This work has been endorsed by leading experts in the Alzheimer's industry and adapted for family caregivers throughout the world.

Carpenter holds a Bachelor of Science degree in family science with a gerontology specialization from the University of Nebraska-Lincoln, and a master's degree in education with a gerontology specialization from the University of Nebraska-Omaha. She is currently enrolled in the Human Sciences/Gerontology Ph.D. program at the University of Nebraska-Omaha. Her personal experiences helping to care for her grandmothers have further inspired her career.

23250270R00095

Made in the USA
Charleston, SC
17 October 2013

Printed in the United States
148512LV00003B/2/A

BRIDGEPORT
PUBLIC LIBRARY

1230196656

CONTENTS

CONFIDENCE
to Care

A Resource for Family Caregivers Providing
Alzheimer's Disease or Other Dementias Care at Home

MOLLY CARPENTER

Home Instead Press

Copyright © 2013 Home Instead, Inc.

All rights reserved.

Published in the United States by Home Instead Press.

First Printing, 2013

ISBN: 978-0-9897833-0-9

Printed in the United States of America

10 9 8 7 6 5 4 3 2 1

First Edition

Disclaimer:

Please note that the content, suggestions and tips included in this resource are provided for informational purposes only. They are not intended to be and should not be construed as being medical advice or a substitute for receiving professional medical advice, diagnosis or treatment. Always seek the advice of a physician or other qualified medical provider for any questions you or a loved one may have regarding a medical condition.

Home Instead Press, LLC, Home Instead, Inc. and the Home Instead Senior Care® franchise and master franchise network do not warrant or guarantee that following any of the suggestions or tips included in this resource will help to prevent, eliminate or alleviate any of the behavioral or other symptoms associated with persons who suffer from dementia, and expressly disclaim any liability with respect to the content, suggestions and tips included in this resource.

Contents

· · · · · · · · · · · · · · · · · ·

Acknowledgments

We gratefully acknowledge the efforts of these individuals without whom this book could not have been possible. Our expert content panel:

Bob Bird M.A., a Home Instead Senior Care® franchise owner from Wilmington, Delaware, who has worked extensively in the field of dementia care; C. Angela Burrow CDP, AP-BC, RN, SCM, a Certified National Trainer at the Learning Community for Person Centered Practices at the University of North Carolina-Chapel Hill and a Nationally Certified Dementia Practitioner; and Kathy Laurenhue M.A., CEO of Wiser Now, Inc., a writer, trainer and curriculum developer.

In addition, our sincere appreciation goes out to our review panel:

Dr. Jane Potter, Professor and Chief of Geriatrics and Gerontology in the Department of Medicine, University of Nebraska Medical Center; David Troxel MPH, internationally known writer and teacher in the fields of Alzheimer's disease and long-term care; Tanya Richmond, Program Coordinator and an Assistant Clinical Professor with the Center for Aging Research and Educational Services; Dr. Amy D'Aprix, M.S.W., Ph.D., CSA, a Life Transition Consultant, author, professional speaker and expert in aging, retirement and caregiving.

Thanks to our creative team who helped consult, coordinate, research, write and design this book, including Jim Beck, Georgene Lahm, Rachel Lambert, Kami Manstedt, Alex McCann and Jenny Witt.

Our thanks also go to The Dilenschneider Group and Significance Press, with special appreciation to Joe Tessitore, Joe Pisani and Patrick Malone for their encouragement and publishing expertise. Thanks also to our editor, Jim Zebora.

We also extend our appreciation to the following Home Instead, Inc., individuals and vendor partners who contributed their advice, assistance and especially encouragement, including Jessie Brumbach, Erin Albers, Greg Skolaut, Dan Wieberg, Albers Communications Group, Fleishman-Hillard U.S. and Canada, and Immersion Active.

In addition, we appreciate the many individuals who shared personal stories about their experience with Alzheimer's disease or other dementias along with care tips from family caregivers, as well as staff and CAREGivers^{SM} throughout the Home Instead Senior Care network.

Finally, our sincere appreciation to Home Instead, Inc., franchisor of the Home Instead Senior Care network, for its vision and thought leadership in bringing this valuable resource to family caregivers.

Foreword

....

As we write this, we can't help but think about the estimated 35 million families around the world facing the realities of caring for someone with Alzheimer's disease. For each, it must seem like the greatest challenge of their lives.

You may be one of them – wondering how to help your gentle father who is suddenly showing fits of anger, or your mother who wanders at night, putting herself at risk and keeping you awake with worry.

For most family caregivers, caring for someone with Alzheimer's disease or other dementias is a new and intimidating experience.

Without knowing what triggers behaviors or some practical techniques to counter them, it's easy to feel overwhelmed.

It has been nearly 20 years now, but our first experience with Alzheimer's disease is still crystal clear in our memories. We had just opened the first Home Instead Senior Care® office to provide in-home care for older people. One of our CAREGivers℠ – very frustrated – called to ask for advice. "How can I get Marion to change clothes?" she wanted to know. "She insists on wearing the same gray pantsuit every day, all day."

How we wish that we knew then what we know now! What a difference it would have made in helping our CAREGiver find a way to get Marion into a fresh set of clothes. We would have simply told her daughter to buy a duplicate of her mother's favorite gray pantsuit.

And that, of course, is why we are publishing this book – to give you practical advice so that you can confidently face caring for someone with Alzheimer's disease at home. It's based on two decades

of experience working with and supporting people with Alzheimer's disease or other dementias. We've also asked some of the most respected experts in dementia care to share their insights so people like you can be successful in providing care for Alzheimer's disease or other dementias at home. Some of the best advice in this book came, not surprisingly, from family caregivers who shared generously from their own experiences to help you.

At this moment, there are two sobering facts about Alzheimer's disease. First, our world is experiencing an Alzheimer's epidemic. Second, in spite of an enormous investment of time, money and medical talent, no cure or prevention for Alzheimer's disease has been found and none is expected in the foreseeable future.

> *But, while there is no cure, there is care!*

For almost every family, that care begins at home and is provided by someone just like you. Without training, most are likely unfamiliar with dementia in any form, and already over-committed with children and a job. Still, they are totally committed to caring for Mom or Dad out of love and a sense of responsibility.

If that's you, then you are exactly the person for whom we've written this book.

Through our work in providing care to tens of thousands of people with dementia, we've learned that the behavioral symptoms sometimes exhibited by those with the disease are also the most frustrating to deal with. So with this book we want to help you understand what may cause those behaviors, how to deal with them, and what you can do to help prevent or alleviate them.

We also understand that there can be emotional and physical consequences for caregivers who often find themselves providing care day after day, month after month and, sometimes, year after year. So, we have included advice about how to care for yourself. Read this chapter first, because you can't care for Mom unless you are taking care of yourself.

If you need or would like additional support or training, we encourage you to make use of the resources listed in the back of this book. Also, the Home Instead Senior Care network offers special training for family caregivers. It's the same Alzheimer's Disease or Other Dementias CARE: Changing Aging Through Research and Education® training that the network provides to its professional CAREGivers. It's free, and you can take advantage of it in two ways. First, just watch the short training videos on our HelpForAlzheimersFamilies.com website. Or you can join one of our family caregiver training classes when it is offered in your area by contacting your local Home Instead Senior Care office.

In the end, we trust that by reading this book you will become a more confident caregiver. Confidence leads to better care and makes the privilege of caring more fulfilling. It is our deepest desire that "Confidence to Care" will help you experience these outcomes.

Finally, thank you for caring. As a family caregiver, you have taken on one of the most rewarding opportunities that life offers. God bless you!

LORI & PAUL HOGAN
Co-Founders
Home Instead Senior Care

INTRODUCTION:
JEDI MIND TRICKS

GLENN KENNY

1: THE DEATH STAR?

In the 1976 film *Network*, William Holden plays Max Schumacher, a veteran television executive who's kind of a last bastion of all those lost broadcasting virtues that the name Edward R. Murrow is regularly trotted out to signify. Schumacher wages a losing battle against declining standards and increasing crassness in TV programming, eventually losing his job for his troubles. This simultaneously prescient and facile satire, written by Paddy Chayefsky and directed by Sidney Lumet, presents Schumacher as a surrogate for the audience—we're meant to feel his frustration and bemoan the imminent death of all the dying values he cherishes. But Chayefsky cannily complicates things by having the aging Max, a married man in the throes, it could be said, of "male menopause" (boy, you don't really hear that phrase too much these days, do you?), fall in love with—or, rather, succumb to the blandishments of—much younger executive Diane Christensen. Venal, hyper, ratings-obsessed, and much more, Christensen is to Schumacher what Charles Foster Kane said he wanted to be to Walter P. Thatcher—"everything you hate." But she's a gurl, and she's played by Faye Dunaway, and Schumacher is going through male menopause, so, you know.

While his best friend, newscaster turned "mad prophet of the airwaves" Howard Beale, is creating a nationwide sensation—and greatly propelling Diane's career trajectory—by going koo-koo for Cocoa Puffs on the air, Schumacher decides to come clean to his wife. Mrs. Schumacher (played by Beatrice Straight, who won a Best Supporting Actress Oscar for her work, which comprises less than four minutes of screen time) has a big go-to-pieces moment, but soon manages to compose herself and asks Schumacher what exactly the deal is with this broad (actually, she doesn't ask, but Schumacher is in such a haze over how he, a man of substance, could have possibly been seduced by such a creature that he can't stop himself from conducting this inquiry in front of the woman he's abandoning). And he basically denounces her and all those of her generation, describing her as "a creature of television." "She learned about life," he practically spits, such is his bitterness, "from Bugs Bunny."

Whoa. I was about sixteen when I saw *Network*, not old enough to really wrap my head around the whole *if-Max-doesn't-even-like-this-woman-how-come-he's-leaving-his-wife-for-her* conundrum (don't worry, I'd learn). Still for most of the movie I was pretty much with the character's program. But I mean, why Bugs Bunny? *Looney Tunes* and *Merrie Melodies* were *awesome*, and here was their most beloved character being dragged into the film's argument to stand in for all the forces that, the movie would have us believe, were about to topple Western Civilization as we knew it and as Edward R. Murrow liked it. And in fact the line still gets my back up. What the hell did Bugs Bunny ever do to Paddy Chayefsky, anyway?

I can only imagine that motion picture enthusiasts younger than I must feel a similar indignation when they dip into, say, Peter Biskind's *Easy Riders, Raging Bulls* or David Thomson's *Biographical Dictionary of Film*, and discover that *Star Wars* killed the movies.

A perhaps dispiriting state of affairs to contemplate, seeing as we live in a world where *Star Wars* is, basically, everywhere. It started out with one movie George Lucas directed in 1977 and has since expanded into a fictional universe. Five features of a proposed six-movie cycle (at one point it was going to be nine, but with Lucas approaching his sixties that seems less and less likely) have been produced thus far. They've made Lucas himself rich beyond his wildest dreams (or maybe not; this is a guy who once boasted to his bossy dad that he'd be a millionaire by the time he was thirty) and he has since put the money he's made from *Star Wars* into what amounts to his own moviemaking empire. I bet that most reasonably comfortable, reasonably media-savvy Americans don't go through a single day without hearing some passing *Star Wars* reference, in conversation or over the television or radio, or without seeing some ad or headline or Internet graphic that refers to it, or without coming upon a piece of *Star Wars*–related merchandise— book, comic, coffee mug, what have you. (Several examples of how *Star Wars* references can be folded into just about any disquisition on any topic can be found in the "Miscellany" at the end of this book.) I suppose for guys like Thomson and Biskind, it must be really fucking irritating. For everybody else, including many of the writers in this book—there are a few who don't remember a world before *Star Wars* existed—to them, it just *is*. At least at first—obviously, it's not the case for those who, in the pages that follow, reflect upon the effect that the *Star Wars* phenomenon has had on their own lives.

Actually, for Thomson—who is, or was, let me get this out of the way right off the bat, one of the finest film critics in the country or, for that matter, the world—George Lucas's friend and sometime collaborator Steven Spielberg is more of a bête noire, but that may well be because he feels more engaged by Spielberg, feels Spielberg possesses a genuine talent that Spielberg's squandered in the service of a blockbuster-hungry Mammon that he and Lucas helped re-create. But, boy, does that Steven ever piss Thomson off. In his inaugural column for *Esquire* back in 1996, cheerily entitled "Who

Killed the Movies?" he wrote of Spielberg: "Even the gravity of *Schindler's List* is like the most popular kid in school taking advantage of his status to recommend education. That's cool. We all know he's the quarterback, too, one heck of a dancer, and—hey! fun! Didn't he make *Jurassic Park* at the same time as *Schindler's List*, just to prove he wasn't one of those dudes who couldn't concentrate?" Only someone who wasn't brought up in the American education system—British-born Thomson now lives in the U.S.— could possibly mistake Steven Spielberg for a quarterback.

When Thomson tackles Lucas in his *Biographical Dictionary of Film*, his palpable distaste for Lucas leads to some fairly wacky pronouncements; of the characters in *Star Wars*, he says, "its people are raised on junk food; they are pink, puffy and anonymous." Perhaps Lucas could have avoided the "pink" problem had he paid more attention to the color timing. Thomson goes on: "Good and evil are reduced to the level of opposing sides in electronic Ping-Pong." As opposed to the relative richness and complexity of a real game of Ping-Pong, I suppose. The usually persuasive Thomson's terminology, the implied eye-rolling over junk food and video games, really give him away here; not to put too fine a point on it, but he basically starts to stink of old-fartdom. Not that I'm a huge fan of such modern or postmodern phenoms as junk food and electronic Ping-Pong myself, but, you know, get over it, Dad. Because when you come right down to it, so many *Star Wars* haters of a certain age won't, or can't, engage *Star Wars* on its own terms; they engage it, rather, as the grave marker for their own glorious youth. It echoes an argument you hear a lot when you talk or read about rock and roll. John Lennon's "Elvis died when he joined the army" remark was the first, and most genuinely provocative, of such throwdowns. They've been coming fast and furious ever since. Kevin Kline's character in *The Big Chill* has a much quoted "no good music since year X" line that I can't bring myself to cite accurately, as it would mean looking at the movie again; but wait, there's critic Jim Miller, in his book *Flowers in the Dustbin*, admitting that he basically lost interest after the Sex Pistols broke up; there's thousands of people probably younger than me, and maybe you, for whom it all ended after Kurt Cobain killed himself; et cetera. My favorite curmudgeon in this respect is the writer Nick Tosches, who will sometimes argue that Elvis himself killed rock and roll, and who will then, elsewhere, extoll the virtues of the latest Iggy Pop release. (And just for the record, movie critics have been trumpeting the death of film since before sound actually, really, killed it.)

Contributor Tom Carson's piece in the January 2002 *Esquire*, entitled "McCabe and Mrs. Kael," beautifully sums up, then upends, the Thomson/Biskind version of history: "The larger fable goes like this: Once, we lived in movie paradise, with one bold masterpiece after another engrossing a public finally willing to grow up. Then George Lucas ruined everything by turning the audience infantile again, abetted by a craven industry that turned off the money tap for the visionaries as soon as the receipts for *Star Wars* rolled in.

"As a product of this era, I can say that just about the only part the myth gets right is that it really was a wonderful time to go to the movies—if, that is, you were part of the relative handful queueing up for *Mean Streets* rather than the hordes waiting to see *Airport*, *Earthquake*, *The Towering Inferno*, or *The Exorcist*. At the time, my friends and I knew we had to catch the movies we were excited about fast, before they flopped."

That lines up about right with my own experience of moviegoing at the time. For me, *Star Wars* didn't register as an earth-shattering experience the first time I saw it; in fact, I didn't even actually see it until a couple of months after its May 1977 release. I saw it with my family while on a vacation at Virginia Beach. I thought it was kind of okay, having pursuaded myself that I was pretty much over sci-fi movies at that point anyway. J. G. Ballard, writing about the movie in 1977, made an interesting point regarding just how sci-fi *Star Wars* really was in the first place: "*Star Wars* in particular seems designed to appeal to that huge untapped audience of people who have never read or been particularly interested in s-f but have absorbed its superficial ideas—space ships, ray guns, blue corridors, the future as anything with a fin on it—from comic strips, TV shows like *Star Trek* and *Thunderbirds*, and the iconography of mass merchandising." Or as one enthusiast of a certain age put it to me: "*Star Wars* actually was the movie we thought we were watching when we went to see those Flash Gordon serials."

A movie I did rush to on opening day was Martin Scorsese's *New York, New York*. At seventeen, I found many elements of its main-character romance a bit befuddling (*why are these two hanging out when they clearly can't stand each other?*—don't worry, I'd learn) but could congratulate myself on recognizing the bits of mise-en-scène that Scorsese had cribbed from Vincente Minnelli, master of Technicolor sumptuousness and father of the movie's costar, Liza Minnelli. Early in Biskind's chapter on *Star Wars*, incidentally, he discusses Lucas's nervousness about releasing *Star Wars* in competition against a number of films, one of them being *New York, New York*. According to Biskind, Lucas's then wife, Marcia, who had been the editor on Scorsese's *Alice Doesn't Live Here Anymore* and was working on *New York, New York*, at one point said to her husband, "*New York, New York* is a film for grown-ups, yours is a kid's movie, and nobody's going to take it seriously." Strangely enough, Lucas remained married to Marcia for six years after she made this statement.

That's where I was coming from. And for the next couple of years, that's pretty much where I stayed—checking out Polanski double features at New York's Cinema Village, getting into Fassbinder, and so on. The big-event movie of the summer of 1980 for me was not *The Empire Strikes Back* but *The Shining*, which I again saw opening day (and thus caught the four minutes of it that Kubrick demanded be cut from every print that very night). In fact, someone told me before I saw *Empire* that it turned out that Vader was Luke's father. The fact that I found the idea a little preposterous—so many of the writers here responded to this revelation by more or less saying, "of course"—is a good indication of how unengaged I was.

But then I actually saw *Empire* and was surprised to find it pretty damn compelling, and to find the Darth-as-Luke's-father gambit quite successfully pulled off. *Empire's* dialogue was a lot snappier than *Star Wars'* (I like to think that a lot of what I enjoyed in *Empire* was due to the participation of veteran screenwriter Leigh Brackett, whose contributions are discussed in Dan Barden's essay here and who made her bones writing sci-fi for the pulps), the varied planetary environments convincing, the increasingly interlacing plotlines intriguing. A really uncanny mixture of the dark and the *neat*, I thought. It made me a fan—a lowercase "f" fan, but a real enough one. Imagine how let down I felt by the preponderance of Ewoks in *Return of the Jedi* (although I knew wishy-washy things were in store when that movie's title was downgraded from *Revenge of the Jedi*).

But regardless of my, or any other critic's, level of engagement with the series, *Star Wars* made, and changed, movie and cultural history, and anybody who wants to make sense of either has to take it on. For the likes of Biskind and Thomson, *Star Wars* not only spoiled the party, it acted as a virus, seeking out and destroying all that was good and true and innovative; it literally blinded all those who came under its spell. Robert Altman, one of the gods, supposedly, of the pre–*Star Wars* second golden age of Hollywood, complains in Biskind's book that today there are no pictures in the multiplexes "that an intelligent person could say, 'Oh I want to see this,'" because of the blockbuster mentality *Star Wars* helped create. But Altman, and William Friedkin, and so many others who didn't become George Lucas are not renowned for their capacity for self-criticism; it's easier for them to point a finger at Spielberg and Lucas than to even conceive that their own indulgences helped destroy the cause of intelligent, mainstream American movie-making. I mean, did Altman make the unspeakable 1979 *Quintet* because someone put a gun to his head and told him "If you don't make a pretentious, incoherent sci-fi thriller that makes *Zardoz* look like . . . hmm, lemme see, that makes *Zardoz* look like *Star Wars*, I'm gonna blow your brains out"? No, I don't think it happened that way at all. Friedkin apparently bullied not one but two major studios to make his highly misbegotten *Sorcerer,* a remake of *The Wages of Fear*—a picture that had gotten made, but good, the first time around. It was a debacle. These crap ideas were the filmmakers' own; they didn't come about because *Star Wars* poisoned the well.

Thomson complains that you couldn't get a film like *Taxi Driver* made in today's Hollywood. Well, then I suppose that we should be glad that it, too, got made when it did, but good. Still . . . *Star Wars* did change Hollywood moviemaking, but it's not a matter of content pure and simple. There are some irrefutable facts here. Mainstream movies today don't get—aren't given—much room to breathe; it's striking today to watch a movie like Paul Mazursky's 1978 *An Unmarried Woman*—not a big favorite of mine, or a picture I'm particularly eager to champion, mind you, but bear with me (and yes, I know it was released a year after *Star Wars,* but these things don't happen overnight)—and note just how relaxed it is in its storytelling, how unconcerned Mazursky is with moving the "plot" forward, as opposed to just letting his characters live onscreen. Similarly, another '70s film that's not routinely trotted out by the lamenters, Clint Eastwood's 1976 *The Outlaw Josey Wales*—which *is* a big favorite of mine, thanks for asking—has a feel as expansive as the big Western sky it's set under. Eastwood tells the story at a pace that lets its events resonate, as opposed to racing for the next set piece. One of Lucas's signature storytelling devices (which has its roots in D. W. Griffith's 1916 *Intolerance*) is the multiple climax wherein, in the last third or fourth of a given picture, four or so plotlines are resolved in action sequences. Sometimes these sequences are woven together tightly enough for the desired rousing effect (the final sequence of *A New Hope,* culminating with the destruction of the Death Star—it's a bit choppy, but it gets the job done; Irvin Kershner did even better with the capture of Han Solo, escape of Leia and company, and battle between Luke and Vader in *The Empire Strikes Back*). But sometimes they're constructed so rotely that the desired effect is merely the result of the audience's desire for said combined with the obvious signals that this is where they should be cheering (that would be the decidedly underwhelming wrap-up of *The Phantom Menace*).

To digress just a little bit: When I was growing up, the movie that was the box office champ of all time was *The Sound of Music*, a movie that had been retitled *The Sound of Mucus* by the film's costar, Christopher Plummer (or so legend has it). Imagine how boys my age, or boys of any age for that matter, must have felt about the fact that this was the most successful motion picture of all time. It gets worse. The movie it supplanted was *Gone with the Wind*. Now granted, *GWTW* is a lavish production with a lot to recommend it, and its humongous popularity is a fascinating and useful and in some cases affection-inducing indicator of just how, um, conflicted U.S. culture is . . . but again, what we've got here is basically what many would term a chick flick with really spectacular Technicolor and gasp-inducing racist undertones or overtones or what have you. I mean, it's a trifle appalling. When *Star Wars* had the top box office spot (it is now occupied by *Titanic*, a movie that, if one looks at it a certain way, grafts *Gone With the Wind* to *Star Wars*, and leaves out the overt racism—I don't know, does Danny Nucci's Chico Marxesque Fabrizio qualify as a demeaning stereotype?), well, I'm sure that Thomson and Biskind et al. would, whenever researching such matters, react in a fashion similar to the way Dracula might recoil from a string of garlic plants; but still, to male movie lovers who grew up with *Creature Features* and *Chiller Theater* as opposed to *Million Dollar Movie*, seeing *Star Wars* occupy the top spot was a bit of a tonic. Even I, despite my detachment from the phenomenon, appreciated that. Sure, I would have preferred, say, *Alphaville* in its place, but, you know, eventually you grow up and realize that that's just not going to happen. (As James Wolcott put it in a *Vanity Fair* riposte to Thomson, "Critics need to get over themselves, and not treat the cinema as their personal cross.")

"*Star Wars* was the film that ate the heart and soul of Hollywood. It created the big-budget comic book mentality." That's Paul Schrader, quoted by Peter Biskind, in the epigraph to Biskind's

"Star Bucks" chapter of *Easy Riders, Raging Bulls*. Biskind's book could easily be used to bolster the argument that one-time American cinematic heroes such as Schrader, Altman, Hal Ashby, Brian De Palma et al. did in fact all commit forms of career suicide. (In the late Ashby's case, we can add to that literal, albeit slow, suicide.) Unlike Thomson, who sounds like a spoilsport and who knows it, Biskind, a tireless interviewer and all-around canny individual, more often than not hands his subjects substantial lengths of rope and lets them do with it what they will. (Biskind's own critical take on *Star Wars* is fairly negative but somewhat dispassionate; his essay "The Last Crusade" in the out-of-print anthology *Seeing Through Movies* is a pretty sharp examination of the links between the Lucas-Spielberg worldview and Reaganism.) A particularly damning pronouncement from George Lucas features on the back of the hardcover edition's dust jacket: "Popcorn pictures have always ruled. Why do people go see them? Why is the public so stupid? That's not my fault." Oooff. Schrader's pronouncement does carry some weight, particularly if you put *Star Wars* up against the dreaded box office champions cited above. *The Sound of Music* and *Gone With the Wind* were monstrous, to be sure, but they were also sui generis. And there's the rub. Schrader is actually absolutely right, in a way. One would have had to have been a fool, even at the heyday of *GWTW* or *Music*'s popularity, to have attempted to pull that particular rabbit out of that particular hat again. (Actually, the fools at 20th Century Fox, which produced *Music*, did try; subsequent musicals like 1967's *Doctor Dolittle* nearly put the studio out of business.) What *Star Wars*, along with *Jaws*, did was provide a kind of template for what my former colleague Howard Karren (a brilliant film thinker who I wish did more writing) calls the "overdetermined" film. The movie wherein every emotional or visceral jolt is calculated like a point on a graph. Such movies do have their pleasures, of course; sitting through a well-made one can be as exhilarating as watching a flawlessly executed gymnastics routine (emphasis on the word "routine"; a case in point, incidentally, would be John McTiernan's morally dubious but quite proficient *Die Hard*). But those don't happen too often, do they? Here's the deal: it's beside the point to complain that *Star Wars* created a Hollywood where *Taxi Driver* couldn't get made today. (And some would argue that making more *Taxi Drivers* is what the indie industry is for.) More germane is the fact that if *Star Wars* hadn't been made, then *Top Gun* could never have been made.

This is weird, because if you look at them side by side (and I don't recommend it), *Star Wars* and *Top Gun* don't seem terribly similar. As a visual storyteller, Lucas has always fancied himself a bit of a classicist. His cinematic god is Akira Kurosawa (Lucas recently endowed a facility at the USC film school with the proviso that the building bear Kurosawa's, and not Lucas's, name), and Kurosawa's idol was John Ford, that most seemingly foursquare (but in fact quite slyly innovative) motion picture tale-spinner. In the movies he's directed, Lucas doesn't handle the camera with anything like the grace with which Kurosawa and Ford did, but boy, can you see him trying. And one of the most weirdly charming things about the initial *Star Wars* movie, a stylistic tic that's been maintained throughout the series, is the use of that hoariest of transitional devices, the optical wipe. (If *Episode I: The Phantom Menace* seemed a trifle slow to contemporary audiences—and did it ever!—it was merely because Lucas himself hadn't been bothering to keep up with trends.)

Top Gun's visual style is all showy freneticism, but its narrative thrust, such as it is (so relentless that its makers had to basically invent a war to get to the dogfight climax), is pure *Jaws/Star Wars*. The visual effects of the film could certainly not have been so easily achieved without Lucas's example, either. But we also have to admit that it was the influence of MTV and video games that helped create this abomination. (Are you getting the idea that *Top Gun* is for me what *Star Wars* is for Thomson?) And indeed, there's a small school of thought that posits that it was MTV and video games that, in fact, killed the movies. But this book isn't about MTV and video games. Although one could argue that *Star Wars* has influenced those cultural phenomena as well. As I've discovered while working on this book, if you think about *Star Wars* too much, you can get caught in a rather unpleasant cultural feedback loop. This could be the most diabolical Jedi Mind Trick of all.

2: PROMETHEUS BOUND

"If I hear about that screening of *Star Wars* one more time, about how everybody was trying to attack George . . . we were rooting for George a hundred percent." That's Brian De Palma, in an interview with Anne Thompson (*Premiere* magazine, September 1998), responding to what's probably the most famous set piece in *Easy Riders, Raging Bulls*, an account of a, in Biskind's telling, disastrous screening of a rough cut of *Star Wars*. At a dinner afterwards ("nobody touched the dumplings," one participant recalls), De Palma is quoted as asking Lucas, "Who are these fuzzy guys? Who are these guys dressed up as the Tin Man from Oz?" While De Palma doesn't out-and-out deny those quotes, he tells Thompson: "I've always had a, shall we say, cutting wit, but everybody who knows me knows I only have their best interest at heart." Fair enough. But it sure does make a far more compelling narrative if you say that after being taunted by many of his peers, and even by his own spouse, for goodness sake, George Lucas suddenly found himself, in the parlance of the movie that knocked *Star Wars* off of the top of the box office, the King of the World. (You remember *Titanic*, right?) He had cannily kept the merchandising rights to all the *Star Wars* characters, not that anyone had necessarily wanted them from him in the first place. They sure did after the movie exploded.

Up until that moment, Lucas's relations with mainstream Hollywood had been, shall we say, strained. Even though he had achieved a substantial box office success with his second fictional feature, 1973's *American Graffiti* (a picture that spun off, sort of, into another '70s cultural phenom, the '50s nostalgia sitcom

Happy Days—I say "sort of" because Lucas had nothing to do with *Happy Days*, but the show did feature *Graffiti* star Ron Howard in a somewhat similar role to his one in the film), he still nursed wounds from what he considered Warner Brothers' mutilation of his first, the rather impenetrable sci-fi dystopia film *THX-1138*. Now Hollywood looked to him. But Lucas realized he didn't have to deal with the type of people who would cut the fingers off his babies anymore. (That's not my analogy, that's his, talking to Biskind about what he went through on *THX*.) "I purchased my freedom from the machine," Lucas told Anne Thompson in the May 1999 issue of *Premiere*. And in doing so he created his own empire. He built Skywalker Ranch, his own, more work-oriented version of Kane's Xanadu. He created ILM, Industrial Light and Magic, the effects concern whose house style was immediately recognizable in scores of increasingly effects-driven movies. With pal Steven Spielberg he created another highly remunerative movie franchise, the Indiana Jones films. His conglomerate of companies includes one devoted to education—Lucas Learning.

He has devoted a considerable amount of effort to changing, for the better, the way we see movies. An audio whiz named Tomlinson Holman lent his name to Lucas's THX (for Tomlinson Holman's Experiment—isn't that cute?) system, which was designed to improve sound in movie theaters. In its early, heavily hyped days, the THX scheme was made much sport of; in one gag in what I recall was an *Animaniacs* cartoon, the "The audience is listening" tag that appeared as part of the very loud announcement that you were sitting in a THX-enhanced theater was changed to "The audience is now deaf." (The very ingenious *Animaniacs* television show was, of course, executive-produced by frequent Lucas collaborator and co-ruiner of movies Spielberg, so this can be interpreted as a chummy bit of in-jokery.) In this dreadful 1990 Leslie Nielsen/Linda Blair/Ned Beatty–starring *Exorcist* parody called *Repossessed*, the letters of the THX logo are replaced with BFD, har de har har. In its early days, THX was intended as the launching pad for a whole slew of movie-watching enhancements; anybody who's recently sat in a multiplex while a movie's image is thrown by an extremely weak projector bulb can tell you the experiment hasn't wholly taken. (Which is probably why Lucas is, these days, so hot on digital video projection as well as digital video production. Talk about killing film—*Episode II: Attack of the Clones* was created entirely without the benefit of celluloid.) In any case, though, it's the work that was done by Lucas's crew that has, in large part, created the whole concept of home theater—surround sound, all that—that the kids are so crazy about today. Ah. George Lucas. Force for Good.

Having control of an empire gives Lucas the privilege that only emperors can enjoy: the privilege of rewriting history. When *Star Wars*, as it was called then, was released in 1977, its opening title crawl did not begin with *Episode IV: A New Hope*. That little bit was first added to the film for the 1979 theatrical rerelease, preparing fans for the imminent release of *Empire*. In 1997 Lucas unveiled "special editions" of the first three films of the trilogy, which were dutifully labeled Episodes IV, V, and VI; the viewing public of course sat still for this display of willful dyslexia, knowing that Episode I would follow in 1999. What some didn't sit still for was Lucas's tinkering with the notorious, and much beloved by fans, face-off between Han Solo and Greedo in the Mos Eisley cantina sequence of—all right, all right—*Episode IV: A New Hope*. Using digital technology, Lucas contrived to have Greedo shoot at Han first, thus recasting Han's under-the-table dispatching of the bounty hunter as an act of self-defense. Thus rendering Solo's charm a lot less, um, roguish. Why, for God's sake? "For the first time," Lucas told Anne Thompson apropos of his experience as a single father (he has three adopted children), "I've been able to see a child's reaction to what I'm doing." And, apparently, tailoring his work to those reactions, or second-guessing himself. This has already created, for longtime devotees, a disturbance in the Force. I recently got this e-mail from a friend in her twenties, addressed to her "*Star Wars* buddies": "So if you haven't heard, *NSYNC has a 'walk on' part in *Star Wars II*. They will be Jedi Knights 'in the background.' They were offered the role after George Lucas' daughter BEGGED him to cast her 'favourite band' in the film. She is ALSO the one responsible for Jar Jar Binks. She's like Fredo Corleone, BAD for the family business." (This friend is Canadian, in case you were wondering about that "favourite.")

Take that, Lucas. To which Lucas might reply, "*Tant pis*. My galaxy, my rules." (Well maybe he wouldn't say "*tant pis*." And as it turns out, the fan protests were heeded; the boy band has been purged from *Clones*.) And there are rules, and there is a continuity at work here. The cultural critic John Seabrook, writing first in the *New Yorker* and then in his book *NoBrow*, provides many fascinating glimpses into the workings of the empire Lucas employs to control his galaxy. "Everyone in the content-creating galaxy of *Star Wars* has a copy of 'The Bible,'" Seabrook writes, "a burgeoning canonical document (currently a hundred and seventy pages long) that is maintained by 'continuity experts' Allan Kausch and Sue Rostoni. It is a chronology of all the events that have happened in the *Star Wars* universe, in all the films, books, CD-ROMs, Nintendo games, comic books, and role-playing guides, and each medium is seamlessly coordinated with the others." It is from this "Bible," of course, that the notorious 1978 *Star Wars* Christmas television special was purged; see the essays by Webster Younce and Tom Bissell in this volume. (And it's rather amusing to note that, all this fuss notwithstanding, sometimes Lucas himself can't keep things straight. In his audio commentary for the DVD of *Episode I: The Phantom Menace*, he for the most part "correctly" refers to his 1977 film as *A New Hope*. But once or twice he messes up and calls it *Star Wars*.)

Now Seabrook gets at least a couple of things wrong in his "The Empire Wins" chapter of *NoBrow*. He says *Star Wars*' "light sabers and Jedi Knights were inspired by Akira Kurosawa's *Hidden Fortress*." I'd love it if he'd explain precisely how; I've watched *Hidden Fortress* a few times since reading that, and, well, no. Actually, what

Star Wars borrows most specifically from *Fortress* is the idea of an epic tale as seen through the eyes of two subordinate characters of dubious intelligence and/or efficacy; of course, *Fortress*'s R2 and 3PO figures are a couple of mercenary cowards who are idiots to boot, while *Star Wars'* robots are for the most part at least loyal, and in the case of 3PO, quite useful. (And yes, Lucas is borrowing from Kurosawa borrowing from Shakespeare here.) *Fortress* of course also boasts a headstrong Princess and a rough-and-ready samurai, loose potential prototypes for Leia and Han. But never mind.

Because Seabrook also grasps an essential point, accurately summing up Lucas as that most enviable of show business clichés (well, at least on the level of lifestyle), the victim-of-his-own-success. "Instead of gaining his independence with the success of *Star Wars*, Lucas had lost it," Seabrook says, having cited Lucas's stated counterculture-styled values and contrasted the innocence of the first *Star Wars* film with the marketing monolith the *Star Wars* franchise had since become. "This was the real lesson of *Star Wars*: In the end, the Empire wins." Purchasing your freedom from the machine, it turns out, means becoming another machine.

And in another way, the victory of the "Empire" is as much Lucas's own fault as anybody's. To wit: here's a guy at the command, basically, of his own studio, a vast technological apparatus, and what are the actual non–*Star Wars* movies that he's chosen to put that apparatus behind, the Indiana Jones movies and Francis Ford Coppola's *Tucker* aside? Um, 1986's *Howard the Duck*; 1994's *Radioland Murders*, for Christ's sake. If Lucas is the only person on Earth who could have made *Star Wars*, just as Disney was the only guy who could have created Mickey Mouse, maybe it's the case that he really can't do anything else.

3: THE FORCE IS WITH YOU, ALWAYS

"A refurbished *Star Wars* is on somewhere or everywhere. I have no intention of revisiting any galaxy. I shrivel inside each time it is mentioned. Twenty years ago, when the film was first shown, it had a freshness, also a sense of moral good and fun. Then I began to be uneasy at the influence it might be having." So notes Sir Alec Guinness, the beloved portrayer of the beloved Obi-Wan Kenobi, in the last volume of his journals, *A Positively Final Appearance* (a quite congenial and enjoyable book, by the way). Guinness then goes on to tell of an encounter in San Francisco with a twelve-year-old who, his mother proudly boasted, had seen *Star Wars* (or *Episode IV: A New Hope*, or what have you) over a hundred times. Guinness burst the little boy's bubble by politely requesting that he never see the film again. The kid, understandably stunned at Obi-Wan's directive to not use the Force, broke out in tears, and the mother registered her disapprobation as well. ("I warned him," Lucas once noted of Guinness's conflicts about playing Obi-Wan. "I told him, 'Hey, you could be Leonard Nimoy.'") "I just hope that the lad," Guinness concludes, "now in his thirties, is not living in a fantasy world of secondhand, childish banalities." (Were Sir Alec alive, he might find Jonathan Lethem's essay in this book instructive.)

Well, one can live in a fantasy world of secondhand, childish banalities and still have time for other pursuits. One of the most eye-opening *Star Wars* references I've encountered while working on this book occurs in the picture *Sky's Day Off*. If you've never heard of it, pat yourself on the back and call yourself a good boy, or girl; it's a porno. It's of the sort-of-free-form, quasi-documentary "gonzo" school of adult entertainment, and it for the most part depicts its title performer, Sky (a rather alarmingly youthful and extremely boisterous woman who could be described as "the Britney Spears of porn," if that weren't midway between an oxymoron and a redundancy), running around at some skateboarding convention and trying to convince any number of young men to let her perform all manner of digital and oral manipulations on their person. (Some of them turn her down!) It begins with a skit in which Sky is about to perform a sex scene for the camera. She and her partner are a trifle conflicted as to positioning. She shoves him off of her and extends her arm. Suddenly a dildo flies through the air and into her hand. Her spurned male partner grabs another such device. Beams emanate from each one. The estranged couple settle their differences with a lightsaber battle. Finally triumphant, she exclaims, "Who's on top now, bitch?" The back cover of the DVD of this title in fact depicts Sky in an Obi-Wan cape, holding the lightsaber. Thank God Guinness didn't live to see *that*. (Then again, it might have pepped him up a bit.) If Lucasfilm is interested in pursuing a lawsuit I'd be delighted to take a finder's fee, thanks. The company is quite tolerant of parodies and unauthorized tributes but don't take too kindly to filthy ones; they recently sued (unsuccessfully) the producers of a hardcore animated cartoon called *Star Ballz* (which I haven't looked at—do I have to?—but am assured is remarkably witless).

The various uses that the tools of *Star Wars* can be put to have a lot to do with the generation with which the film made, perhaps, its most meaningful contact. Such *Star Wars* aficionados are used to taking the good with the bad, the stirring with the stupid, because they're fully accustomed to what we have come to call the postmodern ironic point of view; hence, rather than being appalled by the music and the creatures in the Mos Eisley cantina scene, the way a good, serious sci-fi proponent such as Ballard was (he likened the bar's denizens to Muppets), they could practically embrace its cheesiness. (And it's easy to forget, when ruminating on the cheesier aspects of this sequence, that it in fact also contains some, you know, ass-kicking Jedi action, what with Obi-Wan's cutting off some reprobate's hand. Not to mention the whole introduction of Han/dispatch of Greedo business.) Their sensibilities, though, did not preclude them from being genuinely moved by the scene where Luke comes back to the farm, such as it is, to discover it in ruins, with his only family dead—a scene that echoes, as all good film geeks know, the post–Indian massacre homecoming scene in John Ford's 1956 Western *The Searchers*.

In his article "An Empire of Their Own" (*Premiere* magazine, October 2001), about the mind-boggling number of *Star Wars* fan films floating around the Internet, Harry Allen (who has an essay in this volume on the intriguing links between *Star Wars* and hip-hop) quotes Chris Moeller, the director of one such film, *Trip-*

ping the Rift: "Watching the [*Star Wars* movies], you get this feeling that you're seeing one part of this huge story that started a long time ago and continued long after the [movies] ended, and with enough unanswered questions that you want to see more." Add to that the rather elemental nature of the moral schema of the films (which Tom Carson addresses, among other things, in his provocative essay), and it becomes clear that a lot of the appeal of the *Star Wars* galaxy has to do with what it lacks as much as what it contains.

"What is it that makes people crave the *Star Wars* brand in so many flavors?" John Seabrook asks in *NoBrow*. "Somewhere between the idea and the stuff, it seemed to me . . . an alchemic transformation was taking place: dreams were being spun into desire, and desire into product." A similar observation was made, somewhat more amusingly, in one of the very few on-target moments in Mel Brooks's mostly tedious *Star Wars* parody, *Spaceballs*, in a scene where Rick Moranis, as a distinctly nebbishy would-be Vader, uses the action figures for the film's characters to enact his triumphant pursuit of the Princess.

For many of the writers collected here, their encounters with *Star Wars* were somehow life-changing; the movie functioned not only as a prism—looking at their own lives refracted through it, they conceived new ways of acting, of being—but also a tabula rasa, something they could inscribe their own experiences on. (This blankness influences critical thinking on the film, too; what some see as innocence in the films, others perceive as ingenuousness—not quite the same thing.) I came to *Star Wars* as a precocious would-be snob, living in close proximity to one of the greatest cultural centers in the world, during a time when my existence didn't seem particularly trying or troubled. Elwood Reid, on the other hand, encountered the movie in a much more challenging environment and wildly different circumstances. I don't believe he's exaggerating too much when he states in his essay that *Star Wars* was "the largest and most formidable cultural event to hit Ohio."

And, as Weird Al Yankovic so memorably put it, "The Saga Continues." (Surely you didn't miss his recasting of *The Phantom Menace*'s plot to the tune of "American Pie" back in 1999? For some it almost made the movie itself worthwhile.) Almost right before this book went to press, I got to see what they call an "all media" screening of *Episode II: Attack of the Clones.* "All media" screenings (well, it wasn't quite "all media"—from the looks of the crowd, there were some very bonafide fans in attendance as well, probably lucky radio contest winners) are rather notorious for the jadedness of their audiences; and sure enough, this crowd tittered furiously at the love scenes between Anakin and Amidala. Of course they might not have had said scenes not been so appallingly written, awkwardly staged, and indifferently (at best) acted. Still . . . that same crowd went predictably nuts when Yoda wielded his light saber.

It's a strange beast, *Clones.* What gives it its juice, for me, is its perversity. The convolutions Lucas has to put his creations through to set up *Episode III* (for instance, Jar Jar Binks winds up an inadvertent quisling, and the Jedi basically become the galaxy's biggest stooges) are likely to inspire as much fervent analysis and heated debate among fans as the Dead Sea Scrolls did among theologians (*Star Wars:* Bigger than Jesus.) That this movie's biggest box office competition is *Spiderman*, rather than something "adult" such as *New York, New York*, is likely to fill Thomson and Biskind with much "you see?"-style rue, and I'd be lying if I didn't say I don't feel any such thing myself. (And I kind of liked *Spiderman*.)

Two of this book's contributors—Toms Bissell and Carson—rank *Clones* qualitatively second in the so-far five-film saga. (Their ways of putting it differ, though; one calls it "the second best *Star Wars* film behind *Empire*," and the other calls it "the least bad *Star Wars* movie since *Empire*." Finish the book and take a guess as to who said what.) And I agree, while falling somewhere between their two poles of enthusiasm. (We should also note here that Bissell's prediction concerning Boba Fett's origin—it's coming up soon—was in fact dead on.) I love the fact that Christopher Lee's in it—a nice dovetail to *Episode I: A New Hope*, which featured

Lee's great friend and fellow Hammer Films icon, the late Peter Cushing. (You can see the *Creature Features* fan in me rearing his twelve-year-old head, can't you?) I love the fact that it quotes not just *The Searchers* (again), but *Lawrence of Arabia*, Cocteau's *La Belle et La Bete*, and Cecil B. DeMille's *The Sign of the Cross*. The CGI worlds contained in the film are, for the most part, mind-boggling—as are some of Natalie Portlan's generally outre costumes, but never mind. Is the Force still with Lucas? Well, as stilted and teeth-grindingly lame as parts of *Clones* are, let's all ask ourselves, aren't we in the least bit curious to see how these meshugina Clone Wars turn out?

And there's your answer.

13, 1977, 21

JONATHAN LETHEM

1. In the summer of 1977 I saw *Star Wars*—the original, which is all I want to discuss here—twenty-one times. Better to blurt this at the start so I'm less tempted to retreat from what still seems to me a sort of raw, howling confession, one I've long hidden in shame. Again, to pin myself like a Nabokovian butterfly (no high-lit reference is going to bail me out here, I know) to my page in geek history: I watched *Star Wars* twenty-one times in the space of four months. I was that kid alone in the ticket line, slipping past ushers who'd begun to recognize me, muttering in impatience at a urinal before finding my favorite seat. That was me, occult as a porn customer, yes, though I've sometimes denied it. Now, a quarter century later, I'm ready for my close-up. Sort of.

2. That year, I was thirteen and likely as ideal an audience member as any mogul could have drooled for. Say every kid in the U.S. with even the passingest fondness for comic books or adventure fiction, *any kid with a television, even,* had bought a ticket for the same film in a single summer: blah, blah, right, that's what happened. So figure that for every hundred kids who traveled an ordinary path—*cool movie, wouldn't mind seeing it again with my*

friends—there might be one who'd make himself ill returning to the cookie jar five or six times—*it's really still good the fourth time, I swear!*—before copping to a tummy ache. Next, figure that for each *five* hundred, one or two would slip into some brain-warped identificatory obsession—*I am* Star Wars, Star Wars *am me, goo goo ga joob*—and return to the primal site often enough to push into the realm of trance and memorization. That's me, with my gaudy *twenty-one*, like DiMaggio's *fifty-six*. But what actually occurred within the secret brackets of that experience? What emotions lurk inside that ludicrous temple of hours? *What the fuck was I thinking?*

3. Every one of those twenty-one viewings took place at the Loew's Astor Plaza on Forty-fourth Street, just off Times Square. I'd never seen a movie there before (and unless you count *The Empire Strikes Back*, I didn't again until three years ago—*The Matrix*). And I've still never seen *Star Wars* anywhere else. The Astor Plaza was a low, deep-stretched hall with a massive screen and state-of-the-art sound, and newly enough renovated to be free of too much soda-rotted carpet, a plague among New York theaters in those days. Though architecturally undistinguished, it was a superior place to see anything, I suppose. But for me it was a shrine meant for just one purpose—I took it as weirdly significant that "Astor" could be rearranged into "astro"—and in a very *New Yorker*–coverish way I believed it to be the only real and right place to see *Star Wars*, the very ground zero of the phenomenon. I felt a dim but not at all urgent pity for any benighted fools stuck watching it elsewhere. I think I associated the Astor Plaza with the Death Star, in a way. Getting in always felt like an accomplishment, both elevating and slightly dangerous.

4. Along those lines, I should say it was vaguely unnerving to be a white kid in spectacles routinely visiting Times Square by subway in the middle of the '70s. Nobody ever said anything clearly about what was wrong or fascinating about that part of the city we lived in—the information was absorbed in hints and mutterings from a polyphony of sources. In fact, though I was conscious of a certain seamy energy in those acres of sex shows and drug dealers and their

sidewalk-lurking customers, I was never once hassled (and this was a time when my home neighborhood, in Brooklyn, was a mine-field). But the zone's reputation ensured I'd always plan my visits to fall wholly within summer's long daylight hours.

5. Problem: it doesn't seem at all likely that I went to the movie alone the first time, but I can't remember who I was with. I've polled a few of my likeliest friends from that period, but they're unable to help. In truth I can't recall a "first time" in any real sense, though I do retain a flash memory of the moment the prologue first began to crawl in titled perspective up the screen, an Alice in Wonderland doorway to dream. I'd been so primed, so attuned and ready to love it (I remember mocking my friend Evan for his thinking that the title meant it was going to be some kind of all-star cavalcade of a comedy, like *It's a Mad Mad Mad Mad World*, or *Smokey and the Bandit*) that my first time was gulped impatiently, then covered quickly in the memory of return visits. From the first I was "seeing it again." I think this memory glitch is significant. I associate it with my practice of bluffing familiarity with various drug experiences, later (not much later). My refusal to recall or admit to a first time was an assertion of maturity: I was *always already* a *Star Wars* fanatic.

6. I didn't buy twenty-one tickets. My count was amassed seeing the movie twice in a day over and over again. And one famous day (famous to myself) I sat through it three times. That practice of seeing a film twice through originated earlier. Somebody—my mother?—had floated the idea that it wasn't important to be on time for a movie, or even to check the screening times before going. Instead, moviegoing in Brooklyn Heights or on Fulton Street with my brother or with friends, we'd pop in at any point in the story, watch to the end, then sit through the break and watch the beginning. Which led naturally, if the film was any good, to staying past the original point of entry to see the end twice. Which itself led to routinely twice-watching a movie we liked, even if we hadn't been late. This was encouraged, partly according to a general "steal this book"–ish anticapitalist imperative for taking freebies in my

parents' circle in the '70s. Of course somebody—my mother?—had also figured out a convenient way to get the kids out of the house for long stretches.

7. I hate arriving late for movies now and would never watch one in this broken fashion. It seems to me, though, that I probably learned something about the construction of narratives from the practice. The lifelong moviegoing habit, which does originate for me with *Star Wars,* is that of sitting in movie theaters alone. I probably only had company in the Loew's Astor Plaza four or five times. The rest of my visits were solitary, which is certainly central to any guesses I'd make about the emotional meanings of the ritual viewings.

8. I still go to the movies alone, all the time. In the absenting of self that results—so different from the quality of solitude at my writing desk—this seems to me as near as I come in my life to any reverent or worshipful or meditational practice. That's not to say it isn't also indulgent, with a frisson of guilt, a stolen privilege every time. I'm acutely conscious of this joyous guilt in the fact that when as a solitary moviegoer I take a break to go to the bathroom *I can return to another part of the theater and watch from a different seat.* I first discovered this thrill during my *Star Wars* summer, and it's one that never diminishes. The rupture of the spectator's contract with perspective feels as transgressive as wife-swapping.

9. The function or dysfunction of my *Star Wars* obsession was paradoxical. I was using the movie as a place to hide, sure. That's obvious. At the same time, this activity of hiding inside the Loew's Astor Plaza, and inside my private, *deeper-than-yours, deeper-than-anyone's* communion with the film itself, was something I boasted widely about. By building my lamebrain world record for screenings (fat chance, I learned later) I was teaching myself to package my own craving for solitude, and my own obsessive tendencies, as something to be admired. *You can't join me inside this box where I hide,* I was saying, *but you sure can praise the box. You're permitted to marvel at me for going inside.*

10. What I was hiding from is easy, though. My parents had separated a couple of years earlier. Then my mother had begun having

seizures, been diagnosed with a brain tumor, and had the first of two surgeries. The summer of *Star Wars* she was five or six months from the second, unsuccessful surgery, and a year from dying.

11. I took my brother, and he stayed through it twice. We may have done that together more than once—neither of us clearly remembers. I took a girl, on a quasi date: Alissa Simon, the sister of my best friend, Joel. I took my mother. I tried to take my grandmother.

12. That same summer I once followed Alissa Simon to a ballet class at Carnegie Hall and hung around the studio, expressing a polite curiosity which was cover for another, less polite curiosity. The instructor was misled or chose to misunderstand—a thirteen-year-old boy willing to set foot inside a ballet studio was a commodity, a raw material. I was offered free classes, and the teacher called my house and strong-armed my parents. I remember vividly my mother's pleasure in refusing on my behalf—I was too much of a coward—and how strongly she fastened on the fact that my visit had had nothing to do with any interest in ballet. For years this seemed to me an inexplicable cruelty in my mother towards the ballet teacher. Later I understood that in those first years of adolescence I was giving off a lot of signals to my parents that I might be gay. I was a delicate, obedient, and bookish kid, a constant teacher's pet. Earlier that year my father had questioned me regarding a series of distended cartoon noses I'd drawn in ballpoint on my loose-leaf binder—they had come out looking a lot like penises. And my proclaimed favorite *Star Wars* character was the tweaking English robot, C-3PO.

13. I did and do find C-3PO sexy. It's as if a strand of DNA from Fritz Lang's fetishized girl robot in *Metropolis* has carried forward to the bland world of *Star Wars*. Also, whereas Carrie Fisher's robes went to her ankles, C-3PO is obviously naked, and ashamed of it.

14. Alissa Simon thought the movie was okay (my overstated claims generally cued a compensating shrug in others) and that was our last date, if it was a date. We're friends now.

15. I don't know how much of an effort it was for my mother to travel by subway to a movie theater in Manhattan by the summer

of '77, but I do know it was unusual, and that she was certainly doing it to oblige me. It might have been one of our last ventures out together, before it was impossible for her. I remember fussing over rituals inside the theater, showing her my favorite seat, and straining not to watch her watch it throughout, not to hang on her every reaction. Afterwards she, too, found the movie just okay. It wasn't her kind of thing, but she could understand why I liked it so much. Those were pretty close to her exact words. Maybe with her characteristic Queens hard-boiled tone: *I see why you like it, kiddo*. Then, in a turn I find difficult to relate, she left me there to watch it a second time, and took the subway home alone. What a heart-breaking rehearsal! I was saying, in effect: *come and see my future, postmom self. Enact with me your parting from it*. Here's the world of cinema and stories and obsessive identification I'm using to survive your going—now go. How generous of her to play in this masquer-ade, if she knew.

16. I spent a certain amount of time that year trying hopelessly to distract my grandmother from the coming loss of her only child—it would mostly wreck her—by pushing my new enthusi-asms at her. For instance she and I had a recurrent argument about rock and roll, one which it now strikes me was probably a faint echo, for her, of struggles over my mother's dropping out of Queens College in favor of a Greenwich Village beatnik-folk lifestyle. I worked to find a hit record she couldn't quibble with, and thought I'd found one in Wings' "Mull of Kintyre," which is really just a strummy Irish folk song. I played it for her at top vol-ume and she grimaced, her displeasure not at the music but at the apparent trump card I'd played. Then, on the fade, Paul McCartney gave out a kind of *whoop-whoop* holler and my grandmother seized on this, with relish: "You hear that? He had to go and scream. It wasn't good enough just to sing, he had to scream like an animal!" Her will was too much for me. So it was that when she resisted being dragged to *Star Wars* I probably didn't mind, being uninter-ested in having her trample on my secret sand castle. She and I were ultimately in a kind of argument about whether or not our

family was a site of tragedy, and I probably sensed I was on the losing end of that one.

17. My father lived in a commune for part of that summer, though my mother's illness sometimes drew him back into the house. There was a man in the commune—call him George Lucas—whose married life, which included two young children, was coming apart. George Lucas was the person I knew who'd seen *Star Wars* the most times, apart from me, and we had a ritualized bond over it. He'd ask me how many times I'd seen the film and I'd report, like an emissary with good news from the front. George Lucas had a copy of the soundtrack and we'd sit in the commune's living room and play it on the stereo, which I seem to remember being somewhat unpopular with the commune's larger membership. George Lucas, who played piano and had some classical training, would always proclaim that the score was *really pretty good symphonic composition*—he'd also play me Gustav Holst's *The Planets* as a kind of primer, and to show me how the Death Star theme came from Holst's "Jupiter"—and I would dutifully parrot this for my friends, with great severity: John Williams's score was *really pretty good symphonic composition*.

18. The movie itself, right: of course, I must have enjoyed it immensely the first few times. That's what I least recall. Instead I recall now how, as I memorized scenes, I fought my impatience and yet fought not to know I was fighting impatience—all that mattered were the winnowed satisfactions of crucial moments occurring once again, like stations of the cross: "Help me Obi-Wan Kenobi, you're my only hope," "These aren't the droids you're looking for," "If you strike me down, I'll become more powerful than you can possibly imagine," and the dunk shot of Luke's missiles entering the Death Star's duct. I hated, absolutely, the sewage scene. I hated not knowing who Biggs was. I hated Han Solo and Princess Leia's flirtation, after a while, feeling I was being manipulated, that it was too mannered and rote: of course they're grumbling now, that's how it *always* goes. I hated the triumphalist ceremony at the end, though the spiffing-up of the robots was a

consolation, a necessary relief. I think I came to hate a lot of the film, but I couldn't permit myself to know it. I even came, within a year or so, to hate the fact that I'd seen the movie twenty-one times.

19. Why that number? Probably I thought it was safely ridiculous and extreme to get my record into the twenties, yet stopping at only twenty seemed too mechanically round. Adding one more felt plausibly arbitrary, more *realistic*. That was likely all I could stand. Perhaps at twenty-one I'd also attained the symbolic number of adulthood, of maturity. By bringing together *thirteen* and *twenty-one* I'd made *Star Wars* my bar mitzvah, a ritual I didn't have and probably could have used that year. Now I was a man.

20. By the time I was fifteen not only had I long since quit boasting about my love of *Star Wars*, but it had become privately crucial to have another favorite movie inscribed in its place. I decided Kubrick's *2001: A Space Odyssey* was a suitably noble and alienated choice, but that in order to make it official I'd have to see it more times than *Star Wars*. An exhausting proposition, but I went right at it. One day at the Thalia on West Ninety-fifth Street I sat alone through *2001* three times in a row in a nearly empty theater, a commitment of some nine hours. That day I brought along a tape recorder in order to whisper notes on this immersion experience to my friend Eliot—I also taped *Also sprach Zarathustra* all six times. If *Star Wars* was my bar mitzvah then *2001* was getting laid, an experience requiring a more persuasive maturity, and one which I more honestly enjoyed, especially fifteen or twenty showings in. Oddly enough, though, I never did completely overwrite *Star Wars* with *2001*. Instead I stuck at precisely twenty-one viewings of the second movie as well, leaving the two in a dead heat. Even that number was only attained years later, at the University theater in Berkeley, California, two days after the 1989 Loma Prieta earthquake. There was a mild aftershock which rumbled the old theater during the Star Gate sequence, a nice touch.

21. I'll never see another film so many times, though I still count. I've seen *The Searchers* twelve times—a cheat, since it was

partly research. Otherwise, I usually peak out at six or seven viewings, as with *Bringing Up Baby* and *3 Women* and *Love Streams* and *Vertigo*, all films I believe I love more than either *Star Wars* or *2001*. But that kid who still can't decide which of the two futuristic epics to let win the struggle for his mortal soul, the kid who left the question hanging, the kid who partly invented himself in the vacuum collision of *Star Wars* and real loss—that kid is me.

PALE STARSHIP, PALE RIDER:
The Ambiguous Appeal of Boba Fett

TOM BISSELL

It is said he fears nothing, and affords his bounties no pity. His weapon of choice is a sawed-off BlasTech EE-3 rifle. His armor—dented, sandblasted, scarred by unimaginable travails—is Mandalorian, the armor of a race that was defeated by the Jedi during the Great Sith War four thousand years ago, though his connection to that mighty people remains unclear. On the upper right side of his olive breastplate, one finds a cryptic, xiphoid insignia stamp. Perhaps this indicates his ultimate group affiliation, though what that might be is anyone's guess. But it is curious. Like so much about him, it begs questions.

His helmet looks likes a fifteenth-century Prussian knight's headgear morphed with that of a twenty-third-century linebacker. No glimpse is allowed of his mouth or eyes, though both are suggested by the helmet's tinted T-visor, which endows him with much of his visual dazzle, as does the helmet's targeting range finder, which lowers and retracts, and gives him the faintly edifying air of a large science project. His cape is short, torn, and perhaps singed from its close proximity to the jetpack strapped to his back. His jetpack is also a functional missile launcher, though we do not question how this could be, and from head-on, a single slender warhead can be seen jutting from behind his helmet, looking like an unusually thick antenna.

His utility pouch holds a sonic knife and a sonic beam weapon. His red wrist gauntlets contain powerful blasters and a utility cable. His shoulderpads, both yellow, are blast plates. The yellow pads on his knees possess small rocket-dart launchers. Around his waist is a red honor sash, though from whom or where this honor derives is, again, unknown. The parts of his body not armored are covered by a reinforced double-layer gray flight suit. His boots are spike-tipped and strangely small. From his right shoulder, most terrifyingly, hang several braided Wookiee scalps.

His services are exorbitantly priced, though no one complains of this when they hire him. Nor should they. He is, the galaxy agrees, quite simply best at what he does. Some say he is a failed Imperial Stormtrooper who murdered his commanding officer and defected to a cause no larger than that of his personal enrichment. Others maintain his real name is Jaster Mereel, a Journeyman Protector from Concord Dawn who, after being convicted of treason and driven from his home galaxy, became the notorious bounty hunter known as Boba Fett.

Of course, none of the above is true. It is not even true in the sense that the *Star Wars* films are true. The technical information concerning Boba Fett's costume and weaponry comes from, of all people, a University of Michigan Ph.D. in archaeology named David West Reynolds, who provided his talents for a strange little endeavor entitled *Star Wars: The Visual Dictionary*, which really needs to be seen to be believed. Everything else is what has been grafted onto Boba Fett by fans and licensed Lucasfilm scribes. This is a lot of mythology to have accrued around a character who, in the films that unleashed him, speaks a grand total of four lines and appears in a grand total of eleven scenes—even if those films are the most popular in history. A quarter of a century after his debut, no one seems to know why Boba Fett has become so popular. Nor does anyone seem to care. He looks "cool," one often hears, and indeed he does. Nevertheless, it brings some small amount of distress, though not much surprise, to think that a stylish visage might be all that is required to secure the imperishable cultural status of American iconhood.

Although everyone wonders where Boba Fett comes from, *Star Wars* creator George Lucas has for years forbidden any of his authorized jobbers to explore that question. Presumably, Lucas would like to answer it himself. Boba Fett is a bounty hunter and a murderer, however, and it is not too difficult to imagine what forces may have begotten him. Most likely, his origin will be like that of a thousand cultural boogiemen: an early trauma, a lost father, an incinerated village, the tortured embers of childhood leading to adulthood's later, more vengeful fires. Or maybe he really is for hire and nothing more, which is of course far more unsettling. When, in *Macbeth*, murderers break into Macduff's home to find Lady Macduff and her young son, they demand to know of her husband's location. "I hope," she answers, "in no place so unsanctified / Where such as thou mayst find him." Perhaps this is the caul from which all such characters are pulled, and perhaps a loss of simple sanctity is the best explanation for those without mercy.

None of which even begins to address the whole "cool" thing.

Boba Fett action figures, statuettes, and trading cards can summon from collectors hundreds of dollars. A recent web site poll found him the second most popular character (behind Han Solo) in the *Star Wars* universe. Type "Boba Fett" into Google's search engine and smooch good-bye to the next few days, exploring the twenty thousand web sites devoted to him. (Warning: Boba Fett porn exists.) To page through the Lucasfilm publishing catalog is to see Fett's unbelievable popularity transubstantiate. No less than *eighteen* books feature Boba Fett as a centerpiece character, even German editions ("*Boba Fett: Die Stunde der Kopfgeldjäger*"). If that doesn't seem like a respectable plenitude, keep in mind that Jane Austen wrote six novels, James Joyce only three. Of course, anyone familiar with the extended world of *Star Wars* knows that one of its cardinal delights is how its minor characters are allowed to enjoy celluloid jailbreaks and emerge as interesting figures in their own right. So while Han Solo remains the most popular major *Star Wars* character to receive extrafilmic consecration (though Liam Neeson's terse, martyred Qui-Gon Jinn seems a definite momentum-gainer), characters like Darth Maul, Mace Windu, and Kyle Katarn (from the "Dark Forces" video games) compete with Boba Fett, mostly ineffectively, for minor character supremacy. (Even Anakin Skywalker's freaking pit droid from *The Phantom Menace* gets its own little book.) What Fett and Maul and Katarn and to a lesser extend Windu (we know he's a good guy, and a Jedi, but he's also Samuel L. Jackson) all have in common is their appeal to fifteen-year-old boys' images of themselves: essentially bad-ass but, you know, honorable about it.

But the richness of Boba Fett compared to similar-seeming characters can be quickly adduced by reading one of the novels devoted to them. I read numerous Boba Fett comics and novels in preparation for this essay, and while I cannot say that in every instance I enjoyed the stories, I was always at least *interested* by them. This is because Boba Fett—like Batman, or King David, or Norman Mailer's Rojack, or Rabbit Angstrom, despite the flaws of each (in order: distant, selfish, buggery-obsessed, obtuse)—is fundamentally interesting. One simply likes reading about Boba Fett.

Darth Maul, who perhaps is my favorite current *Star Wars* character, stars in the 2001 novel *Shadow Hunter,* which I picked up overtly to write this essay and covertly because I had enjoyed Maul so much in *The Phantom Menace,* initially regarding him as a figure of Fettlike intrigue. Both are mysterious, tough, and visually compelling. But *Shadow Hunter* is a miserable reading experience. It makes *The Bridges of Madison County* look like *Blood Meridian.* I am not even able to imagine a twelve-year-old boy with a drawerful of Darth Maul T-shirts finding much enjoyment here. (It is fascinating, as a side note, to read these books from a purely literary standpoint and see how language becomes another special effect: "Collaborating with Darth Sidious was about as safe as being trapped in a cave on Tatooine with a hungry krayt dragon." There exists here a conundrum of Lacanian proportions: How can a simile be a simile if the reader has absolutely no goddamn idea what the simile is referring to? And these novels have *pages* of this baloney.) I mean no disrespect to *Shadow Hunter*'s author, one Michael Reaves, and I believe it is ultimately the fault of Maul and not Reaves that *Shadow Hunter* is such a stinking pile. Because here it is: *Darth Maul is irretrievably evil and therefore uninteresting from a dramatic point of view*. The fizzless language the novel uses in describing Maul makes this plain: "Darth Maul exhaled, relaxed his stance, and nodded. His heart rate had accelerated perhaps five beats above normal at most. There was the faintest sheen of perspiration on his forehead. . . . Maul frowned slightly. Not his personal best, by any means. It was one thing to face and defeat droids. Jedi were a different matter." (The Darth Maul Workout cannot be far behind.) What makes Maul so compelling on film—coolness, impenetrability, calm—makes him ludicrous on the page. There is no struggle in an evil character. One can be tormented and do evil things—Raskolnikov is the supreme example forever—and retain dramatic interest, but one's evil nature cannot be a foregone conclusion. Fett may lack struggle at a certain fundamental level of the soul, but he does not seem irretrievably evil. After all, our hero Han Solo worked for the repulsive asshole Jabba the Hutt and was once, long ago, a cadet in the Imperial Academy—and just what exactly were those "spices" he is smuggling around the galaxy in *A New Hope*? Han Solo, under different circumstances, on a different day, could be Boba Fett, and Fett, given the right tweaks of conscience, could be Solo. This is what drapes both characters with their many fascinations. Darth Maul—and even, I daresay, Darth Vader, despite his turn at the end of *Jedi*, which is infuriating in that it is never even suggested before that film—simply cannot command the deep, artesian interest of a Boba Fett.

It is apt that Boba Fett, in all his dark, beclouded glory, debuts in *The Empire Strikes Back*, the only *Star Wars* film that might reasonably be called dark and beclouded. *Empire* begins on frozen barrens and ends on a faraway view of a desolately beautiful solar system. Between these bookends, the forces of good are routed and evil enjoys unquestioned triumph. (Not that this is good or praiseworthy in itself, as some who love *Empire* seem to think. It is merely unusual, especially for a film of *Empire*'s box office ambition.) The film's most joyous moment—R2-D2's repair of the *Millennium Falcon*'s hyperdrive—is not one of victory but rather terrified escape. And *Empire* is filled with moody pronouncements: General Rieekan's "A death mark's not an easy thing to live with"; Han Solo's nihilistic cry, "Then I'll see you in hell!" A recent re-viewing of *Empire* resuscitated moments of even heavier darkness: Solo gutting a tauntaun with Luke's lightsaber, Vader's played-for-laughs garrotings of Admiral Ozzel and Captain Needa, R2's traumatic whistling as he is devoured by a swamp monster, the *unbelievably* visceral Han Solo torture scene, and the still-shocking lopping off of Luke Skywalker's hand in his duel with Vader. Conversely, the film in which Boba Fett is dispensed with without ceremony or honor and indeed for nothing more than a burp joke, *Return of the Jedi*, features a neutered Han Solo, a mincing and unbearable C-3PO, the shameless scenery-devouring of Ian McDiarmid's Emperor, the bathetic neo-Elizabethan dialogue between Luke and Leia on Endor, and the exciting, innovative inclusion of a Death Star.

Originally, Boba Fett was conceived by *Star Wars* art director Joe Johnston and concept artist Ralph McQuarrie as the prototype of a counterinsurgency force called Super Troopers, though the idea was soon spurned in favor of a single character. Some of Boba Fett's other elements were salvaged from early, rejected Darth Vader concepts. "I painted Boba's outfit and tried to make it look like it was made of different pieces of armor," Johnston has said. "It was a symmetrical design, but I painted it in such a way that it looked like he had scavenged parts and done some personalizing of his costume." This is fitting. Boba Fett is a mercenary, and mercenaries are typically equipped with the weaponry of spendthrift nations unwilling to splash blood upon their own hands. Mercenaries also often "personalize" their uniforms. In, say, Latin America, they have been known to do so with human ears. Such supranational audacity is precisely what makes mercenaries like Boba Fett so terrifying and so cool. It is also what, in many cases, makes mercenaries appealing to those without any identifiable sense of nationalism, which includes a huge number of Americans, especially young people and especially those on the Left. One can wrap economic determinism, political revolution, and social justice around one armed, irresistible fulcrum.

But might not Boba Fett actually be a completely brutal prick? *Star Wars: The Visual Dictionary* holds that "Fett's services are famously expensive, but his honor cannot be bought. He only accepts missions which meet his harsh sense of justice." As though "a harsh sense of justice" somehow exculpates the disintegration of people whose crimes are no worse than crossing the Empire or embezzling some Imperial credits from an evil Hutt. It may seem silly to question why there exists such widespread devotion to a character of such moral obscurity—this is, after all, the nation of Billy the Kid, Jesse James, Bonnie and Clyde, and Bernard Goetz— but I would hold, sorry, it's just not.

Boba Fett is cool because he was designed to be cool. He was designed to be cool because, like Milton's Satan and *Othello*'s Iago, he is a character of wicked ambiguity, and those who put Boba Fett together created that ambiguity with care and expertise. Darth Vader is intimidating and at times emotionally overpowering, but that is not the same thing as cool. Consequently, he is not beloved by fans in the same way. The films' ostensible hero, Luke Skywalker, appealing in *A New Hope* and an insufferable pretentious druid in *Jedi*, is not cool either. Nor is he supposed to be.

Here, for the record, are Boba Fett's lines:

1) "As you wish."
2) "He's no good to me dead."

3)   "What if he doesn't survive? He's worth a lot to me."

4)   "Put Captain Solo in the cargo hold."

And here, for the record, are Boba Fett's scenes:

1) The Bounty Hunter Scene, *The Empire Strikes Back*. This is Boba Fett's first and most visually memorable appearance in the films. Devoutly loved by *Star Wars* fans, this amazingly vivid sequence, which lasts less than forty seconds, seeks less to introduce the bounty hunters than to develop the character of Admiral Piett—Imperial first officer, Vader lapdog, and efficient failure— who is himself one of the films' most likable and sympathetic characters. Piett, standing subjacent to the bounty hunters on the deck of the Super-class Star Destroyer *Executor*, is made uncomfortable by this motley assortment of interstellar vigilantism and shares that discomfort with one of his subalterns. "Scum," is actually what Piett calls the bounty hunters. "Yes, sir," the junior officer says, obviously not listening. Piett turns to find himself eye-to-toe with a saurian bounty hunter, who looks down at Piett and snarls. Piett quickly but politely excuses himself. (It is this kind of gentle character touch that makes *Empire* the superior film it is.) We close, then, on the bounty hunters, as Vader debriefs them about capturing Han Solo and the *Millennium Falcon*. Although the *Star Wars* universe putatively crawls with bounty hunters, only six are fully established in the films (not counting the ill-fatedly oblivious Greedo or Princess Leia's Boushh disguise). The six standard orthodox bounty hunters, then, are: Dengar, a squat, half-armored and half-mummy-wrapped killer whose computerized brain allows him perfect detachment; IG-88, a slender and metallic assassin droid, purportedly one of five identical robots that massacred their creators moments after activation and who, unfortunately, looks about as deadly as a pipe cleaner; Boba Fett; Bossk, the aforementioned saurian bounty hunter, a Trandoshan able to regenerate lost limbs and given to skinning his quarry alive; 4-LOM, an insectoid former protocol droid whose programming has degenerated into a

murderous fog; and 4-LOM's partner, Zuckuss, a short, enrobed, gas-masked "findsman" from the planet Gand. Save for Boba Fett, not one of these bounty hunters makes another appearance in the films, though all have turned up in extrafilmic incarnations (including an unexpectedly terrifying IG-88 in the Nintendo 64 game "Shadows of the Empire," in which one must hunt or be hunted by the whisper-thin assassin in a junkyard on the planet Kessel—a real Depends moment, believe me). It is Boba Fett, however, who stands out in the scene. So much of his effortless authority is established merely by his stance—he cradles rather than holds his blaster, his head slightly cocked (these innovations are directly attributable to Jeremy Bulloch, the actor who portrayed Fett)— and it is not surprising at all when Vader stops to address Fett directly, as though his fellow bounty hunters are not even deserving of the *assumption* that they will be able to collar Solo and the *Falcon*. Here, too, we get Fett's first line. Considering how emblematic the bounty hunter sequence has become, it is surprising to learn that almost all of the characters were thrown together only days before *Empire* director Irvin Kershner had to shoot the scene. Dengar's costume is a piecemeal agglomeration of Imperial Storm- and Snowtrooper armor, spray-painted brown. Bossk is wearing a slightly modified version of an X-wing pilot's uniform, dyed yellow. 4-LOM is a C-3PO body beneath a standard FX-shop bug-creature head. Zuckuss is like a thalidomide Tusken Raider. IG-88 is the most obvious casualty of last-secondness, and if one looks at this scene carefully one can see that IG-88's feet remain hidden. This is because the droid was impossible to balance without some sort of broad pedestal beneath him. (Anyone who has seen these movies as many times as I have—don't ask—knows of any number of such lapses, most of which reveal understandable budgetary limitations. For instance, a few moments after Greedo is shot in *A New Hope*, he walks past the camera in a crowd scene. In *Empire*, the junked IG-88 prop can be seen in the background while Chewbacca fights Cloud City's Ugnaughts for 3PO's blasted body parts. *The Star Wars Visual Dictionary* ingeniously explains the latter by claiming that an IG-88 droid followed Boba Fett to Cloud City only to be ambushed and slain by Fett "in the scrap processing levels.")

2) The Space Trash Scene, *The Empire Strikes Back*. Here Boba Fett picks up the trail of the *Millennium Falcon*, which has daringly evaded an entire fleet of Star Destroyers by attaching itself to one of them. The Star Destroyers dump their garbage (this is, according to Han Solo, standard Imperial procedure and an interesting nugget of long-ago, faraway anthropology), and the suddenly detached *Falcon* uses the jettisoned flotsam as camouflage. Unfortunately for its crew, so does Boba Fett, now piloting his starship *Slave 1* (which Industrial Light & Magic artists modeled on a street-lamp). In this scene we also hear the debut of Boba Fett's theme music. It is not a theme in the sense that the "Imperial March" (probably John Williams's most impressive composition for the films) is the theme of the Empire, or "Han Solo and the Princess" is the love theme of Han and Leia, though it is distinctive and belongs to Boba Fett alone. But it is not music, exactly. It is more of a gurgly, viola-and-bassoon thing aurally cross-pollinated with some obscure static sounds. (This scene was expanded upon in the Special Edition of *Empire*, giving *Slave 1* a bit more flying time.)

3) The Refreshments-with-Lando Scene, *The Empire Strikes Back*. This is, to my mind, the most spectacular scene in the *Star Wars* films. Here, Lando Calrissian escorts an unwitting Han, Leia, and Chewbacca to their doom within a Cloud City banquet hall. When the doors to the hall open, Han sees Vader sitting at the table's head like some sort of demonic paterfamilias. Vader rises only to have Solo unholster his DL-44 pistol and open fire, the blasts of which Vader blocks *with his freaking palm*. He then uses the Force to suck the pistol from Solo's hand to his own. (One should point out how *good* Harrison Ford is in the scene. The anger, terror, shock, and resignation in his eyes in this brief sequence equals anything he does in *Witness* or in the interrogation scene in *The Fugitive*.) Cut to Boba Fett, lightly bobbing down some nearby steps, his rifle pointed in casual menace. Wow. Really. (Though it

seems a direly missed opportunity that the actual lunch was apparently never scripted or filmed.)

4) The Torture Scene, *The Empire Strikes Back*. Here Han Solo is lowered onto an electrified thingamajig—it looks convincingly painful—while Vader looks monstrously on. Then Vader is tracked outside the torture chamber and he converses with Fett and a pensive, worried Lando. Meanwhile, in the background, Solo can he heard to be really pretty effectively screaming over the negotiations concerning his and his crew's fate. At this point Boba Fett speaks his second line. In doing so he also stands up to Darth Vader, a moment much remarked upon in *Star Wars* fandom, since Vader neglects to confront him, the only non-Emperor instance of a quailing Vader in any of the films.

5) The Carbon Freeze Scene, *The Empire Strikes Back*. Line three of Boba Fett's can be heard here, and like "He's no good to me dead," "What if he doesn't survive? He's worth a lot to me" seems a pretty ballsy thing to say to Darth Vader. Boba Fett actually does very little in this scene—another classic, another triumph for Harrison Ford—other than stand around and look steam-shrouded and inscrutably evil.

6) The Ambush Scene, *The Empire Strikes Back*. Here Luke Skywalker stumbles across Boba Fett and some Cloud City guards escorting Solo's carbonite-encased body through the cool, white hallways of Bespin. Luke hangs back, letting the small caravan pass, though it is unclear whether he is aware that the body within the carbonite is Solo's (and if Luke does know this, his subsequent doing nothing about it makes him a dick of hitherto unknown, albeit not entirely unimaginable, proportions). Once Fett and his retinue are safely avoided, Luke jogs up for a closer look, a beeping R2 rolling up behind him. Luke wisely silences R2, then steps around the corner—only to see that Boba Fett has backtracked and opened fire. Luke's eyes saucerize as he jumps back behind the corner, two of Fett's very loud, very explosive shots barely missing him. Left in Fett's assaultive wake are two big smoking holes and a light veil of smoke, which he then uses to cover his escape.

7) The "Cargo Hold" Scene, *The Empire Strikes Back*. This final, brief sequence shows Boba Fett standing on a landing platform, backlit by the molten dusk of a Cloud City sunset, as he oversees Solo's body as it is stevedored into the back of *Slave 1*. Cue line four.

Actor Jeremy Bulloch tells a funny story about this scene. Bulloch, who does not provide Fett's voice, was, like David Prowse, who played Darth Vader's body, required to say Fett's lines during filming in order to provide guidance during the postproduction redubbing process. Rather than the scripted line, Bulloch accidentally said, "Put Captain cargo in the Solo hold," and the rough cut was printed that way.

8) The "Lapti Nek"/"Jedi Rocks" Scene, *Return of the Jedi*. The most unspeakable sequence in all the films, almost too depressing to discuss at any length, finds Boba Fett at Jabba the Hutt's palace on Tatooine, listening to the Max Rebo Band and, in the expanded *Jedi* Special Edition footage, flirting with the humanoid tarts who make up Jabba's dancing troupe. In the original *Jedi*, the band's song was a *Flashdance*-grade number called "Lapti Nek." It was horrible. In the new *Jedi*, the song is called "Jedi Rocks." It is a million times worse. The computer-generated imagery is terrible, the characters ridiculous, the humor that particular brand of unfunny George Lucas humor for which *Jedi* owns the trademark.

9) The Boushh Scene, *Return of the Jedi*. Here, in another bottomlessly bad *Jedi* sequence, Princess Leia, disguised as the bounty hunter Boushh, muscles her way into Jabba's palace, Chewbacca in handcuffed tow, and threatens to blow herself and everyone else to smithereens if her demand of a fifty-thousand-credit bounty is not met. Boba Fett does two things in this scene, first raising his rifle when Boushh unveils her thermal detonator and second nodding at her respectfully when Jabba's offer of thirty thousand credits is accepted and the danger has passed. There is, needless to say, a lot wrong with this scene (including the linguistically unprecedented idea that in Boushhese "Yoto, yoto" can mean "Fifty thousand, no less"), but the most pressing issue is the strangeness of the plan the

Rebels have ginned up to free Han. First, 3PO and R2 arrive at Jabba's palace and surrender, as per Luke Skywalker's instruction. But Lando is already working there, somehow, a fact of which no one seems quite aware. Then Leia shows up, gets Chewie thrown in the pokey, and is then herself imprisoned when she blockheadedly frees Han while a dozen of the palace's freeloaders are snoozing nearby. (How *were* they going to spring Chewie?) Luke, at this point, decides to arrive, promptly gets *himself* arrested, is nearly eaten by the rancor, and then pretends that the whole cockamamie process is part of a preordained *plan*. One suspects that this plan was not given the closest eyeballing by its participants, none of whom seem to have the slightest fucking clue who is supposed to be doing what. Not that this has much to do with Boba Fett, admittedly.

10) The Skiff Fight Scene, *Return of the Jedi*. Here we find Fett jetpacking from Jabba's sail barge to one of the smaller skiffs to join battle with Luke Skywalker above the dunes of Tatooine and the sarlaac pit. It is the only instance of Fett using his jetpack in the films, and the special effect that depicts its use is bad, but forgivably so. Upon Fett's arrival at the melee, Luke chops his blaster in half. Fett, in another display of gadgetry, wraps up Luke with what looks to be grappling cable. Luke, however, does something with his wrist, which forces Boba Fett to fall, with a clatter, to the skiff's deck. (It is very tough to discern what exactly is happening in the more action-based portions of this scene, especially if you're watching an unletterboxed video of the movie.) Luke jumps to another skiff, and a groggy Fett, rising, trains his wrist blaster on Luke and prepares to fire. The blind, useless Han Solo is finally informed by Chewie that Boba Fett is in the immediate area, and Solo turns wildly, swinging a vibro-ax and hitting Fett's jetpack ignition switch. Fett is, for some reason, unable to control himself, and he flies screamingly past Luke's ongoing scuffle, bashes into the side of Jabba's sail barge—again with a nicely clattery sound effect—and rolls into the mouth of the waiting sarlaac. Not a good death. In fact, quite a stupid death, and were I one of those frothing

Boba Fett fans I would feel a little cheated by it myself. An interesting thing about this sequence is that Boba Fett seems more interested in fighting Luke than he does Han Solo, his supposed bête noire. Boba Fett actually fights Luke on *two* occasions in the films, whereas the number of blows he trades with Solo is exactly none. One would think that if the most pitiless bounty hunter in the galaxy had his archenemy blind, helpless, and three feet away from him, he might move in for the kill, but Boba Fett does no such thing.

11) The Jabba Scene, *A New Hope* Special Edition. In this bafflingly added exchange between Han Solo and Jabba the Hutt, Boba Fett makes a scene-concluding money-shot appearance: he walks across the screen, pauses, and meaningfully glances around. (We also get here a nice reprise of the weird and little-used Boba Fett theme music.) The audience with whom I saw the Special Edition burst into completely spontaneous and absolutely ecstatic joy when Fett unexpectedly stepped back into their imaginations. It was a strange response, I thought, and an amazing one in that I had little idea of how powerfully the Fett character still gripped the minds of many *Star Wars* fans. Furthermore, Fett is, significantly, the only *Star Wars* character to receive *three* CGI benefactions in the Special Editions, even when, as here, it is inappropriate and actually kind of illogical. What *is* Boba Fett doing hanging around with all these low-grade Jabba bootlicks, anyway? But Fett, it seems, is as popular with the films' creators as he is with the films' civilian fans. No one can resist him.

Searching the Web diligently enough leads to some strongholds of anti-Fett dissent. The most sustained attack on Fett's reputation can be found at www.piett.org. (This is a web site devoted to Admiral Piett, which should give a sense of the unlikely nooks and crannies the films' fans will crawl into for originality's sake.) In the site's "Fett File—Legend or Loser," purportedly written by Piett as an Imperial debriefing, the case against Boba Fett is assembled. "Fett," one file reads, "was given great praise for having captured

Solo and delivering him to the crimelord, Jabba the Hutt. In fact, it was Lord Vader who encased Solo in carbonite—all Fett did was deliver him, a task even a messenger droid could accomplish." In another file, its compiler wonders, not unreasonably: "What kind of idiot leaves an activation switch carelessly exposed on the back of his jetpack anyway?" But even this dissent carries with it the pesty self-awareness that Fett's popularity is, like glaciers or sunlight, all but impossible to thwart.

Boba Fett's cultural durability is unusually resilient for a character whose nativity came not, in fact, in *The Empire Strikes Back*, but rather by way of the animated portion of the tragically bad 1978 *Star Wars* Christmas television special. Interestingly, Fett is presented in the eleven-minute cartoon as Darth Vader's aide-de-camp rather than an independent bounty hunter. Fett, working as Vader's spy, first saves Luke Skywalker from a monster and then attempts to trick him into spilling the beans about the location of the Rebels' secret base. Meanwhile, Han and Chewie are attempting to steal some talisman or something that makes people fall asleep. Everyone meets up, Boba Fett is fingered as a spy, and that is pretty much that. Some points of interest: Fett's voice in the cartoon is not at all similar to the one he will have two years later in *Empire*, and many aspects of his overall mien have yet to be perfected; also, he first appears riding a large apatosaurus and brandishing what looks to be a mammoth tuning fork; also, while the cartoon and its Christmas special integument have apparently been purged from the canonical *Star Wars* "Bible," the enjoyably nerdy starwars.com notes in its Boba Fett file that "one report had [Boba Fett] allowing Rebel agents to capture a mystical talisman infected with an Imperial sleeping virus, though records of the event remain classified and cannot be confirmed," which at the very least shows that the folks curating Lucas's *musée imaginaire* have a pretty wicked sense of humor about themselves and what they do.

Boba Fett's second appearance was, again, not in *The Empire Strikes Back* but as a Kenner action figure. In 1979, it was announced that one could receive in the mail a new *Star Wars* figure, *one not available in stores*, by sending in several Kenner proof-of-purchase labels from other *Star Wars* merchandise. (Fett had a roughly concomitant appearance in the *Star Wars* daily comic strip—which, sadly, no one seems to remember—in a story line called "The Frozen World of Ota.") Since my mother had purchased for me every single available *Star Wars* item manufactured to that point, I had dozens of such proofs-of-purchase. I followed the given directions and a few weeks later received my figure, someone or something called Boba Fett. I did not seem to remember him from the Christmas special, which I know I must have watched, and I could only guess whether he was intended to be a villain or a hero or a robot or a man. Here was a perplexing fusion of elements: Boba Fett wore a jetpack (only a hero would possess such an inherently heroic device) but also a spooky helmet (only a villain would have a spooky helmet), a short, medieval cape (hero) but also a personal missile launcher (villain). Now, I was a highly particular boy when it came to my toys. I did not enjoy playing with other children because other children did not play correctly. They did not know the rules. They broke character. Worse, they were not even aware when they broke character. They did plainly stupid things, such as forcing Leia to hump Chewbacca or allowing Darth Vader to make ridiculous undignified statements or, worst of all, they would put *swears* in the mouths of my action figures. (I once ended a friendship when a playmate had an Imperial Stormtrooper inexcusably if accurately refer to C-3PO as a "Rebel faggot.") The only curses used in the films were "damn" and "hell"—Han Solo, both times—and thus "damn" and "hell" were the only swears I would allow to intrude into my insanely meticulous re-creation of the *Star Wars* universe. I suspect, then, that I took my Boba Fett action figure and placed it somewhere appropriately reverent, uncertain yet of Boba Fett's power or allegiance, waiting for the new film—only one year away now!—to guide my use of it.

(Many remember this Boba Fett action figure with similar lucidity. Many even remember its gnarliest feature: the ability to shoot the red plastic missile from the personal missile launcher strapped to Fett's back. The problem with this memory is that one could *not* shoot the missile from Boba Fett's personal missile launcher. I have friends who claim to remember launching Boba Fett's missile as clearly as they remember the attempted Reagan assassination, their maiden voyage upon two bicycle wheels, and their nervous breakdown upon first seeing *Gremlins*. I am sorry, but the rocket did not fire. It is apparently enough of an urban legend to have moved starwars.com to issue a public statement denying that Kenner *ever* released a missile-launching Boba Fett. Kenner had *planned* to do so until some similar rocket-launching *Battlestar Galactica* toys appeared the season before Boba Fett's unveiling and raised an unholy child-safety ruckus.)

For all this, who or what exactly Boba Fett is remains unclear. *Episode II: Attack of the Clones* will, reportedly, clear up many such questions and feature a long sequence of Boba Fett as a child, revealing his human identity. (Also, in what is almost certainly one of the perfectly baseless rumors in which the Internet specializes in spawning, martial artist–cum–action star Jet Li is said to be slated to play Fett in *Episode III*.) Fett's past and origins are so inchoate, in fact, that he is less a blank slate than a nonexistent slate: one does not overwrite the little that exists but creates a new template from imaginative scratch. One strange bit of essayistic driftwood floating through the Internet is entitled "On Behalf of a Female Boba Fett," which argues that *Star Wars* "needs another female and that . . . female can and should be Boba Fett." To cross such a casting Rubicon, the unsigned essay holds, would "provide evidence that women can serve a cinematic purpose other than romance and reproduction." One wonders if it is despite of or due to Fett's marginality that he has come to be regarded by some of *Star Wars'* loonier fans as a figure of nearly messianic importance.

The writer Susan Mayse, in her brief but insightful essay "The Tao of Boba Fett," remarks that Fett is "the unknowable *Star Wars* character—we learn nothing about his part, we never see his face, he spends minutes on the screen . . . yet he delivers mythic presence." Unlike the "other marquee characters the marketers carefully groomed for stardom," Fett has unexpectedly emerged as a figure Mayse nicely calls "the polarizing neutral." And if by mythic Mayse means a character whose utility is outpaced by portrayal, which is in turn outpaced by public reception, Boba Fett has indeed become mythic. Perhaps most shocked by Boba Fett's unlikely popularity is his creator, George Lucas: "I'm mystified by it," Lucas once said. But we should not read too much into Lucas's mystification. After all, for every Boba Fett and Han Solo and Darth Maul to spill brilliantly from Lucas's skull, there has come behind them a Droopy McCool, a Jar Jar Binks, a Salacious Crumb. An imagination of such off-the-charts inconsistency should hardly be asked to judge, much less surmise, the popularity of its own creations.

Though no less an authority than Lucas himself has maintained that Boba Fett was killed when he plunged into the belly of the sarlaac, the bounty hunter quickly saw extrafilmic resurrection following *Return of the Jedi*. (Though it *is* a little hard to imagine, given the sarlaac's CGI enhancements in the *Jedi* Special Edition, how one could survive being swallowed by its beaky and altogether nasty-looking new mouth.) But as the Gospel According to Mark says that the two Marys arrived at Jesus' tomb to find a young man in a white robe inside, whereas the Gospel According to Luke says that the Marys were greeted by *two angels* inside the tomb, whereas the Gospel According to John has Mary Magdalene arriving at the tomb *alone* and going back to fetch Simon-Peter without even *looking* inside, the resurrection of Boba Fett has seen its own mutually exclusive permutations. Fett's first resurrection, back in #81 of the old Marvel *Star Wars* comic book and inexactly recalled here from memory, came when the sarlaac, unable to digest Mandalorian armor, vomited up Boba Fett onto the sands of Tatooine. Fett wandered into a nearby settlement and ran into Han Solo—Solo was on Tatooine doing one thing or another—and Fett, in a badly amnesiac state, befriended Solo and aided him in his mission. That is, until Fett regained his memory and tried to kill Solo as they were charging out-of-control in a Jawa sandcrawler toward (wouldn't you know it!) the sarlaac. Solo tried to save Fett, but understandably gave up when Fett started shooting at him. Solo jumped off the sandcrawler, leaving Fett trapped inside, and the whole megillah plunged into that most oddly vaginal of *Star Wars* monsters. (Though if the sarlaac was too dainty to digest some freaking armor, how on earth is it supposed to digest an entire all-terrain vehicle?) Fett's file at starwars.com provides Resurrection Number Two. Here, we learn that Fett was seized by the sarlaac's numerous suckers and fiendishly kept alive while being digested, thus explaining *Jedi*'s theoretically impossible punishment of being digested by the sarlaac for "over a thousand years." Fett nearly lost his mind, it is related, as his body flooded with the sarlaac's toxins, but soon managed to blast his way out, get rescued and nursed back to health by fellow bounty hunter Dengar, and return to hunt Han Solo again, most significantly in the groundbreaking Dark Horse Comics series *Dark Empire*, which is almost certainly too good to be spoiled for readers here.

In fact, the numerous comic books devoted to Boba Fett's bounty-hunting exploits is where he has achieved his greatest popularity. It is in these stories, more importantly, where Fett grows closest to what his fans most want him to be. In Dark Horse Comics' *Death, Lies, & Treachery* (story by John Wagner, art by Cam Kennedy), we find Fett at an undisclosed point in the *Star Wars* time line, presumably before *A New Hope*. Someone called Gorga the Hutt, perhaps an ancestral relation of Jabba the Hutt's and a gangster with whom Fett shares a professional attachment, falls in love with Anarcho, the daughter of Orko the H'uun—a sworn enemy of Gorga's, unfortunately. What is a H'uun? We are told they are of a "low caste"—lower, that is, than the Hutts. Well, whatever, but Orko and Anarcho look more or less exactly like Gorga. (One really misses George Lucas's gigantic gift for nomenclature in these comics. *Gorga? Anarcho?*) At any rate, Gorga the Hutt decides that to win Anarcho's small, chubby hand he will need Orko the H'uun's blessing. As it happens, one of Orko's merchant vessels has recently been raided and robbed by a galactic pirate known as Bar-Kooda. How better than to secure Orko's badly needed connubial approval than to provide him with Bar-Kooda's scalp? And who else to serve as the tomahawk but the trusted Boba Fett?

Cut to Fett in a speeder-bike chase through some anonymous wasteland peopled by lots of runty little creatures. (In the *Star Wars* universe—whether film or comic or video game—there are precious few modes of production design: the clean totalitarianism of Imperial milieus, the naturalistically gritty mode of worlds like Hoth and Dagobah, and the repellent-muppet mode of Mos Eisley and Jabba's palace. To imagine the particulars of the latter one needs only to summon the snot-glistening nostrils of a Gamorrean Guard or the slobbering jaws of the rancor. This *Dark Crystal*ish mode also unfortunately tends to be really overused and its entertainment value *really* overestimated in the *Star Wars* universe, and it is a shame that in his exploits Boba Fett is so often exiled to the environs least appreciated by *Star Wars* fans born before 1990.) Fett's prey in this chase are, apparently, four intergalactic hoboes, the first three of whom Fett finishes off, effortlessly, on the fly. The last of them he chases into a bar, whereupon entering Fett announces: "I trust no one has given this fugitive succor?" Anyone with an even shallow understanding of Boba Fett would not be blamed for thinking, "Succor?" A few panels later Fett barks, "Guard your tongue!" This high-strung bitchiness makes him sound less like the most fearsome headhunter in the galaxy and more like he has just stepped out of Ben Jonson's *Volpone*.

It should be said that Boba Fett kills a lot of people in these comics, and that they are always scared, awful, ugly, *bad* people. The mercenary code, when elucidated by a mercenary we are clearly intended to root for, invariably holds that murder is a chilly, unthrilling business best left to professionals. (For a more compelling rendering of this tiresome stance, see Luc Besson's film *The Professional*.) Fett is introduced in one comic thusly: "Throughout the vast reaches of the galaxy—wherever fugitives met or lawbreakers conspired—one name was always uttered in hushed tones." Cut to Boba Fett shooting a whole bunch of people ("Ah!

Boba Fett!"). In *The Empire Strikes Back* and *Return of the Jedi*, though, Boba Fett is not presented this way at all. Han Solo even calls Boba Fett a "twerp" in *A New Hope*'s Special Edition. Boba Fett is, in fact, clearly and most definitely a villain, responsible for stealing away the films' most appealing character (that is, until his monumentally crappy showing in *Jedi*): Han Solo. I, for one, as a Solo-loving six-year-old, *hated* Boba Fett. I did not find him interesting. He was not forbidden fruit. He was, rather, an admittedly cool-looking but completely evil scalawag who had, to my trauma, frozen and abducted my favorite character in all of film and kept him on ice *for three fucking years*.

That is not the Boba Fett at issue here. Fett in extrafilmic appearances is, again, rather like Christ in his extrabiblical stories. Both are always more manly, more purposeful, their meaning more evident. If Jesus' message can barely be grasped from a lone reading of, say, the Gospel According to Mark, then Boba Fett's essential nature is as difficult to understand based on *Empire* and *Jedi* alone. In the comics, though, everyone knows Boba Fett on sight ("Boba Fett! Oh no!"), just as everyone instantly knows Jesus, which is not necessarily the case in the gospels. Whether consciously or unconsciously, these stories seem most interested in addressing how their central character has grown beyond the demarcations of the original narrative. Some fictional characters, it seems, are simply too *big*. They welcome addition, subtraction, clarification, filigree. One thinks of Beowulf, or Ahab, or Huck Finn. Artists and writers go back and reanimate and enlarge these characters time and again because, through some magic confluence, they mean so much *more* than the typographical marks that signify them. This is a rare and magical thing, and it is interesting that science fiction in general and the *Star Wars* films in particular are, for whatever reason, blessed with a surfeit of such characters.

In *Death, Lies, & Treachery*, Fett eventually makes his way to Bar-Kooda with the help of a character named Magwit the Magician. Magwit is a former employee of Bar-Kooda—who as it turns out is a gigantic, sperm whale–headed dude and, I think, completely visually inappropriate for the *Star Wars* universe, at least as I understand it—and Fett cunningly uses that connection to smuggle himself aboard Bar-Kooda's ship, the *Bloodstar*. After a series of magic-related adventures too tedious to recount, Fett fights and kills Bar-Kooda. (Unfortunately not before Bar-Kooda yells, "You're dead meat, Boba Fett!" "Many have tried," Fett answers while simultaneously dealing Bar-Kooda his mortal blow, "none have succeeded!") Fett turns Bar-Kooda in to Gorga the Hutt, and this strand of the story ends on a really unbelievably grisly note: Bar-Kooda's parboiled, smoking, ready-to-be-eaten-yet-still-recognizably-humanoid body on Gorga the Hutt's table. He has even got an apple wedged in his mouth. George Lucas, meet Peter Greenaway.

The story continues: Ry-Kooda, Bar-Kooda's brother, comes after Fett for revenge, but Fett, of course, dispatches him too. Gorga then wants Orko killed, but Fett gets inexplicably squeamish. "You mean murder?" Fett asks. Gorga presses him: "You *do* do exterminations?" Fett: "If the terms are to my liking . . . perhaps." Earlier in the comic the guy whacks anyone who looks at him funny, and suddenly he has developed some rabbinically elaborate murder code?

Of course, Boba Fett is not squeamish. What is happening here is typical to the development of the mercenary, and this phony heavyheartedness is introduced not to preserve the fidelity of Boba Fett's character but to provide the audience with a reminder that our hero is, in fact, a decent sort, underneath it all. It is this *Soldier of Fortune*-type bullshit that endows the likes of Bo Gritz and Randy Weaver and Timothy McVeigh with such a knuckleheaded combination of bloodthirsty fanaticism and blubbery sentimentality. Fett, at any rate, declines to kill Orko the H'uun, letting the vengeful Ry-Kooda do it for him. He then kills Ry-Kooda ("A worthy foe. In many ways, to be admired.") and sneakily keeps the down payment on Orko's murder that Gorga already proffered. That's our boy.

Another of Boba Fett's more well known comic exploits can be found in *Enemy of the Empire* (story by John Wagner, art by Ian

Gibson, John Nadeau, and Jim Amash). This is another pre–*A New Hope* story that culminates in what an average *Star Wars* fan should regard as a wet dream. As the comic itself has it, this is "the never-before-told" story of that "murderous tryst" between Boba Fett and Darth Vader. ("Murderous tryst" sounds a little less apocalyptic than what one suspects the folks at Dark Horse were going for.) Before Vader and Fett are driven to gladiatorial combat, though, the pair meet to discuss the ostensible errand Vader would like Fett to complete. (It is unclear if this story accepts as canonical Fett's first appearance in the *Star Wars* Christmas special.) Vader explains to Fett that his quarry is one Abal Karda, a colonel in the Imperial Lightning Brigade. It seems Karda has pulled a Kurtz and is hiding out somewhere with a small trunk whose contents Vader very much needs. He asks that Fett eliminate Karda and bring the trunk to him, unopened. "Sometimes," Vader says, "ignorance is wisdom, Fett." Fett, for his part, senses that his own death is pretty much preordained in this entire scenario, and quickly figures out how he will double-cross Vader and keep the trunk and its contents for himself.

After Fett leaves, Vader hires some assassins to track Fett and kill him when he attains the trunk. (Even a character as evil as Darth Vader develops in these comics some antihero scruples, berating the assassins for killing "innocent bystanders" on their prior mission. Nowhere else, of course, does Vader express the tiniest worries about innocent bystanders. Perhaps evil needs qualms when, as here, evil and its gradations are a story's focus. Without placing a small moral speed bump across the antihero's dark consciousness, it seems, one is left with *Henry: Portrait of a Serial Killer*.) After the assassins leave to hunt Boba Fett, Vader justifies to himself his strangely roundabout method of obtaining this valuable trunk by thinking: "Little do you dream of the value of what you seek, Boba Fett—and when you learn, you will never wish to part with it. That is why you must die." Uh, yeah.

Anyhow, Fett tracks Karda to a planet called Port Esta. Here, as in other such comic books, we have some very non–*Star Wars*–

looking art. The Wookiee that Fett kills at Port Esta looks like nothing so much as a large yellow gerbil. The Imperial Lightning Brigade wears fatigues that do not at all jibe with standard Imperial design. The double lightning bolt chevron running down their sleeves is the most obvious howler. This manages (a) the impressive feat of making the Imperials-as-Nazis allegory even less subtle, and more significantly it is (b) a total break with the established methodology of Imperial ranking. Imperial Stormtroopers, it seems pretty clear, determine rank by whoever happens to be wearing the big orange shoulder pad. Imperial officers, on the other hand, determine rank by the red and blue (and in the case of a brass hat like Grand Moff Tarkin, red, blue, and yellow) insignia plaque on their chests. Admirals and Grand Moffs get twelve blocks, generals get eight blocks, captains and Moffs get six, and so on. (Rebel echelons are a little harder to make out, since they seem, by and large, a lot less uptight about the whole "rank" thing. Lando, remember, became a general after doing absolutely nothing. Although, in *Empire*, General Rieekan does wear an insignia plaque that bears a striking resemblance to the Ralston-Purina corporate logo.)

On Port Esta Fett learns of Karda's location and the probable contents of his trunk: it has something to do with a race of people called the Icarii, who are both precognitive and can, more interestingly, survive dismemberment. (I will spoil it for you: the trunk contains the head of a female Icarii—a really annoying one—and Vader wants this head to tell him the future, in particular how it relates to his and the Emperor's relationship, which from the looks of it had sprung some serious leaks long before Luke was even thinking about telling Uncle Owen to take one of his moisture vaporators and cram it sidewise.) The story then follows Fett as he procures the trunk from Karda. In the process of fighting Karda for the trunk and its prophetic head, Fett tosses the colonel into a pool of boiling slag. Karda's death is handled pretty graphically, which goes along with the comic's uncommonly brutal depiction of Fett's ruthlessness: other than the face-shot Wookiee and the smelted Abal Karda, Fett scores no less than six kills (four of which are the assassins Vader has hired to track Fett), including two out-and-out, face-to-face, gangland-style liquidations that move one to wonder just what is the appropriate age for these little funny books, anyhow?

Then Vader shows up, and the *real* story—the story promised in the title and on the cover—begins. Boba Fett in two-fisted, gadget-laden glory is a topic of near fetishistic fascination in *Star Wars* comics and novels. One can see why, as the films' only extended instance of Boba Fett in combat occurs in the already addressed sarlaac scene, which is, again, filmed by the late Richard Marquand in such a cramped, incompetent style that the scene, like drunken sex, quickly degenerates into something boundlessly disappointing, no matter how can't-miss an idea it must have initially seemed.

But before getting to *Enemy of the Empire*'s Vader-Fett battle, I should really underscore *how* obsessed with a fighting Fett fans generally seem to be. In the *vastly* underrated Sony Playstation game "*Star Wars*: Masters of Tëras Käsi," one can take control of one of twelve different *Star Wars* characters and basically beat the snot out of one's opponent, who is controlled by either the computer or a couchside companion. In a sociological triumph, the game keeps track of how often each character is selected. On my console, in ascending order of popularity, Darth Vader is selected 8 percent of the time, a Tusken Raider is selected 13 percent of the time, and Boba Fett is selected 57 percent of the time—and I am not even a qualified Boba Fett *fan*. Less anecdotally, this fascination extends into the Internet's oddest corners. One site (www.grudge-match.com) enshrines an interesting debate that argues, *Crossfire*-style, what would happen if Boba Fett and the Predator ever met in a dark alley. (The Predator, for those who don't remember, is the eponymous villain of the terrific 1987 John McTiernan film which starred Arnold Schwarzenegger, and a highly underrated 1990 sequel, a Danny Glover vehicle directed by Stephen Hopkins.) The argument provides a fascinating porthole into the extremely knowledgeable, developmentally arrested intellects of the sort of people who go in for this stuff, and deserves to be addressed at some length. Fett's champion, Dave, feels that "Pred needs to check in with the optometrist. What kind of fool has thermal vision, but no *regular* vision? He's sure going to have trouble seeing Boba Fett. . . . Now, don't go telling me about how Predators fight Aliens and all that [*Predator* v. *Alien*, apparently the *Roe* v. *Wade* of www.grudge-match.com, has also been the subject of several comic books]. The *first* Alien was scary, but since then I see those things get mowed down in baker's dozens, by Winona Ryder no less." Joe, the site's Predator partisan, wonders how Dave "can say that having the skull of an ALIEN is not that big of a deal. These things have **ACID FOR BLOOD**. . . . The only time Aliens were EVER mowed down . . . was when they were up against an elite team of Marines and even then only one survived (this, of course, was due to the fact that he was Michael Biehn who is arguably the coolest person on the planet)." Joe, perhaps sensing how argumentatively rudderless things have gotten, resorts to more limpid logic: Boba Fett, he points out, has two accomplishments, one being that he "alertly points out that the *Millennium Falcon* is not a piece of trash" and "falls into that [sarlaac] pit thing." The Predator, on the other hand, in the first film "carves up an elite unit of special forces . . . and then destroys Mexico with a bomb on his arm," and in the second film "emasculates drug dealers, cops, federal agents AND Bill Paxton. . . . He is finally hurt badly (but not killed) by Sgt. Murtaugh." Dave sallies with the following: "Boba Fett: Defeated by combined forces of Jedi Knight, Indiana Jones, massive enraged Wookiee and smooth-talking con man. . . . Predator: defeated by *Jingle All the Way* costar. Defeated again by *Gone Fishin'* costar." Fett goes on to win 60 percent of the site's fan vote.

Now, before actually venturing into battle with Vader, Fett notes to himself that he "doesn't fear the Dark Lord, but only a fool seeks close combat with Darth Vader." It is hard to tell whether this is meant as a tongue-in-cheek moment—the clauses cancel each other out—but the fact remains that anything Fett does in comics such as *Enemy of the Empire* is typically lavished with every sort of justification and asterisk. His fight with Vader is no exception. It may be that these types of maneuvers seek to prove Fett's essential thoughtfulness, or it may be that Fett needs to be shown as one who is constantly sizing up his given situation. But it is hard to imagine many other *Star Wars* characters whose motives need to be so relentlessly autopsied. In *Enemy of the Empire* Darth Vader is able to behave however he pleases. The comic versions of Han Solo or Luke Skywalker may think excessively to themselves—the interminable contents of thought bubbles is by far these comics' worst aspect—but those thoughts never come in the spirit of pushy authorial justification. Boba Fett seems not a character in so many of these stories but a series of affected poses. Perhaps this is the curse of a character of polarizing neutrality: his studied nature is both what makes him interesting and ultimately restricts his fictional possibilities.

Vader opens his battle with Boba Fett by using his lightsaber to chop Fett's speeder cycle in half ("Let us remove escape from the equation"), whereupon Fett opens fire upon Vader with his wrist blaster. Vader, in turn, blocks the shots with his lightsaber. Finally, Vader ricochets one of Fett's wrist blasts back at him, winging him in the head. Behind the combatants is a cliff overlooking a magmatic ocean of slag, and Fett—holding the trunk while fighting off a sudden burst of Vader's Jedi mind trickery—jumps backwards off the cliff's edge, which recalls Luke's suicide fall in *Empire*. "The fool!" Vader calls, rushing to the edge. Fett, of course, is hovering there, jetpack blazing. He shoots Vader in the face, and Vader drops his lightsaber and collapses. "I win," Fett says, alighting beside Vader. Vader, who at this point is done fucking around, begins to crush Fett's heart with Jedi telekinetics. Fett, for once, turns contrite: "My Lord, we should not be at odds. . . . Let us remove the cause of our dispute." With that, Boba Fett kicks the head-containing trunk off the side of the cliff. Vader, who has only so much Force to go around, it seems, levitates the trunk back into his arms while Fett gets away. The fight is all for naught, however, in that Vader has to crush the decapitated, truth-telling Icariian head when she prophesizes that her power will come between Vader and the Emperor, while Fett, for his part, has a chance to kill Vader as he is levitating the trunk, but as he himself says at story's end, "Where's the profit in that?"

A lot of these Fett stories end on such relentlessly ambivalent notes. Fett doesn't quite win, doesn't quite lose. There is always a lot of drollery about how Fett has secretly managed to steal some tiny spoil of war, winkingly revealed in the final panel ("And his time had not been entirely wasted," concludes one; "And he doubts his owner will miss it," concludes another). Why, one wonders, such narratively hedged bets? I think it is because the victory of the mercenary means the loss of civilization, since mercenaries can be bought and civilization at its most ideal exists beyond such taxable realms. If history teaches us anything about mercenaries, it is that mercenaries are admirable in the abstract and totally awful in the actual, Hessians and Contras being two vivid cases in point. The ambivalence of art devoted to mercenaries is best shown in how it can never seem to actually award them a brimming war chest. By withholding nothing from mercenaries but decisive victory, such art places its visible loyalties on the side of civilization but its deeper sympathies on the side of the mercenary. One sees this sort of thing all the time in the thought of the Too Left: the same people who frame posters of Che Guevara, admire the Cossack-executing Lenin, and read without blinking Marx's most egregious justifications of class-based violence will gnash and foam at the thought of the United States using force to pursue its interests or secure its protection. Not that they feel strongly enough about it to revolt, mind you. By doing nothing but complaining they remain citizens of civilization, but in the weathered backpack of the mercenary their truest, most secret hearts travel. The nice thing about this psychological arrangement is that the mercenary so rarely wins that one's final loyalty is left blissfully unchallenged, and it is upon this vexing moral seam where Boba Fett gains his admirers and popularity. We are *happy* that he bested Darth Vader, happy that he got away, and happy, most of all, that he didn't actually win.

∗ ∗ ∗

Star Wars is many things to many people. Some see it as an antifascist fable. Some see it—inexplicably, in my view—as a *proto*fascist fable, evidenced by the Force-as-controlling-influence and especially by Luke's rejection of soulless technology in his bid to destroy the Death Star at the conclusion of *A New Hope*. But what no one seems to comment upon are the films' many excursions into the grayer world between these two poles. Lucas very clearly loves the world of "scum and villainy" Alec Guinness's Ben Kenobi derides: bounty hunters, smugglers, and the Bedouinlike Tusken Raiders all send his imagination into hyperspace and reap some of its most substantial visual rewards. The mighty Force is of scant comfort in such chaotic realms, as Luke discovers in the Mos Eisley saloon, watching gentle, kindly old Ben use his lightsaber to disembowel one fellow and dismember another. Lingering in the gray seems like a very American fascination, and while Fett's Japanese fans see him essentially as an honorable samurai, Jeremy Bulloch, the British actor who portrayed him, feels that Fett's stock is more strictly Western, in both senses: "I modeled Boba very seriously on Clint Eastwood in *A Fistful of Dollars*," he told the Web magazine the *11th Hour* a few years ago. "It's exactly that, but in armor. . . . I found with Boba Fett, the less I do, the better. He stands in a certain way. He cradles his gun—he loves it. And he's always ready."

Bulloch has had some time to think about this. Despite a long career—including playing Hamlet at nineteen, serving as Q's assistant in the James Bond films, and a recurring role in the inexplicably popular British sci-fi series *Doctor Who*—Bulloch has accepted that the basis of his fame is a character whose amazing voice doesn't even belong to him but to an actor named Jason Wingreen, whose face we never see and whom Bulloch spent a two-film total of four weeks before a camera portraying. (In the Special Edition of *A New Hope*, it is not Bulloch but various Industrial Light & Magic artists within Fett's armor.) "When I got it," Bulloch has explained, "I knew it was . . . not a very big part. And then Irvin Kershner said, 'Now this is your big scene with the bounty hunters. You've got

Dengar and Bossk and the others, but Boba Fett is the main one.' And I said, 'Oh, is he?'" (More rabid fans of Boba Fett might be interested to know that the man who portrayed him pays his bills in lean acting times by interior decorating.) Bulloch has also lamented how heavy and awkward Fett's backpack was, how Fett's helmet largely eliminated human vision, and how he had to count his steps in every scene in order to hit his marks and not fall down, which he did anyway, repeatedly. Do such disintegrating particulars change our thoughts about Boba Fett? Do they somehow leach away his mythic stature?

American intellectuals from Emerson to Dwight Macdonald to Susan Sontag have pissed and moaned about the refusal of mass culture to indulge in the messy questions of True Art. Mass culture, Macdonald wrote in his landmark essay "Masscult & Midcult," "offers its customers neither an emotional experience nor an aesthetic experience, for these demand effort. . . . It asks nothing of its audience . . . and it gives nothing." But what is one to make of a culture that loves pop movies and pop novels and pop music and pop art devoted to the exploits of the loose cannon, the mercenary, the murderer-poet, the bounty hunter, the Batcave vigilante? Such art actually asks quite a lot of its audience, I think: What kind of a hero do we really want? Does it matter if he or she violates agreed-upon social contracts? What is justice, and by whom is it best executed? Are those who administer justice according to some private cosmology ever to be trusted? While the *Star Wars* films may themselves never directly pose such questions, Boba Fett and his strange popularity certainly do, and they are not insignificant in a culture of teenage suburban assassins, death- and ducat-worshiping gangbangers, an extreme Right which kills to protect unborn life and kills to revenge those killed, and an extreme Left either unwilling or unable to imagine a situation in which the justice of a democratic nation-state is preferable to that of fascist Islamists. One finds particles of mercenary romance in each of the above scenarios, and in each the mercenary becomes the vicarious dark half of otherwise polite society.

And if society tends to get the government, architecture, and mercenaries it deserves, it is all the more reason to think hard about those homegrown renegades we most esteem. If Boba Fett serves as a lightning rod for anything more significant than admiration of his arresting costume and four gritty lines of dialogue, perhaps it is as the embodiment of our third-wave, superpowerless anxiety, which long predates the events of September 11, 2001. Here, our politics do not begin to address our fears, our fears can no longer be held at bay by money and distance, and we know that there exists someone, somewhere, not that far away and not at all long ago, capable of inflicting upon us massive amounts of pain or securing for us a ferocious measure of justice. The trouble is, only he gets to decide which one we have coming.

DAGOBAH, NEBRASKA

DAN BARDEN

[1]

I remember the summer of 1980 for two reasons. It was when *The Empire Strikes Back* was released, and it was when my friend Andy (not his real name) and I hitchhiked from California to Boston. We saw *Empire* near the middle of our trip, in Salt Lake City, and forever in my mind the two things will be connected: hitchhiking with Andy and Luke's journey toward discovering that Darth Vader is his father.

My traveling buddy was something of a Wookiee: with Andy at 6'6" and me at 6'3", I sometimes wonder why anyone picked us up. We set out on a beautiful day, our first ride across the Sierras in the back of a pickup. Andy had seen *Empire* the day before we left, and he tortured me for two days before Utah over "the secret."

The end of our first day was at the Mustang Ranch, a legal brothel near Reno. I'd like to believe that it was then, sleeping beside the brothel parking lot, when Andy first mentioned it. Andy had enjoyed himself at the whorehouse—he was actually *whistling a happy tune*—but I'd had a problem with, ah, *finishing*. I've never been, thank God, to a prostitute again. We threw down our sleeping bags beside the road and he asked me something like *Do you want to know something about the movie that you might not want to know?* I'm certain the sentence was convoluted by his desire to both tell the secret and keep it.

Andy had been having trouble before I invited him on the trip. A brilliant young man and the best basketball player I've ever known, he'd been to something like five colleges without getting a degree. I had originally planned to take the trip by myself, but at my sister's high school graduation, while, no doubt, promoting my new adventure, I realized exactly how scared I was. California coastal roads were one thing, but the Midwest was quite another. I've seen pictures of my twenty-year-old self on that day and I looked *manic*. When I found Andy I'm sure I presented the idea as a way to end his troubles. I think I got him at exactly the right moment. The Force was strong with me.

[2]

Leigh Brackett is credited as a screenwriter of *Empire*, working from a story by Lucas. In the continuing colonization of my imagination, an important flag was planted by Howard Hawks with *Rio Bravo*. Brackett—a woman—wrote that script as well, and the movie is one I think about as much as I think about *Empire*. She is also credited (along with William Faulkner) on Hawks's *The Big Sleep* as well as Robert Altman's revisionist look at Raymond Chandler's *The Long Goodbye*. She wrote the first draft of *Empire* just before she died of cancer. (Subsequent drafts were written by then–young buck Lawrence Kasdan.)

Rio Bravo is a Western about a drunk—played brilliantly by Dean Martin—who redeems himself. It's also a story about the strength of his friends who *allow him* to redeem himself. It's a great action movie—one of the best ever—but it essentially comes down to John Wayne wondering whether his best buddy has the *cojones* to put down the bottle while both of them are besieged by bad guys. I enjoy thinking that this was Leigh Brackett's contribution to the script because it seems like a womanly concern—watching men support each other—but Brackett has said that Hawks wanted that, too.

[3]

Wookiees that we were, we spent many hours on the side of the road. Hitchhiking compels you to find new places within yourself. A few months before this trip, I had heard God's voice beside a road in Ukiah simply because there was nothing else to do *but* hear God's voice (He told me what He often tells me: *you'll be okay*). After Andy and I had talked about everything we could possibly talk about, we talked about everything else. We made up silly songs about hitching a ride. We decided that I would try to guess the secret of *Empire*.

I tried. I got stuck on the notion that it must be about Princess Leia or that it involved the death of a major character. We had agreed that Andy would not give me any hints, though, and I ran out of ideas pretty quickly.

In spite of my frustration, those first days of our trip were blissful. There's no other word for it. For a while, too, it seemed like I'd put an end to Andy's troubles. On the road, it turned out, he had a light spirit. We wrote a song about it that I still remember:

Happy to ride
In the back of your truck
It's a long hard haul
But we're fucked up
We've got bourbon
Enough for three
If you'll just stop
To let us pee

Finally, in the day before we saw *The Empire Strikes Back* in Salt Lake City, I gave Andy permission to ruin the movie for me. *Go head, tell me.* I never would have guessed it, and yet it made perfect sense. Even as we waited in line on those impossibly clean streets with those impossibly well-mannered teenagers, that thought balloon was still hovering above my head: *Darth Vader is Luke's father?* Andy had robbed me of the surprise, but he had left me with the majesty. He had tried to explain to me the context of the "there is another" bit, but he screwed that up, and I didn't understand until I saw the movie.

The Empire Strikes Back, however, was not a joyous experience for me. Which is not to say that it was a *bad* experience. Walking from the theater, I felt like my imagination had been imploded. And this had nothing to do with the "secret" of the movie. I had been disturbed by the way the movie started, and I was even more disturbed by the way it ended. Luke begins maimed and ends up even more maimed. Did we really have to wait three years for all this to be resolved? There's a *reality* at work in *Empire* that is absent—and *should be* absent—from the rest of the trilogy. Cutting off Luke's hand, I have to say, wouldn't have been any more shocking to me if it had been his penis.

[4]

In some sense, it *was* Luke's penis. *Empire* was the film, remember, where Luke is revealed as a eunuch. Was there any doubt left that our boy would not be getting the only girl left in the galaxy? That look on Carrie Fisher's face when Han is frozen always kills me. It's clear that Skywalker is alone with nothing to look forward to but completing his Jedi training. Without a hand. And with a face that doesn't look quite right.

That's another thing. Let's talk about Mark Hamill's face. As legend has it, he suffered a car accident between the filming of *Star Wars* and *Empire*. I say "legend" because the Internet message boards are divided on this issue. The way I heard it, the wampa sequence at the start of *Empire* was necessary because it accounted for the changes in Luke's face. *Something* happened. Hamill's skin looked like it had been scoured by bad dreams, as though he had been melted and recast in a different form. His cheekbones were in different places. He looked damaged.

The Empire Strikes Back is a story about failure. In Luke's case, a very particular kind of failure. He loses sight of the big picture and therefore jeopardizes the entire rebellion. He abandons his Jedi training in order to help his friends, and his friends end up in *worse* shape. The movie ends with Han in the clutches of Boba Fett, and it's a real question as to whether Luke's going to pull his head out enough to help him. *Join me, Luke. It is your destiny.*

[5]

A few days after watching *The Empire Strikes Back* in Salt Lake City, we got picked up by two pretty girls from the University of Wyoming who were returning home to Nebraska. As soon as we got into that car, we knew we'd made a mistake. They offered us pot and they offered us booze. And then they offered us more of both. And then more. And then even more. I have a foggy memory of one of them leaning over the bench seat of their old car—a Fairlane or a Rambler or something—and asking us if we were "lightweights." There was nothing on that Nebraska horizon for hours but that horrible question. *Are you guys lightweights? I didn't think there were any lightweights in California.* Andy and I smoked and smoked, drank and drank, smoked and smoked. But then, at a certain point, we had to stop. This part of the story still embarrasses me. In some ways, I remain that twenty-year-old who was proudest of his capacity for self-abuse. I don't remember us ever *stopping* before. And then they asked us the question again. *Are you guys lightweights?* Maybe it was the half week on the road. Maybe it was all the drugs and drinking we'd *already* done. We just had to say, "no more."

We immediately began plotting our escape. We both did that

lifted-eyebrows, these-chicks-are-crazy thing which was inadequate camouflage for the fact that we both knew we *were* punking
out on the drugs and booze, that they had emasculated us, fragile
creatures, by insisting that we do more.

We ended up at some huge Gilley's-like country-western bar, a
warehouse filled with drinking and dancing Stetsons. We had eaten
hamburgers, and it was already dark. The girls seemed to *like* us,
but in some perverse way that I did not understand. They kept asking us bizarre questions that were in some distant way pertinent:
*You guys aren't Democrats, are you? Do you know any homosexuals?
What's the deal with that?* They never left us alone long enough to
talk, and Andy and I were trying to be gentlemen by not just ditching them. Our situation, I have to imagine, was complicated by
extreme drunkenness. *Listen, Ladies, it's been nice to meet you, but
we'd love to go sleep under that freeway bridge now.* We tried to get
each other alone. I winked and went to the bathroom, but Andy
didn't follow me. I came back from the bathroom and then Andy
went. So, then *I* followed *him.* But he was gone. I couldn't find him.
Anywhere.

[6]

A comparison between Dean Martin and Mark Hamill might seem
a stretch, but there's nothing more shocking to me in *Empire* than
what a prick Luke turns out to be. His contempt for Yoda, his
wimpiness during his Jedi training, his terrible defiance of his master in leaving Dagobah—it's really quite shocking. Lucas must have
imagined that the clouds of glory trailing from the destruction of
the Death Star would get young Skywalker over the hump, but I
remain unconvinced.

The Empire Strikes Back, it seems to me, has similar concerns as
Rio Bravo. Yoda does what he can to see that Luke will recover
from his selfishness and shortsighted goals to become the man who
can save the galaxy from Darth Vader, but whereas John Wayne
was successful with Dean Martin, Yoda was *not* successful with

Luke. Luke leaves the Dagobah system on his dubious quest to keep his friends from pain as Yoda warns him that "he would destroy all for which they have fought and suffered." And then, if that weren't enough, we're given the conversation between Yoda and the ghost of Ben Kenobi in the moment after Luke leaves: *there is another*. Forgive me for complaining about a movie that I dearly love, but wouldn't that be a little like John Wayne sobering up Dean Martin, sending him into a gunfight, and then telling Walter Brennan, "Don't worry about it, if this guy doesn't pan out, we can always get Sinatra"?

[7]

I looked everywhere for Andy. And then I went back for the girls and *we all* looked everywhere for Andy. I don't remember the name of that Nebraska town, but it was small, and it *scared me* that we couldn't find him. His mother had given me this look at my sister's graduation—a look of *please don't*—and I was already imagining having to call her. I felt like I was down behind enemy lines, and I couldn't help but think that some redneck had forced Andy to admit he'd voted for Carter. And then bashed his head in.

After we'd searched the town until we couldn't stand, I spent the night at the girls' house. Their concern for Andy had instantly humanized them for me. When I woke up the next morning, I had the simple epiphany that if Andy were still alive, there was only one place he would likely be: *in a motel*.

When I walked into the motel room to find Andy lying in a comfortable bed, watching cartoons, I was filled with such rage and righteousness. He explained that he'd wandered off because he thought that I wanted to sleep with one of the girls, and he just needed to get away from them. And then he got lost.

There's a moment near the start of *Rio Bravo* when John Wayne looks at Dean Martin with deep disgust. Yoda also does a pretty good job—for a puppet—of showing his disappointment with Luke. This was my moment with Andy. I think I imagined that I had done him a great favor by bringing him on the trip. Was this how he repaid me? Andy's new happiness was fragile—I must have known that—but I ignored his fragility. I needed to punish him.

I shouted. I asked him what the *hell* he thought he was doing. I asked him how he could be so *stupid*. I told him that we couldn't continue the trip because I couldn't *depend* on him. Because I couldn't *trust* him. I said it again: *I can't trust you.* I told myself that I was protecting him from his own stupidity, but it was much more disgusting than that. I had offered him the Jedi training, I had given him the Deputy Sheriff's badge, and now I was telling him that he didn't deserve either. I was such an unbelievable dick. I don't think I ever realized what a dick I was until this moment.

So we hitched one last ride to Omaha, and from there we took a bus to Boston. My friendship with Andy ended at the same moment as our trip. We pretended we were friends for about a decade after that, but it was never the same—no more "happy to ride." Eventually, he stopped talking to me, and he refused to tell me why. I knew why.

[8]

Return of the Jedi was downgraded, you remember, from *Revenge of the Jedi.* I couldn't help but see it as a recognition of Luke's diminished power. Does anyone remember what Luke did in that movie? As the new title suggests, his main job seems to be *showing up*. At the end of the trilogy, he is even more spectral than Ben Kenobi. Ultimately, it's the Ewoks who destroy the empire.

[9]

In the days after Salt Lake City, I felt betrayed to discover that my impulse to make Luke the hope of the galaxy may have been misplaced. *That* bit of information—"there is another"—ruined my day even more than the idea that Luke had washed out of Jedi training or that Darth was his father. For me, that was the most radical thing about the film. Not that Luke might be turned to the dark side (that might have been *cool*). What bothered me was the idea that he might no longer be the protagonist. That didn't seem right to me. So much had depended on him.

I teach creative writing, and there's nothing that my students love more than a trick ending, although I do my best to dissuade them. Looking at *The Empire Strikes Back* from a distance of twenty-one years, I'm much more surprised by Luke's defiance of Yoda than I am by Luke's father. I'm happy to be able to report to my students that the big secret of *Empire* doesn't amount to much. The reason that none of the actors guessed it is because it's not essential to the structure of the story. At best, it's a sideshow to the real questions, which will *not* be answered by the end of the movie: does Luke have the *cojones* to save the galaxy? And if he doesn't, who will?

CELEBRATING THE FIFTIETH ANNIVERSARY OF CATCHER IN THE RED-EYE:
Episode IV:
A New Goddamn Hope

NEAL POLLACK

[EDITOR'S NOTE: *Since nameless parties within the Republic may be conspiring against this story, which is a parody, we have opted to change the names of the central characters, and of almost everything else, lest we face a lawsuit that will rob us of everything we've worked so hard to achieve. So remember that if the names seem like rip-offs of an old* Mad *magazine cartoon, but lamer, it's not our fault. May the Farce be with you.*]

If you really want to hear this story, the first thing you should know is that it takes place during a period of civil war, for Chrissake. Rebel spaceships, striking from a crappy hidden base on some phony planet, have won their first victory against the evil Galactic Empire, but the whole thing bores me, if you want to know the truth. As for me, you sure as hell don't want to hear *my* whole goddamn tale of woe or all that Clown Wars hero crap. So I'll spare you most of the details. I'll just tell you about the stuff that happened around the time I met old Osama bin Kenobi, which eventually led to the part where my father cut off my hand and I had to come down to this crumby floating space hospital to take it easy. Sure, I could be flying around the goddamn galaxy, trying to exercise my Red-Eye *powers* and all that kind of garbage, but who needs the hassle? Sometimes, I swear I'm smarter than everyone else in the universe.

Anyway, where I want to start telling is the day Uncle Omen and I bought a couple of goddamn androids. We lived on Tattooyou. You've probably heard of it, especially if you read magazines about godforsaken desert planets where there's nothing to do all day. That planet is strictly for the birds, I'm telling you. If there's a bright center of the universe, then Tattooyou is the planet that it's farthest from. Nobody good has ever come from there, except for maybe me, but like I'm so goddamn special.

This big enormous thing pulls up outside our house, sort of like a truck but it doesn't have any wheels, and all these Jewas start swarming around, wearing their little brown burlap sacks. I swear, sometimes Jewas bug the hell out of me, they really do. Then my Aunt Beirut says, "Puke, tell Uncle Omen if he gets a translator, make sure he speaks Bocce." I had to take Bocce in school for three years, and I never saw any goddamn use for it. Why can't people all just speak English, like the rest of the galaxy? That's what I say, and anyone who disagrees with me is full of horse manure.

So we get down there, and Uncle Omen says he needs an android who understands the binary language of moisture vaporators. Whatever the hell those are. He picks out this golden one, P-PBO, standing there with his big eyes, all scrawny and faggy. That android had this really awful English accent. It was a put-on, I'm telling you. He was a big phony. I can't stand phony androids, I swear. Most of them are so fake, you can't trust a word they're saying. Then my uncle picks out another android, a little red R-P-OO unit, and it just blows up right there in my face! Goddamn cheap Jewas. So we take this other one, this blue one, and then my uncle tells me to take them to the garage and clean them up. I was all excited to go into Toshi station and pick up some power converters. Instead I had to spend a whole night with a couple of goddamn faggy androids. I sure was sore.

★ ★ ★

So there I was, sitting with these androids in my crummy garage. It just wasn't fair! Ol' Jiggs was right, I was never gonna get out of there, not unless I could alter time or some crap like that, or speed up the goddamn harvest. Then that blue android starts playing a movie or something.

I swear to God, the girl in that movie was the best-looking goddamn girl I've ever seen, and I've seen some doozies, I'm telling you. I've never had sexual intercourse, except with my pillow, but I've thought about it a lot. One time I was necking with a girl out back of the greenhouse, and I swear I was going to have sexual intercourse with her or some such thing, but then Uncle Omen hit me on the back of the knee with a hoe and told me to get back to work.

But let's talk about this girl. She was a peach! I'm a sucker for a girl in a veil. So I asked that phony yellow android who she was, but he said he didn't know. I sat there and watched her say, "Help me, Osama bin Kenobi, you're my only hope," over and over again. I didn't know who this Osama bin Kenobi was. There was Old Bin Kenobi, this strange hermit who lived over by the Dune Sea, but why the hell would he have two names anyway?

The girl was pretty, and I really wanted to have sex with her. I had a big boner, actually, if you just have to know. I think about having sex all the time. I swear I do.

Then the movie stopped.

"Where'd she go?" I asked, but that stupid android just bleeped and bleeped, like a goddamn bleeping android.

That night at dinner, I asked Uncle Omen and Aunt Beirut if they knew Osama bin Kenobi. My uncle just about had two heart attacks when I mentioned his name. He said Osama bin Kenobi was dead, like my father. My aunt and uncle were nice and all, but they got awfully touchy when I talked about my father, like he was some sort of madman bent on ruling the universe or some such crap.

Anyway, Uncle Omen told me not to go looking for old Osama bin, that he wanted me on the south ridge working the credenzas.

"Aw, hell," I said. "If those androids work out, I wanna go to the Academy!"

I didn't eat another bite of dinner, I swear. Later I went to stand outside in the wind, like I do sometimes in the evenings. I had a pretty good tan and nice hair and all that, and I was wearing my favorite tunic, but who cares, for Chrissake? I wanted some adventure. This planet had two suns, but they were both stupid and boring.

I'm the most terrific driver you ever saw in your life. It's awful how good I am. If I'm on my way to town to pick up some irrigation equipment, I usually take my landspeeder through a canyon or some such place. If somebody tries to stop me, I'm liable to run him over like a womp rat. It's terrible.

When I woke up the next morning, I sure had a lot of goddamn driving to do. You see, that damn phony British android was all tizzied up because his little blue friend had split during the night.

"How's that?" I asked.

He was Master Puke-ing me and all that suck-up crap, but I just stuck him in the landspeeder and made tracks. That blue android was gonna cause me a lotta trouble. It may sound corny, but I cared about the cute little guy, really I did.

So we found him sure enough in the middle of this canyon, but there were all these sandpeople tracks around and I could see a couple of Mentos. Why those damn sandpeople don't just ride horses is beyond me, I thought. Then this stinky sandperson was on top of me. Goddamn it, they were always barging in on me, trying to hit me with their sticks. They have all these stupid bandages on their face because they have acne something fierce. It's disgusting, really it is.

"For Chrissake, get off of me!" I said.

But the damn thing kept hitting me. What a pain in the ass. The sandpeople are a buncha phonies, and they knocked me out.

I swear to God I must have been unconscious for *days*. But when I came to, Bin Kenobi was hovering over me. He was about seventy years old, but he looked older than that, and he was wearing the same burlap sack that he'd had forever, it seemed like. Sometimes I wondered what old Bin was living for. He was all stooped over, and he had very terrible posture, and he didn't even have a woman by his side. When I'm old and living in the desert, I sure as hell am going to find a girl to cook me dinner. And she won't be a phony, neither. No sir.

"Boy, am I glad to see you!" I said.

"Tell me, young Puke," he said. "What brings you this way?"

"Of course, sir. Well, this goddamn android here says he was sent to look for Osama bin Kenobi."

Bin started going into this nodding routine. You never saw anyone nod in your whole entire life as much as old Bin Kenobi. I could never tell if it was because he was thinking, or because he was just a crazy old fart.

"Osama bin Kenobi," he said. "Osama. Now that's a name I've not heard in a long time."

Now, I didn't understand what he was talking about, partly because I was young and partly because I had a lousy education. You should know that I'm older now than I used to be, but I'm still just as good-looking. People say I still act like a kid, but I know I'm a kid, and I don't see what the hell is wrong with that. Just because I'm a Red-Eye Knight and all doesn't mean I can't act my age, for Chrissake.

So we went back to Bin's place to get away from the sandpeople and all that. He was reading *Tattooyou Week in Review* and there were all these mentholated nose drops all over the place. It was pretty depressing, like most places where old people live.

"Have a seat over here, boy," he said.

He meant next to him on the bed.

"I was once a Red-Eye Knight same as your father," he said.

"No shit?"

"Watch your language, young Puke."

"Yes, sir."

"He was the best star pilot in the galaxy. A good man."

Then all of a sudden Osama bin Kenobi, or whatever the hell his name is, went into this cabinet and gave me this goddamn sword made of light, and he told me that it was an elegant weapon for a more civilized age nonsense or some other guardian of the galaxy crap. Then he started going on about Ralph Nader, his former pupil, who betrayed and killed my father, blah blah, and he was seduced by the dark side of the Farce, which is some goddamn energy field that surrounds us and penetrates us and binds us together. Old people are always going on about history and how important the past is, but I don't see how any of it relates to me at all. Because my only goals are to fly a starfighter and have sex with as many women as possible before I die.

"What a load of crap!" I said.

That little android starting playing the video of that girl again, and I had to stand behind a pillar, my boner got so big. She was some sort of damn princess or something, and she needed Osama's help in the rebellion and wanted him to come to Alderman and save the universe, which is a bunch of nonsense if you stop to think about it.

Anyway, it took me about ten minutes to cool down after that, especially when I saw that she wore her hair in a bun. That look always drove me wild, I swear. Osama bin Kenobi said to me that I needed to learn the ways of the Farce and come with him to Alderman.

"Get lost, pal-o-buddy," I said. "Now don't get me wrong. I don't like the Empire. I hate it. But Alderman is such a long way from here. And besides, I hear it's full of phonies."

Well, you know what happened next. The goddamn imperial Stormdrainers killed a bunch of Jewas and burnt down my house and turned my aunt and uncle into a couple of stinking skeletons. What a stupid mess it all was. So I said to Osama bin Kenobi, "Sure, I'll come with you to Alderman. There's nothing here for me now." He actually seemed excited. You kind of had to feel sorry for the crazy sonofabitch.

It was still pretty early. I'm not sure what time it was, actually, because I don't have a watch. But it was definitely early enough for us to find a pilot to take us to Alderman. What the hell, Bin and I thought, and we went down to the Mos Def spaceport. I swear you won't find a more wretched hive of scum and villainy in the galaxy than Mos Def. What a dump! Bin said it could be rough, but I'm always ready for anything, so I fixed my hair and went in to see what was going on.

The cantina wasn't very crowded, but they gave us a lousy table in the back anyway. You should have seen what was in there! I was surrounded by jerky monsters, I'm not kidding. All those wolf-creatures, devils, and green globs of goo were a bunch of losers, if you ask me. At this other table, practically on *top* of us, this hammerhead kept trying to hit on some creature that looked like a penis covered with hair. What a disgusting phony, I swear. Some people have no taste. And the band was bad. I mean really putrid. They were just a bunch of cheap-looking dudes with big eyes playing their clarinets, as far as I could tell. I knew the song they were playing, "Little Shirley Beans," and it was a swell song, but they were just *murdering* it. They played it really brassy, but not good brassy, more like corny brassy, if you know what I mean.

I could tell right away that the bartender was a phony, too. He was one of those really suck-up bartenders who will kiss your ass if you're a bounty hunter or some kind of intergalactic criminal, but if you're just a guy who wants a drink, you might as well not exist. So it figures that he'd let a walrus-man and this guy who kinda looked like a pig come up to me and start hassling. The piggy was really stuck-up and funny-looking; he went on and on about how he had the death sentence on twelve systems and he was gonna kill me and all that.

He just went at me and pushed me over. I would have pushed him over back, I swear. Sometimes I just drink, but I don't feel drunk. I guess I was drunk then, though, because I fell on the floor and couldn't get back up. I sure as hell didn't feel like fighting at the moment, and I was just sitting there, blocking the whole god-damn aisle. Thank God good old Bin cut off his arm with a lightsaber. That saved me a whole lot of mess, really it did. Some-times I hate walrus-men and pig-monsters. I swear.

All of a sudden, we were sitting at a table with this space pilot and a really tall guy, Jewbacca, all covered in hair. I swear to god, you never saw a hairier guy in all your life. He was all right, I guess, but he kept growling like someone was scratching him behind the ear or something. I thought he seemed kinda faggy, but I didn't say anything because he also seemed kinda strong.

This pilot, though, his name was Don Hoho, and was another case altogether. He looked all right, though you could tell he was kind of a mama's boy at heart. His hair was all tousled and all that crap. But you could also tell that he was madly in love with himself. He thought he was the handsomest guy in the Western half of the universe. He *was* pretty handsome too—I'll admit it. But he was the kind of handsome that turns a guy into a big lame movie star. I knew a lot of guys on Tattooyou who were handsomer than Don Hoho. Or at least not as stuck up.

So he said he wanted ten thousand to fly us to Alderman. I said, that's a lot of money, pal. I mean, whoo-eeee, I had a lot of dough on me, but it went pretty fast. Sometimes I don't even know where all my dough goes. I'm a big spender, I'm telling you. He said, "Who's gonna fly it, kid? You?"

Goddamn. I hate arrogant phonies.

"You bet I could," I said.

Later, we went to the spaceport and Don Hoho showed us his spaceship, the goddamn Post-Millennium Fuck-Up. What a piece of junk! I swear to God. Some people don't know how to pick their spaceships for anything. I read a lot of spaceship magazines, and I've seen some good custom jobs, and this one was strictly for phonies and losers. But Hoho said that he'd made all these goddamn adjustments himself, for Chrissake! Anyway, we got on board the ship, but these damn Stormdrainers were shooting at us and all that nonsense. I hate laser fights, really I do, but at least none of the people on my side ever die. The big hairy guy was good with a gun, and he kept growling. That phony British android was babbling all over the place. I swear to God, that guy never shuts up. Then we were in the air, and the ship was just clunking along, really slow. I didn't have anything better to do, so I started bothering Hoho.

"Hey," I said. "How old do you think I am?"

"I don't care how old you are, kid!"

"Yeah, well, I'm older than you think! And I can fly this thing! Sure I can!"

"Travelin' through hyperspace ain't like dustin' crops, kid," he said.

What a big jerk! This Hoho was so corny. I hate guys like him.

After I had my breakfast, it was only around noon, and we weren't getting to Alderman till two o'clock, so Bin put a goddamn helmet on my head and told me to stretch out my feelings. What a buncha hooey! Then Bin started holding his head and crying, like. I kept trying to imagine him as a Red-Eye Knight saving the universe, but it was hard to picture. "I felt a great disturbance in the Farce," he said, whatever the hell that meant.

So anyway, this stupid ball was flying around and shooting lasers at me. Bin told me to try and hit the lasers with my lightsaber, for Chrissake! I was doing pretty well, actually, pretty terrific, and Bin started singing this song, this old song, and he was singing the hell out of it, too. He had a pretty little voice, and it went, "If a Red-Eye catch a Red-Eye coming through the warp." If any singer's any good, you can always tell, and Bin was pretty good. He was a helluva singer. That song made me feel not so depressed anymore, and I really deflected those lasers, I'm telling you!

Then we got to Alderman, or where Alderman used to be, because now it was just a buncha goddamn rocks floating around in space or something stupid like that. I had a lousy feeling about the whole situation, if you want to know the truth. This big goddamn space station was coming up on us really fast, and for Chrissake, it caught us up in a stinking *tractor beam*!

After we got sucked into the space station, Don made us hide so Ralph Nader wouldn't find us. I didn't see what the big deal was, though. Anyway, after they searched the ship and all that, I said to Don, "Boy, it's lucky you had these compartments," and I meant it! Then we killed two Stormdrainers and all, and Don and I ended up wearing these goddamn *costumes*. They were really putrid, and they smelled bad. Good old Stormdrainer costumes, though! I looked like I had a ton of muscles. I mean, I was really stacked, and I had a big gun. Then Bin went to look for the tractor beam. I wanted to go with him. It might be hard for you to understand this, but I liked the old guy, really I did. He was the only one who ever talked straight with me. Most people are a bunch of goddamn phonies. But Bin said some crap like my destiny lies on a different path than his, so I had to stay with Don Hoho and that stinky hairy guy.

That little blue android, good old R-P-OO, what a swell android, he stuck his little android wanger into the ship's computer, and found out the goddamn princess was going to be executed, for Chrissake! I figured they couldn't kill her, because she's the only girl who ever really gave me a big boner. Don didn't care about her at all. I had to tell him that she was rich, and that if he rescued her, he'd get a lot of money. I swear that's all some people ever think about. I don't care if Slobba the Butt does have a bounty on your head! Sometimes, there are more important things than money, and anyone who says otherwise is a goddamn phony.

So there I went to rescue Princess Layme, and she was asleep on a slab without a pillow or anything! "Aren't you a little short for a Stormdrainer?" she said. Haw, haw! Good old Layme! "I'm Puke Skybarfer," I said. "I've come to rescue you." You should have seen her. You never saw a princess so pretty and smart in your whole life. She was really smart. I mean, she was an Imperial ambassador and feisty battle strategist, and she knew her way around a toolbox, too! As a matter of fact, she was smarter than all of us put together, and that's saying something. You ought to have seen old Layme. She had this brown hair that she could braid a thousand different ways. I'm not kidding. She could stick it behind her eyes or it could hang down like a bunch of goddamn snakes or something, and she looked good in a vest, too. She's pretty skinny, like me, but nice skinny. Like riding an air scooter through the forest moon of Ensor skinny. That kind of skinny. You'd like her, I swear. I mean if you gave old Layme the blueprints to an Imperial Star Destroyer, she'd never show them to you if you were a bad guy. She always knows exactly what you're talking about. She's the kind of girl I want to marry someday. In all seriousness.

So then we got caught up in this goddamn firefight, Don and Layme and Jewbacca and me, and there were crummy Storm-drainers to either side. So we shot a hole in the wall to get away from them, and ended up in some goddamn trash compactor. Now, I've lived in space my whole life, and I've been some pretty stinky places, because I'm not afraid of anything and I used to ride my landspeeder all around. But that trash compactor was the stinkiest place I've ever been by far. It just stank and stank, and then it stank some more. I swear to God. Then we heard a goddamn moan. There was definitely something alive in there, I'm telling you. Before I knew it, a big tentacle had wrapped itself around my waist and pulled me under that godforsaken garbage. It was all slimy and hairy and stuff, and it dragged me all around underwater. I was swallowing all this bilge, and I really wanted to throw up, I'm telling you. I started to shiver there under the water and I realized I was going to get pneumonia and die if the thing didn't squeeze me to death. I pictured millions of jerks coming to my funeral and all.

For no good reason, the thing split and I could breathe again, for Chrissake. The walls started closing in and I started screaming to that goddamn phony android to shut off all the trash compactors on the detention level. "Goddamn it to hell, PPO, come in, for Chrissake!" I shouted. It was really squeezing us hard, and we were going to die in a damn trash compactor. At that moment, I'll admit, I felt awfully sorry for myself, and I promised I'd do something good for the universe if I survived. I really would, if the trash compactor stopped.

We got out OK, or else I wouldn't be writing this, I guess, and then Layme and I got caught at a retractable walkway that didn't move because I'd blasted the controls, but fortunately I had some dental floss in my belt buckle that I'd packed before I left home and all that, so we got across, but the big news is that before we did, she said "good luck," and she kissed me, I swear, and I got a big boner right through my goddamn shorts.

So then we're running for the ship, and Bin is having a lightsaber battle with that crummy Ralph Nader. What a big black phony he is! And Bin just folded up and let Nader slice him open, and then he vanished. I guess I must have really lost it then, because I heard Bin in my head saying, "Run, Puke, run!" I did, but I totally lost it. Later, on the ship, I was crying and all that, because I'm a sensitive guy. Really, I am. I was telling Layme, "I can't believe he's gone," because I couldn't. Good old Bin. He's dead now. You'd have liked him. He was terrifically intelligent and could do things like wave his hand and make people say things that were the opposite of what they meant. He was ironic like that. God, he was a nice guy. What else can you say about someone who taught you to lift objects with your mind? Right after he died, I tried to break all the windows in the Post-Millennium Fuck-Up, but Jewbacca hit me on the head and they gave me a sedative. My head still hurts a little right now, but it's not like I'm trying to write a *novel* or anything like that, for Chrissake.

"It's OK," Layme said to me. "He'd want you to carry on."

I wasn't listening, though. I was thinking about something crazy. "You know what the goddamn hell I'd like to be," I said, " for Chrissake, if I had my motherfucking choice?"

"What?" Layme said. "Stop *swearing*."

"You know that song 'If a Red-Eye catch a Red-Eye comin' through the warp?' I'd like—"

"It's 'If a Red-Eye *meet* a Red-Eye coming through the warp!' old Layme said. "It's a poem. By Boba *Burns*."

"I *know* it's a poem by Boba Burns," I said. "I thought it was 'if a Red-Eye catch a Red-Eye.' Anyway, I keep picturing all these Red-Eyes running around and pretending to fight each other in this magical swamp and all. Thousands of Red-Eyes from around the universe, and nobody's around to watch them, except me. And I'm standing on the edge of some crazy cave. What I have to do, I have to catch all the Red-Eyes when they want to come into that cave and face their darkest fears. I mean, I have to *catch* them before they fall. That's all I'd do all day. I'd be the catcher in the Red-Eye and all. I know it's crazy, but that's the only thing I'd like to be."

Old Layme didn't say anything for a long time. Then, when she said something, all she said was, "Puke, don't be a goddamn pussy."

That's all I'm going to tell about. I could probably tell you how we met up with the rebel fleet and how Layme kissed me on the cheek and I flew my starfighter into the Breath Star and heard Bin telling me to use the goddamn Farce and trust my feelings. About how I turned off my computer and let the Farce guide me and blew up the whole space station by myself, and how when it blew up, I swear I had an orgasm right there in my spacesuit and Bin said to me that the Farce would be with me always. But I don't feel like it. Really I don't. That stuff doesn't interest me too much right now.

I mean, it's all a bunch of baloney, if you think about it too hard. Me and Don Hoho and Jewbacca parading in front of all these people and Layme with her phony hairstyle smiling at us like she rules the universe benignly or some such crap. When I think about it, I wish I'd just stayed at home and had never gotten involved. Who needs to grow up, anyway? All for a lousy *medal*, for Chrissake!

A NIGHT OUT AT
THE MEMEPLEX

ARION BERGER

Any dictator can tell you that the most effective way to control the masses is through the selective withholding of information. By 1999, George Lucas had perfected his impersonation of a strutting, banana-republic tyrant. His partial-unveiling techniques kept the public salivating for tidbits from *Star Wars: Episode I: The Phantom Menace* as they were rolled out under silver domes—the first trailer, the second trailer, the toys, the tickets.

Not only did Lucas control the accessibility of the film and film-related goodies, but he orchestrated a mouthy information campaign worthy of Gabriele D'Annunzio. Whipping the masses to a froth of righteousness, Lucas stated repeatedly in interviews that he expected snotty critics to greet his latest *SW* venture with the same Luke-warmth with which they had met the first three. That stance was a giveaway that it wasn't just greed, but reflexive ass-covering that motivated Lucas—his manufactured and spurious outsider positioning meant that anyone who subsequently rendered a verdict that didn't collaborate with Lucas's self-generated sense of importance would be proving himself a knee-jerk antifun jaded elitist insider. The idea was to paint any objectors, rather than his lathered public, as brainwashed ghouls.

In the end, it wasn't the critics or even the fanboys who decided that *The Phantom Menace* came up way short; it was the second tier of fans and the interested public. But in the year or so leading up to the film's release, the hype juggernaut rolled on unabated and virtually unquestioned. Fanboys and get-a-lifers rabid to stand in line—not for the film, but for tickets for the film, for toys related to the film, for the soundtrack to the film, and for the book (one book sold under cash-generating multiple covers) of the film—weren't left with any reflection on why these pursuits (and expenses) might be a good idea. Even the interested public's explanation is about the *stuff* about the thing, the thing itself being practically nonexistent, or at least irrelevant. "It's *Star Wars*, man!" was not only an acceptable response, it was the only possible response.

That's why the reviews wouldn't matter, and Lucas knew it—responding to his movie meant responding to his careful positioning.

Not long ago naysayers and naked-emperor-spotters would have wondered if everyone else was "brainwashed," a marvelous old-fashioned word. In fact, Lucas's demand that we all participate in his vision of himself and his work, that all citizens should want to see it, that its levels of quality, coherence, and entertainment value should be of no significance, did take the shape of what Charles McKay defined in his excellent 1841 book called *Extraordinary Popular Delusions and the Madness of Crowds*. (Where's the band called Tulipmania, is what I want to know?) But as irksome as it may have been to people who wanted to actually see the movie before falling in love with it, there are harmless possible factors that can account for this.

For one thing, it's fun to participate in some cultural swoon. People need community, thrive on finding or establishing common interests, and thrill to novelty. Ask anyone who stood in line the night of July 8, 2000, waiting to pick up their preordered copies of the fourth Harry Potter book. While the kids busied themselves swirling their capes, the grown-ups—and most of them, us, were grown-ups—traded the handout stickers and swapped genial moanings along the lines of "what are we doing up this late?" before scurrying home with our two or three copies of *The Goblet of Fire*.

Then again, no one has to be brainwashed into having a good time by hopping on a crowded train. In elitist terms—and counter-culturists are always elitists; that's the only way they can keep their numbers satisfyingly small—believing the hype is the ultimate gullibility. But the distinction between cultish and popular has been all but obliterated as the culture flattens out and information is disseminated at a lightning pace to a generally far more savvy populace than that of even fifteen years ago. To align oneself with a subculture is to be part of a widespread movement; nothing happens in the dark of a counterculture anymore. Conversely, joining in a popular wave is a subcultural identification in itself. The structure of taste has shifted from a geologic one—strata of varying widths, with the widest nearest the surface—to a columnar model, with bars of special interests side by side, of approximately equal height.

So when postmodernism proper first washed over U.S. shores on a wave of French theory and snarky Lettermanisms, it identified itself popularly as subsets of references. These references identified the elite audience that it addressed as one conversant with a whole shadow realm of texts and entertainments, which in turn reflected a system of values, beliefs, and standards cherished by the audience and the postmodernist, thus titillating it. The more obscure the reference, the more vigorous a mix of high and low, the more elite the presumed audience.

If God was dead for these appropriative filchers, Hegel wasn't, and neither was Ronald Reagan. Trickle-down culture fed a wider and more middlebrow range of references to the bulky midstratum (Ginger or Mary Ann, anyone?), and antithesis made appropriation the standard by which a piece of art defined itself. I used to joke that the film business had become such a red-meat purveyor that the inevitable next step was a *Star Wars* film that consisted of nothing but a super-digitally-enhanced cantina scene. Soon enough, that joke wasn't funny anymore. Films like *Shrek* turned Lucas's meta-marketing strategy into creative empiricism: a film that is only marginally the thing itself (in *Shrek*'s case, a fairy tale) but depends largely for its definition as that-thingness on a desultory barrage of that-thing-derived references. Without reflecting a set of values, beliefs, or judgments; without exposing inconsistencies, ironies, or hypocrisies; without taking a satirical or parodic stance; a series of random swats in the direction of already monumentally popular jokes, riffs, and entertainments, is just that—"attitude" without the attitude.

Star Wars itself is partially responsible for this vertical shift, and in part a victim of it. It was one of the first movies to become simultaneously a cult artifact and a staggeringly popular phenomenon. It also inaugurated a new way of looking at films—that is, repeatedly. Children who have grown up with the commonplace of video take for granted the practice of watching a movie over and over, or treating it like wallpaper. Not long before, revival houses and art houses existed to keep old films in circulation. As for mainstream or foreign contemporary films, the audience had no access to them once their theater run closed. In 1977, kids returned to the theater in droves, keeping *Star Wars* on the screen for unprecedented runs and whipping up waves of renewed enthusiasm. Repeated viewings were the cult behavior of a huge audience. For all of *Star Wars*' hoary adventure-serial precedent, simplistic message and wha-hoo thrills, it functioned like a specialist taste.

The *Star Wars* cult is a crossover success of massive proportions, but the idea of an internal machine generating fodder for fans is not new, particularly in science fiction. *Star Trek* fleshed out the TV expediencies of its universe with back stories and extraterrestrial trivia (look, kids, a Klingon-language dictionary!) to sate its insiders; prerelease *Phantom Menace* and *Attack of the Clones* web sites fill in the series' plot holes and speculate on the connecting threads among the films, as if it is all meant to make sense. Unlike the appeal of other areas of commerce, in which artificially limited supply generates value—Beanie Babies and other self-appointed collectibles—the mystique of *Star Wars* isn't economic but psychological: How close can the consumer get to the coveted object? After late-'90s audiences were hardened into skepticism by the psych-out gag trailers for—to cite just a few examples—the *South Park* movie, Howard Stern's *Private Parts*, and *The Spy Who Shagged Me*—they were honored with a peek at the real thing, when *The Phantom Menace* trailer opened wide, and they were hard-pressed not to somehow feel lucky.

The old objection to being helplessly ground under the wheels of hype in service of (what turned out to be) such an unimaginative rip-off would be that the Empire has no clothes, but there is a school of thought that would argue that it's more pernicious even than our old friend the washed brain. Said school consists of Memetic theorists; they posit the existence of a "meme," a unit of cultural inheritance that replicates itself, brain to brain, the way genes replicate from body to body down generations. Although the theory has been scoffed at by those in the scientific establishment who hold that the human being is the apotheosis of biological organization (Stephen Jay Gould and Jonathan Miller, for example), meme-theory popularists like Richard Dawkins and the University of London's Susan Blackmore see it as a viable explanation for our continuing cultural evolution, such as it is.

Memes can be "good ideas, good tunes, good poems, or driveling mantras"—paging Bobby McFerrin—". . . spread by imitation as genes spread by bodily reproduction or viral infection," Dawkins writes in *Unweaving the Rainbow: Science, Delusion, and the Appetite for Wonder*. "[T]he conspiracy-theory meme has a built-in response to the objection that there is no good evidence for the conspiracy: Of course not, that's how powerful the conspiracy is." He goes on to say, "Just as a species' gene pool becomes a cooperative cartel of genes—a 'culture,' a 'tradition'—becomes a cooperative cartel of memes, a memeplex, it has been called." Again, as with genes, the conditions must be in place for the transfering of memes to happen. Dawkins cites conspiracy theory because we are familiar with the environment in which it arose—a post-industrial society, an increasingly politically skeptical populace, a distrust of power, and previous solid evidence of conspiratorial misdeeds. But the meme, if it exists, also infected northern Europe's tulip freaks, and makes a very nice case for the Victorian mania for spiritualism that morphed into the New Age foolishness we still live with.

In crude terms, what has made judgment impossible for those relatively uninfected by the meme is the hype, although hype isn't quite the concept in this case. Hype pumps up interest in a venture (usually an entertainment venture) with mass accessibility as the goal. Lucas, on the other hand, controls accessibility as a way of manufacturing interest, among not just the moviegoing public but the toy-buying, burger-eating, Internet-cruising, dinner party–chatting, Western civilization–existing public. His horizontal integration is perfectly suited for modern conditions, the flattened landscape.

When the hype—the mass cultural participation—reaches this level, movies are no longer entertainment. Dawkins argues that while genes build instruments like bodies—an elephant, say—memes manipulate existing bodies. Genes have no purpose in absence of their goal. We are almost at the point, however, that memes do. As units of information, they can exist as satellites without a central planet—that is, the elephant doesn't need to exist for us to harbor a wealth of elephant information. *Shrek*'s fairy tale DNA is in evidence in every frame of a film that was not actually a fairy tale, and Lucas, naively, expected that *The Phantom Menace* could pass for an elephant by displaying a holographic series of units of *Star Wars* information.

Movies never were solely entertainment delivery systems; it's useful and necessary for a culture, or many subcultures, to descry meaning and importance in entertainment products, but the fulcrum of the products' existence used to be their role as pleasures. With that core purpose removed, there's nothing left but a galaxy of merchandise, fictional lore, ticket-scrambling, and reportage of the above that revolves mindlessly around a great black hole.

All the publications that participated with varying degrees of gullibility take, by now reflexively, postmodern attitudes to the subject—the more skeptical, the more they can pose as critics of the hype while fueling it. *Newsweek*'s cover story on "The Selling of *Star Wars*" related in grotesque detail how Lucas and his flying monkeys controlled public interest and retail methods on the way to *Phantom Menace*'s release, but signed off by noting that if "Phantomania has gotten out of hand," *Newsweek* is as culpable as anyone—nudge nudge, wink wink. (They then revved up the machine for the release of the subsequent bomb *Pearl Harbor*.) It was a clever and meaningless escape route to pseudo-news respectability, exposing the entire enterprise as a way of striking a critical pose without genuine critical content.

The trouble with meme theory is, ironically, also the trouble with the *Star Wars* phenomenon—neither makes enough sense when observed too closely, and neither considers the quirks and idiosyncrasies of the audience it seeks to account for. Nor does meme theory, specifically, cover the question of why many audience members remain psychologically unevolved. Sometimes people like stuff because they like it, and sometimes an accidental or purposeful collusion of media, cash-hungry string pullers, and the cultural climate results in what looks like mass hypnotism to the immune observer. It would be nice if there were a Darwinian basis for our occasional inexplicable swoons, because it would provide a rationale for the random, disorderly tastes of the public. (Not unlike the way conspiracy theory accounts for the random, disorderly behavior of those in power; it stems from a deep need for order and reason and, in the absence of these, it attributes motive.) But the theory, like the *Phantom* frenzy, lays a heavy hand on one's decision-making faculties: You have no choice but to buy it. You've been brainwashed. Lucas can chalk up all the grousing to *Star Wars* backlash if he wants, but he doesn't understand that even in his world of Manichaean destiny and chosen ones, a little free will would go a long way.

MARRIED TO THE FORCE

KEVIN SMITH

A brother just can't escape being a *Star Wars* dork sometimes.

It was at the Cannes Film Festival in 1994 that I first realized this, and took note of just how much resonance the long-dormant *Star Wars* phenomenon still had in my life.

Return of the Jedi had come out eons prior, in 1983, and the saga had seemed to breathe its last when the made-for-television movie *The Ewok Adventure* and the subequent *Ewoks* and *Droids* cartoons had hit the air in the late '80s/early '90s. George Lucas, once the mythology-builder and mastermind behind the series of movies that preoccupied so much of my youth, was nowhere to be seen anymore—with the exception of his periodic forays back into producing, on films like *Tucker* and *Radioland Murders*. That he'd gone from envisioning Tusken Raiders riding proudly atop Banthas to creating THX and the Avid editing system forefather, the Edit-Droid, seemed to make sense. Set for life, thanks to the brilliant stroke of foresight in securing the licensing rights to the trilogy, Lucas could kick back and spend the rest of his days dreaming up and developing new advances in the technology of filmmaking that future filmmakers and the next generation of myth builders could benefit from.

So I'm sitting down with a French journalist to talk about my debut film, *Clerks*. We'd already been to Sundance at this point, where Miramax had acquired the picture for worldwide distribution, and the early reviews of our shitty-looking amateur-hour effort were head-scratchingly positive in the states. This, however, was Europe, the cradle of culture, and we were at Cannes, the most well known film festival in the universe. Surely, the film aesthetes in attendance here would see through our overpraised dick-and-fart joke picture and declare that this emperor had no clothes. And the very French journo I was sitting across from, who wore the expression of someone who'd have much rather been interviewing Bruce Willis for his palooka turn in the festival's unequivocal hit of that year, *Pulp Fiction*, seemed as though he was prepared to charge me as a charlatan and spend the next few minutes lecturing me on the visual language of film and dressing me down in Franglais for shitting all over that language with the potty-mouthed antics of our convenience-store confection.

After staring at me for a long beat, this is what he said:

"The foul-mouth boy an' ze fat man outside ze shop . . . are zey the Artoo De-too an' See-Threepio of zis strange universe you 'ave created?"

I slowly, cautiously opened my eyes, which had been grimaced-winced closed in preparation for the barrage of French vulgarities I assumed I was about to be on the receiving end of, and offered the now-smiling cancaner a puzzled, yet relieved look.

"I hadn't . . . really thought of them as such," I said, though it was probably far less well worded at the time. "But . . . I guess they could be construed as Artoo and Threepio, yeah."

"No one has said zis to you yet?" he inquired, kinda pleased with himself.

"No one who's not a friend has talked to me about *Star Wars* since 1983," I volunteered.

And thus began the start of a half hour conversation with this very excited boulangerie regular not just about the parallels between *Clerks* and *Star Wars*, but about how great the *Star Wars* saga was in general, including our favorite moments and characters, and how we both wished Lucas would get off his ass and make the then-remaining six episodes.

Years later, *Star Wars* would assault the public consciousness again in a big, big way, but back in '94 it was a rare delight to hear someone throw those two terms together in reference to the movies I grew up on. In '94, the rerelease of the Holy Trilogy was but a glint in Lucas's eye, not to mention the unveiling to the world of Jar Jar Binks. In '94, it felt like *I* was the only one talking about *Star Wars* anymore.

And talk about it I would—for the next four movies we'd make, a de rigueur *Star Wars* conversational dissection or homage became one of the leitmotifs of View Askew's body of work.

From that first discussion in *Clerks* on the topic of whether or not those hired to build the second Death Star were innocent casualties of war or justly slaughtered coconspirators in the Rebel attack on the work-in-progress space station in *Return of the Jedi*, to how hell-bent Silent Bob was to move a cigarette with only the power of his would-be Jedi mind in *Mallrats;* from Hooper's assertion in *Chasing Amy* that the revelation of a crusty, old, white Anakin Skywalker under the powerful black helmet (and voice) of Darth Vader was a cloying, racist message, to a full-blown Bong-saber duel in *Jay and Silent Bob Strike Back*, the *Star Wars* saga has been as much a part of our films as the wall-to-wall pseudo-intellectual potty talk.

But while every nod to the Trilogy *became* a device we'd incorporate to pander to a Gen X audience as nostalgic as we were for the days when Vader was much more than just a shill for Energizer batteries (a great commercial, but c'mon . . .), it didn't *start out* as that. The origins of the *Star Wars* riffs in our flicks were not born out of demographic data or studio-mandated attempts at hipness; they were born out of a childhood love affair with three movies that were the cinematic equivalent of a prepubescent first marriage.

I *was* married to *Star Wars* when I was a kid. I had all the toys, wallpapered my bedroom with the posters and images cut out of magazines, action figure card-backs, and Burger King giveaways. Every Christmas and birthday from 1977 to 1983, I was the easiest person in the world to shop for. John Williams's scores were the soundtracks of my youth, before pop and rap would edge them out, and Carrie Fisher was my one true love . . . even though she was the bride of Paul Simon.

And whether I wanted it to or not, *Star Wars* influenced—and sometimes *defined*—important epochs of my life, teaching me how to conduct myself in a galaxy not very far away at all.

It's June of 1977, and I'm in second grade at Our Lady of Perpetual Help, the Catholic School of my youth. John Kovic brings in the Kenner *Star Wars* Early Bird Set, a collection of five action figures that would spawn a merchandising empire. The set, comprising Luke Skywalker, Artoo Detoo, Ben Kenobi, Darth Vader, and a Jawa, is the envy of all in class—even me, who has not yet even seen *Star Wars* at this point. I go home and immediately beg my parents to send away for the Early Bird Set, as it was a mail-order-only promotion, and then take me to see the movie that spawned the toys.

I got half of what I wanted. My parents took me to see *Star Wars*, but money being tight in our family, I never did get an Early Bird Set of my own. Seeing how crushed I was by this, my parents endeavored, over the course of the next six years, to provide me with all the essential *Star Wars* figures, play sets, and vehicles. And it was through these purchases that my parents taught me to respect the value of things—because shelling out $1.99 for each figure wasn't easy for our tightly budgeted family to manage. My parents insisted that if they were going to pay for such extravagances, I would have to treat my toys with care. So unlike everyone else I knew, I never took my little guys, gals, and aliens out into the yard to reenact the films; there were no sandy driveways doubling for Tatooine, no snowy curbsides standing in for Hoth. All the settings for the adventures I'd create were crafted around the furniture and crevices found on the floors of the kitchen, the enclosed front porch, or my bedroom.

Because of this care for my *Star Wars* toys, I would eventually amass a collection of figures that would become legendary among my peers, as I was the only kid in O.L.P.H. who could claim he had all the tiny guns and lightsabers the action figures were packaged with—even Han Solo's blaster, which was notorious for being the easiest to lose. And later in life, when adolescent boredom got the best of other fly-by-night fans and they started blowing up their figures with Cherry Bombs and M-80s, my collection could always be found safely tucked under my bed, in a pair of Darth Vader–head carrying cases (today, they reside in a closet in my house).

It was that penchant for keeping things in good condition and never throwing anything out that would eventually lead to Jay and Silent Bob's Secret Stash, our comic book store in Red Bank, New Jersey. Having kept props and costumes from even our first film in safe, guarded condition, the Secret Stash went from being a simple comic book store to a View Askew museum of sorts, with artifacts from all our films decorating the walls and glass cases. Anything that doesn't find a home in the store gets sold off at our web site's auction page, dubbed "EJay," and usually fetches a pretty amazing price for what most would've left for garbage. Had I not been instructed, via my *Star Wars* figures, to treat my belongings with care, neither the store nor "EJay" would be possible.

But perhaps the biggest crossover from the *Star Wars* galaxy to mine would have to be the year we mixed *Dogma* at Skywalker Ranch. Known to house only the premier sound-mixing facilities and best talent in the industry, we were flabbergasted when our faux-blasphemous flick secured a stage and a bona fide Skywalker Sound mix. While there, *Episode I* (and later, *Episode II*) producer Rick McCallum even popped by one of our sessions and invited me to watch the as-yet-unreleased trailer for *The Phantom Menace*, as its mix had just been finished and they were going to screen it in the big theater. And remember, this is during a period when people were lining up months in advance to see *Star Wars* on opening weekend, so there was none of this "Lucas sold out!" or

"Fuck Jar Jar!" backlash. Getting an early glimpse at that trailer was a die-hard fan's dream come true.

I, however, could no longer be considered a die-hard fan. While I still had mountains of respect for what Lucas had created, and enough affection for what I felt were just some old movies that meant a lot to me growing up to keep referencing them in the movies I now found myself making, I'd long since gotten divorced from my childhood marriage to *Star Wars*.

Ironically, though, *Star Wars* would figure prominently in my *next* marriage—this one to a flesh-and-blood partner.

Jennifer and I had met when she interviewed me for *USA Today*. Our courtship and whirlwind romance were cut short by what can only be described as an apparently very healthy sperm count on my behalf. While deep in postproduction on *Dogma*, Jen got pregnant—which was no big deal, as we'd already fallen in love and were musing about marriage. However, getting around to tying the knot prior to the arrival of our first kid was proving extremely difficult, as the demands of *Dogma* made for a very hectic year. I'd secured a big fuck-off ring from Tiffany and proposed to Jen, but we couldn't really find a date to do the deed that wasn't already occupied by some stage of postproduction.

So we're up at Skywalker, in the midst of our mix, and Jen is about seven to eight months pregnant. While I was on the mixing stage all day, she was either resting in the sumptuous lodgings at the Ranch-run inn, or walking the grounds, taking in the beauty of what is truly God's country. And on one particular evening, when I'd come back to the room after mixing, she said:

"It's really so beautiful up here. This would be a nice place to get married."

"Yeah," I said. Because, y'know—she was right.

"Would you want to?" she asked.

"Get married? Of course."

"Up here."

"Sure. I mean, I don't know if they allow for that here, but if they did, it'd be a better place than most to do it."

"It would, wouldn't it?"

And as I sat there on a bed in a room of the Skywalker Ranch Inn (that might've even been partly financed by the money my parents blew on all that *Star Wars* paraphernalia eons ago), gazing at my very patient and even more pregnant girlfriend, a person I didn't even know existed back when I was just a *Star Wars*–obsessed youth, I was moved by what I can only assume was . . . well, *the Force*. Because the next thing that came out of my mouth was:

"Let's do it this weekend."

So, on April 25, 1999, I did what most hard-core fans of *Star Wars* only dream of doing, and got married at Skywalker Ranch.

Lest you think I'm a total *Star Wars* dork in denial, though, I'd like to point out for the record that I finally extricated myself from the stranglehold *Star Wars* seemed to have on my life by *not* naming our kid Leia or Boba, tempting as that might have been. I mean, sooner or later, you've gotta grow up, right? So we named our daughter Harley Quinn.

After a *Batman* villainess.

WORKS EVERY TIME

ELVIS MITCHELL

When *The Empire Strikes Back* was rereleased in its Special Edition in 1997, Lando Calrissian's first line to Princess Leia, "What have we here?"—delivered with a cooled-out, I'll-see-you-in-my-room-for-a-Romulan-Rum-and-Coke assurance—got the same reaction as the piece of dialogue received during the picture's initial release in 1980: the standing ovation due the first interstellar Mack ever spotted on-screen. And Billy Dee Williams's ridiculously suave rogue-trader is given a lavish entrance, striding across the screen in his full swerve-on, 47-degree-angle walk, trailed by a cape and an entourage; all that was missing was James Brown's manager snatching the cloak off Lando's shoulders and proclaiming the brother The Hardest Working Man in Space Business. Revisiting Lando in this context brought to mind the sepia-remake-of-*Casablanca* sketch from *In Living Color,* in which Keenen Ivory Wayans broke out his Williams impression—the heavy-lidded you-belong-to-me stare, the lazy magnetism and liquid seductiveness of Williams's speaking rhythms—and Jimmy-jammed Billy Dee into the Humphrey Bogart role. A canny piece of comedy, because for filmgoers of a certain generation and disposition, Williams presented that potential, and when the *Color* sketch ran in 1990, Williams's *suavecito* was being employed to extol the virtues of Colt 45 Malt Liquor, a mighty-mighty comedown. (This wasn't the first time Williams's silken machismo had been parodied. In the 1972 TV movie *Truman Capote's The Glass House*—a prison drama that could have been a necessarily milder precursor of HBO's *Oz*—white-trash fellow inmate Vic Morrow mocked Williams's predatory amble—but Morrow also kept his distance.) Williams's fox-slaying addition to the *Star Wars* mythos—besides making one wonder if Lando kept Teddy Pendergrass's "Turn Out the Lights" going on the *Millennium Falcon*'s in-dash eight-track player—went a long way towards removing the bad taste that *Star Wars* left in the mouths of African-American filmgoers in 1977. It was hard to ignore the presence of the lone Brother from Another Planet in the first picture—because he was an extra who turned up twice. The unmistakable signifier of intergalactic racism—the hardworking extra's dashing from one set to another—brought to mind the joke that both Arsenio Hall and Godfrey Cambridge spun variations on: a black astronaut choking on the phrases "Yes, NASA" and "No, NASA." And the bullying vigor of James Earl Jones's vocal presence—recognizable instantly to a black audience—giving a malevolent elegance to Darth Vader, begged another question. Although, to be frank, given that Vader was about the coolest thing going in the first *Star Wars*, it made the possibility that he was black perfectly acceptable. (And when it turned out he was Luke's father it was cooler still—I only wish there had been chat rooms back in that day so I could have scanned all of the cyberspace clamor such a revelation provoked—at least until the movie itself had been widely enough seen that everyone knew it wasn't Jones's head beneath the helmet.)

Williams's addition to the cast of *Empire* showed an admirable sensitivity on Lucas's part, an empathy that few filmmakers would've displayed. In his Lucas biography, *Skywalking*, Dale Pollock details the early casting sessions for the first *Star Wars* film and mentions the two other actors up for the role of Han Solo:

Christopher Walken, whose "audition" from the lost "Screen Tests" was the subject of one of the best *Saturday Night Live* sketches ever (Kevin Spacey expertly parroting Walken's spooked, oblivious vocal rhythms), and Glynn Turman. Turman is probably best known as the ROTC commander on the instantly forgettable *Cosby Show* spin-off, *A Different World*. But he cut an impressive swath through the blaxploitation era, starring in the wily, straight-up ghetto comedy *Cooley High* (which ended up getting a small-screen conversion into the pop-locking sitcom *What's Happening?*). Turman was revered by hard-core black action fans for the lead role in the black, exorcist drama *J. D.'s Revenge*, in which he played a decent young dude possessed by the spirit of an O.G. determined to stick it to the Man even from the Grave.

Lucas passed on Walken because . . . well, it's easy to see why; the movie was going to be spacy enough as it was. The rationale behind his refusal to use Turman is, unfortunately, easier to understand than the elimination of Walken. Knowing—if he ever got to make his planned sequels—that a romance for Han and Leia was planned, Lucas didn't want the controversial, and probably noncommercial, element of an interracial relationship, a love that in the mid-'70s still barely dared to speak its name. "I didn't want to make *Guess Who's Coming to Dinner?* at that point, so I sort of backed off," Lucas told Pollock. To compensate for his moment of cowardice and the complaints of racism lodged against the first *Star Wars*—a benign racism that was part of a continuous and hilarious tradition to some black movie fans and slap in the face to others—Lucas conjured up the sleek Calrissian and contoured him to Williams's contours. According to *Skywalking*, "George conceived Lando as 'a suave, dashing black man in his thirties,'" and Williams, whom Lucas had been impressed by in *Lady Sings the Blues*, was Lucas's man from the outset.

What's important to remember is that Williams by that point had done his time in blaxploitation film, too, and with the exception of *Lady*—where the camera lingers over his Louis McKay, the chocolate-drenched piece of wish fulfillment, so that all of the young black women in the audience were given ample time to swoon—opportunities were scarce. The 1971 TV movie *Brian's Song* put Williams on the map, though it was just another way station in costar James Caan's trajectory. Caan's career took off shortly thereafter with *The Godfather*, and it had to be abundantly clear to Williams how few chances black actors get for leading roles. He knew there'd be no *Godfather* in his future, and in those days, crossover was something that Kool and the Gang and Barry White had more of a chance to exploit than he would.

His sculpted, male beauty and leading-man presence lashed to polished acting skills probably got in the way after a while; he would have been as out of place kicking down doors in a pair of leather pants alongside of Jim Brown and Fred Williamson as Harrison Ford would. The country-boy slyness of his performance as Gale Sayers in *Brian's Song* showed what he could do when given the material, and Motown honcho Berry Gordy—who put the actor in *Lady Sings the Blues*, which he produced as a vehicle for Diana Ross—labored to make a place for Williams in the movies. *Hit!*, a revenge picture in which Williams plays a Fed determined to bring down a drug cartel after his daughter dies of a smack overdose, was originally to star Steve McQueen, and Gordy grabbed the script for his Dark Gable. Gordy reunited Williams with several of his *Lady* collaborators, like director Sidney J. Furie and Richard Pryor. *Skywalking* details Williams's dawning ambivalence as he approaches Lando, reluctant because he didn't want an affirmative-action role. Eventually, he came to believe that the part could have been played by anyone.

Williams was wrong, though—no one else could've inhabited the part, not as he did. The actor's velveteen pride—smooth to the touch, but raging beneath the skin nonetheless—informed the turn. More than anything, Williams's underplayed relish—the pleasure he can radiate—give his scenes in *The Empire Strikes Back* the feel that they're in a movie for grown-ups, much like the brief scenes highlighting Alec Guinness's bespoke authority do. It's true, Lando is kind of a roué cliché, but Williams dances through his lines—he's never been an actor to rush a speech. When he's on-screen, the material doesn't seem carved from Smithfield ham; well, not so *obviously* carved from Smithfield ham, anyway. As Han and Leia fly out of the blocks in an attitude-laced sprint, Williams's blissful cool—part of his charm—adds to the enjoyment; his Chilly Willy Player's contrast to Harrison Ford's revved-up Solo gives Han something to do. Solo is no longer just grinding out third-rate banter with Leia. He's suspicious, and slightly envious, of Lando.

To some extent, Williams was right about Lando's token possibilities, as no one ever believed he had a Stormtrooper's chance with Leia. And such a romance would've been a huge turnoff to the black audience. The enthralled black female segment would never have forgiven him for depriving them of a fantasy held since he smoothed out his pinstriped lapels in *Lady*. And Lucas knew that having Lando spend too much time sniffing around Leia—given the presexual atmosphere of the films—would have raised too many questions. A lot of the fun, though, comes from what can only be described as Williams's worldly-anachronistic quality. Just who was hooking up Lando's perm in outer space, anyway? Williams's appearance became part of a compact with African-American audiences, a conspiratorial smirk with the black actors who don't really make sense in certain on-screen situations. Lucas's comprehension of balance had to inspire actors like the young Samuel L. Jackson. Jackson was in school in Atlanta at Morehouse College at the time of *Empire*'s release, and for him to witness not just some pleasant but anonymous performer, but an actor with Billy Dee Williams's iconic cool being employed to do what he does and not just function as well-meaning wallpaper (he was far too Mack-tastic to be consigned to such a place) must have been a trip. And the circle went unbroken when Jackson became a part of the *Star Wars* mythos himself, representing a presence as potent in its ramifications as Lando Calrissian offered in 1980. Williams is an undeniably stylized presence in the movies; he's larger than life, which means that he's not overwhelmed by the grandiosity that Lucas constructed. A lesser figure might have been daunted, if not consumed, in the Worlds Beyond tableaux. Williams's ease speaks for itself; it must've been responsible for a whole suburban-warrior class of young would-be Landos of all races, training to ply their bravado on the cuties sitting in front of them in homeroom.

Williams fell victim to his own carefully maintained stylization, though—the underslung glissandos of urbanity didn't give him much room to operate; he was not considered to be an actor with much range outside of the urban sophistication that became his bailiwick the first time he marcelled his hair. Once he went Mack, he could never go back. The same closed system mired Richard Roundtree and Ron O'Neal, actors who showed promise beyond the circumscribed worlds of *Shaft* and *Superfly*. Since black actors of the period were allowed so few chances, Williams couldn't even use his role in *Empire* to knock down a few walls and fashion a future for himself within that rather limited purview of the sci-fi genre. A year after *Empire*, he was running two steps behind Sylvester Stallone, as the terse sidekick in the worthless cop drama *Nighthawks*.

The swell of pride in theaters when Lando sidled onto the screen—I can testify to the reaction in Detroit when *Empire* first played—caused an attendant ripple of applause, the quieter version of a shout-out. By placing Williams in the picture, Lucas guaranteed that black audiences would connect with the *Star Wars* galaxy in a way that they never had with fantasy and science fiction before. But his inclusiveness seems to have been lost on productions that have come in the *Star Wars* films' wake. Most distressingly, the lesson that Lucas put into practice by creating Lando has been at least partially negated, Samuel L. Jackson or no Samuel L. Jackson, by the Jar Jar Binks controversy—that name even sounds like it belongs on the Mantan Moreland of space, and his comportment did as much for intergalactic brothers as *Homeboys from Outer Space*.

In the fantasy world, it looked like Williams would get up to the plate one more time. His peerless urbanity loomed large in 1989's *Batman*, where he played the crusader who didn't wear a cape:

District Attorney Harvey Dent. Flashing that razor-sharp smile gleaming with promise, Williams hung back, and those of us aware of the Batman undercurrent figured that it meant there was more to come for him—and director Tim Burton planted that seed. In the comics, Harvey Dent has acid flung in his face by an angry victim of the prosecutor's talent; Dent marshals the remains of his scarred psyche and deteriorates into the conflicted villain Two-Face, one of the few bad Batman nemeses who didn't seem like a pathetic mental patient in a Halloween costume, as in, well . . . the Riddler, the Penguin, Mr. Freeze . . . all of the other Batman foes besides the Joker. In the comics, Two-Face had the damaged back-story of a character out of a particularly malignant film noir: he was the Janus of thugs, with his godlike handsomeness on one side of his face, and a dense, repellent mass of scar tissue on the other, so crazy he was reduced to flipping a coin—one side scratched with a knife—to decide his actions. And Williams, with his glowing good looks, was a logical choice—after all, wouldn't any guy go goofy after being deprived of that particular brand of matinee-idol patina? A patina that, incidentally, Time the Avenger had done a poor job of diminishing. By 1989, the fifty-two-year-old Williams still looked robust and well-preserved. And his potential Two-Face triumph seemed prefigured in another way; in *Nighthawks* his face gets slashed and he spends the last third of the picture with a gauze bandage covering his stalwart jawline.

Williams's Dent was nowhere to be seen in the 1992 sequel *Batman Returns*, though the picture barely bothered to make any time for the title character, either; it could've been called *Batman Returns for About Twenty Minutes*. His—Williams's, I mean—excision was a bad sign, since the regulars from the previous *Batman* movie all got screen time except for Dent and Vicki Vale. Vicki's absence could be explained by the fact that no one had any idea what to do with the character once Bruce Wayne revealed his secret identity to her. Williams's absence from *Batman Returns* was part of an odd summer for African-Americans. That same season, one critic noted that in the Eddie Murphy romantic comedy

Boomerang, no white characters were in the picture. The same writer didn't point out that few speaking roles for African-Americans existed in *Batman Returns,* a movie set in Gotham City, provisionally a fictional version of Manhattan. By the time Two-Face was added to a Batman movie—*Batman Forever*—Harvey Dent had been recast. He was now played by Tommy Lee Jones, who already looked like he hadn't quite got out of the way of a vial of acid flung in his direction. (You almost wondered if director Joel Schumacher wouldn't have wanted to supervise the *unharmed* side of Two-Face's visage with makeup prosthetics and CGI.) Few mentioned that Williams had gotten the bum's rush, since more attention was focused on new Batman Val Kilmer (stepping in for Michael Keaton) and his brand-new PG-13 costume—with its amply rounded booty compartment and anatomically correct nipples, the suit looked like it had been made in a West Village shop for the lamest of rough trade. As for Jones, he had become a part of the Warner Brothers stable—he single-handedly rescued the studio's Steven Seagal programmer *Under Siege,* and rode *The Fugitive* into a Best Supporting Actor Oscar win. Obviously, giving the Two-Face role to Jones was Warner's idea of loyalty. Yet, Lucas proved how cheap loyalty comes in the firmament of the American cinema. He made his stand to eschew the inertia that functions as racism in the movie-studio world and, with Williams, pursue a casting choice that both sent a signal and united audiences. By welcoming a black character into a series of films that would forever alter the way the world viewed fantasy, Lucas's generosity and shrewdness showed that a bigger worldview doesn't have to be an afterthought. If you want to contemplate how little has changed since *The Empire Strikes Back,* all you have to do is look at *Harry Potter and the Sorcerer's Stone,* or *Lord of the Rings,* or any of the pile of films that use science-fiction fantasy as coin of the realm, to see that Jim Crow is a part, unintentional or not, of otherworldly stories of heroes.

Two years after the ignominy of *Batman Forever*—with a title that seemed to describe the picture's running time—Lucas rereleased the *Star Wars* trilogy, celebrating the twentieth anniversary of the theatrical debut of the first picture. When I saw *The Empire Strikes Back* at the Cinema Dome in Los Angeles, the crowd's full-throated cheers, voicing its unanimous approval for the most down brother ever to blast into hyper-drive, erased, for just a moment, the embarrassment of the Colt 45 commercials, the endless string of straight-to-cable misadventures Williams endured, and Lucas's subsequent misfires. And for a beat, Lando Calrissian, the first owner of the *Millennium Falcon*—before he dropped the spacecraft's pink slip to Han Solo in a card game—was back where he belonged, in the captain's seat of the galaxy's most beloved freedom ride. Williams's bemused charisma was literally far-flung, and the endless skies of the many planets twinkling behind him seemed bountiful, full of dreams for him and the audience members who saw his very presence there as a glimpse of a future that still, as yet, has not really come to be. But, for a little over two hours, all seemed right in a world a long time ago, in a galaxy far, far away.

THE CHRYSANTHEMUM
AND THE LIGHTSABER

ERIKA KROUSE

[1]

I was having a beer with my karate dojo after practice one night when I raised the question, "Are you a *Star Trek* person or a *Star Wars* person?"

"Do you have to be one or the other?" one man asked.

"Yes."

They didn't even pause to think about it. "*Star Wars*." "*Star Wars*." "*Star Wars*." "*Star Wars*." "*Star Wars*." "*Star Wars*." "*Star Wars*." "*Star Wars*." "*Star Trek*" (he was a computer programmer). "*Star Wars*."

"Why?" I asked. "Why *Star Wars*?"

Nobody spoke for a few seconds. Then my *sensei* shrugged and said, "It's the hero's journey."

That seemed to say it all, and the subject was changed to football.

[II]

The hero's journey begins at home, when he's just fledgling potential. He is a special child, a leader. He could save the world. Or something could go wrong, and he could blow up the World Trade Center. What makes him change into something mighty, or something horrible? Nature, nurture, or neither?

[III]

It's no secret that George Lucas was in love with samurai films, as am I. Akira Kurosawa's *Hidden Fortress* is a near montage of *Star Wars* scenes, from the two lost strangelings arguing in the desert at the beginning of *Star Wars* to an equine replica of Princess Leia chasing the Stormtroopers through the forest in *Return of the Jedi*. The characters are prototypes—there's even a samurai version of Han Solo.

Star Wars' costumes alone establish this samurai influence. Vader's helmet is nearly identical to *kabuto* bowl-like samurai helmets, with the sides winging out at angles and a *mempo* faceplate to hide emotions and terrify enemies. Stormtrooper uniforms (which always looked uncomfortable to me, and hard to keep clean) were also modeled after samurai armor. Samurai Vaderesque robes were originally designed by the Japanese to disguise the movement of feet. When Vader moves, he floats.

Vader is pure warrior; he has mastered himself, his sword (lightsaber, whatever), and his emotions. But if Vader is a twisted samurai, the Jedi Knights are more in the spirit of the samurai ideal. Take *Phantom Menace*—Qui-Gon Jinn and Obi-Wan Kenobi wear long samurai robes and obi (wide belts), with samurai topknots in their long hair. They also use (neon) swords, the soul weapon of the samurai warrior class. As guiding spiritual ideologies, the samurai had Zen, and the Jedi have the Force.

I am fascinated by warriors, fighters. In karate class, I pile my hair into a samurai topknot. I have necrophiliac crushes on Che Guevara and Bruce Lee, and my very first child-love was Muhammad Ali. While actual strategic war never thrilled me, I love the renegade warrior—his independence, his instant decisions, his cohesive moral code. I love how the drawing of one weapon necessitates the drawing of another. I love how the ethical battle is always decided by the outcome of the physical one.

Sick, perhaps. Or maybe just a bid for simplicity in a weird world where death can come by opening a letter. I want ethics in arms. I want a world where battles are fought by fighters, not computers or terrorists. I want the bad guy to wear black, and the good guy to save the day.

[IV]

I had decided to take karate lessons because I was afraid of violence. Violence, not pain—I never had a problem with pain. I often looked down at my legs, surprised to find a deep, crusty gash, or a purple bruise blooming untended. It's still that way, except now parts of my body refuse to bruise, the way abused children refuse to cry. Sometimes I'll notice blood on the floor of the dojo and call out, "Someone's bleeding!" Everyone will stop and check their toes, their arms, their noses. But it will be me.

Yet I dissolved into sudden tears when my friend Lisa threw an ice cube in my face. Ditto when a lover's sleeping fist collided with my eye. Ditto when my father turned on me in a sudden rage, even from a distance. Or when I bent down to pet a stranger's puffy chow chow, and he bit me, softly but cruelly.

I started taking karate classes in 1998, during a particularly nasty breakup. I had been crying convulsively for four days, and I only stopped to go to my first karate class. Halfway into it, the *sen-*

sei gave us pads to practice punching and kicking. I was paired with the only other woman, who was a black belt. I thought, *She's a little skinny chick like me. No problem.* I held a large pad for her and she kicked it, once. My left contact lens stayed where it was while the rest of my body flew backwards into the wall.

We found the contact lens, and I hurried to the bathroom to poke it back into my eye. I looked through the mirror at my chapped eyes, rabbity around the edges, dirty lens stuck to my finger, and thought, *What the hell am I doing?*

[V]

When a samurai warrior wanted to further his training, he didn't seek out other fighters. He instead found a Zen master to teach him how to meditate. Zen Master Hakuin Ekaku (1686–1768) said, "Meditation in the midst of action is a billion times superior to meditation in stillness." Conversely, the samurai believed that action in the midst of meditation was a billion times superior to action in the midst of anything else.

The samurai were attracted to Zen Buddhism with its emphasis on simplicity and self-control, full awareness of each moment, and tranquillity in the face of death. Zen Buddhism was also infused with Shinto, the Japanese national religion. Shinto is a sophisticated form of animism, in which all of nature is imbued with spirit (*shin*), very similar to Yoda's somewhat muddled animism.

Samurai and Jedi ideologies are nearly identical. Zen Master Taisen Deshimaru defined Zen spirituality in the following manner:

> Our life is not just *in* our body, it is a perpetual exchange with the life of the universe. Understanding this interdependence comes with the perception of *ku* or nothingness, vacuity. . . . The manifestation of *ku* is infinite, limitless energy, which is accessible to us when we are in harmony with universal life; we are invested by it unconsciously, naturally, without any resistance.

Compare with Yoda's Force:

> Life creates it. Makes it grow. Its energy surrounds us and binds us. Luminous beings are we—not this crude matter. You must feel the force around you—here, between you, me, the tree, the rock, everywhere. Yes! Even between the land and the ship.

Yoda is the archetypal martial arts teacher. He's small, old, and ugly. He looks like someone you'd push off a bar stool. He's more powerful than his physical capacity, which is the point of martial arts. Speaks funny English he does. He knows secrets about you, and he keeps them from you, until he doesn't. He is cranky. He eats disgusting food. He catches you at your assumptions.

Like Zen masters who only teach focus and meditation, Yoda didn't teach Luke any fighting technique at all. He never once matched swords with Luke. Instead, Luke had to condition his body and mind, standing on one hand, balancing Yoda on his foot, levitating rocks and neatly piling them on top of each other. He strapped Yoda onto his back and did acrobatics through the jungle, while Yoda yammered in his ear about the Force.

Particulars aside, this approach is actually very similar to traditional martial arts training—physical and spiritual conditioning through seemingly unrelated tasks. There are tales of fighters retreating to the woods to punch trees for two years, or you might have seen people hitting the *makiwara* (wooden post wrapped in padding), or shoving their hands into buckets of sand. In *The Karate Kid*, waxing a car. I know men who punch walls, and one man who bashes his big toe against the ground every day, building the muscle in his feet. He can now toe-kick a person to death, if he's ever attacked while barefoot.

A typical training in my dojo begins with sit-ups, push-ups, lunges, running, exercises, basics (punching, blocking, kicking), and star jumps (be glad that you don't know what these are). Once we're tired, we do kata (forms), and *bunkai* (full-contact kata-based fights), trying to keep our focus and technique in the face of physical depletion. The idea is, this is when karate counts—when you're at a loss.

Still, we don't train in a swamp, or prepare to fight Osama bin Laden. Nine-hundred-year-old Yoda is not our *sensei*. My *sensei*'s name is Paul. He is a buff, good-looking man, thirty-four years old, with a job in Internet sales. Barbara-*sensei*, his beautiful and brutal wife, is a professional comedian and teaches karate class when *sensei* is on business trips. The two of them are open, generous, and a lot of fun. There are no swamp creatures, no yelling. They don't make us enter dark caves with a lightsaber, or lift aircraft with our minds. Barbara-*sensei* is Canadian. I have it pretty easy, comparatively.

[VI]

There has always been an element of mystique in the martial arts, for good reason. Many artists demonstrate seemingly miraculous feats—extinguishing flames with the "energy" of their strike, brushing aside multiple attackers while seated, killing charging bulls with one punch. In *The Phantom Menace*, the prospect of two Jedi armed with lightsabers was more daunting than an army of murderous blaster-toting droids.

If you break martial arts down into technique, the mystique doesn't fade—it gets stronger. You can know exactly how a fighter moved—reproduce it, even—but never achieve the same effect. As it is impossible to break a work of art into a formula of techniques, a martial art also surpasses such explanation. Even so, technique is the only means we have to understanding a martial theory. Let's look at the fighting technique of the Jedi.

Rules of engagement don't preclude multiple attackers, but *Star Wars* preserves the old tradition (both Western and Eastern) of single combat between leaders of opposing forces deciding an issue. In *Star Wars*, these hand-to-hand battles serve as a microcosm for the fights in space, but they also demonstrate how the spirits of these two leaders—Darth Vader and Luke—provide a foundation for the fight as a whole.

In these battles, Darth and Luke both prefer the same weapons—the lightsaber and the Force. Regarding their actual combat technique, the fighters depart from Western fighting styles and embrace the Eastern. The most popular Western style of swordplay is fencing, using a light lance for duels. Fencers mostly keep a low stance with both legs bent, occasionally lunging for strikes. They thrust and parry with one arm, the other arm free for balance, their bodies turned fully sideways to eliminate most of the targets on their bodies. They move sideways like crabs, traversing the same line to exhibit control and to force the sword to do most of the evasion work. Parries and strikes are very controlled, using small circles and direct thrusts with the tip of the sword.

Although the Jedi do use some fencing techniques, their style of fighting most closely resembles Japanese kendo, an ancient style of swordplay dating from as early as 400 C.E. Jedi Knights grip the lightsaber with both hands, facing their opponent frontally, rather than sideways. They trade the speed of fencing for the mighty blows of kendo, deflecting blaster fire and cutting through metal with their force. As the *Star Wars* trilogy progresses, the fighting becomes more cohesive, with more dynamic moves. Most of their strikes are swipes from the side or over the head, striking with the edge rather than the tip of the weapon. The Jedi allow gravity and the momentum of their swings to move their sabers diagonally from side to side, often in a shallow figure-eight fashion.

Although they sometimes balance themselves in the center between two bent legs, it seems that the Jedi's basic stance is the lunge or the half lunge, with the front leg bent and the rear leg nearly straight, allowing the forward motion of their bodies to augment the force of their strokes. When they strike, they don't poke at a dainty target—they swipe *through* the opponent, following through on their stroke the way golfers do. They don't aim for the target necessarily—they aim for a point beyond the target. This is a technique emphasized in most of the Asian martial arts—striking through your target to the space beyond it, in order to penetrate the target fully.

This technique is what makes martial arts so powerful. Fighters of the Asian martial arts usually commit their body weight to a stroke, delivering few blows of force, rather than a multitude of lighter strokes. The martial artist is more apt to give up ground than the fighters of Western arts (boxing, fencing, etc.), realizing that it only takes one successful blow to end the conflict forever. For this reason, many martial artists do not engage in tournament fights, which focus on the accumulation of points by striking a target repeatedly in a fight, lightly or otherwise. For the purists (and the Jedi), the aim of engaging in conflict is to end the argument quickly, with one killing blow.

[VII]

So why, why, why, why, why do this strange thing? As Han Solo said, "Hokey religions and ancient weapons are no match for a good blaster at your side." If I'm learning karate for self-defense, why not save time and buy a gun?

I guess I'm not studying karate for self-defense after all, although that was why I started. I had the illusion that I would be invulnerable if I knew how to protect myself. Like Luke, I came from bad stock, a line of men gone wrong. My grandfather chased my grandmother around with a knife, beat his children. One uncle pulled out a gun when he was angry, beat his children. My father, when he was around, beat his children.

Often, people who had rough childhoods study martial arts when they grow up. You couldn't toss a throwing star across a dojo (if anyone actually knew how to do that anymore) without catching one such person on each prong. Beaten boys, raped girls, bully-fodder, short people—many of them grow up and study karate, tae kwon do, kung fu, or jiujitsu. Some of these people come to my dojo. They understand violence; they understand survival. They are usually the ones who have the easiest time learning karate, and the hardest time controlling themselves.

One talented fighter (we'll call him Han) had grown up with a terrible father of the extinguishing-cigarettes-on-son's-skin caliber. He taught martial arts at a dojo I sometimes visited to learn new techniques.

One day in class Han ordered a student to hit him. The student promptly punched Han in the nose. His nose visibly broke. Han said, "Hit me again." The student did. Blood everywhere. "Again." The student balked. "Again," Han insisted, ignoring the thickness of his voice, as if he only had a head cold. The student said, "Um, I don't . . . I think . . ." Han looked at him, blood waterfalling down his face. Then he said, "You pussy."

This is not the Force. Nor is it the Dark Side, really. This is the stuff of kamikaze pilots, of gladiators, of heroin addicts. This is Generation X violence, Camus violence, shooting an Arab because, hey, why not? This is the stuff that happens when you've seen tragedy, and you're half-fascinated, half-bored with the way that nothing, anymore, is unimaginable.

[VIII]

As fathers go, I think Darth Vader wasn't atypical for my father's generation. Menacing, uncommunicative, prone to wild violences. Obsessed with his career, rotten to his family. So, okay, Luke's father happened to be the menace of the universe, and mine just worked for IBM. But I could tell that the nasty things both of them did with their days filled them with impotence and rage, and at evenings at my house, those two things created an explosive mixture.

I'm sure Darth Vader thought he was doing his best. After all, he doesn't even know he has a son, and when he finds out, he tries to teach him the tricks of the trade, adopt him into the family business. He doesn't want to hurt his son, necessarily.

But time goes on, and Luke is stubborn, defiant. He won't turn. Darth Vader looks at his progeny and thinks, *Why isn't he more like me? And yet he is so much like me.* The two elements together are infuriating. He wants answers. He thinks, *I gave this boy life, and I can take it away, too. Who will stop me?*

I saw *Star Wars* for the first time in a drive-in when I was eight, on vacation in Cape Cod with my family. It was after a fight between my father and me, and I brooded in the back seat of the car while the screen flashed pale, soggy images and the speaker barked dialogue, sounding like a person shouting into a tin can far, far away. Space, yeah. Death Star, so what. The robots were okay. I wasn't into it.

And then, right behind my father's head, I saw Darth Vader floating down a white hallway. Black robes, helmet, asthma. Brutal, invulnerable, accountable for nothing. His black eyes were opaque, his expression permanently grim, ready to hurt without any thought of consequences or control. It was the lack of remorse that told me everything. Even then, long before the release of *The Empire Strikes Back*, I knew who he was. I knew he was somebody's father.

[IX]

After I had studied martial arts for a while, I became reckless. I insisted on walking along East Colfax in Denver at night sometimes, alone in a short skirt. Crackheads veered toward me, whispering in my ear. I heard the word "pussy" a lot. One man slowed down his low rider until it kept pace with me. "How much?" he asked, and then cracked his door to see what I'd do. A prostitute chased me off her corner, screaming in pink glitter heels. Alleys. Abandoned lots in Five Points, smoking a cigarette by a fence. Men with scary bulges in their pockets. "Hey little girl, hey, hey, come over here." Once I passed a cop car with three cuffed men slumping forward on the hood. The cop turned to me and said slowly, "Ma'am. Get out of this neighborhood. Now."

In *Beyond Good and Evil,* Nietzsche warns: "Under conditions of peace, the warlike man attacks himself."

I danced with dangerous-looking men in dive bars, disappointed when they turned out polite, kind.

I'd daydream at work, playing imaginary fights in my head. I'd stare at the wall, thinking of what I'd do, and what I'd do next.

I left my apartment door unlocked. I undressed in front of my open window, lights on, shutter up. I lay alone in the dark, heart ticking, thinking, OK, *come and get me. Try it.*

[X]

Justice, courage, compassion, courtesy, truthfulness, honor, and loyalty: this is the code of the samurai warrior. Sounds simple. But each of these ideals is its own *koan,* or unsolvable riddle—should Luke be loyal to his friends or to his father? How can Luke show compassion toward his father if it renders him unable to kill Vader and defeat the evil that is inherent in him? How can Luke be truthful to a deceptive liar? What is courage without fear? And what the hell is honor anyway?

When a samurai had dishonored himself (and therefore his family, his lord, his clan, his prefecture, etc.), he was given the option of seppuku, or self-immolation. He performed a ritual commonly known as hara-kiri, where the warrior disemboweled himself with a sword shortly before an executioner incompletely severed his head from his body, leaving it dangling from a flap of skin. Although seppuku was formally banned in the 1600s, Japanese people often still commit suicide today when they fear dishonor: students throw themselves in front of trains if their test scores are too low, and girls with unplanned pregnancies slash their wrists. Bloody and vicious, seppuku was considered to be the honorable last resort, when there were no other options left.

The samurai neither ran from nor embraced his death. He conditioned himself until he accepted death as a part of his life. He was ready at any moment for death to come. If the warrior accepted death, his life was qualitatively stronger. Only then could he realize his full potential as a warrior, willing to die for his cause.

At two points in the trilogy, Luke commits incomplete acts of seppuku to preserve his honor. The first is during a lightsaber fight with Darth Vader in *Empire Strikes Back*, when Vader reveals that he is Luke's father. Vader holds out an open hand, asking Luke to join him so they can rule the Empire together, as father and son. Luke is dangling from a pole. He realizes that to live, he will have to take the gloved hand and embrace the Dark Side. Instead, Luke releases the pole and falls through space, deciding to die rather than succumb. But of course Leia rescues him and Luke lives to fight again as a Jedi.

The other act of seppuku occurs in *Return of the Jedi*, when Luke surrenders to the Empire and enters the Death Star to save his father's soul, knowing that it will soon be bombed by the Alliance. He is ready to die. When the Emperor says that Luke will turn to the Dark Side, Luke says, "You're wrong. Soon I'll be dead. And you with me." Luke does not choose to fight (except for some gratuitous lightsaber scenes with Vader) and refuses to kill his father, surrendering his own life instead. Luke relies on the reemergence of "good" in his father to save his own life, in spite of the fact that he had never seen any evidence of this "good" in Vader before. Vader is an evil monster. But Luke believes in him anyway. Because Darth Vader is his father.

[XI]

My black belt test wasn't a mighty battle. I didn't have to face my father, my demons, my worst fears. I didn't have to enter a cave, combat evil, fight intergalactic terrorism, or explode a Death Star. I had to do a lot of kata and fight everyone in the dojo. All of them were bigger than me, up to twice my weight. It was hard. It was long. I remember at one point casually wondering whether I was going to pass out, throw up, or both at once. The test took place over two days, and when it was over I was physically, mentally, and emotionally exhausted.

Even so, after I passed the test, got the belt, and wore it, I thought, *That's it?* I had thought that maybe getting a black belt would mean that I could now do great things. Fight crime! Walk on water! But I'm still clumsy. I still occasionally punch myself in the eye (hard to do, but possible). I'm still lifetimes away from what I want to be.

Maybe I had thought that it would cleanse me, birth me anew into a purer world. Where I came from would no longer matter. I wouldn't feel the way I do, like I come from something violent and cruel, and that maybe I've got that same thing lurking inside of me.

[XII]

Enemies have changed. I grew up in the Cold War, thinking that your enemies were distant and untouchable. They hid behind nuclear weapons, which allow a soldier to kill without the inconvenience of seeing the victim.

But things are coming full circle. Nuclear weapons have rendered themselves useless in their potential for total annihilation. So our enemies are creeping closer, laying down their missiles. They're using the old-fashioned tools of war—poison, blades, fists, and the will to die.

We'd all like to think the Force is with us. Nobody wants to be evil. But it's not so simple in real life. Greed is ambition with a twist, and vengeance is nearly interchangeable with justice. Violence is justified as self-defense, or survival of the fittest. Forgiveness is often just weak desperation. The Dark Side is relative— plenty of people own stock in Exxon, eat veal, put razor blades in apples. Think of arsonists, or people who write anonymous hate mail, people who throw lit cigarettes at dogs. Even unresolved issues can make you a candidate for succumbing to the Dark Side.

Most of us are never given the luxury of a showdown, or an opportunity to save the world. Of course, we would try, given the chance—we'd have nothing to lose. But most of our battles are smaller, and there's plenty to lose. I don't know the difference between being brave and fighting for the sake of fighting. You can believe in something so much that you just inflict your own personal war on people of peace.

[XIII]

Luke is training at Yoda's outdoor dojo and notices a dark cave. Yoda says, "In you must go."

Luke asks, "What's in there?"

"Only what you take with you," Yoda answers.

Yoda tells Luke to leave his weapons outside. Luke gives him a long look and then brings them anyway. Upon entering the cave, he encounters Vader and draws his weapon first. The fight is over in a few cursory strokes, and Luke lops Vader's head off. It rolls to a stop, and then explodes, revealing Luke's own head, his own face.

Zen Master Deshimaru wrote, "You must not take out your sword because if you try to kill someone, you must die for it yourself. What you must do instead is kill yourself, kill your own mind. . . . You are the strongest and the others keep their distance. It is no longer necessary to win victories over them."

But can I do this thing myself? Is the Force with me? I suspect No. I can hang a spoon from the tip of my nose, but that's about it as far as levitation is concerned. Can I fight without fighting? Could I close my eyes to land a torpedo in the belly of the Death Star? I have always had the sinking suspicion that if I were a character in a movie, I'd be the first unnecessary death, the first plane to go down, the first person to be deceived by the enemy in disguise.

To fight is to plunge into the unknown, armed only with your skills and liabilities, which are often identical. Questions to ask before you fight: What do you bring with you into that cave? How

do you let it go? And most important, how do you survive once
you do?

[XIV]

The thing is, I don't want to let go. I don't want Luke's capacity for
forgiveness, Ben's objective respect, Yoda's Zen. They're not practical. Yoda told Luke that he'll never be a Jedi until he confronts his
father. But things are simple in *Star Wars*. It's a movie. What do you
do with a person who has no remorse? Luke used his own life as
bait to save his father. Will I do the same?

Really, no.

I believe in the power of compassion, I do. But I also believe in
Nietzsche, who wrote, "He who fights with monsters should look
to it that he himself does not become a monster. And when you
gaze long into an abyss the abyss also gazes into you."

It's hard for a Jewish girl to say this, but I've suffered enough.
The last time my father and I did anything noncombative together
was when I was eighteen. To bond or whatever, he took me to a
Mets game. Even just sitting in the plastic seat next to him felt dangerous, like being sucked into the undertow of a tidal wave. I didn't
know what to do. I was so nervous, I ate five hot dogs in the first
two innings and then threw up in the stadium bathroom at the
bottom of the fourth. The Mets lost.

After a long war, it's hard to stop fighting. It's what you're
trained to do, what you're good at. I, however, am tired of it. I don't
want to fight my father anymore. So I fight everything else.

I haven't been without a bruise in four years. When I wear
shorts, people look at my legs with concern. Look at that battered
girl. Look at her arms. Sometimes I have a fat lip, and I suck on it. I
limp without noticing. Nothing really hurts anymore.

All this damage says to me: I can handle anything, and I can
handle the price I have to pay in order to handle it. My shins are
ridged with scar tissue. My jaw still clicks from the time it was

dislocated—likewise with both of my thumbs. My body is sore 100 percent of the time. My friends make fun of me, jumping in the air and shouting "Wotcha!" Some of them think I'm sick, calling karate "your macho theatrics."

But it feels real, what I do in the dojo against another person. It doesn't feel violent. It feels like the opposite of violence. Everything blends together into a pure focus. I forget everything except for what I'm doing in that moment. There's a point where my body's so tired, it's like slow dying. And there's something there, some Force, which makes me feel most alive while I'm taking this mock journey toward death.

But I know this isn't what they mean at all.

It's hard to realize that I'm just not strong enough. I want the hero's journey. But I doubt the integrity of my battles. When I fight, I still see my own face in my opponent's, my own fears reflected. I'm still looking for clues as to what I'm made of, trying to understand the nature of this war I've invented for myself. And to prepare for a future victory—to see which side, if any, will win.

THE FORCE VISITS
WILLOUGHBY, OHIO

ELWOOD REID

The summer *Star Wars* hit, I was, for lack of a better word, a pussy.
And although I was large for my age, recent growth spurts had left
me mushy and awkward, body shy in a neighborhood full of delin-
quents, gas huffers, S.P.E.D.s (older and unpredictably violent Special Ed kids or short bussers, who after years of torture had turned
mean), brave turn-the-other-cheek Christians, thug jocks, burn-
outs, and pre-ADD nutjobs whose favorite trick was to ask if you'd
ever met the Jackson Five and when you answered "no" they would
then show you five knuckles, punch you in the mouth, and laugh at
your fat-lipped stupidity.

I'd been in only one real fistfight and lost—chipped tooth,
bloody nose, and a face full of snow. The noble peacenik wisdom of
"Run and live to fight another day" didn't mean shit in northeast
Ohio. You either avoided conflict altogether or you joined the fray,
took your lumps, and picked your spots. The trick was to survive
until you could defend yourself. One way to keep the bullies and
thrill-seeking sadists from circling was to strike a pose—model
yourself on some widely understood tough guy and hope the powers that be bought the act long enough for you to actually grow

balls and stand up to them. A few kids opted to be Steve Austin—The Six Million Dollar Man (a complicated act, involving lots of slow-motion running and odd sound effects), others modeled themselves on Jack Lambert—the Pittsburgh Steeler's viscous mook of a linebacker who along with Mean Joe Greene (another model tough guy until the Pepsi commercial) regularly destroyed our beloved Cleveland Browns. There were even a few kids who went around talking and acting like Muhammad Ali, dazzling their would-be intimidators and upsetting their vaguely racist fathers with butchered white-boy versions of The Greatest's poetic taunts. Then *Star Wars* arrived, and with it a whole new set of other-worldly heroes.

I remember dashing out of the packed theater still in the grips of the film—fists clenched and heart racing as kids made thrumming lightsaber sounds, panted like Darth Vader, and proclaimed the movie cool. I took out the small finger-shaped piece of meteorite I carried with me at all times and held it to the sky wanting very badly to be called away to a planet far, far away and launched on some great adventure. (I believed in aliens and UFOs, and the discovery of the large meteorite earlier that spring and its subsequent confiscation by NASA lab rats—another story—had only reinforced my irrational hope that if and when aliens landed they would know me by the piece of meteorite that I carried, slept with, and stroked.) But nothing happened, and as I walked across the bright parking lot, the movie magic fading fast, I pondered my own rapidly changing place in the neighborhood. Like Luke, I would have to master my fears and strike out on the dark adventures of adolescence, without the benefit of lightsabers or the Force.

We lived on a dead-end street in a town called Willoughby on the outskirts of Cleveland. Behind our house sat a massive abandoned polo field, once part of an exclusive country club that was perched on a lush green hill. The Club, with its wrought-iron gate and rarely glimpsed clubhouse, was a constant reminder that there were people out there who ate shrimp cocktail more than once a year, drove silent German sedans, vacationed in Europe, and talked knowledgeably of horses and stock portfolios. Nobody in our neighborhood was a member of the Club and, except for a few lucky kids who caddied, nobody even knew a member of the Club. Even the adults sneaked onto its impossibly green golf course to fish for bass or look for lost golf balls, only to be chased off by the greenkeeper or chewed out by some white-haired rich guy as he lined up his tee shot. But through some Robin Hoodlike justice of subdivision, the polo field and surrounding woods had been orphaned by the new interstate, leaving its use and rule to the strip of "have not" families whose houses bordered its edges.

The woods were full of swamps, small creeks, abandoned cars, interstate trash, a power relay station, and dozens of forts that had been built, destroyed, and rebuilt by the various and sundry gangs. For better or worse every last one of us were Willo-Billies. We played baseball, smear-the-queer, and nasty war games in the field using any and all weapons at our disposal—BB guns, wrist rockets, stick swords, tent stakes, mud balls (with or without rocks), Polish cannons, sharpened lawn darts, golf balls, Pepsi bottle bombs, etc.

The bullies of the moment were Sharon and Richard Moros (not their real names), or the Morons if you dared. They lived just down the street in a seedy red ranch house, the front yard decorated with beer cans, busted lawn chairs, and a partially disassembled white Chevy Ranchero. Richard had thick black glasses, yellow teeth, a laugh like Woody the Woodpecker, and an endless supply of M-80s which he tossed down sewers or at unsuspecting fat kids who were too slow and trusting to know when they were being fired upon. As bullies go, Richard wasn't big or particularly strong, just crazy and unpredictable. Most importantly he loved to fight and did not care if he won or lost. Whenever there was a shortage of pansies to pound on, Richard would fight older jocks, his sister, and even the occasional stray dog with equal gusto and disregard for his own well-being. Older kids, who at first had easily whipped Richard, gave up after the third or fourth rematch and refused to fight him because he didn't fight by any of the rules. He bit, kicked, spit, threw knives, grabbed balls, poked eyes—anything. And if you tried to run, Richard would chase you down on his lime green banana bike, riding no hands as he launched buckeyes from his trusty wrist rocket, lost in the thrill of the hunt.

Sharon was two years older than her brother and looked like some butch version of Peppermint Patty. She had red hair, crooked teeth, biceps, and unfortunately large freckles which she made up for with the handjobs she was rumored to dispense with alarming regularity in dark scrap-carpeted fort rooms and damp basements. You called her Red Baron at great risk, because her boyfriends, large army-jacketed stoners, would grab and hold you down while Sharon burned you with her Led Zeppelin lighter or forced you to sniff Rush until you passed out.

The summer of *Star Wars*, the Morons and their band ruled the woods and polo field. They wrecked our forts, destroyed bikes, and frequently broke up baseball games because, according to Richard, baseball was "for faggots." But as the summer wore on I knew that I would have to make a stand against the Moron gang or else be forced to abandon the small corners of woods and polo field my brother and our group of friends had managed to claim as our own. I didn't know how I was going to do this. But avoiding conflict in a neighborhood built on conflict was becoming increasingly difficult.

Unlike many of my peers I didn't geekily obsess over the robots or cool X-wing fighters. C-3PO was annoying (or gay, in the pre-PC parlance of the times) and would have been immediately beaten and pulped were he to ever crash-land in our neighborhood. And R2-D2 reminded me of the shop-vac my father rolled out for us during the weekly and dreaded garage cleanings, which due to his pack-rat mentality became our own Aegean stables. Instead, in my search for heroes I focused on the old-fashioned swashbuckling bravery and the struggle between good and evil waged by Luke, Darth, and Han Solo in *Star Wars*—the largest and most formidable cultural event to hit Ohio.

My first impression was that Luke was a bit of a wuss, always doubting and worried. Of course I admired the cocky cool of Han Solo even though I knew I did not possess the tousled bravado or flair for snappy comebacks required to pull off such an act. So I settled on Darth because he was a man of few words and taller than everybody else. Darth did not take any shit. Darth knew what he wanted and would kill to get it. I practiced on the smaller members of our gang, randomly strangling Scott Legan when he refused to play right field or whacking his older brother John with a stick when he insisted on harassing the opposing batter in his Spock voice, "That was an illogical swing, Lugnuts," etc.

There was a problem with my Darth act, though. It only worked on friends—the weak, the halt, and the lame. It had yet to be tested on my foes. So when Richard Moros and his pyromaniac sidekick, Julius, attacked our fort one day, I stood my ground, Darthlike, waiting for the moment to strike. My refusal to run momentarily confused Richard and Julius. Normal operating procedure called for me to retreat behind the rickety plywood walls and let the siege begin.

After huddling with Julius, Richard shouted, "You retarded or something Reid?"

When I didn't answer, Richard directed Julius to lob a chunk of concrete at my head. It missed and for a moment the power of the Dark Side convinced me to take a few steps toward them, thinking I could get close enough to slap the Darth clamp on their dirty throats. From the safety of the fort my crew began to shout encouragement. But then Richard, eager to preserve custom, pulled out his wrist rocket and bounced a golf ball off my shin. I quickly crawled back to the fort, trying to hold back the tears of pain as my gang launched a volley of mud balls, sticks, and stones at the invaders until Richard and Julius lost interest and left to steal cigarettes from the 7-Eleven.

I'd been brave, but it was no consolation for the purple knot on my shin or the fact that I had now officially entered the Moroses' radar as a potential roadblock in their campaign of terror.

I went home that night and reconsidered the Darth act, finally admitting to myself that wuss or no wuss I had far more in common with Luke than I did with Vader or the rock-star cool Han Solo.

A second viewing of *Star Wars* with John Legan confirmed this fact. As we left the theater John pulled up his hooded sweatshirt and began talking like Obi-Wan Kenobi, calling me Luke and raising his fingers mystically to indicate some errant bit of the Force that had found its way to Ohio and was waiting for me to tap into it.

If Luke had the Force to wrestle with, I had to master my own fears, not just of the Moroses and their gang, but of serial killers. The summer of 1977 was not just the summer of *Stars Wars*, it was also the Summer of Sam. Additionally, I'd spent way too much time reading a copy of Vincent Bugliosi's account of the Manson family murders, *Helter Skelter*, which I'd stolen from my parents' bedroom. I obsessed over Charles Manson and his swastika-ed followers the way other kids geeked out over Spider Man comic books or Wacky Packs. I memorized the crime-scene photos—the word PIG scrawled in blood, ropes used to bind the victims, and of course the beautiful, but already dead, Sharon Tate. I sometimes dreamed of rescuing her only to be overwhelmed by the band of murderous hippies.

Serial killers were not just something that happened other places. Two weeks after I'd seen *Star Wars* again and had decided to drop the Darth act, our morning game of baseball was interrupted by a long line of police cars and unmarked FBI sedans pulling down the overgrown cinder road on the far side the polo field.

"It's the cops," Lugnuts shouted. A few older kids tossed cigarettes, grabbed mitts and bats, and sped away on stolen bikes, squealing like pigs, bravely flipping off the distant policemen.

The rest of us quickly followed suit and scattered, convinced that the police had finally figured out the source of the rocks dropped off the overpass at oncoming cars or the petty acts of arson and vandalism in and around the neighborhood, not to mention the thousands of prank and obscene phone calls.

I retreated to the woodpile and waited for the sirens. But after ten minutes the police were still out there talking and pointing. Curious, I snuck back, threading my way through the undergrowth until I was no more than twenty feet from the police officers and FBI agents. They were studying a map spread on the hood of a car. After a brief discussion, one of the officers opened the back of a cruiser and hauled a man from the back seat. He was dressed in a blaze orange jumpsuit, his legs and hands bound in long chains. He had shaggy black hair, a patchy beard, and a series of muddled tattoos on his powerful forearms. But it was his eyes that got me. They were featureless black slots chopped into his heavy brow, rimmed with dark circles that seemed to suck in all of the available light. He muttered something to his captors, pointed at the leg chain, and seemed to test them. I knew in an instant he'd done something bad and that here in my own backyard was the sum of all my *Helter Skelter* fears.

As I strained to get a closer look, one of the officers spotted me.

"Get out of there, kid," he said, parting the bushes with his nightstick.

I knew enough not to run and so I rose from my hiding place slowly, sure that at any moment he'd slap the cuffs on me and toss me into the backseat next to the man in the orange jumpsuit.

He asked me what I was doing.

"Nothing," I replied in a quivering voice.

He smiled and helped me out of the bushes and asked me how well I knew the woods.

I shrugged and said, "Pretty good."

"Ever find anything unusual?"

"Like what?"

"Oh, I don't know," he said. "We're just looking is all. Look kid, you'd better . . ."

Just then the man in the orange jumpsuit stopped his catatonic pacing and stared at me. We locked eyes and I felt the cold stab of fear as he shuffled across a small ditch toward me, muttering in an agitated rumble about my presence. Transfixed, I stood my ground and returned his stare. I did not run or drop to the ground in a quivering heap. Sure, I was scared but as the man got closer I swallowed my fear and felt strong and brave for having done so, even as one of the officers jerked him back and pointed at the barbed-wire fence running alongside the interstate.

"You better go home now," the officer said, patting me on the shoulder and sending me on my way.

Later I learned that the man had killed several women and remembered burying one of their bodies in a field next to the freeway. The search of the polo field turned up nothing, but that didn't stop us from scouring the field for unmarked graves and discarded murder weapons. Next to the freeway we found an old blue Samsonite suitcase somebody had tossed from a car. We took the suitcase back to our fort and bashed it open with a rock. Inside were several heavily soiled men's dress shirts, pairs of mismatched socks, a metal nail file, Alka-Seltzer tablets, and dozens of foil-packed Trojan condoms. On one of the shirts we found what looked like bloodstains and we all knew in the twisted logic of ten-, eleven-, and twelve-years-olds that the suitcase belonged to the man in the orange jumpsuit. We burned the shirts, kept the condoms, and vowed to tell no one of our discovery.

I also stopped reading *Helter Skelter* and, in retelling the story of how I'd stood my ground as the psycho had come after me, my role grew more and more heroic even though I'd yet to stand up to the relatively harmless Moroses. I had, however, learned to face my fears.

By the time I saw *Star Wars* for a third and final time (again with John Legan who had now combined his Spock act with a reasonably good Obi-Wan imitation), the Moroses had completed construction of their Death Star—a massive two-story fort built from the remnants of our recently destroyed fort and loads of lumber pinched from a nearby subdivision. They'd furnished the inside with discarded sofas and orange shag carpeting, ashtrays, and blacklight Blue Oyster Cult and Boston posters. The surrounding area was littered with beer cans, old tires, cigarette butts, and even a condom wrapper.

On one of our reconnaissance missions we watched as Sharon Moros spray-painted ZEPPELIN RULES in drippy red scrawl across the front of the fort while her boyfriend of the moment, a tall pale thug we called Lurch, looked on, smoking cigarettes and fingering the Daisy pellet gun he held in his lap. Richard emerged, saw us watching, and tapped his sister on the shoulder, pointing. Sharon flipped us off while Richard mooned us, shouting, "Thanks for the wood ya homos."

He laughed his Woody the Woodpecker laugh as Lurch loaded his gun and began pumping it methodically. We quickly retreated, vowing to knock the fort down after they'd gone home for dinner.

We discussed our options, which included tricking Johnny the Retard (too unpredictable and liable to rat us out later under inter-rogation from Sharon) into knocking the fort down, or stealing some of my father's gasoline and setting fire to it (too risky—earlier that year we'd nearly set the whole woods on fire), or we could simply attempt the unthinkable and knock it down ourselves and face the consequences. As it got darker our numbers dwindled so that by the time we set off for the Death Star there were only four of us—my brother Jeff, John and Scott Legan, and myself. John wisely assumed the role of sage adviser and in his Obi-Wan voice gave us what amounted to a preattack pep talk.

When we arrived at the Death Star we waited patiently for signs of activity before tossing a rock against the door. Nothing happened. We tossed another rock and still no reaction.

We looked at each other. The time had come for us to agree to a mutual chickening out. Scott turned to go. My brother looked at me, waiting for the green light to sprint the dark paths back home.

"Let's do it," I said. "Screw the Morons. They wrecked our fort."

John nodded in agreement and, as I rose to attack the fort, said in his grave Obi-Wan voice, "Now, Luke, now!"

And so I led the charge and the others followed, shoving at the surprisingly sturdy walls of the fort. The Morons, unlike most of us, believed in nails. It took all of us to topple it and as we stood back marveling at our own bravery I heard the all too familiar sound of a pellet gun being pumped and primed.

Then I heard Richard cackle moments before Sharon streaked out of nowhere and chased us out of the woods and into the polo field.

Halfway across the field Sharon dashed after Scott as Richard leaped onto my back.

I snapped and without thinking fought back, clamping Richard in a headlock and twisting as hard as I could until I felt his body whip over and land with a thump on the ground. I was filled with some dark force as I squeezed him harder and harder. His glasses pinched off his face and broke. When I looked down he was crying and gasping for breath.

The force began to ebb and I loosened my grip and told him I was going to let him go and that he'd better not do anything. He blinked in agreement and so I released him.

He sprang to his feet, rubbing his throat and staring at me. Sharon and Lurch arrived on the scene, took one look at Richard's tear-streaked face, and shook their heads.

"You're gonna die, Reid," Richard said.

Lurch put a protective arm around Sharon and pointed the pellet gun at me. "Do something, Richie," Lurch said. "You'd better do something before I shoot him."

Richard lunged and again I caught him in a headlock and we went to the ground. He thrashed for a minute and tried to gouge my eyes as Sharon circled shouting, "Kill him, kill him."

But I had him and the louder she yelled the harder I squeezed until I could feel the fight go out of Richard. He went limp and looked up at me with pleading, fearful eyes.

I let him go again and stood, half expecting Lurch to pepper me with pellets or for Sharon to jump me. Richard stayed on the ground crying softly and clutching at his swollen throat. Lurch drew a bead on me and I stood there, staring him down until he lost his nerve and lowered the gun.

I turned and walked away as Sharon, in a rare moment of tenderness, actually helped her brother to his feet and found his broken glasses for him.

I didn't see Richard until several days later when he came by our rebuilt fort with Julius in tow. I didn't run and hide, even as Richard began to throw lit matches at me and taunt me. Instead I walked up to him and made a fist.

Julius backed away and Richard flinched.

"Get outta here," I said.

Richard mustered the last of his bravery and said, "What are you gonna do about it ya queer?"

"I'll kill you," I said.

And I meant it.

ANAKIN, GET YOUR GUN

JOE QUEENAN

From the very beginning of the *Star Wars* saga, the moviegoing public has engaged in an intellectually duplicitous relationship with Darth Vader and the Galactic Empire. On the one hand, Vader is widely viewed as one of the most satanic figures in the history of motion pictures, occupying the same vaunted position as Dracula, Freddy Krueger, Michael Corleone, and others of this ilk. On the other hand, much like Dracula, Freddy Krueger, and Michael Corleone, Vader is considered to be resourceful, energetic, resilient, and endowed with an unrivaled ability to get things done. Finally, just like Dracula, Freddy Krueger, and Michael Corleone, Vader is an extremely impressive, attention-getting dresser. A master of monochromatic menace in his jet-black, Astral Armani threads, Vader has perfected a look that is never out of place, no matter how formal the interstellar occasion.

Whatever else he may be criticized for, Vader is certainly not dull, which brings us back to my initial argument. As much as audiences fear Vader and ostensibly yearn for his destruction, there can be no denying that the least interesting sequences in the *Star Wars* movies are the ones that he is not in. Whenever the camera lingers too long on Princess Leia, Luke Skywalker, Yoda, Obi-Wan Kenobi, Qui-Gon Jinn, Chewbacca, C-3PO, or the insufferable Jar Jar Binks, the story tends to get slack, mushy, or camp. Like Jack Palance in *Shane* or the great white shark in *Jaws*, Darth Vader is almost never seen on-screen, yet whenever he disappears for any length of time, the audiences that ostensibly dread his machinations cannot wait for him to come back and pep things up. If only because of his theme song.

In short, Darth Vader is the fulcrum, the focal point, the emotional epicenter of the *Star Wars* saga, as has become clear since the release of *The Phantom Menace*. Though phenomenally successful at the box office, *The Phantom Menace* is by far the least satisfying and least exciting of the *Star War* movies, and there is a simple reason why: Darth Vader isn't in it. What's more, it is now generally agreed by *Star Wars* aficionados that his able though short-lived successor, Darth Maul, is not in it nearly enough.

There is nothing unusual or disturbing about the public's mixed and perhaps even dishonest feelings toward a terrifying villain. By and large, villains, whether fictional or real, are more fascinating than their virtuous counterparts. (This is especially true if the villain is played by someone like Dennis Hopper or Alan Rickman and his nemesis is played by someone like Kevin Costner or Kyle MacLachlan. Or if the villain is a gigantic shark locked in mortal combat with Richard Dreyfuss.) This is the reason St. Augustine viewed acting as sinful, since it required decent human beings to impersonate evildoers, and conceivably be seduced by their power.

Nowhere is the allure of the classic villain more apparent than in the works of the Immortal Bard: Iago is more compelling than Othello, Richard III more fascinating a figure than Henry VII, Macbeth more commanding a presence than Macduff. Similarly, in real life, Geronimo is more riveting than the interchangeable white men who pursue him, Al Capone more captivating than Eliot Ness, Richard Nixon more electrifying than George McGovern. Since George Lucas relied heavily on such legendary archetypes in writing *Star Wars*, it is hardly surprising that Darth Vader should be more interesting than his son, Luke Skywalker, or his daughter, Princess Leia. In her case, a *lot* more interesting. Leia is so dull and predictable it's hard to believe these two come from the same gene pool.

But in *Star Wars*, there is another important dynamic at work. Though many might deem this heresy, there can be no denying that the general public has consistently misunderstood the underlying theme of these films. Because of a childlike, gap-toothed, wide-eyed affection for the lovable man-child Luke Skywalker, the damsel-in-distress Princess Leia, the swashbuckling corsair Han Solo, and this unlikely trio's mongrel entourage of precocious druids, fey robots, and cuddly marsupials, the public has overlooked the real message of the *Star Wars* epic.

That message is this: It is the Empire, not the Rebel Alliance, that offers the best hope for the future of the race. It is the Empire, not the Rebel Alliance, that is best equipped to bring peace and prosperity to this troubled galaxy. It is the Empire, not the Rebel Alliance, that is on the cutting edge of technology. By resisting, subverting, and ultimately destroying the Empire, the rebels have bequeathed their children a chaotic, primitive, technologically retrograde society that will almost certainly collapse into anarchy within a generation. By lending their enthusiastic support to the rebels in this well-intentioned but self-destructive jihad, the public is indulging in an unprecedented level of hypocrisy. Cheering for the Rebel Alliance is like rooting for Paraguay against England, like rooting for Chad against Sweden. Worse, it is like rooting for Afghanistan against America.

In essence, I am presenting three cognate arguments here. First, I am making the nonearthshaking assertion that Darth Vader and his cohorts in the Empire are infinitely more charismatic—or to use the modern vernacular, *cooler*—than the rebels, and therefore worthy of a certain grudging admiration. Second, I am making the more controversial claim that the Empire (which because of its overall technical efficiency and unilateral nuclear dominance bears a strong resemblance to the United States of America) occupies the moral high ground in the *Star Wars* saga. Third, I am issuing the admittedly incendiary declaration that by mistakenly rooting for the Rebel Alliance in *Star Wars*, moviegoers not only confuse good with evil, but also fail to see their own pellucid reflection in Darth Vader and the Empire. This is a situation that I hope to see corrected.

From the beginning of time, human evolution has been a painful, bloody process in which the old reluctantly gives way to the new. Men of the Ice Age resented the men of the Bronze Age with their newfangled weapons and attitudes; men of the Bronze Age despised the hotshots of the Iron Age, viewing their technological prowess as a sign of moral putrescence. Yet human life would not be what it is today were it not for the triumph of technologically advanced societies over primitive ones. Any effort to obstruct this progress, no matter how pure the motives of the saboteurs, frustrates the dialectical process of history and is bad for humanity.

Economists have known this for centuries. When news of George Armstrong Custer's epic miscalculation at the Battle of the Little Bighorn reached Karl Marx's ears in London, he found himself faced with a troubling conundrum. On the one hand, he was happy to see Sitting Bull and Crazy Horse pull off one of the great upsets in the history of Anglo-Indian warfare. On the other hand, the triumph of a Stone Age society over a modern society was bad for everyone, because it interrupted the march of progress, delaying the inevitable triumph of socialism over capitalism. And anything that delayed the arrival of the future—i.e., the past—was a bad thing. It is not merely Marx who believed this. Hegel, from whom Marx pilfered most of his great ideas, had the same opinion.

The same logic can be applied to *Star Wars*. Because they are so helpless, so innocent, so sweet, so peace-loving, so klutzy, the rebels inevitably beguile an unsuspecting public into supporting their cause. But once we get past their seductive Tinkerbell qualities, it becomes obvious that the rebels stand for everything modern people despise. They are inefficient. They are disorganized. They do not finish what they start. They are incapable of making quick decisions. They cannot keep their eyes on the prize. In fact, it is not going too far to say that they are complete and utter fuckups.

For starters, they are dinky. The first insurgents that we see in *A New Hope* are the slapdash droid R2-D2 and the prissy, fuddy-duddy robot C-3PO, a slightly less fey version of the gay butler who camped it up in Woody Allen's 1973 film *Sleeper*. This pair of electronic nerds look like hastily assembled props at a poorly attended Mensa Halloween bash. By comparison, the first villains that we see are the nattily attired Imperial Stormtroopers and the peerless fashion plate Darth Vader. The contrast is remarkable; from the very beginning, it is evident that we are dealing with a duel to the death between seasoned professionals and rank amateurs, between dapper sophisticates and third-rate clowns.

This dichotomy becomes steadily more apparent as the series continues. Unlike the villains, whose spiffy haberdashery is characterized by a decided thematic unity, the rebels have a raffish, thrift-shop look. Luke and his family dress in what is best described as southern California neo-biblical loungewear: bathrobes, sheaths, smocks, muumuus. Princess Leia is usually seen wearing sweatpants or worse. The rebel aviators cavort in orange jumpsuits that make them look like the dorks that roll out the tarp during rain delays at Shea Stadium. Yoda appears to be a slimy, nine-hundred-year-old amphibian prototype of Mickey Rooney. Chewbacca closely resembles an orangutan, and not an especially good-looking one. Even the refined, elegant Obi-Wan Kenobi has a foolish, retro getup, and could easily be mistaken for a Trappist monk deported to Deep Space for unspecified monastic offenses.

Things steadily deteriorate as the series wends its way toward the Empire's unfortunate demise. For example, in *Return of the Jedi*, when Luke and Leia visit the planet inhabited by the Ewoks, they wear ridiculous helmets that look like toilet seats with Rolodexes glued on top of them. Throughout the saga, the rebels turn up for battle wearing glorified pajamas or outfits they bought cheap at a Franciscan brothers garage sale, while the Empire's suave, debonair operatives always come dressed to kill. The rebels simply have no sense of occasion.

The insurgents' hair is also a problem, and gets worse as the series unravels. Purists may argue that this was unavoidable, that with the passage of time, the anachronistic '70s hairstyles of the rebels would inevitably come to seem démodé and ridiculous, while the helmeted Darth Vader would never be subjected to the remorseless vicissitudes of fashion. I disagree. Whether we are talking about Luke's boyish bangs, Leia's girlish curls, Qui-Gon Jinn's Motley Crue locks, or the young Obi-Wan Kenobi's irksome pigtail, the rebels always look like burned-out hippies in search of the Lost Bong. Their natural environment is not long ago and far away in a place called Alderaan. It's long ago and far way in a place called Haight-Ashbury.

Rebel ordinance and transport are also resolutely third rate. As if Luke's slapdash airborne go-cart were not tacky enough, Han Solo tools around the galaxy in a cheesy spaceship that rocks back and forth like a crummy old Mazda. When they need to go on patrol in Arctic climes, the rebels saddle up a hybrid creature that looks like a disastrous fusion between a camel and a yak. By comparison, the Imperial legions rely on a breathtaking fleet of state-of-the-art spacecraft, not the least of which is the Death Star. And once the original Death Star is destroyed, Vader and the Emperor, rather than sitting around pouting, build a fully operational replacement almost overnight. Love 'em or hate 'em, there's one thing you have to concede about this pair: *They take a licking, but keep on ticking.*

The fact of the matter is, the rebels are out-and-out Luddites, fecklessly resisting the Empire's bold technological breakthroughs at every turn. Tellingly, when the insurgents enter the Götterdämmerung phase of their struggle at the conclusion of *Return of the Jedi*, they are armed with slingshots, tree trunks, and feudal-era catapults owned and operated by a battalion of diminutive fur balls who look like Chewbacca's precocious nephews. And yet, it's worth remembering that had this hideously downscale uber-Wookiee not commandeered one of the Empire's cutting-edge All Terrain Scout Transports, the rebels would never have been able to dismantle the Death Star's protective shield—and the entire Rebel fleet would have been destroyed. Proving that when you have a choice between an ax and an AK-47, go with the heaviest firepower every time.

Such basic efficiencies as just-in-time inventory are not among the Rebel Alliance's strong points. For example, *The Phantom Menace* takes forever to get going because the roving Jedi Knights Qui-Gon Jinn and Obi-Wan Kenobi cannot obtain spare parts for their vehicle and must hang around town until an eight-year-old boy wins a junior spaceship race and secures the parts they need. The Empire would have never put up with this nonsense. A Sith Lord would have simply told the parts distributor to fork over the merchandise or get sliced and diced by a lightsaber. Had Darth Vader or Darth Maul been on the job, the spaceship could have been repaired in three shakes of a cat's tail and the movie would have been fifty minutes shorter.

It is hardly surprising that *Star Wars* appeared in 1977, the year President Jimmy Carter took office, for the Rebel Alliance is a perfect metaphor for the Carter administration: a bunch of well-meaning, badly dressed rubes with terrible hair who simply could not do anything right. By contrast, the Empire closely resembles the dark forces of the Reagan administration, renowned for its ruthless efficiency. (It is also no accident that Ronald Reagan referred to his proposed antiballistic missile shield as "Star Wars," just as it has become increasingly clear over the years that the seemingly innocuous term "Trade Federation" is secretly a code word for "Republican.")

In the years since he was driven from office with his cracker tail between his legs, Carter has made strenuous efforts to rehabilitate his image, portraying himself as a selfless moral crusader who got blindsided by a reeling economy, soaring interest rates, and an unprecedented level of collusion among the assorted forces of evil. In fact, just like the Rebel Alliance, his administration was filled with incompetent ding-dongs who wrecked the American economy and ruined our image in the eyes of friends and foes alike.

The stunning similarities between the Rebel Alliance and the

Carter administration do not stop there. Just as the Carter White House was humiliated when a bunch of feisty Iranian students seized our embassy in Tehran, the Rebel Alliance (originally the Old Republic) gets humiliated when its leaders are deposed by the insurgent Trade Federation (with support from the fledgling Empire). The speed with which Princess Amidala is deposed and taken into custody provides incontrovertible proof that the Republic has crummy security, deficient intelligence, and is run by bozos. How could a self-respecting potentate allow herself to get run out of office by a bunch of glorified Space Teamsters? And what does it say about her military advisers that no one saw this coming?

Some may argue that in defending Darth Vader and the Empire I am being deliberately argumentative and mischaracterizing Lucas's real beliefs. Far from it. As the *Star Wars* epic works its way back to the beginning, it becomes evident that the youthful Vader had legitimate reasons for crossing over to the putatively "dark" side. Let us recall that when we first meet young Anakin Skywalker (Kid Darth) at the beginning of *The Phantom Menace*, he is a hard-working slave on the outlying planet of Tatooine. Indeed, his dream is to one day become a Jedi Knight so that he can free his fellow slaves. Yet it immediately becomes obvious that the existing Jedi Knights do not share his idealism, that in fact nobody in the Republic cares one way or the other about the plight of juvenile slaves on a far-flung planet.

"Can you help him?" asks Mrs. Skywalker when she confers with Qui-Gon Jinn, the mysterious interstellar Celt played by the dour Liam Neeson.

"I don't know," he replies. "I didn't actually come here to free slaves."

Well, thank you very much, Mr. Jedi Knight! Yes, it's precisely that kind of attitude that got the Republic in trouble in the first place. This is the point at which the Republic starts to resemble the Clinton administration: all talk, no action. Deplore slavery, but never make a serious effort to eliminate it. No wonder the Empire succeeds in overthrowing the Republic with such ease; who wants to be governed by phonies like this?

That's certainly the way Vader will ultimately come to look at things. Since the Jedi Knights make no effort to aid him and his enslaved mother until he helps them get the spare parts for their spaceship, it is easy to understand why he eventually develops such a terrible attitude. But that will come much later; at this point in his life he is still idealistic and pure. As he says to his mother, "Mom, you said the biggest problem in this universe is nobody helps each other." And helping people is what he sets out to do, even if his methods are occasionally harsh. But as the man once said, "If you want to make an omelet, you've got to break a few eggs." And break them he does. Like Napoleon Bonaparte, a brilliant warrior and revolutionary statesman whose innovations gave birth to the modern world but whose reputation has been unjustly besmirched by the cabal of reactionaries who ultimately prevailed against him, Vader is a man more sinned against than sinning, an unjustly maligned visionary whose daring new ideas could bring stability to a galaxy that badly needs it.

And I mean *badly*. By the time *Return of the Jedi* begins, it is clear that the entire galaxy is a mess, with lawless thugs like Jabba the Hutt disrupting the natural order. Only a strong central authority like the Empire can restore sanity to the universe. Which is why Vader holds out the hand of peace to his son: "With our combined strength, we can end this destructive conflict," he says to Luke during one of their confrontations. Admittedly, it's a bit tricky to hold out the hand of friendship to someone whose hand you have just cut off, but in not abusing his son further Vader manifests admirable restraint, leaving the door open for future negotiations.

The set-to between the Empire and the Rebel Alliance is a textbook example of what happens when a feudal society crosses swords with a modern one. Instead of accepting the inevitability of modernization, the feudal society becomes testy and sulks. Nobody wins in this situation. But this conflict also illustrates the psychological discord that plagues most modern people when faced with situations such as this. On the one hand, people living in the twenty-first century typically exhibit a knee-jerk sympathy for colorful aboriginals with their primitive weapons, garish attire, and unsophisticated economic systems. On the other hand, these same modernites secretly admire efficient, ruthless, well-dressed leaders with cutting-edge technology and terrific organizational skills.

At the beginning of this essay, I mentioned the intellectual duplicity of the American people in their relationship with Darth Vader. This has become increasingly true as we distance ourselves from the '60s, an era when corporate leaders were almost universally vilified. Since that time, the American people have developed a love affair with tough-as-nails, shoot-from-the-hip, can-do corporate honchos like Lee Iacocca, Donald Trump, and Chainsaw Al Dunlap. Vader (which rhymes with "raider") is the perfect embodiment of one of America's most beloved folk heroes, the take-no-prisoners corporate raider. With his ruthless demeanor and ability to make snap decisions, Darth Vader is a lot like Disney's Michael Eisner or General Electric's Jack Welch. Sometimes he even resembles Michael Milken. To men such as this, using the firepower of the Death Star to destroy an entire planet would never be construed as annihilation; they would merely describe it as a highly sophisticated form of *downsizing*. The rebels, by contrast, are soft and indecisive. They have trouble pulling the trigger. They have no single, charismatic leader; power is dispersed among a handful of people. This is a terrible organizational model.

One of the things Americans most admire about the Trumps and Welches is their ability to cut through the crap. Darth Vader shares this ability to dispense with the small talk and cut to the chase. And his message is never ambiguous. While the rebels tend to trade wisecracks or resort to New Age gobbledygook, Vader speaks in the clear, precise lingo of the seasoned Fortune 500 CEO. Consider the difference: Whenever Luke Skywalker appeals to his mentors for guidance they respond with enigmatic, impenetrable hooey about "the Force." The biggest problem with Kenobi and Yoda is that you can never get a straight answer out of them. "Stretch out with your feelings," is a typical Obi-Wan Kenobism. As if anyone could possibly figure out what *that* means. And Yoda, with his syntactically ravaged sentences, is even worse. You would have thought that in nine hundred years of being a Jedi Master he might have taken a few months off to learn that the noun goes before the verb, that sentences like "Help you I will" are ungrammatical. But no.

By contrast, Imperial speech is always terse, direct, nonelliptical. Consider this classic exchange between Vader and one of his subordinates:

> ADMIRAL: "Our ships have sighted the *Millennium Falcon*, Lord. But it has entered an asteroid field, and we cannot risk . . .
>
> VADER: "Asteroids do not concern me, Admiral. I want that ship— not excuses."
>
> ADMIRAL: "Yes, Lord."

Here we have the watertight, nonsense-free speech of the seasoned CEO. Get the job done, ass face. And spare me the goddamn details.

"He will join us or die, master," says Darth Vader when the Emperor demands how his efforts to recruit Luke are progressing. Here, Vader sounds like Bill Gates at the top of his game. Sure, Apple Computer devotees can make fun of Microsoft by referring to it as the Evil Empire. Well, who cares? Unlike Apple, which was determined to sell high-priced computers to a magic circle of geeks who thought they were better than everyone else, Microsoft set out to sell inexpensive, standardized systems to anyone who wanted them. Like Vader, Gates was determined to bring order to a fragmented universe. This is anathema to Apple enthusiasts; like the rebels, they prefer an anachronistic, anarchic, nonauthoritarian system.

Well, look where it got Steve Jobs.

Namby-pamby believers in the Rebel cause both loathe and dread the blunt Imperial style of speech. It unnerves them when the Emperor says things like: "Use your aggressive feelings, boy. Let the heat flow through you." But the Emperor is right. Why shouldn't we let the heat flow through us? It's ridiculous to pretend that there is anything morally wrong with this philosophy. It is the philosophy of George S. Patton. It is the philosophy of William Tecumseh Sherman. It is the philosophy of Michael Jordan. It is a philosophy that has stood this great Republic in good stead lo these many years. This wonderful nation was founded on the principle of using your aggressive feelings and letting the heat flow through you. The last person to not use his aggressive feelings and let the heat flow through him was Mahatma Gandhi. Look where it got him.

One of the things that makes Darth Vader so admirable is that he does not wear out his welcome. Film buffs generally agree that Francis Ford Coppola made a colossal mistake when he went back and shot *Godfather III*, that by the time Mario Puzo's Italian-American *Fall of the House of Atreus* had run its course, the depraved Michael Corleone had lost his edge. Much the same can be said of Pacino's despicable character in *Scarface*, where, by the end of the three-hour film, his bag of tricks has been emptied and the audience is happy to see the back of him. The *Friday the 13th*, *Halloween*, and *Nightmare on Elm Street* series also fall prey to the battle-fatigue syndrome; after a while the audience simply loses interest in the latest depredations of Michael, Jason, and Freddy and would prefer to see them die. Like any guest who has overstayed his visit, they deserve to be put to the sword.

Vader, by contrast, never loses that special something. He never surrenders that ineffable star quality that makes him so unique. He never becomes a caricature of himself. And he never descends into camp. That's why the audience is always glad to have him back. Other directors can learn much from this series—even the great ones. Let's face it, Steven Spielberg made a big mistake when he killed off the shark at the end of *Jaws*; in the three sequels, its substandard replacements were never equal to the task. George Lucas did not make the same mistake with Vader.

At this point, I would like to devote a few minutes to the subject of *image*. Foreigners looking at Americans invariably assume that the only thing we care about is money. Close, but no cigar.

While it is true that Americans care more about money than any people in the history of mankind, the one thing they care about even more is being perceived as *cool*. Americans have a pathological fear of being viewed as bad dressers or owning records that have fallen out of fashion or using outdated terminology in conversations with peers. Such gaucheries fall under the general rubric of *lameness*. This is another reason why I find the public's alleged affection for the Rebels so implausible. Look at the way they dress. More tellingly, look at the way they talk.

"I don't know where you get your delusions, laser brain," Princess Leia sneers at Han Solo at one juncture. When he responds with one of his typically inane comebacks, Leia ripostes: "Why, you stuck-up, half-witted, scruffy-looking Nerf Herder."

Why, you stuck-up, half-witted, scruffy-looking Nerf Herder?

Like I said: lame.

In filing this admittedly controversial *amicus curiae* brief on behalf of the Empire, I am not suggesting that Darth Vader and the Emperor are entirely flawless, or that they make untrammeled, unblemished role models for the youth of today. Far from it. Both men have rough edges and could profit from a long weekend at the local Charm School. Vader has a bit of the bully in him and can get chippy when riled, and the Emperor does not interface well with subordinates. But as leaders and managers, this pair are peerless. And when they fail, the blame cannot be laid at their doorsteps.

Indeed, it is ironic that throughout the *Star Wars* cycle, the "villains" rely on brains, cunning, and superior technology, while the "heroes" rely on luck and the occasional electrodynamic intercession of a mysterious dead man with a Japanese name and an English accent. Vader, by contrast, is a brilliant tactician whose strategy is ultimately foiled not because it is ill conceived, nor because of personal failings on his part, but because of bad luck and the incompetence of a few underlings. It's the same old story: *You can't get good help anywhere.*

Most historians agree that the worst event in the history of mankind was the collapse of the Roman Empire because it created a vacuum of power in central Europe that persists to this day. Machiavelli, devil's advocate for the Medicis, understood this and so does George Lucas. He understands that a rough, tough central authority, whatever its shortcomings, is infinitely superior to a rudderless, passive confederacy, that more people will be happy under an efficient authoritarian regime they fear than under a passive, incompetent regime they love. Yet for a quarter century now, the public has completely missed the point of this remarkable series of films. Foolishly, they assume that the message at the end of *Return of the Jedi* is that primitive societies are superior to modern ones. From our own life experiences, we know this is not the case. This is the sort of thing that people believed back in the turn-down-your-thermostats-and-die Jimmy Carter Era. What the Rebel Alliance represents is the fractured dream of the '60s, a phantasmagoric, free-floating society with minimal police presence, an informal political structure, and a deliberately inert economy.

The Ewoks' victory dance at the end of *Return of the Jedi* gives us a pretty good idea of where this galaxy is headed. Yes, the victorious Ewoks are undeniably cute. But a society built upon cuteness cannot long survive. Look at Camelot. Or Holland. The peppy, bouncy Ewoks theme song sounds like that reprehensible Up With People! music they used to play at Super Bowl halftime shows. As the furry creatures cavort merrily, Lucas is giving us a clear idea of what lies ahead for citizens of the galaxy. Chaos. Which brings to mind something Obi-Wan Kenobi once said to Luke all the way back in the very first film. "Who is the greater fool?" wondered Obi, philosophically. "The fool, or the fool that follows him?"

Only Yoda could answer that one.

Clue got haven't a I.

BECOMING DARTH VADER

LYDIA MILLET

The year of *Star Wars* I was eight. It may have been the year I worshiped my classmate Pam, who wore train tracks on her teeth and large, round glasses with peach-colored plastic frames. I had neither braces nor glasses then but I believed that if I had both I might also have a chance of recapturing, in my own lesser person, the magic that was Pam. My own large front teeth were unrestrained by orthodontics and therefore crossed over each other to create an impression I will call "chortling rabbit." I spoke loudly and laughed often, producing a sound that my mother implied, with a measure of disapproval, resembled the honking bray of a donkey.

Rabbits, donkeys; I was approachable and familiar, the opposite of lovely and serene. I wanted to be liked by everyone. Pam, on the other hand, had a placid, laid-back demeanor. She rarely seemed eager to please. She had her own pantheon, of course, her own personal altar of proud and lofty figures, chief among them, at that time, Farrah Fawcett. Although my long-term memory is poor, I remember clearly one of Pam's shirts, which was white with red and orange horizontal stripes. It was cotton and had a hood that hung down her back; the drawstring at the collar was red to match the stripes. Come to think of it, the shirt I remember so clearly may have been my shirt, bought to emulate one of Pam's shirts. My mother says I used to come home from school in tears, sobbing the ragged-voiced refrain *Pam hates me. Pam hates me.* There were days, apparently, when that was all I said.

But it may not have been that year. It may have been the year when dimpled Anka from Romania and I went behind the green wooden shed in the copse beside the school to kiss boys. We were entrepreneurs. For each kiss we demanded as payment either a candy necklace or a handful of gum, which to me was contraband since my father—who at that time, I believe, may have smoked a meerschaum pipe—had outlawed gum-chewing in the house. Or maybe it was the year when I took a swing at Cary, the redheaded boy who I seem to recall was already planning, in fifth grade, to be an architect when he grew up. I hit Cary, thinking I was the boss of him and possibly even swaggering away with a boastful air. Not much later he sauntered up to me on the street and swiftly punched me in the stomach. I ran home crying.

I think I was a crybaby.

Or then it also may have been the year I won the long jump, or the year I slipped on the track running the 400 and filled my right knee with deep grooves of black gravel, which it still carries. It may have been the year when Cary and his cronies, with nary a care for cliché, actually did put earthworms in my hair, causing me to emit piercing shrieks. We had what they called a *healthy antagonism*, Cary and I. It may even have been the year when, at a Brownies meeting—within our Brownies hierarchy there were various bands of fairies, and in my time I had been leader of both the red-and-yellow Kelpies and the emerald green Pixies—I was discovered to be harboring head lice. My mother, a practical, cautious person not given to frivolous embellishment, insists to this day that the lice were the size of cockroaches. The way she tells it they were running around in circles on the top of my head like prize fillies at the Kentucky Derby.

Whether all of these were in fact just one year, and whether that was the year of *Star Wars,* is lost to me forever. At some point my brother got a lightsaber, I know that much. In previous years, for Halloween, he had been a pirate named Don Dirk of Dowdee, with a plume in his cap. I had always been a fairy-princess-queen, a triple whammy of bet-hedging. Should some insufficiently humble unbeliever say, glancing at the delicate silver-and-gold crown my father had fashioned for me out of a mesh of pipe cleaners and bulbous Christmas ornaments, *What are you? A princess?* implying, I knew even then, *a rank pretender to the throne?* I could wave my scepter and scoff: *Not just a princess. Also a queen.* For obvious reasons, I could not be only a queen; queens were old, and often ugly.

Should the same arrogant unbeliever further say, *Oh, you're just a princess-queen?* I could point to my wings, made of white nylons decorated with glued-on glitter and stretched over artfully molded clothes hangers, and say, *I am, in addition, a fairy.* I ruled over the land and sea, but when the chips were down I could also turn you into a toad. I was a spiritual as well as a secular leader. Let mortals beware.

There we were, Josh a pirate, me a fairy-princess-queen, and my little sister Mandy the Frankenstein monster. And then the loud starry darkness in the theater, the action figures, the lightsabers, and Josh went from pirate to Luke Skywalker. He would go swashbuckling around the house sowing the seeds of fear. The lightsaber wavered and sliced, warbled and swooped precariously near tabletops and shelves, a threat to trinkets everywhere. I wish, for the sake of narrative, that I could say it was the lightsaber that struck my sister in the eye, prompting a panicked run to the Hospital for Sick Children in the family Toyota. In fact it was a plastic medieval sword that Josh wielded while encased in his plastic knight's armor, a menacing combination. Half-blinded by the visor of the helmet, he would stagger around stabbing at the air with a poignant desperation. My sister paid the price.

(She was not permanently maimed, though; of the three of us, as I write this, she is the only one who still has 20/20 vision.)

★ ★ ★

I was bored by the lightsabers, being a girl, even though, as a girl, I was also a tomboy, skinny, dirty, stringy-haired. I was the kind of tomboy who threw tantrums when she didn't win. (As a result she often won.) This was the lesson learned: You can try to strong-arm them, as I did with Cary, and that may be effective as a temporary measure, a brutish demonstration of force. But then what happens is they walk up to you later, when you've grown lazy and compla- cent, and cave in your stomach with a fist. Or you can *whine* them into submission, a tack taken by many a desperate wife over the centuries. There's the iron fist and there's the velvet whine, with its sinister, deadening stamina. The superior efficacy of the whine, over the long term, has yet to be understood by U.S. foreign-policy makers.

I was bored by the lightsabers then and I am bored by them now, after a quarter century. Watching the movies as an adult, the light- saber fights were the only parts through which I fast-forwarded. I like my symbolism more covert.

As a prepubescent it was easy to identify with Princess Leia, so obviously virginal, so obviously disinterested, and always being saved. Object not subject, she was saved right and left; though she did occasionally fire off a gun, she never did much saving herself. She did, however, remain calm. No girlish squeals for Princess Leia. Earthworms would have presented no challenge to her composure. She was a better, more seamless tomboy than I was but still, of course, only ornamental, window dressing in the shining world of the heroes.

It was easy to remain Princess Leia across and beyond the years spanned by *The Empire Strikes Back* and *Return of the Jedi*. I went from tomboy to jock and gone were childish things like dress-up, potions, and singing *The Sound of Music*; almost overnight the looseness of play vanished and the strictures of competition took its place, the channeled rigor of performance. My high school was determined to make children into pillars of the establishment, determined first and foremost to instill in children the unswerving conviction that they were *born to lead*. In its defense, it taught Latin and Greek and *Beowulf* and Chaucer in Middle English, and there were teachers there, some of them gentle fossils, others eager newcomers, who honestly believed they could instill a *passion for learning* and who, in so believing, themselves became romantics and were loved.

This was when we first grew familiar with nonfood brand names, when clothing was identified with manufacturers, and video games and portable technologies began their triumphant emergence into the mass market and were instantly known by their trademarks, Sony Walkman, JVC, Pac-Man. Now it happens much earlier, needless to say; infants formulate their first phrases to include the words *Sega* and *Microsoft*, but the early '80s were only the first glimmer of dawn in the era of personal electronics and universal branding.

Still, despite being told I had been born to lead, which meant, chiefly, growing up to be a banker, a lawyer, or a captain of industry, I remembered what I had learned: there is safety in distance, safety in remove. While it was true that, as a fairy-princess-queen, I had been a world leader, it had always been an inherited title. Striving for such a position was out of the question. A royal is not a politician. I was perfect and unimpaired as an observer; I left it to the imperfect, the frantic, the boisterous to do the hard, messy work of empire-building.

One speaks with unchallenged authority only about oneself. This is why so many writers, seeking authority, write only about familiar things; it is why, contrary to popular opinion, the bravest writers are those who take as their subject matter that about which they know almost nothing. It is why I, in writing about *Star Wars*, actually write only about myself, why, in fact, I, like many who attempt the so-called personal essay, seize upon any outside stimulus as carte blanche to expose myself to all and sundry, naked, writhing, and frankly none too clean. Clearly the personal essay is an ideal venue for the airing of dirty laundry, the foisting of self-indulgent reminiscences upon an unsuspecting, innocent readership. In writing a personal essay I remind myself of a cat, proudly depositing at its owner's feet a small, pink baby mouse with no head.

If we were not all voyeurs at heart the personal essay would have no home. But luckily our culture's love of stories is firmly entrenched, and any love of stories is a love of voyeurism, since to read a story is automatically to become a voyeur, to savor the act of seeing from a secret place. If we could, we would watch the *whole lives* of strangers bundled into two hours—that is, those parts of their lives that would fill us with a mad compulsion to express ourselves, be fulfilled, and seek glory, not those parts that would send us back to bed whimpering.

Quite often when I leave a multiplex after seeing a movie I have the distinct sensation it has taught me nothing I did not already know, shown me nothing I could not have imagined for myself, but has exhorted me, mostly through its soundtrack and cinematography, to *express yourself, be fulfilled, and seek glory*. By contrast, I seldom leave a multiplex thinking I have been encouraged to *contemplate, empathize, and share all you have*. It's apparent that Hollywood has given itself the job—rhetorical, propagandistic, full of ecstasy—of pressing all citizens into the service of advancement. It is not certain what kind of advancement is generally being urged upon us, (the specifics are vague) but I'd hazard a guess it's something in the American Dream family: self-love, self-improvement, the massive personal accumulation of wealth.

Sometimes it's simpler: I leave the theater with the heartfelt conviction that I should be better groomed.

But it's noteworthy that *Star Wars*—with its childish yet prophetic vision of smart-aleck boy wonders, monsters both cuddly and ugly but always integrated into daily life, and everlasting, intergalactic human-race diaspora—emerged at a moment in the late '70s when Hollywood had, for a time, been turning away from exaltation, setting itself a grittier, more realistic task. Its ebullience subdued by the cultural disillusionments of Vietnam and Watergate, Hollywood was suffering from a sort of erectile dysfunction of the urge to propagandize, and as a result producing subtle and exceptional art on film. For the most part, the actors of the '70s were less immaculate than those of decades before or since; the heroes were less superhuman, the villains less subhuman, the soundtracks less hysterical with grandeur, and the cumulative effect certainly less self-congratulatory and patriotic. (Outer space, as a setting for movies, attracts the most grandiose soundtracks—*Thus Spake Zarathustra*, for example—which is natural since it is, of course, both the final frontier and a long time ago, in a galaxy far, far away. Outer space gets to be both ancient history, lost in the boundless void of the universe, and the prophetic vision of a future of infinite dispersal: tiny we roam across the sands, ten million light-years hence.) So *Star Wars* came, both through and despite its intended message about virtuous small rebellions, to tell both '70s Hollywood and the viewing public: *No. Let there be an end to this foolishness.*

This is no way to prop up an empire.

That the world of *Star Wars* was also a prepubescent world, where the heroes were clean, earnest, and sexless, and the truths about good and evil simple, made it the perfect propaganda for all ages. In the far distant past and the far distant future, good American boys with mom-and-pop values, gay English butler robots for companions, and apes for copilots will save the universe from merciless domination by ruthless, impersonal forces. There is hope yet, my friends, for despite what you see outside these cinema walls, in the far distant past and in the far distant future we, you, I, all of us, will save America from itself.

Darth Vader, dark *Vater, dark father,* unmistakably, was the most erotic figure in the *Star Wars* family and the only tragic one, and because of this he had a terrible beauty.

To state the obvious about Vader, he was a faceless man behind a ferocious black mask, protected by his anonymity. Endlessly a cipher, endlessly an intrigue, he was the only question *Star Wars* posed to its audience, the only mystery presented. We might imagine behind the mask the face of Hitler, the face of a monster, the face of a machine, a skull with gaping eye sockets, or far, far more, something horrifying and primeval, beyond words as well as beyond sight, unspeakable. There was no end to what we could imagine, and for that reason the mask was, needless to say, far more compelling than anything that could ever be behind it, as is the way with masks. And, arguably on a more mundane level, Vader was also the ultimate sellout: possessed of all the powers of the Force, holding the key to enlightenment itself, he chose to use his genius for evil. He was, among other things, a lampoon of Adam Smithian enlightened self-interest: in a preview of '80s ideology, he made selling out look sexy. At the helm of the expansionist Empire, he was untrammeled id, an embodiment of lust for power and for domination.

But Vader also seemed absurdly trapped in his throatbox and his cloak of gloom. He prowled around self-consciously, almost, it seemed, wearing his mask in public shame, or wearing his shame in the form of a mask. It was as though he was too discreet to show himself, perhaps out of simple reluctance to inspire repulsion. And, as many suspected and as was finally confirmed, all he was really hiding was a maimed face. I always had an inkling, watching him stride around in glum determination, that Vader wore the mask because he was vain, and chose to inspire fear rather than repel desire. Alternately, I speculated, maybe his face was not awe-inspiring at all. Maybe it was just a plain face with a flattened nose, a weak chin, and rabbit teeth. Maybe Vader needed the mask because without it he was just a man you passed casually on the street.

Lord Vader was an aristocrat, and as such he had poise, elegance, and good manners. Even when inflicting the death grip he was calm and composed. He kept his counsel; a man of few words, he chose them carefully, played his cards close to his chest. His mystique was dependent upon it. A voluble Vader could not have commanded the Empire; a chatty Vader would not have caused military men to quake in their boots. There are those who can smile and smile and be a villain, but Vader was not one of them. His power was the power of silence.

But silence does not come easily to all of us. For me there is only one answer to all social problems and irritants: nervous, trapped, irritated, or bored, I talk. In addition, thrilled, overjoyed, pleasantly content among friends, I talk. Confused, ambivalent, hesitant, agitated, I talk; I also talk when scared, angry, hurt, anxious, impatient, restless, morose, despondent, smug, curious, contemplative, playful—in a word, awake. When the back-and-forth of talk is good, I listen, too, of course, and when the talk is shallow or predictable I float, registering the words and idly foreseeing a response but not listening deeply, thinking not about the past but about the future: what will be said next, how it should be said, and more often what will likely not be said, whether the difficult things to say and to hear should be said and by whom, and what should never be said at all. Sometimes the daydreams of conversation are not as relevant as this, and talk produces a landscape far away, a landscape shimmering with the fragments of words, the suggestions of words, the memory of words gone by.

It seems to me sometimes that I am surrounded by Vaders. The Vaders are the ones who do not wear their hearts on their sleeves, who protect themselves from exposure. They do not display themselves in all their weakness to disarm would-be detractors, adopt a deceptively submissive pose to fool fearsome opponents. They do not broadcast their flaws, do not reach out to others by seeking and embracing a communion of weakness, of understandable frailty. (Many is the friend I have made this way, when we saw, in the turn of an instant, talking, that we knew each other best not through our successes but through our failures and our wry awareness of them.) Vaders do not make inappropriate remarks at dinner parties, let down their guard in drunken moments to reveal the wanting soul within. The Vaders are too smart for that, and they know which side their bread is buttered on.

The Vaders know about masks. They use them well.

And of course, the strongest of the Vaders rule the world.

If what is sought first and foremost is empathy, it is hard to be Vader. A Vader must seek, before love and often to the exclusion of love, authority. A Vader is a formalist, who must be persuasive not in content but in form: he doesn't have to persuade you he's correct in a matter, but he does have to persuade you to act as though he is. Might does make right, in fact, insofar as end effects are concerned, and this is something Vader knows. Quibbling over details is for children; ethics themselves are for children, an elaborate game played by the powerless. The powerful have little use for morality except as it applies to their lackeys, and possibly as a pet aesthetic, a pretty and self-legitimating idea of rectitude; hence, as cynics know so well, the social compact of the law restricts the actions of all of us except those who are, neatly, beyond it.

Vader has an erotic charge just because he gets what he wants. Others may protest that when they think of *Star Wars* and *sexy* they think of young Harrison Ford, who as Han Solo played the part of a Harlequin romance hero, a rough-talking mercenary who treats our heroine Leia with gruff, arrogant disrespect before revealing, at the eleventh hour, a heart of gold beneath the leathery macho facade. But for me, the Han Solos of the entertainment world are old hat. In the first place they're predictable; in the second, they want nothing, finally, but a good obedient girl for a wife. Sassy back talk is only an aphrodisiac.

Vader, on the other hand, does not have any transparent desires, except, one assumes, ruthlessly to command, judge, and punish. Vader is opaque save for his menace, his propensity for killing underachievers on the spot and destroying whole planets by remote control. If it weren't for his genocidal tendencies Vader would be a laughing matter, and admittedly I don't really personally believe he blew up that whole planet.

And the silent man breaks our hearts as he dies, as we watch him—bound up in the tragedy of his own silence—leave a world that, after all, barely even knew him. Remember the poignancy of Vader as he lay dying, having sacrificed himself for his son, finally exposed as a father, a human, a mortal, his now horrible but once handsome face ravaged and half eaten up by machine. For Vader, exposure could only mean death.

At a certain point in my twenties I began to wonder if it was possible to be relentlessly exposed and still command respect. I saw how some of the women and men I encountered would hold themselves in check, how they, unlike me, would not tell every*one* every*thing* about themselves at their earliest convenience. These people were cagey about their desires and their foibles, with whole libraries of secrets and aces up their sleeves. Instead of riotous storytelling and rushes of disclosure, they had a style that was deliberate and reserved; they designed the way they presented themselves to others, carefully doling out tidbits of self over time like so much Pez from a collectible dispenser. Their masks were well wrought. And these people could not be taken for granted. As friends or as acquaintances, they were islands in a chilling sea whose treacherous shoals had to be navigated with care. Intriguing but untouchable, they could be seen and heard but not felt or known; they were perennial strangers with whom one could fall in love again and again but never be intimate. And they tended to be people whose names, in their professional lives, had about them an aura of the sacrosanct, inspiring awe, trepidation, and sometimes seven-figure movie deals.

And also at a certain point it became clear to me that there are no meritocracies in the world; that in the arena of cultural production, as in any industry, power goes very simply to those who demand it.

When I realized that—an easy lesson for many, but apparently a difficult one for me, raised by loving parents and sheltered from threats both large and small—I came to understand that I was not a contender in the action-packed galaxy. I had carved out for myself a comfortable and ultimately passive niche. Although I did not resemble a princess in any particular, did not live like a princess, had no poise or austerity, no subjects, no servants, and no white gown, I was still a princess wannabe: I watched from a point outside the field, waiting eternally for the true games to begin, waiting to ascend a private and, of course, imaginary throne.

It is no simple task to become Darth Vader. For one thing, what happens to the people who knew you before you wore the mask? How do you face them in your newly forbidding garb? It takes years to build a house of friends, a house of kindness, warmth, familiar sympathy. If you become Darth Vader overnight, does the house stay well lit, its welcoming rooms suddenly rendered alien by the presence of a prowling and enigmatic host? Surely the friends will laugh when you don the black facepiece, when you begin to hold yourself aloof and wander, cloaked in darkness, up and down the house's shadowy corridors.

Or you can transform yourself slowly into Vader, acquiring, bit by bit, the habits and accoutrements of mastery and distance. First the cloak, then the boots, next the gloves and lightsaber, and finally the helmet; first the pregnant pauses, then the brevity of speech, and finally the heavy breathing. This way your friends will have time to adjust to the metamorphosis, and though increasingly uneasy, even alarmed or outright frightened, they may not resort to ridicule. You will inspire distaste, you will receive referrals to mental-health professionals, the house may grow quiet and dim, with dust along the tabletops and sofas, but the laughter that comes of shock at the absurd will probably be absent.

Some of us, it would seem, are unable to bring ourselves to cultivate distant mystique. Some of us, in the end, hold our friends dearer than cloaks and daggers, hold the houses we live in closer than the sprawling and holy temples we might like to build; some of us stay forever on the brink of being Darth Vader, dreaming of the power we might, in some other galaxy, command, but finally, perpetually, forlornly abdicate. Some of us wait eternally for that moment when, inspired by rage or desperation or pride, we will emerge from ourselves like butterflies from cocoons, our colors lit brightly for all to behold in the radiant space of the air. We wait to become something we have never been; we wait, like almost everyone else, for a sudden and redeeming grace.

And then, needless to say, there is the question, *Why?* Why is it desirable to be Darth Vader instead of a quiet watcher from the balcony or the cheap seats? Are weakness and fear of anonymity at the bottom of it all, at the base of every struggle for power and renown? Or can a poignant idealism light the sacred fire of ego, as Hollywood and free-market capitalism often wish to tell us, and somehow propel us flailing into the realm of greater good? Is the will to leave an imprint on the universe always a shallow and selfish will?

About a mile from my house in the Arizona desert, on the other side of a straight, fast, two-lane road that rushes with eighteen-wheelers and jacked-up pickups decorated with shotgun racks, there is a towering mound of petroglyphs, pictures of suns and antelope etched on stone by natives now gone for many hundreds of years. When I see them I do not think of the will to power, the clinging, striving, individual soul that wants to promote itself beyond its fellows. When I think of the desire to make markings on rocks that will outlast us all, I think of solitude and sadness; I think of those who have gone before and those who will follow us. I think of a soft finger touching a rough stone, and the stunning light of a star I can see in the night sky, a star that died thousands of human lifetimes ago.

IT'S A WONDERFUL LIFE DAY,
or How I Learned to Stop Worrying and
Love the *Star Wars Holiday Special*

WEBSTER YOUNCE

I don't remember when I first heard about the existence of the "lost" *Star Wars Holiday Special*, but some surreptitious whisper, some furtive murmur, or sotto voce allusion must have initially brought it to my attention. I do remember that rumors floated among my friends of a television extravaganza, featuring all the stars of the original movie, which was broadcast in the fall of 1978 and never aired again. Unfortunately, though, no one I knew had actually seen the thing, though some had vague recollections of its original broadcast and others were certain that bootleg copies of it existed. But I couldn't really confirm anything about it, and so like all things rooted in supposition and innuendo, the *Special* eventually assumed a talismanic status in my imagination. It became something like the medieval philosopher's stone or the fountain of youth, a shimmering, chimerical objective, forever just out of reach, into which I poured great hope, inordinate expectation, and an irrational amount of psychic energy. The entire matter seemed to be shrouded in mystery, including the explanation for the *Special*'s disappearance. I gave no credence whatsoever to the most oft-cited reason, which held that the *Special* was so awful, so horrific a debacle, that George Lucas had banned it from the airwaves, refused to acknowledge its existence, and would under no circumstances allow it to be released on video. This seemed highly unlikely to me. It wasn't that I was convinced that Lucas was incapable of producing a cinematic embarrassment; after all, I had seen *Howard the Duck*. Moreover, Lucas seemed perfectly at ease with the video release of two other infamous television spin-offs, the stupendously bad *An Ewok Adventure* and the execrable *Ewoks: The Battle for Endor*. The very fact that these three calamities blithely remained available to anyone with the poor judgment to seek them out seemed evidence enough that there was another explanation for the air of mystery that Lucas had draped around the *Special*—assuming, of course, that the show ever existed. After all, I had only heard rumors of it, usually along the lines of the "my cousin's roommate's best friend saw a copy at a party." So I was left with little more than conjecture and surmise, both of the show's actuality and of its putative suppression. What I knew beyond a shadow of doubt, though, was that if the show did exist, the likelihood that I would ever actually see it was virtually nil.

As I say, the *Special* had come to occupy a rarefied, near-mythic status in my imagination, and I knew from extensive childhood fantasy reading that the surest way to prevent any hoped-for event from occurring was to expect it. At a more rational level, it seemed perfectly clear that if Lucas himself did not want the *Special* to surface, the only way I would ever discover the truth about it would involve some kind of dark ops mission, a cloak-and-dagger scenario involving a succession of anonymous phone calls, dead-letter drops, and coded messages culminating in a midnight rendezvous in a parking garage with a scratchy-voiced figure in a trench coat who, in the process of sliding a brown-paper package toward me from the shadows, would gravely inform me that many Bothans had died to bring me this information.

Reality, however, turned out to be far more inexplicable. In the mid-1990s I moved to a new city and into an apartment with a roommate who, I discovered one afternoon while rifling through his belongings, had a bootleg copy of the *Special* crammed in his video collection amid his collection of Japanese *anime* and several episodes of *Friends*. Bathetic shelving aside, the knowledge that the *Special* was in my apartment had a weirdly chilling effect. I simply couldn't bring myself to watch it. I had visions of loading the tape into the VCR as the apartment door burst open and smoke billowed into the room. In would pour a legion of white-helmet-and-codpiece-wearing soldiers who would take me to a secluded room, strap me to a mechanical gurney, and slowly lower me toward an evil-looking, multiple-needle contraption while demanding I reveal the whereabouts of a man named Solo. (My paranoia may, in fact, be congenital. I have a brother who for years slept with a heavy, three-foot-long iron pipe in his bed to defend himself against attack from the Black Riders of Tolkien's *The Lord of the Rings* saga. Then again we did live in Mississippi, an exceedingly strange and mythic part of the world where people speak in archaic locutions and where hairy feet are not uncommon. A confusion of the state with Middle Earth is not as odd as it might initially appear.) Eventually, though, my curiosity got the better of me. I double locked and chained the apartment door, closed the blinds, turned off the ringer on my phone, and sat down to watch the show. If only I had heeded my fears.

The *Star Wars Holiday Special* is the most excruciatingly bad piece of television ever to air on that vast wasteland. And in saying so, I am at risk of understatement. The *Special* is worse than any description of it can possibly convey; as with stories of war, famine, or pestilence, language fails. But standing in the grand tradition of those who bear witness, I will relate (briefly, for pity's sake) what came across the airwaves that Day of Infamy, November 18, 1978. The story line, such as it is, is relatively straightforward. On the Wookiee planet of Kashyyyk, Chewbacca's nuclear family anxiously awaits his return for the family observance of Life Day, the Wookiee holiday reserved for the celebration of, well, Life. Or something, since the arcana surrounding the holiday is never actually explained. The Aristotelian complication in this high drama is an Imperial blockade in place around Kashyyyk. Han Solo and Chewie are late, much to the dismay and distress of Chewbacca's wife, Malla, his father, Itchy, and his son, Lumpy. (Yes, Itchy and Lumpy.) And so the family waits, killing time in ways that would drive Beckett's Didi and Gogo to suicide. So what exactly transpires during this absurdist tragicomedy? A '70s-era variety show.

Seeking to allay her fears about her husband, Malla contacts, via a secret video communicator, a cosmetic-slathered Luke Skywalker (you hope this is a consequence of Mark Hamill's notorious 1977 automobile accident), and an apparently heavily medicated Princess Leia (of course, Carrie Fisher's own writings make superfluous any conjecture about her appearance). Both Luke and Leia assure Malla that Chewbacca will make it home safely, a belief seconded by a local trader named Saundan, played by Art Carney in the first of many "special guest star" appearances, who arrives bearing Life Day gifts. Saundan is responsible for the creepiest part of the *Special*, a segment that makes you wonder what happened to the network's Standards and Practices department. If there was one thing that you would expect to raise an objection from the censors, it would be Wookiee porn.

Saundan tells Itchy that he's brought the pater familia a "proton pack" for the "mind evaporator," a term that at this point in the *Special* made me wonder if I had become snarled in a cleverly contrived Möbius strip of self-referentiality. But alas, the capacity for irony has yet to evolve on Kashyyyk, which one should recall existed a long, long time ago in a galaxy far, far away. Itchy settles himself in the mind evaporator, which resembles a Barcalounger with attached helmet and visor, as Saundan inserts the proton pack. A swirl of vintage '70s disco lights swims across the screen as a woman's husky voice begins speaking urgently: "I know you're searching for me. Searching, searching. . . . I exist for you alone. I am in your mind as you create me. Oh, yes . . . I can feel my creation. . . . I'm getting your message. Are you getting mine?" Itchy certainly is, emitting a sound somewhere between a moan and a growl. Slowly a woman with pink strands of hair comes into focus. I regret to report that it is Diahann Carroll. "Oh, oh. . . . We *are* excited, aren't we? Well, just relax. Just relax. . . . You see, I am your fantasy. I am your experience. So experience me. I am your pleasure. Enjoy me." This continues for far, far too long, Itchy moaning on cue, until some perfunctory disco-space music begins, and Ms. Carroll sings about the ecstasy of the moment. At long last, the ecstatic moment is gone, and her image fades back into the swirl of light in which it began. This entire segment is profoundly objectionable on any number of grounds, of course, but one offense in particular deserves attention: How worried could Itchy be about his son's safety if he's able to be so easily distracted by a woman with pink hair?

At this point, a valiant effort begins on the part of the screenwriters to restore the dramatic tension dispersed by the porn segment. (This begs the question of whether or not the credited screenwriters actually existed, since the entire affair has the decided whiff of improvisation.) Without warning, a team of Stormtroopers arrives at the house and, in an egregious violation of Fourth Amendment guarantees, begin to ransack the home searching for Rebel sympathizers and Alliance propaganda. These constitutional scofflaws overturn furniture, rifle through drawers, and in one feel-the-evil moment rip apart Lumpy's stuffed toy Bantha. Never one to stand idly by, Saundan entices an Imperial Guard with an object that looks like a boom box–cum–sewing machine. Twisting a couple of knobs amid a flurry of twitches and spasms taken straight from Carney's time on *The Honeymooners*, Saundan activates his box, subjecting the guard to a performance by none other than Jefferson Starship. The musicians, dressed in costumes that would embarrass Devo, dutifully flail away on their instruments while Marty Balin sings into what can only be described as a fluorescent sexual aid. The Diahann Carroll segment is positively restrained in comparison, and you half expect the Imperial Guard to order the entire home razed as a defense measure.

As the terrifying search continues, Lumpy wanders over to an out-of-the-way video screen and begins watching a cartoon. This is, believe it or not, the highlight of the *Special* and the only reason, apart from curiosity of the rubbernecking-at-car-crash sort, that the *Special* has any credibility among *Star Wars* fans. Created by the Nelvana Studios of Canada, the cartoon is of primary interest for comprising the first appearance of *Star Wars'* most popular villain, the notorious bounty hunter Boba Fett. Why such a cartoon (a) exists and (b) is in Chewbacca's home, no one ever explains, but you could reasonably assume that the cartoon is some kind of Alliance propaganda designed to bolster the morale of the good people caught beneath the boot heel of Empire. That it never occurs to Lumpy that this is exactly the kind of thing the Stormtroopers are wrecking his house to find, and that perhaps he should watch something else at this particular juncture, bodes ill for the long-term future of the Rebellion. But since every child needs his father to be a hero, and in the cartoon, Chewie lives up to the billing, we can forgive little Lumpy his foolishness.

The cartoon holds up pretty well, even apart from its interest as Boba Fett's debut. On a secret mission to find a magical amulet, Han and Chewie lose contact with their home base and go missing in a strange, watery world. Luke sets off in search of them and, after crash-landing on the planet, is rescued from a hungry sea monster by none other than Fett himself, looking remarkably like Space Ghost, riding an animal from Land of the Lost and armed with a utensil from a Brobdingnagian sewing kit. Fett takes Luke to the *Millennium Falcon*, where first Han and then Luke fall victim to a "sleeping virus," for which Fett offers to procure the antidote. Chewie, ever the intuitive judge of character, senses something amiss and insists on accompanying the enigmatic bounty hunter. Good thing, too, since Fett turns out to be in the employ of Darth Vader and is conspiring to turn the Rebels over to the Empire. The plot, however, is quickly foiled, and although Fett escapes, our heroes have a good chuckle at his expense as the cartoon concludes. Lumpy applauds.

Before we can take a moment to reflect upon the implications of the cartoon (Fett works for Vader? What magical amulet?), the *Special* rushes headlong into its unintentional—so we assume—apologia for the Empire. A video screen on the wall flickers into life, depicting a view of Tatooine from space while a stentorian voice informs viewers that the following unexpurgated vision of life on the planet is offered to Imperial citizens "in the hope that our own lives may be uplifted by the comparison and enriched with the gratitude of relief." (If someone can explain what "the gratitude of relief" means, I would probably feel it.) The monitor cuts to the interior of Mos Eisley Cantina, the most popular bar in the galaxy, presided over here by tough-broad bartender Ackmena, who is courted by a smitten and hapless Krelman. In a casting choice that continues to haunt viewers, Ackmena is played by Beatrice Arthur, Krelman by Harvey Korman. Ackmena and Krelman indulge in some agonizingly protracted repartee before the real pain begins: a stunning musical number in which Ackmena (as a reminder, this is Bea Arthur) dances with Cantina patrons while singing about the sweet sorrow of closing time: "One more chorus, one more tune. It's not the end, friend. If you're a friend, friend. Then you come back to me, pal. To celebrate, pal. You have to wait, pal." The bar empties, and as the video screen fades to black, we are left with a tableau of Krelman offering Ackmena a flower. What's fascinating is that as an instance of propaganda and indoctrination, the whole scene is really quite effective. After seeing what goes on in Mos Eisley after-hours, a universe of fascistic repression looks pretty good.

Finding nothing incriminating in the apartment, the bad guys move on, leaving one ill-fated trooper, in the grand tradition of doomed and anonymous military flunkies, to stand guard alone. Soon Han and Chewie arrive, make short work of the Stormtrooper, and enter the home to much rejoicing and hugs all around. After some cringe-inducing chitchat (a typical example has Han kneeling in front of Lumpy and saying, "I think his voice is changin'. [Pause.] Come on, I'm just teasin' ya."), Han takes his leave in order to give the family peace in which to observe their holiday. The rituals of Life Day apparently involve transportation to an astral plane, for soon the family stands amid the firmament, dressed in the long, red robes later used by Stanley Kubrick in *Eyes Wide Shut*, and join a procession of Wookiees marching into a ceremony hall. The celebration itself has a surprisingly sparse turnout, with only a dozen or so Wookiees in evidence, but the numbers are bolstered by the arrival of R2-D2 and C-3PO, and soon thereafter, Han, Luke, and Leia. The culmination of the Wookiee holy day has arrived, and we reach what is the most hallowed moment in the liturgical calendar of an entire species, the fulcrum around which its spiritual life spins: Leia singing "The Life Day Song." This sacred litany, sung to a lugubrious version of John Williams's ubiquitous theme, is an impassioned hymn to Life Day itself. "A day that brings the promise that one day we'll be free to live, to laugh, to dream, to grow, to trust, to love, to be." In other words, "The Life Day Song" is a paean to the day that brings the promise of another day. Life Day is a holiday with modest claims, it seems. As Leia concludes, a close-up of Chewbacca dissolves into a series of flashbacks of scenes from the movie before cutting to Chewie and the family seated around the dinner table, joining hands and bowing their heads. And on this peaceful scene of Wookiee domestic harmony, the *Special* mercifully concludes.

It should be clear from this brief and edited synopsis that watching the *Special* is an agonizing experience. The suffering, however, is not merely the result of it being the most abominable piece of "entertainment" as has ever been foisted upon television viewers. What is particularly painful is the way in which the *Special* manages to obliterate the quicksilver magic that inhabited the original movie. The wonder and awe that the film evoked—from the stunning shot tracking the terrifyingly immense underbelly of an Imperial warship to the stirring pomp and circumstance of the regal ceremony honoring Han and Luke's triumphant heroism—is an essential part of that mysterious alchemy Lucas performed in transforming a hodgepodge of inherited mythologies and legends into an immutable touchstone of twentieth-century pop-cultural consciousness. What the first film conveyed was nothing less than a sense of the sublime, that aboriginal emotional and psychological response that the Romantic poets revered and sought so desperately in their poetry. Lucas managed to capture it in *Star Wars*, and twenty minutes of the *Holiday Special* is enough to snuff it out completely. Viewer response to the *Special* on that notorious evening in 1978 is impossible to reconstruct, but I suspect Obi-Wan neatly summarized the effect the *Special* had upon the American viewing public: "I felt a great disturbance in the Force, as if one million souls cried out in torment and were silenced at once." Oh, the humanity.

Once you move beyond the shocked, appalled silence the *Special* invariably induces, the question for the *Star Wars* fan is how to deal with the brute fact of its existence. How do we account for this monstrosity, this great blight in the cinematic universe? You could do what Lucas himself is said to have done, at least for a time, which is simply not to acknowledge the *Special*'s existence. Unfortunately, not even the formidable power of Skywalker Ranch is enough to sustain the Stalinist suppression necessary for such a denial, particularly as samizdat, in the form of bootleg videos, kept cropping up. So Lucas eventually began publicly acknowledging the *Special*, the story goes, by expressing the understandable desire to see every copy of it destroyed. But unlike Henry II's wish to be rid of Beckett, the thorn in King George's side has never been removed: the *Special* continues to sit in video collections around the world, not to mention residing amid the psychic scar tissue of those unfortunate enough to see it. Milan Kundera once observed that "the struggle of man against power is the struggle of memory against forgetting." There are times, though, in which the capacity to forget, rather than to remember, is the more liberating, as anyone who has seen the *Special* can attest. But try as you might, the debacle is impossible to erase from memory, and so the pain continues.

In the end, there is nothing to be done but acknowledge the *Special*'s existence. So the pressing question for devotees then becomes how to account for it. The problem has two components, the first falling into the realm of theodicy: how could a benevolent Lucas be responsible for something so contemptible? As I noted earlier, following the "Well, have you seen *Howard the Duck?*" line of reasoning, I have no difficulty in assigning him blame, but for others the question can be more problematic. We want our heroes to be perfect, and when they fail us, the impulse is to reject them completely. Once you grant Lucas's responsibility for the *Special*, then veneration of him may be a bit tricky to maintain. "After such knowledge, what forgiveness?" T. S. Eliot asked, and fans who have fallen into knowledge of the *Special* must wrestle with the dilemma. In practice, though, most either ignore the question or just concede that the *Special* was a colossal blunder and try to move on. But moving on is not actually so easy to do because of the peculiar nature of Lucas's creation. What made *Star Wars* so compelling from the start was the sense that we were getting a glimpse into a unique, self-contained universe, one that existed apart from our own but with a historical and temporal continuity every bit as ordered and coherent as the universe in which we live. (I know, I know, technically speaking everything occurred in another galaxy—one that was far, far away, right?—and not in an alternate universe, but the effect is what I'm referring to here.) The Empire, the Rebellion, Tatooine, Jedi Masters, Mos Eisley Cantina, rogue smugglers—all these things existed *out there* somewhere, and we had stumbled upon them.

Since *Episode IV: A New Hope* first appeared, tremendous effort has gone into maintaining this sense of authenticity, of the reality of an extant *Star Wars* universe. The sweated labor involved in maintaining this pretense is quite impressive. The difficulty arises from the sheer volume of *Star Wars* materials. In addition to the feature films, there have been a dizzying number of novels, comic books, television specials, radio dramas, board games, action figures, cartoons, and other media, all of which carry with them their own idiosyncratic part of the grand narrative of the *Star Wars* universe. And since all these products were created in a relatively haphazard fashion, all sorts of contradictions and discontinuities have arisen that must be reconciled in order for the coherence of the *Star Wars* universe to be maintained. One result is that great and intense debate rages in the realms of fandom over what constitutes *Star Wars* "canon." And of course, little highlights the problematic nature of determining canonicity more than an attempt to deal with the *Holiday Special*.

The very fact that the word "canon" arises in attempting to sort out these matters is telling, for it speaks to the unique, if not downright weird, relationship *Star Wars* fans have with the object of their devotion. The entire subject almost always assumes the trappings of the religious. The word "canon" is of course most often used within a religious context, and although even there it has multiple meanings, its primary use is as a referent to a collection or body of texts recognized as authoritative and universally binding within a worshiping community. In the Judeo-Christian tradition, the word is customarily defined as the list of writings acknowledged as genuine and inspired. The word itself comes to us through the sacred linguistic triumvirate of Latin, Greek, and Hebrew. Like the Latin word *canna*, the Greek word *kanon* is probably derived from, or at least associated with, the Hebrew word *qaneh*, which means reed or rod. *Kanon*, then, means rod, specifically a straight rod used as a rule, which is the place from which the other English meaning of canon—"rule" or "standard"—takes its origin. Since a rod used as a rule can be subdivided into smaller units and marked appropriately, *kanon* came to mean a series of marks, and thus was also used to mean a "list" or "series." And this underlies the meaning that "canon" conveys today.

The word, though, is not restricted to a sacral meaning, as any English major can attest after having received his sixth or seventh gift copy of Harold Bloom's imperious *The Western Canon*. But it is the religious freight the word carries that is of particular interest here, for in almost any discussion of *Star Wars*, you will encounter religious terminology, concepts, and methodology. This essay—this entire volume, in fact—is no exception. You could argue that these gestures toward the religious are related to the innate human longing for something beyond the empirically verifiable, which in turn goes some way in explaining that *frisson* of recognition and delight that accompanied the debut of *Episode IV*. But whatever its origin and implications, the religious impulse is undeniably woven into the fabric of the *Star Wars* universe and into the discourse surrounding it. Upon reflection, then, it seems almost inevitable that a web site dedicated to piecing together information about *Episode I* before its release had as its webmaster a Roman Catholic priest. The priesthood is, after all, the intermediary office between the material and the metaphysical, between things seen and unseen. Nor is it surprising that discussions continue unabated to this day as to which fictions bearing the *Star Wars* imprimatur constitute canon and which ones are, well, "apocryphal." Debates over the matter are a staple on a number of *Star Wars* web sites, with arbiters offering rubrics of canonicity that range from the simple and severe (feature films only) to the scrupulously calibrated (a hierarchy involving fourteen gradations of reliability). I wouldn't be surprised to learn that somewhere there exists a rigorous calculus for determining the number of Wookiees that can dance on the head of a pin—cavorting that is undoubtedly choreographed to "The Life Day Song." As far as I know, that particular instance of scholastic hairsplitting has not yet occurred, but a number of efforts have been made to legitimize, for lack of a better word, other aspects of the *Holiday Special*. The attempt to justify the ways of George to men, or at least to incorporate the disaster that is the *Special* into the warp and woof of his universe, is arguably noble in intent, but the truth is that the *Special* is too great a debacle to allow for anything more than feeble half gestures at justification. The members of Chewbacca's family, for example, make appearances in both the *Star Wars Encyclopedia* and the *Star Wars Character Log*, where we are given explanations for the embarrassment of their *Holiday Special* names. "Itchy," we learn, is actually the old porn-fiend's nickname, taken from his given name, Attichitcuk, while "Malla" is the shortened form of Mallatobuck. And "Lumpy," it turns out, comes from Lumpawarrump, which admittedly isn't much of an improvement but is at least consistent with the rest of the family's appellatory methodology.

None of this really does much in the way of accounting for the *Special*, but then no one has ever had much success in explaining cosmic catastrophe. At best, one just accepts it, somewhat like the existence of a Dark Side to the Force. But we can take solace in the fact that both the official and unofficial guardians of the *Star Wars* Industrial Complex will continue their battle to safeguard the coherence and integrity of the *Star Wars* universe. Even in the face of a calamity like the *Holiday Special*, the troops keep soldiering on, adjusting histories, realigning narratives, expanding appellations, and, in the case of Ackmena and Krelman's romance, practicing an essentially benign neglect. And that is reassuring, giving fans a new hope that, perhaps, one day we'll be free to live, to laugh, to dream, to grow, to trust, to love, to be.

PLANET ROCK:
Star Wars and Hip-Hop

It's hard to overstate the impact of *Star Wars* on mass culture. Beyond, even, its then breakthrough visuals, this ultimate sleeper film thoroughly revolutionized the movie business—from how much a film could be expected to gross, to how widely it opened in theaters, to how it was marketed, to those areas from which revenue could be derived—practically inventing movie merchandising in the process.

However, hip-hop has been no slouch, either. Riding onto the cultural landscape just a few short years before Lucas's triumphant May 1977 juggernaut, hip-hop basically grew up with the Force and, like it, also largely transformed everything it touched. Perhaps by virtue of their mutually ignominious births, hip-hop and *Star Wars* also initially shared salient themes—that of principled innovators going up against entrenched opposition—that rang true for millions, resounding with unlimited cultural impact, leaving no one untouched.

Well, no one, except Luke Skyywalker. Not the Jedi, but the forty-one-year-old Miami-based purveyor of butt-bobbing bass, aka Luther Campbell. Sure, *hip-hop* affected him. But *Star Wars?*

"I saw the first one—the shootin' and all that—but I don't know what was going on. I saw the girl in there. I didn't get it," he says.

That Lucasfilm sued and won a $500,000 suit against Campbell in the late '80s over the use of the Skyywalker name certainly doesn't aid the love lack. And while Campbell says his indifference preceded the court's decision by a decade, he admits that the lawsuit purified his distaste: He won't be going to see *Attack of the Clones*, much as he avoided *The Phantom Menace*, despite the presence of Jedi Master Mace Windu, played by his favorite actor, Samuel L. Jackson, whose movies he watches "religiously." "Not this one."

Plus, "I had the name before the character," Campbell avers. Back in 1975 at Miami Beach Senior High, people started calling him Luke Skyywalker "'cause I played basketball good. Dunks and shit. Just like the other guy: Remember Kenny 'Sky' Walker, who played for the Knicks?"

For his apathy, Campbell credits *Star Wars'* FM-rock-blow-dryed Trans-Am-halo, which he deems "totally white-oriented. [For me to get into it] it's gotta have some kind of blackness in it."

Reginald C. Dennis, thirty-five, former editor at *The Source*, *XXL*, and the editor-in-chief at *Manifest*, a GQ-like black men's magazine he's developing with partners, concurs on *Star Wars'* pastiness, noting that, in the original, "There's no black person with a speaking role. Watching *Star Wars* was like watching *Robin Hood*. And [yet] you couldn't stop black kids from going to see *Star Wars*."

Indeed, Dennis saw the movie at least five times the summer of '77, having, that previous winter, fervently consumed the pre-released *Star Wars* comic books. The film's ethos locked neatly into his own youthful, hip-hop one. "That you could go on an adventure filled with mindless destruction was very appealing to kids. And *Star Wars* was a movie where scores of people were killed, you saw an entire planet of people blow up—which *I'd* never seen before—and there was no blood. So, the movie's called *Star* Wars, and it made war fun, and so soon after Vietnam. Every kid I knew wanted a laser gun and a lightsaber. It's no mistake that my generation is the most violent generation."

Did *Star Wars* have something to do with that? "I don't know, but when I saw *Star Wars*, I *liked* Luke Skywalker, but *Darth Vader* . . . if I was a Jedi Knight, I'd have been on the Dark Side as soon as I heard about it."

But what Dennis considers his destiny, Bronx-born and -raised rapper Q-Unique, of the hip-hop crew the Arsonists, is still attempting to resist. "*Star Wars* was possibly the most overwhelming movie I've ever seen in my life," he affirms. Seven years old when the first film was released, today he says he's collectively seen all four movies "about a thousand times."

For this artist, then, attempting to fashion a more politically conscious, antimaterialistic, countercorporate kind of hip-hop (in direct opposition to the variety that has seemingly seized control of all the nation's transmitters), the metaphors of *Star Wars* have direct bearing. "The Empire reminds me so much of the music industry itself, and of the underground artists that are fighting so much to stand up for the pure and what's righteous." These concerns have, then, seeped their way into the artist's work, fashioning a rich extended metaphor that analogizes the Empire and the $15 billion-a-year U.S. record biz.

For example, on his track "Respect the Unexpected," quoth Q: "I'm the one who is predicted to lead the underground to victory / Over the evil industry." In his *Star Wars*/music business matrix, "the Stormtroopers would be the A&Rs, the CEOs would be the higher-ranked officers, and, at this point, there's *too* many Darth Vaders. Me, being well trained in the ways of hip-hop by the masters, such as [hip-hop founder] Afrika Bambaataa and [b-boy legend] Crazy Legs—who I would look at as Obi-Wan Kenobi and Yoda—I just gotta keep on going up against these evil industry people, and moving with the rebellion." And Q promises to further develop the theme of his training under these hip-hop Jedi Masters in an upcoming record to be called—what else?—*Star Wars*.

It's not just Q who considers the Force. The use of the *Star Wars* corpus as a rich lode of metaphor is widespread in hip-hop. "Comin' back / Like *Return of the Jedi*" on Kool Moe Dee's 1987 "How You Like Now?" may or may not be the earliest such reference to the 1983 film, but it's by no means the only one:

"The fly guy with the Force like Luke Sky"; "I set shit off like Boba Fett" (Redman, "Can't Wait")

"Well I'm the Chief Rocka / Rips up like Chewbacca" (Do It All, Lords of the Underground, "L.O.T.U.G.")

"No doubt, under the influence of the *Falcon / Millennium* spaceship" (Black Thought, The Roots, "Without a Doubt")

"And never see three P.O.s!!!" (Lord Have Mercy, "Flipmode Is Da Squad")

"You know that I'm the man like Chewbacca knows Han . . . Solo" (House of Pain, "Feel It")

"Voices speak to me from long-gone Jedi Knights" (U.K. rapper Lewis Parker, "Rise")

"Phone home, or return like Jedi" (Rock, Fab 5 [Heltah Skeltah & O.G.C.], "Lefleur, Lefar, Eshoshka")

"*Star Wars* moving in like Han Solo" (Busta Rhymes, "Woo Hah! Got You All in Check")

"I get down with the Force of Luke Sky/Chewbacca, R2-D2 and the crew" (Erick Sermon, "Welcome")

"Meanwhile the goverment bring *Star Wars* from glock to glockers/C.O.P. has an APB out on Chewbacca" (Wyclef Jean, The Fugees, "The Beast")

"Obi-Wan Kenobi swore before me" (Rza, Killarmy, "And Justice for All")

"With the Force like Luke Skywalker" (Inspektah Deck, Wu-Tang Clan, "Hellz Wind Staff")

"In flight / Counterattack like a Jedi Knight" (Q-Tip, Busta Rhymes, "Wild Hot")

"Black starship control / I walk like I'm Darth Vader" (Kool Keith, "Dark Vadar")

"I have something for you here / What is it? Your father's TURNTABLES / The weapon of a Jedi Knight" (D. J. Stoic, "3PM Migraine")

Whew! Now add a dash of crews with names like Jedi and Jedi Mind Tricks. Sprinkle in a taste of "Fortruss," the track by the Tampa-based Walkmen that carpets the "Imperial March" theme with lyrics thickly knotted by *Star Wars* references and samples. The Force will be with hip-hop culture—always—and vice versa. But this makes sense. Both *Star Wars* and hip-hop are realms of myth; trenchantly, though not exclusively, male in viewpoint; filled with colorful, often heroic, characters; and formally structured by stringent rites of passage.

These parallels are not invisible to everyday fans, either, especially those who are fans of both subcultures. Londoner Ossie Hirst—who, at twenty-one, doesn't remember a time before either *Star Wars* or hip-hop, having grown up in the age of both—notes, "I see parallels between the strict skills of learning some aspect of hip-hop and learning to be a Jedi. Both are very technique-based. When Luke is learning to use the lightsaber, while on the *Millennium Falcon*, it's like learning to [turntable] scratch or something. He keeps getting burned, but he's learning, and the same kind of dedication is needed in hip-hop." Agrees Philly native Steve S. Jackson, twenty-five, "I look at the lightsaber fights, and I think of moves that would be nice while b-boying," as breakdancing is organically known by those within the culture. Meanwhile, Troy Frazier, twenty-five, of Atlanta says the two worlds share core values, best summarized as, "Stand up for what you believe in, even in the face of seemingly insurmountable odds. Or as [the Roots'] Black Thought said 'Either stand tall or sit the fuck down.'"

Others derive different lessons from the films. Richard Quitevis, aka D.J. QBert, is former front man for the defunct Frisco Bay–based dj team Invisibl Skratch Piklz. Known to wield two Technics the way Sith Lord Darth Maul wields a double-bladed lightsaber, QBert's seen the films "maybe twenty-five times each. I even have a Darth Vader computer mouse."

As the Piklz raided Earth's sounds for their own line of dj-battle records, George Lucas widely ravaged the planet's imagery to create *Star Wars'* unique retro-futuristic, otherworldly look. In *Episode IV: A New Hope*, Luke's seeker—the softball-like training sphere—was partially forged from truck-model-kit parts. The radiating shafts of the Death Star's fusion reactor in *The Return of the Jedi* were made from fifteen hundred fishing rods. Lucas incubated the rest of his films with other rich visual sources, sampled from as far and wide as Japanese samurai culture, cheap Republic movie serials, German fascism, Middle Eastern architecture, the Westerns of John Ford, *2001: A Space Odyssey*, West African sculpture, and American art deco.

Of Lucas's panoramas, says QBert, "He teases you with spurts of beauty." (Perhaps D.J. Premier and Guru's Gang Starr felt the same way; hence their liberal evocation of Lucas's feature film, *THX-1138* for their "You Know My Steez" video.) And indeed, QBert's solo debut, *Wave Twisters: Episode 7 Million: Sonic Wars within the Protons*, on his own as-innocuously-titled Galactic Butt Hair Records, pays homage to Lucas via its narrative of a dj-ing, b-boying dentist and his robot, out to save a beautiful woman—and the galaxy—from a masked villain called the Red Worm. In fact, when asked hypothetically what hip-hop track he would blast in his X-wing's sound system during a trench run on the Death Star, QBert cites "Cosmic Assassins," from his own album . . . and a recording composed with exactly such a scene in mind.

Still, "I didn't like the fact that the music in *Star Wars* didn't sound as futuristic as it should. Like in the Cantina scene?" he says, referring to the swing-styled melodies of that most memorable sequence. "I think some hip-hop music sounds *way* more advanced than what they were playing in the Cantina."

QBert's implicit question—What would *Star Wars* become, were it to be reimagined through the mind of hip-hop?—is answered noisily by Supergenius, aka Morgan Phillips, thirty-three. Like Q-Unique, seeing *Star Wars* at seven, he says, "was the beginning of my whole aesthetic world." On *Star Wars Breakbeats*, his own Suckadelic Records label bootleg, the sounds of the film series—racing TIE fighters, firing blasters, whirring machinery, and spirited human and alien vernaculars—get locked in step over fluid and funky grooves and percussion.

So, says Supergenius, instead of having Puffy rap defiantly in the maw of Godzilla—QBert's nominee for what he'd most want to shoot with the Death Star's turbo laser—"I thought, if you wanna put out a full-length record that's a compliment to a movie, why not just remix the movie itself, rather than have a bunch of corny bands trying to slap together a compilation? Why not really go into the sound of the movie and try to make tracks out of it?"

So he did, fashioning bruisers like "Trials of a Jedi," "One Smooth Character," "Greedo Plays Himself," and "Your Powers Are Weak Old Man"—that last track composed of the noise from Obi-Wan Kenobi and Darth Vader's crackling lightsaber battle over Zapp's "More Bounce to the Ounce," as Darth breathes menacingly, uttering and reuttering the title. Listening, it's easy to imagine that you're watching that alternate-universe version of *Star Wars* where, as Steve S. Jackson said, "Dr. Dre would be Vader (he just seems Vader-ish), Princess Leia would have to be Bahamdia (simply because I don't think there's any woman that's nicer than her), and Han Solo would be played by KRS-One."

But if you're still having a hard time picturing such entertainment, then just check out Supergenius's animated, fifty-second short, *Look, Sir: Droids*, in which b-boying Stormtrooper Kenner action figures windmill in Tatooine's ochre dust, under the watchful eye of an approving, head-nodding dewback.

JEDI UBER ALLES

TOM CARSON

Clocking in several years ahead of the political reality, the release of *Star Wars* in 1977 marked the cultural beginning of the Reagan era. I don't know if Jimmy Carter ever even saw the movie, much less grasped its significance. But one look at it ought to have been enough to tell him he was a goner. From his gingerly acceptance of the Sandinista revolution in Nicaragua to the dispirited-looking cardigans that symbolized his energy policy, Carter hoped to induce Americans to come to terms with an age of diminished swagger and reduced gratification, no easy job even for a president less charmless and unpersuasive than he turned out to be. While his bug-eyed ineffectuality would most likely have doomed the case no matter what, the opening blasts of the *Star Wars* theme—not-so-incidentally the first symphonic movie score to become a recognizable hit since the counterculture's advent—were the sound of Santa Anna's trumpeters playing the "Deguello" outside Carter's Alamo. The lines around the block at every theater showing the movie were a figurative declaration that the country had had it up to here with second thoughts. Like Tennessee Williams's Blanche DuBois, we didn't want realism; we wanted certitudes, and triumphalism, and whooshing pomp. That's why it's always seemed appropriate that the Strategic Defense Initiative, the Reagan policy most at odds with observable fact—and in a competitive field, too—ended up borrowing its nickname from George Lucas's fantasy.

One reason fans bristle at the notion that their fanhood might have a larger cultural or sociological significance, of course, is that they consider their relationship to the movie to be paramountly meaningful for its own sake—calling it symptomatic of anything else diminishes rather than elevates it. Another reason is that Americans compartmentalize their politics like nobody else on earth, and get exasperated fast when anyone suggests that there's any overlap at all between how they vote and what they do for fun. In other words, discussing the politics of *Star Wars* is no very quick road to seeming engaging. And just to make things worse for myself, I'll put you on notice up front that I'm going to feel obliged to resort to a term that '60s radical chic-sters abused with such blithe abandon that it's triggered nothing but eye-rolling ever since. The word in question—look, I'm trying to get this over with, all right?—is fascism. Why, sure, you say, relieved. Everybody knows the bad guys are totalitarians, from those faceless Kitchen Aid storm troopers up through heavy-breathing, Nazi-helmeted Darth Vader himself. That's why, when Reagan wiped all the shades of gray out of the Cold War by calling the Soviet Union an "evil empire," everyone recognized the phrase as yet another *Star Wars* derivation; that nobody dismissed such talk as fit for a comic book may be the ultimate example of the movie's seepage from pure fantasy into people's real-world attitudes.

Now let's consider the good guys. They're the valiant rebels fighting to overthrow tyranny, which in movie terms is enough to guarantee their virtue (hey, that's what *we'd* do). In fact, though, their own authoritarian mystique beats the Empire's all hollow, just because it's much loftier and more stirring. What we have here is a heroic brotherhood of knights empowered by that reductio ad absurdum of comic-book Wagnerianism, "the Force," whose appeal as primitivist, suprarational mumbo jumbo gets laid on with a trowel in the later films—even as it's gradually made clear that eligibility for the club is a matter of superior bloodlines; not the most democratic notion. Face it, it's not too hard to imagine that well-known cinema addict Hitler watching *Star Wars* with tears dripping down his cheeks until they soaked his mustache. He'd simply equate the Jedi with the Aryans, and the Empire with Jewish capitalists and the powers that imposed the Treaty of Versailles on Germany after World War I. The contending absolutes of "Good" and "Evil" are so free of definable content here—what makes good good? It fights evil; thanks, George—that nothing in the movie's schema would prevent him from doing so. In fact, a number of its ingredients might downright encourage him to do so.

This is partly a matter of imagery—most famously, Luke Skywalker's apotheosis in the final victory march, whose staging and lighting blatantly mimics Leni Riefenstahl's lionizing photography of Nazi rallies in *Triumph of the Will*. (That Lucas himself was the first to draw attention to this, with an air of pride that he hadn't wasted his time in film class, just proves that his own political naivete leaves the average koala bear looking like Cardinal Richelieu.) But the protofascist side of *Star Wars* is also built right into the film's premise, and the paradox is that the propaganda is ingenuous, not cunning. The attitudes are ingrained in the artistic DNA of the simpleminded pulp adventure tales of another age that Lucas's movie derives from, and whose disquieting gist he inadvertently made explicit simply by reproducing their appeal with such unthinking fidelity. Sometimes a naif ends up drawing a clearer map than a critic ever could.

The basic wish fulfillment in adventure stories for adolescent boys is twofold. On one side, they're often fantasies of community—either a heroic comradeship of like-minded souls ("No Gurls Allowed") or a fiefdom populated by willing satraps ("Cheetah Allowed," you might say). At the same time, they're also fantasies of power—not just heroic behavior but dominance of one's environment, a logical enough dream inversion of a real-world environment that most youths experience as dominating them. All this is frequently mixed up with notions of service to some higher ideal or gnomic but righteous organization, because boys are entranced with the concept of duty; it makes them feel *recognized*. Make those values the hallmarks of a whole society, as Lucas innocently does, and suddenly, ending *Star Wars* with a nonjudgment at Nuremberg doesn't seem—as indeed it doesn't—at all inappropriate.

We like to call the appeal of such tales "perennial"—with Joseph Campbell's *Hero with a Thousand Faces*, that blunderbuss placed in the hands of the semiliterate, getting hauled out to endorse their permanence as myths. And yes, of course at some level they do derive from medieval romances, Nordic warrior legends, and so on—as does Nazism, at least in the self-romanticizing aspect so vital to its sales pitch. Even so, Lucas's more immediate source, the pulp adventure story specifically tailored for adolescent males, didn't really emerge as a distinct literary genre until the latter part of the nineteenth century, when one of its cultural functions was to help mold European boys for their imperial mission and American ones for manifest destiny.

The reason that the durable ingredients of such stories don't strike us as sinister even today is simply that they *predate fascism*; they originated in an era when attitudes we'd later learn to call fascistic in other contexts seemed benign and indeed admirable. Even when the real thing reared its head in the '20s and '30s, any number of Western intellectuals—though few in the countries that were actually experiencing it—were rather taken with this bold stuff, most notoriously that sucker for drawing-room absolutism George Bernard Shaw; that it was hotly debated just proves that it hadn't yet been decisively judged evil, which indeed it wouldn't be until the outbreak of World War II. At the pop-culture level, the very name of Superman—dreamed up in 1938 by two bright Jewish kids, who presumably knew that his moniker was English for *Ubermensch*—is proof that, far from setting off alarm bells, concepts later tainted by their association with the Nazis were simply part and parcel of Western culture's available usages (and thrills). In fact, it could be argued that the release of *Star Wars* was a milestone in the process of cultural forgetfulness by which damaged goods become undamaged—that is, innocuous—again; only a few years earlier, people's awareness of the real-world connotations of its particular mythology would still have been too vivid for Lucas's idealization of righteous, ritualistic young Siegfrieds to be looked on all that kindly.

Particularly since *Star Wars* is a kids' movie, it's reasonable to wonder just how tainted those concepts actually are, or should be. (You know, sheesh—are you going to let Hitler ruin *everything*?) Even back in the '60s, when I was the approximate age of Lucas's original target audience, my friends and I always found being the Germans alluring in our World War II games, and I don't believe that made us wicked. At an even earlier age, I was cuckoo for Kipling's *The Jungle Book*, and only recognized decades later that I'd lapped up some of the damndest kiddie-book propaganda for subjugation to racial hierarchies ever written. But while that's turned my understanding of Mowgli and his four-footed sepoys more piquant, it hasn't made my affection for them—which is now, of course, affection for my own childhood—one whit less tranquil. On an adult level, if you've defended something like Madonna's "Justify My Love" by arguing that pop gives its audiences leeway to indulge sexual fantasies that they wouldn't dream of acting out in real life, it's hard not to concede that that should go for their political fantasies, too. No left-winger who loves John Wayne like I do should assume that there's necessarily a direct equivalence between the credos that thrill people in the dark and the ones they try to live by outside the theater. Try this as a syllogism: we live in a democracy, and movies are escapist. Doesn't it make sense that one of the things they offer us an escape from is democracy?

It's also undeniable that I would find the politics of *Star Wars* less off-putting if I responded to the movie with more delight at the level I'm supposed to, namely, entertainment. But I don't, probably reason enough—if they even need one—for fans to take everything else I say with about a pound of salt. It bored me half senseless the first time I saw it, on a double bill with *Barbarella* at the old St. Mark's Theater in New York; the friend who took me insisted that we sit through *Star Wars* first, since he knew that otherwise I'd split as soon as *Barbarella* was over. (He was right, and it pissed me off that he had my number.) Ever since, I've begrudged George Lucas all the time I've had to put in thinking about *Star Wars* and its progeny; as a movie critic, I can't help feeling that I've got better things to do. But—well, he won: I may have very little use for the *Star Wars* movies as movies, but their magnitude as a cultural phenomenon compels my reluctantly respectful fascination just the same.

The main reason I'll never be a fan, though, is just that Lucas strikes me as so fundamentally humorless. There's a lot of crowd-pleasing horsing around in the *Star Wars* movies, but few glimmers of real cleverness or wit. Audiences may think the byplay between R2-D2 and C-3PO is proof Noel Coward has nothing on us, but they dote on the dopey earnestness of the trilogy's overarching concept, even when they're perfectly aware it's dopey. The real test of humor is the role you let it play in what you take seriously, and Lucas's comedy passages are always ghettoized diversions. They never impinge on the solemnity of the thematic stuff about the Force—and the Dark Father, and yadda-yadda-yadda—and, for him, the act of filmmaking itself isn't exactly imbued with merriment. Or style either, but many fans who know that tend to feel a tolerant affection for Lucas's clumsiness. Recognizing how inane he can be is what humanizes him for them. Maybe he helped inaugurate the age of sleek, hi-tech special-effects spectaculars but, *The Phantom Menace* aside, people love the *Star Wars* movies for their *homeliness*—the clunky, straightforward, sophistication-allergic sincerity of it all.

Needless to say, that includes an allergy to political sophistication. It's worth emphasizing again that Lucas's relationship to his own material's dark side is unwitting, if not stubbornly ignorant.

Pleased though he may have been to learn that his tale fit Joseph Campbell's recipe for mythic alphabet soup, a thinker he isn't; indeeed, he actively mistrusts reflectiveness. If his actual political views remain gnomic, that's largely because politics are unimportant to him. The only overt allusion to current events in any *Star Wars* movie is a perfunctory gesture to conventional Hollywood liberalism; reflecting Bill Clinton's then recent impeachment crisis, *The Phantom Menace* finds room for a very silly pro-Clinton subplot that luckily goes by in an eyeblink. (It's damn near the only thing in that crawling movie that does.) Otherwise, though, Lucas's fundamental worldview apparently remains that of the Modesto shopkeeper he might well have become if he hadn't discovered movies—in which arena, of course, he's the most successful businessman-artist since Disney. Very little really matters to him except his own product, and like a good salesman, he believes in it absolutely.

Whether Lucas would find the kinship grating or gratifying (and who knows?), it's this combined know-nothingism and faith that gives him common ground with another great salesman, Ronald Reagan—who was also, of course, a fellow storyteller. Both, in their way, urged us to become as children again, and invested that condition with a moral superiority that more than made up for being uninformed. Melding tomorrow with a yesterday that never was, Lucas's invitation to the audience to return to the comforting simplicities of an earlier era of entertainment was as ideologically loaded as Reagan's summons to hark back to an earlier state of historical ignorance-as-bliss, because you can't uncritically revive the pulp narratives of another age without also replicating their values. Famously, Reagan once spoke wistfully of a time when "Americans didn't even know they had a racial problem"—meaning, of course, *white* Americans, since those of color had presumably been well posted on its existence since 1492. With the possible exception of David Lynch, who's like his twin brother gone bad, Lucas may be about the whitest—and most goyish—American filmmaker alive, and he's always balked at admitting that the fairy tales he loves have a racial problem, too.

It's a trickier one than it at first appears to be. Back in 1977, it missed the point to complain about the first *Star Wars* movie's all-vanilla human cast, and Lucas's stopgap attempt at a remedy—plunking Billy Dee Williams into *The Empire Strikes Back* and later Samuel L. Jackson into *The Phantom Menace* without ever finding much for either to do—was equally irrelevant. As I would bet everyone had intuitively grasped without articulating it, nonwhite characters had been depicted in the series from the start. It's just that they appeared as Wookiees, Ewoks, funny robots, Jawas, and so on, leading up to the ultimate insult of that calypso-spouting, pan-galactic Stepin Fetchit, Jar Jar Binks. Without seeming quite aware of what he was saying, Lucas once even talked up Chewbacca as a plug for multiculturalism (what was he, Canadian?). When you learn that the Jawas' twittering jabberwocky was actually doctored Swahili, you can't help wondering how this filmmaker can stay so blandly oblivious to the distasteful implications of what he's doing, if he really is.

All this goes back to Lucas's sources—the adolescent fables of an age when white superiority was taken for granted and swash-buckling adventure in exotic lands dramatized the imperial mission at its sexiest, a genre whose stereotypes got transplanted lock, stock, and barrel to sci-fi once all those H. Rider Haggard heroes started running short on places to romp here on earth. (As the inventor of both Tarzan and John-Carter-on-Mars, Edgar Rice Burroughs is an almost literally pivotal figure here.) Every sci-fi fan understands that depicting alien creatures on other planets is usually a way—conscious or not—of talking about alien peoples on our own, and the form is basically so open-ended that it can accommodate enlightened propaganda as easily as the benighted kind. After all, television's most lasting monument to the Great Society's liberal optimism is the original *Star Trek*, with its endless lobbying for multiculturalism and vision of a pan-galactic UN; that many Trekkies choose to identify more with Vulcans or even Klingons than their fellow earthlings is, in a way, Gene Roddenberry's ultimate triumph. Lucas, however, reverts to the most retrograde version of the fantasy; one type of relationship never featured in the *Star Wars* movies is nonhuman characters interacting with human ones as equals. From that hairy, seven-foot-tall Gunga Din Chewbacca to Yoda, the Jedi's answer to Jiminy Cricket, they're our heroes' adorable helpmeets and servants if friendly, and repulsive, comic grotesques or menacing, emotionless machines if not. (If you want to protest that Yoda is a superior being, not a lesser one, well—try to imagine him having a sex life. Try to imagine him up and deciding that he's got better things to do than dispense comically phrased fortune-cookie wisdom to young ofays.)

It suggests how ingrained this sense of hierarchy is that audiences respond to its "rightness" as the natural order of things without, presumably, realizing what they're responding to. Viewers without particular memories of Stepin Fetchit or Butterfly McQueen are probably serenely unaware of the offensive tradition that Jar Jar Binks revives. (Uh-uh: they hated Jar Jar for his own sake.) Modern moviegoers, being fortunately unfamiliar with what an old-fashioned anti-Semitic caricature looks like, undoubtedly don't recognize that *The Phantom Menace*'s grasping, mercenary junkyard trader is one. Since his own nostalgia, like Reagan's, is partly a rebellion against the critical spirit that insisted on looking behind such things, Lucas himself may not recognize it either. What helps him get away with reviving stereotypes like these is that he seems to relate to them purely as entertaining pop conventions, without the faintest notion of their import. Yet that's just why his unnerved inclusion of token African-American actors in the later *Star Wars* episodes is more a betrayal of his vision than the correction of a mere oversight. His cosmos's old-fashioned racial schema— equating white people with human beings, and depicting everybody else as Other—is in fact so organic to the concept that the presence of black faces in the human cast registers as, quite simply, an aesthetic flaw.

The blackest visage of all, of course, is Darth Vader's mask, and I don't think it's entirely coincidental that the villain's voice was contributed by James Earl Jones—a black actor so commanding that white Americans have actually felt most comfortable with him as a disembodied voice. In Lucas's sexless universe, Darth Vader is also something that only Han Solo, otherwise, is implicitly allowed to be, namely, virile; that's part of what makes him threatening, like King Kong. I think it's indisputable that, at some level, audiences did perceive Darth Vader as black. Wasn't that why there was such a sense of letdown when his features were finally revealed, as if Lucas had pulled a bait-and-switch by substituting some schlubby white actor for the imposing black man we knew was inside that helmet? America's racial pathology is such a stew that appeals to it don't need to be either conscious or coherent to resonate, and from this angle the fact that Darth Vader turns out to be Luke's father is less important than the way Luke experiences it as a taint. It's hard to suggest this at all without seeming to overstate it, but I can't help suspecting that part of what makes the whole Dark Father business powerful is the way we register it, subliminally, as a projection of what used to be Western culture's idea of the ultimate sexual horror: miscegenation. Lucas has certainly toyed with this elsewhere in the series; at the beginning of *Return of the Jedi*, when Princess Leia is in captivity, it's unmistakably the outer-space version of that classic darkest-Africa pulp fantasy: the white girl about to be despoiled by slobbering savages. Revealingly, the sequence is also the only time our heroine gets to exhibit any erotic allure—who'd have guessed that, under that bland pie-face, Carrie Fisher was pure hubba-hubba below the neck?

All the same, Lucas's great advantage over other would-be genre revivalists—that is, his fellow boomer film-school nebbishes, most of whom attempted at one time or another to make self-conscious pastiches of the films they'd loved in their youth—is that these throwbacks and reversions to primitive movie tropes never seem premeditated, much less arch. Programmatic he isn't, at least not in this series. It's interesting that, despite their huge popularity at the time, the Indiana Jones movies haven't retained anything like the hold the *Star Wars* trilogy has on the public's affection, perhaps because—was this Spielberg's influence?—their old-timey thrills do seem mechanically contrived. But Lucas's ace in the hole is that he's suggestible, not calculating, and his almost eerie absence of preconceptions—which is what he shares with David Lynch—is the most interesting thing about him. Before he dreamed up Luke Skywalker, he was on board at one point to direct *Apocalypse Now*, and what drew him to the material was fascination with the idea of a tiny country bringing a superpower to its knees. If this rings a bell for *Star Wars* fans, it should; the Ewoks are the oddest cinematic tribute that the Vietcong are ever likely to get.

Instead, needless to say, *Apocalypse Now* ended up being directed by Francis Ford Coppola, whose complex relationship to his onetime protégé—half the hare and the tortoise, and half Mozart and Salieri playing musical chairs—is likely to end up as the richest moveable feast for budding dissertation writers since Hemingway and Fitzgerald. Meanwhile, ironically enough, *Star Wars* and its sequels became Hollywood's metaphorical cure for America's post-Vietnam trauma, turning Coppola's (willfully) tormented reexamination of the conflict into an anachronism by the time it appeared. Not long afterward, Reagan entered the White House, holding out the heartening promise that the simpleminded Manichaeanism of Lucas's imaginary universe wasn't just fit for fantasy, but a perfectly valid approach to real-world problems.

One obvious reason that *Star Wars* chimes so well with Reaganism is that, like Lucas, Reagan got most of his ideas about the world from old movies. In their separate realms, though, they both also expressed one of this country's most cherished conceptions of itself, benignly endorsing American exceptionalism in all its ahistorical innocence and sense of virtuous, sanctified mission. Among resonances closer to home, while the Jedi may be rebels, they're also *conservative* underdogs; they aren't fighting to bring about a new order, but to restore an old one, making them far more palatable to mainstream Americans than revolutionaries would be. The conviction that they were on a mission to wrest the country back from people who had traduced it was what made Reaganism a romantic cause to its adherents, too; that was why they never considered themselves radicals.

It's as a fairy-tale projection of how Americans view the world and their own role in it that *Star Wars* is most fascinating. Lucas invents other cultures, but, partly because his imagination doesn't exactly thrive on details, he's remarkably uninterested in making them seem valid or organic. He just wants them to be picturesque—either cute or frightening. He's equally indifferent when it comes to getting us to feel any compassion for the Empire's victims; it's as if that would just be a distraction from his heroes' gallantry, rather than helping to motivate it. When a whole planet gets destroyed, it's with nary a hint of death or suffering—which, right, would only upset the kiddies. But would at least a hint that they *ought* to find the sight upsetting really come amiss? The galaxy's only function seems to be to provide an arena for righteous derring-do, and its nonhuman inhabitants are, first and foremost, disposable—conveniences, but never characters.

If American audiences don't find this bothersome, that's because they find it natural—or did, until September 11, 2001, jolted us out of our tendency to see the rest of the world as little more than a theme park. But these jolts have never been permanent. *Star Wars* is a perfect fable for America's sense of its own goodness, but it also shows how unreflective that sense can be.

A BIG DUMB MOVIE
ABOUT SPACE WIZARDS:
Struggling to Cope with *The Phantom Menace*

TODD HANSON

Go ahead and make fun of me all you want, I've heard it all before. But here's the thing:

We waited a good half our lives for it to come out, and when it did, it was as if the destructive power of a fully operational battle station had been unleashed on the childhood hopes and dreams, accumulated over more than two decades of unwillingly delayed gratification, of pretty much a whole generation (and yes, I realize how pretentious those five words sound in this context, but seriously, I mean it—*pretty much a whole generation*, or at least a particular sociocultural subset sizable enough to constitute a really, really big chunk of one)—shot down like a bullseyed womp rat back in Beggar's Canyon back home; sliced open like the stinking underbelly of a frostbite-eviscerated tauntaun in the vast and unforgiving Hoth tundra; exploded into a trillion shimmering fragments of rubble and debris in the skies over the Forest Moon of Endor or the (similarly forested) Fourth Moon of Yavin.

Except that it wasn't: Although one cannot help but be drawn to such bombastic and overblown metaphors to describe, looking back dazed and bewildered on the experience, what the hell exactly happened, in truth there was nothing dramatic or sensational about it. Instead, what it evoked were far less interesting childhood memories: standing for forty-five minutes, wondering what to do, in a parking lot outside of a locked grade school, because your big sister forgot to pick you up after band practice; sitting through the crushing boredom of Vacation Church School on a Saturday morning while knowing that each excruciating minute you were there you were missing Captain Kool and the Kongs on the *Kroft SuperShow*; or wanting to sneak out back and have your first cigarette with the Ozzy-worshiping lowlifes from shop class but having instead to listen to your toupeed English teacher drone on about T. S. Eliot's point in saying "this is the way the world ends / not with a bang but a whimper."

The Inevitable Anticlimax: It's an old story. The eventual fall from an ecstatic flight into escapism back to the mundanity of real life. There's nothing surprising about that—it happens, literally, all the time, by which I mean to say *every* time: every single escapist daydream, since Cro-Magnons first dreamed up names for the people whose shapes they saw in the stars and made up stories about the wars these gods fought with one another in the heavens, has ended the exact same way—not with bang, but a whimper. This one hurt, though. This one hit us where we lived (or wished we did)—sure, it was underwhelming, but that word doesn't even come close to conveying what we're talking about here because, for most people who saw it, it was underwhelming *in the extreme*, if such an oxymoronic phrase can even be said to make any sense at all. And it wasn't just the hard-core geeks who reacted this way, either (although they, poor souls, were the hardest hit, and as of this writing, almost three years since it happened, it still looks as if many of them will never recover, sitting motionless in their parents' basements, staring mournfully at their vast collections of R5-D4 and Dewback-Mounted Desert Stormtrooper figures with blank, wounded expressions, wondering what it all *means* anymore), but the regular normal-person populace as well: conditioned by months of hype and speculation and Taco Bell promotions and all the rest of the Vast Insidious Machineries of Consumerism to expect nothing less than some messianic Second Coming, however—many millions of them stood up from their overpriced seats in the multiplex as the lights came up on opening weekend and said to each other, "It was okay, I guess, but . . . uh . . . that's it?"

Yep, that was it all right: despite all the goings-on-and-on about the "magic" and "wizardry" of the Vaunted Auteur's "visionary creative genius" and what-have-you, at the end of the day what *Star Wars Episode I: The Phantom Menace* all came down to was a Big Dumb Movie About Space Wizards, for what it's worth, and nothing more.

It may seem silly (and rightly so, I suppose—hey, don't ask me to intellectually justify any of this, because, efforts of countless sociocultural commentators to the contrary notwithstanding, if you ask me, the whole concept of approaching the *Star Wars* phenomenon from an "intellectual" standpoint still strikes me as barking up the wrong tree) that the spectacularly underspectacular failure of *The Phantom Menace* to achieve the same hold on the public imagination as the films it prequeled should be seen as some sort of Significant Cultural Event. I guess that's fair. Still and all, though, it was one, and why exactly this should be the case is a matter that takes some explaining, and indeed making sense of *The Phantom Menace* is a much more complicated Gordian (or should I say Mandalorian?) knot than one would at first think a Big Dumb Movie About Space Wizards would have any right to be.

It's sort of embarrassing to admit this, but the fact of the matter is that the release of *Star Wars Episode I* was, for me, a profoundly personal sort of Really Big Deal that set off a full-blown shitstorm in my head, starting well before the film even came out and which has really yet to subside to this day. And I wasn't alone in this: everybody who bought into the prerelease excitement (and let's face it, pretty much everybody did, even the most cynical and media-weary members of a generation conditioned by thirty-plus years of mass media hoo-ha to react with smart-ass dismissal to any sort of Giant Mainstream Media Event at all, people normally impervious to such mass manipulation from the marketplace, who actually *pride* themselves in not caring about stuff they're told to want to consume) felt like they got took. Different people reacted differently to the feeling, but everybody felt it. The way I personally dealt with this humiliation (and, believe me, the endless ribbing I took from friends and loved ones continues unabated, even now, three years later) may not be a very pretty picture, but if nothing else, it does, hopefully anyway, make for a funny story at my own expense.

Go ahead and make fun of me all you want, but for me, grappling with *Star Wars Episode I: The Phantom Menace* involves trying to get at the heart of some really bizarre shit.

Shit, *to wit* (and these are just a few of the more obvious questions, off the top of my head):

1. Jesus, how bad could this movie possibly be anyway?
2. Man, weren't those first ones great, though?
3. Why, then, wasn't this one?
4. If it's so bad, why does everybody keep going to see it?
5. Why would anybody even care about these questions in the first place anyhow?
6. What the hell is the deal with those Japanese accents?
7. If, in the entire history of cinematic vocabulary, there had never before existed any such thing as a Tragicomic Bumbling Space Frog Archetype, why the fuck would anybody, least of all a supposed Vaunted Auteur whose visionary creative genius and deep insight into Joseph Campbell's *Power of Myth* had made a profound impact on pretty much a whole generation, ever, ever want to create one?
8. And why, in God's name, would a thirty-year-old, reasonably intelligent adult want to walk around in public dressed in the robes of a Jedi Knight?

We may never know the answers to these questions.

Let me get one thing straight, right off the bat here, right now: I am not a *Star Wars* geek. Yeah, yeah, I know—you think I doth protest too much—but honestly, for me, *Star Wars* appreciation is not some kind of lifestyle, the way it is for the sort of person who actually sits down with another human being to debate issues like whether or not *Slave 1* could outrace the *Millennium Falcon* in a fair fight, or the backstories of Admiral Piett and General Veers, or whether or not the digestive tract of an asteroid-belt-dwelling Giant Space Worm would have Earth-type gravity so that people who accidentally flew into it thinking it was just a cave could walk around inside it without knowing they were not actually in a cave at all but were, rather, inside an asteroid-belt-dwelling Giant Space Worm instead. I do not consider any of these things even remotely important at all. God bless them, but to me, all the *Star Wars* geeks are committing the same essential error as those intellectual socio-cultural commentators that I would argue are barking up the wrong tree—that is, they are taking all of this Space Opera Non-sense way, way too seriously. No, I am not a *Star Wars* geek, but I do understand them, because I have a lot of *Star Wars* geek friends.

Not to put too fine a point on it, the apoplexy of these people in the face of the release of *Episode I* was truly a sight to behold. They were stunned, then shocked, then stunned again at how unthink-able it was that the movie was something less than what they'd expected. They were gap-mouthed with incredulity. One such friend of mine, Vebber, was willing (this is not a joke) to pay One Thousand Actual U.S. Dollars (he writes for TV, so he can afford to do stuff like that) for the privilege of seeing the film three days early, that's how excited he was. (The screening was a charity event, and when I told him that if nothing else, at least the money was going for a good cause, he was silent, and when I asked him what the cause was, he said, "I have no idea. Probably crack babies or something. What do I care?") He actually told me he was afraid he might wet his pants when the film started, and knowing him very well, I believed it. Though Vebber didn't end up seeing this screening after all (pitilessly leaving, presumably, the crack babies to their own devices), his equally rabid friend Mark did get to one of the advance showings (Mark is I guess what you'd call a

Professional Science Fiction Fan Community Luminary—I believe he was once described in print as "one of the world's leading Treksperts"—I didn't even know that was a word—and so probably has as much loyalty to the overall concept of Space Opera Nonsense as any man alive), and he was so incensed, so outraged, that he stormed out afterward shouting angry warnings to the people waiting in line for the next screening. As they yelled at him not to give anything away, and the die-hard loyalists in the crowd remained rooted in denial, insisting that he could not possibly be right, he must have looked like a crazed doomsday prophet running amok in the streets, like Kevin McCarthy in that incredible scene at the end of the original *Invasion of the Body Snatchers*. "It's terrible!" he shouted in a panic, his entire worldview, he would later say, collapsing around him. "It's absolutely terrible!"

And it really just sort of undeniably is.

The best description I ever heard of why was from that same guy, Mark, who said, "Think of it from a storytelling perspective. Instead of a mythological saga of good versus evil, almost all of the plot is about two guys whose spaceship breaks down and they need to get parts to repair it," and he is completely correct. The script is, to put it baldly, totally fucked. The epic elements at the beginning and end—an invasion of a virtuous planet by a corrupt merchant class, a gigantic, Kurosawa-style battle between an underdog insurrection and a relentless mechanized army they cannot possibly defeat, a noble and idealistic young queen, interplanetary politics on a grand scale, the resurrection of the ancient and unspeakable evil along with a quasi-Messianic saga of biblical import, as well as a full-blown space-navy battle and, of course, the chance to see the once-great Jedi Knights, wiped out into extinction by the start of *Episode IV* back in 1977, in all their antediluvian glory—are inexplicably rushed through with palpable impatience, while the film's bloated middle section is as saggy and ponderous as Lucas's own middle-aged billionaire gut must surely by now be.

The sheer incompetence of the pacing and structure is nothing short of bewildering, and even simple, obvious things that could have been done to even the structure along are just bypassed, almost as if Lucas had chosen to make the film appear intentionally amateurish. Take, for example, Sith lord Darth Maul's first attempted attack on the principals. We get only a few shots of what is apparently supposed to consist of menace and suspense as he lands on Tatooine and begins to hunt the Jedis there with probe droids—I don't believe I'm exaggerating when I say that there have been episodes of TV's *The Equalizer* that contained more ominous buildup than Lucas manages to achieve with these barely-there sequences. Then, when he does finally attack, the entire battle between him and the Jedi master Qui-Gon Jinn lasts all of thirty or so seconds. Jesus, you want to yell at the screen, why even bother setting up the cameras for a lightsaber battle if you're only going to have it last less than a minute? Might as well just include thirty more seconds of tedious pans across the Tunisian desert and shave a couple of million dollars off the budget, making it possible to manufacture several hundred thousand additional toys.

Another great example of this confusing inattention to detail is the droid ships that we see in the Trade Federation hangar bay in the beginning scene, pictured walking around on four legs and swiveling their elongated heads around ominously to look at the landing ambassador's ship as Obi-Wan and Qui-Gon arrive. Apparently—not that you'd know this by watching the film—these four-legged droids fold up into planes and are the same things that we later see the Naboo fighter pilots dogfighting with at the end. Lucas bothered to have the things designed, and he must have decided to film that introductory establishing shot of them—it's in the final edit of the film, after all—so why not include even one simple example of them folding up so the audience can realize what's going on? It's just ridiculous, and there's no explanation ever offered as to why we don't see them again until they're in midair.

Watching these kinds of glaringly obvious mistakes makes it seem like the filmmakers weren't even bothering to try—the whole thing starts to scan like a term paper written at the last minute by a drunk frat guy pulling a halfhearted all-nighter. It's especially hard to take when juxtaposed with the seeming hours of publicity footage of Lucas droning on and on about why he made this choice or that in the creative process of forming and molding his unique vision to the screen. Who does he think he's fooling, one asks? Is he completely delusional? What's with all the auteur-talk when the finished product appears to be slapped together at the last minute? No wonder the nerds' worldviews started to crack.

Watching this stuff, obsessing over it during that odd summer of 1999, I kept assuming that they'd simply screwed up the editing somehow, and that the film might someday be returned to its original state by simply reinserting some of these sequences later on. Sadly, one look at the extra scenes included in the DVD release reveals that this is not the case. Take the example of the movie's much-rumored Greedo-wrestling-with-Anakin scene, in which Qui-Gon catches the two youngsters scuffling in the street and then upbraids Anakin for fighting. The sequence is obviously missing because it's where Anakin gets the scratch that Qui-Gon later gets the blood sample from that reveals the child's abnormally high midichlorian levels. The nerd word on the street was that this scene had Qui-Gon telling Anakin "You must learn to control your anger!" which would make perfect narrative sense as foreshadowing of the boy's later descent into evil and conversion to the dark side of the Force. As it turns out, though, there's nothing remotely like it in the scene! It's enough to make the midichlorians in anyone's blood boil just thinking about it—that's how frustrating it is.

There are many theories about why the second *Star Wars* movie Lucas directed compares so poorly to the first one; mine is that he really needs a good editor, and his first one—his now-ex-wife, Marcia Lucas, by all reports one of the finest in the business—whose cutaways, timing, and deft touch with pacing and suspense lent so much of the excitement to the original, isn't with him (or, in fact, the business) anymore. But like I said, it doesn't make sense to approach this film from an academic standpoint, so these observations are all really beside the point.

Question: How hard can it be to make a Big Dumb Movie About Space Wizards and have it turn it out reasonably well? After all, it's not as if there are a lot of subtle character shadings to flesh out—if you want to establish that some guy is evil, all you've got to do is paint his head an abstract pattern of red and black and put horns on his head.

So why did everybody end up feeling so let down by this thing, this by all accounts what should have been simple, straightforward (albeit bombastic, huge, and overblown, but still) piece of unambitiously lowbrow entertainment? Especially when they were all so willing to like it, even to the point, for some, of actually dressing up like a Jedi Knight, if you can believe it?

Why would anybody do anything that stupid? I mean, what kind of a complete moron would a person have to be?

The answer to that question—why would anybody care that much in the first place—is really pretty simple (and for those of you who were there, I'm sure I don't even need to explain) and it's this: for anyone who saw it, as a little kid, growing up in 1977 suburban America, *Star Wars* was—indisputably, without question—the Coolest Thing They Had Ever Seen in Their Entire Life So Far. Nothing else that came before it—I mean nothing—prepared us, going into those darkened theaters with our dads, for the full-on, go-for-broke, all-out Mind-Blowing we were about to receive. For kids of that time, raised as we all were (and our parents too, and as all subsequent generations of suburban Americans have been as well) on the concept of consumer entertainment as the whole raison d'être of your little-kid-existence (I'm talking here about paging through the Sears Catalog's pre-Christmas edition, the Sears Wish Book I believe it was actually called, and gazing lustfully at the various G.I. Joe figures, knowing that if only you could somehow get them all, your life would be complete; watching Godzilla movies or the hammy Adam West version of *Batman* on TV after school and knowing that you were set for hours of pure bliss because the *Spider-Man* cartoon was coming on next, and then *Prince Planet*, and then *Speed Racer*, watching the commercials for multicolored plastic Whammo! Products that parents hooked garden hoses up to and which then spun wildly around and thinking *if only I had that*; watching the adults get plastered and play Jarts in the backyard and thinking *man those things are so neato*—at least for those of us who didn't *die* that way; just being so spaced out on the sheer whiz-bang wonderment of it all—on what I would, if I wanted to get a lot more pretentious here than I actually do, call by French Situationist Guy Debord's term the society of the spectacle—that you actually thought all those shitty, shitty Scooby-Doo-derivative-mystery-solving-kids-plus-cartoon-mascot cartoons like *Goober and the Ghost Chasers* or *Captain Caveman and the Teen Angels*, for cryin' out loud, were cool), well, in that environment, when *Star Wars* came out, it was the equivalent of some sort of SALT II–era thermonuclear weapons (which you'd perhaps just begun to get the tiniest clue about but which would occupy a whole lot of mental space in your life later on) having gone off in your head.

I was born in the autumn of that head-spinning year 1968, the year that everything went to hell, and as it turns out it was a great time to be born, because it meant that I was exactly eight years old going nine in the summer of 1977—really just the exact perfect age to be when *Star Wars* came out. It was as plain as day, a truism that didn't need to be justified, an axiomatic *fact of nature*, that *Star Wars* was better than anything else you'd previously encountered. It was just *obvious*, kids didn't even need to say it to each other: it was just Known, it was Understood. And not just better, but way better: ten, twenty times cooler than whatever the last coolest thing we'd ever seen had been. Not even the really, really great stuff we'd seen and experienced—the very best of it, like, say, the WGN-TV five-day "Gorilla Thrilla Week" lineup of *King Kong, Son of Kong, Mighty Joe Young, King Kong Versus Godzilla*, and the original *Planet of the Apes* on the after-school 3:30 movie—could compare. It dwarfed whatever it was it had put into second place—you couldn't even *see* second place. Second place was somewhere off the bottom of the page.

I had one of those stupid cardboard-stand things that Mattel made available for the Christmas shopping season that you had to wait several months to get the action figures to go with because they didn't have the toys made yet—still perhaps the record holder for most ludicrous consumer frenzy item ever—and it was the best gift I got that year and maybe even ever, even though it was, literally, nothing. I copied terrible versions of the Ralph McQuarrie production drawings from *The Star Wars Sketchbook* onto huge sheets of construction paper in my room and hung them on my walls—what a cool book that thing was (man, I wish I still had it, but it eventually became a pile of loose papers falling out of a collapsed binding after too many page-throughs—I loved that book so much I physically destroyed it with love). I had never shown any interest in baseball cards but I collected with relish all sixty-three of the initial *Star Wars* bubblegum cards, the ones with the light blue borders, and it took me a whole summer of intense effort to get the complete set (and no, I don't have that anymore, either).

So no I'm not a *Star Wars* geek, at least not anymore I'm not, but I was then—if you define the term "*Star Wars* geek" as "person for whom *Star Wars* is so ridiculously cool that it's become a central aspect of their existence," which is what most people, I assume, take it to mean. But the thing is: so was *everyone*—every single last eight-year-old I knew of, to greater or lesser degree. There weren't any *Star Wars* geeks back then because in 1977, the words "*Star Wars* geek" and "little kid" meant the exact same thing. For anyone who grew up at the right time for it, the validity, power, and sheer significance of *Star Wars* had a kind of emotional undeniability that bypassed the intellect and defied any need for rational or analytical explanation: That's the reason there are so many *Star Wars* geeks today (and that I know so many of them, and that I know you do, too)—they remain transfixed, even now, well into their thirties, all over the place, dotting the landscape; the same reason that kids (if they had the means) went to see it dozens of times that summer (like the samizdat cartridge in *Infinite Jest*, it was so entertaining that it inspired the immediate desire to see it again); that's why Alec Empire, founder of the Berlin digital hard-core scene and frontman of the band Atari Teenage Riot, has an entire instrumental album called *Generation Star Wars*. It was an a priori given in your life. That's the reason all this stuff means so much to the people for whom it means so much.

It may sound ludicrous that a childhood-defining experience would come out of something as banal and shallow as our base consumer culture, but we were growing up in a base consumer culture, so it actually makes sense. Waiting for the stupid little Luke and Leia and Darth and the other toys to finally show up in the mail was an eternity. But that was nothing compared to that other, more impossible eternity, the one I just couldn't wrap my head around, because it was too big: I had read (and saved, and read again) the *Time* magazine article about George Lucas's future plans (I no longer remember when this was, it may have been as late as 1980, but I'm thinking it was more like 1978) and it said there was not only going to be *a* sequel, there were going to be *nine* films . . . nine! . . . and after the first three, there would be three that took place a generation earlier . . . and I thought to myself, sitting in my little kid room alone, *oh my God, someday I'm going to see a movie with Obi-Wan as a young Jedi, and the story of Luke's fighter pilot* father, *the one who died before he ever knew him, and I'll see the Clone Wars, with my own eyes. But its not going to come out for years and years and* years, *so long that, God, though I can't even imagine this yet, I might even be an* adult *by then.*

(And hey, what happened to that smarmy comedic tone, funnyman? How did this smart-ass essay get so maudlin and sentimental all of a sudden? Could it be that you were actually writing, for a second there, *without irony?*)

Go ahead and make fun of me all you want, but man, I gotta tell you, it freaks me out to even think about this, even now.

★ ★ ★

I finally did get those stupid toys in the mail (with the lightsabers that went up the inside of the arms—stupid!) but when I did get them, I felt the first twinge of what would eventually become a familiar feeling: the Inevitable Anticlimax. They were cool, obviously, but they somehow didn't feel like they'd been worth the wait. They couldn't have been; for little kids, a few months' wait means a huge percentage of their conscious life. I remember the chill I felt in my bones when I opened up my first pack of the new, second series of *Star Wars* cards, the ones with the red borders, and I realized that I was looking at number 237, and knew that there was no way I could ever possibly get all of these; it had taken me forever just to get the first sixty-three.

Thus began what would become a lifetime of disillusionment and disappointment with the aforementioned Vast Insidious Machineries of Consumerism. We're all familiar with this tired refrain by now—that cynical awareness of the Big Lie has become emblematic of, again, pretty much a whole generation, and the sociocultural commentators say that The Ironic Voice has become the Dominant Mode of Cultural Discourse, and blah blah blah, and wow, they even go so far as to call this the Age of Irony (ooooh!)— the Jaded Age. You've heard all this before so there's no need to go into it; you know what I'm talking about. I myself have been plugging away in the comedy mines writing in The Ironic Voice for over a decade (and now, after twelve years, and even I can hardly believe this myself some days, I even make a *living* doing it) and the point being that at some stage *Star Wars* got replaced as the Official Touchstone of a Generation, as everybody with even half a clue knows, by Merrill Markoe and David Letterman and their mid-'80s paradigm-shifter *Late Night With* etc., and pretty soon everybody was thumbing their nose at the Vast Insidious Machineries of Consumerism (even the people, like Letterman, who were/are *inside* same), and where does that leave the thrilled little kid in his room, waiting for the Clone Wars movies to finally come out in twenty years?

You didn't exactly have to be a rocket scientist to figure out what was going to happen. As soon as the publicity engines started cranking out the news that *The Phantom Menace* was going to come out, for real this time, that it was actually being made (it had been such a long delay since the third sequel that most of us had given up on ever seeing it at all), I knew two things straight off: first, that this movie's release was going to be the biggest thing to come down the pike since, well, ever. And second: everybody was going to hate it.

How could they not? There was no way any *Star Wars* prequel could possibly live up to their expectations, and besides, the whole Big Prerelease Merchandise Roll-Out phenomenon, which had seemed so significant, so full of gravitas and awesome promise and all of that, when it was established by the first two sequels in '80 and '83, had become so commonplace that everything from That Forgotten Thing Where Jamie Lee Curtis Fights a Robot on a Boat to That One Michael Crichton Movie with the Super-Intelligent Apes That Nobody Went to See had a whole slew of consumer products to go with them (and yes, they did make action figures for those films, and the A-V Club editors at *The Onion*, proud own-ers of what must be by this point one of the most impressive collections of Extremely Lame Promotional Kitsch-Objects ever assembled in North America, have the little plastic Donald Suther-land as Half-Human/Half-Robot and Super-Intelliegent Talking Gorilla with Detachable Cyber-Backpack dolls to prove it). Not only were people no longer impressed by that sort of thing, they had actually grown to despise it with a passion. Still, for this one exception, people forgave the flash flood of Lucasfilm-franchised products that swamped retailers coast to coast—it seemed like *Star Wars* had, in some way, sort of *earned* it—and waited in line just to get the products, let alone see the actual film. Yet I knew in the long run it wouldn't work, and all those poor schmucks who bought all four covers of the hardcover edition of the novelization (I mean, really. Come on, guys. Summon up a little dignity.) would end up angry and hurt and disappointed—to use a word Christian Gore, cult filmmaker, editor of *Film Threat*, and complete *Star Wars* nut, would eventually use in a vicious (and accurate) attack shortly after the film's release, *betrayed*. People actually felt personally betrayed, if you can imagine it, by *The Phantom Menace*, and whatever else might be said about that Jamie Lee Curtis/Robot/Boat movie, at least nobody ever accused it of betrayal.

And so, as the release date loomed closer and closer and the attendant anticipatory furor steadily built, I thought to myself, with increasing frustration: what to do about *The Phantom Menace* menace? It was clear that a gigantic, even epic, letdown was on the horizon; that there was no way that something as old-fashioned, as willingly, gleefully even, nonironic as a new *Star Wars* movie would match the late-'90s atmosphere of hypercritical, media-savvy, self-aware yadda yadda yadda; that there would be no place for Space Opera Nonsense in the embittered zeitgeist of the Jaded Age. What had, in 1977, been an a priori given of Cool would become, in 1999, an equivalent a priori given of Anticool. What I finally decided (after what, okay, I'll admit, was probably way too much thinking—go ahead, make fun of me) was this:

I constructed an argument that held it didn't make any sense— that it was beside the point—to view the prerelease hype, or the subsequent letdown, or even the content of the upcoming film itself, with any sort of ironic distance or critical awareness at all. In other words, it didn't matter that Lucas was only going to give us a Big Dumb Movie About Space Wizards, because *that's all he ever wanted to give us in the first place*. In other words, it seemed stupid to let my hypercritical self-awareness blah blah blah get in the way of my having a good time. That's probably not such good advice all the time, because after all, I could make that same argument about the Jamie Lee Curtis/Robot/Boat movie, and everything else on the big empty plate the Vast Insidious Machineries of Consumerism keep serving up time and time again, and I'd be a simp to do so. But this case was different. I decided I was going all-out for this one— despite the palpably looming Inevitable Anticlimax I was going to cast caution to the wind, leap willfully into the abyss, and fully Geek Out for *The Phantom Menace*. In other words, like one of those full-grown men dressed up, in public, like a freakin' Jedi Knight, for crying out loud, I decided to *commit*.

And so that's what I did. I'll probably never be allowed to live it down for as long as I live.

This decision—embarrassing as it may have been and as dumb as it made me look in front of my friends, who naturally hated the film, and who, again naturally, thought I was out of my mind for continuing to insist, against all logic, that it was cool—was nevertheless sound, and I stand by it. The reasoning was simple: there's nothing wrong with a Big Dumb Movie About Space Wizards, even if it's a bad movie, because its supposed to be that way—because it's like that *on purpose*. Why was the original *Star Wars* so great in the first place? Because of the script, or the mechanics of the plot, or Marcia Lucas's editing? We were kids, for chrissakes, we weren't film buffs . . . there was, and there *still* is, no *point* in analyzing the movie on the basis of its merits *as a film*. The reason it was so great was that it had a Pirate in it, and a Princess, and Gunslingers, and WWII-movie-style Fighter Plane Dogfights, and yes, Space Wizards. You want to judge the original *Star Wars* movies on their merits as actual films, you run into a wall really quick—yes, they are awesome movies, without question, no argument there, but don't kid yourself that they somehow aren't *bad* movies as well. Think about it: the just-ludicrous-beyond-belief *lame* humor (come on, that corny-ass "Nerf herder" banter between Han and Leia where she calls him a whole string of insulting adjectives, one of which is "scruffy-looking," and then he responds with "who's scruffy-looking?" Puh-leeze!), the ham-handed, plothole-ridden storytelling (oh, yeah, Luke gets all his Jedi training from Yoda in parallel-time with the *Millennium Falcon*'s extended chase scene to Bespin? What, were they chased for months, or did he get trained in hours?), the terrible, terrible acting (as Pauline Kael said in her 1977 review of the original, "you never catch the actors acting badly deliberately, they just *seem* to be bad actors"), the cloying cuteness (I don't even want to go into this one), and on and on ad nauseam.

The fact is, *all* the arguments that stand against *The Phantom Menace* (and Lord knows, there are many) can be made against any one of the original films, but there's no reason to make them, because that would be *beside the whole friggin' point of the movies in the first place*, which is that Lucas, after doing his Orwellian-Dystopia Serious Statement About Society Movie just out of film school (*THX-1138*, which is a *great* Orwellian-Dystopia Serious Statement About Society Movie, by the way) and his subsequent Retro-Adolescent Coming-of-Age Movie (*American Graffiti*, which is not as good as *THX-1138* but is a pretty great Retro-Adolescent Coming-of-Age Movie nonetheless, especially in the subplot about trying to find Wolfman Jack), was tired of all this artistic filmic film-talk and was trying to get back to the whole reason he fell in love with the movies to begin with: yes, Space Opera Nonsense, in the form of the Flash Gordon and Buck Rogers and *Tom Corbett Space Cadet* serials *he* loved when *he* was a little kid, and have you ever seen one of *those* things? They're *terrible!* It doesn't matter though, because they're not supposed to not be terrible, they're just supposed to be cool. And guess what? They are, and Lucas doesn't need to justify this: for him, it is just Known.

That's why when Lucas, in interviews, dismisses the criticisms of *The Phantom Menace* (and surely the same criticisms are on the horizon for *Attack of the Clones*, and he will no doubt have the same reaction then) by saying he doesn't care, they said the same things about all the other movies too, well, it may seem as if he could not possibly be any further out to lunch, but the thing is, get this: he's not delusional, he's not lying, and he's not just making a misguided attempt to rationalize his way out of admitting he fucked up, because, as hard as it may be to believe, *he's not wrong*. He's absolutely correct in dismissing his critics, because they did say all those things about the original films, and the whole Inevitable Anticlimax notwithstanding, Lucas was right!

So, after mulling all of these contradictions over in my mind for the few years it took between Lucasfilm announcing the pre-production of the megaprequels and finally releasing *Episode I*, I arrived at the conclusion that the proper response to the question on everybody's lips—"Yeah, I can't wait, but what if it's bad?"—was (and this was my Official Stated Position on the matter):

"I don't care how bad it turns out to be. I've been waiting to see it since I was eight, and as long as it has Space Wizards in it, I'm going to love this movie with all my heart."

Because ultimately, to the little kid in his room, waiting for the Clone Wars movies to come out in twenty years was just about as elusive a fantasy as actually *being* a Pirate, or a Princess, or a Cowboy, or a Space Wizard, it was just about equally removed from reality. Only there was a difference: unlike all those other childhood fantasies (who among us ever did get to really *be* a Pirate, or a Princess, or a Cowboy, when we grew up?) the getting-to-finally-see-the-Clone-Wars fantasy, as it turned out, was something that *was actually going to come true.*

At least, that's what I convinced myself of in the spring of 1999. How, after all this thinking about what to do, I somehow ended up talking myself into the extremely embarrassing position of having to defend what just about everybody on Earth has by now dismissed as one of the worst movies ever made, I may never fully understand. Looking back on it now, I realize I dealt with the problem like the guy in *The Caine Mutiny* who aims the ship directly at the heart of the hurricane. Was I right to do what I did? Well, the argument seemed sound at the time, and yes, I stuck to my guns on it. At least give me credit for that, even if it did get me ending up looking about as stupid as, um, er, well, as one of those full-grown men dressed up like a Jedi Knight. I've got to admit though, even with a fully thought-out defense ahead of time, the reality of the Inevitable Anticlimax strained the credibility of my position way, way beyond even the worst of my worst-case scenario predictions. I guess if one is foolhardy enough to try and pit himself against an entire zeitgeist like that, it's only to be expected that you're gonna get your ass kicked—it's sort of a Captain Ahab versus the Whale That Cannot Be Defeated Because It Symbolizes Nature situation—but as prepared as I was to defend my decision, even I had a hard time dealing with the aftermath once I saw a twenty-five-foot moving and talking image of Jar Jar fucking Binks for the first time.

Though it seems clear that no discussion of *The Phantom Menace* would be complete without it, I hesitate to even mention the name Jar Jar Binks at all, if only out of an overwhelming desire on my part to never again, for the rest of my life, have to think about the fact that he exists. But, of course he does, and there is nothing any of us can do to change that. He is part of the permanent record of our culture now, and it may be decades before his grinning, hideous visage is erased from the collective unconsciousness. What sadistic fever-dream dredged him up from Lucas's mind to be created is thankfully beyond the power of any but the Vaunted Auteur himself to know. The larger question of why anyone would want to go that extra step and actually unleash this behemoth upon an unsuspecting and trusting public is beyond all rational consideration.

Amazingly, not only does Lucas *not admit to this day* that Jar Jar Binks is, to put it in the most polite possible terms, the shall we say weakest element of the first *Star Wars* episode, he goes on, unbelievably, to actually cite Jar Jar as the one thing that he is the *most proud of* in the whole film. "Why?" you ask, aghast? Because he is the first completely digital construct ever to appear as a main character in a major motion picture, and as such, he represents (I'm saying that Lucas thinks this, not me) the most significant contribution that Lucas has yet made to the craft of filmmaking, the highest technical achievement so far, the greatest innovation: His Proudest Moment.

Well, I guess Lucas can go ahead and continue thinking that if he wants. Me, myself personally, I've typed the name "Jar Jar Binks" only three times so far (four counting that last one) and I've already done it more times than I can bear. Therefore, I will henceforth refer to him instead only as He Who Shall Not Be Named (HWSNBN for short). Why the people at Lucasfilm felt they needed a commercially accessible, marketable character like HWSNBN in the movie, presumably for the really small, small kids—like age two, maybe—to relate to, I have no idea: they already had two Rosencrantz and Guildenstern comic relief characters, the droids, and in case they were worried about not hitting the Teletubbies crowd, maybe somebody could have reminded them that one of these droids already speaks in bip-bop-beep baby talk. Ultimately, it's not that the character design and animation of HWSNBN are even all that bad, really. With a different voice and a completely new set of dialogue and actions, he could have been just fine. What's so atrociously, unwatchably cringe-worthy about him is his personality: a grotesque caricature of marketability, an UberBarney with the Voice from Beyond Elmo. Actor Ahmed Best, who is said to have pursued the role with great fervor, presumably thought that this part was going to be his ticket to immortality. The universal response to the character has been so vehement, virulent, and vitriolic, however, that he may be better off removing it from his résumé entirely, leaving a gaping hole in his job history right after the part about the off-Broadway sensation *Stomp*.

This shambling, misshapen Lovecraftian vision has been the bane of my existence since his arrival on this planet, first in movie form, and then in his far more nightmarish, real-life, *true* form: as merchandise.

For that summer, everywhere you went across these United States, HWSNBN was there. I know this because my girlfriend and I went on a long road trip that year, no matter what state we were in, any time we stopped the car, wherever we looked, we saw HWSNBN looking back at us, in life-size cardboard cutout form, a friendly smile on his face gesturing with outstretched flipper/paw toward a conveniently located display case of Pepsi products, as if to say "Wah-na so-da?" He was the personalized embodiment of the Vast Insidious Machineries of Consumerism, he was the symbol of everything we'd grown to despise about our commercial society made CGI flesh, and, in that, perhaps the argument could be made that *The Phantom Menace* was actually the most culturally relevant of the all the *Star Wars* films, because it is the failure of these Machineries to deliver on their empty promises, more so than said promises themselves, that our culture is really all about. That, of course, more so than his annoying cuteness or his insipid voice, was the most depressing thing about him.

With this in mind, I might have at least found some consolation in watching these machineries sputter and falter, as the full economic impact of the Inevitable Anticlimax slowly became more and more apparent following the movie's launch. Companies lost fortunes as books and toys that had been expensively licensed from Lucasfilm piled up unsold in stores for months on end. The Taco Bell promotion was reportedly a record setter for the least successful fast-food promotion in fast-food history, and merchandising deals of every stripe fared little better. Though the film itself, on the strength of its hype and despite the negative reaction it got from just about the whole country, still managed to become the fourth-highest box office moneymaker in movie history, the implosion of the merchandising bubble told the true story. I think it is worth mentioning that, as of this writing, in March of 2002, a full three years since the post–*Phantom Menace* merchandise implosion, with the trailers for *Episode II* already in theaters (and those same *Star Wars* geeks who professed to hate the new movie with every fiber of their being currently the *same people* who are getting all excited about it), this long after the fact, I *still*, when I went down to my local drugstore to buy a new toothbrush last week, found a HWSNBN toothbrush staring back at me from the shelf: that's a true story.

Sadly, I was unable to take any pleasure in this (our nation taking collective revenge upon HWSNBN's smug, sardonic face by *not* buying him) because the sudden, drastic drop in the cost of all this crap (90% Off! Everything Must Go!) made it instantly affordable for seemingly everyone I knew—knowing as they did that I had signed on whole hog and gone all out for *The Phantom Menace* and had stubbornly refused to back down despite all evidence to the contrary, and who, of course, wanted to give me as much shit as humanly possible about my doing so—to buy said crap for me, as humiliating gag gifts, in vast quantities, at dollar-store prices, for the next couple of years. I soon had more *Star Wars Episode I* bullshit heaped on me, with sarcastic smiles and knowing explanations of "I knew you liked this stuff, it was only two dollars and sixty cents, can you believe it?" than any mortal man deserves. I had Anakin Skywalker cereal bowls. I had Queen Amidala–shaped soap. I had little spiral notepads with Sebulba on them, and I had them all by the ton. I had never been so mortified in all my days. But most of all, I had reams and reams of HWSNBNs—on stickers, bean bag toys, throw pillows, towels, posters, pencils, and shoelaces—my friends cut out his picture from the countless ads he appeared in and taped them to my walls, my desk, my computer, so I could never get away from his countless, ubiquitous faces—each one looking back at my stubborn support for *Episode I* with a silent, grinning rebuke.

I still have all this crap, by the way. It overflows bags and boxes in my closets.

You want it? No? That's what I figured: I can't unload this shit on anybody.

So then anyway, was it worth it? I don't mean for the nation (for the nation, no, obviously not worth it), but for me: in the face of that silent rebuke, did my argument stand up? I'm still not sure about that one: sometimes I think so, and other times not. I'd never been able to indulge in multiple viewings of *Star Wars* as a kid, and now, at thirty, I had a job, my rent was paid, and the theater showing *The Phantom Menace* was only a two-minute walk down the street from where I worked. I saw the movie at least eight times that summer, and I've seen it on video and DVD a couple times since, so that means that all in all I have, voluntarily and of my own free will, sat through *Star Wars Episode I* probably a good dozen times at least. Each time, the two contradictory halves of my own personal take on the film battled, like the light and dark sides of the Force, in my neurotic little media-addled head. But anyway, for what its worth, here stands my defense of *The Phantom Menace*, a movie that I am the only person I know of who professes to actually like; even, on some level, to sort of deeply love. Go ahead and make fun of me all you want, because believe me, I've heard it all before. But here's the thing:

It still seems to me that no matter what one may say, if you're honest with yourself, and accept the movie on its own terms (which is to say, on the same level as you took in the Space Opera Nonsense that so stirred you as a kid) you cannot deny that *Star Wars Episode I: The Phantom Menace* has elements in it that are as cool or cooler than anything we've seen in any of the *Star Wars* movies period. Ask yourself, "Would I have liked this movie if I got to see it when I was eight?"—not if you were eight years old in 1999 (in 1999 the Place To Be was definitely not eight years old. I can't imagine an eight-year-old of today being affected in anywhere near the same way by the *Star Wars* mythos as we all were back in 1977, because they've seen all this sort of stuff before, and back then, we hadn't. In 1999, the Place To Be was fourteen years old, and male, and watching *The Matrix*, which is, come to think of it, another example of just what I'm talking about, an undeniably *bad* movie, a B movie, a cheesy-as-hell movie by any kind of Informed Film Criticism standards, but an undeniably *awesome* one nonetheless) but rather if you were eight years old *again*, back then, in that fairy-tale summer. If you say no, I say you're lying.

What about Senator Palpatine? The Emperor is one of the very greatest characters in the *Star Wars* mythos (and for all the bitching the purists do about *Return of the Jedi* because of all those horrible friggin' Ewoks, we should remember that of the whole first trilogy, the Emperor was only in the last one), brilliantly played by Ian McDiarmid in what I would argue is the best performance of any in the series; his every move, gesture, and weird-half-speech-impediment-ish pronunciation oozing *pure evil*. As an audience we react to the Emperor with visceral repulsion, mirroring the way people naturally react to the palpable presence of actual evil: our skin crawls at the sight of him. He is just *awesome*, and in *Episode I* we get to watch him, the titular menace, at his most loathsome: bald-facedly lying to those who trust him (telling the Queen's court, "The negotiations haven't started? But how can that be true? I have assurances from the Chancellor that the Ambassadors have arrived," when we just saw him, not two minutes before, in his Sith Lord alter ego, ordering their *deaths*) and working his deceitful machinations behind the scenes. ("The Council will appoint a new Chancellor . . . a *strong* Chancellor.") No? What about that great moment (twisting those around him to make them more evil than they already are) when the Trade Federation Viceroy says to him "But Lord Sidious . . . is that . . . *legal?*" and he replies with sheer hatred in his voice—just so *evil!*—"I will *make* it legal!"

No? Not buying this? Okay, what about Queen Amidala, striding forward to address the Galactic Congress with "I was not elected to watch my people suffer and die while you discuss this invasion in a committee!" Or that beautiful shot of her standing contemplatively at the Theed Palace window, her head sorrowfully lowered as she watches the occupational force seize the city square? Like her daughter Princess Leia, she functions as a damsel-in-distress for the plot purposes of fairy-tale archetypes, but she is a super-bad-ass female heroine as well, brandishing a laser blaster shoulder-to-shoulder alongside frontline infantry soldiers, while in other scenes maintaining a regal aura of nobility and leadership with a painted face as immobile, formal, and dignified as a feudal Japanese noblewoman. And she's only fourteen! What about that close-up of her, saying with doomed idealism, in stern, measured tones, "I will not condone a course of action that will lead us to war." That alone makes the film worth seeing again!

No? Okay, what about Anakin Skywalker, eight years of age, looking Qui-Gon in the eye after being told that pod-racing is dangerous, and saying, with the pride that will eventually be his downfall into darkness, "I'm the only human who can do it." Just try telling me that's not awesome! Or the scene where he openly hits on the Queen, calling her one of the most beautiful creatures in the universe? Princess Leia was one of my first crushes (after the scantily clad Caroline Munro in the awesome Ray Harryhausen flick *The Golden Voyage of Sinbad*) and it's strange to remember that presexual version of desire, when you were awed by and drawn to physical beauty, aching for the unapproachable object of your affections from the impossible distance of being too young, but you didn't fantasize about sex, you just wanted to *marry* them. (I had a whole new layer added to this early Princess Leia fantasy-imprint in my early twenties, when I learned that, in real life, in 1977 Carrie Fisher was a nineteen-year-old hard-partying Hollywood Wild Child who, when told by Lucas she had to tape her breasts down to keep them from jiggling too much on the set, rebelled by starting a tradition, at the end of each shooting day, of letting a different guy from the crew *rip the tape off*—hoo-mama, help me.) And it is that exact feeling of childhood longing that's evoked by Anakin's little-boy crush on Padme, the handmaiden that he is not yet aware is not only a queen, but also the future mother of his son and daughter.

No? Well, what about the fact that she's, apparently, also his future *victim*, come to think of it (since there's no Queen Amidala still around in old age at the start of *Episode IV*), and that is, after all, the film's central conceit: that we, the viewer, already *know* that this boy is doomed to be the greatest villain in the universe, that he will grow up to cut off his son's hand, to blow up his daughter's adopted planet, that the Good Space Wizards are going to be wiped out, and the Evil Space Wizard, the central character of it all, will triumph—and yet, that he will ultimately be redeemed at the very end—*awesome!* Seriously, you've got to admit that with all these doubling-back narrative structural effects, Lucas is, in some ways, getting at the very heart of something about those childhood fantasies, and what it's like to grow up from them, and then look back on them after having grown up; on innocence, and experience, and the difference. You can't admit that at the very least that's *kind of* cool? No? Come on, you're sort of starting to piss me off now.

Okay then, well what about the scene there at the very end, where the Queen and the Jedis are storming the Palace, and the hangar bay door opens, and the music kicks in, with as awesome a theme as John Williams ever wrote, and a whole classical chorus of voices starts belting out *ancient Sanskrit* for chrissakes—to reveal Darth Maul, Lord of the Sith, in all his terrible splendor, and the three Force-wielding principles silently drop their outer robes to the floor, and the stage is set for what can only be described, unquestionably, indisputably, as the greatest lightsaber fight, *by far*, that *anybody's* ever seen? Jesus, it makes all the other lightsaber battles, thrilling as they were at the time, nothing less than excruciatingly boring to watch now by comparison, that's how fucking great it is, with Darth Maul simultaneously attacking two full-on prime-of-their-lives Jedi Knights, all three of them spinning and flipping in superhuman leaps and parries and *Jesus*—when Obi-Wan finally gets out from behind the force field, after helplessly watching his Master slaughtered before his eyes, and he runs forward into the fray and just busts out *swinging*, and you just want to stand up in your seat and go *yeah!*—like people did at the end of the first trilogy when Vader grabs the Emperor and lifts him above the edge of the pit and they stood up and yelled *throw him over!*— and I mean, *man*, it just makes you want to name your *kid* Obi-Wan, if you had a kid, it's so cool. Look me in the face and tell me you're gonna deny that's awesome! Seriously! You don't think so? Really? You don't think that moment, that supreme awesome moment of Space Opera Nonsense Writ Larger Than Large (and hey, there's that nonironic tone again, funnyman), when the Good Space Wizard takes on the Bad Space Wizard with total, unstoppable, righteous *fury*, is worth getting excited enough about to want to see again and again?

No? Well, fuck you then! The hell with you if you can't set aside your self-awareness long enough to embrace that moment! What good does it do anybody not to allow yourself to appreciate something that life-affirming?

Fuck you and your smartass ironic distance! What about that little kid in his room, so long ago, waiting for his chance to see the Clone Wars movies someday! What about him, huh? Don't his feelings matter at all, you cynical bastards? All you sons of bitches can kiss my ass! And while you're at it, I suppose this is as good a time as any to say, yeah, by the way, that was *me* in the homemade Jedi Knight costume on opening weekend, motherfuckers, and yeah, I had one of those toy lightsabers in my belt, and yeah, I knew I looked stupid, but you know what, I didn't care, and I'm not ashamed, and fuck you if you can't take a non-joke. Picture me wearing it now, why don't you, grabbing my nutsack and flipping you the bird.

Okay, so I'm a little defensive about this.

After waiting for more than twenty years, I finally saw *Star Wars Episode I: The Phantom Menace* at a beautiful gigantic old theater called the Orpheum, on State Street in Madison, Wisconsin. The theater had been struggling financially and was kind of dilapidated (it was built before movies originally, for touring stage acts and vaudeville and the like) and had almost got converted and remodeled into something strange and modern and horrible but had just, at that point in time, been saved by a community outreach campaign and a guy who came in and bought it at the last minute to preserve it and restore it to the way it was. He had been working hard to get the restorations done in time for the opening, had put in new seats and restored the vending area and had acquired a brand-new state-of-the-art THX sound system (these were required for any theater that wanted to show the film), and so the whole mood surrounding the theater was optimistic and hopeful in that rare way that sometimes happens.

The theater, because it was originally intended as a stage theater, sat way more people than any movie house could ever expect to draw. It was huge, with seventeen hundred seats, and it was therefore never full, which meant that no matter how popular a movie was, you could always see it if it was playing there, because it would never sell out, but they completely filled it all the way up that night, even the huge and grand old balcony, packing them in to the rafters. For the *Star Wars* premiere, all the tickets were sold in advance, and they sold out a week ahead of time at all the other theaters in town, and people had to wait in line for them, and even then they sometimes couldn't get a ticket, but the situation at the Orpheum was perfect because it was so big they still had tickets available right up until the showing itself, so nobody had to wait in line.

They chose to anyway. There was a carnival atmosphere in the street outside for hours before the first showing, which was at midnight on opening day. I could hear the chatter and laughter and crowd noises from where the old offices of *The Onion* were, a block away from The Orpheum, before we moved to New York. I had gathered with a large group of friends and coworkers who were all going to see the movie together that night and, having changed into my Jedi Knight outfit, I was swinging around the really cool lightsaber I bought earlier that week at Toys-"R"-Us—much cooler than any of the versions available to me when I was a kid, this one actually made the awesome lightsaber humming sound when you turned it on, and was pressure sensitive, so that when it connected with something, it made the sound effects of a lightsaber clash. The writers' room in the old offices was filled, like most comedy staffers' rooms, with a bunch of goofy and offensive shit—dumb posters people had defaced to comic effect, a whole wall of dumb pseudo-humorous monkey photos we called "The Wall of Chimp," funny clippings from insipid celebrity-profile magazines, and other detritus of the Jaded Age—one of which was a child's baby doll dressed in a bunny costume that some wiseacre or other had hung from the ceiling by a noose. Swinging the lightsaber at it, I kept sending the fake dead baby swinging in wide arcs and parabolas around the room. Though I knew in the back of my mind that the Inevitable Anticlimax was just around the corner, I was in great spirits.

I'd been thinking about maybe wearing Jedi Knight robes ever since someone had pointed out that I had the same hair and beard as Liam Neeson wore in the prequel and put the idea in my head. Finally I figured, what the hell, there's no point in being self-conscious about looking stupid—*come on man, show some balls.* Since the Inevitable Anticlimax was on the way, I'd end up getting made fun of anyway, so I guess I figured that hey, maybe just going all-out into uncoolness, for this one occasion, would be almost sort of punk rock or something. My girlfriend's sister Pam, who's a home economics teacher, *and a damn good one,* had sewn it for me, so it was awesome-looking. Even better, my roommate at the time, Jeffrey, decided he was going in costume too, but he wore a borrowed *Star Trek: The Next Generation* uniform (Jeffrey is not a *Star Trek* geek, he just thought it'd be funny) and just *confused and bothered* people: now *that* was punk rock.

When we finally went down and joined the line, there was a brief moment of panic as a policeman, apparently worried that the horseplay in the crowd was getting out of hand, started striding over to us to tell us to behave, but luckily my coworker John, in his usual wiseass mode, defused the situation by singing the Darth Vader "Imperial March" theme as the cop approached, drawing a huge laugh from the crowd as others took up the refrain and sang along and effectively robbing the policeman of any authority he might have otherwise commanded. People passed food and beverages around; a few people, as they always are in Madison, were passing joints. It was a beautiful, temperate spring night and the weather was perfect, and everybody was having a great time, and the weird thing is: almost all of the people there, really, were not *Star Wars* geeks either (although there was a comparatively small contingent of them—you could sort of, um, really easily tell which ones were), mostly they were all just a really big crowd of former eight-year-olds like me.

At some point, the local news showed up. Because I was wearing a costume, a reporter singled me out and asked, "Why are you wearing that?" I was speechless. I had no real answer prepared. I was not the sort of person who would ever normally do stuff like this, so I was unable to explain why this one night I had. I thought about it, and realized that although I am not really a *Star Wars* geek (at least not in the sense that most people take it to mean) I certainly could relate to the idea of being a Normal Regular geek, if by "Normal Regular geek" you mean "guy who didn't really fit in in junior high, and ended up spending a lot time alone in his room, looking at *Mad* magazine, watching movies, drawing cartoons, and reading books," which is what I, anyway, would take it to mean. So after a brief pause, I said, "Why do you think? Because I'm a big freakin' geek! This is our day. Geek nation!" and then I turned around to the people standing behind me and yelled "Geek nation!" and they all started yelling it too. I don't think the reporter understood what we were trying to say.

I am not making this up.

At the last minute, I spotted my friend Rob, who was also not a *Star Wars* geek, he was a stoner musician guy who played in a surf rock outfit in town, but had been enough of a lifelong *Star Wars* fan to name his band "The Mandalorians" and actually get Boba Fett's shoulder insignia tattooed on his own shoulder. I waved him over and he came with us as we made our way into the huge theater for the show. I knew him from around town as kind of a tough-guy rocker type, but his face, as we all sat there, was lit up with an expression of pure little-kid delight. As the crowd waited for the movie to start, shouting out wisecracks, I realized that something strange was happening. As often happens with excited crowds of that size, it had spontaneously burst into a kind of tribal chant-type thing. Normally, I never experience this, because I don't go to any of the places where crowds that large usually form—I'm not a sports fan, so I don't go to ball games; I'm not a hippie, so I don't go to Phish shows; I'm not a Republican, so I don't go to political conventions. I'm usually always on the outside of crowds that large, living in the Jaded Age. But then the chant changed, and I realized they were all singing the Main Title Theme from *Star Wars* and I thought *Oh my God, man . . . I can't believe this is actually happening, for real.*

At some point some joker stepped out to introduce the film and yelled, "Are you ready to see *Star Wars?*" and Jeffrey stood up and said, "I thought this was gonna be *Star Trek!*" and that got a big laugh. And then the lights went down and everybody cheered, and the previews came on and they booed, and the 20th Century Fox logo came up and they cheered, and the Lucasfilm logo came up and everybody cheered again. And then, the words "A long time ago," etc. came up, and everybody went "Shhh! Shh!" until the whole place, all seventeen hundred of them, was totally, and completely silent.

I knew the Inevitable Anticimax part was coming, and that sort of made me sad, but in the meantime, there was still this. That coming disappointment would be the biggest impact on our collective cultural consciousness until a year and a half later, election night 2000, which was really going to freak everybody out, until of course the following autumn after that, which was *really* going to, and this, right now, was sort of the Last Perfect Moment before all the bad stuff started to go down. And go ahead and make fun of me all you want, because I've heard it all before, but here's the thing: then there was a sudden blast of brass fanfare, exactly like the one we all knew by heart, and the screen filled with light, and from the foundations to the roof the building shook as the whole place went absolutely apeshit.

STAR WARS TALE

KATE BERNHEIMER

Once there was a little girl and an older sister, and they had this game they played, and in the game they played Princess Leia and Darth Vader and Luke Skywalker. The younger sister played Princess Leia and the older sister played Darth Vader and Luke Skywalker. This all took place in the kitchen, papered metallic silver with yellow flowers.

First the sister who played Princess Leia rolled her hair into balls on the sides of her head and was locked in the pantry, but as the pantry didn't really lock it was pretend-locked by the other sister who, at the time in the game when the locking took place, played Darth Vader. The Darth Vader sister had a black plastic garbage bag over her shoulders like a cape and spoke with a raspy voice. This Darth Vader sister would say, "You must be locked inside this soundproof room because you were very, very bad and you will never, ever get to see the handsome Luke Skywalker again." And always the Darth Vader sister would threaten the Princess Leia sister with "beating, rape, and other forms of torture."

While threatening Princess Leia, the Darth Vader sister would sometimes close herself into the pantry too. She would stretch her

arms imposingly across the door. This was a cue for the Princess
Leia sister to throw her arms around the Darth Vader sister and
cling to her in thrilled terror. Then the Darth Vader sister would tilt
back her head and cackle in the raspy voice. She'd leave the pantry,
fake-locking the door. Back in the kitchen she would pretend to
pluck a yellow flower from the papered walls and stomp on its
bloom. Rasping, she'd cackle again.

Now the sister playing Princess Leia became terrified, and
screamed "Help! Help me Luke!" and the sister who was playing
Luke Skywalker, who had just been playing Darth Vader, would
quickly, quickly remove the garbage-bag cape from her shoulders
and put on a white shirt of the father's (which the mother used for
baking) and say, in a voice full of passion, "Princess Leia!" But
because the pantry was sealed off from sound, being "soundproof,"
Princess Leia couldn't hear Luke Skywalker, even though Luke
Skywalker out in the kitchen could hear Princess Leia calling for
him. "Help! Help me Luke," Princess Leia sobbed again and again.
Yet Luke Skywalker, abjectly, only could listen.

Pacing the kitchen, Luke would wave his arms in their long
white sleeves to the rhythm of Leia's cries. That he could hear her
at all was an auditory curiosity, a miracle of sorts, a fatal glitch
Darth Vader had not predicted when he had locked the Princess in
the room. At this very moment in the crisis, each and every time
the game was played, Luke could hear Leia cry for help from
inside the soundproof room. In fact the game hinged on his hearing
her. How else would he know to promise to save her from rape,
beating, and other forms of torture?

Yet as Princess Leia could not hear Luke from inside the pantry,
telling her how he would save her (which would prove that he
loved her), Luke Skywalker would make tapes for her to listen to
on a cassette recorder. He would speak into the microphone as he
paced around the silver kitchen professing his "deep and unfath-
omable love for you, Princess Leia, my only sister—I mean lover—
who is locked away right now and can never hear my voice again
and might be beaten, raped, or tortured!" He would then rewind to

the beginning of his message and open the door to the soundproof room, hand Princess Leia the cassette recorder and slam the door shut again, hard. The Luke Skywalker sister often forgot whether to be tender or mean, having to juggle so many roles.

Princess Leia, clutching the machine to her chest, would hit "play," listen to his message, and then record one of her own. She whispered close to the machine. "Luke Skywalker, I love you with all my heart, all my heart, you are my one and only lover and I will love you for all time even from inside this soundproof room in which the wicked Darth Vader has locked me for all time, and where I will be punished again and again in so many unspeakable ways." She would attach a yellow flower from the wallpaper to her message, placing the flower on the recorder with care. After rewinding meticulously to the beginning of her message, Princess Leia would open the door and hand the recorder to Luke. Sniffing the flower with great fervor, the young Luke would cry.

So it continued along. Back and forth Luke and Leia would pass the recorder and profess their love with only occasional interruptions by a garbage-bagged Darth and his threats of beating and rape. And though it made the sisters glow, no one ever got saved.

A *STAR WARS* MISCELLANY:
Extracts Culled from Various Media

COMPILED BY AIMEE AGRESTI

In *Star Wars*, there's a scene in which R2-D2 spews out a three-dimensional image of Princess Leia into the middle of the room. "Unfortunately, it doesn't work that way," says Mr. Benton, one of the foremost researchers in the field. "I'm amazed at how even scientists who should know better get angry when they are told we can't violate the simple rules of light moving in straight lines. You can't spit out light and have it turn around without a reflector."

> —Steve Benton, chief holographic researcher for Polaroid Corp., in the article "Holography Remains Elusive Dream," Walter Immen, *Globe and Mail* 12/01/1980

Yes, the *Star Wars* gang has released its very own Christmas album, entitled *Christmas in the Stars*. It features such standard fare as "Sleigh Ride" and " 'Twas the Night before Christmas," as well as a few cosmic extras such as "Christmas in the Stars." Darth Vadar would absolutely hate it.

> —"Spaced-out Yule from C-3PO & Co.," *Globe and Mail* 11/19/1980
> (*I wonder if this artifact is still in the "Bible"?*—Ed.)

In nooks and corners, the author may be glimpsed striking a rich variety of pompous attitudes, interlarding the narratives with a McInerny-esque and rather gratuitous litany of hipness-establishing buzz words (Burberry, *Star Wars*, Jerry Falwell, MOMA, Karen Black, the Food Emporium, Cadillac Broughams [in two stories], the New York Helmsley Hotel, et al.).

—Review of Harlan Ellison book *Angry Candy*, Mitch Berman, *Los Angeles Times* 01/01/1989

DIRTY ROTTEN SCOUNDRELS—A long time ago, before *Star Wars* brought about the age of technology and *National Lampoon's Animal House* brought about the age of bathroom humor, comedies were almost always elegant.

—"Top Attractions," Philip Wuntch, *Dallas Morning News*, 12/30/1988,

Henry Kurtz (director of the collectibles department at the Phillips auction gallery in Manhattan): If I had a warehouse, I would start stocking Michael Jackson, Cher, and Bruce Springsteen memorabilia; *Star Wars* toys, particularly the original series of Empire commandos and Darth Vader figures; E.T. toys, and any personal items from entertainment or sports celebrities.

—"Spotting the Icons of the '80s: Experts tell what will show future generations the way we were," Patricia Leigh Brown, *Dallas Morning News* 12/20/1988

John Remillard is wearing the kind of headset used by telephone operators. He's sitting at a table that holds what looks like an ordinary personal computer, which is hooked up to an electronic device the size of a stereo tuner. He speaks into the tiny microphone that is an inch from his mouth and attached to the headset. "Four," he says. He presses a key on the computer keyboard and a large orange circle appears on the computer screen. Underneath the circle is the word . . . "four." Remillard beams. . . . But people who have watched C-3PO exchange witticisms with Luke Skywalker and his pals on the silver screen will find it hard to get

excited by hearing Remillard say "four" and watching the word pop
up on a computer screen.

> —"Say Hello to a 'True' Talking Computer,"
> Paul Galloway, *Chicago Tribune* 12/18/1988

"You have to parody movies at just the point where they finish
making them. We didn't think it was a good idea to do another
horror-movie spoof, for instance, because they aren't taken that
seriously any more. The same with sci-fi. It was Mel Brooks' intention to spoof *Star Wars* in *Spaceballs*. But *Star Wars* was already a
spoof."—David Zucker, director.

> —"The 'Naked' Guys: Exposing a trio of film makers who take spoofs
> quite seriously," Jay Carr, *Boston Globe* 12/12/1988

[Charles] Prosek's own collection has 10,000 troops featuring
armies from the Egyptian, Assyrian, Greek, Persian, Carthage, Roman,
English Civil, Hungarian, Renaissance, Mexican-American, American Revolutionary and assorted colonial wars and World War II.
This is only a small sample of what's available from ancient wars all
the way up to Star Wars, he said.

> —"This Is War! And the Battleground Is Prosek's,"
> S. R. Carroll, *Chicago Tribune* 12/11/1988

Byrne Piven, who plays Macbeth and directs *Macbeth*, writes in a
program note that the germ of an idea for this staging came to him
three years ago when he saw a university production of *Julius
Caesar* that was set on another planet. Another source of inspiration is surely *Star Wars*, with Macbeth as Darth Vader and Macduff
as a more adult Luke Skywalker who definitely has The Force
with him.

> —"Piven 'Macbeth' Just Like Arousing Mad Maxbeth,"
> Richard Christiansen, *Chicago Tribune* 11/11/1988

He's funny. He's weird. He's great. At least that's how students at
H.E. Charles Middle School describe science teacher Tim Holt. . . .

Holt may tell about a little town. As he spins the yarn, the towns-people evolve into characters in the day's real lesson: the components and functions of microscopic cells. "Then they remember the point," Holt said. "You can't use boring stuff with them. They're used to special effects. They've been to *Star Wars*. It's got to be hands-on for these kids. They've got to touch it."

> —"Teacher Makes Science Lively: Tim Holt piques seventh-graders' interest in funny ways," Jim Conley, *El Paso Times* 11/10/1988

What follows over the next three hours plus intermission is a highly technical, inside-joke-ridden, masterful performance. It is to product demonstrations what Vatican II was to church meetings. To reach the grasp of "mere mortals" who might have stumbled in amid the chosen, [Steve] Jobs invokes images as well as numbers and technology. He illustrates the power and precision and digital-sound quality of his NeXT computer by summoning up the sights and sounds of *Star Wars, 2001: A Space Odyssey*, John F. Kennedy, Martin Luther King Jr. and Moon-walking astronauts.

> —"The Cult of Steve: All Hail the Prophet of the Personal Computer," Wes Smith, *Chicago Tribune* 10/23/1988

Today, our collective robotic fantasies are measured against the kindly androids R2-D2 and C-3PO, George Lucas' classic creations in *Star Wars*. Lucas was creating science fiction, but Engelberger's vision is for real. . . . Home robots, in contrast, while utilizing the technology, will be more anthropomorphic and voice-activated. Engelberger describes Homebot, visually, as a cross between R2-D2 and C-3PO. "It's gonna live in your home with you—it's got to be friendly."

> —"At Home With Robots Experts Developing Kindly Androids That Will Dust, Scrub, Vacuum and, Yes, Even Do Windows," Series: Reshaping the Future, Connie Koenenn, *Los Angeles Times* 10/17/1988

In artists' renderings, it looks a bit like a spaceship that landed on the west side of downtown Houston. Actually, it's only the old

Albert Thomas Convention Center as it would look in 1992 if a redevelopment plan drafted by a team directed by *Star Wars* filmmaker George Lucas becomes reality. The city of Houston is negotiating with Houston-based Century Development Corp. and Lucas' Skywalker Development Co. to turn the Thomas center into a beehive of downtown nightlife, with restaurants, clubs, theaters and shops, similar to Dallas' West End MarketPlace.

> —"Houston Seeks Livelier Nightlife: *Star Wars* creator
> offers 'bold idea' to boost downtown," Bruce Nichols,
> *Dallas Morning News* 10/16/1988

Michael Kudesh keeps on his desk a few sets of clear Lucite balls. The customized balls are only used at special parties for play on the club's table—a sort of *Star Wars* model with stainless-steel rails.

> —"Pool Is Cool Again 'It's Very Social, Very Sexy'—
> and It's Going Downright Upscale All Over Town,"
> Marla Donato, *Chicago Tribune* 10/05/1988

Chains . . . black sleeveless "Megadeath" T-shirts . . . leather pants . . . fish-net stockings . . . pink Tina Turner hair. . . . As one sober hotel guest put it, the cocktail lounge at the Sheraton Universal on Saturday night looked like the bar scene from *Star Wars*.

> —"Heavy Metal Rockers Say They Want More Respect,"
> Dennis McDougal, *Los Angeles Times* 10/03/1988

Skeeter redesigned the console of its SK 2000 this year and the new design seems to make more efficient use of space. The boat still bears a striking resemblance to Luke Skywalker's hovercraft in the movie *Star Wars* but the 1,400-pound bass boat is selling as fast as Skeeter can turn them out.

> —"Power Boating: Innovative designs cater to fishing, recreational needs,"
> Ray Sasser, *Dallas Morning News* 09/22/1988

The front entrance is a *Star Wars* pergola framing a semicircular courtyard, beyond which stands an entry facade shaped like an open book and inscribed with an American flag and an inspirational message from former Columbia University president Grayson Kirk.

> —"Cool Schools: El Paso proves bright, fresh design doesn't have to cost a fortune," David Dillon, *Dallas Morning News* 09/18/1988

At its worst, the new *Ring* suffered from stylistic inconsistency, visual gimmickry, hectic, even distracting, dramatic choreography, and a frustrating vagueness of intention. When Kupfer and his designers appeared to run out of ideas, they simply filled the stage with *Star Wars*-style laser effects, or hauled out the smoke pots. Too often, what one saw confused, or, worse, contradicted, what one heard.

> —"High-Tech Wagner: A Provocative New *Ring* Ignites Passions at Bayreuth," John von Rhein, *Chicago Tribune* 08/14/1988

"A lot of people want to know what our homes are going to be like in the year 2000," said Joy Schrage, a spokesman for the Michigan-based appliance firm. "I think many of us have watched too many *Star Wars* movies. We are not going to see any plastic bubble cities and space-age homes."

> —"High Tech Finally Coming Home," Steve Brown, *Dallas Morning News* 09/28/1984

I think the reason the concept of the personal robot is so appealing is that too many people have seen *Star Wars* and have fallen in love with the idea of having a cute little robot to boss around. Indeed, the idea of a digital batman that makes your bed or consoles you when you're feeling down or fetches your slippers appeals to the part of us that wants to be pampered.

> —"Personal Computers: Personal Robot: A Cute Idea, but No Cigar," Michael Schrage, *Washington Post* 09/24/1984

The scene was of innocence and fantasy, more Ringling Bros. than rock 'n' roll, more *Star Wars* than *Gimme Shelter*. Children tugged their parents from one concession stand to another. A few fell asleep as the Jacksons shifted from funk to lullaby.

—"The Jacksons! Wizards of Awe for 'Victory Tour' Fans,"
David Remnick, *Washington Post* 09/22/1984

Something else was happening, too, to fuel interest in the classics. The age of relevance was being replaced by an age of fantasy. Computers and high technology were all the rage, and movies like *Star Wars* and *Close Encounters of the Third Kind*, with their traditional heroes of light and antagonists of darkness, along with bizarre creatures, were grabbing the minds of young people. "The myths often deal with a hero who is separated from his parents who has to go off to some kind of test, encounters the parents and then returns as a grown-up person. This is what happens in *Star Wars* when [Luke] Skywalker encounters his father Darth Vader," said Coogan. "It's the pattern of the Greek hero. . . . The Greek myths offer a kind of escape from the kind of positivism and rationalism that is in the rest of the students' program. It's a relief for them."

—"Dead Language Very Much Alive:
Latin and the Classics Making a Comeback in U.S. Schools,"
Elsa Walsh, *Washington Post* 07/22/1984

From a distance, it looks like something out of *Star Wars*: a crazy quilt of geometric structures dumped in the middle of a lush, well-tended park. Close up, the mystery deepens: plants grow out of the sides of plastic boxes and cylinders that have been stacked every which way.

—"Circus of Color: The Arboretum's Country Garden,"
Charles Fenyvesi, *Washington Post* 06/07/1984

Warren Moon is so deliberative that Steinberg calls him "Yoda," after the wise character in the Star Wars trilogy. But he finally ignored Houston's poor recent records and chose the security of the Oilers' deal.

—"Stars Were Right for Moon's Ascent to $6 Million Deal,"
Paul Attner, *Washington Post* 02/17/1984

"It was like meeting Jesus. All I could say was, 'Thank you on behalf of my generation. I wouldn't be doing what I'm doing if it wasn't for you.' I based my entire life on using the Force."—Fran Healy of the rock group Travis to the *Toronto Sun*, on recently meeting his idol, *Star Wars* creator George Lucas.

—"Lifeline: The Force is with Rock Group Travis,"
Cesar G. Soriano, *USA Today*

What was the highlight of 2001?

"Meeting George Lucas. I made myself look a complete arse, but it was still cool. We were supporting Dido in America and he came with his daughters. I met him afterwards and I'm a big *Star Wars* fan. I said, 'I've always tried to let my life be guided by the Force,' and he said 'That's nice,' in the most blank way imaginable."

—Fran Healy of Travis, interviewed in Q magazine, issue 184

You're in a square, transparent pod underneath the stage at London's Earls Court. The point man is staring at you, waiting for a thumbs-up. . . . If you are ready—if thumbs-ups are exchanged—then seconds later you're cavorting with Madonna in front of 17,598 fans. "It's like going from one world to the next," says guitarist Monte Pittman. "Under the stage it's like a hidden city. It's like something in *Star Wars*. Then you go up and there's just a sea of people screaming."

—"What it Feels Like in a Whirl: Madonna and 'Family' Deal with Acute
Labor Pains in Delivering the You-Know-What of All Pop Tours,"
Jeff Gordinier, *Entertainment Weekly* 07/27/2001

[Carson] Daly deals with this level of pop-cultural cluelessness daily. "With somebody like Prince, I might have to say, 'Standing next to me is a guy who has sold over 200 million records worldwide,'" he explains. "This is my childhood, so it's weird. These kids haven't seen *Star Wars*. Nobody had any idea who Chewbacca was."

—"'Total' World Domination: EW Dives into the Adolescent Abyss
Surrounding MTV's Countdown Phenom, 'Total Request Live,'"
Caroline Kepnes, *Entertainment Weekly* 02/23/2001

Kelly Wiglesworth was born one month after *Star Wars* opened in 1977. And in one of her darkest hours on *Survivor*—that late-series stretch where it seemed like Rich, Sue, and Rudy would swoop down like merciless storm troopers and vote her off—the feisty 22-year-old river guide (who stayed alive with stunning immunity wins) invoked her generation's mythological touchstone. "I feel like Luke Skywalker," she said, conveniently renouncing her alliance with Tagi's shiftiest members when they were no longer useful. "I crossed over to the dark side for a moment." A moment? Honey, when would you say you crossed back?

—"*Survivor* Wrap-Up," *Entertainment Weekly* 09/01/2000

Trust us. Even if your kid has the entire scrolling text from the opening of *Star Wars* memorized, even if he collects coins and stamps, even if he wants to be a CPA, even if all that—if the Xterra is his first car, he's going to be cool.

—The Year 2000 *Esquire* Auto Awards 01/01/2000

REED ROTHCHILD: Have you seen that *Star Wars* movie?

EDDIE ADAMS: Yeah, I've seen it four times.

REED ROTHCHILD: You know, people tell me I kind of look like Han Solo.

—From the film *Boogie Nights*, 1997,
written and directed by Paul Thomas Anderson

"This is storybook stuff," said Cardinal teammate Ron Gant after McGwire's 61st home run. "I mean, there can be movies written about things like this. It's like *Star Wars* with Luke Skywalker. The Force was with Mark McGwire."

—"A Truly Grand Slam," *People* 09/21/1998

POLICEMAN (*questioning Nathan Arizona, whose infant has just been kidnapped*): What did the pajamas look like?

NATHAN ARIZONA: Oh, I don't know, they were jammies! They had Yodas and shit on 'em!

—From the film *Raising Arizona*, 1987,
written by Joel and Ethan Coen, directed by Joel Coen

Actor Adam Goldberg, who plays Private Mellish, one of Tom Hanks's men in *Saving Private Ryan*, says he was a bit apprehensive about meeting director Steven Spielberg. "When I met him, I had already gotten the part, so I basically went in there praying he wouldn't take it away," recalls Goldberg, 27. "Spielberg was playing a Star Wars video game on his computer, and he said, 'I'll be with you in a moment.' So that immediately put me at ease." Goldberg's only regret? "I didn't get to play the *Star Wars* game with him. But I don't know if he allows other people to touch it."

—"Chatter," Chuck Arnold, *People* 08/17/1998

STIFFLER: Ozzy, go long.

Oz runs toward the beach.

JIM (to Stiffler): What are you doing?

STIFFLER: (*preparing to throw a football*): Fishing.

Stiffler deliberately overthrows the ball and Oz falls, stumbling onto a blanket populated by several attractive young women. As Oz sheepishly apologizes, it's clear that the girls are delighted to have met him.

JIM (*in awe*): Amazing.

STIFFLER: The Force is strong in that one.

—From the film *American Pie II*, 2001,
written by Adam Herz, directed by J.B. Rogers

COMMENTATOR MORTON KONDRACKE: I've likened Afghanistan to the meanest bar in the universe in *Star Wars*.

COHOST AND "WEATHER GUY" STEVE DOOCY: Mort, I've been to that bar. They don't serve Wookiees, as I remember.

—"Fox and Friends," *Fox News* 1/4/02

The Force may not be with Enron Corp. these days, but it was implied by the *Star Wars*–related names of some of the fallen energy company's financial vehicles. JEDI LP and Chewco Investments LP, inspired by Chewbacca the faithful Wookiee in the *Star Wars* movies, are among the limited partnerships that have been associated with Houston-based Enron, which descended into bank-ruptcy in December. It's unclear who the big *Star Wars* fans were at Enron, but Lucasfilm Ltd. said this week it was an unwilling participant. "Until it surfaced in the [Enron Collapse] press, Lucasfilm was unaware of possible use of our protected trademarks by Enron, and any actual use by Enron of such trademarks was without our permission," Lucasfilm spokeswoman Jeanne Cole said.

—"Lucasfilm Frowns on Enron's *Star Wars*," Associated Press 2/7/2002

ACKNOWLEDGMENTS

I wish I could take credit for coming up with the idea for this volume, but in fact this book was the brainchild of Tom Bissell, who was an editor at Henry Holt at the time. While he was casting about for writers, he contacted my friend David Foster Wallace, who demurred—he had only seen *Star Wars* once, in French as it happens (long story), and in any case he was much more of a *Lord of the Rings* man—but who recommended that Tom get in touch with me. For that, I owe many, many thanks to Dave, despite the fact that I couldn't wheedle him into contributing.

When circumstances made it impossible for Tom to do the day-to-day work of putting the book together, he very kindly entrusted that task to me, for which I am very grateful. Tom has since left Holt to pursue his writing muse (his splendid essay on Boba Fett in this book is, I think, a clear validation of his choice), but during all this time I have regarded him as a close collaborator. I would like to say that this book is as much his as it is mine; I can only hope that I was able to live up to his vision of it.

Elizabeth Stein at Holt picked up the ball after Tom left the company, and she has been a joy to work with. Her patience, good humor, and understanding are very much appreciated.

Of course I have to thank each of the contributors. All compilations of this sort come together under trying circumstances; with this book, the circumstances got a little more trying than usual. The events of September 11, 2001, caused a few people who had initially signed on to reconsider, feeling that this was no time to be thinking about *Star Wars*. I respect their decision while regretting their absence from the book. But it makes my gratitude to those who hung in there that much stronger. They (and their various representatives) have been remarkably kind, patient, and diligent, not to mention brilliant and perceptive.

My colleagues at *Premiere* magazine, past and present, are the best group of people one could ever hope to work with, and their companionship and support mean the world to me. Many thanks to editor-in-chief Peter Herbst, who I think of more as a coconspirator than a boss. Respect also to his predecessors: Michael Solomon, always a class act, and my buddy Jim Meigs, who gave me the gig here in the first place. Much love to the delightful Rachel Clarke, the indefatigable Kathy Heintzelman, my editor and homeboy Tom Roston, Susannah "The Wind Beneath My Wings" Gora, Chris Cronis, Cheryl Maday, Victoria Crosby, Jill Bernstein, Andrew Gillings, David Carthas, Leslie Dela Vega, Richard Baker, Christine Cuccuza, and Brooke Hauser. These are people who, no kidding, actually make you want to get out of bed and go to the office in the morning.

West Coast editor Anne Thompson's penetrating interviews with the likes of George Lucas and Brian De Palma saved me a lot of legwork; I'm indebted to her not just for her industry savvy but for her perceptive insights. The rest of the LA office is full of friends who I don't see enough of: Sean M. Smith, Fred Schreurs, Kristin Lootens. My former colleague and very dear friend Howard Karren was great in helping me clarify many of the ideas in my introduction. And another former colleague, the much missed Aimee Agresti, was a real trouper in compiling the miscellany at the close of this book.

A lot of people ask me how someone becomes a movie critic. Hell if I know, but all movie critics, I suppose, start off by talking about the pictures they've seen with the people they've seen them with. I've been seeing and talking about movies with my friend Joe Failla for more than three decades; with Ron Goldberg for more than two. Their insights inform my introduction; their friendship helped make it possible. In a similar vein, I need to thank Doug Brod, Ed Hulse, Brian Koppelman, David Levien, Stewart Wolpin, Kent Jones, Francesca Doria, Patricia Sener, Beth "the Shermanator" Sherman, Alex Lewin, Christina Lem, and Davitt Sigerson. The chicken parmesan at Kevin St. James in Manhattan was a hearty source of sustenance during the final stages of putting this book together; I should also give a holler to The Whole Sick Crew at the late Finn bar in Carroll Gardens. Several trusted advisers have urged me not to use this page to say anything about my cat, and I can certainly see their point. Nevertheless, said cat, Pinky, is a really good one. Among his salutory qualities is a disinclination to sit on my keyboard. And I would like to thank my family: my parents Allan and Amelia, my sister Kathleen, and my brother Michael. This book's dedicatee, my cousin Mark, died of lymphoma earlier this year; even when I would see him at his weakest, he always asked me how this book was coming along. I really wish he was here to see it.

CONTRIBUTORS

AIMEE AGRESTI is a writer living in Washington, D.C. Her work has appeared in *Premiere, People, Travel Holiday,* and the *Washington City Paper*.

HARRY ALLEN, hip-hop activist and media assassin, writes for *Vibe, Premiere,* and other publications and is also a segment producer for radio station WBAI. He lives in New York.

DAN BARDEN is the author of *John Wayne: A Novel*.

ARION BERGER is a freelance writer whose work has appeared in *Rolling Stone, The Washington Post, Esquire, The New Republic, Entertainment Weekly,* and the *Washington City Paper,* among other publications. Her essays have appeared in *Madonna: The* Rolling Stone *Files* and *The* Rolling Stone *Book of Women in Rock;* her book *Hardcore Rap* was published in 2001. She is an adjunct professor of English at Georgetown University and the winner of the Society of Professional Journalists' Washington Dateline award for arts criticism in 1999.

KATE BERNHEIMER is the author of a novel, *The Complete Tales of Ketzia Gold,* and the editor of an essay collection, *Mirror, Mirror on the Wall: Women Writers Explore Their Favorite Fairy Tales*. She is at work on a new novel, *The Complete Tales of Merry Gold*, and a collection of short fiction, *A Cageling Tale and Other Stories*. She lives in Portland, Oregon.

Tom Bissell was born in 1974, and his first memory is of seeing *Star Wars* with his family at a drive-in in Escanaba, Michigan, in 1977. He has reported on filmmaking, space exploration, ecological disaster, and the war in Afghanistan, among other topics. He is also a fiction writer and a critic whose work has been nominated for the Pushcart Prize and two National Magazine Awards and has appeared in *Agni, The Alaska Quarterly Review, Bomb, The Boston Review, Esquire, Harper's,* and *Men's Journal*. His first book, a travel narrative about Central Asia, will appear next year. He lives in New York City.

Tom Carson is the "Screen" columnist at *Esquire,* where his work won an ASME award in 2000. A longtime contributor to the *Village Voice,* he is also a former staff writer at the *LA Weekly*. Over the years, he has written for a number of publications, including *Rolling Stone, The Boston Phoenix, The New York Times,* and others. His novel *Gilligan's Wake* will be published in 2003.

Todd Hanson is the head writer of *The Onion, America's Finest News Source,* and was in that capacity a co-recipient of the 1999 Thurber Prize for American Humor. He has also written for *Slate, Space Ghost,* and *The Oxford American*. After many years in Madison, Wisconsin, the Second City of Slack, he now lives in Brooklyn.

Erika Krouse is the author of *Come Up and See Me Sometime,* a collection of short stories. She lives in Boulder, Colorado.

Jonathan Lethem is the author of *Girl in Landscape, Motherless Brooklyn,* and other novels. He lives in Brooklyn and Toronto.

Lydia Millet is the author of three novels: *My Happy Life; George Bush, Dark Prince of Love;* and *Omnivores*. She also writes for the Natural Resources Defense Council and the Center for Biological

Diversity, and divides her time between Tucson, Arizona, and New York City.

ELVIS MITCHELL is a film critic for *The New York Times*. He lives in New York.

NEAL POLLACK is the greatest living American writer. *The Neal Pollack Anthology of American Literature* was recently issued in paperback, and he is currently working on a novel. He lives in Philadelphia.

JOE QUEENAN is the author of seven books, including several on the cinema. His most recent book is *Balsamic Dreams: A Short but Self-Important History of the Baby-Boomer Generation*. A frequent contributor to GQ and *Movieline*, he lives in Tarrytown, New York.

ELWOOD REID is the author of a short story collection and two novels; the most recent is *Midnight Sun*. He lives in Montana.

KEVIN SMITH has written, directed, and appeared in the films *Clerks, Mallrats, Chasing Amy, Dogma*, and *Jay and Silent Bob Strike Back*. He writes a column for the U.K. magazine *Arena* and contributes short films to *The Tonight Show with Jay Leno*. His next feature is *Jersey Girl*. He lives in Los Angeles and New Jersey.

WEBSTER YOUNCE saw *Star Wars* five times in 1977. Only the protective innocence and naivete of childhood spared him from the horrors of the *Star Wars Holiday Special* the following year. An editor in New York City, his journalism and criticism have appeared in *Harper's, Time Out New York, Beliefnet,* and New York Citysearch.

Glenn Kenny is a senior editor and chief film critic for *Premiere* magazine. He lives in Brooklyn.